CASE STUDIES IN SPORT MARKETING

Brenda G. Pitts, Ed.D.
Editor
Florida State University

Fitness Information Technology
A Division of the International Center for Performance Excellence
262 Coliseum, WVU-PE
PO Box 6116
Morgantown, WV 26506-6116 USA

Library of Congress Card Catalog Number: 2002115155

ISBN: 1-885693-47-8

ISBN 13: 978-1-885693-47-1

Copyeditor: Sandra R. Woods
Cover design: Jamie Merlavage
Developmental Editor: Geoff Fuller
Printed by: Publishers' Graphics

10 9 8 7 6 5 4 3

Fitness Information Technology
A Division of the International Center for Performance Excellence
262 Coliseum, WVU-PE, PO Box 6116
Morgantown, WV 26506-6116
800.477.4348 (toll free)
304.293.6888 (phone)
304.293.6658 (fax)
Email: icpe@mail.wvu.com
Website: www.fitinfotech.com

Sport Management Library

The Sport Management Library is an integrative textbook series targeted toward undergraduate students. The titles included in the library are reflective of the content areas prescribed by the NASPE/NASSM curriculum standards for the undergraduate sport management programs.

Editorial Board

Titles in the Sport Management Library

Ethics in Sport Management
Financing Sport
Fundamentals of Sport Marketing
Legal Aspects of Sport Entrepreneurship
Sport Facility Planning and Management
Sport Governance in the Global Community
Sport Management Field Experiences

Forthcoming Titles

Communication in Sport Organizations
Economics of Sport

ABOUT THE EDITOR

Dr. Brenda G. Pitts is a graduate of the University of Alabama. She is currently with the faculty of sport management at the Florida State University. She teaches undergraduate and graduate courses including Sport Marketing, Sport Administration, and Research in Sport Administration. She has taught Sport Marketing around the world including Hong Kong, Singapore and Malaysia. Her research has been published in numerous journals including the *Journal of Sport Management, Sport Marketing Quarterly, Journal of Sport and Social Issues, Leisure Information Quarterly, Journal of Legal Aspects of Sport,* and *Women in Sport and Physical Activity Journal.* She is the co-author for the *Fundamentals of Sport Marketing* textbook, co-authored a chapter title "Strategic Sport Marketing: Case Analysis," is currently working on two books on the lesbian and gay sport market, and has given numerous scholarly presentations at national and international conferences. Her research foci include sport marketing, sport management curriculum, and sport and sport management in the lesbian and gay community.

Dr. Pitts' professional service contributions have included serving the North American Society for Sport Management as an officer for five years and in other various capacities, serving as Co-Chair of the NASPE-NASSM Task Force on Sport Management Curriculum Standards for seven years, as a member of the Sport Management Program Review Council for three years, and organized the first research conference on lesbian and gay people and sport held in conjunction with the Gay Games IV in New York in 1994.

A former collegiate and professional basketball player, Dr. Pitts is a member of the Huntsville-Madison County Sports Hall of Fame and continues to pursue her lifelong interests in sport and sport management through participation and occasionally managing sports such as soccer, golf, boating, softball, camping, and volleyball.

ABOUT THE CONTRIBUTING AUTHORS

F. Wayne Blann earned a doctor of education degree from Boston University, and currently serves as professor of sport sciences and coordinator of sport management at Ithaca College. Dr. Blann pioneered research on American collegiate and professional athletes' career transitions and Australian elite amateur and professional athletes' and coaches' career transitions. He has served as consultant to the National Basketball Association, National Football League, National Hockey League Players' Association, and Major League Baseball Players' Association regarding players' development programs. Beginning in 1996, the "Professional Athletes Career Transition Program" (PACTP) developed by Dr. Blann has served as the model for athlete career education programs being implemented by the Australian Institute of Sport and at each of the Australian state institutes of sport. He has given numerous presentations at national and international conferences and has published articles in sport management, applied sport psychology, sport sociology, and applied research in coaching and athletics journals and newsletters. As a former collegiate athlete, coach, and athletic director, Dr. Blann is an honorary member of the Jouhnson State College, Vermont, Sports Hall of Fame.

Jacquelyn Cuneen, Ed. D., is a Sport Management Field Experience Coordinator at Bowling Green State University. Her primary research foci are professional preparation in sport management and sport and event marketing. She has authored or co-authored articles appearing in the *Journal of Sport Management, Sex Roles, Sport Marketing Quarterly, Journal of Physical Education, Recreation, and Dance, Schole*, and others. Prior to coming to BGSU, she was Account Executive, Continuity

Director and Director of Women's Programming for two ABC Radio affiliates in New York's Capitol District, and Southern Tier. She has been a member of the NASSM Executive Council, the Graduate Sport Management Program Advisory Board for West Virginia University, and various other professional committees. Dr. Cuneen was a visiting scholar for the North Carolina Center for Independent Higher Education in 1992.

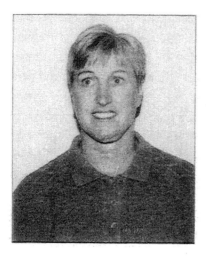

Dianna P. Gray, Ph.D., Associate Professor, University of Northern Colorado, Greeley, Colorado

Dianna Gray received her B.S. from James Madison University and her M.S. and Ph.D. from The Ohio State University. Currently, she is a faculty member in the sport administration graduate program at the University of Northern Colorado. She is also a consultant and author in the areas of sport marketing and public relations. She has presented at NASSM, EASM, AAHPERD, and at various international conferences. Dr. Gray currently serves on the advisory board of the Women's Sport Foundation and the Sport and Entertainment Academy, Indiana University.

Richard L. Irwin, Ed.D., Associate Professor University of Memphis.

Dr. Irwin joined the University of Memphis Department of Human Movement Sciences & Education faculty in 1994 following four years as an assistant professor at Kent State Univeristy. In addition to serving as coordinator for the Recreation, Leisure & Sport Studies Unit (comprising of the undergraduate sport and leisure studies and graduate sport and leisure commerce degree programs), Dr. Irwin is also the director of the Bureau of Sport and Leisure Commerce at the University of Memphis. As director of the University of Memphis Bureau of Sport & Leisure Commerce, Dr. Irwin has been responsible for generating over a quarter of a million dollars in external funding. Funded research and service projects have been conducted on behalf of local and national sponsors such as the National Collegiate Athletic Association, Women's Basketball Association, Memphis Convention and Visitors Bureau, FedEx St. Jude Golf Classic, and Memphis AAA Baseball. Additionally, Dr. Irwin is co-principal of Audience Analysts, a sport market research company, which has consulted with several professional sport franchises including the Orlando Magic, Cleveland Cavaliers, Philadelphia 76ers, and Indiana Pacers. His scholarly research track has typically focused on sport and leisure marketing management as reflected by published works on the topics of sport sponsorship, and licensing, as well as consumer behavior and servicing. Dr. Irwin also serves as a member of the North American Society of Sport Management Executive Council, the *Sport Marketing Quarterly* Editorial Board, and the AXA/Equitable Liberty Bowl Board of Directors.

Dr. David K. Stotlar has a Doctor of Education degree from the University of Utah and teaches on the faculty at the University of Northern Colorado in the areas of sport management and sport law. He has had over 40 articles published in professional journals and has written several textbooks and book chapters in sport, fitness, and physical education. He has made numerous presentations at international and national professional conferences. On several occasions, he has served as a consultant to fitness and sport professionals and, in the area of sport law, to attorneys and international sport administrations. He was selected by the USOC as a delegate to the International Olympic Academy in Greece and the World University Games Forum in Italy. He has conducted international seminars in sport management for the Hong Kong Olympic Committee, the National Sport Council of Malaysia, Mauritius National Sports Council, the National Sports Council of Zimbabwe, the Singapore Sports Council, the Chinese Taipei University Sport Federation, the Bahrain Sport Institute, the government of Saudi Arabia, the South African National Sports Congress, and the Association of Sport Sciences in South Africa. Dr. Stotlar's contribution to the profession includes having served as the chair of the Council on Facilities and Equipment of the American Alliance for Health, Physical Education, Recreation and Dance as a board member and later as president of the North American Society for Sport Management.

TABLE OF CONTENTS

THE SPORT MANAGEMENT LIBRARY iii

ABOUT THE EDITOR v

ABOUT THE CONTRIBUTING AUTHORS vii

FOREWORD xiii

PREFACE xv

ACKNOWLEDGMENTS xix

I. **An Introduction to the Case Study Method** 1
    Chapter 1 — An Introduction to the Case Study Method 2
    Chapter 2 — A Strategic Sport Marketing Case Analysis Model ... 14

II. **The Cases** 27
    How the Sport Marketing Case Studies Are Organized 29

Section One: The Sport Performance Industry Segment 30
    The Sport Performance Industry Segment: An Overview 31
Cases:
    (1) Every Game's a Big Event: The Toledo Mud Hens Baseball Club
    — Jacquelyn Cuneen 33
    (2) Gender Equity Achieved Through Strategic Marketing
    — Richard L. Irwin 55
    (3) Marketing a Basketball Tournament
    — Wayne Blann 61
    (4) Colorado Xplosion of the American Basketball League
    — Dianna P. Gray 65
    (5) Filling Your Football Facility With Fans—17,000 or Bust!
    — Dianna P. Gray 73

Section Two: The Sport Production Industry Segment 80
    The Sport Production Industry Segment: An Overview 81
Cases:
    (1) Modern Turn for a Traditional Product: Cygnet Turf & Equipment
    — Jacquelyn Cuneen 83

(2) Northern Lights, Inc.

— David Stotlar 95

(3) Big Mountain Corporation

 — David Stotlar 103

(4) Football Helmets and the Concussion Dilemma

— Wayne Blann 109

(5) Adidas: Making a Comeback

— Dianna P. Gray 113

Section Three: The Sport Promotion Industry Segment 122
The Sport Promotion Industry Segment: An Overview 123

Cases:

(1) The Sinking of the America's Cup

— David Stotlar 125

(2) National Express, Inc. — Assessing Sport Sponsorship Effectivenes

— Richard L. Irwin 133

(3) Starting a Sport Marketing Firm

— Wayne Blann 139

(4) Call Your Own Game: TRZ Sports Services, Inc.

— Jacquelyn Cuneen 143

(5) Catch That Championship Fever!

— Richard L. Irwin 163

APPENDIX 173
Pitts, B. G., Fielding, L. W., & Miller, L. K. (1994).
Industry segmentation theory and the sport industry:
Developing a sport industry segment model. *Sport
Marketing Quarterly,* 3(1), 15–24.

FOREWORD

The use of case studies in sport management education is a growing trend. This is exemplified by this publication specifically relating to a series of sport marketing case studies. Case study teaching is a popular method of teaching within business schools throughout the world. This is a significant point as I note the alignment of sport management education towards business schools and associated management and business teaching methodologies. As the author points out in this text, case study teaching offers the opportunity to simulate the real world in the classroom. Based on the information presented in the case, students are able to exercise and apply their problem-solving skills in the same way managers do within businesses and sporting organisations.

This text highlights the emphasis on preparing students for managerial decision making within an increasingly business oriented sports sector. It is difficult to provide students with living, breathing organisations to study for obvious reasons. Case study analysis simulates, as best we can as educators, the business and managerial framework within which decisions are formulated. There are no right or wrong answers to arise from case study analysis, only those that appear to be better argued and logically presented given the circumstances confronting the manager. The text does an excellent job in extolling the benefits of case study analysis. The value of the cases presented in this text are further reinforced via the link to the text *Fundamentals of Sport Marketing* by Pitts and Stotlar (1996) which provides the theoretical bases upon which the case studies can be evaluated.

Another feature of the text is the industry segmentation model used to group the case studies, further demonstrating our increasing understanding of the diversity and complexity of organisations comprising the sport industry. There are five cases in each section covering a variety of sports and related organisations, perspectives and dilemmas confronting the sport marketing manager. In the sports performance industry segment the nuances of marketing events are developed, as is the importance of gender equity in participatory programs, the use of situation analysis and its importance in determining marketing strategies and finally the challenges of filling stadia for sporting events. The sport production industry segment provides a more traditional application of marketing theory. This section reinforces the challenges of marketing goods as opposed to services as outlined in the first five case studies. Students should note the subtle differences in marketing theory as it applies to services and marketing sport, in contrast to marketing goods such as football helmets, turf and associated equipment and the important sporting goods industry.

The final segment is the sport promotion industry which allows students the opportunity to examine how sport acts as a conduit for organisations to promote and subsequently sell product. Sponsorship is central to this sector. As an Australian fortunate enough to be in the USA when Australia wrested the America's Cup from the U.S. in 1983 I enjoyed reading this case study. Prior to 1983 the America's Cup had never been won by any other nation other than the USA. The event is steeped in tradition, as was the New York Yacht Club, responsible for the conduct of the event until 1983. This case study is interesting because it demonstrates how the America's Cup became more attractive to sponsors as the conservative traditions of the New York Yacht Club dissipated. It also highlights the challenges of sponsoring sport when the outcome can never be guaranteed.

This textbook is a welcome addition to the range of sport management related resources designed to improve the level of instruction in the classroom. As indicated it covers an interesting array of case studies specific to sport marketing. The organisation of the case studies and the supporting theory available through *Fundamentals of Sport Marketing* provide a comprehensive package for the instructor and student. Students are also provided with extensive advice on how to analyse and use case studies in the classroom. I urge students to carefully read this section before embarking on the exploration of solutions. Students should also use the knowledge and guidance provided by their instructors to assist their analysis and learn to appreciate the evolution of solutions to emerge from working with their fellow students in the analysis of the case studies. Even in a changing world of corporate organisation, information sharing and discussion form the basis of solid managerial decision making. I wish students and instructors well in their use of this valuable resource and recommend its use to all those studying sport marketing. I also congratulate Dr. Brenda Pitts as editor, responsible for bringing together five contributing authors whose dedication to providing the very best in sport management educational resources will be appreciated by many students.

David Shilbury, Ph.D.
Coordinator Sport Management Program
Deakin University
221 Burwood Highway
Burwood 3125
Melbourne, Australia
shilbury@deakin.edu.au

PREFACE

The sport business industry is a challenging and exciting business. It is a multibillion-dollar industry and ranks as the 11th largest industry in the United States. In this large and complex industry, the need for specially educated sport management professionals is at an all-time high. Based on the popularity of sport and its pervasive place in our daily lives, the industry will continue to grow and develop. The need for sport management professionals will increase in relation to this growth. Moreover, as the sport industry continues to grow in variety, scope, and specialty, there will be an increased need for sport management professionals with specializations. The need for specialization exists today.

There are a variety of careers one may pursue. This is the topic of an entire book edited by Parks, Zanger and Quarterman (1998). In the future, sport management degree programs will offer specializations such as sport marketing, management in the fitness industry, sport information, athletic administration, sporting goods industry, resort and country club management, sport law and others. Although a few colleges and universities already offer some of these specializations, more will be added as programs develop.

In the past, sport professionals enjoyed the popularity and growth of sport without having to acquire a specialized education. A person with at least a degree in physical education or recreation seemed to be best prepared. However, those were the days of simplicity. The highly competitive nature of the sport business industry today requires that a person seeking a career in the sport industry acquire a complex mix of talents and a wealth of specialized knowledge and skills. From this need grows our new field of study, sport management. This involves degree programs designed specifically to prepare individuals for the sport business industry. The knowledge base of sport management includes financial management in sport, sport marketing, sport sociology, economics of the sport business, personnel management in sport, computer applications in sport, legal aspects of sport, and other important subject areas.

This book is for individuals interested in a career in sport management and in particular in sport marketing. Sport marketing is an important specialization. Marketing is the one aspect of a business that makes it or breaks it. Sport marketing personnel must make educated and strategic decisions in today's rapidly changing local, national, and world markets. One of the most successful methods for teaching students to critically analyze sport business situations and make educated decisions is the case study method.

This book is a sport marketing case study book. The primary purpose for this book is for students to apply what they have learned about sport marketing principles and concepts to simulated sport business situations. Further, it was written to help the student obtain a high level of competency in critical analysis, problem identification, decision making, and solution development.

In addition, this book was written for the sport marketing instructor. Sport management and sport marketing instructors are always searching for course material and sport business case studies and for ways to make their courses a more meaningful learning experience for their students. The objective is to make the course material more relevant by using real situations. This book provides a key resource and will help the instructor by serving as a model for new courses and as a tool for existing courses.

Features

The book is divided into two parts. Part One contains two chapters. They are written as overview chapters and should not be considered conclusive. They provide a starting point. There are many case analysis models in general marketing literature that could be used in sport marketing case analysis. The reader is encouraged to try more than one model in order to find one that works best for her or him.

Part Two contains the cases in three sections. The sections reflect the three industry segments developed in sport marketing research in an industry segmentation model by Pitts, Fielding, and Miller (1994) (see appendix). This model offers a unique way of looking at the sport industry by categorizing products according to product function. A sport marketer needs to understand the functions, utility and benefits that a consumer is looking for in a product. For example, Erin wants a better batting average, more hits and home runs, and better hitting control in softball. Erin must have a product that will provide those functions and benefits. Therefore, the marketer must understand that the company is providing a product whose functions will be to increase batting average, hits, home runs, and improve hitting control.

The cases in this book were selected based on reality, various marketing problems in different marketing areas, and a variety of sport industry settings. Some contain issues that challenge sport management professionals. Some issues today that affect the sport business industry include environmental concern, human rights, economics, politics, the world as market place, global humanity, and others. The intent is to place the student in situations that depict the world today and in the future.

The cases vary in length and complexity. This does not mean that a short case is a simple case. A case of any length may challenge the student's knowledge of basic sport marketing principles and the student's creative and analytical skills.

None of the cases contain all the facts relevant to or existing in the specific situation presented. This challenges the student to learn to detect "black holes" in information and then to make educated assumptions.

How to Use This Book

This book may be used as a single text for a class or may be used in conjunction with other textbooks or course materials. In many situations, the instructor has already prepared case study materials and has no textbook. I believe the instructor will find this book useful as a text and as a secondary resource.

In addition, although this book is intended for use in undergraduate sport marketing and sport marketing case study courses, it may be used in a variety of classes and may even be useful to practitioners. The reader is encouraged to review its content for potential use in a variety of situations.

Finally, this book was written to be a companion book to *Fundamentals of Sport Marketing* (Pitts and Stotlar, 1996). All cases are based on those basic fundamentals of sport marketing as found in Pitts and Stotlar. The book could also be used for graduate seminar courses on sport marketing. There are 15 cases, which would allow the use of one case per week in a typical 15-week semester.

References

Parks, J. B., Zanger, B., & Quarterman, J. (1998). *Contemporary sport management.* Champaign, IL: Human Kinetics.

Pitts, B. G., Fielding, L. W., & Miller, L. K. (1994). Industry segmentation theory and the sport industry: Developing a sport industry segment model. *Sport Marketing Quarterly, 3* (1), 15–24.

Pitts, B. G., & Stotlar, D. K. (1996). *Fundamentals of sport marketing.* Morgantown, WV: Fitness Information Technology.

ACKNOWLEDGMENTS

There are many people to be recognized for their help and contributions in a variety of capacities to bring this book to reality. Each person's contributions are appreciated, and I would like to recognize them. First, I want to thank the contributing authors. They are some of the best faculty in sport marketing, all of whom are well known in sport management in the United States, some of whom are recognized around the world for their expertise. They have worked long and hard to bring to the field the first case study book in sport marketing. I think the reader will agree that the cases are extraordinary.

I want to thank Janet Parks and the editorial board of the Sport Management Library (SML). The SML is a significant contribution to sport management. Many of the books are the first of their kind and will serve as the foundation upon which future books are written. Dr. Parks has been the guiding force for the SML and deserves our highest recognition for her vision, leadership, and work.

Charlie Song (San Jose State University) and Denny Ruth Kelley (University of Tennessee) provided exceptional critical reviews of earlier drafts of this manuscript. Their analysis and vision for changes toward creating a much better and more user-friendly book were significant. The contributing authors join me in thanking them.

Earlier versions and drafts of this manuscript were tested in one of my courses and by Denny Ruth Kelley in one of her courses. Our students' evaluations and feedback were very helpful. I appreciate their help and appreciate Dr. Kelley's willingness to test the cases. Thank you.

Karen Groves, a computer graphics design specialist, turned the tables and graphs into neat and professional works of art. Thank you, Karen.

Finally, I want to thank the real companies who gave us permission to write about their businesses and who have released their information for this book. We hope this partnership between sport management education and the sport industry will continue and we will work with other companies in future editions of this book.

PART I

An Introduction to the Case Study Method

CHAPTER 1

An Introduction to the Case Study Method

The Sport Industry, Sport Management, and Sport Marketing 3

Introduction to Case Study 3

Objectives of Case Study 4

Purposes of Case Study in Sport Marketing 6

Help for the Student 7

    Group Work 9

    Communication 10

    Research 11

The Instructor's Role 11

    Group Work 12

    Communication 13

    Research 13

Suggested Further Reading 13

The Sport Industry, Sport Management, and Sport Marketing

The sport industry is "the market in which the products offered to its buyers are sport, fitness, recreation, or leisure-related and may be activities, goods, services, people, places, or ideas" (Pitts & Stotlar, 1996, p. 3). The sport industry is enormous and varied, consisting of a great variety of companies, organizations, and products. Students who want a career in the sport industry are majoring in sport management, the young and emerging field of study that prepares one to enter the sport industry. Sport management is "all people, activities, businesses, and organizations involved in producing, facilitating, promoting, or organizing sports, fitness, and recreation products" (Pitts & Stotlar, 1996, p. 2). The sport industry consists of much more than people who are directly involved with managing sports. For example, the industry includes those companies that manufacture equipment or promotional merchandise; those businesses that produce uniforms and other apparel or shoes; services such as racket stringing, golf club cleaning, or laundry; professional services such as legal advice, promotional advice, or advertising; and those companies that design, build, or manage sports facilities.

Sport marketing is one aspect of sport management and is "the process of designing and implementing activities for the production, pricing, promotion, and distribution of a sport product to satisfy the needs or desires of consumers and to achieve the company's objectives" (Pitts & Stotlar, 1996, p. 80). It is a major management function for any sport business and requires continual strategic planning. A student in sport management must acquire sport management, including sport marketing, skills and knowledge. Using case studies is a method for gaining some of the knowledge and skill needed. It allows the student a real look at situations that exist in the sport business industry. The cases involve a variety of sport business settings and include a variety of marketing problems that the student may face.

Introduction to Case Study

In sport management curricula, students are expected to learn a base of knowledge, master analytical and conceptual thinking, become prepared to successfully meet the challenges of the real world and the sport business industry, and develop the ability to deal with the daily issues and problems to be confronted in their profession and at their workplace. Most curricula in sport management provide the field experience as a way for students to apply what they are learning, be exposed to and learn about a real sport business, and gain practical experience. Additionally, many instructors in sport management are increasingly using case study. Using cases, students practice the fundamentals of sport management in the classroom and learn to analyze a situation and recommend appropriate action if needed. One of the primary differences between field experience and case analysis is that field experience takes place outside the classroom in actual sport business settings. Case study takes place inside the classroom. The two methods complement each other. In case study, the students learn from situations that may or may not be real. Therefore, if mistakes are made, they can be corrected without consequences to a real sport business. The students are guided by the instructor toward better thinking, analyzing, and developing solutions.

In many sport marketing courses, students practice the fundamentals of sport marketing using case study. A case puts forth sport marketing circumstances in a particular situation in a sport business. A case might involve one sport marketing element and a single product, or many elements and issues and an entire company. The student's task is to analyze the factors and issues, develop appropriate courses of action or strategies, estimate possible consequences, and determine a best strategy or plan of action.

Case study provides the student experience in wrestling with a variety of problems and issues, honing analytical skills, explaining and defending assessments, and formulating strategies that are feasible and that should work. Many times, cases used in the classroom are presented without a complete set of facts. This is a more realistic portrayal of the real world. The purpose for this is to encourage students to develop some realistic assumptions about the incomplete information and the situation presented. This becomes a part of the student's assessment of the situation and eventually may become part of the proposed course of action.

Objectives of Case Study

The primary objective of using case studies in sport marketing is to provide classroom experience in which the student may apply the theory and principles of sport marketing to simulated sport business situations. In using case analysis, emphasis should be placed on the process of analylzing situation and arriving at decisions, not the final decision. The student should understand this and should not expect to be trying to find a "right answer or solution."

The process includes conducting research and the objective critical analysis of various information. The student learns the process with the guidance of the sport marketing course instructor. Through this practice the student will form an analytical and decision-making framework for approaching a situation, analyzing it, and formulating decisions and solution strategies.

Perhaps the greatest objective of case study is to teach the student to think critically and independently. Of course, the student must be given the full opportunity to develop that skill. The instructor provides a decision-making framework. The student uses the framework to identify problems, if there are any. Then, the student uses the framework to analyze the situation, begin to formulate possible strategies for handling the situation, identify the consequences of those strategies, and determine a best course of action.

If the instructor provides too much direction, the student will simply follow the instructor toward the answers. The student must be allowed to develop work on a case completely even if the instructor knows that the student's plan will not work. Afterward the instructor should point out to the student the weaknesses and strengths of the plan, why they are weaknesses and strengths, and why it most likely is not the best plan of action. In most cases the student's plan is not one that will not work at all. It might be that the student's plan is one that has too many weaknesses or one that will create ineffective or negative consequences to work effectively and successfully. This teaches the student to predict the possible consequences of the solutions.

In trying to predict consequences of solutions, the student tries to determine if, how, and why something will or will not work best for a given situation and what will be the effect of the solutions on people, the environment, or other factors. Based on these predictions the student may make changes in order to strengthen the plan of action or in order to impact the effect the actions may have on people, the environment, or other factors.

Case study requires a lot of work from the student and the instructor. Each must come to the class well prepared in order to effect success. Case study requires that the student become an analytical thinker, and this can be demanding. The student must learn how to determine if problems exist in a case, formulate objectives from which a solution plan will be developed, predict outcomes and consequences, change parts of the plan if needed, and defend decisions and strategies.

It requires the instructor to be a guide, not a lecturer with all the answers. The instructor must allow the student to think independently and yet appropriately question the student's decisions as a means of helping the student foresee the consequences of decisions. This brings reality into the classroom. The student is required to think and act as a responsible employee faced with a real problem.

On the other hand, case study does not replace actual work experience, nor should case study be regarded as a means of providing a student with all of the tools needed to analyze and solve problems. The student is preparing for the day she or he holds a fully responsible professional position in the sport industry. The skills developed in sport marketing case study — research methods, critical analysis, consequence analysis, and strategy development — are critical tools to take into the sport business industry.

Purposes of Case Study in Sport Marketing

Theory is merged into reality. The case study method offers an opportunity to apply classroom theory and fundamentals to case situations in order to test one's understanding of the theory and to determine its usefulness. The case study method allows the testing of ideas that look good in theory, but might not be practical in an actual situation. Students will draw from their knowledge of theories and fundamentals gained from courses in sport management and sport marketing to analyze the situations and develop strategies.

Attention is focused on the multiple factors and issues that can influence decisions. The case study method focuses attention on the infinite variety of goals, problems, facts, conditions (internal and external), conflicts, and personalities that exist in sport industry businesses and organizations. The student must determine what these factors and issues are in a particular case, give them consideration in analysis of the problems in a situation, and give them consideration when developing plans and strategies.

Critical thinking and decision-making abilities are developed. Critical thinking involves objective analysis. In case study, the student is required to study situations objectively and without jumping to conclusions, determine if problems exist, identify and analyze them in order to determine the root of the problems, recommend specific actions to be taken to correct or improve the situation, analyze and forecast the possible consequences of decisions, and determine a way to evaluate the entire situation and solutions.

The student should learn not to jump to conclusions. This requires the student to develop patience until the situation can be studied. Case study helps the student develop the ability to suspend making a decision until a full understanding of the situation has been developed, all elements that may be affected have been identified, all facts — directly and indirectly related — have been gathered, all consequences of any course of action have been predicted, the best course of action for that situation and for that time has been selected, and all was done in an educated and objective manner.

This helps the student develop intellectual and emotional poise.

Sport marketing elements are identified and utilized in the decision-making process. The cases used in this book vary in content, cover a variety of sport industry settings and products, and involve a variety of issues. Some of these are sport marketing research, consumer analysis, product management, pricing, organizational structure, promotional methods, leadership issues, cultural diversity issues, legal issues, and distribution. Most of the cases involve more than one element and issue. This helps the student develop the ability to identify which marketing elements are involved. This then helps the student to develop educated strategies.

Objectivity, sensitivity, and professional ethics are developed. Today's society consists of people with great diversity in lifestyles, race, values, opinions, age, handicap, and many other elements. Additionally, there are many issues and concerns in society that bring about heated debate. It is important to understand that personal beliefs, attitudes, or values toward an issue or a person may influence decisions, and that those decisions will have either a negative or positive impact. Therefore, the student should be certain that those decisions reflect attention to law, discrimination, professional ethics, and other considerations. Through case study, students can begin to develop objectivity, sensitivity, and a code of professional ethics that will help guide them in developing strategies and making decisions.

Help for the Student

Working with cases can be fun and challenging. It can also be frustrating. Let's talk about the enjoyable and challenging side of case study first. While you, the student, assume the role of a sport marketing director, or an associated role, you are given a free hand to study the case, try to discover and unlock any problems in the case, and to develop strategies about how to correct or radically change a situation according to what you believe will work. This freedom takes some time to get used to. In most all other courses, you sit and take lecture notes with the purpose of memorizing them for an exam. In using case study, there are practically no lecture notes to memorize. The purpose of case study is to teach you to think, to analyze critically and objectively, and to develop decisions and strategies that will work best for a particular situation.

There is no one correct answer in case study. There are different ideas, solutions, and strategies that can work effectively. In each situation, you develop a plan of action that will probably work best for that situation and will probably reach the objectives you formulated. There are many facts, issues, and other factors to be considered in a case. There are almost always people involved. It is your job to analyze the situation, determine if there are problems needing attention, formulate objectives that will guide you through developing a plan of action, and develop solutions or a plan of action that will work best for that particular situation.

Your plan should be discussed and analyzed by the instructor and the class. Through this process, you will learn whether or not your idea will work. If it is found that the idea will not work very well, this does not mean that it is a wrong answer, it is just one that will not work very well for that particular situation. This, of course, is when the process becomes frustrating. You believe you have uncovered all the problems in a case. You spend countless hours putting together what you believe is the greatest plan around. You believe the plan is perfect. Then your bubble is popped! The instructor or other students in the course point out that a few of the problems you uncovered are not really problems needing immediate attention. You missed the most pertinent problems in the case. Others also point out that some of your solution objectives are self-serving and will probably offend a particular population. Finally, they question the solution strategies on which you worked very hard. They point out that a few of these strategies will have more negative consequences than positive and that it would be best that you drop those strategies and develop different ones.

You must remember in these situations that the instructor and the other students are not attacking you personally! Therefore, do not throw away your work. Make notes on what others have discussed about your work. Listen to them and seriously consider their perspectives and ideas. Remember this: After one case study, you simply are not going to be able to think as critically and completely as you will after you have worked on many case studies. In other words, with lots of practice, you will learn to identify most of the problems in a case and how your decisions will affect various populations, to think of many more solution options from which to choose, and to predict the consequences of your plans.

In addition, you will learn that your work will go through many changes. Initially, this is hard to take. People tend to be afraid of change. This is because we spend so much time trying to get everything around us set in some sensible order and never change it. We also tend to think that change is weakness. Further, we are conditioned to make decisions based on our own personal beliefs, preferences, prejudices, and ideas about what is right and wrong. Keep in mind that this is exactly what you should not do. For example, think about what would happen if a judge were to use her or his personal religious beliefs in making decisions in the courtroom. Of course, this does not mean that you must change your personal beliefs. It means that as a professional person in a position making decisions that will affect a company, employees, customers, and many other things you must try your best to make sure those decisions are entirely objective, the best and most appropriate for that situation. In that capacity, you carry the responsibility for the consequences of your decisions. Therefore, it is in your best interest to make decisions that are best and appropriate and will have mostly positive consequences. When you consider making changes to your plans in this context, you will realize that change is better. Your plan will be stronger, better, and a more appropriate plan for that situation.

Group Work

There should be assignments in which you will work on a case or a project with a group. Learning to work with a group is important. There will be many times in your career in which you will work with a group or a team. In a real workplace, groups are given official titles like committees, task forces, or commissions. You should capitalize on the opportunity to experience group work and learn how to work in a group.

The first skill you must learn when working with a group is listening. You have a responsibility to listen. You never know when someone will have the idea that will be the best idea for a case. Therefore, rule number one is that you should take each person in your group seriously. This can be tough to do. There will certainly be individuals in your group with whom you disagree on many points, who is different from you in many ways, who simply gets on your nerves, or any number of factors. You must be intelligent enough and professional enough to leave those factors outside the group project. Stay professional and objective.

There will be a different perspective about a case from each individual in the group. Listen to each one. A single individual simply cannot think of every possible perspective, idea, solution idea, objective, or other factor to consider in a case. Each perspective will help you obtain a better and more complete understanding about the case. Each will help you understand how ideas and decisions can affect people in different ways. Through this process, the end result will be a project that is stronger than many projects completed by a single individual.

Another rule of group work is that each person in the group must participate equally. Actually this will practically be impossible as each person's characteristics are different, and some will contribute more work than others will. However, it never hurts to try. Try to learn what each person's skills are and how those skills can be best utilized in the group to complete the task. Do not be afraid to communicate your thoughts, ideas, and perspective about any item being discussed in the group. Encourage others to do the same.

Another goal of group work is for the group to learn how to organize a group, manage a group, assign tasks within the group, and keep the group on the right track. You will notice that in a group some individuals will tend to take charge more easily and more often than others. There are advantages and disadvantages to this. An advantage is that there is someone in the group with natural management skill. That is good for the group. There is someone who will manage the group. A disadvantage is that this person might not be the appropriate leader for the group or for the project. Someone must recognize this and move to change the leader. Another disadvantage is that if one person is always taking charge, then others never have a chance to be the leader. Again, someone must recognize this and specifically appoint those individuals who need the practice.

Communication

Communication is very important. If you cannot communicate your ideas, thoughts, suggestions, or critical analyses, no one will understand what you are trying to say. Therefore, you must learn to communicate orally and in writing. Oral communication is usually very different from communication in writing. Writing typically requires proper English grammar and composition and correct spelling. In your career, there will be plenty of times when you will be required to prepare reports or projects in writing. Imagine what your boss will think about you if you cannot communicate your ideas, if your English is poor, or if you can not spell correctly. The time to learn to communicate is now, not when you are on the job.

The skills of negotiation and persuasion as forms of communication are important. You already possess these skills although they are probably very limited. For example, have you ever argued with a parent to raise your allowance? Have you ever tried to convince a friend to see a particular movie even though the friend has stubbornly refused? In these conversations, you most likely used a number of arguments and reasons why your proposal should be accepted. Now it is time for you to improve those skills. In case study, consider your arguments and reasons that will support your ideas. Develop those reasons that show why you have made particular decisions. Use research and communication skills to make your arguments stronger.

Research

Don't be afraid of the word "research." Research does not always mean setting up an elaborate study and conducting it for a long period of time. It also does not always mean spending countless hours in a library reading everything there. Research, in its most rudimentary forms, involves experimenting, investigating, studying, exploring, examining, gathering information, and searching for answers. As a sport marketer you will be conducting research. Your research will involve many methods depending on your purpose: conducting surveys, conducting consumer analysis, test marketing a product, searching for information to support a marketing proposal to the boss, and many other forms.

You should use research in case study. The information you find for a case will help you develop stronger strategies. For example, if there are legal matters to attend to in a case, you could seek help from an attorney, or you could go to a law library and find information there that would help. The result is that you have researched for answers or for data and found what you needed, and the information becomes a strong part of your case.

The Instructor's Role

Teaching with case studies can be fun. Keep in mind that this approach is definitely challenging. You now enter into an instructor-student relationship that is different from lecture-only classes because using case studies is different from delivering lectures.

The atmosphere you will develop in the classroom is very important. The atmosphere must be one that is nonthreatening to any student. This can be done by establishing rules to which the students must adhere when participating in discussion, group work, and individual work. The students must be encouraged to be open and forthright with their ideas. It is a scary moment for most students when they present their work for analysis. They are afraid of failure, nonacceptance, mockery, or other factors. You must establish an atmosphere that is open, accepting of, and objective about each student's work. The student must know that no idea is a stupid idea. It could possibly be the very best idea, or it is simply one that is not the best for that particular situation.

The student will ask you for the right answers. You must be prepared to help the student understand why you believe the idea is not right for that particular situation. This involves analyzing and predicting the effects or consequences of the student's ideas. All decisions have consequences, and most have both positive and negative consequences. Point out those positive and negative consequences.

You might feel an overwhelming urge to tell your students what you would do in the cases. The students might beg you to tell them. Remember, most of the students are looking for what you would do because they believe the instructor's solution is the "right" one. Therefore, if the student learns how you would approach a situation and how you tend to develop solutions for the situations, that is exactly what they will try to copy.

Keep in mind that sometimes you might be wrong about your analysis of a student's work. Therefore, do not judge a student's plan too quickly. Always allow the student plenty of time to discuss the reasoning behind decisions and actions. Allow time for a discussion of the student's predictions of the consequences of the plan. You will find that for every student in your class there will be that many ideas about what to do in a situation.

Keep in mind that the case study method of learning is not an infallible one. The direction and guidance you offer will have a profound effect on the student's developing attitude and professionalism. It is important, therefore, that you make every effort to use the case study method in an appropriate manner. You must take an objective role and allow the student to present her or his arguments in full, after which, you and the student should analyze the student's work for strengths and weaknesses in light of appropriate actions, ethical actions, and actions and strategies that are best for the situation presented.

Philosophies and attitudes the student learns throughout the case study experience will most likely stay with the students well into their first job. This experience undoubtedly increases the student's capacity to approach a situation, analyze it effectively and finally to develop objectives and strategies for action if needed. In this approach you must guide the student in such a way that she or he arrives at decisions through careful and objective analysis: the examining and reexamining of all the facts and other information pertinent to the situation.

Group Work

One goal of case study should be to develop the ability to work in a group. The objective here should be to teach the student to learn to listen to others in a group, organize and assign tasks, and work effectively with others. Therefore, use some case studies as group projects. Discuss the importance of learning to work in a group. Develop some guidelines for working in a group. Develop a method for evaluating each individual's contribution to the group work.

Communication

Communication is important. The student must learn to communicate orally and in writing. Develop assignments and projects that require the student to communicate orally and in writing. For example, use assignments and activities in which the student must make oral presentations and assignments and activities that require the student to perform written tasks with the case studies.

Find ways to develop the student's ability to negotiate and to persuade. The skills of negotiation and persuasion are important to the sport marketer. Communication and research are the necessary skills to be effective at negotiation and persuasion. Encourage the student's use of these skills. Develop assignments and activities that require the use of them.

Research

Research is important in sport marketing. The student must learn to do research. Finding answers and information is necessary for a sport marketer to do a successful job. Encourage research with the cases as a means of obtaining information, using information, and supporting decisions.

Suggested Further Reading

Bannon, J. J., & Busser, J. A. (1992). *Problem solving in recreation and parks.* Champaign, IL: Sagamore Publishing Inc.

Culkin, D. F., & Kirsch, S. L. (1986). *Managing human resources in recreation, parks, and leisure services.* New York: Macmillan Publishing Company.

DeSensi, J. T., & Rosenberg, D. (1996). *Ethics in sport management.* Morgantown, WV: Fitness Information Technology, Inc.

Kraus, R. (1994). *Leisure in a changing America: Multicultural perspectives.* New York: Macmillan Publishing Company.

Moody, P. E. (1983). *Decision making.* New York: McGraw-Hill Book Company.

Pitts, B. G., & Stotlar, D. K. (1996). *Fundamentals of sport marketing.* Morgantown, WV: Fitness Information Technology, Inc.

Thoma, J. E., & Chalip, L. (1996). *Sport governance in the global community.* Morgantown, WV: Fitness Information Technology, Inc.

Zeigler, E. F. (1982). *Decision-making in physical education and athletics administration: A case method approach.* Champaign, IL: Stipes Publishing Company.

CHAPTER 2

A Strategic Sport Marketing
Case Analysis Model

Overview of the Strategic Sport Marketing Case Analysis Model 15

Phase One: Situation Analysis and Problem Identification 16

Phase Two: Sport Marketing Analysis 19

Phase Three: Sport Marketing Solution Development 20

Suggestions for Activities and Assignments 22

Overview of the Strategic Sport Marketing Case Analysis Model

The strategic sport marketing case analysis model presented in this book is the result of many years of searching for the complete case analysis model. It was developed from various case analysis models (see the "Suggested Reading" section at the end of this chapter)

The strategic sport marketing case analysis model presented here consists of three phases (see Figure 1). In Phase One, Situation Analysis and Problem Identification, the student must examine the situation, determine if problems exist, and identify those problems. In Phase Two, Sport Marketing Analysis, the consumer and product markets must be analyzed. Phase Three is the Marketing Program Development. In Phase Three, solution objectives are formulated, and strategies and plans of action are developed.

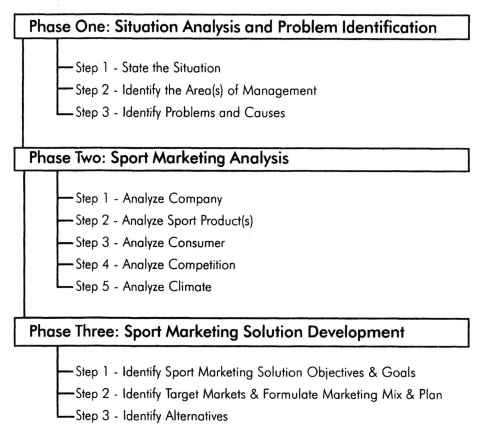

Figure 1
Sport marketing case analysis model

You should study the model to understand the complete model and each of its steps. Practice using the model on a case or two. If you find it hard to remember some of the sport marketing concepts you learned in sport marketing class, take out your notes from that class and your textbook, and refer to them when needed.

In some cases you may not be able to apply every step. Remember that the cases vary in length, situation, and the amount and type of information given. In this situation you are expected to make educated assumptions about the missing information. That is, it is not a good analysis to simply state that the information is missing. The good analysis will point out that certain information is missing and will make intelligent assumptions about the voids.

Phase One:
Situation Analysis
and Problem Identification

The first step in analyzing a given situation is to examine the facts, evidence and all other pertinent information available. If you determine there are problems, then you must determine the underlying root of the problems.

One of the purposes of Phase One is for you to learn how to seek and identify the facts in a given situation. You should not make immediate conclusions or assumptions without all of the facts. You will learn how to recognize all of the facts pertinent to a situation in order to make educated decisions.

Another purpose of Phase One is for you to learn to analyze a situation according to specific factors in order to determine if there are any problems. Do not assume that there are problems just because you are given a case to analyze. Analysis means that one must examine and reexamine the entire situation from all angles and from all viewpoints, consider the damages, identify the consequences, and determine if these are really problems that need correcting.

Remember that every situation is unique. The facts, information available, people involved, and other factors within any given sport business situation can be different from other situations. You may draw upon past situations and experience and study the analysis and decisions made in those cases that are similar to a present situation. This will help in analyzing and developing strategies and solutions for problems. There is, however, a danger in referring to how you solved a prior problem. The danger arises when the problem solver does not study the new situation, compare it to the old one, and analyze it properly. The necessary time to study the new situation is not taken, and a quick and easy answer is given: "Let's do that again. It worked the first time."

Another method that is helpful to analyze and develop solutions is to study other businesses and what strategies are being used. A sport marketer should always study other businesses, sport and nonsport. There may be strategies that will work for the company or solutions that will work for your problems. Another reason for studying your competition is to understand them. You may use this knowledge in many different ways to help your success.

The intelligent decision maker will not simply apply a solution plan from a prior situation even though it may be the easy way out. The extra amount of time spent to properly analyze a situation and arrive at educated decisions can often be the difference between success and failure.

One approach to analyzing and solving problems is to hire a sport marketing consultant. This, of course, will cost money and in some cases, quite a bit of money. The knowledge gained from a sport marketing case study course will not give all the answers but should provide an analytical framework that may be used in most problem situations. Using that framework as a foundation you will have a basic knowledge with which to approach a situation.

There are three steps in Phase One. Study each one carefully. Discuss it with your instructor and other students in class in order to understand it thoroughly before using it.

Step 1: State the Situation. The purpose of Step 1 is to study and understand a situation. You will objectively identify all the pertinent facts, people, and other factors in a situation. You must seek to really understand what has happened, what might happen, who is involved, and the personalities of those involved. Resist the temptation to proclaim you already know the problems in a case. You have only just begun to get to know the case.

In Step 1 you will act as a detective. You will gather all the facts and evidence in the case. You will study the case until you can state the situation in your own words. Here are some ideas on working through Step 1.

Read the case several times. Make notes about certain facts and information given and about information you believe is missing. Describe the situation in your own words orally and in writing. Read the case again. Check your description of the case with the actual case again. Add to it if needed. Do not identify any problems at this point.

Identify any and all marketing elements readily apparent in the situation, such as, research, product, price, place, and promotion strategies given, product development, and market or industry analysis.

Step 2: Identify the Area(s) of Management. Determining what management areas the situation falls into will help you determine problems and will help you develop solutions for those problems. This guides you to resources that may be used if needed. It also guides you to the individuals within those management areas on whom you might need to call for help either in identifying problems and/or in determining solutions for the problems. Does the situation seem to be a legal one? Might it be a personnel one? Has the situation come about because of something in the area of facilities? Is it a pricing strategy situation? There are also other areas of management and marketing to consider, such as program management, distribution, consumer behavior, advertising, product policy, legislation, and licensing.

Once you have identified the areas within which you believe the situation falls, identify resources available. For example, if one area is personnel management, a resource you will probably want to use is the personnel policy manual. If the situation seems to fall into the new product development area, you will want to know what the company policies are on new product development and who works on those policies.

Step 3: Identify Problems and Causes. It is now time to try to determine if there are any problems in the case, what the problems are and the causes of those problems. First refer to your work in Step 1. Ask this question: What brought about this situation? Your answers to this question will be your first list of problems for the case. Now ask this question about each problem you listed: Is this really a problem? The answer to that is whether or not the situation brought about is a negative one or a positive one. If the situation is negative for the company or for the people involved, then you have a situation in which something needs to be addressed. If it seems to be a positive one, then perhaps nothing needs to be changed.

Ask many more questions about the situation. For every question you ask, ask an opposite question. For example, if you ask this question, Why didn't sales of the new golf clubs increase in May?, an opposite question would be Why did new golf club sales increase in months other than May?

For every problem you identify, consider the opposite. In other words, do not be satisfied with one line of questioning or examination. Ask questions or cross-examine from another perspective. This will help you to see many more sides of the situation and will help you to really uncover the real problems and causes of those problems.

The purpose for identifying the causes of problems is that herein lies the real root of the problem. If the root of the problem is not corrected, then the problem is likely to recur. Do everything you can to uncover the causes of your list of problems. These are the factors for which your solutions will be developed.

Phase Two: Sport Marketing Analysis

After thorough analysis and discussion of a situation to the point that you are satisfied and you have identified objectively the problems and causes in a situation, it is time to analyze the situation from a marketing perspective. This is done after the situation analysis because you must understand the situation from an overall perspective first and then from a marketing perspective. Keep in mind that marketing is only one facet of an organization and must not be considered in a vacuum. All areas of a company are linked.

After identifying the problems in a case, you will analyze the case from a marketing perspective. This is done after determining the problems because it will help you make educated decisions concerning solutions for the case.

Step 1: Analyze the Company. Analyze the company or organization according to the following: history, growth of company, location, population, number of employees, strengths of the company, weaknesses of the company, and financial situation and financial resources.

Step 2: Analyze the Sport Product(s). List and describe the sport product(s) offered by the company or organization. Describe the products' functions, utilities, and benefits. Identify the current and historical product life cycle stages. Identify the sport industry segment according to the Pitts, Fielding, & Miller (1994) model (refer to the appendix). Describe the strengths and weaknesses of the product(s). Describe the present price and cost structure.

Step 3: Analyze the Consumer. Identify the consumer markets the company targets currently. Describe them in detail (if given in the case). Describe the nature of the demand for the company's existing products. Describe the extent of demand. Describe the strengths and weaknesses of the current markets. Identify potential new markets.

Step 4: Analyze the Competition. Identify the competition and describe them in detail. Estimate the number of competitors and their market shares, financial resources, and marketing resources. Describe the strengths and weaknesses of the competition. Identify potential future competition.

Step 5: Analyze the Climate. Identify environmental factors affecting the situation, such as social, legal, and political environments. Discuss the possibility of future changes in environmental factors that might affect the situation.

Phase Three:
Sport Marketing Solution Development

The development of solution objectives and the marketing plan is the final phase in the case analysis model.

Step 1: Identify Sport Marketing Solution Objectives and Goals. You will need to consider if you need objectives that are long-range, short-range and stop-gap. Long-range objectives might be objectives that could take a year or 10 years to complete. Short-range objectives might take a month or more. Stop-gap objectives exist to remedy a situation immediately until other short — or long-range solution objectives can be developed.

How will you know which type of objectives you need? There is no specific formula. Objectives are developed out of how you want to solve problems and what you want to accomplish through those solutions.

Based on your complete analysis of the situation, the problems and their causes, what do you want to accomplish through your solutions for this case? Do you simply want to remedy a problem, or do you want to go further and turn the problem into a new opportunity for the company? Is it a problem that requires a stop-gap solution? Are the problems ones that require complex solutions and quite a length of time to pursue? What will you need in order to pursue solution objectives you set? Do you have those resources? If not, how might you obtain them?

Before moving on to the next step, you should consider the possible consequences of your solution objectives. This is difficult to do. Try to predict the outcome of your objectives based on the problems and the situation of the company. What can you estimate will be the positive consequences, and what will be the negative consequences? For example, a positive consequence is that a particular solution objective will be achieved. A negative consequence of the same objective is that you might lose a particular consumer segment. Now consider the impact of each of the consequences. What are the overall advantages and disadvantages of each of the consequences for the company in many respects? You might decide that the negative consequence will not have a great impact on the company. Therefore, the solution objective is one that will mostly positively affect the company. Your decision is to keep the objective.

Step 2: Identify Target Market(s), Formulate Marketing Mix and Marketing Plan. Not every one of your sport marketing problems will require a complete sport marketing plan. However, if your solution objectives calls for changing a marketing plan or creating a new one, then you must know the process of developing a marketing plan.

After making final decisions on your marketing solution objectives, it is time to identify your target market(s) and to develop the marketing mix and marketing plan. These decisions should be based on your objectives. This is the plan of action to be used to achieve your objectives.

Your first step is to identify your target market(s). This may already exist if you are working within an existing marketing plan. If not, this process begins with the identification of your consumer market segments. If you don't remember how to do this, refer to material from your sport marketing class and textbook.

Your next step is to develop the marketing mix: product, price, promotion, and place. Make your decisions based on your objectives and target markets. Again, if you need help, refer to your sport marketing class notes and textbook.

After making decisions on your marketing mix components, plan strategies for the achievement of them. Your strategies should include decisions on factors such as, but not limited to, time schedules, financial resources available, financial resources attainment, people needed to work on the plan, work schedules, other materials needed, deadlines, contracts, licensing if needed, and legal counsel if needed.

You now should try to predict the consequences of your plan of action. Just as you did for your objectives, try to determine what the positive and negative consequences of these actions will be for your consumer and your company. If necessary, change segments of your plan until you reach a point that you are satisfied with the consequences and the effect on the consumer and the company.

Step 3: Identify Alternatives. Do not throw away all of the ideas you developed earlier. Keep those ideas. You might be able to use them as alternatives if something goes wrong with your original plan. In other words, this step can be thought of as Plan B to back up Plan A if it does not work as you anticipated.

Suggestions for Activities and Assignments

Each instructor who uses case studies has most likely developed an individual style for this method of instruction, has probably developed case studies, and might have a variety of activities and assignments that she or he uses with case studies. If you are that instructor, the following activities and assignments are offered to add to your possibilities. For those instructors who are using case studies for the first time, the following activities and assignments and the case analysis model will help you have an easier start.

Questions. For each case, there is a set of questions that may be used in many ways. Here are a few examples: Choose specific questions or use all of them; discuss the questions in class; divide the class into groups and have each group discuss the questions; have the groups discuss one or two of the questions and present their discussion to the class; assign the questions as an out-of-class written assignment; use the questions as exam study guides; use the questions as exam questions.

Use the case analysis model in a variety of ways. Here are a few suggestions: Have the students apply only one phase of the model; use selected steps of the model; assign a case for out-of-class analysis, and have the students turn in a written analysis of the case using the model; use the model in class for analysis and discussion; use the model for the final exam; have the students give oral presentations of their analysis with the model.

Use the case analysis model as the framework for the semester. There are three phases in the model. Use one phase for the first third of the semester, the second phase for the second third, and the third phase for the last third. During the second third of the semester, the student uses both Phases One and Two. In the last third of the semester, use all three. This gives the student time to master one phase at a time.

Team Projects. Divide the class into small teams. Have the teams use the model or certain parts of the model with a case. Have each team present its work to the class for analysis.

Role Play. Choose a case you believe will lend itself well for role play. Assign parts and roles. Have the students act out the case and their solutions in class.

Other outside assignments. Ask the student to find a sport industry case study in another marketing case book and bring it to class for discussion.

Develop a list of basic marketing questions. Ask the students to find and bring to class sport magazine or newspaper articles about the sport industry. Use the list of questions in number 4 below to discuss the article from a sport marketing perspective. Sample questions might include:

- What is the sport product discussed in the article?
- Are the consumer markets discussed? If so, who are they? If not, what do you believe they are?
- Are marketing or advertising or promotions discussed in the article? If so, identify them.
- Do you believe these promotions are appropriate for the product and the consumer? If not, what would you do?
- Who are the competitors?
- What is the sport industry segment?
- What is the nature of this segment?

Brief Case Analysis for Small Group Work. In class, this activity is best used at the beginning of the semester (or quarter) as a lead-up activity for later in-depth case study. Following are the steps for the activity:

1. Prior to the class, select cases. The number of cases will depend on how many groups you will establish, how many cases you want each group to discuss, and if you want each group to use the same case or different cases. The time needed for this is approximately 75–90 minutes. (As an incentive for thorough discussion, have each group give a presentation of their case and discussion. This usually takes about 5 to 10 minutes per group.)
2. Establish groups of 4 to 5 and assign a leader of each group.
3. The students should have their sport marketing course notes and text available for reference during the discussion.
4. Give the following list of discussion questions to each member of each group, and begin.

(1)

Briefly describe the sport business/organization. Include business type, company location, and general background information about the business.

(2)

Are business objectives given? What are they? Discuss.

(3)

Who are the consumer target markets? Discuss the demographics and psychographics of the consumer markets for this company.

(4)

What is (are) the product(s) offered by this company (product market and industry analysis)? What is (are) the product line(s)? What are the product items in the product line(s)? Analyze all facets of the product(s), such as what function does(do) the product(s) fulfill for the consumer?

(5)

Determine which sport industry segment the product(s) may be categorized as (refer to the appendix).

(6)

Discuss the demand for these products. What is the market share of this company?

(7)

What are internal and external factors in the sport industry segment that might affect the business?

(8)

What are the prices for the products? What are the pricing strategies? Do you believe the product will sell for the set price?

(9)

What is the distribution system of the company? Is it effective? Would you suggest another distribution strategy?

(10)

What are the promotional mix and promotional strategies of the company?

(11)

Do you see any opportunities or problems of the company in this situation? What are the factors you believe are causing the problems? Discuss the problems and opportunities and discuss possible solutions for them.

(12)

What is your complete analysis of this company and your solutions for its problems/opportunities?

References and Suggested Reading

Bannon, J. J. (1987). *Problem solving in recreation and parks.* Champaign, IL: Management Learning Laboratories.

Bannon, J. J., & Busser, J. A. (1992). *Problem solving in recreation and parks.* Champaign, IL: Sagamore Publishing Inc.

Bernhardt, K. L. & Kinnear, T. C. (1985). *Cases in marketing management.* Plano, TX: Business Publications, Inc.

Pitts, B. G., & Fielding, L. W. (1991). Strategic sport marketing: Case analysis. In Parkhouse, B. L. (Ed.), *The management of sport: Its foundation and application.* St. Louis: Mosby Year Book.

Zeigler, E. F. (1982). *Decision-making in physical education and athletics administration: A case method approach.* Champaign, IL: Stipes Publishing Company.

PART II

The Cases

How the Sport Marketing Case Studies Are Organized

Case study does not require that the case studies be organized or categorized in any particular method. However, it is common that case studies are organized in some manner to help the instructor and student in using the cases in a more productive way. In marketing, case study textbooks sometime organize the cases according to marketing tasks, such as promotion, pricing, or distribution. Some are organized according to type of industry, such as service industry, entertainment industry, or music industry.

The case studies in this book are organized according to research involving sport industry segmentation. In their study, Pitts, Fielding, and Miller (1994) suggest that the sport industry can be divided into three industry segments: the sport performance industry segment, the sport production industry segment, and the sport promotion industry segment. Pitts et al. argue that all products in or related to the sport business industry can be categorized into one of these three segments. Understanding the sport industry as a whole and in parts — industry segments — can provide guidance for the sport administrator in decision making. The sport marketer must understand product functions, utility, and benefits to be able to truly give the consumer what the consumer wants. Read the study provided in the appendix in order to understand the segments. In addition, study chapter 8 in the Pitts and Stotlar (1996) textbook for a better understanding of product functions, utility, and benefits.

The cases are divided into three sections. The sections are titled by the three sport industry segments as developed in the Pitts, Fielding, & Miller Industry Segment Model (1994). The purposes for using a research study as a framework for this book are to apply research to the industry and to provide a guideline to ensure that you have opportunity to work on a variety of sport business case studies. The article and model are reprinted in the Appendix. You will want to refer to it often.

This book is also written to be a companion book to *Fundamentals of Sport Marketing* (Pitts & Stotlar, 1996). You will want to use the principles of sport marketing in working on the cases. You may also want to use other textbooks specific to sport marketing and sport management as references. There are some selected ones in the sections titled "Suggested Reading" at the end of each case.

References

Pitts, B. G., Fielding, L. W., & Miller, L. K. (1994). Industry segmentation theory and the sport industry: Developing a sport industry segment model. *Sport Marketing Quarterly, 3* (1), 15–24.

Pitts, B. G., & Stotlar, D. K. (1996). *Fundamentals of sport marketing.* Morgantown, WV: Fitness Information Technology.

SECTION 1

THE SPORT PERFORMANCE INDUSTRY SEGMENT

The Sport Performance Industry Segment: An Overview

In this segment of the industry, sports performance is the product for sale. Sports performance products include sports, recreation, leisure, and fitness activities. These all have one thing in common: They are activity products. Activity products in the sport industry are sold to consumers in two broad categories: participation and spectatorial.

The consumer can purchase participation products including participating in a basketball tournament, joining a fitness center to work out, hiking in the Himalayas, scuba diving at Cozumel, camping in the Smokey Mountains, canoeing on the Mississippi River, and running in a marathon. All of these products are participation products.

The product for sale is sport performance as a participation product. The sport marketer selling this product must understand the special product attributes of participation in order to enhance success of properly promoting the product and selling it. People participate in sports for many reasons, some of which are fun, recreation, entertainment, competition, social, love of the sport, fitness, and weight maintenance or weight reduction. Therefore, as with any other product, if sport marketers understand these product functions, they can communicate more effectively through advertising and other promotional methods to enhance their chances of selling the product. To see this in practice, find advertisements for fitness centers in your local newspaper. Read them and notice the language used in the ads. Do you see any of the product functions mentioned here, such as lose weight, get in shape, have fun, meet people?

Sport performance is also sold in a very different way in the sport industry. It can be sold as an entertainment, or spectatorial, product. Some of these include college soccer matches, body-building contests, and basketball games. Today, many sports events are created almost solely for the purpose of entertainment. Consider, for example, the American Gladiators, boxing, and men's arena football. Why would a person pay an admission fee to watch a basketball game? There are many reasons, most of which are related to entertainment. Some of these are, to have something to do, to have fun with friends, to support the team, to try to get on television, to be a part of the action, or to watch a known player perform. Therefore, the sport marketer needs to study and understand the consumer to determine why the consumer buys the product. This knowledge is used for specific marketing strategies, such as advertising, pricing, and scheduling. Again, watch for newspaper advertisements or television commercials about a sports event. You will notice the way the ad or commercial communicates to you in that it attempts to make the event attractive to you enough that you want to attend. One example to consider is the advertising for the annual Super Bowl. The marketers are trying to make the event sound appealing enough to entice you to go to the event, or at least to watch it on TV.

The common element is sport performance, and the sport marketing person must concentrate on the functions and benefits of either participating in or watching an activity. As the sport marketing person better understands the utilities, functions, and benefits of these products, chances for communicating with the consumer about the product are increased. Refer to chapter 8 in the Pitts and Stotlar (1996) textbook.

The cases in this section include two participation and three spectatorial cases. There are professional and ethical issues to consider in some cases as well as the many other marketing elements.

EVERY GAME'S A BIG EVENT: THE TOLEDO MUD HENS BASEBALL CLUB

Jacquelyn Cuneen, Bowling Green State University

Professional baseball has been played at various sites in Toledo, Ohio, since 1883. Teams had a variety of names such as White Stockings, Swamp Angels, Black Pirates, and Glass Sox. Bay View Park was the home site in 1896. Bay View was situated near a marshland that was brimming with peculiar-looking birds with short wings and long legs known as marsh hens, rails, or mud hens. The abundance of the birds near their park gave the Toledo Mud Hens Baseball Club their enduring nickname (Toledo Mud Hens Baseball Club, Inc., 1994e).

The Mud Hens are currently a beloved Toledo tradition. Residents of northwest Ohio and southeast Michigan consider the Hens to be a local treasure. Fans check Hens' scores and standings regularly; advertising signs at various fast-food restaurants and other surrounding businesses support the Hens throughout the year by posting messages related to the Hens' schedule and record; infants, children, and adults can be seen attired in Mud Hens clothing routinely; and names of Mud Hens players are as recognizable to Toledoans as those of any currently popular major league phenomenon.

The Mud Hens are one of the few minor league baseball teams to have achieved international fame. Toledo native Jamie Farr was frequently attired in a Mud Hens' cap and game shirt while portraying Maxwell Klinger on the M*A*S*H television situation comedy when the program aired regularly on CBS-TV. Currently, Farr can be seen wearing the Mud Hens clothing in M*A*S*H syndication worldwide. The team's unusual opportunities for publicity through Farr's portrayal of Klinger seem to have reaped rewards; *Baseball America* ("Reader Survey," 1994) reader survey results indicated that Mud Hens was the favorite minor league team nickname among baseball fans. The current popularity of collecting minor league baseball merchandise has also favored the Mud Hens; Rousselot (1992) identified the Hens' cap as #4 of the top 10 favorite minor league baseball caps to own. Mud Hens baseball contributes much to Toledo commerce, travel, and tourism. Many tourists traveling in the region call the Hens ticket office requesting tickets to see Klinger's favorite team.

City of Toledo Activities

Toledo, Ohio (population 332,900), is located on U. S. Routes 75 and 80/90, and State Routes 23 and 25 approximately one hour south of Detroit, Michigan, two hours west of Cleveland, and three hours north of Cincinnati. The city is situated on the western end of Lake Erie at the mouth of the Maumee (the largest river flowing into the Great Lakes). Toledo is one of the world's busiest freshwater ports and the third busiest port on the Great Lakes. The Maumee's natural harbor has 35 miles of frontage (Greater Toledo Convention and Visitors Bureau, 1994).

Toledo is predominantly an industrial city with several national manu-facturing plants including Chrysler, Jeep, Libbey, Inc., Libbey-Owens-Ford, Owens-Corning, Owens-Illinois, Dana Corporation, and others. Nu-merous crude oil and gas pipelines are directed to Toledo, making the city a major refining center. The city is also world famous for glass production.

During the spring, summer, and autumn, when the Mud Hens play, there are several citywide events at staggered intervals, or other Toledo perma-nent tourist or resident attractions (Greater Toledo Convention and Visitors Bureau) that would interest groups and individuals:

1. Toledo's major annual celebration is a Rock Rhythm 'n' Blues Festi-val held during Memorial Day weekend. Food, beverages, games, and other activities are part of the festival.
2. An annual Northwest Ohio Rib-Off (cooking contest) is held on the waterfront in early spring. Food, beverages, games, and other activi-ties are part of the festival.
3. Rally By the River featuring specialty foods, beverages and profes-sional entertainment is held on the waterfront each Friday night.
4. A 2-day German-American Food Festival is held in late August.
5. Toledofest Celebration of the Arts is staged on the waterfront over Labor Day weekend. Food, beverages, games, and other activities are part of the festival.
6. Raceway Park interests many tourists and residents for harness rac-ing events.
7. The Toledo Storm minor league hockey club (Riley Cup champion in 1993) plays at the Sports Arena from late autumn to late spring.
8. The LPGA-Jamie Farr Toledo Classic golf tournament is played at an area golf course for one week at the beginning of July.
9. The University of Toledo (UT) sponsors professional entertainment and concerts in its Glassbowl Stadium periodically. UT also conducts

an NCAA Division I sports program from late summer to late spring.

10. Fort Meigs, a reconstructed fort from the War of 1812 era, is open daily until 5:00 PM.

11. The 57-acre Toledo Botanical Gardens is open daily from 8:00 AM to 9:00 PM.

12. The Toledo Museum of Art contains more than 700 paintings by celebrated European and American artists as well as books, manuscripts, sculptures, medieval ivories, prints, tapestries, and glass. Admission to the museum is free except for special exhibits.

13. The 30-acre Toledo Zoo, containing more than 450 species of mammals, birds and reptiles in natural habitats or aquariums, is open daily from 9:00 AM to 5:00 PM.

14. The S. S. Willis B. Boyer is docked at Toledo's International Park. The Boyer is a 1911 era freighter that was the largest, most modern Great Lakes ship of its time. It is now a museum depicting freighter history and is open Wednesday to Sunday from 10:00 AM to 5:00 PM.

15. Toledo has a nationally respected symphony and ballet. Symphony and ballet seasons begin in late autumn and conclude in late spring.

16. Numerous other activities, such as ethnic festivals, riverfests, amateur theater, and various sporting activities, such as fishing, and golf are available.

Toledo's central location both as a port and major highway thoroughfare draws many travelers for overnight or extended visits. The city is also beginning to develop some distinction as a convention city. The Seagate Center is the site for larger conferences; Seagate features a 75,000 square foot exposition/trade show hall and 25 large meeting rooms.

Immediate proximity to Detroit and Cleveland sport and culture creates a natural competition for any Toledo event, and the Mud Hens understand the multiple competition rooted in both Toledo events and those originating in the surrounding area. The primary marketing objective for the Mud Hens is to maintain high attendance yearly and to continue to break the previous year's attendance records. The Hens have framed their primary marketing strategy to draw consumers by positioning baseball games in a product line that features other types of concurrent entertainment. Their theme involves making "Every Game A Big Event" for fans; each game is characterized by a special occasion or giveaway.

Product

The Mud Hens are owned by the County of Lucas, and the baseball club is a nonprofit, but self-supportive organization (i.e., no owners or shareholders gain dividends, but the baseball club must generate its own revenue in order to operate). The club is administered by a six-member board of directors (president, vice president, secretary-treasurer, two board members, and general manager) who receive no remuneration for their services. A 10-member advisory board works with the board of directors. The advisory board comprises local leaders and business executives who confer with the board of directors on various issues.

Mud Hens management consists of three assistant general managers (Community Relations, Media Relations, Ticket Operations). Other front office staff include directors for (a) marketing and entertainment, (b) marketing and sales, and (c) marketing and promotions as well as a business manager, ticket manager, clubhouse manager, head groundskeeper, stadium maintenance coordinator, and office secretary. There are various other staff positions, such as bookkeeper, public address announcer, club physician, trainer, official scorers, radio announcers, ticket manager, maintenance crew chief, and the field and coaching staff (Toledo Mud Hens Baseball Club, Inc., 1994f).

The Mud Hens' home field is Ned Skeldon Stadium located in Maumee, Ohio, a convenient suburb of Toledo. Skeldon Stadium is easily accessible from Interstate Routes 75 and 80, and State Routes 23 and 25. The stadium is 29 years old and is in excellent condition. Seating capacity is 10,025 with 2,587 box seats, 1,238 reserved seats, and 6,200 general admission seats. Skeldon Stadium has a special section designated for family seating; no alcohol is permitted in the family section. Capacity of the family section is 650.

The Hens have been a minor league farm club for five different Major League Baseball teams since their inception, but currently are an AAA team whose players are "one step away" from the Detroit Tigers. Several "name" athletes have played for the Mud Hens: Ray Chapman, Jim Thorpe, Hack Wilson, Casey Stengel, Pete Gray, Joe Niekro, Rick Cerone, Kirby Puckett, Frank Viola, Willie Hernandez, and others are Mud Hens veterans. According to *Baseball America* ("American League East," 1994a), 4 of the Tiger's top 10 future prospects currently play for the Mud Hens.

The team has been affiliated with the International League since 1965. The Hens play up to 144 games per year. All official (i.e., not exhibition) games feature other AAA opponents exclusively; teams that visit Skeldon Stadium bring numerous top 10 prospects representing their major league affiliates. Table 1 shows International League teams, locations, and major league affiliations (International Baseball League, 1994).

Table 1
Mud Hens Record Since 1965

Year	Wins	Losses	Percentage	Finish	Team Affiliation
1965	68	78	.466	7th	New York Yankees
1966	71	75	.486	6th	New York Yankees
1967	73	66	.525	3rd	Detroit Tigers
1968	83	64	.565	1st	Detroit Tigers
1969	68	72	.486	6th	Detroit Tigers
1970	51	89	.364	8th	Detroit Tigers
1971	60	80	.429	7th	Detroit Tigers
1972	75	69	.521	5th	Detroit Tigers
1973	65	81	.445	4th	Detroit Tigers
1974	70	74	.486	3rd	Philadelphia Phillies
1975	62	78	.443	7th	Philadelphia Phillies
1976	55	85	.393	8th	Cleveland Indians
1977	56	84	.400	8th	Cleveland Indians
1978	74	66	.529	3rd	Minnesota Twins
1979	63	76	.453	7th	Minnesota Twins
1980	77	63	.550	2nd	Minnesota Twins
1981	53	87	.379	8th	Minnesota Twins
1982	60	80	.429	7th	Minnesota Twins
1983	68	72	.486	5th	Minnesota Twins
1984	74	63	.540	3rd	Minnesota Twins
1985	71	68	.511	6th	Minnesota Twins
1986	62	77	.446	6th	Minnesota Twins
1987	70	70	.500	5th	Detroit Tigers
1988	58	84	.408	4th	Detroit Tigers
1989	69	76	.476	4th	Detroit Tigers
1990	58	86	.403	4th	Detroit Tigers
1991	74	70	.514	3rd	Detroit Tigers
1992	64	80	.444	3rd	Detroit Tigers
1993	65	77	.458	5th	Detroit Tigers

Note. Adapted from *Toledo Mud Hens 1994 Media Guide*, p. 26, by Toledo Mud Hens Baseball Club Inc., 1994. Copyright 1994 by The Toledo Mud Hens Baseball Club, Inc. Adapted with permission of the author.

The International League competes with two divisions: Eastern (Rochester, Ottawa, Scranton/Wilkes-Barre, Pawtucket, Syracuse) and Western (Charlotte, Richmond, Columbus, Norfolk, Toledo). The Mud Hens have posted various records against division opponents over past years (see Table 2).

Table 2
International League Teams and Major League Affiliations

Team	Location	Affiliations
Charlotte Knights	Charlotte, NC	Cleveland Indians
Columbus Clippers	Columbus, OH	New York Yankees
Norfolk Tides	Norfolk, VA	New York Mets
Ottawa Lynx	Ottawa, Ontario, Canada	Montreal Expos
Pawtucket Red Sox	Pawtucket, RI	Boston Red Sox
Richmond Braves	Richmond, VA	Atlanta Braves
Rochester Red Wings	Rochester, NY	Baltimore Orioles
Scranton/Wilkes-Barre Red Barons	Moosic, PA	Philadelphia Phillies
Syracuse Chiefs	Syracuse, NY	Toronto Blue Jays
Toledo Mud Hens	Toledo, OH	Detroit Tigers

Note. Adapted from *International League Record Book 1994*, pp. 36-73, by the International League of Professional Baseball Clubs, 1994. Copyright 1994 by International League of Professional Baseball Clubs. Adapted with permission of author.

In the past 7 years, the team has posted .500 records twice. Generally, the team plays .400 level baseball. Performance records do not appear to affect attendance substantially.

The Mud Hens have broken single-season attendance records each year since 1991 (Toledo Mud Hens Baseball Club, Inc., 1994f). Average daily attendance is 3,553; average nightly attendance is 4,271. Final figures for the 1993 season indicated that 285,155 fans attended Mud Hens baseball games.

Unique Features of Mud Hens Baseball

Numerous activities and pranks involving the fans make attendance at Mud Hens games different from attendance at other baseball games. Hens management attributes some attendance successes to unique game features that make attendance fun for spectators by involving them in high-jinks between or during baseball innings. Fans sign up at the Hens Customer Service Desk (located near the entrance gates, souvenir and concessions stands) to participate in various activities and contests such as:

Dancin' with Muddy: The Mud Hens team mascot is Muddy the Mud Hen. Muddy circulates throughout the stadium during games and randomly appears somewhere in the stands in the middle of the third inning to lead the section in a dance to a favorite tune of the day.

Homerun Inning: If the Hens hit a home run during the fourth inning, a fan whose name is drawn wins a brand-name cellular phone.

Safe at Home Dash: Children age 14 and under may be selected to race Muddy around the bases before the start of each game. If children reach home safely before Muddy, they are eligible for a drawing to win season-ticket coupon books to use the following year. The contest is sponsored by a local home security firm; Muddy has yet to win the dash.

Superfan: Fans may complete an essay of 25 words or fewer explaining why they should be the game's "Superfan." The superfan winner is announced at the end of the fifth inning; winners receive a Hens cap and T-shirt compliments of the daily Toledo newspaper.

Singers in the Stands: Fans may sign up to sing "Take Me Out to the Ballgame" during the seventh-inning stretch. A cordless microphone is delivered to their seats, and singers win free hot dogs compliments of a brand-name food distributor.

Car & Boat Race: Skeldon Stadium owns a sophisticated score and message board capable of generating unique graphics. Chad, the Hens' scoreboard operator, has achieved some local celebrity by generating creative graphics and contests. For instance, the message board shows a daily or nightly race between a car and a boat. Fans on the first-base line cheer for the car while fans on the third-base line cheer for the boat; fans behind home base cheer for a tie. Randomly selected fans on the winning side receive various products compliments of a local waste management firm.

Hens' Jukebox: Lists of songs are displayed on the message board at the end of the seventh inning, and fans cheer for the song they wish to hear. Chad's noise-meter determines the winning song according to cheers, and fans sing along with the recording.

Various other events and comical giveaways are featured. Several lotteries are held during the game using those halves of spectators' tickets that have been retained by gate attendants. When numbers are announced, spectators report to the Hens Information Desk to claim their unannounced prize. Prizes are donated by local enterprises and may include a used tire, a movie marquee poster, a bookstore display, bicycle handlebars, or numerous other whimsical prizes. Prizes and winners are displayed to the crowd via Chad's message board.

Single Game Attendance Incentives

The Mud Hens and various sponsors stage numerous promotions and giveaways (Toledo Mud Hens Baseball Club, Inc., 1994f). Giveaways range from standard to unique. Typical giveaways such as cap nights or photo nights, are sponsored by locally owned or franchised enterprises. The Mud Hens also provide humorous or useful novelties or special appearances for nearly each game. Table 3 contains a partial list of single-game incentives.

Normal ticket prices apply for all giveaway games. There is no age limit restricting the giveaway of novelties. All promotions and giveaways are advertised heavily by the Hens; Mud Hens' estimates show that giveaway sponsors are featured in advertising packages worth approximately $9,148 (Toledo Mud Hens Baseball Club, Inc., 1994c).

Famous Mascot

Muddy the Mud Hen received national-level press coverage from *Sports Illustrated* (O'Brian, 1993) when James G. Konecny, Assistant General Manager and Media Relations Director, secured a shoe contract for Muddy through a regional representative for Converse. Muddy is present for all Mud Hens games and events. The mascot moves around each section of Skeldon Stadium but always returns periodically to Muddy's Nest atop the Hens' dugout. Muddy may be armed with any number of gadgets, such as a large, plastic children's baseball bat used as a conductor's baton to prompt the crowd, or a super size water shooter used to heckle.

Muddy attends various community functions and is frequently an invited guest to local children's and adult's birthday parties. The Hens and a national-franchise ice cream retailer sponsor an annual "birthday bash" for Muddy as a pre-game event each July. Muddy's friends, including Yogi Bear and other famous characters, attend to celebrate with the fans.

Photographs of Muddy are popular in the Toledo area, especially if they are personally autographed. Muddy is also featured on a line of baseball cards that have the mascot posed in various comic or athletic positions.

Concessions and Souvenirs

Concessions and souvenir stands are located in the large concourse immediately inside the entrance gates. The Mud Hens offer traditional baseball-

Table 3
Partial Listing of Mud Hens' Special Game Incentives

Sponsor and Event	Sponsor's Origin
Mud Hens Opening Day	Local (Mud Hens)
Pepsi Night 1	Regional-National
CableSystem Night	Local
Detroit Tigers Exhibition	Local (Mud Hens)
Anderson's/Eveready Battery Night	Local-National
Martian Antenna Night	Local (Mud Hens)
Sherwin Williams Painters Caps Night	Local-National
Famous Chicken	Local (Mud Hens)
U. A .W. Night	Local
NW Ohio Chiropractor Night	Regional
Shriners' Night Parade	Regional
Friendly's-Muddy's Birthday Bash	Local-National
Detroit Tigers/Toledo Tussle	Regional (Mud Hens)
Mud Hens Banner Day	Local (Mud Hens)
Toledo Blade Reader's Night	Local
Ramada Inn Team Photo Night	Local-National
Turn Back the Clock Weekend	Local (Mud Hens)
Burger King/TV 5 Kids Clinic	Local
Manwich Cap Night	National
Famous Chicken 2	Local (Mud Hens)
Ohio Baseball Hall of Fame Induction	Regional (Mud Hens)
Baseball Card Show	Local (Mud Hens)
Food Town Family Sunday	Regional
Karaoke Night	Local (Mud Hens)
Disco Night	Local
Sports Illustrated for Kids Give-away	National
Toledo Blade "Dawn-Patrol" Carriers Day	Local
Hens Fans Appreciation Weekend	Local (Mud Hens)
Kids Club Activities	Local (Mud Hens)
Little League Parade	Local (Mud Hens)
Arrow Thru the Head Give-away	Local (Mud Hens)
Advertisers Appreciation Night	Local (Mud Hens)

Note. Adapted from 1994 Mud Hens Schedule: *Every Game's a Big Event*, p. 6 by Toledo Mud Hens Baseball Club, Inc. Copyright 1994 by The Toledo Mud Hens Baseball Club, Inc. Adapted with permission of author.

park-type foods, snacks, and beverages at two concessions stands. Mud Hens Pizza and Hens Ice Cream Sandwiches are specialty exclusive concession foods (i. e., specially blended and/or prepared ingredients) and are available only at Skeldon Stadium. Mud Hens Pizza is not sold at regional chain or independent grocery outlets. Hawkers (15–20 per game) circulate the stands with food, snacks, and beverages. Concessions are prepared and managed by a local catering firm. Prices of food and beverages at Skeldon Stadium vary but are below typical ballpark prices.

Souvenirs are sold at the Hens' Nest, a large store located in the concourse under the third-base grandstand. A full line of Mud Hens clothing, accessories, and novelties is available; Detroit Tiger merchandise is also sold. Prices of clothing and other souvenirs are comparable to typical ballpark prices.

Mud Hens merchandise is also sold by local retailers (chain and local department stores, discount stores, convenience stores, specialty shops, and so forth). The Hens have no merchandise catalog, but do produce a product and price listing of merchandise for mail-order customers. Information is sent upon customer request; there is no mailing list.

Place

Skeldon Stadium is part of the 180-acre Lucas County Recreation Center complex. The Toledo Mud Hens Baseball Club, Inc., rents the baseball facility from Lucas County at an annual rate of $1.00. In addition to Skeldon Stadium, the complex contains the Lucas County Fair grounds, the County Recreation Center, and the Ohio Baseball Hall of Fame. The Hall of Fame is a smaller version of the National Baseball Hall and features memorabilia honoring Major League Baseball players who are Ohio natives. The Ohio Hall holds inductions each fall during a Mud Hens game. There are 35 acres of free parking at the recreation complex; parking capacity is 21,000 vehicles.

Hens home games are broadcast via WFRO-AM and WMTR-FM radio. Listenership statistics and radio user demography have not been ascertained by the stations.

All International League teams are granted permission to originate radio broadcasts from Skeldon Stadium. The local cable system televises at least five Hens games per season using a four-camera set-up.

Price

The regular price per ticket to regular season Mud Hen's games is $5.00 for box seating, $4.00 for reserved seating, and $3.00 for general admission.

Children age 14 and under and senior citizens receive discounts of $1.00. Single-game tickets for designated special events, such as a Detroit Tigers exhibition game, and an annual "Toledo Tussle," an exhibition game featuring Tigers alumni, are $8.00, $7.00, and $3.00.

Season Tickets or Trade-In-Coupons

Mud Hens season tickets are called Trade-In-Coupons or TICs (Toledo Mud Hens Baseball Club, Inc., 1994g). Unlike traditional season tickets that entitle customers to attend each home game, TICs are redeemed for the games of their choice. TICs books contain 70 coupons, each worth one Mud Hens ticket. Holders of coupons have the option of calling to reserve their seat for any particular game or exchanging a coupon at the Hens' ticket office upon arrival. TICs books are available for box seating (guaranteed seating located within 50 feet of the playing field) at a rate of $210 or reserved seating (guaranteed seating located within 100 feet of the playing field) at a $180. rate. TICs books offer customers savings of nearly 50% off regularly priced tickets, and holders receive preferred parking passes. TICs are restricted for use at the Detroit Tigers Exhibition and Old Timers' games, Famous Chicken and Phillie Phanatic appearances, playoffs, and other special events games.

Mud Hens Trade-In-Coupons are sold by the Diamond Club, a group comprising baseball fans and other volunteers representing the civic, business, corporate, labor, and industrial leaders of Toledo. There are currently 100 Diamond Club members. For the past 16 years, the Diamond Club has sold over 1,000 TICs each season (Toledo Mud Hens Baseball Club, Inc., 1994f)

Diamond Club members are entitled to view Hens games from a modern skybox located behind home base. The skybox contains a food and beverage bar, lounge seating and tables, and enclosed box-seating. The Diamond Club box is also used for pregame parties for up to 30 guests. There are three methods by which interested persons may become Diamond Club members: (a) sell 15 season tickets (Trade-In-Coupon books), (b) purchase a radio advertising package for their businesses , or (c) purchase advertising and promotions packages amounting to $8,000.

Group Sales

Increases in group sales increases are a continuous marketing objective for the Hens, and some options are offered to attract groups and corporations to the games (Toledo Mud Hens Baseball Club, Inc., 1994d). Groups of 25 or more receive reduced-price tickets, same-location seating on pre-ferred sides (i.e., first, third, or home bases); entrance to Ned Skeldon Sta-dium two hours prior to game time; recognition on the message-score board; eligibility for Group Prize-Giveaways; box-seat tickets for future use for group's leader; and a special visit from Muddy. Groups of 100 or more may elect a group member to participate in a ceremonial first pitch. Group ticket sales are promoted through use of a brochure distributed at various high-traffic businesses (e. g., banks, restaurants, and gasoline stations) and by limited mailing (i. e., selected large and small businesses, industries, fans, and so forth). Pricing for group tickets is incremental depending on group size. Table 4 shows the rates for group and hospitality tickets.

Table 4
Rates for Toledo Mud Hens
Group Outings and Corporate Hospitality

Group Size	Box Seat	Reserved Seat	General Admission
25 - 99	$4.50	$3.50	$2.50
100 +	$4.00	$3.00	$2.00

Note. Adapted from *Toledo Mud Hens Group Outing Information*, p. 1, by Toledo Mud Hens Baseball Club Inc. Copyright 1994 by The Toledo Mud Hens Baseball Club, Inc. Adapted with permission of author.

The Mud Hens would like to increase reservations for certain types of group outings. The Mud Hens will work with customers to design individ-ually prescribed packages for special groups events. Events that have been popular in recent years that the Hens would like to stage for each home game are:

Pre-Game Picnics: The Mud Hens offer catered picnics, or "ballpark buffets," for any group. The picnics are targeted toward businesses, indus-tries, schools, families, sororities and fraternities, local or regional service groups, and so forth. The Mud Hens make picnics easy for groups by han-dling all arrangements for food and service. Muddy also visits and entertains at each picnic. There are two picnic areas in Skeldon Stadium: one located behind the extreme left field fence and another behind extreme right field.

Birthday Parties: The Mud Hens offer children's or adults' birthday cel-ebrations at Skeldon Stadium. All arrangements are made on an individual basis by the Mud Hens staff. Ticket pricing for adults' parties are off the rate card; food and beverage pricing is based on amounts and types of catering required. Pricing for children's birthday parties depends on the number of children and adults.

Corporate Hospitality: The Hens can accommodate corporation parties and outings (Toledo Mud Hens Baseball Club, Inc., 1994d). Group size is 25 minimum, but the Hens have cooperated on company parties of 2,000 guests. Ticket prices are determined with the regular group rate card, and amenities such as the first pitch, welcome message, and visit from Muddy and the players are offered.

There is no sales representative assigned specifically to groups acquisition, although an assistant general manager responsible for ticket operations handles all group requests not addressed by the Diamond Club. Groups order tickets by calling or faxing the Mud Hens box office. Payment is made by check, major credit card, or money order, and payment must be received by the Mud Hens no later than 2 days prior to game day. Tickets can be mailed to group leaders or may be obtained at the stadium. Rain checks for groups are provided in two ways: (a) groups may reschedule their outing, or (b) individuals may exchange their tickets for a future game. No refunds are available. Groups may receive special pricing considerations for all Mud Hens games except the Tigers Exhibition, Tigers Old Timers, Phillie Phanatic, Famous Chicken, and other such special-event games.

Summer Fun Packs

The Mud Hens offer two types of Summer Fun Packs to attract spectators to special events and the "bigger" Mud Hens games at Skeldon Stadium (Toledo Mud Hens Baseball, Inc., 1994b). Each Summer Fun Pack contains a different series of tickets. Table 5 shows the ticket contents of each Summer Fun pack.

Table 5
Contents of Mud Hens Summer Fun Packs

Summer Fun Pack # 1	Summer Fun Pack # 2
Mud Hens Opening Day (April 15)	Tigers Exhibition (May 9)
Tigers Exhibition Game (May 9)	Famous Chicken Night (June 9)
Famous Chicken Night (June 9)	Toledo Tussle (July 9)
Toledo Tussle (July 9)	Phillie Phanatic Night (August 13)
Phillie Phanatic Night (August 13)	Hall of Fame Game (August 19)

Note. Adapted from *Mud Hens Summer Fun Packs '94*, p. 1, by Toledo Mud Hens Baseball Club Inc. Copyright 1994 by The Toledo Mud Hens Baseball Club, Inc. Adapted with permission of author.

Summer Fun Packs cost $30.00 for box seats, $25.00 for reserved seating. Summer Fun Packs are marketed in the same way as group tickets (i.e., there is no specially assigned ticket agent, brochures are placed strategically throughout the region, sales are processed as received via phone or fax, and so forth).

Promotion

The Mud Hens promote their product through public service, community activism, and commercial means. A mix of public relations activities, paid advertising and commercial associations takes place throughout the calendar year.

Youth Camp

The Hens and a local sports medicine clinic sponsor a yearly Mud Hens Baseball Camp for girls and boys aged 8–13. The camp is held at Skeldon Stadium, and Mud Hens players and coaches teach fundamental skills. Enrollment is limited to 100 campers. Price of the 2-day camp is $50.00 (Toledo Mud Hens Baseball Club, Inc., 1994a).

Personalizing the Players

The Mud Hens organization collects feature-interest type information relative to Mud Hens players and uses it to help bring the players closer to fans and help player visibility within the community and media. Dossiers listing likes, dislikes, favorite movies, TV shows, vacations, and music preferences of players (and Muddy) are distributed to local media and are used by reporters in their news and feature stories about the Hens.

The management also encourages players to be active in the greater Toledo community by attending public service events; participating in pregame picnic appearances, autograph signings, children's contests and interviews, and making the rounds on morning radio and television shows.

Media Coverage and News Features

Toledo affiliates for ABC, CBS, and NBC television report Mud Hens scores and/or highlights on nightly sports newscasts, and each radio station in northwest Ohio and southeast Michigan reports Hens scores regularly on nightly or morning news broadcasts. It is not unusual for Toledo radio and television stations to report the Mud Hens scores ahead of major league scores, including those of the locally popular Tigers and Indians.

The fans' game-time activities (see section "Unique Features of Mud

Hens Baseball") are frequently reported in Toledo's major daily newspaper. Pictures of fans wearing their giveaway items on Martian Antennae Night or Funny Nose and Glasses Night or pictures of Muddy leading the bleacher section dance or rounding the bases in the children's baserunning contest appear prominently in either the sports or features section of the paper.

Frequent news releases are also prepared by the Hens media department. For instance, when the Hens return to Toledo after extended road trips, their return is announced by listing game dates, times, and the event of the game (such as a home run hitting contest for fans, Independence Day fireworks, Banner Day, and so forth).

Some celebrities playing in the Pro-Am Tournament associated with the LPGA Jamie Farr Toledo Classic have worn Mud Hens clothing during play. Professional basketball player Charles Barkley was the most recent Pro-Am player to be pictured in the daily newspaper wearing a Mud Hens cap.

Industrial Goods

Part of the Hens' plan to generate self-supporting revenue involves sale of advertising to local, regional, and national enterprise and numerous businesses use the Mud Hens' popularity to promote their own products and services (Toledo Baseball Club, Inc., 1994c). Signage is available on left- and right-field fences, scoreboard in center field, concourse, walkways into the stadium from the concourse, picnic and birthday party areas, and customer service desk. Rates for signs vary according to location and preparation. (Costs are increased if the Hens create and paint the signs.)

Prices for outfield signs range generally from $1,600 to $2,000 for a 10' by 14' sign or $3,200 to $4,000 for a 10' by 28' sign. Currently, there are 68 signs in the outfields. Concourse and walkway signs range in price from $600 to $800; there are four concourse signs and three walkway signs.

Advertising on the message center (Chad's scoreboard) is sold on a seasonal basis. Cost per season is $1,080 to show at least one commercial per game or $1,800 to show at least two per game.

Print advertising is also available in Hens' souvenir programs and scorecards. The *Ned Skeldon Stadium Souvenir Program* is 110 pages in length. Program ad costs are based on color, size, and/or location. Table 6 shows rates for program advertising. Costs of advertising are not subject to drastic increases from season to season. In fact, 1993 and 1994 advertising costs are identical. All program advertisers receive free general admission tickets for two special advertisers' nights held in June.

During each game, fans are invited to turn to specific ads in the program

Table 6
Rates for Toledo Mud Hens Souvenir Program Advertising

Back Cover	$2,500	Inside Front	$2,000	Inside Back	$2,000
Full Page	$2,000	Full Page*	$1,200		
Half Page	$1,750	Half Page*	$700		
Quarter Page*	$500	Eighth Page*	$300		

* Denotes black and white advertisement

Note. Adapted from *Toledo Mud Hens Baseball Club Advertising Rates*, p. 1, by Toledo Mud Hens Baseball Club Inc. Copyright 1994 by The Toledo Mud Hens Baseball Club, Inc. Adapted with permission of author.

to search for a lucky number. Special prizes are awarded to those fans who have the lucky numbers. Souvenir programs sell out each season. The Mud Hens' marketing department indicates that at least four other people besides the buyer read each program, and programs are saved for future value (Toledo Mud Hens Baseball Club, Inc., 1994c).

All scorecard ads are black and white; scorecards are contained in the Mud Hens program, which costs $2.00. Full-page score ads cost $1,200, half pages cost $700, and quarter pages cost $500.

Additional Advertising Opportunities for Sponsors

The Mud Hens also offer advertisers the opportunity to advertise on ticket backs, pocket schedules, special events postcards, and other mass distribution vehicles. Rates are negotiated independently.

Games are broadcast via WFRO-AM and WMTR-FM radio. Signals of both stations cover a critical radius encompassing all of northwest Ohio and southeast Michigan. Potential market size of these areas is 19 counties exceeding 3,000,000 persons (Toledo Mud Hens Baseball Club, Inc., 1994c). Giveaway merchandise and services are also awarded to listeners. Contests are conducted in ways similar to stadium contests except call-ins are required. Listeners win free cellular phones, weekend getaways, cash, free clothing, and so forth. Advertising space is available for pre- or postgame sponsorship, scoreboard shows, game MVP, and other. The Mud Hens also cooperate with advertisers by tailoring radio advertising programs specifically for their companies or services.

The Mud Hens offer various radio sponsorship packages to advertisers ranging from Flagship coverage (see Table 7; spots on all 144 Hens games broadcast on WMTR FM) to Network coverage (see Table 8; spots on all 144 games broadcast on WFRO-AM and WMTR-FM).

Table 7
1994 Mud Hens Radio Packages
and Costs for Flagship Coverage on WMTR-FM

Plan # 1 ($17,280)	Plan # 2 ($13,824)
Eight 30-second spots per game	Six 30-second spots per game
Opening & closing billboards	Opening and closing billboards
Twelve 30-second promo spots per week	Nine 30-second promo spots per week
2 season box-seat exchange tickets	2 season box-seat exchange tickets
Diamond Club membership	Diamond Club membership
Plan # 3 ($10,368)	**Plan # 4 ($5,760)**
Four 30-second spots per game	Two 30-second spots per game
Opening & closing billboards	Opening & closing billboards
Six 30-second promo spots per week	Three 30-second promo spots per week
1 season box-seat exchange ticket	1 season box-seat exchange ticket
Diamond Club membership	Diamond Club membership

Total costs per game:		Total cost per spot:	
Plan #1 =	$120	Plan #1 =	$15
Plan #2 =	$96	Plan #2 =	$16
Plan #3 =	$72	Plan #3 =	$18
Plan #4 =	$40	Plan #4 =	$20

Note. Adapted from 1994 *Toledo Mud Hens Radio Packages*, p. 1, by Toledo Mud Hens Baseball Club Inc. Copyright 1994 by The Toledo Mud Hens Baseball Club, Inc. Adapted with permission of author.

Different packages apply for each type of coverage with costs ranging from $5,760 to $17,280 for 30-second commercials.

Advertisers can also purchase commercial time under three different contract rates for Mud Hens radio broadcasts. Table 9 shows the rates per season, month, or limited-time basis.

The Hens receive remuneration from the stations, but stations sell advertising and retain profits from advertising sales.

Table 8
1994 Mud Hens Radio Packages and Costs
for Network Coverage on WMTR-FM and WFRO-AM

Plan # 1 ($18,432)	Plan # 2 ($9,792)
Four 30-second spots per game	Two 30-second spots per game
Opening & closing billboards	Opening and closing billboards
2 season box-seat exchange tickets	1 season box-seat exchange tickets
Diamond Club membership	Diamond Club membership
Total costs per game: Plan #1 = $128 Plan #2 = $68	Total cost per spot: Plan #1 = $32 Plan #2 = $34

Note. Adapted from *1994 Toledo Mud Hens Radio Packages*, p. 1, by Toledo Mud Hens Baseball Club Inc. Copyright 1994 by The Toledo Mud Hens Baseball Club, Inc. Adapted with permission of author.

The Ballpark Is Open: The Hens WWW Page

The Mud Hens maintain a complete, updated World Wide Web page that reports both the latest and total-season game scores, records, and statistics (Toledo Mud Hens Baseball Club, Inc., 1997). Named "The Ballpark is Open," the page contains links that take Web visitors to the (a) Hens Press Box (for specific player information), (b) Mud Hens Store (to purchase souvenirs), (c) 24-hour access ticket office (with encryption for security), (d) Mud Hens Gallery (for a panorama of current and historic photographs), (e) business office (to answer FAQs), (f) Muddy's Buddies page (of special interest for children), (g) Hens library (for historical research), (h) Web Friends page (for Hens discussion groups), and (i) Hens mailroom (for interactive purposes and customer interface). The Hens page also provides linkages for TICs holders to use in making reservations. The Hens make advertising space available on each of the links.

Note: The preceding case as written deliberately contains some information that is directly related to marketing problem solving and some information that may be irrelevant and/or unrelated. Readers must glean appropriate data in order to successfully complete a case study; different types of information will be useful for different questions and/or solutions.

Table 9

1994 Mud Hens Costs for Advertising on WMTR-FM & WFRO-AM.

Seasonal Spots	WMTR-FM		WMTR-FM & WFRO-AM	
	1 Spot	2 Spots	1 Spot	2 Spots
Half Season	$2,016	$3,744	$3,168	$5,760
Third of Season	$1,440	$2,688	$2,112	$4,032
Quarter Season	$1,080	$2,016	$1,584	$3,024
Monthly Spots	WMTR-FM		WMTR-FM & WFRO-AM	
	1 Spot	2 Spots	1 Spot	2 Spots
April	$690	$1,380	$1,012	$2,024
May	$900	$1,680	$1,320	$2,520
June	$840	$1,568	$1,232	$2,352
July	$900	$1,624	$1,276	$2,436
August/September	$990	$1,848	$1,452	$2,772
Individual Spots	1-50	51-100	Over 100	
WMTR-FM	$30	$28	$26	
WMTR-FM & WFRO-AM	$44	$42	$40	

Note. Adapted from *1994 Toledo Mud Hens Radio Packages*, p. 2, by Toledo Mud Hens Baseball Club Inc. Copyright 1994 by The Toledo Mud Hens Baseball Club, Inc. Adapted with permission of author.

Study Questions

1. What (who) are the Mud Hens' target markets relative to the primary marketing objective of maintaining attendance? What key elements in their current marketing strategy address the target markets?
2. Why do the Mud Hens continue to break attendance records? What makes the Hens unique in the Toledo market, and why do they retain their position?
3. As long as the Mud Hens continue to break yearly attendance records, will a lack of consumer demographic data have a substantial effect on the Mud Hens' marketing plan(s)? Why? What advantages would the

Hens gain if they had more complete data on their primary consumers (i.e., those who attend games)?

4. What elements of marketing should the Mud Hens consider in any research to maintain attendance status? What effects should the elements have on marketing strategy?

5. Identify those elements of Mud Hens games that may attract consumers (individual, group, family). What elements may be expanded, or what other elements may be developed to meet the attendance maintenance objective?

6. Which Toledo activities are direct competitors to the Mud Hens? Which are not? What data exist to show that events and activities of those types draw or do not draw similar consumers? Where are the data available? How should the Mud Hens deal with the competitors?

7. Identify some strategies and/or incentives that would help the Mud Hens meet their objective of more group ticket sales. How could Toledo's convention, travel, and tourism trade be accessed by the Hens?

8. Is it realistic for the Hens to expect that pre-game picnics, birthday parties, and corporate hospitality parties would be booked for each home game? Why? How could the Hens market those group sales more effectively?

9. With the success of the Diamond Club relative to season tickets sales (i.e., TICs), should the Hens continue to sell TICs through the Diamond Club? Why? What would be an advantage of hiring a TICs sales staff? Disadvantages?

10. What would be the Mud Hens' advantages of changing from TICs to traditional season tickets? Disadvantages?

11. Identify the strengths and weaknesses of the Mud Hens' per-game pricing structure. Should the Hens increase ticket prices? What does marketing literature indicate about price increases and their effects on consumption relative to sport commodities?

12. Do meaningful preliminary data exist to justify large expansion into secondary consumer markets (i.e., collectors or those with interest but who may not attend)? Should the Mud Hens take advantage of their national celebrity?

13. If they were to take advantage of their national celebrity, what types of marketing and promotion should the Mud Hens use in obtaining national consumer bases? What elements of their product line could be marketed nationally?

14. Would there be any advantage to making Hens' concessions products

(such as Mud Hens Pizza or Hens Ice Cream Sandwiches) available in local or regional stores? Any disadvantages? Should the Hens make the products available?

15. What ways can the Mud Hens justify their pricing of signage although lacking current demographic data? Should the Hens commit to defining their primary users? How should the Hens determine their fan base?

16. Design a demographic data collection for the Mud Hens that would reflect information from the entire season. Design the collection to be currently useful for a 7-year period (i.e., futuristic questions should be included; consider collecting data relative to information super-highways, computer ownership, access to Internet, and so forth, in addition to television, radio, newspaper usage).

17. Determine if the Mud Hens' radio/television broadcast arrangements with the local stations are satisfactory. If yes, explain why. If no, explain why, and outline a more suitable arrangement.

18. Formulate local and regional strategies to promote the Mud Hens and their product(s) during the off-season.

19. Suggest some additional promotional activities and giveaways for the Mud Hens.

20. Suggest some ways in which teams in the International League could cooperate in marketing strategies.

Suggested Readings

Bigelow, C. (1989, January). Spicing up your concessions profits. *Athletic Business*, 42.

Carolin, R. (1989, October). Involving local leaders generates community goodwill. *Athletic Business*, 24.

Ferguson, M. (1990, January). Reaping concessions profits. *Athletic Business*, 36.

Gordon, C. (1987, August). Taking a grassroots approach to research. *Marketing News*, 22.

Hofacre, S., & Burman, T.K. (1992). Industry segmentation theory and the sport industry: Developing a sport industry segmentation model. *Sport Marketing Quarterly*, *1*(1), 31–36.

Peppers, D., & Rogers, M. (1993). *The one to one future: Building relationships one customer at a time*. New York: Doubleday.

Pitts, B. G., Fielding, L. W., & Miller, L. K. (1994). Industry segmentation theory and the sport industry: Developing a sport industry segmentation model. *Sport Marketing Quarterly, 3*(1), 15–24.

Pitts, B. G., & Stotlar, D. K. (1996). *Fundamentals of sport marketing.* Morgantown, WV: Fitness Information Technology, Inc.

Stotlar, D. K., & Johnson, D. A. (1989, September). Stadium ads get a boost. *Athletic Business*, 49.

References

American League East: Top 10 prospects. (1994, February 7–20). *Baseball America*, p. 27.

Greater Toledo Convention and Visitors Bureau. (1994). *1994 official visitor's guide.* Toledo, OH.

International Baseball League. (1994). *International league record book 1994.* Dublin, OH.

O'Brian, R. (1993, March 15). Hen picked. *Sports Illustrated, 78* (10), 10.

Reader survey results: Teams, dollars and sense, executive/non-player. (1994, January 10–23). *Baseball America*, p. 24.

Rousselot, C. (1992, January). No minor passion. *Future Stars*, pp. 22–23.

Toledo Mud Hens Baseball Club, Inc. (1994a). *Mud Hens and sports care present the Toledo Mud Hens 1994 Baseball Camp.* Maumee, OH: Author.

Toledo Mud Hens Baseball Club, Inc. (1994b). *Mud Hens summer fun packs '94.* Maumee, OH: Author.

Toledo Mud Hens Baseball Club, Inc. (1994c). *Toledo Mud Hens baseball: Every game's a big event.* Maumee, OH: Author.

Toledo Mud Hens Baseball Club, Inc. (1994d). *Toledo Mud Hens: group outing information.* Maumee, OH: Author.

Toledo Mud Hens Baseball Club, Inc. (1994e). *Toledo Mud Hens: History in the making* Maumee, OH: Author.

Toledo Mud Hens Baseball Club, Inc. (1994f). *Toledo Mud Hens 1994 media guide* Maumee, OH: Toledo Mud Hens Baseball Club, Inc.

Toledo Mud Hens Baseball Club, Inc. (1994g). *Toledo Mud Hens season ticket information.* Maumee, OH: Author.

Toledo Mud Hens Baseball Club, Inc. (1997). *The ballpark is open.* [Online] Available: World Wide Web http://www.mudhens.com/

Related Professional Associations

National Association of Professional Baseball Leagues
201 Bayshore Drive SE
St. Petersburg, FL 33701
Phone: 813-822-6937
Fax: 813-821-5819
Internet: http://www.minorleaguebaseball.com/info/about.html

Acknowledgment

The author gratefully acknowledges James G. Konecny, Assistant General Manager and Media Relations Director for the Toledo Mud Hens, for his valuable contributions to this project.

Gender Equity Achieved Through Strategic Marketing

Richard L. Irwin, University of Memphis

● ●

Middle State University (MSU) was established in 1910 as a land-grant institution in the north central region of Minnesota. The university has a current enrollment of approximately 16,874 full-time students, 86% of whom are pursuing undergraduate degrees. Recently, the athletic program, which competes as a Division I independent, has encountered thorough scrutiny from the National American Collegiate Athletic Association (NACAA) for illegal activities by university alumnae. The review revealed that several overzealous alumni were providing male athletes with free use of automobiles and housing as well as cash payments with no services rendered. The 2-year investigation resulted in the football program's receiving a 3-year "Death Penalty" sentence as well as the firing of the athletic director, Howard Murphy, and the entire football coaching staff including two-time National Coach of the Year, Payton Fox.

Following an extensive national search, lasting over 6 months, Lu Ming was hired as the new athletic director for MSU. A former Olympic gymnast, Dr. Ming previously served as the Athletic Director at Eastern State University (ESU), an NACAA Division II school in New York City, for the past 5 years. Dr. Ming was considered a perfect candidate for the MSU position as a result of her accomplishments at ESU. During her tenure at ESU, the athletic department gained national acclaim for their gender equity achievements while maintaining a competitive position within the Northeast Athletic Conference (NAC). After inheriting an athletic program almost exclusively composed of males, Dr. Ming was able to balance participation rates that accurately reflected the composition of the university student body, which necessitated a 576% increase in females athletes' participation. Astonishingly, within the same time frame, participation among men increased 4% as well. Furthermore, Dr. Ming was able to secure over $1 million in athletic endowments to help support this valuable institutional mission while maintaining a competitive program.

Not everyone agreed with the hiring of Dr. Ming. There is a large group of male alumni who believe Dr. Ming is not the person for the job. Their contention is that MSU is a big-time athletic program in need of a big-time administrator. This group had a candidate of their own, Mr. Gerald "Jumbo"

Mitchell, a former MSU football star who has been serving as the assistant athletic director at the University of Central Minnesota for the past 3 years. Although Mr. Mitchell was interviewed for the position, it was the contention of the search committee that Dr. Ming not only possessed the skills necessary for "righting the ship" but was described as an "athletic marketing specialist," also a characteristic considered of great importance to the selection group.

Immediately following the hiring of Dr. Ming, Dr. Leonard Smith, an ardent supporter of the athletic department and close personal friend of Mr. Murphy, stepped down as university president citing personal health. Subsequently, Dr. Carol Davis, formerly President/CEO with BMI, a worldwide business machine corporation, was hired by the board of trustees to replace Dr. Smith. It was the opinion of the board that Dr. Davis, with a doctoral degree in marketing, possessed the requisite knowledge and skill to guide the institution into the 21st century. However, throughout the interview process and after the position was accepted, it was made abundantly clear to Dr. Davis that her first priority was to "clean up" the athletic department.

Adding salt to the existing wounds, within the first week of her presidency, an office aide provided Dr. Davis with an article from *US-Today*, a nationally popular daily news magazine, highlighting that MSU ranked at the bottom of all Division I intercollegiate athletic programs with regard to Title IX compliance. Unfortunately, Dr. Davis was not completely familiar with all of the issues related to Title IX. Although she knew the legislation had something to do with equal opportunities for males and females in educational programs, she was unsure how it related to athletics. As a result, she enlisted the help of Dr. Ming in addressing the situation. At the meeting, Dr. Ming provided Dr. Davis with several resources for enhancing her knowledge of the subject area. These included the actual Education Amendments Act of 1972, which included Title IX, Title IX Review Documents from the Office of Civil Rights, National Association for Girls and Women in Sport (NAGWS) Title IX Tool Box, and a variety of articles from *The NACAA News* on the topic of gender equity.

Dr. Ming indicated that the status of the MSU athletic program mirrored the situation she encountered at ESU, which eased Dr. Davis's mind considerably. Dr. Ming only had one request — that the President initiate the indicated actions. It was Dr. Ming's belief that a directive from the institutional CEO would command the attention of all athletic personnel. Dr. Davis was more than willing to fulfill this request after studying the provided materials.

Following the input from Dr. Ming and review of the materials, Dr. Davis called a mandatory meeting of all athletic personnel to deliver the following message: There will be no reinstatement of football, and within 3 years the athletic department WILL achieve complete equity with the following parameters:

1. Participation rates among male and female athletes as well as budgetary allocations accurately reflect gender-based enrollment rates which for the past 5-year period has been female dominated (48% male and 52% female);
2. There will be an equal number of men's and women's teams;
3. Current participation rates among male athletes must remain stable;
4. All promotional efforts aimed at attracting participants as well as spectators will be equitable as required under the provisions of Title IX; and,
5. All external funding opportunities such as sponsorships, booster donations, and endowments will be appropriated equitably among all athletic programs.

Without football, MSU will have 251 males participating in the following sports: soccer (32 athletes), wrestling (25 athletes), track and field (44 athletes), cross-country (28 athletes), baseball (35 athletes), basketball (14 athletes), hockey (27 athletes), lacrosse (24 athletes), and swimming (22 athletes). The women's athletic program has 115 athletes participating in field hockey (26 athletes), basketball (12 athletes), softball (16 athletes), track and field (23 athletes), cross country (15 athletes), and volleyball (12 athletes).

It now becomes the primary responsibility of all athletic department administrative personnel to develop an action plan that addresses the President's athletic equity mandate. Dr. Davis' only request is that the submitted plan follow a typical product-planning procedure, which, according to her, can be found in any fundamental marketing textbook and generally consists of (a) market research yielding product offerings, (b) product test marketing, (c) product modification, (d) production and product availability, (e) marketing mix manipulation, and (f) evaluation and feedback.

According to the President, it is imperative that the strategic plan address the following:

1. Recommendations for women's sports that are to be added to the MSU program complete with supportive rationale for inclusion;
2. Recommendations for the retention of all or some selected men's sports using an approach similar to the one described above;

3. Delineation of marketing strategies with supportive tactics that will be implemented for increasing as well as maintaining participation rates of both the male and female athletes at MSU. This should be done for each sport that is to be added/retained including information on the appropriate market growth vector to be employed (e.g., new market development) and the proposed marketing communications mix to be employed.

At this point the President has not indicated any budgetary limitations except for the fact that expenditures must be equitable. Therefore, possible acceptance of any plan appears to be based on the rationale with which it is presented.

Learning Exercise

In groups of four to five, develop a two-phase strategic plan as requested by Dr. Davis. For the purposes of this assignment, your plan need only consider equity relative to anticipated team participation rates. Be sure to construct strategy based on sound rationale.

Discussion Questions

1. Why is this a sport *marketing* case?
2. What should Dr. Ming's role be in this process? How should she delegate responsibility to her administrative and coaching staff?
3. How important is it that the President's background was in marketing?
4. Are there other groups or consumers in the community who will be affected by theses changes? Who? How?
5. What are some short-term consequences to be expected with this action? What are some long-term consequences to be expected? How should these be handled?

Suggested Readings

Branch, D., & Crow, R. B. (1994). Intercollegiate athletics: Back to the future? *Sport Marketing Quarterly, 3* (3), 13–21.

Carter, D. M. (1996). *Keeping score.* Grants Pass, OR: Oasis Press.

Frankel, E. (1992, November). Gender equity. *Athletic Management,* 15–19.

Mullin, B. J., Hardy, S., & Sutton, W. A. (1993). *Sport Marketing.* Champaign, IL: Human Kinetics Publishers.

NAGWS Tool Box. (1992). American Alliance for Health, Physical Education, Recreation, & Dance.

Sutton, W. A. (1987). Developing an initial marketing plan for intercollegiate athletic programs. *Journal of Sport Management, 1,* 146–158.

Professional Associations

National Association of Collegiate Directors of Athletics (NACDA)
P. O. Box 16428
Cleveland, OH 44126
(216)892-4000
http://www.nacda.com

National Association of Collegiate Marketers of Athletics (NACMA)
(440)892-4000, http://www.nacda.com/about/member/nacmomem.html

National Association for Girls and Women in Sport (NAGWS)
1900 Association Drive
Reston, VA 20191
(800)213-7193
http://www.aahperd.org/nagws/new-nagws.html

Women's Sports Foundation (WSF)
Eisenhower Park
East Meadow, NY 11554
(800)227-3988
http://www.lifetimetv.com/WoSport

Marketing a Basketball Tournament

Wayne Blann, Ithaca College

Background

During the early 1990s student-athletes of color at State University believed they were not being treated fairly with regard to selection and participation on varsity intercollegiate athletic teams, especially on the basketball teams. The student-athletes of color discussed this situation with members of the African-American and Latino Society (ALS) at one of the regularly scheduled meetings. The student-athletes of color expressed their view that the sports environment was hostile toward them and they were experiencing institutionalized ostracism. Because the student-athletes of color believed they were not being afforded fair opportunities to compete on intercollegiate sports teams, especially the basketball teams, they suggested that they wanted to work with the ALS to establish a basketball tournament for students of color.

In 1991 the State University African-American and Latino Society founded The Bringing Brothers Together Basketball Tournament. The purpose of the event was to offer a highly competitive basketball tournament for students of color (women and men) with a positive and supportive sports environment where the players' skills and talents would be appreciated and recognized by the community. During 1991–93, The Bringing Brothers Together Basketball Tournament was successful in developing competitive men's basketball games with a good number of participants/teams and some spectators. The women's basketball participants, however, were small in number, with few teams and few spectators. The participants and spectators comprised women and men of color who were students in the university. Because the ALS marketed the tournament only to students of color on campus, the event was limited in its scope and did not grow in size or popularity.

During 1991–93, the university's Educational Opportunity Program (EOP) Director, staff, and activities committee worked with The Bringing Brothers Together Basketball Tournament as a strategy for bringing EOP alumni back to the campus. The EOP Office made the basketball tournament the focal point of an EOP student and alumni weekend that included other activities to appeal to a larger and more diverse group of people. The EOP Office became a cosponsor with ALS of the newly named The Bringing

Brothers Together Basketball Weekend. The additional resources and leadership provided the ALS by the EOP office broadened the scope of the event, which was now marketed to all students, faculty, administration, staff, and EOP alumni. Those who participated and watched the basketball games were still primarily women and men of color, but some participants and spectators were white. The expanded market resulted in a larger number of men's basketball participants/teams with the games becoming highly competitive and very popular with the spectators. Likewise, the women's basketball participants/teams increased in number, became more popular, and were better attended. Other activities held in conjunction with the basketball tournament included a dinner/dance on Saturday night and a formal basketball awards banquet with a speaker on Sunday night.

Between 1991 and 1993, the event increased in size and popularity. However, between 1994 and 1996, the number of participants and spectators decreased with a significant decrease among women participants and spectators. In 1996 the men's basketball games were heavily marketed and somewhat successful, whereas little was done to market the women's games. There were so few women participants that it was not possible to organize games, so 3-on-3 basketball contests were held for women in place of the games.

Current Situation

In 1997 the university's Diversity Awareness Committee was consulting with the Office of Multiculturalism to identify ways to promote multicultural education and positive relationships among different groups of people in the university and the community. Representatives of the Diversity Awareness Committee and the Office of Multiculturalism met with representatives of the ALS and the EOP Office to discuss the possibility of reorganizing The Bringing Brothers Together Basketball Weekend to achieve these purposes. All groups agreed that changing the event so that it would promote positive relations among diverse groups of people and provide multicultural education programs was a worthwhile endeavor.

Developing a Marketing Plan

A task force composed of representatives of the ALS, EOP Office, Diversity Awareness Committee and Office of Multiculturalism was established to develop a proposal for The Bringing Brothers Together Weekend that would (a) clarify the mission, (b) establish clear objectives derived from the mission, and (c) identify programs/activities that could be marketed to specific targeted audiences to fulfill the objectives and mission.

The task force agreed that the basketball tournament would continue to be the focal point of the marketing strategy. It was further agreed that a special focus would be to increase women's involvement in the event, especially in light of gender-equity concerns currently being addressed by the athletic department. Finally, the task force agreed to consult with sport marketing experts (you and your classmates) to obtain their help in developing a marketing plan within the context of unifying the community and furthering social justice.

Questions for Study

1. Write a marketing mission statement.
2. Write specific marketing objectives derived from and linked to the marketing statement.
3. Describe specific marketing/promotions programs and activities that might be implemented to reach specific target audiences in carrying out the marketing objectives and achieving the marketing mission statement.

Suggested Reading

Blann, F. W. (1998). Sport marketing. In J. B. Parks, B. R. K. Zanger, & J. Quarterman (Eds.), *Contemporary sport management* (pp. 171–184). Champaign, IL: Human Kinetics.

Covey, S. R. (1989). *The seven habits of highly effective people.* New York, NY: Simon and Schuster.

DeSensi, J. T. (1994). Multiculturalism as an issue in sport management. *Journal of Sport Management, 8,* 63–74.

Grunig, J. E., & White, R. (1992). Communication, public relations and effective organizations. In J. E. Grunig (Ed.). *Excellence in public relations and communications management.* Hillsdale, NJ: Erlbaum.

Related Professional Associations

African-American Athletic Association

African-Latino Society, 953 Danby Road, Ithaca, NY 14850, (607)375-2538, http://www.ithaca.edu/admin/cca/cca2/als.html

Association of Black Women in Higher Education, c/o Nassau Community

College, Nassau Hall, Room 19, One Education Drive, Garden City, NY 11530-6793

Black Coaches Association, P. O. Box 4040, Culver City, CA 90231-4040, (888)667-3222, http://www.bca.org
Diversity awareness programs/offices on campuses
Minority affairs programs/offices on campuses

COLORADO XPLOSION OF THE AMERICAN BASKETBALL LEAGUE

Dianna P. Gray, University of Northern Colorado

●●●

Introduction and Problem Statement

Lark Birdsong, General Manager of the Colorado Xplosion, and Anne Price, Director of Marketing for the Xplosion, were concerned about the problem of promoting the second-year franchise in a city that hosts five other professional sports teams. Given the success of the Women's National Basketball Association (WNBA) inaugural season, the task of positioning the Xplosion as a "major league" team in Denver was daunting. Even though the league office had done a great deal in getting the ABL off the ground, it was obvious to Birdsong and Price that the burden of promoting the team and attracting fans rested squarely on each franchise's shoulders.

Although Denver, with a metropolitan area population of approximately three million people, enthusiastically supports the Broncos (NFL), Rockies (MLB), and Avalanche (NHL), attendance at Nuggets (NBA) and Rapids (MSL) games has been spotty. Sold-out stadia are the norm for the Broncos and Rockies, and during the Avalanche's initial season in Denver, the winners of the 1996 Stanley Cup drew an average of 12,350 fans at McNichols Arena. McNichols, with a seating capacity of 14,500, is home for both the Nuggets and the Avalanche. The Nuggets, who struggled during the 1996 season and did not make the playoffs, were in the bottom third of the NBA in attendance figures for the 1995–96 season. The Colorado Rapids, a Major Soccer League franchise, had the lowest attendance figures in the league's inaugural year.

The ABL was established in 1995 to provide postcollegiate competition for elite female basketball players, build on the growing popularity of the women's college game, showcase the premier women's basketball players in the United States, and once the league began playing, take advantage of the tremendous success of the USA Women's Olympic team, winners of the gold medal in Atlanta in 1996. Colorado received one of the eight initial teams, making the Xplosion Denver's newest professional sports franchise. However, Birdsong and Price do not consider Denver's other professional sport teams as their primary competition. The University of Colorado's women's basketball team, perennially ranked among the top women's collegiate programs in the country, and the Women's National Basketball

Association (WNBA), the NBA-backed women's professional league that debuted in the summer of 1997, are direct competitors for a share of the women's basketball fan. In addition, Price sees the Xplosion competing with other entertainment options (attending movies, "malling," outdoor activities, etc.) for customers.

The American Basketball League

The American Basketball League (ABL) made its debut in the fall of 1996 with a 40-game regular season schedule and four playoff games. The league entered the market at a time when women's basketball was at its zenith in the United States, with the NCAA Women's Final Four selling out in advance for the fourth consecutive year and a gold-medal performance at the 1996 summer Olympic games still fresh in fans' minds. More than 13.5 million women play basketball regularly, nearly 25% more than in 1985.

In spite of the fact that the NBA-sponsored WNBA played to record crowds and enjoyed considerably greater attendance success than expected, ABL co-founder and VP Gary Cavalli believes that the ABL will be successful. Cavalli says, "We believe we have the right plan. We are just going to push forward" (Lister, 1996a, p. 3C). Table 1 profiles the eight teams competing during the ABL's inaugural season.

The Players for the First Season

Seven members of the U.S. Olympic team — Azzi, Edwards, Lacey, McCray, McGhee, Staley, and Steding — signed to play in the ABL. Unfortunately, not all of the Olympic team members chose to affiliate with the ABL. Some are playing in Europe or Asia, or chose to sign with the WNBA. Three of the most prominent Olympians — Lisa Leslie, Rebecca Lobo, and Sheryl Swoopes — opted to play with the WNBA. Although Cavalli would have liked to have signed all of the Olympic team's players, he is happy with the players who did commit to the ABL. "We actually got 80% of the people we wanted and a couple we hadn't anticipated" (Lister, 1996b, p. 3C). The average player's salary is $70,000; however, some players may earn as much as $250,000.

In an effort to generate more local and regional interest, the former Olympians and other marquee players were distributed among the eight franchises. Shelley Sheetz, an All-American at the University of Colorado, is just such a player for the Colorado Xplosion. Sheetz is joined by a number of other marquee players, including Charlotte Smith (Final Four MVP, All-American), Sylvia Crawley (1996 U.S. Olympic Team alternate, 1995

Table 1
American Basketball League Teams for the 1996 Inaugural Season

Team	Arena/Seating	Premier Player(s)	Coach
ATLANTA GLORY	Norcross (GA) 3,000 seats	Teresa Edwards (U of Georgia)	Trish Roberts
COLORADO XPLOSION	Denver Coliseum (16 games) 9,300 seats McNichols Arena (4 games) 14,500 seats	Edna Campbell (Texas) Sylvia Crawley, Charlotte Smith (North Carolina)	Sheryl Estes
COLUMBUS QUEST	Battelle Hall (OH) 6,700 seats	Nikki McCray, Carla McGhee (Tenn.)	Brian Agler
NEW ENGLAND BLIZZARD	Hartford Civic Center (Conn.) (8 games) 15,418 seats Springfield Civic Center (Mass) (12 games) 8,712 seats	Shanda Berry (Iowa)	Cliffa Foster
PORTLAND POWER	Memorial Coliseum 12,888 seats	Katy Steding (Stanford) Natalie Williams (UCLA)	Greg Bruce
RICHMOND RAGE	Richmond Coliseum (14 games) 11,992 seats Univ. of Richmond Robbins Center (6 games) 9,171 seats	Dawn Staley (U Virginia) Jackie Joyner-Kersee (UCLA)	Lisa Boyer
SAN JOSE LASERS	San Jose State Univ. Event Center 4,550 seats	Jennifer Azzi, Val Whiting (Stanford)	Jan Lowrey
SEATTLE REIGN	Mercer Arena 4,623 seats	Venus Lacey (Louisianna Tech) Cindy Brown (Long Beach State)	Jacquie Hullah

Source: *USA Today*, September 19, 1996, p. 3C.

USA Basketball Player of the Year), and Edna Campbell (1996 U.S. Olympic Team alternate, Pan-Am, & Jones Cup member).

The Competition:
The Women's National Basketball Association

The WNBA is the second new women's professional basketball league in the United States established during the 1990s. Unlike the ABL, the WNBA is a summer league and enjoys the support of its established parent, the National Basketball Association. The WNBA is also an eight-team league, all of the teams owned by the 29 NBA teams. During its first season, WNBA games were nationally telecast three times a week on NBC and cable channels ESPN and Lifetime, a first for any start-up league.

In addition to the backing of the NBA and a lucrative national television agreement, the WNBA signed some influential sponsors, including American Express, Coca-Cola, Bud Light, Champion, Nike, Sears, and Spalding. All have multiyear marketing partnerships with the league.

ABL Sponsors

Reebok, Lady Foot Locker, Nissan, First USA Bank, Phoenix Home Life Mutual Insurance, and Baden Sports Inc. are the ABL's national sponsors. Other companies are being courted, particularly in the women's athletic apparel category. During its first 2 years, the ABL negotiated about $10 million in league sponsorship agreements.

On the local level, businesses ranging from grocery stores and quick-serve restaurants to banks, hotels, and airlines are signing on as sponsors. In Colorado, *The Rocky Mountain News*, Norwest Bank, and Coors brewing have signed on with the Xplosion as local sponsors.

Table 2
ABL Profit/Loss Projections

Year	Projection
1996/97	$3 million loss
1997/98	$2 million loss
1998/99	$2 million profit

Source: USA Today, October 18, 1996, p. 2B

National Television

During the inaugural season of the ABL (1996), SportsChannel Regional Network televised 12 regular-season Sunday night games, as well as the ABL's All-Star Game, two playoff games, and the championship series.

The Xplosion appeared in three national broadcasts (Sunday night games) and five regional broadcasts (on Prime) as part of the national television package. For its second season (1997), the ABL signed a national television agreement with Fox Sports, and Nike has signed on to conduct a national advertising campaign highlighting various ABL players.

Marketing and Promotions

Xplosion Director of Marketing, Anne Price and her colleagues at the Xplosion are positioning the team as "superior entertainment value for the dollar" (A. Price, personal communication, October 8, 1996). There is a growing concern among sports fans that the major spectator sports leagues are pricing the product beyond the range of the average fan. Cognizant of this issue, yet not wanting to underprice and compromise the perceived value of the product, the Xplosion is offering a series of ticket packages and prices that will accommodate the majority of fans. Tables 3 and 4 list the season ticket packages and pricing chart for Xplosion games.

Table 3
Xplosion Season-Ticket Packages (per 20-Game Schedule)

Plan	Adult	Jr. (to 15) Sr. (60+)	Family (4 tickets)
Courtside A	$700	NA	NA
Courtside B	$400	NA	NA
Gold	$240	$220	$860
Silver	$200	$180	$700
Bronze	$160	$140	$540

Source: Colorado Xplosion 1996-1997 Ticket Information

In addition to the traditional marketing and advertising strategies (television, radio, outdoor, and print advertising), the Xplosion is conducting a grassroots promotional campaign. In an effort to introduce Denver to the ABL and the Xplosion, Birdsong, Price, and Xplosion players have been making a number of public appearances and accepting speaking engagements. In an effort to attract Denver's business community, the franchise has sponsored a weekly Hoops Cocktail Hour. Each week members of the business community are invited to the Xplosion's front office to meet the players and "talk hoops" with General Manager Birdsong and other front-office per-

Table 4
Xplosion Partial Season and Individual Game Ticket Information

Plan	Adult	Jr. (to 15) Sr. (60+)	Family (4 tickets)	Group (10+)	7-Game Price*	11-Game Price*
Courtside A	$36	NA	NA	NA	NA	NA
Courtside B	$21	NA	NA	NA	NA	NA
Gold	$13	$12	$47	$11	NA	NA
Silver	$11	$10	$39	$9	$74	$116
Bronze	$9	$8	$31	$7	$60	$94

Source: *Colorado Xplosion 1996-1997 Ticket Information*

* ABL Sampler partial season-ticket packages. The 7-game package exposes the ticket holder to every team in the league. The 11-game package is the equivalent to a half-season package. "Partial packages...the expense is small, the value extraordinary." (Colorado Xplosion 1996-1997 Ticket Information brochure).

sonnel. The initial response to the cocktail hour has been very positive.

Price is also working hard to get the public to know the Xplosion's players. Each week a different player is highlighted in *The Rocky Mountain News* (an Xplosion sponsor and print media partner) and the focus of game-day promotions.

Although it is well-known in professional sport circles that the foundation of a team's promotional program rests on close public relations work with all the news media in the region — television and radio stations, and newspapers — this is not as easy to achieve as it might appear. Given the number of professional and college teams in the Denver metropolitan area, competition for air time and print space is fierce. Additionally, the costs associated with a new franchise are enormous, and funds allotted for promotional purposes are limited. Birdsong and Price definitely have their work cut out in trying to market and promote the Colorado Xplosion.

Case Study Questions

1. Using information on situational analysis from chapter 4 of the Pitts and Stotlar (1996) text, analyze the Xplosion's situation in relation to its competitive, economic, and social environments.

2. What would you recommend Birdsong and Price do to market and promote the Colorado Xplosion for its second season of competition? Be specific in your sport marketing mix strategies (the four Ps).

3. At what stage are the ABL and, specifically, the Colorado Xplosion, on the sport product life cycle? What does this mean for promoting the ABL? the Xplosion?

4. How would you position the team? Justify your answer.

5. Do you think that the United States can support two women's professional basketball leagues? Be able to justify and defend your position.

Related Activities

1. Log onto the ABL's and WNBA's Internet sites, and evaluate how each league is promoting its teams on-line.

2. Compare the markets of ABL and WNBA teams. What does this tell you about each league's marketing strategies?

3. Contact an ABL and WNBA franchise and request a ticket-sales brochure from each. Compare how each league and team market and sell their product.

4. Conduct some focus group research with a group of 10 to 15 students on your campus to determine attitudes toward women's college basketball, the ABL, and the WNBA. Use your findings to help determine how you would market women's basketball.

5. Using your institution's library resources, determine the audience profiles for men's and women's basketball. Given this information, how would you segment consumers of women's basketball?

6. Develop an annual marketing plan for an ABL or a WNBA team. The development of a marketing plan for the upcoming season may help you to identify some of the emerging problems, opportunities, and threats associated with a relatively new sports league.

Related Readings

Carter, D. M. (1996). *Keeping score: An inside look at sports marketing.* Grants Pass, OR: The Oasis Press.

Cohen, W. A. (1995). *The marketing plan.* New York: John Wiley & Sons.

Colorado Xplosion 1996–1997 Ticket information brochure.

Horovitz, B. (1996, October 18). A basketball league of their own. *USA Today,* p. 1–2B.

Pearce, A. (1996, October 19). Women's team lives up to name. *Rocky Mountain News,* pp. 1C, 6C.

Pitts, B. G., & Stotlar, D. K. (1996). *Fundamentals of sport marketing.* Morgantown, WV: Fitness Information Technology, Inc.

Schaaf, P. (1995). *Sports marketing: It's not just a game anymore.* Amherst, NY: Prometheus Books.

Schlossberg, H. (1996). *Sports marketing.* Cambridge, MA: Blackwell Publishers, Inc.

Settle, R. B., & Alreck, P. L. (1986). *Why they buy: American consumers inside and out.* New York: John Wiley & Sons.

Stotlar, D. (1993). *Successful sport marketing.* Madison, WI: WCB Brown & Benchmark.

Suggested Trade Newsletters and Publications to Read

Advertising Age	*Brandweek*
Adweek	*Marketing News*
American Demographics	*Sports Business Daily*
Amusement Business	*Team Marketing Report*

References

Lister, V. (1996, September 19). ABL tries to court success. *USA Today,* p. 3C.

Lister, V. (1996, October 17). Pro game gets another go. *USA Today,* p. 3C.

FILLING YOUR FOOTBALL FACILITY WITH FANS — 17,000 OR BUST!

Dianna P. Gray, University of Northern Colorado

Introduction and Problem

Sitting in her office, Linda McLaughlin, the recently hired marketing director for Northern University Intercollegiate Athletics, and her assistant director, Mike Williams, contemplated their charge. McLaughlin had just been instructed by the Director of Intercollegiate Athletics to devise a plan to insure that attendance at home football games averaged 17,000 by 1999 and 20,000 fans per contest by the 2000 season. One of the primary reasons for setting this attendance goal was due to an NCAA requirement that Division I-A teams with a stadium capacity of greater than 30,000 average more than 17,000 in paid attendance per home football game at least one year in the immediate past 4-year period. Northern last fulfilled this attendance requirement in 1995 when they drew 86,685 fans in five home dates — an average of 17,337 fans per game. Because Northern failed to average greater than 17,000 fans per game for either the 1996 or 1997 seasons, the requirement must be fulfilled in one of the upcoming two seasons. As a first step to tackling this task, Linda asked Mike to gather information regarding the university, the Department of Intercollegiate Athletics, the Northern football program, and the environment in which the university operated.

Northern University

Northern University is a 4-year public institution located in northeastern Ohio in a town of 43,000. The University has an enrollment of approximately 23,000 students and offers nine different baccalaureate degrees in over 150 different career fields and 15 graduate degrees in 50 areas of study. Approximately 25% of the students reside on campus. Of those who commute, most live within a half hour to an hour drive of the main campus.

Northern University is located in the center of four major urban areas: Akron, Cleveland, Canton, and Youngstown. The University is easily accessible from these areas as well as a number of other major cities in Ohio and Pennsylvania. Its campus is attractive and nicely landscaped. The University recently celebrated its 87th anniversary as it was founded in 1910.

The Department of Intercollegiate Athletics

The Department of Intercollegiate Athletics at Northern University believes that its main purpose is "to plan and provide the best program possible for the students and community of Northern University." The department takes the position that it is but one part of the University and that it is committed to serving the institution. The department views its responsibility to foster and develop an atmosphere that allows the student-athlete to meet personal and professional goals, as well as career objectives.

Northern offers 20 Division I sports for its athletes — 11 for men and 9 for women. The Eagles are a member of the Mid-American Conference, a nine-school league that has produced champions in a variety of major sports. Northern University alumni include Jack Lambert, former All-Pro with the Pittsburgh Steelers and the late Thurman Munson, captain of the New York Yankees.

Facilities for the athletic program include Mix Stadium, an indoor fieldhouse and practice facility, ice arena, 18-hole golf course, all-weather outdoor track, and Memorial Gymnasium, which houses a 5,000-seat basketball and volleyball facility, gymnastics center, training rooms, and administrative offices. Mix Stadium is the largest in the Mid-American Conference, with seating for more than 30,000 fans. The stadium was constructed in 1969 as part of a $5.3 million bond program.

Northern University Football

The 1990s have not been easy for Northern University football. Most of the time Northern finds itself at the bottom of the standings in the MAC. In 1992, the Eagles went winless for the entire season and in 1993 and 1994 earned but one victory. In 1995, the team compiled a 4-7 win-loss record with a 3-6 record in the MAC. The combination of an intensive promotional campaign to increase attendance, including an extensive direct-mail campaign, Dallas Cowboy Cheerleaders half-time promotion at the homecoming game, and other attendance incentives, as well as improved on-the-field performance by the team, resulted in an increase in average home attendance to 17,337 (see Table 1). However, in 1996, absent a specific promotional campaign and a lack of further improvement in the team's win/loss record, average attendance figures again dropped to 7,014 fans per game, as the team posted a season record of 3 victories and 8 defeats. McLaughlin has reason to be encouraged, though, with the attendance figures for the 1997 season, with a 38% increase to a season average of 9,665. A combination of a greater emphasis on promoting the football team and a .500 season

Table 1
Football Attendance Breakdown by Year

Year	Avg. Student Attendance	Season Ticket Sales	Avg. Public Sales	Avg. Total Sales
1997	4,400	1,573	3,692	9,665
1996	3,381	1,441	2,192	7,014
1995	9,873	4,179	3,285	17,337
1994	2,725	1,848	5,717	10,290
1993	4,074	1,579	7,266	12,919
1992	6,556	665	2,437	9,658
1991	1,221	739	1,643	3,603

resulted in these improved attendance figures.

Competition for the Entertainment Dollar

The Northern football program has direct competition from a variety of small and medium collegiate athletic programs and other entertainment events in the Akron-Cleveland area. In addition, northeastern Ohio supports the Cleveland Indians and Cavaliers professional baseball and basketball teams, as well as a professional indoor soccer franchise, The Cleveland Crunch. Indirect competition from several other forms of entertainment, such as the Cleveland Orchestra, Cleveland Ballet, Rock-n-Roll Hall of Fame, and the flats (a popular, upscale revitalized area of Cleveland, which offers a variety of eateries and boutiques), among others, are factors that McLaughlin must also consider.

Ticket Information

At Northern, students with a valid ID card are admitted free to Eagle football games. This is possible because a portion of the general fee paid by all NU students is allocated to the Department of Intercollegiate Athletics.

Brochures regarding season-ticket packages are mailed in the spring to all previous season ticket holders, faculty and staff, Varsity N members, and Black & Gold club members. Season tickets are available at the cost of $60 for reserved seating and $85 for chairback seats (seats with a back between the 40-yard lines).

For the general public, general admission tickets are sold at the price of

$11.00 per game. Interested customers can obtain tickets in advance at the Northern ticket office, Memorial Gymnasium, via the telephone with a credit card, or at the stadium on the day of the game.

Demographic and Attendance Information

McLaughlin and Williams knew that they could not rely alone on a successful football season to attract fans. The football program, although working hard to try to get out of the MAC basement, probably would not be in the top of the conference standings, much less win the conference championship. However, both felt certain that given the success of previous promotional campaigns in increasing attendance, and the improvement in attendance figures for 1996 and 1997, achieving the attendance goal was possible in the next 2 years. Although the potential for increased season-ticket sales and increased attendance appeared to be attainable, McLaughlin realized that she needed more information before developing an appropriate marketing plan. After reviewing the demographic and statistical data currently available on the football program (see Tables 1 & 2), McLaughlin felt confident that there was potential for attendance growth at Northern's home football games.

Case Study Questions

1. Is Northern's football attendance problem unique? Why or why not? You should be able to support your answer with data.
2. What marketing mix strategies would you recommend to McLaughlin and Williams to help achieve not only the necessary average attendance figure of 17,000 but also a consistently near-capacity audience for future seasons?
3. What are the NCAA's regulations on football ticket sales promotions? How will these restrictions affect McLaughlin's ticket-pricing strategy(ies)?
4. What do the data Williams gathered tell you about the audience profile of Northern's fans? How can this information benefit McLaughlin as she develops a marketing strategy for the upcoming season(s)? What additional or different information would you include in the next audience analysis questionnaire?
5. What is a strategic analysis? Be specific in defining the components of a strategic analysis.
6. How can conducting a SWOT analysis assist McLaughlin and Williams in developing both short- and long-range marketing plans?

Table 2
Audience Profile of Northern University Football Attendees

Demographic	FB Season Ticket Holder	General Public	Students
Males	88%	90%	62%
Females	12%	10%	38%
White	78%	90%	72%
Black	22%	10%	28%
Married	83%	80%	NA
Single	17%	20%	NA
Average Age	49 years	38 years	19 years
Median Age	48 years	41 years	NA
Average Income	$39,571	$44,000	NA
Average Household Size	2.66	3.00	NA
College Educated	77%	40%	NA
NU Graduate	55%	20%	NA
Residence	NE Ohio	NE Ohio (Cleveland suburbs)	NA
Average yrs. Attending	9.4	4.1	NA
Attend with Friends	55%	40%	100%
Attend with Family	45%	60%	0%
Reason for Attending	Loyalty to NU	Like football Know a player	Know a player Fun
Like Most re: NU FB	Overall program	Excitement	NA
Like Least re: NU FB	Losing/No fans	Lack of fans	NA
Have Cable TV	77%	50%	37%
Listen To NU FB on Radio	77%	40%	20%

7. What marketing recommendations would you make to McLaughlin for the Northern football program? Be specific in terms of the relevant components of the marketing mix.

Related Activities

1. Find the NCAA News in your university library or the NCAA's home page on the World Wide Web. Periodically check for updated college football attendance figures. What are the trends regarding college football attendance?

2. Conduct some focus group research with a group of 10 to 15 students on your campus to determine their attitudes toward the university's football program. Use your findings to help determine how you might develop a promotional campaign that would attract more students to football games.

3. Work with the athletic department's director of marketing to develop an audience profile questionnaire and administer it at your institution (for any of the sports sponsored by the institution). Working in teams of three or four, analyze the data and prepare a written report for the Director of Marketing.

Related Readings

Carter, D. M. (1996). *Keeping score: An inside look at sports marketing.* Grants Pass, OR: The Oasis Press.

Gray, D. P. (1996). Sport marketing: A strategic approach. In B. L. Parkhouse (Ed.), *The management of sport: Its foundation and application* (2nd ed.) (pp. 251–289). St. Louis: Mosby.

Pitts, B. G., & Stotlar, D. K. (1996). *Fundamentals of sport marketing.* Morgantown, WV: Fitness Information Technology, Inc.

Schaaf, P. (1995). *Sports marketing: It's not just a game anymore.* Amherst, NY: Prometheus Books.

Schlossberg, H. (1996). *Sports marketing.* Cambridge, MA: Blackwell Publishers, Inc.

Settle, R. B., & Alreck, P. L. (1986). *Why they buy: American consumers inside and out.* New York: John Wiley & Sons.

Suggested Newsletters and Publications

Advertising Age	*Marketing News*
Adweek	*NCAA News*
American Demographics	*Sports Business Daily*
Amusement Business	*Sport Marketing Quarterly*
Brandweek	*Team Marketing Report*

SECTION 2

THE SPORT PRODUCTION INDUSTRY SEGMENT

The Sport Production Industry Segment:
An Overview

There are many different products — goods, services, people, places, and ideas — needed to produce sports, recreation, leisure, or fitness activities. Some of these include facilities, equipment, clothing, shoes, officials, coaches, trainers, rulebooks, and governing associations. There are also many different products desired to influence performance in activity. Some of these include personal trainers, managers, fitness-enhancing equipment, performance-enhancing products, psychological training, first-class facilities and equipment, and specially designed clothing and shoes.

This segment of the sport industry contains those products needed or desired to produce a sports event or to produce or influence the level of performance of the participant. As such, some examples of products in this segment include sports equipment, sports facilities, sports officials, athletic trainers, and sports governing bodies. All of these are needed in order for a sports event to take place. Some of these are desired to influence the level of the event or the level of the athlete's performance. For example, we play softball with a softball, a softball glove, a softball bat, and softball shoes — equipment needed to play softball. We can possibly influence the level of our performance if we use a selected bat and glove and even cleats. Sport marketers of these products know that softball equipment will sell to those of us who want to participate in softball. They also know that there are some softball players who believe that their level of performance can be enhanced if they purchase and use specific equipment. Therefore, softball bats, for example, can range from a basic model with little promise of performance to a very expensive model with promises of enhanced performance — improved batting average, control, and distance.

Sport marketers need to know what the consumer wants the product to do in order to develop and design the product. The sport marketer can also use this information in promoting the product. Check your local newspaper for an advertisement for sporting goods or watch for commercials on television for a specific product. You can also go to a sporting goods store and look for in-store advertising, such as a sign next to the equipment. You will note that the ads speak to exactly what the consumer expects from the product.

The cases in this section include a variety of sport production products and involve several different marketing elements. In addition, the student will be challenged with ethical and professional issues relative to sport marketing.

Modern Turn for a Traditional Product: Cygnet Turf & Equipment

Jacquelyn Cuneen, Bowling Green State University

Cygnet Turf & Equipment is a 5-year-old company owned and operated as the secondary pursuit of a successful physician who has an interest in farming and inventing. Douglas S. Hess, M. D., founded Cygnet because he could pursue his farming avocation and meet the demand for superior sod in commercial and residential landscape use. Cygnet began by growing a blue-grass product line and harvested the sod using the second most popular harvester machine in the industry. Cygnet also offered an added incentive to turf products buyers: Cygnet Turf would also install the sod (99.5% of sod farmers grow and deliver but do not install turf).

As business flourished, Hess found that a major problem in installing turf on large jobs is the ripping, tearing, and stretching damage that occurs due to tension when the sod is pulled during unrolling; pulling on heavy lengths of sod causes the sod to stretch and fit improperly. Also, forklifts were used to place the sod rolls; forklift placement proficiency is correlated to the proficiency of the forklift operator. If sod must be tugged into place because of an operator's misjudgment, seams, gaps, and weak spots result. To protect the sod from stretching and gapping, installers fixed mesh netting on the underside of the sod to protect it. After installation and settling, the netting tends to work its way up through the sod causing footing problems and injuries.

In 1988, Hess devised the plans for a sod-installation machine that would turn out sod without tearing or stretching it. Hess's blueprints resulted in several machines that are self-propelled with small engines, or require use of small tractors to install large rolls of sod in a short time, yet do not harm the sod because the sod is merely being turned into place. Machinery is calibrated so that rolls of sod (4 inches x 36 inches x 2 feet or 4 inches x 70 inches x 1 foot) are placed adjacent to each other with little or no manual adjustment. Cygnet Turf & Equipment holds U. S. and Canadian patents on the machinery; no other company in either of these countries may use the sod-installation machines.

The Sod and Turf Industry

Industry figures show that sales for nursery and greenhouse crops reached $8.4 billion in 1991, outselling wheat, cotton, tobacco, peanuts, sugar, and rice (American Sod Producers Association, 1993). The sod and landscape component of the farming industry caters to a niche market, yet Cygnet market research shows that there are 1,400 sod farms totaling 304, 200 acres in the United States. Typically, sod farms are 300 acres with most turf products distributed to landscape contractors in rolls or slabs. Cygnet Turf & Equipment grows, harvests, and installs only rolls. An American Sod Producers Association (1993) membership profile shows that the typical sod farm has been producing for 15 years; 67.8% are incorporated, 16.1% are owned by one person, and 16.1% are partnerships. Most sod farmers (57.5%) operate as cool-season growers (growing periods are interrupted due to harsh winters); 25.5% are transition growers (some interruptions occur) whereas 17.2% are warm-season growers (farms produce sod on a year-round basis).

Industry average shipping capacity is 25 tons carrying 1,080 yards of sod. Most growers deliver to sites between 31 and 75 miles of their growing sites (American Sod Producers Association, 1993). Table 1 shows the typical current market radius of sod growers, as well as the typical radius serviced 5 years ago.

Table 1
Typical Market Radius of Sod Growers

Miles Traveled for Delivery	% of Growers: 1988	% of Growers: 1993
1 - 30	21.7%	14.4%
31 - 75	40.2%	57.8%
76 Miles or Over	38.1%	27.7%

Note. Adapted from *ASPA Membership Profile Survey,* p. 2, by American Sod Producers Association. Copyright 1994 by ASPA. Adapted with permission of author.

Although just 80% of the acreage from a typical sod farm is allocated specifically for sod growth, 98% of the farm's income (increased from 95% in 1988) is traced to sod sales (American Sod Producers Association, 1993). Sales have increased slightly over the past 5 years (from 92 acres sold in 1988 to 100 acres sold in 1993). Industry median income for growers was $480,000 in 1992 against $443,150 in expenses. Industry average expenses were $622,050; net worth of the average sod farm was $1,929,667. Over one third (33.5%; Median percentage = 41.5%) of sod growers' budgets are used for salaries (average salary budget = $153,000.).

Landscaping contractors have been the largest market for the sod industry over the past 5 years, but Cygnet Turf & Equipment has found a smaller niche market in sport facilities. Cygnet market research projects that artificial practice and playing surfaces for collegiate and professional football, baseball, softball, field hockey, soccer, and other outdoor sports will be replaced by natural turf surfaces as innovative forms of natural, durable sods are developed (Mazzeo, 1994).

Product

Cygnet grows, harvests, delivers, and installs large rolls of sod for sport, recreational, commercial, or residential use. Cygnet's primary product of sod is unique because of the technology developed to install it: The usual thickness of sod to be installed for sport, commercial, or residential use is slightly less than one inch. Cygnet's patented installation machinery enables sod rolls to be as thick as two inches and as wide as four feet. Thicker, larger rolls of sod are desirable for playing fields for several reasons, including (a) they are usable just days after installation; (b) they are more durable because of the thicker sod bed; and (c) fewer injuries occur because there are fewer seams, and the surfaces are more "fixed."

Cygnet technicians are able to grow specially ordered sod for use in certain climates or for special purposes. For instance, clients may have unique specifications such as (a) sod must be durable enough to withstand concerts, practices, and games; (b) it must have no excessively spongy or firm spots; (c) it must drain quickly; and (d) it must be able to withstand yearly extremes in weather and temperatures. Cygnet sod technicians will plant, test, and nurture different grass-types, then harvest, transport, and install the sod.

Cygnet Machinery: A Sole-Source Installer

Cygnet's overriding advantage in the sod product line is their proficiency at harvesting and installing larger rolls of sod. Cygnet farm-grown sod is installed by Cygnet's own technicians, who know the properties of the sod and have intricate knowledge of the patented sod-installation machinery; workers harvest, transport, and install sod with minimal damage to the product. Sod is harvested by lifting and rolling it into giant cylinder-type rolls (sod rolls are not unlike rolls of carpet in a warehouse). Rolls are transported to their destination, then removed and installed using Cygnet's patented installation machines. Because Cygnet's machines merely unroll the sod into place, workers do not pull and stretch the sod in order to create a good fit between pieces. Crews of four workers can install 4–5,000 yards (the equivalent of 1.5 football fields) of sod in one day using Cygnet's machinery, and fields are ready for use in a few days because of Cygnet's particular installation method (when Cygnet installed 15, 600 yards of new sod in Cleveland Municipal Stadium, the Browns practiced on the playing surface 5 days later).

Product Competition: Sod Installation

Cygnet market research shows six direct competitors for sod sales:

1. An Eastern-based company that also specializes large rolls. The company furnished the sod for a major league ballpark and an NCAA Division I-A football stadium, both located in the eastern United States. The company uses forklifts to place the rolls; forklift placing proficiency is correlated to the proficiency of the forklift operator. Seams, gaps, and weak spots result if the sod has to be tugged or pulled into place because the operator misjudged the placement.
2. A large, Midwestern multiservice farm (offering other greenhouse and nursery products) that installed sod in a newly constructed Midwestern Major League Baseball park. This company is more centrally located to Cygnet than to other competitors.
3. A sod grower in Cygnet's state that specializes in large roll bluegrass installations. This company has installed sod for a Major League Baseball stadium.
4. A sod grower in Cygnet's region that specializes in residential customers.
5. A small sod farm in an adjacent northern state, also specializing in residential and smaller commercial sites.
6. A sod grower in an adjacent northern state specializing in peat sod for sport installations. This company installed sod for an NCAA Division I-A football stadium.

Product Competition: Modern Installation Machinery

Cygnet market research identified just two North American competitors related to modern installation techniques:

1. A Midwest company that produces an installer comparable to one of Cygnet's. However, although Cygnet's installer permits rolls to turn

out sod smoothly, this company's installer is designed in such a way that workers must pull the rolls in order for them to unwind. Mesh netting must be attached on the underside of the sod to protect the sod from tearing. The company is very visible in the marketplace because it advertises heavily on the national level.

2. A southern-based company that produces an installer model comparable to one of Cygnet's. Like the machine used by Cygnet's in-state competitor, this company's installer is designed so that sod must be pulled from rolls. The southern-based company does not advertise extensively on national levels.

Forms of Cygnet equipment are being used currently in the United Kingdom. Cygnet Turf & Equipment is investigating the feasibility of producing and manufacturing their patented equipment for retail sale in North America.

Place

Cygnet Turf & Equipment is located in Cygnet and North Baltimore, Ohio, small communities located approximately 40–50 miles south of Toledo on Interstate 75. Cygnet plants 150 acres of land; 100% of land production is devoted to developing and perfecting sod. Cygnet has expansion capacity to 1,500 acres.

Sod products are shipped to sites via interstate highway from North Baltimore using flatbed trucks contracted by Cygnet. Cygnet is in constant touch with drivers and technicians at the site to monitor and time deliveries. Deliveries arrive at the site every hour and 10 minutes. Using this "pipeline" system, machinery handles sod rolls just once when sod is removed directly from the flatbed and placed on the installation machine. Many Cygnet competitors deliver entire orders of sod in one trip; machinery removes the sod from the truck, stores it in advantageous places on the ground; then machinery lifts the sod again when it is time for placement. Cygnet's system is "kinder" to the product. Consistent with industry averages, most of Cygnet's sod products are sold to landscape contractors. Table 2 shows the industry averages for types of sod sales.

Currently, Cygnet's main distribution relative to sport markets is primarily regional. Cleveland Municipal Stadium (prior to its destruction), the University of Michigan, The Ohio State University, the University of Findlay, and Defiance College all have Cygnet-grown and -installed sod in their stadia. However, Cygnet has the resources to deliver and install their products anywhere in the United States and was the major grower and installer

Table 2
Sod and Turf Product Customers for 1988 and 1993

Customer	1988	1993
Landscape Contractors	44.6%	40.0%
Homeowners	15.0%	14.0%
Nurseries or Garden Centers	7.9%	12.0%
Builders	12.0%	9.0%
Golf Courses	4.7%	8.0%

Note. Adapted from *ASPA Membership Profile Survey*, p. 3, by American Sod Producers Association. Copyright 1994 by ASPA. Adapted with permission of author.

for the sod in Miami's Joe Robbie Stadium (NFL Dolphins). Distribution is arranged by contract and dependent on order size and distance traveled. Average truck capacity for the industry is 25 tons; average load transported is 1,080 yards of sod (American Sod producers Association, 1993). Cygnet figures are consistent with industry averages.

When customers wish to purchase sod products from other sod vendors, they may contract with Cygnet to install the sod with their patented installation system. Trucking is arranged by Cygnet, and the pipeline delivery method is used. This accounts for a small portion of Cygnet's business; most contracts call for Cygnet to both supply and install sod.

Promotion

Industry average advertising expenses were $15,029 (median = $6,125; 1.6% of total operating budgets). Table 3 shows the typical advertising venues for the turf industry.

Cygnet figures show that their advertising and promotion expenditures exceed industry averages. Currently, Cygnet's sole promotional strategy involves advertising in various trade journals and participating in turf industry and related trade shows.

Cygnet has relied heavily on word-of-mouth promotion. Cygnet has earned an exemplary reputation among sod customers and has obtained many contracts due to satisfied customers. Many sod growers and installers have had to replace or reinstall their products due to substandard products or insufficient installation; no Cygnet job has had to be redone due to faulty growing or installation methods.

Table 3
Typical Promotional Media Used by Sod Growers

Media	1988	1993
Customer Referral	82.0%	86.0%
Yellow Pages	79.5%	86.0%
Direct Mail	42.5%	44.2%
Newspaper	35.0%	41.9%
Trade Shows	35.0%	39.5%
Trade Journals	20.0%	33.7%
Radio	10.0%	14.0%

Note. Adapted from *ASPA Membership Profile Survey*, p. 2, by American Sod Producers Association. Copyright 1994 by ASPA. Adapted with permission of author.

Immediate Promotional Plans

In 1994, Cygnet obtained the services of Mary Beth Mazzeo, an independent marketing researcher, who proposed a marketing plan for the company (Mazzeo, 1994). She identified several immediate needs for promotional success:

1. Cygnet should use a standard logo in all promotional efforts. The logo created shows a cygnet swan outlined in a solid oval with the company name integrated prominently with the artwork.
2. A stationery system (logo letterhead, envelopes, etc.) should be created and used for all company correspondence.
3. Uniform business cards using the logo should be designed for each company representative.
4. A professionally produced videotape showing Cygnet's harvesting and installation procedures should be prepared and sent to inquiring customers.
5. Succinct brochures and other promotional materials should be prepared.
6. Direct mail advertising should be used four times per year for smaller clients and more frequently for larger accounts.
7. Cooperative arrangements should be made with multiproducts nursery and garden retailers. Cygnet literature should be available to a "do-it-yourself" market, as well as large sport and commercial markets.
8. Databases should be established in order for Cygnet to conduct large

business on an individualized level. Databanks will help Cygnet market on a personalized level.

9. A newsletter should be published quarterly in order to maintain contact with customers. The newsletter that was created ("Cygnet Sod Turf Times") contains information about Cygnet's latest inventions, grass recycling, sodding, and a question and answer column.

10. Cygnet should increase their associations with industry trade shows.

11. Camera-ready artwork should be created, and preproduction print should be completed by Cygnet in order to offset advertising costs.

12. Specialty advertising items (novelties, pens, pencils, notepads, and so forth) using Cygnet's logo should be created and distributed at trade shows and with each inquiry.

13. Cygnet's print advertising should be of display rather than classified type. Print advertising should be placed in U. S. and Canadian markets.

14. Radio should be used as an advertising medium in spring and summer. Cable TV should also be used as an advertising medium.

15. Media lists should be compiled and retained, and records of ads and expenditures should be analyzed regularly.

Strategic Objectives

Cygnet's management and marketing executives have identified several short- or long-term goals (Mazzeo, 1994) related to market penetration (new users of new products) or market development (reselling newly developed or additional products to current customers):

1. Build and sell the best machinery on the market (long term).

2. Sell 70 acres of sod locally (short term).

3. Complete four major installations (short term).

4. Sell ten 30-inch layers of sod in inventory currently (short term).

5. Complete negotiations with an engineering firm to build and install machines domestically (short term).

6. Build a loyal customer base (short and long term).

7. Develop a solid promotional plan (short term).

8. Develop a system of dealerships for 30-inch machines (long term).

Price

Price of sod rolls varies according to types and amounts of sod and dimensions of grounds. Price for Cygnet machinery installation varies as a function of the same variables. Residential and landscape contractor accounts comprised 96.9% of Cygnet's business in 1993. Sport field sales and installation contracts accounted for 3.1% of business, yet Cygnet's income statement translations showed that these contracts accounted for one quarter of 1993 cash receipts. Large-roll installation accounted for most overall receipts in 1993 (54.3%), with 31.2% of income derived from machine sales, and 4.1% from small-roll sales (Mazzeo, 1994).

Industry averages indicate that 85% of sales are to wholesale markets with 15% to retail sales. Cygnet's sod prices do not vary according to wholesale or retail trade: All buyers pay the same price for sod products. Cygnet has no records to show if wholesale buyers of their products increase prices in resale on the retail market.

Note: The preceding case as written deliberately contains some information that is directly related to marketing problem solving and some information that may be irrelevant and/or unrelated. Readers must glean appropriate data in order to successfully complete a case study; different types of information will be useful for different questions and/or solutions.

Questions for Study

1. The average market radius for the turf growers has decreased relative to longer distance jobs over a 5-year period, and increased for some shorter distance contract sites (see Table 1). What effect will this have on the turf industry? What measures could turf growers and sellers take if their farms are longer distances from the larger jobs available?

2. Cygnet's larger jobs relative to sport complexes have been completed at various distances from North Baltimore (from a half hour away to 48 hours away). Does Cygnet need to be concerned about market trends relative to distance? What factors should Cygnet consider in assessing the distance trends?

3. What are Cygnet's prospects for gaining an entire North American rather than regional market? What factors should Cygnet consider in international promotions?

4. Cygnet is unique due to its sole-source installation status. Describe the benefits of being a sole source for installation. Should Cygnet concentrate on installations exclusively? What benefits would Cygnet have if they were exclusively an installation company ?

5. How will Cygnet be affected if other growers decide to install as well as grow sod? What ramifications will Cygnet feel if other growers use

Cygnet's machinery to install sod? Will Cygnet's long-term goal relating to manufacturing equipment affect their market advantage? How should Cygnet distribute sod-installation machinery without depleting their own markets?

6. What factors should Cygnet consider in identifying their primary markets? Should Cygnet abandon the residential and commercial market and concentrate on the sport and recreational market? Should their decision be based on job type? That is, what factors should Cygnet consider in maintaining a local residential and commercial sales base, but a national sport and recreation sales base?

7. Market trends for the turf industry show that sales to typical buyers have declined slightly over the past 5 years (see Table 2), yet Cygnet's frequency of sales has increased relative to commercial, residential, and sport facility customers. What factors have contributed to Cygnet's atypical growth during a declining period for the turf industry?

8. Analyze Cygnet's competition base. Does Cygnet's competition base merely relate to growing? Does Cygnet have any genuine current competition for installation?

9. What are the trends in outdoor sport and recreational facility construction relative to playing surfaces? Are newer stadia and parks installing artificial or natural turf? What factors are considered in field construction? What are the construction trends in stadium and park renovation?

10. Devise plans that will enable Cygnet to meet its strategic marketing goals in the short and long term.

Suggested Readings

Graham, J. R. (1994, January/February). Marketing turfgrass sod: Use value added to increase business. *ASPA Turf News*, pp. 14–15.

Peppers, D., & Rogers, M.. (1993). *The one to one future: Building relationships one customer at a time*. New York: Doubleday.

Pitts, B. G., & Stotlar, D. K. (1996). *Fundamentals of sport marketing*. Morgantown, WV: Fitness Information technology, Inc.

Surviving the storm: Dealing with price wars, competition and the economy. (1993, September/October). *ASPA Turf News*, pp. 52–58.

Wildmon, J. (1993, May). Turfgrass renovation: Measures for success. *Sports Turf*, 14–17.

References

American Sod Producers Association. (1993, November/December). *1993 ASPA membership profile survey*. Author.

Mazzeo, M. B. (1994). *Cygnet Turf & Equipment: Strategies of success*. Cygnet, OH: Cygnet Turf & Equipment.

Related Professional Associations

Turfgrass Producers International (TPI)

1855-A Hicks Road

Rolling Meadows, IL 60008

Phone: 708-705-9898

Fax: 708-705-8347

Note. Effective July 24, 1994, the American Sod Producers Association (ASPA) membership voted to change the name of the organization to Turfgrass Producers International.

Acknowledgments

The author gratefully acknowledges Mary Beth Mazzeo, Marketing Consultant, and Richard Mazzeo, Business Manager for Cygnet Turf & Equipment, for their valuable contributions to this project.

Northern Lights, Inc.

David Stotlar, Northern Colorado University

Directions

As the marketing team for Northern Lights, Inc. (NLI), this case will help you become aware of the challenges facing the start-up of a new company and in developing a respectable presence in several market areas. Careful monitoring of market conditions, evaluation of market needs, rapid response to market requests, and adjustment of marketing techniques must all be recognized as mandatory and included in market planning and research. These are all predicated on high-quality market research.

You are a member of a four-person marketing team that is in place and functioning full time. Initial product development is in the final stage with units scheduled for release during the first quarter of the coming year. Marketing goals, definition of strategies, selling activities, and budgets are all being completed. Extensive business and financial planning activities have been completed. Your task is to complete the market research for implementation of the marketing plan.

Introduction

Northern Lights, Inc. (NLI) has recently been incorporated under the laws of the State of Colorado as an applied technology company specializing in the development, manufacturing, and marketing of lighting products for sport utility vehicles (Jeeps, Blazers, Explorers, etc.). The overall company management, including marketing activities, is handled by Mr. Juan Hernandez, President and Chief Executive Officer, who has over 22 years' management and sales experience. Product design, purchasing, production, and quality control are managed by Ms. Althea Hayward, Vice President of Engineering and designer of NLI products. She is the owner of seven patents on various mechanical and electromechanical devices.

The immediate goals of the company include (a) short-term capitalization, (b) initial product introduction, (c) product sales, and (d) breaking even within the first year's operation. Guidelines for product development indicate that the product concepts must be market driven in an identifiable market. Long term goals include (a) expansion of the product lines, (b) expanded distribution, (c) research and development of new products, and (d) custom product development through a subsidiary division.

None of the NLI's products are presently being marketed; however, the initial product has been developed and can be seen in Figure 1. Manufacturing cost estimates indicate that the primary auxiliary lighting system can be priced to sell in the $50 range. Market surveys also verify the price as acceptable. At this level, NLI will have a strong initial net profit margin of $25 per unit over the first 100,000 units. All sales over this figure generate a profit of $35 per unit. Projected sales must quickly establish a healthy cash position to aid in absorbing the necessarily higher marketing costs accrued during the start-up period. In the succeeding year, reductions in costs resulting from improvements in manufacturing processes and possibly better component purchases are projected to increase profit margins by 10%.

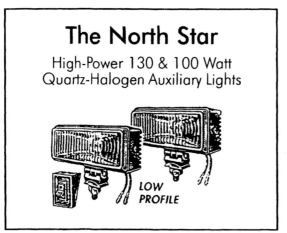

Figure 1

To determine the feasibility and marketability of the NLI line of products, many demonstrations were conducted during the development period to assess consumer interest. Particular attention was paid to comments regarding consumer acceptability and changes were instituted to improve operation and/or design. Included in the market survey was participation in last year's Specialty Equipment Market Association (SEMA/AI) show held in Las Vegas, Nevada, which attracted 29,672 domestic buyers and 6,643 from international markets. SEMA is a support organization for the majority of the after-market automotive manufacturers and suppliers. Comments from this show were most favorable, and contacts with many potential wholesale and catalog suppliers were established.

The trade show and general market research indicate that the typical user benefits of auxiliary lighting systems fall into three categories: functional, economical, and psychological. More specifically these comprise

Functional

1. The mounting framework provides a secure location for the lighting system without defacing the vehicle.
2. A lighting system is an auxiliary device that enhances the vehicle's

factory-installed lighting and road illumination.

3. The interchangeable colored lenses permit expanded marketability — that is, red/red for firefighters, red/blue/clear for law enforcement, and amber/amber for construction and public utility vehicles.

Economical

1. According to the *NADA Official Used Car Guide*, auxiliary lighting enhances the resale value of sport utility vehicles approximately $125.00 at wholesale and $150.00 on the retail market.

2. If used for business purposes, that is, volunteer fire use, construction, or law enforcement, the unit may be deductible as a business expense and the cost added to the value of the vehicle and included in the depreciation of that vehicle.

3. The units can be removed from the vehicle being sold or traded and reinstalled on a replacement vehicle with only minor effort.

Psychological

1. Confidence of superior visibility leads to added safety.

2. Feeling of being contemporary; "having the latest gadget." (Market studies indicate that 14% of Americans want to be first in line for a new product.)

3. Satisfaction of having increased the value of the vehicle.

4. Satisfaction of minimizing income taxes if (purchase price is tax deductible and unit can be depreciated with vehicle), in accordance with federal tax laws.

NLI intends to operate as a customer-oriented company and build a favorable industry reputation. The company offers and honors a one-year limited warranty against defects in workmanship and material. Financial projections include a warranty expense generated by the outright replacement of .5% of all units sold at retail costs. Defective units will be held with no repair action taken. Information obtained from units returned will be monitored, and as indicated, design or production changes will be considered. The establishment of a system for repair of defective units will be considered when indicated by economics. The cycle of market development and sales activities is consistent with historical norms for successful introduction of vehicular lighting systems.

NLI may wish to increase marketing activities across the broad potential market base of long-term and fleet users. This might be accomplished by expanding the refined direct selling approaches into additional segments within the broad market as well as wholesale distributions through established mail order and mass merchandising outlets. Fleet markets are considered long term because of the amount of official red tape involved in establishing product acceptance by municipalities purchasing from fleet operations.

The company has retained financial and business planning counsel from Bankers International Corporation, which is an experienced business planning and development firm, in order to be poised for an initial public offering (IPO) when it is most beneficial to the company and its stockholders. Your management team must carefully consider the areas in which strength is required to successfully compete and develop beyond the initial product introduction. The company has selected financial, legal, and business planning counsel capable of serving as an integral part of the management team throughout the planned growth.

Financial projections indicate that NLI should quickly become a cash-strong company. It is recognized, however, that the company may wish to expand its marketing and new product releases more rapidly than can be supported by sales alone. NLI may, therefore, strive to position the company as an attractive candidate for an IPO during the first years of operation. This option may be exercised as a function of the IPO market and the company's expansion needs to meet market demands or competition. Management is also developing strategies that will position the company as an attractive candidate for acquisition or merger on the strength of its market position.

Question: What financial and legal decisions in the interim should be made with the IPO option in mind?

Initially NLI will purchase its inventory requirements in the United States to maximize its control of all facets of manufacturing and marketing. The company, to ensure its competitive edge, may actively pursue alternate component and subassembly sources including possible overseas suppliers. Preliminary discussions are presently in process with several overseas importers and liaison firms. The results of this investigation provide valuable input for any planned NLI expansion into international markets.

The ability to compete successfully in the long term is based on the company's continued efforts in thorough planning, attention to customer needs, product quality, realistic assessments of marketing challenges, and updating and implementation of stated goals.

Question: What profit is needed to generate a positive cash flow through product sales within the first year following the national introduction of the initial product?

Question: What percent of the available market will be needed to achieve this goal?

Question: Which market strategies or techniques need to be implemented during the year to achieve these goals?

Marketing Environment

Last year, aftermarket sales of sport utility vehicle off-road and recreational lighting systems were, according to published figures, in excess of $894,000,000. This rather sizable amount covers a broad market of recreational and off-road equipment purchasers and includes specific and targetable submarket groups, such as volunteer firefighters, construction companies, public and private security companies, and law enforcement entities. Additional market extensions include government and military users. There are in excess of 30 domestic manufacturers of aftermarket vehicular lighting devices. Twenty of the manufacturers are classified as large corporations and account for 88% of the business generated. The general market for aftermarket vehicle lighting has been growing at a rate of about 15% per year.

Question: In the domestic market, approximately how many vehicles are currently equipped with some type of auxiliary lighting device?

Question: What does your research indicate as a market size for additional, unique lighting products in previously untapped or inadequately supplied markets?

Company research indicates that the international potential for NLI products appears to be considerably larger than that of the domestic market.

Question: Do your data support this finding?

Question: What steps should be taken to secure foreign patents and to develop long-range plans to penetrate those markets?

Immediate goals, objectives, and activities for your marketing team include:

- Generate a positive cash flow through product sales by the seventh month following the national introduction of the initial product.
- Penetrate one and one-half percent (1 1/2%) of the available market for the entire product line by the end of 3 years.
- Define market strategies (media uses, direct mail programs, and tradeshow selection) or the wholesale marketing techniques, or both, to beimplemented during the coming year.
- Complete the agreements necessary to implement product sales through at least one nationwide distributorship catering to sport utility vehicle auxiliary lighting products.
- Complete offshore production analysis and locate potential sources for subcontract or joint venture production.

Long-term objectives for your marketing team include:

- Enhance product-line development and implement revised and tested marketing strategies.
- Expand and refine product marketing with the addition of wholesale outlets.
- Solidify marketing arrangements with mail order and catalog firms initially contacted. The goal is to have catalog advertising circulating to five million household and/or consumer outlets within 5 years.
- Complete marketing arrangements with at least five fleet operations with combined sales of 100 or more vehicles.
- Position NLI as an attractive candidate for an IPO initial public offering, merger, or   acquisition during the next 3 years.
- Positioning NLI, through continued expansion nationally and internationally, as a leading supplier for the aftermarket demands for sport utility vehicle lighting products.

Market Size and Identity

Question: How many people in the United States own and use sport utility vehicles in some type of recreational or business activity?

Some business activities require the use of some sort of vehicle-mounted safety or emergency lighting device as well as sport and recreational use. In addition to the primary target market identified above, there may be discreet and targetable submarket groups, such as fire departments with both municipal fire-fighting professionals and volunteer firefighters. Construction companies and private security companies also utilize similar vehicles and trucks, many of which could be equipped with your products.

Question: What data is necessary to project market size based on the primary and secondary markets you select?

Market Characteristics

General trade journal reports indicate that a substantial portion of the personal market for these lighting systems comprises individuals characterized as "affluent" consumers (households with incomes greater than $75,000 in 1998), who have been the subject of extensive studies regarding attitudes and buying habits. This affluent market is growing at 8.6% per year in the 1990s. These studies have found that this market's primary purchase motivators are convenience and quality.

Question: Can you present data that either support or refute these general findings?

NLI may wish to increase marketing activities across the broad potential market base of long-term and fleet users. These markets include sales for private and public utilities trucks, forestry and lumber trucks, military and border patrol/immigration vehicles, municipal and volunteer fire equipment, and the large number of law enforcement vehicles throughout the United States.

Question: Should NLI increase its market activities across the broad potential base by expanding the refined direct selling approaches, by increasing the number of wholesale distributors, and by adding mail order and mass merchandising outlets?

Custom-Design Markets

Through a subsidiary corporation, NLI has the ability to custom design vehicular lighting systems for entire police forces, fire and rescue, highway patrol, security patrol, municipal fire departments, and any other group utilizing vehicular lighting systems similar to existing products. Custom-designed products for this market, developed in the future, are expected to be highly profitable additions to the current product.

Question: When would be the best timing for initiation of these activities?

The marketing environment consists of 30 domestic manufacturers of aftermarket vehicular lighting devices with the top 20 accounting for 88% of the market. To analyze each of the competitive manufacturers is cost prohibitive. Therefore, analysis of the competition should be directed mainly at the products being offered with a closer look at *one* of the large and successful companies now operating.

Question: Through an analysis on the major competitor, what is their existing product competition and what might be future competing products?

The International Market

NLI considers international marketing of its products to be similar to that of the domestic market in that there are definable and targetable areas. Assistance and cooperation from the international representatives will be necessary to ensure successful market penetration. As stated earlier, NLI will proceed with attempts to obtain foreign patents on its devices and to expand its operations worldwide as capabilities and funds become available.

Question: What actions are required to commit to the international market?

Last-Minute CEO Directive

In support of NLI's goal to quickly generate a positive cash flow, the CEO has dictated that initial marketing efforts be concentrated in segments where quick buying decisions are made and where orders are on a cash basis (credit cards, money orders, or certified funds). He considers direct sales, through trade publication advertisements and direct mail, the least costly and most lucrative methods to penetrate the market. Therefore, your initial strategies must now include direct mailing of order form/brochures and ad placements in selected automotive-related publications.

Question: Based on your data collection, what is the most lucrative publication for ad placement with mailing-list parameters that would be most desirable for inclusion in your marketing initiatives?

Related Professional Associations

Specialty Equipment Market Association (SEMA) located at www.sema.org provides information and market research on the specialty equipment and automotive aftermarket industry.

BIG MOUNTAIN CORPORATION

David Stotlar, Northern Colorado University

● ●

Descriptive Information for the Big Mountain Corporation

Big Mountain Corporation, located in a large western city, is a small to medium-sized manufacturer of consumer goods relating to hiking, backpacking, and climbing activities. It is a family-controlled organization begun about 25 years ago. Big Mountain is considering a major expansion of facilities and product lines to tap the rapidly growing and diversified market. The 5-year outlook for obtaining and developing key managerial personnel poses a problem in light of the technological changes and corporate expansion plans that would require considerable technical expertise and innovative ability. Basically, the production techniques, the products, and the consumers themselves have grown very sophisticated in the last decade. In order to maintain a competitive advantage in an industry dominated by huge companies, Big Mountain has to be extremely creative and current regarding the technology required to produce its products. The plan for modernizing and expanding existing facilities indicated that reorganization would be needed. It has been predicted that business expansion and new-product development needs would create demands for new specializations and hiring (particularly in engineering and marketing).

Currently, Big Mountain has 105 persons in managerial positions. The managers are divided among departments as shown in Table 1.

Table 1
Big Mountain Market and Production Expansion

	Number of managers	Present average salary (without 21% fringes)	Projected Increase
Executive Staff	5	$83,121	10%
Manufacturing	34	$36,065	50%
Accounting	17	$38,454	30%
Finance	6	$39,140	20%
Marketing	13	$57,900	40%
Engineering	21	$38,731	30%
Personnel	5	$36,248	20%
TOTAL	105		

The problem before you is whether Big Mountain should still plan to significantly increase its productive capacity, based on continued optimistic demand data for hiking, backpacking, and climbing products. The company will need to add human resources in some areas and perhaps decrease them in other areas within the next 2 years in order to facilitate the expansion.

Specifically, Big Mountain is considering an increase in production capacity within the next 2 years. Market research, new-product development, financial planning, personnel, production planning, and scheduling will each have to conduct independent analyses to determine if expansion is feasible and desirable at this time. The planned expansion includes additions to the engineering department for new product development and prototypes, to manufacturing for new work processes and scheduling, and to marketing for added sales capability and advertising. Of course, because new products will be designed, manufactured, and (it is hoped) sold, these areas must grow. In addition, support areas would also need to grow to serve the needs of the larger manufacturing organization.

Within the next 2 years, productive capacity could be increased by 50%. Physical facilities are already being finished to house manufacturing and administration expansion. With this expansion, the executive committee's estimate of sales 2 years from now, allowing for inflation, is $54,000,000.

The financial picture of Big Mountain has been consistently bright and improving. The organization, witnessed by the historical balance sheet (see Table 2), has a sound capital structure and relatively small debt obligations. Sales volume and net income have also increased in 8 of the last 10 years.

Additional information on Big Mountain concerns its specific departments. These are reasonably autonomous units, and their director or vice president typically has considerable authority for the departments' activities. Information about each department follows.

Manufacturing. This is the largest and most powerful department; however, the department lacks direction, as its senior people must take charge of the entire operation, and they are reluctant to delegate any authority in manufacturing, which is a reason for their failure to promote anyone to challenge their authority in the manufacturing department. Equipment is modern, but expertise in production planning and control is shallow. Ties to engineering are weak.

Accounting. Accounting is not a large group, but is professional. It boasts graduates from prestigious business schools and people from major public accounting firms. The goals of the department are to educate managers in accounting practices and set up Big Mountain as an example in the

Table 2
Historical Abbreviated Financial Data
for Big Mountain Corporation (in thousands of dollars)

Assets	Two years ago	Last year	This year
Cash	49	48	53
Marketable securities	150	165	170
Receivables, net	199	205	208
Inventories	300	310	324
Net plant and equipment	1,300	1,280	1,273
Total assets	2,000	2,008	2,028
Claims on Assets			
Accounts payable	60	59	63
Notes payable	100	97	106
Accruals	9	9	9
Federal income taxes accrued	131	135	140
Mortgage bonds	500	495	500
Stock	600	620	632
Retained earnings	600	593	578
Total claims on assets	1,998	2,008	2,028
Net sales volume	30,000	32,500	36,000
Net income (after taxes)	921	1,235	1,386

industry of an organization that is able to implement the latest accounting conventions and rules correctly and efficiently.

Finance. This department is quite small, perhaps due to the family-owned nature of the company. One member of the department is a member of the family of the founders and owners of Big Mountain. The remainder of the department consists of managers with little power.

Marketing. This department is viable and visible. It has a pool of creative people who have developed a effective sales network. Their goals are to expand and begin to develop in-house advertising capability.

Engineering. The engineering department is large, but contains many people who direct the maintenance system for machinery and other tangible assets. Liaison with the manufacturing department is poor, and this hinders morale in engineering. The best people hope for transfers to manufacturing where things actually happen. Engineering contains a small research and development (R-and-D) group who are given excellent physical resources and who are quite visible. However, their work is seldom advanced through manufacturing where the ideas for new products always seem to originate. R-and-D has been called a public-relations gimmick by some. The director of engineering was recently hired to develop the department into a viable force, particularly R-and-D, but is having problems retaining people.

Personnel. Personnel is the smallest department as far as number of managers, but has several clerks because of its record-keeping functions. Personnel is involved in an affirmative-action program, in union negotiations, and in contract administration almost exclusively. Selection and training are primarily decentralized (i.e., left to line managers). Performance appraisal and career development are the department's strong points.

Case Problem

The decision being considered is the addition of a third shift to join the existing two (hence the 50% increase in manufacturing). Assume a span of control from management to labor at 1 to 5 with an average salary for labor at $21,000 with fringe benefits at 18%. Inflation will exist at 5% per year across the board.

> Your task is to determine if market and production expansion is warranted within the stated parameters. Will the increased labor costs be covered by the increase in sales (it will be assumed that all other expense data remain fixed)? Is this a wise move for Big Mountain Corporation? Justify your answer.

Suggested Readings

Blankenship, A. B., & Breen, G. (1995). *State of the art marketing research*. Chicago: American Marketing Association.

Breen, G., & Blankenship, A. B. (1989). *Do-it-yourself marketing research*. New York: McGraw-Hill.

Cohen, W. A. (1991). *The practice of marketing management*. New York: Macmillan.

Author's Note: A solution for Big Mountain is presented in Table 3.

Table 3
Solution for Big Mountain Case

		Avg. Salary	Total Salary		Expansion	New Avg. Salary	Total Salary
Executive Staff	5	$83,121	$415,605		5	$87,277	$436,385
Accounting	17	$38,454	$653,718		22	$40,377	$888,287
Manufacturing	34	$36,065	$1,226,210		51	$37,868	$1,931,281
Finance	6	$39,140	$234,840		7	$41,097	$287,679
Marketing	13	$57,900	$752,700		18	$60,795	$1,094,310
Engineering	21	$38,731	$813,351		27	$40,668	$1,098,024
Personnel	5	$36,248	$181,240		6	$38,060	$228,362
			$4,277,664		$346,142	$5,964,329	
Fringes at .21			$5,175,973	Total Cost Mgmt	Fringes at .21		$7,216,838
Work force	505	$21,000	$10,605,000		680	$22,050	$14,994,000
Fringes at .18			$12,513,900	Total Cost Labor	Fringes at .18		$17,692,920
		Total Personnel Costs	$17,689,873	Total Personnel Costs			$24,909,758
		Old Sales Vol.	$36,000,000	New Sales Vol.			$54,000,000
				Net gain Sales		$18,000,000	
				Net Pers. Exp. Increase		$7,219,884	
				Difference		$10,780,116	
				With $10 million increase, they should expand.			

FOOTBALL HELMETS AND THE CONCUSSION DILEMMA

Wayne Blann, Ithaca College

Background

In a December 19, 1994, *Sports Illustrated* article by Peter King titled "Halt the Head Hunting," Buffalo Bills defensive end Bruce Smith said of pass rushing: "It's an art. It's also a car accident" (p. 29). King also reported on how Los Angeles Rams defensive end Fred Stokes felt about plowing through Atlanta Falcons quarterback Jeff George after he released the ball. Stokes said, "It sounds animalistic but I got such a rush, I was slobbering. That's the game. It might be crazy, but it goes back to Pop Warner football. At every level, the harder you hit, the more you get patted on the back and the happier you are" (p. 29). According to King, that is the culture of the game. Data supplied by the 28 National Football League teams showed that 445 concussions were suffered by 341 players between 1989 and 1993. This represents about four concussions per weekend and about 2.5 concussions for every 1,000 plays. King reported other evidence that indicates that concussions are the silent epidemic of football:

- 250,000 out of 1.5 million high school football players suffer concussions during any given season
- Players who have already suffered concussions are four times more likely to suffer another concussion than players who have not suffered concussions
- Concussions are under-reported at all levels of football because players do not admit to the injuries and trainers cannot readily diagnose mild concussions
- NFL guidelines for allowing players to return to play after suffering concussions are too lenient and in some cases more lenient than professional boxing's guidelines
- Post concussion syndrome among NFL players and former players is more widespread than believed because players do not want to admit to their conditions." (pp. 40, 45)

The Effects of Hard-Hitting in Football

Football is a contact sport that involves clean, hard hitting, but it should not allow cheap shots, unnecessary or intentionally rough hits to be carried out by players against other players. Allowing unnecessary rough hits by players increases the chances that players will suffer from concussions. Neuropsychologists agree that individuals who have concussions tend to have more concussions, more easily, and that repeated insults to the brain cause neuropsychological damage. However, little information exists regarding the effects of football concussions at any level in the game. Neither administrators, coaches, athletic trainers, nor players really want to know what effects concussions have had on players or the extent to which players have incurred neurological problems.

Developing A Marketing Plan

The manufacturers of the padded football helmets recognize that their product might be better than existing helmets in protecting players from suffering concussions from some hard hits. The evidence that exists about concussions suffered by football players clearly allows the manufacturers an opportunity to market the padded helmets as a "safety precaution" for all players, at all levels of the game. However, the manufacturers also recognize that marketing the padded helmets solely on the basis that they provide a "safety precaution" for players ignores the ethical issues that exist within the context of the culture of the game and society (i.e, encouraging, endorsing, and even cheering violence). Indeed, the manufacturers believe that if players think their product better protects them from concussions, they will try to hit even harder, because the culture of the game values such tactics.

Historically, as the sports equipment manufacturing industry develops improved protective equipment, other kinds of player injuries emerge as a result of the new equipment. The record shows that sports equipment manufacturers are ultimately sued by players for injuries they incur that are linked to protective sports equipment. Given this reality, it is likely that manufacturing, marketing, and selling the new padded football helmets might result in product liability lawsuits. Consequently, the manufacturers might also confront this product liability issue.

The manufacturers recognize they have both a legal and ethical responsibility to properly protect players' health in the long term, not simply make them somewhat better protected (possibly) from concussions in the short term.

The manufacturers realize that marketing their product on the basis that it provides players better protection from concussions fails to address the causes of the problem that threatens players' health in the long term. The manufacturers believe they have a social responsibility to market their product in ways that will help change not only the rules of the game but also, indeed, the culture of the game. It is their perspective that a marketing plan for padded helmets must include strategies that will encourage football governing bodies and rules committees to take actions that will actually reduce, if not eliminate, the incidence of player concussions in the game.

The manufacturers of the padded football helmets decided to consult with sport marketing experts (you and your classmates) to develop a marketing plan that addresses the ethical issues involved in this situation and that, when implemented, will result in the product's being marketed in socially responsible ways. The manufacturers have requested that you develop a marketing proposal that (a) establishes a clear mission, (b) identifies specific objectives derived from the mission, (c) sets forth marketing strategies that reach targeted audiences at all levels of the game and will carry out the objectives and mission, (d) clearly identifies the ethical issues that exist in the culture of the game and in society and how they influence the marketing strategies, and (e) demonstrates the ways in which the marketing plan addresses the ethical issues and is socially responsible.

Questions for Study

1. Discuss the legal issues in the game of football that relate to this marketing problem.
2. Discuss the ethical issues in the game of football that relate to this marketing problem.
3. Write a marketing mission statement.
4. Write specific marketing objectives derived from and linked to the mission statement.
5. Describe specific marketing/promotions programs/activities that might be implemented to reach specific target audiences in carrying out the marketing objectives and to achieve the marketing mission statement.
6. Explain how the marketing plan you recommend be implemented will address the legal and ethical issues in the game of football.

Suggested Readings

Blann, F.W. (1998). Sport marketing. In J. B. Parks, B. R. K. Zanger, & J. Quarterman (Eds.), *Contemporary sport management* (pp. 171–184). Champaign, IL: Human Kinetics.

Covey, S. R. (1989). *The seven habits of highly effective people.* New York: Simon and Schuster.

Grunig, J. E., & White, R. (1992). Communication, public relations and effective organizations. In J. E. Grunig (Ed.), *Excellence in public relations and communications management*. Hillsdale, NJ: Erlbaum.

Slack, T. (1997). *Understanding sport organizations: The application of organizational theory*. Champaign IL: Human Kinetics.

Related Professional Associations

American Marketing Association
250 South Wacker Drive, Suite 200
Chicago, IL 60606
(800)AMA-1150
http://www.ama.org

National Collegiate Athletic Association
6201 College Boulevard
Overland Park, KS 66211-2422
(913)339-1906
http://www.ncaa.org

National Football League
http://www.nfl.com

National Football League Players Association
http://www.sportsline.com/u/NFLPlayers

Sporting Goods Manufacturers Association
200 Castlewood Drive
North Palm Beach, FL 33408
(561)842-4100
http://www.sportlink.com

ADIDAS: MAKING A COMEBACK

Dianna P. Gray, University of Northern Colorado

• •

Background

Adidas had its beginnings in the 1920s, in Herzogenaurach, Germany, shortly after the end of World War I, when Adi Dassler and his brother, Rudolf, began making athletic shoes especially for runners and soccer players. Adi Dassler realized that to be credible with consumers, his product must be credible with athletes. By the 1950s, Adidas, so named for Adi Dassler's first and last names, had established an image as the premier athletic footwear company. This image was created primarily by the number of track and field athletes who won Olympic medals in Dassler's shoes, the most notable being American Jesse Owens, who won an unprecedented four gold medals at the 1936 Berlin Olympic Games. This early success established Adidas as a market leader in the athletic footwear industry and, by the 1970s, helped turn the firm into the world's top athletic shoe company.

Although Adidas invented the modern athletic shoe and dominated the industry for many years, it has fallen from its leadership position in the last two decades. After Adi Dassler's death in 1978, the company, faced with increased competition from U.S.-based companies Nike and Reebok, and more recently, Fila, has struggled. Adidas' philosophy of making excellent shoes for real athletes was compromised during the 1970s when the trend of athletic shoes as fashion statements for "weekend warriors" emerged. Slow to react to market changes, and badly underestimating the U.S. market, Adidas was left in the marketing dust of Nike, which, by emphasizing research and development, aggressive marketing, and shifting manufacturing to the Far East, was able to bring new products to the marketplace more quickly and cheaply than Adidas did. Once the market leader, Adidas fell to fourth in the U.S. athletic shoe market (see Table 1).

Though Adidas remained relatively strong in the international markets, its shoe sales in the United States lagged behind. In an effort to strengthen its U.S. position, in 1986 Adidas AG created Adidas USA, Inc., by buying out the four independent Adidas distributorships in the United States. The consolidation of the U.S. distributors was an important move by Adidas if it expected to make inroads in the $8 billion U.S. market, where more than half of the world's athletic shoe sales occur.

In 1990, with the company still struggling and faced with the death of Horst Dassler, Adi's son and Adidas CEO, the Dasslers sold the company to

Table 1
Percentage of U.S. Athletic Shoe Market, 1990

Company	Percent of Total US Market
Nike	33%
Reebok	24%
L.A. Gear	12%
Adidas	2%
Converse	2%

Source: *USA Today*. 1991

French corporate raider Bernard Tapie. For a brief period, things began to look up. In 1991 a new line of performance-oriented functional shoes and apparel, called Equipment, was developed, and company executives began to feel more optimistic about the chances of gaining in the U.S. market. In 1993, Adidas America was created, and along with its parent, Adidas AG, was purchased by an investment group, led by Robert Louis-Dreyfus. Louis-Dreyfus, former head of the British advertising group Saatchi & Saatchi, felt that only a couple of changes were needed to turn the company around.

How did Adidas lose its commanding lead in the athletic footwear market and get to its current status? What can Adidas do to try and recapture market share and bolster a sagging brand image? A review of Adidas, past and current marketing strategies should shed some light on this situation.

Marketing Strategy

The marketing strategies pioneered by Adidas influenced the entire athletic footwear industry. By having Olympic athletes wear Adidas products during international competition, the ultimate testing ground for its athletic footwear, the company received tremendous visibility and was able to obtain feedback from athletes, which led to continuous design changes and improvements. Endorsement contracts were made with the national sports associations, rather than with individual athletes, as is the case now. It is because of Adidas' early use of endorsement contracts that now virtually every athlete, Olympic and professional alike, has an endorsement contract with a footwear company. College players, and in some cases high school players, drafted by the National Basketball Association end up with lucrative endorsement contracts before they have played a single professional game!

In addition to its success with Olympic athletes, early in its history, Adidas established itself as the foremost provider of quality soccer shoes for elite players. The company is responsible for the development of several advances in soccer-shoe technology. The 1954 German team won the World Cup wearing Adidas shoes, and little has changed since to challenge the company's dominance in soccer.

To establish an easily recognized brand image, Adidas developed and marketed its distinctive, three stripes logo. It is essential for the effectiveness of endorsement contracts that the company's logo (mark) be easily recognized by fans and potential customers. This is the primary reason for paying an athlete to wear a particular product: Customers who see the product worn by an elite athlete want to associate with the athlete's success or image by wearing the same shoe. Another benefit of a highly recognizable and distinctive logo is its use with other product lines, such as equipment, apparel, and related products.

During the late 1970s and early 1980s, Adidas led the athletic footwear industry in offering the widest variety of running shoes. Shoes for every type of foot and running style — more than a hundred styles and models — made up Adidas' inventory. Only Nike would later eclipse Adidas in the number of styles and models of running shoes offered.

Where Did Adidas Go Wrong?

How could a company with such a commanding share of the athletic footwear market in 1980 and, on the face of it, a successful marketing strategy, let its market advantage slip away? Without doubt, Adidas underestimated both the potential growth of the athletic shoe market (in the late 1970s and early 1980s) and Nike's aggressiveness in seeking to dominate the U.S. marketplace. Adidas enjoyed many years of relatively little competition in the United States, and it was not until Nike and Reebok exploited the fitness craze of the 1970s that Adidas was faced with any significant rivals. Certainly, Adidas' slow recognition of the market conditions in the United States is evidence of marketing myopia.

Clearly the barriers to entering the market were not insurmountable, as Nike and Reebok, and a host of other smaller firms demonstrated. Neither the technology nor the money needed to begin production was enough to prevent a number of competing companies from entering the market. Should not Adidas have been more aware of this fact? Why did the company not aggressively discourage the development of competing companies by expanding the channels of distribution and adding retail outlets?

There were, however, other factors besides Nike's emergence in the athletic footwear industry that contributed to Adidas' undoing, not the least of which were its high production costs. Most of Adidas shoes were produced in Germany and France, where labor costs were considerably higher than if the company manufactured its shoes in the Far East. In addition, there were distribution problems faced by the company's four U.S.-based distributorships. Many retailers lost confidence in the company when it did not fulfill orders in a timely fashion.

However, the main problem probably was that the company lost its focus on products made for serious athletes. The move away from catering to the serious athletes and diversifying into fashion proved disastrous.

Making a Comeback

Since Louis-Dreyfus' arrival as CEO, he has pared staff drastically and doubled the marketing spending to 11% of sales, realizing that running shoes are running shoes, and image is all (Levine, 1996). Another Louis-Dreyfus move was to sell Adidas' factories in Europe and move production to the Far East, where most of the factories that manufacture athletic shoes exist. The result was the outsourcing of all production and the creation of a new logistics department to manage these new business relationships in Asia.

Another change in Adidas strategy was to reduce the number of product lines it offered. Historically the company produced shoes and apparel for every conceivable sport. As mentioned previously, at one time the company offered the second-largest selection of running shoes — over a hundred different styles and models — exceeded only by Nike. By eliminating the production of some items, particularly those with low demand, and focusing on the production of high-demand shoes, profitability has increased.

Under Louis-Dreyfus, the company is also refocusing and concentrating again on developing footwear for athletes. Adidas' heritage, successfully copied by Nike, is one of innovating and designing performance products. Adidas is returning to its original positioning as a company that makes products for the serious athlete. Adidas is also heavily involved in sponsorship as part of its sport marketing strategy. Table 2 lists Adidas' various sponsorship commitments.

In an effort to deal with the shipping and on-time delivery problems, issues that have historically plagued Adidas, sourcing and distribution have been restructured. Like other athletic footwear manufacturers, Adidas ships product from the factory to a regional warehouse before shipment to local retailers. Improved logistics, along with better relations with the factory,

Table 2
Adidas' Sponsorship Activities

Event	Sport/Level	Sponsorship Level
National High School Coaches Assn. National Basketball Championship	Amateur	Sponsor
NASCAR Winston Cup Series	Auto Sports	Associate Car Sponsor
Adidas/MetLife Soccer Classic at Indiana University	College	Title Sponsor
National Cycle League	Cycling	Sponsor
Boston Marathon (Official Footwear & Apparel)	Endurance	Official Sponsor
U.S. Soccer USA Boxing U.S. Weightlifting	Olympic	Official Sponsor
World Cup USA 1994	Soccer/ International	Official Sponsor
U.S. Soccer	Olympic	Official Sponsor
U.S. Amateur Soccer Association	Soccer/Amateur	Title Sponsor: Adidas U.S. Open Cup
ATP Senior Tour	Tennis	Official Sponsor Sponsor: Thriftway ATP Championship

Source: *Sports Sponsor Fact Book (1995)*

better quality control, and more timely delivery from the factory to the warehouse, has improved the company's delivery record and helped change retailers' attitudes toward the company and its products.

Adidas has also made a commitment to increased marketing of its products and the restoration of its brand image. The company was founded on the philosophy of making superior shoes for elite athletes. Nike, however, with Michael Jordan as its prime endorser, has taken the athletic footwear market to new levels. Adidas' reputation as the footwear of choice for professional and elite athletes has been usurped by Nike, particularly in the U.S. market, and Nike continues to gain market share internationally. It will be difficult for Adidas to return to its former status as the industry leader in athletic footwear, no matter how many marketing dollars the company is willing to spend in its fight against Nike and Reebok.

In an effort to capture some of the youth and Generation X markets, Adidas is placing a greater emphasis on grassroots activities and focusing some of its advertising on attracting teenaged, urban consumers away from the established Nike and Reebok brands. Rather than focus its marketing efforts solely on top-level, big-dollar marketing tactics, Adidas is doing a lot of guerrilla marketing activities at the lower levels of sports. An event that has attracted considerable attention outside the United States is a 3-on-3 outdoor basketball tournament, developed to give youngsters in Europe, South America, Africa, and Asia an opportunity to compete with each other. The first world championships were held in 1995 in Barcelona. Over 200,000 people were on hand during the 2-day event to watch teams from 51 countries compete.

Because the company cannot compete head-on with the marketing and advertising expenditures of Nike and Reebok, Adidas has decided to target key metropolitan areas in the United States, rather than attempt to blanket the entire country. New York City and Miami were identified as prime areas. Subway car cards and graffiti-style painted walls are among the advertising tactics being used to build up Adidas' brand image, particularly among the 12-24 demographic.

Conclusion

Even though Adidas has not regained its previous position as the most respected brand of athletic footwear, it is making a comeback. From less than 2% of the U.S. market in 1991, to approximately 6.5% in 1997, Adidas is gradually making up lost ground.

Table 3
Percentage of U.S. Athletic Shoe Market, 1995

Company	Percent of Total US Market
Nike	36.8%
Reebok	20.5%
Adidas	6.2%
Fila	5.8%
Keds	3.6%
Converse	2.9%

Source: USA Today, September 17, 1996, p. 3B

Six and a half percent may not seem like much, especially when compared with Nike's 36.8%. However, with the U.S. market accounting for over half of the $14 billion world market, a shift of four percentage points can mean nearly a quarter billion dollars of incremental sales.

Furthermore, according to analysts, the trend should continue. The projected growth for Adidas in the U.S. is 8% by 1998. On top of that, Adidas continues to be a dominant player internationally, based primarily on its leadership position in Germany, Japan, and Argentina, as well as its dominance in the rapidly growing Eastern European markets.

Case Study Questions

What happened in U.S. markets during the 1960s and 1970s that later had a profound impact on Adidas' market share?

Why did Adidas lose its commanding position in the U.S. athletic footwear market? Could this have been prevented? How?

What should Adidas have done to protect its market position from competing companies, Nike, Reebok, and L.A. Gear?

How has Adidas regained its brand image and become a competitive player in the U.S. athletic footwear market? What would you recommend Adidas do to continue its comeback? Would you build on the current strategies or recommend new ones? Justify your recommendations.

Related Activities

1. You can find Adidas on the World Wide Web at http://www.adidas.com. Periodically check their income statement (at http://www.adidas.com/finance/financial.htm) to see if the company is continuing its comeback.

2. Where is Adidas ranked currently with respect to its percentage of the U.S. shoe market? The international shoe market?

3. Compare Adidas' 1995 sponsorship activities (Table 2) with its current sponsorship commitments. Has Adidas changed the sports it is targeting? What does this tell you about Adidas' marketing strategy?

4. Conduct some focus group research with a group of 10 to 15 students on your campus to determine the level of brand recognition and loyalty for different footwear and apparel companies. You might compare Nike, Adidas, Reebok, Fila, and Converse. Use your findings to help determine how you would continue Adidas' comeback.

Related Readings

Carter, D. M. (1996). *Keeping score: An inside look at sports marketing.*

Grants Pass, OR: The Oasis Press.

Friedman, A. (1995). *Sports sponsor fact book*. Chicago, IL: Team Marketing Report.

Gwin, P. (1996, June). Adidas jumps back into the race. *Europe, 357,* 22–24.

Gelsi, S. (1995, December 4). Sneaking into third. *Brandweek, 36,* 24–25.

Hartley, R. F. (1986). Adidas — Letting market advantage slip away. In *Marketing mistakes* (3rd ed.). New York: John Wiley & Sons.

Jensen, J. (1994, July 25). Adidas continues to play hard. *Advertising Age, 65,* 42.

Jones, D. (1996, September 17). Nike orders secure industry foothold. *USA Today,* p. 3B.

Kindel, S. (1996, February). Making a run for the money: Adidas AG. *Hemispheres,* 47–48, 50.

Mussey, D. (1995, February 13). Adidas strides on its own path. *Advertising Age, 66,* 6.

Pitts, B. G., & Stotlar, D. K. (1996). *Fundamentals of sport marketing.* Morgantown, WV: Fitness Information Technology, Inc.

Schaaf, P. (1995). *Sports marketing: It's not just a game anymore.* Amherst, NY: Prometheus Books.

Schlossberg, H. (1996). *Sports marketing.* Cambridge, MA: Blackwell Publishers, Inc.

Sandomir, R. (1996, May 22). Bryant a pitchman before he's a pro. *The New York Times,* pp. B9, B13.

Strasser, J. B., & Becklund, L. (1991). *Swoosh: The unauthorized story of Nike and the men who played there.* New York: Harcourt Brace Jovanovich, Publishers.

Sullivan, R. (1996, July). Sneaker wars. *Vogue, 186,* 138–141, 173.

Suggested Trade Newsletters and Publications

Advertising Age
Adweek
American Demographics
Brandweek
Consumer Reports

Marketing News
New Product News
Sports Business Daily
Team Marketing Report

References

Levine, J. (1996, March 25). Adidas flies again. *Forbes, 157,* 44–45.

SECTION 3

THE SPORT PROMOTION INDUSTRY SEGMENT

The Sport Promotion Industry Segment: An Overview

There are products needed or desired for the purpose of promoting a sport product. Therefore, any product — goods, services, people, places, or ideas — created for the function of promotion fits into this industry segment. This part of the sport industry is composed of products that are used as promotional tools to sell products in the sport industry. Sports team souvenir T-shirts fall into this category. Advertising is in this category. Advertising is a product to be sold. Therefore, if a fitness center wants to advertise its products, it must purchase advertising.

Promotional methods in the sport industry include a large variety of products. This includes souvenirs, pregame giveaways, endorsement advertising, sponsorship, and media relations.

Sports is also a promotional tool used by companies to sell their products. In other words, there are businesses that use sports as an advertising tool. Therefore, many sports businesses must consider their sports events in this way — how the sports event can be used to help sell another product. This usually comes in the form of sponsorship or endorsement. Here are some examples. A cereal company puts a famous athlete's picture on the cereal box hoping that more cereal will be sold. This is called endorsement advertising. The athlete's picture suggests that the athlete supports, or endorses, the cereal. In another example, a prestigious car company helps fund a professional women's golf tournament. This is sponsorship. The car company is suggesting the notion that those who drive the car participate in or are fans of a prestigious sport. The company is attempting to appeal to the consumers of the event and of the sport.

The cases in this section involve promotional products — those products used to promote a sport product. Refer to chapters 11–15 in the Pitts and Stotlar (1996) textbook for help.

THE SINKING OF THE AMERICA'S CUP

David Stotlar, Northern Colorado University

● ●

Sponsoring sporting events has gained popularity in the past several years as corporations attempt to break through advertising clutter. Considerable attention is focused on successful campaigns, but not all sponsorship deals provide the result anticipated by event owners or corporate sponsors. The following report from the IEG Sponsorship Report (June 1, 1992, reprinted with permission) chronicles some of the problems encountered during a sponsored sailing event.

America's Cup Players

America's Cup Organizing Committee (ACOC): Responsible for defending Cup and staging event. Formed from Sail America Foundation, which ran Dennis Conner's '87 and '88 Cup efforts. Prohibited by a self-imposed "defense plan" from selling sponsorship to commercial entities until October 1990. Finishes race with $11 million in sponsorship and $3 million in debt. Major sponsors: San Diego Unified Port District, AT&T, Coors Brewing Co. and TGI Friday's Inc.

Malin Burnham: ACOC president, San Diego banker and San Diego Yacht Club (SDYC) member and former commodore. Founder of Sail America. Lent $4 million to ACOC, forgiving $2 million in '91.

Tom Ehman: San Diego Yacht Club (SDYC) member tapped by Burnham as ACOC executive vice president/general manager. Executive director of New York Yacht Club's (NYYC) America II challenge in 1986–87.

David McGuigan: ACOC vice president marketing; former head of IMG's Chicago office and former vice president of sales at Dennis Conner Sports. Hired IMG and Arlen Marketing.

Ernie Taylor: Executive director of the Challenger of Record Committee (CORC) that conducted the America's Cup challenger races.

International Management Group (IMG): Agency that has represented Conner's personal licensing and merchandising since '87. TV subsidiary TWI won contact to advise on and sell ACOC TV rights. Hired by ACOC to sell international licensing. Later retained to sell ACOC sponsorship in joint venture with Arlen Marketing.

Arlen Marketing: Agency hired to sell ACOC domestic licensing. Formed joint venture with IMG to sell ACOC sponsorship. Headed by former Dennis Conner Sports executive vice president Doug Augustine.

Marketing and Promotion Group: Agency hired by McGuigan to manage $1 million America's Cup Village (a special event and tourist festival center built and run in conjunction with the America's Cup Event) during May 1991 Int'l America's Cup Class World Championships.

The Omnis Co.: Hired by ACOC on Arlen/IMG's recommendation in October 1991 to manage America's Cup International Centre (for hospitality and tourism). Fired by ACOC in March 1992, when Arlen/IMG took over management.

Team Dennis Conner: Syndicate that raised $10.5 million in sponsorship, led by American Airlines, General Motors Corp.'s Cadillac Motor Car Division and Pepsi-Cola Co., which anteed up to $3 million each.

America 3: Syndicate formed by multimillionaire Bill Koch that set sail with $6 million in sponsorship, primarily from Coors Brewing Co., General Motors' Corvette, AT&T and Digital Equipment Corp., each of which spent $500,000 to $1.5 million. Successfully defended the Cup in May 1992.

In the Beginning

From a historical standpoint, the America's Cup has been embroiled in controversy since its inception. In 1851 New York business leaders were invited to send a New York harbor pilot boat to London to participate in the World Trade Exhibition. In responding, the Commodore of the New York Yacht Club, built an extremely fast boat for the event and christened it "America." The race victory for America brought the Royal Squadron Cup to the United States and it has been known as the America's Cup ever since. Significant legal battles over the America's Cup continued from 1871 through the 1983 series with arguments over the design and length of challenger's ships and race schedules. It was in 1983 that U.S. skipper Dennis Conner lost the Cup to Australia II of the Royal Perth Yacht Club. The succeeding race in 1987 off the shores of Perth brought additional turmoil. Considerable discussion occurred over the ownership of the television rights for the Cup race with the Royal Perth Yacht Club (as owner of the Cup) eventually coming out in control. However, the series, through the efforts of Dennis Connor and the crew of the Stars and Stripes, brought the Cup and its controversies back to the United States and the San Diego Yacht

Club. This is where the current case study of the 1992 America's Cup event begins.

As the America's Cup Organizing Committee faced a $3 million debt and a bevy of unhappy sponsors in the wake of its 1992 event, preparing for 1995 seemed to be the least of its problems.

Debt and discontent stemmed from a string of missteps by ACOC. Among them:

- Badly misreading the sponsorship market
- Relying on overly optimistic forecasts of income from TV rights fees, then losing those rights when a cash crunch hampered its ability to cover TV production costs.
- Overestimating the number of potential attendees and the event's economic impact.

"From the beginning, ACOC didn't understand how to package the event and sell it to corporate America," said Mary Reiling, staff manager, national event marketing for AT&T, the low-seven-figure presenting sponsor of ACOC's America's Cup Int'l Centre. "Once we signed on, it was evident that although ACOC and San Diego Yacht Club could run the races, they did not know how to run an event. We did not receive the value we expected."

"After we came aboard and started asking questions, we saw ACOC didn't have the infrastructure to handle it," said Paul Leroue, Coors Brewing Co.'s assistant brand manager, Coors Light, which sponsored the Centre and eventual defender America.

Sponsors who refused the organizing committee's proposals say they did so after sensing potential problems. "We're not the least bit surprised things didn't turn out the way ACOC wanted," said Ladd Biro, director, world-wide sales promotion for American Airlines, which turned down ACOC in favor of renewing with Team Dennis Conner. "The organization was not particularly well run. We felt it was better to steer clear, and I'm glad we did."

Packaged Goods

Disgruntled sponsors were the last thing ACOC president Malin Burnham and executive vice president Tom Ehman expected to confront. "Our number-one goal was to defend the Cup, and the best way to do that was to see that the syndicates were funded, so we decided not to sell sponsorship," said Tom Mitchell, ACOC's senior vice president of operations.

The event's "defense plan" gave the syndicates first crack at sponsor dollars and prohibited ACOC from seeking backers until October 1990, and then only with its board's approval. Instead, ACOC's $33 million budget was to come from TV rights fees-projected at $22 million — as well as license agreements, in-kind commitments, memberships and merchandise sales.

However, supporting a syndicate was not ideal for every potential sponsor. Tying into the right syndicate might offer a windfall of on-camera visibility, but tying into a loser meant watching investment sail out of view.

"Why spend money backing the wrong horse?" said Warner Canto, senior vice president, worldwide marketing development, American Express TRS Co (AmEx).

Faced with that dilemma in 1987, AmEx sought to guarantee presence with whichever syndicate ended up defending the Cup in 1988. It offered six syndicates a total of $750,000, with the largest portion earmarked for the top finisher. The syndicates, cutthroat competitors on land and sea, would not cooperate. "One called a press conference denouncing the whole thing," Canto said. "We pulled the program."

Leading up to this year's event, potential sponsors again pushed for a sponsorship program that made sense for them. Many turned to ACOC in hopes of a unified Cup package. "From day one, we told ACOC we wanted the event, not the syndicates," Reiling said. "It wouldn't put together the package for us." Even some within the America's Cup camp pushed to consolidate competing interests by developing a package that would have included syndicate and event sponsorship, as well as ad time on event TV broadcasts.

"I was in Ehman's office three years ago and said 'Let's market this together,' " said Ernie Taylor, executive director of the Challenger of Record Committee (CORC), which conducted the America's Cup challenger races. "He said, 'Yeah, yeah, sure,' and went off and did all these deals without us."

Unplugged

ACOC retained Trans World Int'l, the broadcast arm of IMG, to sell the event's foreign TV rights and consult on the sale of domestic rights. In October 1990, ACOC struck a deal with ESPN: $3 million for U.S. broadcast rights and another $5 million toward production.

Although Taylor said ACOC did not consult with CORC until the ESPN deal was signed, the committees agreed to share subsequent production risks and rewards on a 55-45 basis in anticipation of TWI's projected $14.5 million in foreign rights. By May 1991, immediately after ACOC staged the Int'l America's Cup Class World Championships, the joint TV deal began to unravel. Excessive production costs put ACOC $2.6 million over budget and overseas rights fees were slow in coming.

"We expected most of the rights payments to come in up front," Burnham said. "Instead, they came in at the end. TWI honestly made cash flow estimates it thought were right, but the economy slid, and I know TWI had difficulty selling foreign rights."

"In June '91, we couldn't get proper accounting from ACOC," Taylor said. "Finally it admitted that more than $1 million that was supposed to be used for TV production had been spent on other areas of the event."

In July, Burnham fired off a letter to CORC nixing the agreement, leaving ACOC holding all TV rights-and risks, Taylor said. As ACOC's cash flow deteriorated, it approached CORC in October and again in November to reinstate the agreement. Taylor refused.

By December, ACOC admitted it could not fund TV production, Taylor said. On Jan. 24, ACOC forfeited broadcast rights to CORC and TWI. The new partners, who then sold $5 million in foreign rights, made it an 80-20 split, minus ACOC's debts.

Village People

Early in '91, ACOC decided to use the 10-day Worlds to "test public interest" in an America's Cup Village, Burnham said. ACOC vice president of marketing Dave McGuigan retained John Peterson, president of Marketing and Promotion Group, to "organize the Village for the Worlds, and if it worked out, to do it for the Cup," Mitchell said. Peterson said his contract extended through May 1992.

Despite the self-imposed ban on sponsorship, in October 1990, ACOC landed an "up to" $8.3 million Village sponsorship from the San Diego Unified Port District, which, as a noncommercial entity, was exempt from the ban.

However, Port District authorities who did not return calls from IEG Sponsorship Report, released funds slowly-and on the condition that they not be used to promote the village, Burnham said. "The district is a quasi-governmental body; we had to operate within the parameters of its legal and political policy."

In lieu of promotion dollars, "Peterson had to work with local radio stations to set up special days in the Village that the stations would promote," Mitchell said. In the end, Peterson's anticipated paid attendance of 100,000 and a $1.7 million net windfall for ACOC never materialized. Even though ACOC eliminated the gate charge, no more than 60,000 people came,

Mitchell said. "We decided we didn't know how to do a Village."

"We overdid it by having an international Village with food and cultural attractions," Burnham said. "The location was not good. It was hard to see, hard to park." Despite these problems, Burnham said he felt "a moral obligation" to build the venue on Port District property.

Death Throes

In August 1991, ACOC was $5 million in debt, despite Burnham having forgiven a $2 million personal loan. It laid off seven of 25 staff members, reduced its budget to $20 million and canceled plans for opening and closing extravaganzas.

In August, ACOC also publicly announced its search for sponsors-to the American syndicates' chagrin — through a joint venture between Arlen Marketing and IMG. ACOC had hired the two firms in August 1990 to sell domestic and international licensing, respectively.

Yet at least two sponsors told IEG Sponsorship Report they had been approached by McGuigan in early 1991 with behind-the-scenes proposals. Russell J. Ford, manager, special market promotions for American Airlines, said ACOC contacted him in January, just as the carrier was preparing to sign with Conner.

"Anything ACOC offered either duplicated Conner or wasn't worth anything to us," Ford said. "We tried to ensure that no other airline ambushed us, and as goodwill we offered to set up travel arrangements to defray expenses a little, but what ACOC was proposing was ridiculous. It needed tickets everywhere. The committee talked about hospitality and logos and PR, but we were already doing hospitality with Dennis' people."

Reiling said ACOC approached AT&T in April 1991. After she requested the syndicates' input, the committee returned with a proposal approved by America and Team Dennis Conner — not quite an umbrella package, but enough to bring her back to the table.

Meanwhile, in an attempt to find a viable sponsor hook, Arlen/IMG convinced ACOC to revive the Village concepts as the America's Cup International Centre. But the proposal lacked specifics, Canto said. "It didn't have anything for us." The Centre's eventual sponsors were dissatisfied even before the venue opened.

For example, The Omnis Co., which Arlen/IMG hired to run the Centre, sent AT&T scrambling to meet a January deadline for delivery of a 90-foot painting that would serve as the site's centerpiece. When Omnis reversed and asked AT&T to delay delivery, Reiling refused.

AT&T was no happier after the Centre opened. "It would have worked for us if attendance had been better," Reiling said. "The crowds didn't start coming until May 9, when the finals began."

ACOC also failed to provide the hospitality it promised AT&T, Reiling said. "We arranged our own and received buoy signage in exchange. Visually, the Centre didn't end up looking like we expected."

Another Centre sponsor, TGI Friday's Inc., went so far as to withhold payment, charging that Omnis failed to insure the venue. James Ishii, Omnis' chief executive, denied the charge, attributing appearances to the contrary to untimely withdrawals and deposits.

The TGI Friday's sent Arlen/IMG a letter outlining conditions for resuming payment, said Arlen president Doug Augustine. "Friday's was disappointed and felt Omnis had to go," Mitchell said. "I went to Friday's headquarters for a week and came to the same conclusion. When I came back, I recommended we cancel Omnis's license." TGI Friday's would not comment on the incident.

Arlen/IMG took over the Centre in March, Augustine said, "to maintain a relationship with sponsors, so we could see as best we could that they got everything they bargained for."

Economic Bust

Along with ACOC's internal economic woes, its event delivered just one-half to one-third of its projected economic impact on San Diego. A May 1990 University of San Diego study commissioned by ACOC estimated that the event would add $911 million to local coffers, but the total likely will be $300 million to $500 million, Mitchell said.

"We've been accused of overhyping the event and failing miserably in attracting people," Burnham said. "But whether it's $500 million or $350 million, that's $500 million or $350 million San Diego wouldn't have had. Previously, the largest event the city hosted was the Super Bowl, which I think had an impact of $131 million. We didn't do too bad."

ACOC remains $3 million in debt, including another $2 million owed to Burnham, Mitchell said. "We have no plans to file for bankruptcy."

*Material reprinted from IEG Sponsorship Report June 1, 1992 with permission from Rick G. Karr, Senior Editor. For additional information or subscriptions contact:

IEG Sponsorship Report
640 North LaSalle, Suite 600
Chicago, IL 60610-3777

Study Questions

1. In chronological order, what were the major errors committed by ACOC, and what actions could have taken to prevent them?
2. What were the major errors committed by organizers of the Village, and what actions could have taken to prevent them?
3. What basic marketing principles were violated (or ignored) by the various parties involved in sponsorship of the America's Cup Challenge?
4. Divide into small groups. Review the situation above. Your group is to present three errors made by the parties involved and identify an alternative course of action for each error that would have produced more desirable results.

Related Association

International Events Group
640 North LaSalle, Suite 600
Chicago, IL 60610-3777

Suggested Readings

IEG Sponsorship Report
International Events Group
640 North LaSalle, Suite 600
Chicago, IL 60610-3777

Other information available at
www.sponsorship.com

NATIONAL EXPRESS, INC.—ASSESSING SPORT SPONSORSHIP EFFECTIVENESS

Richard L. Irwin, University of Memphis

• •

Over the past 20 years National Express, Inc., has established a strong reputation as a leader in the express shipping business. As the second largest shipper nationwide National Express, based in Newport, Tennessee, is always seeking means for improving market share and challenging their competition.

Disappointed at the company's inability to overtake their leading competitor, Allied Parcel Company, David Stone, founder and owner of National Express, replaced a majority of the executive staff including Tae-Ho Chin, Director of Sport & Event Marketing. Tae-Ho was a very likable man with great staff rapport. Not one person had ever been replaced within the unit since he assumed the position of director in 1985. The staff were very comfortable with him, and the unit was actively involved in a variety of sport events ranging from local youth leagues to sponsorship of "The National," a premiere event on the Professional Golf Association (PGA) Tour. However, in David's mind, Tae-Ho had failed to keep up with the times yielding the unit complacent. Make no mistake about it: The severance package offered to Tae-Ho provided for a comfortable retirement with 3 years' pay on top of the company retirement plan as well as bonus stock options.

Unfortunately, the department staff was leery of their new director, Jenny McDowell, who was recently hired from International Sports, Inc., a sport marketing agency in Phoenix, Arizona, where she spent 8 years assisting with several accounts including Coca-Cola's Olympic and National Football League sponsorships. Jenny had a wonderful reputation in the field and was seen as creative as well as articulate yet tough when needed. According to David, "she had it all." He was very confident that she was the right person for moving the department forward. The staff was pleased to hear that Jenny believed in laissez-faire management. Her philosophy was to assign, mentor when called upon, treat the staff in a mature manner, and evaluate.

Under Jenny's direction were five staff members, three men and two women, all of whom had been with the company for at least 8 years. They were a collegial bunch who spent a lot of their free time together. They all seemed to think alike and were considered great "PR types."

Within her first week on the job, Jenny called a staff meeting and requested that over the next 12 months a thorough assessment of each sponsorship activity be initiated with documentation supplied supporting the sponsorship investment. As she put it, the unit was spending in excess of $30 million dollars annually with little evidence of return on investment. Actually the directive was coming from David, who had grown frustrated with what he thought was frivolous spending within the Sport & Event Marketing unit. Although he, as much or more than anyone else, enjoyed attending the numerous events sponsored by National Express, he had grown concerned about the value obtained from each. Jenny challenged each staff member to design a sponsorship assessment protocol that would yield quantitative results that could be reviewed by all interested parties at sponsorship renewal time. At the conclusion she distributed some materials for the staff to review and offered a reminder that each sponsorship activity was intended to generate business for the company.

Oscar Montoya had been a staff member within National's Sport & Event Marketing unit for 10 years. A native of Newport, Oscar had volunteered to assist with The National every year since his senior year at Newport High. Upon completion of his undergraduate degree (B.A. in marketing) at Western Tennessee University, Oscar was hired by National as department representative. In his 10 years in that capacity, the tournament had experienced phenomenal growth. Annually record numbers were in attendance, television ratings were up, and leading tour money winners consistently participated. Oscar left the meeting certain these evaluation materials would not be all that difficult, but he only had 2 months to prepare. He also viewed this as a critical project as the event title sponsorship agreement was up for renewal. Because his job was directly linked to this specific event, it was imperative that he generate and forward favorable information.

Within a week Oscar did what all brilliant marketers would do: He called his former professor at Western Tennessee University and requested to meet with some students who might like to help with a research project. He wanted to employ two methodologies for collecting the quantitative-type data requested by Jenny. He proposed that one small group of students tape record the telecast of the event and calculate the total on-air exposure time received by National Express. This included in-focus viewing of coarse signage, pin flags, tee boxes, and National Express on-screen logo burn-ins, as well as oral mentions of National Express by the broadcasters. The second group was to execute exit interviews of event patrons simply seeking to know who they thought was the title sponsor of the event and the sponsors' business. To Oscar's delight, 15 students volunteered to assist with the event research.

As the title sponsor, National Express receives 1,000 tickets to the event as well as a provision to host a hospitality tent along the 18th fairway. Each year that Oscar had been associated with The National, all tickets had been distributed with many going to employees and the remainder to sales staff, and the hospitality tent, at an additional cost of $250,000 for catering, was always packed. With their share of the tickets, sales staff were encouraged to invite customers who they felt were deserving. Meanwhile, management typically invited 100 customers from across the country who spent more than $100,000 in shipping within the past year.

As the event approached, Oscar felt he had assembled a solid assessment of the event. His research crew was ready, all tickets had been distributed, no cancellations had occurred, and the television ad spots were set. Now if only Mother Nature would cooperate!

The event was a beauty. Jose Galdez birdied the final six holes to capture the lead from Chin Wei, who had led from the start. The fantastic charge by Galdez led to an impromptu plunge in the lake on Hole #18, which provided an ideal photo opportunity generating excitement among guests as well as extra exposure on sports pages and highlight shows all across the country. Jenny had attended and upon departure congratulated Oscar for providing a great hospitality environment. She demonstrated genuine enthusiasm for his report.

Now for Oscar's assessment responsibilities. As previously noted, all tickets had been successfully distributed and were in fact used for admission to the event. Overall attendance was up a record 13% with television ratings holding steady with the past 2 years.

Oscar chose to present a scrapbook-style bound copy of his findings to Jenny. He divided the results into the following sections: (a) attendance, (b) television, (c) additional media, (d) invited guests, and (e) general atmosphere. To his credit, Oscar believed he had compiled some rather convincing data that he provided in the report summary as follows:

- The on-site research revealed that 88% of the sample (N=1,000) correctly cited National Express as the title sponsor and 65% were familiar with their business category.
- Stabilized television ratings (3.1 with an 8 share) for the Saturday and Sunday rounds.
- Over 15 minutes (15:14) in on-air exposure time representing more than $3 million in commercial air time ($200, 000 per minute ad rate).
- Selected photos from national publications (e.g., *Sports Illustrated*, *Golf*, & *USA Today*).

- A comprehensive list of all invited guests who attended and their shipping performance over the past year.
- Photographs of the hospitality tent.

Within 21 days after the event's conclusion, Oscar submitted his report to Jenny. He anxiously awaited her comments as he assisted Betty Bowers with her preparations for the upcoming trade show.

Upon arriving at the office 2 days later, Oscar turned on his computer which notified him that he had an e-mail message from Jenny. He hurriedly clicked to view the following message:

Interoffice Memo

TO: Oscar Montoya
FROM: Jenny McDowell, Director
         Sport & Event Marketing
RE: "The National" Sponsorship Assessment

Initially, allow me to commend you for your evaluative initiatives related to our sponsorship of The National. You have provided some valuable, insightful data from which we can all derive a sense of accomplishment. Unfortunately, you have failed to provide concrete data that demonstrate we have accomplished our primary sponsorship goal(s)/objectives(s) via this sport sponsorship agreement. Without such facts our association with this event may be in jeopardy. It is imperative that we meet to discuss this situation this morning. Please be sure to bring the Guide to National Express Sponsorship Activity (distributed at our first staff meeting) with you.

Discussion Questions

1. What information might Oscar be lacking in his report?
2. How would he generate the additional information necessary to assess the sponsorship effectiveness?
3. Where did the problems start?
4. What should Jenny have done differently?
5. If you were hired as Oscar's replacement, how would you complete this task?
6. What resources are necessary?
7. What information is still accessible?

Suggested Readings/Resources

Crompton, J. L. (1994). Benefits and risk associated with sponsorship of major events. *Festival Management & Event Tourism, 2*, 65–74.

IEG Newsletter

Mullin, B. J., Hardy, S., & Sutton, W. A. (1993). *Sport marketing.* Champaign, IL: Human Kinetics Publishers.

Schaaf, P. (1995). *Sports marketing.* Amherst, BY: Prometheus.

Sponsor's Report

Related Professional Organization of Interest

International Events Group (IEG)
640 North LaSalle, Suite 600
Chicago, IL 60610-3777
(800)334-4850
http://www.sponsorship.com

STARTING A SPORT MARKETING FIRM

Wayne Blann, Ithaca College

● ●

Background

A group of male and female African-American and Latino entrepreneurs identified what they believed to be an opportunity for establishing a sport marketing firm that could develop its own niche in the marketplace. The entrepreneurs recognized that predominantly white-owned and -managed sport marketing firms were currently serving African-American, Latino, and other ethnic minority athletes using traditional (white-oriented) marketing strategies. It was their perspective that these traditionally white-owned and -managed sport marketing firms gave little, if any, consideration to their clients' race and ethnic or cultural backgrounds in developing marketing strategies. A further concern of these entrepreneurs was their view that minority athletes were, in some cases, being misrepresented and, perhaps, even exploited by the traditional approaches used to promote athletes. The African-American and Latino entrepreneurs also recognized that promotional programs involving minority athletes most often benefited events, organizations, and businesses that were already well established and controlled or owned by the dominant financial (white) classes of people. This was viewed negatively by the entrepreneurs because they believed that successful and highly visible athletes, especially minority athletes, should be encouraged to take actions to help businesses and people in the communities from which they came.

The African-American and Latino entrepreneurs wanted to establish a sport marketing firm owned and managed primarily by African-American, Latino, and other ethnic minorities that would develop promotional programs based upon an understanding and appreciation of their clients' race and ethnic and cultural backgrounds and needs. The entrepreneurs were also committed to developing promotional programs for their clients that would help address the financial, social, and moral issues faced by their communities.

Developing a Proposal for a Sport Marketing Firm

The entrepreneurs recognized that a first step in establishing a sport marketing firm was to obtain adequate financial support to support recruiting clients and initiating programs to serve clients during the first 3 years of operation and also to ensure financial stability for the future. It was decided that in order to identify and attract corporate sponsors, the entrepreneurs needed to develop a marketing plan that would (a) establish a distinctive mission; (b) establish clear objectives derived from the mission; (c) identify strategies for recruiting clients; (d) develop unique marketing activities/programs that would best serve the clients and, by so doing, distinguish the firm and differentiate it from its competitors in the marketplace; and (e) develop sponsorship packages that would appeal to and benefit both traditional (white-owned) corporations and African-American, Latino, and ethnic minority-owned businesses.

Developing a Marketing Plan

The entrepreneurs decided to consult with sport marketing experts (e.g., you and your classmates) in developing a marketing plan. Listed below are some of the questions they wanted help with in developing a plan.

Questions for Study

1. What market research do you recommend be undertaken to obtain the best possible data to assess the merits of this idea and to develop a marketing plan? Who should be surveyed? What information should be collected? What factors/trends in the marketplace need to be considered when interpreting the data? What ethical and social responsibility concerns need to be considered?
2. What purposes do you believe should be set forth in the mission statement? Explain how each purpose demonstrates ethical actions or social responsibility on the part of the firm.
3. What objectives do you recommend be written to carry out the mission?
4. What marketing activities/programs do you recommend be implemented to serve specific targeted audiences? How will these activities/programs help achieve the marketing objectives and fulfill the mission?
5. What steps would you take to identify corporate sponsors for the various marketing activities/programs?
6. What kind of sponsorship packages would you develop to appeal to and benefit different types of corporations?
7. What other questions do you believe need to be examined in order to successfully implement a marketing plan?

Educational Purposes of the Starting-a-Sport Marketing Firm Case Study

1. To develop students' understanding of how a sport marketing plan is derived from the mission and objectives of an organization.

2. To develop students' understanding of how sport marketing plans are developed within a sociocultural context.

3. To develop students' understanding of multiculturalism issues in developing sport marketing strategies.

4. To develop students' critical thinking skills in identifying ethical and social responsibility issues that exist within the broader social context and that influence how sport marketing strategies are developed.

Suggested Readings

Blann, F.W. (1998). Sport marketing. In J. B. Parks., B. R. K. Zanger, & J. Quarterman (Eds.), *Contemporary sport management* (pp.171–184). Champaign, IL: Human Kinetics.

Covey, S. R. (1989). *The seven habits of highly effective people.* New York: Simon and Schuster.

DeSensi, J. T. (1994). Multiculturalism as an issue in sport management. *Journal of Sport Management, 8,* 63–74.

Grunig, J. E,. & White, R. (1992). Communication, public relations, and effective organizations. In J.E. Grunig (Ed.), *Excellence in public relations and communications management.* Hillsdale, NJ: Erlbaum.

McCarville, R. E., & Copeland, R. P. (1994). Understanding sport sponsorship through exchange theory. *Journal of Sport Management, 8,* 102–114.

Slack. T. (1997). *Understanding sport organizations: The application of organization theory.* Champaign, IL: Human Kinetics.

Related Professional Organizations

African-American Athletic Association

Association of Black Women in Higher Education

Black Coaches Association
P. O. Box 4040
Culver City, CA 90231-4040
http://www.bca.org

National Alliance for Black School Educators
National Association for the Advancement of Colored People
(410)521-4939
http://www.naacp.org

National Chicano Council for Higher Education
National Network of Hispanic Women
12021 Wilshire Boulevard, Suite 353
Los Angeles, CA 90025
(213)225-9895

The National Urban League
http://www.nul.org

CALL YOUR OWN GAME: TRZ SPORTS SERVICES, INC.

Jacquelyn Cuneen, Bowling Green State University

● ●

TRZ Communications Services, Inc. (incorporated in 1984 as TRZ Sports Services, Inc.) was founded in 1982 in Akron, Ohio, to assist colleges, professional teams, and other sport organizations with fund-raising, ticket-sales program development, computer installation and instruction, broadcast network development, special event management and promotion, and other marketing, advertising, and public relation activities. While framing TRZ's various marketing, promotional, and sales activities, founder and Chief Executive Officer Thomas Zawistowski continued to work on a vision to develop a cost-efficient distribution system designed to bring college athletics games of all kinds to those graduates, boosters, and parents who were too widely dispersed to be reached by traditional radio and television broadcasts (TRZ Sports Services, 1994b).

Zawistowski's solution was to broadcast games using telephone services (TRZ Sports Services, 1994b). By March 1990, TRZ had arranged to broadcast all 32 games of the National Invitation (basketball) Tournament using a Kansas City, Missouri, service bureau owned and operated by a national long-distance carrier. The venture was a marketing achievement but a technical and financial disaster. Satisfied that the right technology could make telephone broadcasting possible and profitable, Zawistowski set out to acquire exclusive rights to distribute audio portions of games using a pay-to-listen concept, and in fall 1990, TRZ was using a service bureau in Omaha, Nebraska, to broadcast games. The Omaha venture was a technical and marketing success, but financial aspects remained problematic due primarily to a telephone-carrier system architecture that constrained profit. TRZ needed a way to provide the broadcast service at a price customers would be willing to pay yet that would generate profit for TRZ.

In December 1991, TRZ acquired a $1,000,000 investment (in exchange for 20% interest in the corporation) that enabled the company to build a propriety technical platform to make telephone broadcasting economically sound by the start of the 1992 college football season. Despite limited advertising and promotion activities (resulting from diminished capital due to the technical developments), the company continued to grow as the first enterprise to use telephone broadcasting.

Easy Access to Every Game in Any Market

TRZ revolutionized sports programming availability when it began TEAMLINE, an electronic medium designed to serve a fragmented market (TRZ Sports Services, 1994i). With TEAMLINE, live, unedited, unfiltered coverage of any sports event can be sent to fans across the country. Using their personal, business, hotel, cellular or pay phones from anywhere in North America, listeners access games, coaches' shows, press conferences, awards banquets, meetings, fundraisers, executive committee meetings, college/university presidential addresses, and sports informational services. Callers outside of North America use international operators and a national long-distance carrier. TEAMLINE operates primarily by feeding off the switchboard of each team's flagship radio station, but it can also feed from an office phone line, audio coupler or portable radio.

College sports are TRZ's primary broadcast stake. Initially, most institutions provided only football and men's basketball games from their radio flagships, but currently lacrosse, field hockey, ice hockey, and other sports that are not usually broadcast nationally are available regularly on TEAM-LINE. In 1993, telephone broadcast sales of college football increased 14%, of college men's basketball increased 55%, coverage of college women's basketball expanded to 32 teams, and college men's baseball sales doubled (TRZ Sports Services, 1994a) from the previous year. In the 1993–94 college seasons, 20,000 separate, live sporting events were broadcast via TRZ telephone lines (TRZ Sports Services, 1994e).

TRZ Targets

Sports "fanatics" were first identified as the target for TEAMLINE. Fans were perceived as an audience that would not be alienated by periodic miscues or service obstructions during initial development (TRZ Sports Services, 1994e); thus, TRZ could test and refine TEAMLINE's technical, interface, billing, and administrative fundamentals. Zawistowski thought fans would use TEAMLINE for three predominant reasons: (a) vast selections of games not scheduled for TV or radio broadcast, (b) opportunities to hear home team announcers, and (c) timeliness. There were four primary markets identified (TRZ Sports Services, 1994e, 1994f):

1. Sports fans who do not have regular geographic access to broadcasts of their favorite teams' contests.
2. Traveling fans who may wish to follow their favorite teams' contests while on the road and/or users who may also use TEAMLINE to listen to events not regularly available to them on local stations.

3. Newspaper, radio, and television reporters who listen to postgame or other programming from distant cities and/or follow distant games of local, regional, or national importance.

4. Individuals who monitor game and/or players' conditions for various reasons.

TEAMLINE Audience

The majority of TEAMLINE callers are male (96%). Average age of callers is 39, but age demography is distributed fairly evenly. Callers' average income is $71,000 (TRZ Sports Services, Inc., 1994c, 1994j), and most callers are college graduates. TEAMLINE audience demographics are shown in Tables 1 (age and income) and 2 (education).

Table 1
Age and Income Demography of TEAMLINE Callers

Age	%	Income	%
40-49	24	Over $50,000	53
30-34	22	$35,000-$50,000	17
35-39	21	$20,000-$35,000	15
18-29	18	Under $20,000	5
Over 50	14		

Note. Adapted from *Connections Magazine Fact Sheet*, p. 1, and *TEAMLINE Caller Demographics and Information Sheet*, p. 1, by TRZ Sports Services, 1994. Copyright 1994 by TRZ Communications Services, Inc. Adapted with permission of author.

Table 2
Education Demography of TEAMLINE Callers

Education	%
College Graduate	54.3
Master's Degree	27.7
Doctorate	6.0
High School Graduate	12.0

Note. Adapted from *TEAMLINE* Caller Demographics and Information Sheet, p. 1, by TRZ Sports Services, 1994. Copyright 1994 by TRZ Communications Services, Inc. Adapted with permission of author.

Income and education statistics are skewed by TEAMLINE promotion characteristics. TEAMLINE is promoted by colleges and universities to their alumnae/i bases. Therefore, listeners are likely to be college graduates with above-average incomes.

TRZ is committed to move telephone broadcasting from a niche market to a mass consumer product. TRZ national survey data indicate that the market contains 71 million consumers, only one tenth of one percent (1/10%) of whom have heard of TRZ's services. A survey conducted for TRZ in 1991 (TRZ Sports Services, 1994e) indicated that sales of audio sports services can reach $100 million annually.

Product

Thousands of people have access to the games of their choice on TEAM-LINE. Games are accessed by calling an 800 number, choosing the event(s) they wish, and listening for as long as they desire. Some users access several games for a few minutes each day or night. TEAMLINE is easy to access; Table 3 shows the procedure that callers use to access the TEAMLINE.

Table 3
Accessing TEAMLINE

- The TEAMLINE 800 number is dialed from any telephone in North America.

- The caller is prompted to punch in a team's 4-digit access code and select the event of choice.

- The caller is prompted to punch in major credit information.

- The credit card is verified, and the caller is connected to the event in seconds.

- Listeners are charged by the minute a declining retroactive rate ranging from $.30 to $.50 per minute. Rates decrease as listening time increases.

- Charges cease when listeners disconnect by hanging up (listeners are charged by time, not event).

Note. Adapted from *Annual report to CoSIDA* membership, p. 5, by TRZ Sports Services, 1994. Copyright 1994 by TRZ Communications Services, Inc. Adapted with permission of author.

Speaker phones and other add-on devices enable users to listen to TEAMLINE broadcasts just as they listen to radio broadcasts. Currently, TRZ holds exclusive pay-to-listen audio-transmission rights agreements with nearly 200 NCAA member schools (1994d). Teams from each major conference such as the Atlantic Coast, Big East, Big Eight, Big Ten, IVY, and Pacific-10, are included on TEAMLINE broadcasts (TRZ Sports Services, 1994o). TRZ also offers access to 28 National Football League teams, 26 teams in the National Hockey League, nearly half of all Major League Baseball, and several minor league baseball teams (TRZ Sports Services, 1994b, 1994e). Customers may call the same game as often as they like and may call different games on the same day or night. There is no set-up fee or minimum length for calls. College football games are the most frequently accessed (see Table 4); however TEAMLINE sales are dependent on the amount of advertising and promotion originated by the college/university, league/conference, and/or team.

Table 4
Sales for TEAMLINE Broadcasts

Sport	% of Caller Requests for Sport
College Football	46.8
NFL Football	21.4
NHL Hockey	21.0
College Basketball	10.8

Note: The information in this table is from *Connections* magazine fact sheet, (Page 1) by TRZ Sports Services, 1994. Akron, OH: TRZ Communications Services, Inc. Copyright 1994 by TRZ Communications Services, Inc. Adapted by permission.

That is, Table 4 shows that college football is the most frequently accessed sport. If colleges and universities promote TEAMLINE college football broadcasts heavily, then TEAMLINE's sales of college football rise; if TEAMLINE's service is not promoted, then sales fall. In other words, if colleges/universities promoted women's or men's basketball heavily, then those sports could supplant football as the most frequently accessed sport.

TRZ holds 1- to 3-year contracts with teams giving exclusive rights to distribute audio services on a pay-to-listen or subscription basis (TRZ Sports Services, 1994e). TRZ is negotiating currently with the National Basketball Association in order to provide scheduled NBA games to callers (TRZ Sports Services, 1994g). Table 5 shows the current status of contracts with TRZ collegiate and professional affiliates.

TRZ has an agreement with another communications and another sports marketing enterprise whereby TEAMLINE callers may order programs

Table 5
Current Status of TRZ Broadcast Contracts

Sport	Contract Terms in Years
Individual Colleges/Universities	3
NFL Football	1
NHL Hockey	2
College Basketball	3
All contracts contain first rights of renewal.	

Note. Adapted from *TEAMLINE Caller Demographics and Information Sheet*, p. 1, by TRZ Sports Services, 1994. Copyright 1994 by TRZ Communications Services, Inc. Adapted with permission of author.

and/or videos from the games they accessed and other events broadcast on TEAMLINE. Merchandise is mailed to customers after the game. Costs are dependent on market value (TRZ Sports Services, 1994a).

Incentives for Teams to Cooperate with TRZ

TRZ's major market goal is to have colleges and universities expand their uses of TEAMLINE by including more broadcasts of their nonrevenue sports, coaches' shows, press conferences, media days, team fundraisers, and other athletics functions (TRZ Sports Services, 1994g). TEAMLINE broadcasts offer sport enterprises several commercial benefits (see Table 6).

TRZ pays affiliates 12% gross of all revenue collected from sales of their events and 15% gross of revenues collected from third-party distributors. When events are offered in multiteam packages, TRZ allocates and distributes payments according to a formula developed by TRZ and the affiliates. Fee payments are made quarterly in December, March, June, and September.

TRZ proposes that TEAMLINE also benefits colleges and universities as a recruitment, retention, and endowment tool (TRZ Sports Services, Inc., 1994l):

1. Recruitment: Because even smaller schools can provide live coverage of any event, local fans, parents, and friends of players can hear every game. Local sports reporters have access to instant information relative to former high school players' performances, so local coverage is easy to disseminate. Institutions have found these elements to

Table 6
TEAMLINE's Benefits to Collegiate Athletics Departments

- TEAMLINE provides national and international access for fans who live beyond an institution's normal critical broadcast radius.

- Institutions receive commissions from TEAMLINE when any revenue is generated as a result of customers ordering their athletics programs events. Institutions receive a percentage of every dollar generated from calls to their events.

- Institutions can reach alumnae/i, fans and media nationally with game broadcasts, voice mail, fax or call transfers.

- Athletics programs receive national exposure for all sports.

- Players' families and the institutions' recruits have access to all live games.

- TRZ fund-raising activities related to long-distance calling are possible for institutions.

Note. The information in this table is from *Annual report to CoSIDA* membership, p. 4, by TRZ Sports Services, 1994. Copyright 1994 by TRZ Communications Services, Inc. Adapted with permission of author.

be important in recruiting athletes to their programs.

2. Retention: Players feel good about their college playing experiences when they know that their parents, friends, and former coaches can listen to their games. TEAMLINE also helps athletes' retention rates because the service can provide live coverage of classes that athletes miss while traveling.

3. Endowment: Colleges and universities have found that graduates respond to financial development needs when they are aware of them. Broadcasts of coaches' shows and live broadcasts of games help endowments by disseminating information relative to program needs.

TRZ Communications Services, Inc. also maintains voice-mail boxes and fax mailboxes, and provides call transfers for affiliated athletics programs. Rate charges for voice-mailboxes are flat fees of $4.95 per call for 5-minute updates. Fax mailboxes cost $2.95 for the first page and 99¢ for each additional page accessed from the mailbox. Users determine the limits for the number of pages contained in the fax boxes (TRZ Sports Services, 1994o).

Fund-Raising Programs

TRZ has continued its active involvement in fund-raising for college and university athletics departments by providing revenue ideas related to communication venues. A current project makes it possible for additional revenue to be generated through already existing donors when donors use

TRZ-issued telephone calling cards for regular long-distance calls (an independent long-distance carrier cooperates on the project). Portions of monthly payments (5% of a customer's collected long-distance dollar amounts) are allocated directly to a customer-designated athletics department. Athletics departments receive the monthly contributions at no extra cost to supporters; subscribers receive special long distance rates far below regular calling card rates (TRZ Sports Services, 1994h, 1994m).

TRZ and the carrier also offer a TEAMLINE debit calling card for travel or business use. The debit card is a prepaid calling card; when funds are depleted, cards are reloaded for the appropriate amount. Subscribers pay an average $.25 per minute with no access, connection, or monthly fees. Costs are approximately 40% less than regular calling cards; users receive a 5% rebate on every dollar of use to support their athletic programs (TRZ Sports Services, 1994a, 1994p).

TRZ Product Concepts for the Future: Worldwide Audio and Video Access

TRZ's major action priority is to seek capital and recruit management talent to increase the scope and capacity of audio sports services (and also move toward nonsports interactive audio). TRZ would like to expand capacity by creating access points worldwide using the information superhighway. Projections show that interactive features and customization options would cut current unit costs 75% (TRZ Sports Services, 1994e). Current TRZ capital has been earmarked to purchase and install prototype hardware and software in major U. S. and Canadian markets. Increased cash flow is needed to help TRZ offset initial operating deficits for up to 18 months in each market. Portions of capital and profits will be used to establish and support national and local sales/marketing efforts.

TRZ' s current technology is able to deliver the audio portion of an unlimited number of live or time-delayed events to any home or business that has access to conventional telephone service and equipment. Only audio and low-to-moderate speed databases can be carried on public switchboard telephone networks (TRZ Sports Communications, 1994e); TRZ is investigating new call processing and bridging that will be capable of interfacing with video and foresees technology that can deliver black- and -white video signals over traditional analog telephone networks. Several manufacturers are developing low-cost customer-premise transceivers that would favor implementation of the system. TRZ research (TRZ Sports Services, 1994e) indicates that current customers are willing to pay up-front for the possibility of expediting black-and-white transceiver availability. Fiber optics can support cable TV, computer connections, and home management systems. When fiber-optic telephone lines become more common, TEAMLINE will be able to provide immense numbers of video events inexpensively.

TRZ projections show that black-and-white video service deployed over telephone lines would require a $1,500,000 investment. Engineering and development costs would use one half to two thirds of the capital for (a) designing and constructing prototype transceivers; (b) identifying, evaluating and selecting a manufacturer; and (c) covering unexpected cost overruns and initial promotional efforts.

Financial projections based on TRZ estimations of sales in new local and nonsports markets show that each expansion of network capacity and capability will require minimum incremental hardware and software investments of $25,000. Reaching each of the 50 largest North American markets would require capitalization of $1,250,000. Primary financing would be secured from cash flow generated by increased sales; overall income would be depressed initially due to operating shortfalls (TRZ Sports Services, 1994e).

Place

TEAMLINE games are delivered via radio broadcast or other audio signals using telephone, cable-television facilities, direct satellite, cellular technology and other electronic transmission methods serving homes, businesses, hotels, mobile phone units, and other locations. Home teams provide TRZ with phone lines for audio access. Broadcast teams are the home-site announcers.

The most recent market research (TRZ Sports Services, 1994c, 1994k) shows that 270,190 calls were placed to TEAMLINE in 1992; total minutes of use were 3,459,097. Average length of a call was 38 minutes with the longest single call lasting 270 minutes (4.5 hours). Reuse rate of first-time callers was 90%. Calls from the longest distance were placed from London, England (to hear California vs. Stanford football, December 17, 1990), and Johannesburg, South Africa (to hear Virginia Tech vs. Georgia Tech football on December 3, 1990).

TRZ has joined with an Atlanta company to provide TEAMLINE through cable telecasts beginning in Fall, 1994. Converters enable the TEAMLINE audio to be played through stereo systems. Test markets are Akron, Orlando, Spokane, and Roanoke. Cable prices begin at $5.00 per game ($19.95 per month); the monthly fee also includes access to 30 Music Choice channels. TRZ plans to expand the cable service nationwide by 1995 (TRZ Sports Services, 1994a).

Promotion

TEAMLINE's primary marketing method has been through joint advertising agreements with the teams (TRZ Sports Services, 1994e). Teams agree to promote TRZ services to fans, alumnae/i, and media through their press releases, game programs, media guides, local news features, booster magazines, arena/stadium signage, announcements in game broadcasts, public-address announcements, scoreboard messages, and so forth. TRZ provides free pictures, negatives, copy, camera-ready artwork for half- or quarter-page advertisements, broadcast quality audio- or videotape, and other materials to use in their promotions. College teams print advertisements at no charge for TRZ. TRZ also has rights to use teams' names, nicknames, and logos in national advertising.

TRZ has also used cooperative and per inquiry advertising with regional sports magazines linked to colleges and universities. The company has been satisfied with response to ads and plans to increase opportunities for cooperative advertising.

TRZ's Publication: Connections Magazine

TEAMLINE *Connections* is a monthly publication that contains daily programming guides, access codes for games, collegiate and professional rankings, news stories, and other features relative to sports teams and TEAMLINE programs. *Connections* is available by subscription for $2.50 per month.

Advertising is accepted in *Connections*. Advertising rates begin at $500 (see Table 7).

Table 7
Advertising Rates for CONNECTIONS Magazine

Full Page	Inside Front	Inside Back	Back	Center Spread
$500	$750	$750	$1,000	$1,000
Circulation: 50,000		Readership: 150,000 per issue		
Rates are for page size of 5" x 7.5".				

Note. Adapted from *Connections Magazine Fact Sheet*, p. 1, by TRZ Sports Services, 1994. Copyright 1994 by TRZ Communications Services, Inc. Adapted with permission of author.

The majority of *Connections* subscribers are from California, New York, and Florida (see Table 8), although *Connections* reaches subscribers in each state and the District of Columbia in some frequency.

Table 8
Geographic Distribution of CONNECTIONS Magazine Users

State	% Users	State	% Users	State	% Users
California	13.3	Alabama	2.0	D. C.	.6
New York	7.2	Maryland	1.9	Oklahoma	.5
Florida	6.9	Washington	1.9	Utah	.5
Illinois	4.6	Missouri	1.7	Nevada	.5
Texas	4.4	Arizona	1.3	Arkansas	.4
Virginia	4.4	Wisconsin	1.2	Nebraska	.4
North Carolina	4.1	Oregon	1.2	Alaska	.4
New Jersey	4.0	Colorado	1.1	New Mexico	.4
Georgia	3.8	Iowa	1.1	Delaware	.4
Ohio	3.5	Kentucky	.9	Idaho	.3
Pennsylvania	3.1	Louisiana	.8	Maine	.3
Tennessee	2.8	Kansas	.7	South Dakota	.3
Massachusetts	2.7	Minnesota	.7	Vermont	.3
Michigan	2.5	West Virginia	.7	Rhode Island	.2
Connecticut	2.5	New Hampshire	.7	Wyoming	.2
Indiana	2.2	Hawaii	.6	Montana	.2
South Carolina	2.1	Mississippi	.6	North Dakota	.1

Note. Adapted from *Connections Magazine Fact Sheet*, p. 1, by TRZ Sports Services, 1994. Copyright 1994 by TRZ Communications Services, Inc. Adapted with permission of author.

Some TEAMLINE affiliates in Ohio, Michigan, and Florida are test schools for a TEAMLINE Season Ticket and Business Boosters fund-raiser. Schools encourage their season ticket holders to use a TRZ company as their long-distance carrier; TRZ then charges the lowest possible long distance rate, and the schools receive monthly commissions from TRZ (commission is based on each dollar spent by holders on long distance). The program generates up to $25,000 per year for institutions.

Promotions for TRZ Fund Raising

TRZ markets their long-distance discount cards using brochures, advertisements in *Connections*, and target mailings. Athletics departments promote the cards to fans, boosters, and students through media of their choice (usually alumnae/i publications, game programs, mailings to boosters, and so forth). TRZ creates, funds and provides brochures to institutions, which distribute them to staff, season-ticket holders, donors, area boosters, and other supporters. Sign-up sheets are available in the brochures, or interested customers call an 800 number to subscribe. TRZ and the long-distance carrier complete the steps for telephone service and bill the customer monthly (TRZ Sports Services, 1994n).

Corporate Sponsorship

Sponsorship opportunities are available for corporations that wish to reach TEAMLINE customers (TRZ Sports Services, 1994p). Billboard commercials (such as "Today's game is brought to you by . . .") are available for each game, coaches' show, or team information line. Logo and theme line tags are also available in game program advertising, newspaper and magazine ads, merchandise, and other promotional items as well as in *Connections* (see Table 7).

Price

TEAMLINE users listen as long as they want from pre- to postgame (TRZ Sports Services, 1994i). Calls are timed from connection to disconnection. Discounts are given for each minute that callers stay on-line. Greatest rate card charge is 50¢ per minute; least charge is 20¢ per minute. A sample TEAMLINE rate card is shown in Table 9.

Average cost for users is 32¢ per minute. Canadian charges are higher due to higher costs of delivering the service, and all applicable charges apply to international calls (TEAMLINE *Connections*, 1994). Users are charged by their credit-card companies; TRZ pays the phone charges for each call and also pays 12% of each dollar generated to those affiliates whose fans call the events.

Initially, TRZ assessed a service charge of 50¢ for each call. Beginning in 1991, a $2.95 set-up fee was charged to cover initial cost, encourage longer calls, and eliminate short calls. When TRZ developed its own technology to access game feeds in 1992, set-up charges were dropped (TRZ Sports Services, 1994n).

Callers who used TEAMLINE beyond a 30¢-per-minute mark during

Table 9
Example Rates for TEAMLINE Broadcast

Minutes	Cost per Minute	Total Cost	Discount
1	$0.50	$ 0.50	- - -
15	$0.47	$ 7.06	6%
30	$0.44	$13.17	12%
45	$0.41	$18.34	18%
60	$0.38	$22.57	25%
75	$0.34	$25.85	31%
90	$0.31	$28.18	37%
105	$0.28	$29.57	44%
120	$0.25	$30.01	50%
135	$0.24	$32.14	52%
150	$0.23	$33.81	55%
165	$0.21	$35.10	57%
180	$0.20	$36.00	60%

Note. Adapted from *Connections*, p. 19, by TRZ Sports Services, 1994. Copyright 1994 by TRZ Communications Services, Inc. Adapted with permission of author.

the previous year and users who do not wish to use major credit cards when accessing games are encouraged to purchase a TEAMLINE season ticket (TRZ Sports Services, 1994i). Season tickets permit users to pay for phone charges in advance and save 25% or more per minute (cost of season-ticket minutes are as low as $.25). TEAMLINE Season Tickets are available at the start of each season. Season tickets are available in two packages (TRZ Sports Services, 1994k):

1. The Gold Season Ticket — a 900-minute credit for $225 (average cost per minute = 25¢).
2. The Silver Season Ticket — a 300-minute credit for $95 (average cost per minute = 32¢).

Users who have purchased season tickets find that hook-ups to games are faster because they only have to enter a 6-digit PIN number and, the team's 4-digit access code and select the event of their choice. Time to access games and events using a 20-digit credit card number and expiration date takes 50% longer. TRZ finds that customers are more likely to use prepaid cards over credit cards because the minutes have already been purchased. Trend examination shows that prepaid minutes are used despite overall season record or the significance of an individual game. Affiliates receive a negotiated percentage of each dollar generated by season-ticket usage.

The Price Incurred by TRZ

TEAMLINE's major costs in delivering games to customers are the long-distance charges incurred by bringing games over the phone lines to Akron, then bridging the call to the customer's phone. Projections show that by sending TEAMLINE directly to customers' local calling areas, TRZ would pay charges for one rather than two calls. TRZ is currently testing local access technology in the Cleveland market. Results will indicate the likelihood of providing local access to 50 cities to meet TRZ's goal of providing local access to 51% of the U. S. population.

TRZ Nonsport Product Interests

Technology proven to be sound by TEAMLINE's success has prompted TRZ to identify viable markets for other interactive audio services (TRZ Sports Services, 1994g).

Business programs: Providing live coverage of company press conferences, product announcements, and so forth for industry analysts, stockholders, and employees. Sales meetings and various restricted announcements could be narrowcast to those who hold security codes, such as institutional investors and vendors.

Entertainment: Providing coverage of daytime or nighttime programming, studio announcements, interviews, concerts, and tape-delayed broadcasts of commercial media programs for those who may have missed them when regularly scheduled.

Science: Providing coverage of presentations at major scientific conventions and announcements from major science centers and agencies.

Medicine: Providing 24-hour billing information to patients, eligibility requirements for state health-care assistance, and so forth with switching mechanisms so callers can code-in for live operators. TRZ is offering this service currently to a health-care corporation in Cleveland.

TRZ also foresees calling access for (a) conferences, (b) education programs, (c) customer and vendor information services, (d) various communications and database services, (e) news programs, (f) foreign language programs, (g) religion programs, (h) business programs, and (i) political programs. TRZ is certified by the Association of Professional Associations to deliver live or prerecorded continuing education events and to administer tests and validate identity of test subjects by using TRZ's interactive voice-response capabilities.

Note: The preceding case as written deliberately contains some information that is directly related to marketing problem solving and some information that may be irrelevant and/or unrelated. Readers must glean appropriate data in order to successfully complete a case study; different types of information will be useful for different questions and/or solutions.

Study Questions

1. Are the four primary markets identified for TEAMLINE still currently valid? That is, should TRZ continue to serve the fragmented market? What other markets might be attracted to TEAMLINE (i.e., what does general trend analysis indicate about the types of individualized, tailored services offered by companies such as TRZ)?

2. Does TEAMLINE really have any direct competition? That is, if fans have a chance to hear their favorite team's games anytime, even if network broadcasting is not carrying the games, what factors would keep them from listening?

3. How can TRZ convince customers that costs of telephone broadcasting are not prohibitive? What should be the focus of a TEAMLINE national promotional campaign in order to attract 51% of the U. S. population?

4. Typical demography for TEAMLINE callers shows that upscale ($71,000 income), 39-year-old, college educated males are TEAMLINE's primary users. What advertising, promotional, and public relations vehicles should TRZ use to attract more callers and enable TEAMLINE to attract the mass market?

5. In what ways should colleges and universities support use of TEAMLINE by their publics? How should colleges and universities promote TEAMLINE to their graduates, fans, boosters, and so forth? How could TRZ encourage colleges and universities to better promote TEAMLINE yet still maintain TRZ profits?

6. How can TRZ meet a major market goal to have colleges and universities provide TEAMLINE access to nonrevenue sports? Who are typical supporters of nonrevenue college and university sports? Should TRZ consider alternative pricing and profit-sharing strategies to encourage colleges and universities to offer more nonrevenue contests via TEAMLINE? Why would this be a sound or unsound strategy?

7. How could TRZ determine the size and scope of the market for listeners

of coaches' shows, press conferences, media days, team fund-raisers, and other functions?

8. TEAMLINE enjoys an exceptional reuse rate. Explain the market advantages of retaining customers. Identify ways in which TRZ could encourage reusers to place calls to TEAMLINE more often.

9. In what ways could TRZ convince numerous public service locations (such as hotels, restaurants/grills/bars, hospitals, and so forth) to promote TEAMLINE in their own advertising or promotional ventures? Design a profit-sharing plan for the location (i.e., teams receive 12% return; consider the percentage that would be justified for TRZ to pay a bar for broadcasting a game, yet would still enable TRZ to clearly make a profit.). Determine if such a market would be sizable enough for TRZ to offer some of its regular long-distance calling discounts to hotel, restaurant, or hospital management. How would TEAMLINE's demographics change if publics other than college/university graduates knew more about TEAMLINE? What advantages are there to a wide demographic base?

10. What advantages does TRZ's future market position (low cost black-and -white transceivers) lend to its current market position? That is, how does TRZ's current and future technological superiority reinforce current market position and dominate future position? How can TRZ use that position in its promotion of TEAMLINE?

11. How can TRZ start market planning in order to recoup the capital investments that will be spent to expand its coverage to video (i. e., how can TEAMLINE make profits and replenish investments from its offset)? What strategies should TRZ use currently to attract a large audience of TEAMLINE video users in the future?

12. In what ways could professional sport support use of TEAMLINE by their publics? How should professional sport promote TEAMLINE to their fans? How could TRZ encourage professional sport to promote TEAMLINE yet still maintain profits?

13. Design strategies by which TEAMLINE Gold or Silver Season Tickets could be promoted better by both colleges/universities and professional sports. What additional incentives could TRZ offer to colleges and universities in exchange for their heightened support?

14. In what ways could *Connections* magazine be used to better promote both TEAMLINE and itself? How could colleges/universities and professional sport alert fans to *Connections*? (Remember that most of *Connections* pages contain program schedules and access codes, but news,

rankings and other stories of interest are also featured.)

15. What states should TRZ target for intense promotional campaigns for TEAMLINE? (See Table 8; assume that *Connections* subscribers and TEAMLINE users are the same customers.) Is it more advantageous to target higher use areas, such as California, New York and Florida, or should TRZ concentrate on lower use areas, such as North Dakota, Montana, and Wyoming? Why? What rationale should determine targets?

16. Considering the overall demographics of TEAMLINE users and *Connections* readers, what enterprises (sport and nonsport) should be interested in using *Connections* as an advertising vehicle?

17. What strategies can TRZ use to convince corporations that sponsorships of broadcasts can reap both monetary and public relations advantages? What pricing structure should apply to sponsorships? Should pricing be based on past frequency of calls for certain teams, or should TRZ's sponsorship rate be based on preseason standings? That is, should the price of sponsoring games featuring Division I football bowl contenders be more expensive than sponsoring games that have proven to be popular yet are "insignificant" in national standings (i.e., should pricing be based on the game, or the number of callers)?

18. How can TRZ encourage college and universities to use the fund-raising components of both TRZ and TEAMLINE? What other TEAMLINE-related fund-raising strategies could TRZ offer to colleges and universities?

19. How can TRZ's plans to enter nonsport-related telephone broadcasting (business, entertainment, science, medicine, and so forth) enhance their market position relative to sport? How can TRZ determine if combination packages (offering cards for exclusive sport and entertainment use, or sport and medicine use, and so forth) would be feasible?

20. Design a promotional strategy showing that costs of TEAMLINE game broadcasts are not prohibitive. That is, convince displaced collegiate and professional sports fans that the cost structure for TEAMLINE differs substantially from regular long-distance charges and suggest ways that fans could use TEAMLINE to follow their favorite games.

Suggested Readings

Balasubramanian, S. K., & Kamakura, W. A. (1989). Measuring consumer attitudes toward the marketplace with tailored interviews. *Journal of Marketing Research, 26,* 311–326.

Gordon, C. (1987, August). Taking a grassroots approach to research. *Marketing News*, 22.

Hofacre, S., & Burman, T. K. (1992). Demographic changes in the U. S. into the twenty-first century: Their impact on sport marketing. *Sport Marketing Quarterly, 1* (1), 31–36.

Park, C. W., Roth, M. S., & Jacques, P. F. (1988). Evaluating the effects of advertising and sales promotion campaigns. *Industrial Marketing Management, 17*, 129–140.

Peppers, D. & Rogers, M. (1993). *The one to one future: Building relationships one customer at a time.* New York: Doubleday.

Pitts, B. G., Fielding, L. W., & Miller, L. K. (1994). Industry segmentation theory and the sport industry: Developing a sport industry segmentation model. *Sport Marketing Quarterly. 3* (1), 15–24.

Pitts, B. G., & Stotlar, D. K. (1996). *Fundamentals of sport marketing.* Morgantown, WV: Fitness Information Technology, Inc.

Stier, W. F. (1992). Understanding fundraising in sport: The conceptual approach. *Sport Marketing Quarterly, 1* (1), 41–46.

Sutton, W. (1987). Developing an initial marketing plan for intercollegiate athletic programs. *Journal of Sport Management, 1*, 146–158.

References

TEAMLINE *Connections.* (1994, November). Akron, OH: TRZ Communications Services, Inc.

TRZ Sports Services. (1994a). *Annual report to CoSIDA membership.* Akron, OH: TRZ Communications Services, Inc.

TRZ Sports Services. (1994b). *Company history.* Akron, OH: TRZ Communications Services, Inc.

TRZ Sports Services. (1994c). *Connections magazine fact sheet.* Akron, OH: TRZ Communications Services, Inc.

TRZ Sports Services. (1994d). *Exclusive pay-to-listen audio transmission rights agreement.* Akron, OH: TRZ Communications Services, Inc.

TRZ Sports Services. (1994e). *Executive summary.* Akron, OH: TRZ Communications Services, Inc.

TRZ Sports Services. (1994f). *The four primary markets for TEAMLINE.* Akron, OH: TRZ Communications Services, Inc.

TRZ Sports Services. (1994g). *The future of TRZ communications services, Inc.* Akron, OH: TRZ Communications Services, Inc.

TRZ Sports Services. (1994h). *Go team.* Akron, OH: TRZ Communications Services, Inc.

TRZ Sports Services. (1994i). *How TEAMLINE works.* Akron, OH: TRZ Communications Services, Inc.

TRZ Sports Services. (1994j). *TEAMLINE caller demographics and information sheet.* Akron, OH: TRZ Communications Services, Inc.

TRZ Sports Services. (1994k). *The TEAMLINE season ticket.* Akron, OH: TRZ Communications Services, Inc.

TRZ Sports Services. (1994l). *Telephone broadcasting.* Akron, OH: TRZ Communications Services, Inc.

TRZ Sports Services. (1994m). *The TRZ/BN1 long distance fund raising program.* Akron, OH: TRZ Communications Services, Inc.

TRZ Sports Services. (1994n). *TRZ TEAMLINE rate card (past and present)*. Akron, OH: TRZ Communications Services, Inc.

TRZ Sports Services. (1994o). *What TEAMLINE has to offer to its corporate sponsor*. Akron, OH: TRZ Communications Services, Inc.

TRZ Sports Services. (1994p). *You make the call*. Akron, OH: TRZ Communications Services, Inc.

Related Professional Associations

National Association of Broadcasters
1771 N Street
Washington, DC 20036
Radio members phone: (800)455-5394 [in the U.S.], (202)429–5400
http://www.nab.org/

Acknowledgments

The author gratefully acknowledges Thomas Zawistowski, Chief Executive Officer, and Kim Snyder, Executive Assistant, TRZ Sports Services, for their valuable contributions to this project.

CATCH THAT CHAMPIONSHIP FEVER!!

Richard L. Irwin, University of Memphis

●●●

Introduction

Ernie English is experiencing one of those weeks that many of us only dream about. Having been recently hired as the Associate Athletic Director for Marketing and Promotions at a university that has qualified for the national championship football game Ernie is prepared to relish the team's recent accomplishments. Hey, it's events like this that typically improve booster donations, corporate sponsorship, and attendance—all responsibilities assigned to Ernie when he accepted this position a short time ago. Life couldn't be better for the rapidly ascending athletic administrator. However, Ernie, as well as his immediate predecessors, has failed to adequately address one critical element of the contemporary sport promotional mix: licensing. This is about to turn Ernie's dream week into a major nightmare.

Background

Ernie English was recently hired as the Associate Athletic Director for Marketing and Promotions at Western Tech in Commerce City, Colorado. Tech is a state-funded institution founded in 1898 with an enrollment of approximately 7,500 full-time students. Commerce City, on the other hand, is a "bedroom" community nestled at the base of the Rocky Mountains (or so it says in the school promotional literature!). A town of approximately 80,000 citizens, Commerce City has many residents who commute daily to work in Denver.

Ernie's official date of employment was December 1 due to an extended search to find the perfect person and the fact that his predecessor departed in the midst of fall sports in order to accept a position with the expansion Rocky Mountain Rockies of the newly formed United States Baseball Association (USBA). Ernie's position has been expanded to include a variety of marketing-related and revenue production-oriented tasks including event and team promotions, ticket sales, corporate sponsorship, booster club management, and licensing. Prior to accepting the Tech position, Ernie had served as the Athletic Marketing Assistant at South Central University, an NCAA Division II school in Broken Arrow, Oklahoma. His primary responsibilities at South Central were associated with team and event management as well as corporate sales. Ernie earned his master's degree in sport management from Midwestern University prior to accepting the position at South Central and after earning a bachelor of arts in business administration at Pacific Western.

His first few weeks on the job have been very exciting as the Western Tech "Techsters" have experienced the most unbelievable football season in school history. The team has advanced unscathed through the NCAA Division II Football Playoffs after finishing the regular season 12-2 and claiming the Mountain States Conference Championship. The Techsters' opponent in the national championship game will be Capitol College from Midland, Texas. Appearing in the title game is nothing new for the Capitol College Statesmen, who have dominated NCAA Division II Football the past 12 years winning eight championships as well as three runner-up trophies.

The Championship Fever

The campus as well as community has been abuzz as the Mighty Techsters have never before qualified for a national playoff, let alone the championship game, in any team sport. Attendance at the one home playoff game against Divinity College was 11,990 after averaging 8,562 during the regular season. Immediately following the semifinal victory over the Midland University Plainsmen this past Saturday, many local businesses began offering "Techster Specials" that ranged from free Techster logo cups with the purchase of a "full meal deal" at the four Bellybuster Cafes in Commerce City to no cover charge at Orville's Hangar, a local student hangout, for anyone wearing Techster logo apparel.

The Call

On the Monday prior to the championship game, slated to be played at the Georgia Dome in Atlanta, when Ernie returns from attending the weekly Techster Booster Club Meeting at the Buckboard Tavern, he has received calls from Angie Ehrhart, Director of Licensing at the NCAA, as well as Rusty Miller, National Sales Director for Specialty Sports of Tunica, Mississippi, the Official Concessionaire of the NCAA.

Each of the callers has requested permission for Ernie, on behalf of Western Tech, to grant Specialty Sports permission to use the WT logo on all championship merchandise to be sold at the championship game in Atlanta. Ernie chooses to return Angie's call first, and she informs him that the NCAA commonly enters into a three-way, short-term joint license agreement with participating institutions for all national championship events. This arrangement entitles all parties involved to share equally in the royalties generated from the sales and distribution of Specialty Sports merchandise. According to Angie, this arrangement has proven quite lucrative for participating institutions in the past with some schools generating several thousand dollars over the championship weekend. To expedite the process, Angie recommends that Ernie forward a short-term license agreement to her and Rusty indicating that the NCAA, Capitol, and Western will act as colicensors and designating Specialty Sports as the exclusive licensee of the arrangement.

This all sounds quite impressive to Ernie, particularly the ability to generate the much-needed revenue. However, when Ernie casually mentions to Angie that Western Tech does not currently have an official licensing program in operation, she expresses a sense of amazement. In fact, she erroneously tells him that this may terminate the possibility of royalty sharing. Although he later finds this not to be true, it does raise some immediate concern, and his stress level is beginning to rise.

Ernie concludes the conversation with Angie indicating that he will request the university legal affairs office draft a contract outlining the specific information needed to appropriately execute the agreement. She allows him until Wednesday to fax to her and Specialty Sports the completed contract. In the meantime he must forward Specialty Sports the Techster logo slicks and PMS colors for printing as well as a standards manual describing how the logos should be displayed.

Immediately following his conversation with Angie, Ernie calls the Office of Legal Affairs in hopes of getting some assistance with this situation. Unfortunately, the University Counsel is out until late in the afternoon. Ernie's next call is to the Office of Sports Information to see if they have a standards manual. Bert Bestgien, the Sports Information Director, who thinks that having a standards manual would be a great idea but has never seen one for Western Tech in his 24 years on campus, refers him to Printing Services. When Ernie reaches the receptionist in Printing Services she indicates that he must obtain the approval of Tim Baake, Printing Services Manager, before she can release an official copy of the standards manual. Unfortunately, Tim is also out of the office but will return at 8 a.m. Tuesday morning.

Finally, at approximately 3:30 p.m. Mountain Standard Time, Glen Gagnon, the university legal counsel, returns Ernie's call. After Ernie explains the problem, Glen indicates that it will not be difficult to draft a *modified* license agreement for the purposes described by Angie; however, he is leaving in the morning for a legal seminar in Santa Clara, California, and will not return until Sunday. He suggests that Ernie call Angie back immediately and ask if they have a copy of a contract that could modified by

Western Tech for this weekend's event. What a great idea! Ernie hangs up immediately and dials the NCAA Headquarters in Overland Park, Kansas, only to be reminded that they are on Central Standard Time and their offices have closed for the day. When Ernie attempts to call Glen, the receptionist relays that he has departed for the day.

Following a stroll to the soft drink machine for a dose of caffeine and a moment to collect his thoughts on this issue, Ernie returns to his office to find a message from Sally Lees, the women's gymnastics coach. When he contacts her, Sally says that she had been to the Student Center for lunch and observed some fraternity brothers distributing T-shirts prominently bearing the Techster athletic logo, which has always been a block-letter-style capital WT as displayed in Figure 1, along with the words *Kick Capitol's Ass*. Sally also said that when she confronted the young men, they indicated that they were selling the shirts as a fraternity fund-raiser. When asked if they had obtained permission to use the school's athletic logo the young men responded negatively and suggested that because they were full-tuition-paying students at the school, they should not need to request such permission. Lastly, one of the more rational young men asked Ms. Lees from whom such permission should have been obtained, and when she expressed uncertainty, her argument with them appeared to be rendered mute.

Figure 1

After listening to her description of the situation Ernie could not help but ask Sally why she has brought this information to him. Her response is "Isn't licensing a part of marketing and promotions? For heaven's sake, what were you hired to do, coordinate bake sales?"

Yes, in fact, Ernie had been told that licensing would eventually become a part of his job responsibilities within the athletic department. The key word was *eventually*. Unfortunately, licensing is not an area in which Ernie has been well trained. He remembers his sport management professor, Dr. Terry Davis, talked about licensing occasionally and indicated to the students that it was emerging as a major marketing and promotional issue as well as revenue source for sport organizations of all types. However, Ernie chose not to actively pursue the topic, a decision that is beginning to haunt him at this moment.

In concluding his conversation with Sally, Ernie requested the name of the involved fraternity. Sally says it was the Alpha Betas, a fraternity that is very supportive of all athletic teams and one that is attempting to organize a group to attend the title game in Atlanta.

Ernie decides to follow Sally's request and contact the AB House. Not sure of exactly what he is going to say, he gets the House answering machine that essentially verbalizes the message contained on the t-shirts for sale at the student center. Ernie leaves a message requesting a house representative contact him at their earliest convenience.

As the time approaches 5 p.m. Ernie remembers that he has set an appointment with Dirk Rosenbaugh, General Manager of Goldsby's Department Store. The meeting is to discuss a possible sponsorship for men's and women's Basketball. Goldsby's has always been a supporter of the athletic department as Dirk was a four-time letter winner in tennis while receiving a bachelor's degree in business administration.

Dirk's office is near the men's section in the store, but Ernie decides to enter through the children's section to see if he can get any Christmas ideas for his 8-year old niece, Samantha. As Ernie approaches the entrance, he notices a huge banner over the entry welcoming all Techster Fans to Goldsby's and wishing the Techsters Good Luck against the Statesmen. Just inside the door is an elaborate display of Techster logo merchandise. Items include T-shirts, sweatshirts, caps, pennants, posters, and windsocks. At first Ernie is overwhelmed with joy—these people really love the Techsters! Then he thinks that this is going to be an easy sell. Finally, as he comes to his senses, he begins to wonder if the school has approved the usage of their logo on any of this merchandise.

Ernie decides to bypass the shopping and head directly for Dirk's office. Along the way he finds several other Techster logo items ranging from seat cushions to writing pads. Because he is relatively new, he is not sure if this is common or due to the Techsters' trip to the national championship. He also begins to wonder who is producing and supplying all this stuff.

When Ernie arrives at Dirk's office, it too is decorated in the blue and gold of Western Tech. Dirk himself proudly wears a tie emblazoned with the Techster logo. Ernie chooses to stick with the issue at hand initially. He discusses with Dirk the potential categories of sponsorship and the various entitlements. Dirk is waffling and making things somewhat difficult. When it appears that Dirk is going to balk at a sponsorship, Ernie blurts out rather unprofessionally, "You either become a sponsor, or remove all the unlicensed merchandise from your store."

Dirk asks Ernie to clarify his comments and define "unlicensed merchandise." Ernie is a bit lost for words. He indicates, similar to Sally's confrontation with the fraternity brothers, that Dirk has not obtained permission to display Techster logo merchandise. Dirk states that he is not the producer of the goods, nor does he need any permission to display the merchandise because there is no existing policy that prohibits this action. Second, he contends that he asked the athletic director, Geri Weaver, on several occasions from whom he should order school logo merchandise and never received a response. Last, Dirk states that the school logos are public property and that all tax-paying citizens have the right to use them if they so wished. He adds that while studying business at Tech, he learned a lot about licensing and that he is well aware of his rights as a tax payer as well as business person.

Ernie asks Dirk whom he is in fact receiving the merchandise from, and Dirk says a variety of imprinting companies but declines to provide any specific information. Somewhat bewildered Ernie decides to conclude the meeting and asks Dirk if he can delay his final decision until after the football game. Dirk agrees and offers Ernie a Techster logo pen as a parting gift. Ernie is well aware that this is a jab from Dirk, who is well known for his arrogant stunts.

Just before leaving Ernie remembers that he needs to pick up an anniversary card for his parents. Because Goldsby's is the anchor store of the Commerce City Megamall, this is the most convenient time to stop at the card shop. Next door to Carl's Cards is The Jocque Shop, which has a full window display of Techster merchandise similar to that found at Goldsby's. Ernie decides to go undercover and obtain key inside information.

He enters the store and appears interested in the Techster merchandise hoping to attract the attention of a sales associate. Eventually, a teenage associate wanders over and offers to help Ernie if he needs it. Ernie expresses his interest in the Techster paraphernalia and asks the teenager if he knows where it was made. The teenager proudly responds, "Right in the back of the store! Isn't it way cool? Do you want to place a big order?" Ernie declines but asks if he could talk to the manager. The teenager sheepishly retrieves the manager from their office and points in the direction of Ernie.

Ernie introduces himself to Mr. Jocque LaBonde, store owner and general manager as well as former All-American ice hockey player for the Techsters during the early 1980s, who turned professional one semester shy of completing his undergraduate degree in marketing. Following a brief stint in the National Hockey League and International Hockey League, Jocque returned to Commerce City to work. He used his signing bonus to start The Jocque Shop, a very lucrative business that now includes franchises in seven Western region cities.

Ernie tells Jocque that he greatly appreciates his support of the school but feels that first permission should have been obtained before Jocque produced items bearing the logo of the school and that the school was entitled to recoup a portion of the revenues generated from this use. At this Jocque bursts into laughter and states, "I've been doing this for well over 10 years, and now you barge in here after the wimpy football team finally achieves a little success and demand that I start paying for this stuff! You must be joking."

Ernie informs Jocque that the wheels are in motion to develop new policies that will disallow unauthorized use of the school athletic logo for commercial purposes. Jocque, who stands 6'3" and looks as if he could still hold his own on the ice, does not appear too intimidated by Ernie's comments. In fact, he responds with, "If you come after me, are you going after the bookstore? Those are the people ripping everyone off!"

With that Ernie heads for home, forgetting about his parents 25th anniversary and his niece's Christmas interests. He is now on a mission.

When Ernie arrives at the office on Tuesday ready to address the situation, he immediately receives an intercampus package from Tim Baake in Printing Services. Inside the package is the standards manual he requested on Monday, a standards manual request form requiring the department head's signature to be returned to Mr. Baake, and a memo from Tim wishing the Techsters good luck this weekend. Ernie breathes a sigh of relief. This licensing stuff isn't going to be all that tough. A good standards manual demonstrating the proper logo presentation requirements, a few solid operational policies, and a hard-nosed approach are all that it is going to take.

Then he opens the manual and discovers it was designed for school stationery letterhead only and has not been updated since the athletic department added gold as an accent color in 1985. That's when the phone rings. On the other end is Angie Ehrhart from the NCAA inquiring about the status of the school standards manual and short-term joint-use license agreement.

Suggested Discussion Issues

Ernie is obviously confronted with a number of licensing-related issues. Please describe in detail how you recommend Ernie deal with the following in the short-term (prior to the championship football game):

- The NCAA & Specialty Sports
- Bellybusters
- The Alpha Betas
- Goldsby's
- The Jocque Shop
- The Bookstore

In your response, please be sure to thoroughly describe your suggested course of action and the rationale for these procedures. Essentially, what grounds does Ernie have for your recommended course of action? Is there any legal or ethical foundation? What consideration must be given to community public relations?

In the long term, do you think that the university should initiate a licensing program? Why or why not? If they should, how would you recommend that Ernie go about establishing such a program?

What type of licensing-program operational policies do you recommend for adoption? What departments on campus should be actively involved in the creation and execution of the licensing operational policies? Should any royalty exemptions be granted to internal or external organizations? How would you suggest Ernie deal with promotional licensing agreements?

Suggested Readings

Irwin, R. (1991). A license to profit. *College Athletic Management, 3* (1), 18–23.

Irwin, R. L., & Stotlar, D. K. (1993). Operational protocol analysis of sport and collegiate licensing programs. *Sport Marketing Quarterly, 2* (1), 7–16.

Irwin, R. L., Stotlar, D. K., & Mulrooney, A. L. (1993). A critical analysis of collegiate licensing policies and procedures. *The Journal of College and University Law, 20* (3), 97–109.

Merchandising Reporter
Team Licensing Business

Professional Associations

Association of Collegiate Licensing Administrators (ACLA)
The Collegiate Licensing Company (TCLC)
Attn. Bruce B. Siegel, Esq.
320 Interstate North, Suite 102
Atlanta, GA 30339
(770)956-0520

Licensing Resource Group (LRG)
426 Century Lane, Suite 100
Holland, MI 49423
(616)395-0676
http://www.lrgusa.com

APPENDIX

Industry Segmentation Theory and the Sport Industry: Developing a Sport Industry Segment Model

Brenda G. Pitts, Ed.D.
Lawrence W. Fielding, Ph.D.
Lori K. Miller, Ed.D.
University of Louisville

ABSTRACT

The purpose of this study was to apply industry segmentation theory to the sport industry and to develop a sport industry segment model. Porter's (1985) theory of industry segmentation was applied. Traditional and contemporary definitions of sport and sport industry as well as lists and descriptions of sport products were used. The results produced three sport industry segments: sport performance, sport production, and sport promotion. In addition, product variety categories and buyer types were identified in each segment.

Drs. Brenda Pitts, Lawrence Fielding, and Lori Miller are faculty members in the Sport Management Program at the University of Louisville.

In planning for competitive advantage, a bat-making firm decides to identify, define, and offer a new product designed specifically for a new target market--a youth market (Fielding, Pitts, & Miller, 1991). The decision is based on two areas of information: the consumer segment and the competition. The consumer segment, or target market, consists of those who are buyers or potential buyers of a product. The competition consists of those firms offering or potentially offering the same product or a substitute product to satisfy consumer need. Analysis of both is critical in the decision-making process for sport marketing strategies.

In the words of Porter (1985), "Competitive advantage is at the heart of a firm's performance in competitive markets" (p. xv). Competition shapes the firm's strategies and activities in its quest for a profitable and sustainable position in an industry (Porter, 1985). Further, Porter points out that industries are not homogeneous. There are various segments within any given industry. Segments differ in many ways, yet boundaries may fluctuate due to a multitude of factors, one of which is product substitutability.

In some cases of industry segmentation, segments are found to be so different that they are reclassified as an industry. The deciding factor, or boundary, may be interrelationships between segments. Where interrelationships between segments are strong, those segments may be considered as true segments of an industry. For example, all sport, recreation, leisure, and fitness activity products (activities for participation) serve to meet specific buyer needs or desires: fun, fitness, competition, entertainment. Where interrelationships between segments are weak, those segments may be considered separate industries. For example, one may argue that recreational soccer—a product offered for participation for beginners, intermediates, and a few advanced players--is so very different from professional soccer--a product offered for the participation of the elite player and primarily for spectating--that they may be considered separate industries. Indeed, many segments of the sport industry may be considered separate and complete industries with no interrelatedness to other segments. The marketing and/or management person must determine the answer to these boundary questions and decide how to position the firm toward gaining and sustaining competitive advantage.

Porter also elaborates that industry segmentation should go beyond accepted models of segmentation. Final decisions on segment boundaries are always a matter of degree. Industry segmentation should be considered a tool in guiding one toward industry structural analysis. Such analysis serves to expose key elements of competitive advantage (Porter, 1985).

> **In pursuit of contributing to the development of a body of knowledge in sport management, and specifically to sport marketing, as fields of study, we believe that academicians, students, and practitioners will benefit from a study of the sport industry through industry segmentation.**

"An industry is a market in which similar or closely related products are sold to buyers" (Porter, 1985, p.233). Some industries may contain just one product variety. It is more typical that an industry contains a variety of product items sold to many existing or potential consumers who vary demographically and psychographically, and who may change in need, want, or demand. Companies within an industry segment "create new product varieties that perform new functions, combine functions in new ways, or split off particular functions into separate products" (Porter, 1985, p. 233). Similarly, new consumers may become part of an industry, existing consumers may change their need, or consumers may drop out of an industry (Porter, 1985).

An industry segment is a combination of a product variety (or varieties) and a group of consumers who purchase it. Industry segmentation is the division of an industry into subunits for purposes of developing competitive strategy (Porter, 1985). The primary reason for industry segmentation is competitive strategy formulation. Other reasons include to identify marketing opportunities and threats within a specific product market, to develop an appropriate marketing mix, and to inform major resource allocation decision making (Day, Shocker, & Srivastava, 1979; McCarthy & Perrault, 1990; Porter, 1985).

Although there is some research on defining and delineating the sport industry, we found no attempts to apply Porter's industry segmentation theory. Current research in defining, delineating, and segmenting the sport industry includes the following: (a) identifying consumer markets in various sports (see consumer marketing reports, such as American Sports Data, Inc., the Sporting Goods Manufacturers Association marketing reports, and the National Golf Foundation's marketing reports); (b) delineating the sport industry according to career segments (see Parks & Zanger, 1990); and (c) defining and delineating the industry according to type of sport setting (see, for example, DeSensi, Kelley, Blanton, & Beitel, 1990). Although the research on consumer markets and sport-setting types may be used by the sport marketer in competitive strategy formulation, the career-setting information is targeted for use by the student of sport management.

In pursuit of contributing to the development of a body of knowledge in sport management, and specifically to sport marketing, as fields of study, we believe that academicians, students, and practitioners will benefit from a study of the sport industry through industry segmentation. In particular, the research may be of value to instructors of courses in sport marketing, sport management, or of similar courses in competitive strategy, strategic planning, or strategic marketing planning and management.

The practitioner may use industry segmentation information to inform decisions concerning where to compete within an industry and where to focus company strategies within an industry; to identify opportunities and threats within an industry segment; to create new industry segments; or to inform decisions concerning exiting a segment. It was, therefore, the purpose of this research to apply Porter's (1985) industry segmentation theory to the sport industry.

The Porter Model

To segment an industry, four segmentation variables are used (for a complete discussion on industry segmentation, see Porter, 1985). Any one or any combination of the variables may be used. Porter's four segmentation variables are presented with a brief discussion of each.

1. **Product Segments:** The discrete product varieties that are, or could be, produced" (Porter, 1985, p.238). Product segments are developed by identifying all the product offerings produced or potentially produced within an industry. Defining characteristics may include physical size, price level, features, functions, technology or design, inputs employed, packaging, performance, new vs. aftermarket or replacement, product vs. ancillary services or equipment, and bundled vs. unbundled. Product de-

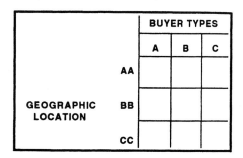

**Figure 1. A simple Industry Segmentation Matrix (top left and right)
and a Combined Matrix of three variables (bottom)**
(Adapted from Porter, 1985)

scriptors may be combined in a variety of ways to define a particular segment.

2. **Buyer Segments:** "The types of end buyers that purchase, or could purchase, the industry's products" (Porter, 1985, p. 238). Buyer, or market, segmentation always produces debate. Boundaries that might determine buyer differences and segments of buyers can differ from marketer to marketer and from company to company. Segmentation should reflect differences among buyers because the goal of segmentation is to expose all these differences. Porter divides buyers into two categories: industrial and commercial buyers and consumer goods buyers. Industrial and commercial buyers may be defined by the following: buyer industry, buyer's strategy, technological sophistication, equipment manufacturers vs. users, vertical integration, decision-making unit or purchasing process, size, ownership, financial strength, and order pattern. Consumer goods buyers may be defined using the following variables: demographics, psychographics or life-style, language, decision-making unit or purchasing process, and purchase occasion.

3. **Channel Segments:** "The alternative distribution channels employed or potentially employed to reach end buyers" (Porter, 1985, p. 238). Differences in channels may include direct vs. distributor, direct mail vs. retail or wholesale, distributors vs. brokers, types of distributors or retailers, and exclusive vs. nonexclusive outlets.

4. **Geographic Segments:** "The geographic location of buyers, defined by locality, region, country, or group of countries" (Porter, 1985, p. 238). Geographic location variables affect product purchase decisions according to product attributes due to differences in weather, customs, government regulations, and other geographical differences. Some variables are localities, regions, or countries, weather zones, and stage of national development or other country groupings.

METHODOLOGY

A comprehensive industry analysis for segmentation requires the development of a matrix using all four segmentation variables and each category that is relevant (Porter, 1985). This may result in a matrix so large and complex that it becomes confusing, unmanageable, and most likely not useful. The task, then, is to aggregate variables into meaningful segments. Segmentation may be achieved using any one of the variables (product, buyer, channel, and geographic location). Some examples are shown in Figure 1.

Definition of Sport and Sport Industry

For our purposes in this research, we used definitions of sport and sport industry from Pitts (1988) and Pitts,

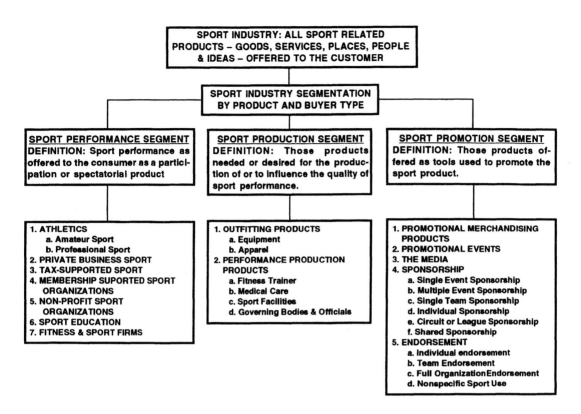

Figure 2. The Sport Industry Segment Model

Fielding, and Miller (1991). Although sport has been defined in many ways, it typically refers to physical activity through some form of organized and regulated game, such as volleyball, basketball, soccer, softball. Pitts uses a broad and diverse definition of "sport." According to this definition, sport is any activity, experience, or enterprise for which the primary focus is fitness, recreation, athletics, and leisure related. Activity and experience are inclusive of the many athletics, fitness, recreation, and leisure-related activities of today: car racing, horse racing, boogey-boarding, knee-boarding, water skiing, golf, walking, camping, hang gliding, throwing the boomerang, horseback riding, participating in rodeos, sailing, and many more. Enterprise is described as the management and business activities necessary for the organization and production of sport.

"Sport industry" is defined as the market in which the products offered to its buyers are fitness, sport, recreation, and leisure related. These products include goods, services, people, places, and ideas. Sport industry products include, but are not necessarily limited to, the following: fitness activity and all fitness-related goods and services; sports activity and all sports-related goods and services; recreation and leisure activity and all recre-

ation- and leisure-related goods and services; and all related management, financial, marketing, and other administration and business goods and services (Pitts, 1988; Pitts, Fielding, & Miller, 1991).

The application of all four variables of the Porter model to the massive sport industry would require quite possibly years of research and analysis. The result could be book length. For this reason, we chose to limit segmentation of the sport industry to two of Porter's variables--product segments and buyer segments. We strongly suggest that further research be conducted utilizing the complete industry segmentation model for a complete sport industry segmentation.

Definitions, descriptions, and functions of the multitude of products offered in the sport industry were collected for analysis (see, for example, the works of Comte & Stogel, 1990; DeSensi et al., 1990; and Stotlar, 1989). From their works, product functions and benefits were identified and grouped homogeneously within groups as well as heterogeneously between groups to form specific product segments. Definitions for the product segments were developed. In addition, sport products within each segment were identified and categorized.

It has been suggested by Mullin (1985) that there are

only two types of buyers of sport products: spectators and participants. Mullin's categories of sport consumers are based on selling "sports" for participation or for spectating and do not include an analysis of the complete sport industry. The findings of our study show that there are more than two categories of sport product consumers. Types of buyers in the sport industry are dependent on product segment, product variety, and product function and benefit.

RESULTS

Three segments were identified in the sport industry, and we have labeled them the Sport Performance Segment, the Sport Production Segment, and the Sport Promotion Segment. Industrial and consumer goods buyer types were identified. Figure 2 illustrates the segments identified in the sport industry.

Sport Performance Segment

As a product, "sport performance" is offered to buyers primarily in two ways: as a product for participants and as a product for spectators. These may be treated as separate industry segments due primarily to the nature of marketing participation and spectatorial products. We have placed them in one industry segment because of similarities in product function and benefit.

As a participation product, sport performance is offered to the buyer in a multitude of product offerings. The consumer may choose to participate in any number of sports or leisure activities, settings, performance (skill) levels, and market segment offerings (demographics segmentation such as an over-30 age group soccer league). Some of the settings are sports leagues, tournaments, one-day events, camps, and education classes. In the development of a list of product varieties, it is important to note that a matrix may be developed for every product variety. Figure 3 demonstrates a segmentation matrix using basketball as a product variant of sport participation and demographics as buyer type variants. With this illustration you can see that developing a complete list of product varieties in this product segment would be highly complex and require much time and paper.

In some industries, as in the sport industry, there are so many products offered that consolidation is necessary to make the list more workable. Although it is true that sports, recreation, and fitness activities can be different in definition and actual activity, almost all provide the buyer with similar functions and benefits: a workout, stress management, fun, competition, activity, or entertainment. We have focused the sport performance segment on formats through which the product may be offered. For example, basketball, volleyball, and martial arts are different activities, yet they may be offered to the buyer in similar formats, such as leagues, tournaments, or one-day events. Within each format, the product may be differentiated as it is structured to attract a particular buyer type.

As a product for spectators, sport performance is offered to consumers in four ways: spectating through personal attendance at a sport event, spectating the event via television, spectating sport event videos, and spectating a sport event indirectly through the images created in the listener's mind by the sense of hearing through radio. Spectating the event in person is considered the purest form of spectating if one considers the standard dictionary's definition of spectating. However, in sport marketing, all forms of the spectatorial product are important as each is essential to the promotion of the event, profits realized, and advertising sales.

Most spectatorial products are offered at no cost to the consumer. Consider the thousands of softball leagues, volleyball leagues, youth baseball leagues, and similar sporting situations where anyone may watch and enjoy the competition. These sporting events will most likely never change. However, recently there has been an increase in the number of events offered at a cost to the consumer, for example, pay-per-view sporting events and pay-per-order cable sports programming. As the number of opportunities to watch sporting events increases, the number of events offered at a cost will also increase as sport spectating continues to enjoy market demand.

Sport spectating in person has changed dramatically over the last twenty years. There have been improvements in facility construction, technology, and design. Before these changes, sport event spectating took place in a basic sport facility designed only for enveloping the court, arena, or field. This meant that the spectator's comfort and other needs were not considered. Seating and other need-fulfilling accommodations were designed into the facility. Today, the spectator has a range of choices: One may watch from low-cost, basic seating or from an expensive "skybox," an enclosed and private climate-controlled room with accoutrements, such as a large-screen TV, a supplied bar, food, newspapers, magazines, phones, facsimile machines, computers, plush seating, a balcony, and a private bath.

Sporting events today are offered in a variety of facilities. An "outdoor" sport, such as football, may now be viewed in an "indoor" enclosed facility. Further, if a spectator doesn't want to be distracted by the children, the sport facility management offers childcare services while the sport event is taking place. The sport facility today typically offers the consumer many accommodations and services. These have become an integral part of the sport event package.

In all sport activity, the marketer must understand that the production and consumption of the sport event or activity take place simultaneously (Mullin, 1985). This is not unique to the sport industry as it is also true of other entertainment industry products, such as live theater, dance performances, opera, and music group performances. However, these types of events require specific marketing strategies, for example, advance offering of tickets. The

BUYER TYPES: SKILL AND AGE									
		BEGINNER				ADVANCED			
		9-12	13-18	19-25	OVER 30	9-12	13-18	19-25	OVER 30
PRODUCT: BASKETBALL TYPES:	LEAGUE								
	TOURNAMENT	YES	YES	YES	YES	YES	YES	YES	YES
	CAMP	YES	YES	NULL	NULL	YES	YES	YES	NULL
	COLLEGE	NULL	NULL	NULL	NULL	NULL	YES	YES	NULL
	PROFESSIONAL	NULL	NULL	YES	YES	NULL	YES	YES	YES

Figure 3. Sport Performance Segment: A matrix using some buyer types and product types shows possibilities

selling of tickets strictly prior to an event, and especially of a limited number of tickets, helps create demand, or the illusion of demand. The marketer must affect buyer action on three levels. At the first level, the marketer must persuade the consumer to buy the tickets needed for admission to the event. At the second level, the marketer must persuade the buyer to attend the event. One might believe that selling tickets is the only job required and assume that the buyer will attend. The marketer must not make this assumption and must work to persuade the consumer to attend. At the third level, the marketer must try to persuade the consumer to purchase other products offered before, during, and after the event. These usually are called product extensions and include items such as valet parking, souvenir merchandise, food, and beverage. The revenue from these products can be a large source of income and help offset the cost of the event.

The substitute products for attending a sport event in person are television, video, and radio. The opposite is also true: The substitute product for watching an event on television or video or listening to it on the radio is attending the event in person. In many instances, however, the owner of the sport event will regulate the ability of a local broadcasting station to televise the event. One reason, of course, is that if the event is televised and is free to the consumer, the consumer may choose not to spend the money to attend the event. Hence, television broadcasting rights contracting has developed. In this instance, a different buyer type is identified--television broadcasting companies. The event management will offer the buyer the opportunity to "buy," or televise, an event. The deals are contingent upon perceived television spectator demand. If demand is sufficient, the company will be able to "sell" advertising time; this partially pays for the cost of televising the event.

Product Segments: The following are the categories of product varieties identified in the Sport Performance Segment:

1. **Athletics:** organized sport under the auspices of organized athletics for schools and professionals that is separate from sport organized outside these two ven-

ues. Athletics includes (a) amateur sport performance as organized in the schools and colleges and (b) professional sport performance for which the performer receives a fee.

2. **Private nonsport business:** sport organized and offered by privately owned firms whose primary product is not sport. These businesses are in business for another reason and add a sport or two, such as a pub that adds a sand volleyball court and now offers leagues. There is a fine line between these firms and the ones built primarily for sports. Typically, a pub will add the sport facility if it is inexpensive and popular. When interest in the trendy sport wanes, the pub closes the sport facility and remodels it as additional pub space.

3. **Tax-supported sport organizations:** sport organized and offered by tax-supported, public organizations. Examples include city parks and recreation offices, state parks and recreation organizations, and a state Olympics organization.

4. **Membership-supported sport organizations:** sport organized and offered by membership-supported clubs or organizations. These may or may not be nonprofit organizations. Some examples are a camping club that organizes camping trips, a rugby organization that offers a rugby league, a soccer organization that offers soccer leagues, and a fencing club that offers fencing competitions.

5. **Nonprofit sport organizations:** sport offered by nonprofit firms. Examples include the International Olympic Committee, which offers the modern Olympics every four years; the Federation of Gay Games, which offers the Gay Games every four years; the Amateur Softball Association, which offers structured softball leagues and tournaments every year; the Special Olympics; the United States Soccer Association, which offers structured soccer leagues and tournaments; the YWCA and the YMCA, which offer a number of fitness and sport activities.

6. **Sport education:** Sport taught to the consumer. Some products are private lessons, clinics, sport camps, fitness camps, coaching clinics, seminars, conferences,

and sport institutes.

7. **Fitness and sport firms:** Fitness, health, wellness, and sport firms that offer participation in sports and fitness in either a single-sport or multisport setting. This includes the privately owned fitness and sports businesses. Examples are fitness centers, tennis clubs, indoor soccer centers, indoor volleyball centers, golf clubs, and resorts.

The product types identified are those products offered to the consumer as sport performance as either a participant product or a spectator product. If the sport marketer understands the benefits and functions of the product, successful sport-marketing strategies will result.

Buyer Segments: Buyer types were identified in this industry segment in both participant and spectatorial product types. Buyer types include both industrial/commercial and consumer goods categories. Some industrial and commercial buyer types identified include the following: companies that contract for fitness/wellness programs for their employees; companies that purchase large numbers of sport event tickets; companies that buy the right to broadcast sporting events; and companies that buy materials to produce sporting goods for sale to retailers or another channel.

Consumer goods buyers identified in this segment include a wide variety of buyers categorized by demographics, psychographics, life-style, language, and other factors. Buyer types of sport as a participant product may be identified using demographics. Basketball may be offered in age-group leagues, such as youth, 16 and under, 18 and under, 19 to 24, 25 to 29, over-30, over-40, and so on. Further, within each age group, more buyer types may be identified, such as female, male, and coed. Figure 3 presents an example of some buyer types of basketball available to the sport marketer using two demographics, skill level and age.

It is also interesting to note that many identifiable populations are organizing and managing their own sports leagues, events, olympics, classes, clinics, and more. Some of them are women, African Americans, Native Americans, the Jewish population, the lesbian and gay populations, and the disabled. Each population is a buyer type. The sport marketer could develop and offer products targeting each buyer type. Further, the marketer could identify even more buyer types by using demographics or psychographics, much like those used as an example in Figure 3.

Buyer types identified in sport performance offered as a spectatorial product consist of those consumers considered spectators. As was identified in sport performance offered as a participant product, the sport marketer may use demographics and psychographics to identify and segment buyer types within each of the four forms of sport event spectating available. For example, spectating the Super Bowl is offered to the following buyer types: corporate buyers with unlimited funds; corporate buyers with limited funds; individual buyers with unlimited funds; and individual buyers with limited funds. Further, within each type, the sport marketer may identify specific buyer types by using demographics and psychographics.

If the sport marketer is successful at identifying all the buyer types that exist for a product, the marketer will succeed in formulating marketing strategies. If the sport marketer can identify potential buyer types, products may be developed to meet the needs of those types.

Sport Production Segment

Definition: This segment comprises those products necessary or desired to produce sport or to influence the level of sport or fitness performance. Some sports cannot be performed at all without certain products. Some sports could not be performed at desired levels without specific products. This creates a demand for a variety of products needed or desired for the production of sport and for influencing the level or quality of sport performance.

For example, in the production of a softball game, a participant needs some specific softball equipment—a glove, a bat, a softball. To participate in an officially organized competition, one will also need a softball facility and umpires. In addition, if participants want to improve or enhance their level of performance, they could purchase specific equipment in the belief that performance will be enhanced. Many products and prices are offered to the consumer. Softball bats are offered in a variety of materials, colors, lengths, weights, and prices. Each is offered to benefit different buyer types and consumer wants and needs. In addition, the softball player may indulge in softball-lover paraphernalia, such as softball keychains, t-shirts, bags, caps, socks, and gloves.

Another example to illustrate this is tennis and Martina Navratilova. It is questionable if Navratilova would be the all-time great champion in women's tennis if she had to use the first type of tennis racket produced, had no personal fitness trainer or weight training equipment, and was confined to playing matches in clothing that almost completely covered her. Although Navratilova is one of the greatest athletes in sports today, her success has been enhanced by high-tech equipment, training methods, and performance-enhancing apparel.

Product Segments: The following are the categories of product varieties identified in this industry segment:

1. **Outfitting products:** the equipment and apparel either required or preferred in the performance/production of sport.

    A. **Equipment:** Required and/or preferred, sport equipment may be inexpensive and fundamental or highly specialized, customized, and expensive.

    B. **Apparel:** Sports clothing and sport shoes required or referred. Again, these products may be basic and inexpensive or specialized, customized, and costly.

2. **Performance production products:** performance production products, other than outfitting products, needed or

desired for the production of sport. Sport may be produced at one of many points along a continuum. This continuum ranges from the highly sophisticated, elite performance in an expensive, high-tech facility to the weekend athlete's performance in a local homespun facility, such as a back yard. This includes the following:

A. **Fitness trainer:** The fitness trainer, whose actual title may be "trainer" or "strength and conditioning coach" or other, designs and coordinates the athlete's fitness, conditioning, and sport training program.

B. **Medical care:** The sport medicine team specializes in the care and rehabilitation of the injured athlete, regardless of level of athleticism. The sports medicine team often works with the fitness trainer in the coordination of the many facets of the athlete's life that affect the level and frequency of performance. This form of medical care used to be offered only to professional, collegiate, and high school athletes. Recently, freestanding sports medicine clinics open to the public have increased primarily due to the demand of the weekend athlete for appropriate and specialized medical care.

C. **Sport facilities:** Research has shown the negative and positive effects of the sport facility on athletic performance. Marketers will also attest to the selling performance of sports facilities. Whether for performance or for the spectator's convenience, the sport facility's condition, materials, and other factors are important in the production of sport performance. These include the sport field, court, track, pool, arena, stadium, and other facilities needed, such as concession areas, parking areas, locker rooms/dressing rooms, media provisions, officials needs, and private boxes or rooms.

D. **Governing bodies and officials:** The growth of sport has demanded a parallel growth of the structure and limits within which the sport may be performed. Governance of sport influences fair play and decreases risk of injury. The organization or sport, regardless of the size of the production or the level of performance, requires rules, regulations, policies, and compliance personnel. The governing body provides the guidelines for the structure and format of the sport and defines all aspects of the sport, such as performance rules, facility requirements, equipment regulation, reward and compensation guidelines, and even performance standards in some cases.

Many rules of sports and sport equipment are modified today to increase the marketability of the sport. Some examples include the Special Olympics, in which almost all rules of sports and equipment have been modified; men's basketball, in which the height of the basket has remained 10 feet to encourage crowd-pleasing dunks; women's basketball, in which the ball is smaller than the men's basketball in order to enhance crowd-pleasing skills; and marathons that include or hold a separate marathon for wheelchair athletes.

Buyer segments: Buyer types include those consumers who need or want outfitting or performance production products. Buyer types identified include both consumer goods buyers and commercial and industrial buyers. Two consumer goods buyer types identified include (a) sport participants of all demographically and psychographically identified segments and (b) gift shoppers--those consumers looking to purchase these kinds of products as gifts for birthday, Christmas, or other occasion. Some commercial and industrial buyers include high school and college athletic departments, professional sport firms, tax-supported sport organizations, membership-supported sport organizations, nonprofit sport organizations, sport educators, fitness and sport firms, private nonsport firms offering sport as a secondary product, and private nonsport firms.

Sport Promotion Segment

Definition: This segment comprises those products used in the promotion of sport industry products. Sport or fitness activity can exist without promotion. However, it is enhanced, promoted, and in some cases partially funded by promotion products. Sales of sport- and fitness-related goods and services are certainly affected by promotion. The competitors in all segments of the sport industry use a variety of promotion products and tactics. This need to compete creates a demand for promotional products, means, methods, and people who specialize in promotion, marketing, public relations, and other related areas.

Product Segments: The following are the categories of product varieties identified in this industry segment;

1. **Promotional merchandising products:** Promotional merchandise is strategically created to promote sport or a sport product. For example, sport managers or marketers use a variety of promotional merchandise products to promote and market sporting events, organizations, and even individual sport celebrities. Included might be t-shirts, cups, key rings, caps, jackets, blankets, and an event program (a printed program). Other examples include lamps, bumper stickers, sweats, decals, and even shoes. Typically, the merchandise is printed with the logo or other identifying mark of the sport organization or product.

2. **Promotional events:** Planned event or events to coincide with or to bring attention to a sporting event or to a sport product. Examples include holding a concert by a popular star or group in conjunction with a sport event; having a sport star appearance in conjunction with a sport event; having a well-known coach or athlete attend the opening of a sport facility; "give-aways," as they are called in sport marketing, wherein the marketer gives away something, such as caps, to people to attend a sporting event or a sport facility; promoting "tailgating" (partying using the tailgate of a vehicle) by offering specific areas in the parking lot and other benefits, such as free ice, to those tailgaters

who arrive during a specific time period; giving a barbecue to sport club members; and giving milestone banquets.

3. **The media:** Marketers of sport and of other sport products use the media as promotional vehicles for the sport, sporting event, or sport product. At the same time, media use sport, sport figures, sporting events, or sport products to promote their product. Sometimes, as in radio and TV, fees are paid for the right to broadcast a sporting event. This may be achieved at a cost to management of the sporting event, an exchange of goods, such as tickets, or by other means. Included here are (a) print media (i.e., newspapers, magazines, trade journals) and (b) audio/visual media (i.e., radio, TV).

4. **Sponsorship:** Full or partial funding of sport-related expenses in return for certain promotional gains. This is an exchange relationship. Sponsorship helps defray the expenses of a sporting event, a sport facility, or an athlete. Promotional gains might include advertising or other promotional means for the sponsor or an exchange of other goods or services. There are various sponsorship avenues, some of which are as follows:

A. **Single event sponsorship:** A single event is sponsored.

B. **Multiple event sponsorship:** Two or more events are sponsored.

C. **Single team sponsorship:** A single team is sponsored.

D. **Individual sponsorship:** One individual is sponsored.

E. **Circuit or league sponsorship:** A full league or an entire circuit is sponsored.

F. **Shared sponsorship:** Two or more sponsors sponsor an event, team, individual, league, or circuit. This has become popular because the total cost of an event is shared and is therefore less expensive for each sponsor.

5. **Endorsement:** A fee is paid, or goods and/or services are traded for the use of an individual or other to endorse—show support for—a product. The product may or may not be a sport product. Use of the endorser brings attention to the product by capitalizing on the popularity of the endorser. Some examples are the use of Chris Evert to promote tennis rackets, the use of Michael Jordan to promote Nike shoes, and the use of Chuck Yeager to promote motor oil. There are different categories of endorsement. Those categories identified are:

A. **Individual endorsement:** Use of an athlete, coach, owner, or other individual person.

B. **Team endorsement:** Use of a full team.

C. **Full organization:** Use of an entire organization, such as the NCAA, the NFL, the IOC, or USOC.

D. **Nonspecific-sport use:** The use of any sport, without the use of well-known figures or teams or organizations, to promote a product.

Buyer Segments: Buyer types include both commercial/industrial and consumer goods buyers. The commercial/industrial buyers include those sport businesses that use promotional methods to promote their products. Some examples are high school athletic departments, college athletic departments, professional sports organizations, private sport businesses, and tax-supported sport organizations. Consumer goods buyers include those who purchase promotional merchandise for individual use. Some examples include gift buyers, those who purchase merchandise as a gift; collector buyers, those who purchase promotional merchandise as a collector item; and "fan" buyers, those who identify themselves as "fans" of a particular team or sport.

SUMMARY and RECOMMENDATIONS

The purpose of this investigation was to apply Porter's industry segmentation theory to the sport industry and to develop an initial sport industry segment model. The model developed in this study, using only a portion of Porter's theory, represents a new perspective of the industry and should be viewed as an initial framework for further investigation.

Although it seems easy to accept traditional definitions and categorization of products and consumers in the sport industry, this acceptance is perhaps the most important catalyst for analyzing the industry from different perspectives. As an example, the addition of an over-30 women's category in a soccer league reflects the identification of a new buyer type. The analysis should show that many female soccer players do not want to stop playing soccer just because they turn 30. Their desire for type of competitor has most likely changed; that is, they may now choose to compete against a similar age group instead of competing against the 20-year-olds. In this example, the use of just one demographic creates a new buyer type and should point to a few more: men's over-30 and coed over-30. This can be taken a step further. Are there 40-year-olds who play soccer? If not today, what about when the 30-year-olds begin to turn 40?

The identification of a new buyer type does not mean, however, that the firm must develop a product for that type. It does mean that the sport marketer knows that the buyer type exists and may begin considering the feasibility of adding a product to meet buyer want.

Challenges to the sport marketer in using segmentation theory are to identify new ways of segmenting the industry and to find new ways of combining segments. This could lead to the discovery of a variety of segments and, perhaps, of more meaningful segments. For example, this may include discovering a new use for an existing product, a new buyer type for an existing product, or a buyer type but no existing product. This kind of analysis will ascertain the future possibilities for the company.

Although we were able to use a portion of Porter's (1985) theory to identify product segments and buyer segments in the sport industry, we recommend an analysis of the sport industry using all of Porter's model. We also recommend investigation of the sport industry using other industry segmentation models. Investigations should build upon the research presented here. Scholarly analysis could result in different and perhaps more complete analysis of the sport industry. The very purpose of industry segmentation is that it is to be used as "an analytical tool, not an end in itself" (Porter, 1985, p.254).

REFERENCES

Comte, E., & Stogel, C. (1990, January 1). Sports: A $63.1 billion industry. *The Sporting News*, pp. 60-61.

Day, G.S., Shocker, A.D., & Srivastava, R.K. (1979). Customer-oriented approaches to identifying product-markets. *Journal of Marketing, 43* (4), 8-19.

DeSensi, J.T., Kelley, D.R., Blanton, M.D., & Beitel, P.A. (1990). Sport management curricular evaluation and needs assessment: A multifaceted approach. *Journal of Sport Management, 4*(1), 31-58.

Fielding, L.W., Pitts, B.G., & Miller, L.K. (1991, February-March). *Learning about market penetration and market development from successful companies: Hillerich and Bradsby from Buster Brown Bat to the Babe Ruth autograph model 1907-1923.* Paper presented at the International Conference for Sport Business, Columbia, SC.

McCarthy, E.J., & Perrault, W.D. (1990). *Basic marketing.* Homewood, IL: Irwin Publishers.

Mullin, B. (1985). Characteristics of sport marketing. In G. Lewis, & H. Appenzeller, (Eds.), *Successful sport management.* Charlottesville, VA: The Michie Company.

Parks, J.B., & Zanger, B.R.K. (Eds.). (1990). *Sport & fitness management: Career strategies and professional content.* Champaign, IL: Human Kinetics Publishers, Inc.

Pitts, B.G. (1988). *Sport product markets.* Unpublished manuscript, University of Louisville.

Pitts, B. G., Fielding, L. W., & Miller, L.K. (1991, June). *Sport product-markets: A conceptual model.* Paper presented at the conference of the North American Society for Sport Management, Ottawa, Canada.

Porter, M.E. (1985). *Competitive advantage: Creating and sustaining superior performance.* New York: The Free Press.

Stotlar, D.K. (1989). *Successful sport marketing and sponsorship plans.* Dubuque, IA: Wm. C. Brown Publishers.

Economics for Business

Fourth Edition

David Begg and Damian Ward

London   Boston   Burr Ridge, IL   Dubuque, IA   Madison, WI   New York
San Francisco   St. Louis   Bangkok   Bogotá   Caracas   Kuala Lumpur
Lisbon   Madrid   Mexico City   Milan   Montreal   New Delhi
Santiago   Seoul   Singapore   Sydney   Taipei   Toronto

Economics for Business
Fourth edition

David Begg and Damian Ward
ISBN-13 9780077139452
ISBN-10 0077139453

 Higher Education

Published by McGraw-Hill Education
Shoppenhangers Road
Maidenhead
Berkshire
SL6 2QL
Telephone: 44 (0) 1628 502 500
Fax: 44 (0) 1628 770 224

Website: www.mcgraw-hill.co.uk

British Library Cataloguing in Publication Data
A catalogue record for this book is available from the British Library

Library of Congress Cataloging in Publication Data
The Library of Congress data for this book has been applied for from the Library of Congress

Executive Editor: Natalie Jacobs
Commissioning Editor: Rebecca Birtwistle
Development Editor: Kiera Jamison
Marketing Manager: Vanessa Boddington
Production Editor: James Bishop

Text Design by Hard Lines
Cover design by Adam Renvoize
Printed and bound in Singapore by Markono Print Media Pte Ltd

ISBN-13 9780077139452
ISBN-10 0077139453

Economics for Business
Fourth Edition

Dedication

For my mum – Margaret Ward
Damian Ward

For my beloved Jen
David Begg

Brief Table of Contents

Detailed table of contents   vii
Preface   xii
Guided tour   xiv
Online resources   xvi
Acknowledgements   xxii
About the authors   xxiii

Section 1   Introduction   2

    1   Economics for business   4

Section 2   Understanding markets   30

    2   Consumers in the marketplace   32
    3   Firms in the marketplace   58
    4   Markets in action   84

Section 3   Competition and profitability   102

    5   Market structure and firm performance   104
    6   Strategic rivalry   135
    7   Growth strategies   164
    8   Governing business   188

Section 4   Domestic macroeconomics   220

    9   Introduction to the macroeconomy   222
    10   Measuring macroeconomic variables and policy issues   247
    11   Expenditure and fiscal policy   274
    12   Money, banking and interest   299
    13   Inflation, output and economic policy   328
    14   Supply-side policies and economic growth   351

Section 5   Global economics   372

    15   Exchange rates and the balance of payments   374
    16   Globalization   399

Glossary   430
Index   441

Detailed Table of Contents

Preface xii
Guided tour xiv
Online resources xvi
Acknowledgements xxii
About the authors xxiii

Section 1 Introduction 2

1 Economics for business 4

Economics for business at a glance 5

1.1 What is economics? 5
1.2 Why study economics for business? 11
1.3 Business data application: understanding the main economic resources within major economies 14
1.4 Appendix: the economist's approach 17
Summary 25
Learning checklist 26
Questions 26
Exercises 27

Section 2 Understanding markets 30

2 Consumers in the marketplace 32

Demand theory at a glance 33

2.1 Business problem: what is the best price? 33
2.2 Introducing demand curves 34
2.3 Factors influencing demand 35
2.4 Measuring the responsiveness of demand 40
2.5 Income and cross-price elasticity 44
2.6 Business application: pricing strategies I – exploiting elasticities 45

2.7 Business application: pricing strategies II – extracting consumer surplus 49
2.8 Business data applications 52
Summary 54
Learning checklist 55
Questions 55
Exercises 56

3 Firms in the marketplace 58

Cost theory at a glance 59

3.1 Business problem: managing fixed and variable costs 59
3.2 The short and long run 60
3.3 The nature of productivity and costs in the short run 61
3.4 Output decisions in the short run 66
3.5 Cost inefficiency 69
3.6 The nature of productivity and costs in the long run 71
3.7 Business application: linking pricing with cost structures 75
3.8 Business application: footballers as sweaty assets 77
3.9 Business data application: wages and productivity 78
Summary 80
Learning checklist 81
Questions 81
Exercises 82

4 Markets in action 84

Market theory at a glance 85

4.1 Business problem: picking a winner 85
4.2 Bringing demand and supply together 86
4.3 Changes in supply and demand 88
4.4 Disequilibrium analysis 91
4.5 Price floors and ceilings 92
4.6 Pooling and separating equilibria 93

4.7   Business application: marketing pop concerts – a case of avoiding the equilibrium price   93
4.8   Business application: labour markets   95
4.9   Business data application: understanding supply and demand in the car market   96
Summary   98
Learning checklist   98
Questions   99
Exercises   99

Section 3   Competition and profitability   102

5   Market structure and firm performance   104

Perfect competition and monopoly at a glance   105

5.1   Business problem: where can you make profits?   105
5.2   Profit maximization   106
5.3   The spectrum of market structures   111
5.4   Perfect competition   112
5.5   Monopoly   119
5.6   When is a monopoly not a monopoly?   125
5.7   Business application: 'Oops, we're in the wrong box' – the case of the airline industry   126
5.8   Business data application: understanding the forces of competition   127
Summary   132
Learning checklist   132
Questions   132
Exercises   133

6   Strategic rivalry   135

Strategic rivalry at a glance   136

6.1   Business problem: will rivals always compete?   136
6.2   Monopolistic competition   137
6.3   Oligopoly theory: natural and strategic entry barriers   139
6.4   Oligopoly theory: competition among the big ones   142

6.5   Competition among rivals   146
6.6   Game theory   148
6.7   Game theory extensions: reaction functions   150
6.8   Business application: compete, co-operate or gain a first-mover advantage?   152
6.9   Business application: managing supply costs – anonymous auctions for supermarket contracts   153
6.10   Business data application: competition in the bus market   154
6.11   Appendix: auction theory   156
Summary   160
Learning checklist   161
Questions   161
Exercises   162

7   Growth strategies   164

Growth strategies at a glance   165

7.1   Business problem: how should companies grow?   165
7.2   Reasons for growth   167
7.3   Horizontal growth   167
7.4   Vertical growth   170
7.5   Diversified growth   177
7.6   Evidence on mergers   178
7.7   Business application: horizontal growth by merger   180
7.8   Business application: vertical growth – moving with the value   181
7.9   Business application: economies of scope   182
7.10   Business data application: trends in mergers and acquisitions   183
Summary   185
Learning checklist   186
Questions   186
Exercises   187

8   Governing business   188

Governing business at a glance   189

8.1   Business problem: managing managers   189
8.2   Profit maximization and the separation of ownership from control   190
8.3   Principal–agent theory   194

8.4   Business application: stock options and the reduction of agency costs   195
8.5   Regulation of business   199
8.6   Externalities   200
8.7   Dealing with externalities   202
8.8   Merit, demerit and public goods   204
8.9   Price volatility   204
8.10 Market power and competition policy   207
8.11 Assessing government interventions   209
8.12 Business application: carbon trading   210
8.13 Business data application: impact analysis and smart metering   213
Summary   215
Learning checklist   216
Questions   216
Exercises   217

Section 4   Domestic macroeconomics   220

9   Introduction to the macroeconomy   222
Macroeconomics at a glance   223

9.1   Business problem: business cycles and economic uncertainty   223
9.2   Macroeconomic issues   224
9.3   The circular flow of income   227
9.4   National income determination and business cycles   230
9.5   Business application: predicting the business cycle   235
9.6   Business application: profiting from recession   238
9.7   Business data application: finding and understanding data on key components of aggregate demand   240
Summary   243
Learning checklist   244
Questions   244
Exercises   245

10   Measuring macroeconomic variables and policy issues   247
Measurement and policy issues at a glance   248

10.1 Business problem: what are the macroeconomic policy issues?   248
10.2 GDP: measurement and policy   249
10.3 Inflation: measurement and policy   255
10.4 Unemployment   260
10.5 Balance of payments   262
10.6 Macroeconomic policies   263
10.7 Business application: international competitiveness and the macroeconomy   264
10.8 Business policy: inflation targeting?   266
10.9 Business data application: accuracy of economic data measurements   269
Summary   270
Learning checklist   271
Questions   271
Exercises   272

11   Expenditure and fiscal policy   274
Economic stability and demand side policies at a glance   275

11.1 Business problem: who's spending and where?   275
11.2 Consumption, investment expenditure and the business cycle   277
11.3 Fiscal policy   281
11.4 Government's approach to managing fiscal policy   283
11.5 Foreign trade and aggregate demand   288
11.6 Business application: debt funding and crowding out   290
11.7 Business application: taxation or government spending?   292

11.8   Business data application:
       understanding the fiscal
       position and the implications
       for business   293
Summary   295
Learning checklist   296
Questions   296
Exercises   297

12 Money, banking and interest   299

Money, banking and interest at
a glance   300

12.1   Business problem:
       understanding how the
       monetary environment
       influences the commercial
       environment   300
12.2   What is money?   301
12.3   The banking system   302
12.4   Regulation   305
12.5   Credit creation and the
       money supply   309
12.6   The demand for money   311
12.7   Money market equilibrium   312
12.8   Monetary policy   315
12.9   Business application:
       monetary policy and
       investment   319
12.10 Business application: the
       importance of banking
       to the economy   321
12.11 Business data application:
       financial markets and the
       impact of quantitative easing   322
Summary   325
Learning checklist   325
Questions   326
Exercises   326

13 Inflation, output and economic policy 328

Inflation, output and economic policy
at a glance   329

13.1   Business problem: following
       a severe economic crisis,
       how does an economy
       return to equilibrium?   329

13.2   Short- and long-run
       macroeconomic equilibrium   331
13.3   Employment, inflation
       and output   333
13.4   Inflation, aggregate
       demand and supply   336
13.5   Short- and long-run
       equilibrium   337
13.6   Monetary policy rules   339
13.7   Adjustment speed   340
13.8   Business application:
       understanding the interest
       rate path   343
13.9   Business application:
       recognizing the importance
       of real business cycles   344
13.10 Business data application:
       understanding the formation
       of inflationary expectations   345
Summary   347
Learning checklist   348
Questions   348
Exercises   349

14 Supply-side policies and economic growth   351

Supply side policies and economic
growth at a glance   352

14.1   Business problem: assessing
       economic growth   352
14.2   Growth and aggregate
       supply   354
14.3   Neoclassical growth theory   358
14.4   Endogenous growth theory   359
14.5   Supply-side policies   360
14.6   Business application:
       how does innovation
       promote business?   364
14.7   Business application:
       the BRIC economies   365
14.8   Business data application:
       digging behind gross
       capital formation   367
Summary   368
Learning checklist   369
Questions   369
Exercises   370

Section 5 Global economics 372

15 Exchange rates and the balance of payments 374

Exchange rates at a glance 375

15.1 Business problem: should the UK be a member of the euro? 375
15.2 Forex markets and exchange rate regimes 376
15.3 Fixed versus floating exchange rates 380
15.4 The balance of payments 382
15.5 Exchange rates and government policy 385
15.6 European monetary union 387
15.7 Business application: monetary sovereignty, exchange rate depreciation and export growth 390
15.8 Business application: hedging 391
15.9 Business data application: real exchange rates within the Eurozone 393
Summary 394
Learning checklist 396
Questions 396
Exercises 397

16 Globalization 399

Globalization at a glance 400

16.1 Business problem: how do we take advantage of the global economy? 400
16.2 Why is the global economy developing? 401
16.3 A closer look at the EU 409
16.4 To what extent are markets becoming global? 413
16.5 Business application: globalization – exploiting comparative advantage 420
16.6 Business application: sources of international competitiveness 421
16.7 Business data application: understanding the scope for low-carbon technologies in a global economy 423
Summary 426
Learning checklist 427
Questions 427
Exercises 428

Glossary 430
Index 441

Preface

This book is for students interested in business. It is not an economics book with some business applications. Instead, we highlight problems faced by real businesses and show how economics can help solve these decision problems.

Our approach

This approach is new, and focuses on what as a business student you really need. It is issue driven, utilizing theories and evidence only after a problem has been identified. Business decisions are the focus on the screen, and economic reasoning is merely the help button to be accessed when necessary. Of course, good help buttons are invaluable.

Our coverage

Our book offers a complete course for business students wanting to appreciate why economics is so often the backup that you require. After a brief introduction, we help you to understand how markets function and how businesses compete, then we train you to evaluate problems posed by the wider economic environment, both nationally and globally.

As a business student, you do not need to know, nor should you want to master, the whole of economics. Your time is scarce and you need to learn how to manage it effectively. *Economics for Business* gets you off to a flying start by focusing only on the essentials.

Cases and examples

Business does not stand still and neither should you. You need a course embracing topical examples from the real world as it evolves. Whether we are discussing the pricing of Madonna's concert tickets, the location of Google's server farms or the collapse of the global banking system, we aim to bring you the business issues of the day and challenge you to think about how you would respond to them.

Strategic learning

Business students want an instant picture of where they are, what the problem is, and how an intelligent response might be devised. Each chapter begins with the executive summary 'at a glance' and concludes with a summary and learning checklist, providing an informative link in the flow of ideas.

You are thus encouraged to become a 'strategic learner', accessing resources that support your particular lifestyle and learning pattern. You can follow the order that we propose, but you can also browse and move from one topic to another, as you might on the Internet. Active learning both engages your interest and helps you remember things.

Online of course

Our online supplements include access to Connect, McGraw-Hill's web-based assignment and assessment platform. Connect allows instructors to assign auto-graded quizzes and tests, view reports on students' results and get a clearer picture of student progress. For students, Connect provides access both to assignments from your lecturer and to resources for independent study. It provides immediate feedback on how well you know each topic from the book and gives you reading suggestions, MP3 revision notes, additional case studies, animations and practice tests to improve your understanding.

In addition, an Online Learning Centre provides key teaching aids for lecturers.

Summing up

We were prompted to write this book because fewer and fewer students are studying economics for its own sake. More and more students are switching to courses that study business as a whole.

This creates a market.

David Begg
Damian Ward
May 2012

Guided Tour

Each chapter opens with a set of **Learning outcomes**, summarizing what you will take away from each chapter.

Learning outcomes

By the end of this chapter you should understand:

Economic theory

LO1 Economics is the study of how society resolves the problem of scarcity

LO2 The concept of opportunity cost

Business application

LO5 How firms operate within microeconomic and macroeconomic

At a glance   Strategic rivalry

The issue

Firms in perfect competition earn normal economic profits. But can firms avoid direct price comp
product differentiation, and, if so, what are the consequences for pricing and profits? In additio
where there are only a small number of large players, should firms compete or try to co-operate wi
Co-operation leads to increased profits; competition does not.

At the start of each chapter, the **'At a glance'** box provides a snapshot of the chapter and what's to come.

Key terms are highlighted and defined in the margins near where they are first mentioned in the text, to solidify your understanding of core concepts. They are also collected together in the **Glossary** at the back of the book and online.

> Inelastic demand is where elasticity $\varepsilon < 1$, or a change in the price will lead to a proportionately smaller change in the quantity demanded.

In economic terms, demand is said to be perfectly **inelastic** whe
does not respond to a change in price. This is detailed in the fi

Clearly, *perfectly inelastic demand* is an extreme situation. So
Table 2.1, we consider the situation where a 10 per cent chang
5 per cent change in demand.

The demand for Coca-Cola may well be inelastic. If Coke in
per cent we might expect it to lose a small, rather than large, nu
demand is not very responsive to a change in price.

Table 6.3	Ten highest EU cartel fines per case since 1969	
Year	**Case name**	**Amount in €million**
2008	Car glass	1,384
2009	Gas	1,106
2007	Elevators and escalators	832
2010	Airfreight	799
2001	Vitamins	791
2008	Candle waxes	676
2010	LCD	648
2010	Bathroom fittings	622
2007	Gas insulated switchgear	539
2007	Flat glass	487
Source: European Competition Commission Cartel Statistics.		

Each chapter provides a number of **Figures** and **Tables**, which will help you to visualize key economic models, and illustrate and summarize important concepts.

Scattered throughout the book, contemporary **Business applications** bring the economic theory to life by applying topics to real business situations.

 5.7 Business application: 'Oops, we're in the wrong box' – the case of the airline industry

Financial performance is essential, or, in other words, profits count. The firm's revenues and costs determine profits. If we look closely at revenues and costs, we find they are both influenced by prices. A firm's revenues are determined by the price it sells its output for and a

---

Box 6.1

Starbucks to open 200 drive-thrus for roadside caffeine fix

Starbucks announced that it will open 200 'drive-thrus' in Britain over the next five years. Car drivers will order their triple-shot frappuccinos or skinny caramel lattés by speaking into a microphone and then drive forward to pick up their coffee from a hatch – all from the seat of their car.

Drive-thrus are big business in America – two-thirds of McDonald's turnover comes from car-based diners and Starbucks has 2500 outlets, but they have had limited success in Britain. Kris Engskov, the new UK managing director of Starbucks, insisted customers had already embraced the idea. It has been experimenting with 10 roadside shops over the last three years.

'This is absolutely about customers asking for this. The drive-thru meets a customer need,' he said, pointing

Mr Engskov said the new outlets were not a sign that the company was abandoning the high street, at a time when many retailers were struggling. 'We'll continue to develop there, but we need to be flexible. Coffee purchase is driven by convenience, be it a drive-thru or a kiosk, or retail.' The company suggested that 100 new shops could be opened in addition to the drive-thrus over the next five years.

Analysts said the move was proof that the high-street coffee market was becoming saturated. Neil Saunders, managing director at Conlumino, said: 'The coffee shop market competition is intense in the UK. If you educate people about drive-thru it is possible they will embrace it.'

Adapted from an article by Harry Wallop in

Lively and engaging **examples** from the world of business are provided throughout the text to demonstrate economic principles in a relevant context.

Summary

The chapter **Summary** consolidates your learning by summarizing the main points discussed throughout each chapter.

1. The profitability of a market is determined by the competitiv

2. Perfect competition is highly competitive. It has no entry bar homogeneous products and buyers and sellers.

3. In the short run, firms in perfect competition can earn super long run, rivals will enter the market and compete away any

---

Learning checklist

You should now be able to:

- Explain why firms maximize profits when marginal co
- Recall the main assumptions behind perfect competiti
- Explain why the demand curve faced by a perfectly co
- Explain the level of profits in the short and long run i

A **Learning checklist** enables you to check your progress against the learning outcomes for each chapter.

Questions and **Exercises** at the end of each chapter test your understanding of the checklist topics, so that you can confidently progress to the next chapter or discover which topics you may need to revisit before moving on. They are grouped by level of difficulty.

Questions

1. If a firm is a profit-maximizer, then marginal cost and ma
   .... (Fill in the blank)

2. A firm discovers that its marginal cost is less than its mar increase or decrease output?

3. Describe the key assumptions that characterize a perfectl

Online Resources

Online Learning Centre

Visit **www.mcgraw-hill.co.uk/textbooks/begg**.

The Online Learning Centre accompanying this book provides a wealth of resources to assist you in your teaching.

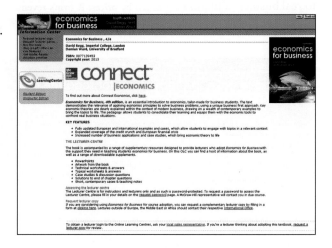

Resources for lecturers:

- Animated PowerPoint presentations
- Artwork from the book
- Technical worksheets and answers
- Case study worksheets and answers

- Topical worksheets and answers
- Case studies and teaching notes
- Guide answers and teaching notes
- Lecture outlines

Test Bank available in McGraw-Hill EZ Test Online

A test bank of over 1000 questions is available to lecturers adopting this book for their module. A range of questions is provided for each chapter, including multiple-choice, true or false, and short-answer or essay questions. The questions are identified by type, difficulty and topic to help you to select questions that best suit your needs and are accessible through an easy-to-use online testing tool, **McGraw-Hill EZ Test Online**.

McGraw-Hill EZ Test Online is accessible to busy academics virtually anywhere – in their office, at home or while travelling – and eliminates the need for software installation. Lecturers can choose from question banks associated with their adopted textbook or easily create their own questions. They also have access to hundreds of banks and thousands of questions created for other McGraw-Hill titles. Multiple versions of tests can be saved for delivery on paper or online through WebCT, Blackboard and other course management systems. When created and delivered though EZ Test Online, students' tests can be immediately marked, saving lecturers time and providing prompt results to students. To register for this FREE resource, visit **www.eztestonline.com**.

Make our content your solution

At McGraw-Hill Education our aim is to help lecturers to find the most suitable content for their needs delivered to their students in the most appropriate way. Our **custom publishing solutions** offer the ideal combination of content delivered in the way which best suits lecturer and students.

Our custom publishing programme offers lecturers the opportunity to select just the chapters or sections of material they wish to deliver to their students from a database called CREATE™ at

www.mcgrawhillcreate.co.uk

CREATE™ contains over two million pages of content from:
- textbooks
- professional books
- case books – Harvard Articles, Insead, Ivey, Darden, Thunderbird and BusinessWeek
- Taking Sides – debate materials

Across the following imprints:
- McGraw-Hill Education
- Open University Press
- Harvard Business Publishing
- US and European material

There is also the option to include additional material authored by lecturers in the custom product – this does not necessarily have to be in English.

We take care of everything from start to finish in the process of developing and delivering a custom product to ensure that lecturers and students receive exactly the material needed in the most suitable way.

With a **Custom Publishing Solution**, students enjoy the best selection of material deemed to be the most suitable for learning everything they need for their courses – something of real value to support their learning. Teachers are able to use exactly the material they want, in the way they want, to support their teaching on the course.

Please contact **your local McGraw-Hill representative** with any questions or alternatively contact Warren Eels e: **warren_eels@mcgraw-hill.com**.

ECONOMICS

STUDENTS...

Want to get **better grades**? *(Who doesn't?)*

Prefer to do your **homework online**? *(After all, you are online anyway...)*

Need **a better way** to **study** before the big test?

(A little peace of mind is a good thing...)

With **McGraw-Hill's** *Connect™* *Plus Economics*,

STUDENTS GET:

- **Easy online access** to homework, tests, and quizzes assigned by your instructor.

- **Immediate feedback** on how you're doing. (No more wishing you could call your instructor at 1 a.m.)

- **Quick access** to lectures, practice materials, eBook, and more. (All the material you need to be successful is right at your fingertips.)

- A Self-Quiz and Study tool that **assesses your knowledge** and **recommends** specific readings, supplemental study materials, and additional practice work. By utilising this resource you end up with a tailor-made study plan to help you where you need it most.

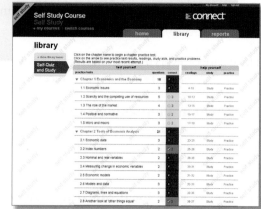

Less managing. More teaching. Greater learning.

 INSTRUCTORS...

Would you like your **students** to show up for class **more prepared**?
(Let's face it, class is much more fun if everyone is engaged and prepared...)

Want an **easy way to assign** homework online and track student **progress**?
(Less time grading means more time teaching...)

Want an **instant view** of student or class performance? *(No more wondering if students understand...)*

Need to **collect data and generate reports** required for administration or accreditation? *(Say goodbye to manually tracking student learning outcomes...)*

Want to **record and post your lectures** for students to view online?

 With McGraw-Hill's *Connect*™ *Plus Economics*,

INSTRUCTORS GET:

- Simple **assignment management**, allowing you to spend more time teaching.

- **Auto-graded** assignments, quizzes, and tests, as well as questions which match end of chapter questions exactly.

- **Detailed Visual Reporting** where student and section results can be viewed and analyzed.

- Sophisticated **online testing** capability.

- A **filtering and reporting** function that allows you to easily assign and report on materials that are correlated to accreditation standards, learning outcomes, and Bloom's taxonomy.

- An easy-to-use **lecture capture** tool.

- The option to **upload course documents** for student access.

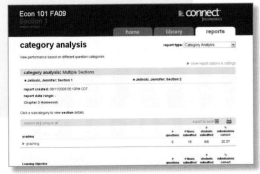

Want an online, **searchable version** of your textbook?

Wish your textbook could be **available online** while you're doing your assignments?

Connect™ Plus Economics eBook

If you choose to use *Connect™ Plus Economics*, you have an affordable and searchable online version of your book integrated with your other online tools.

Connect™ Plus Economics eBook offers a media-rich version of the book, including:

- Topic search
- Direct links from assignments
- Adjustable text size
- Jump to page number
- Print by section

- Embedded videos
- Note-taking
- Book-marking
- Highlighting

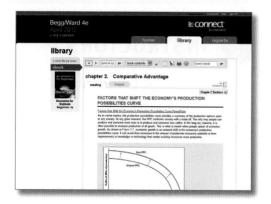

Want to use **Connect™** even if your **instructor isn't**?

Even if your instructor is not utilising Connect™ in their course, you can still benefit.

The Self-Quiz and Study tool is available for you to use on your own via http://connect.mcgraw-hill.com/selfstudy.
You can register here if your instructor is not using Connect and the tool will help assess your knowledge, then recommend specific readings, study materials and practice questions to help you learn.

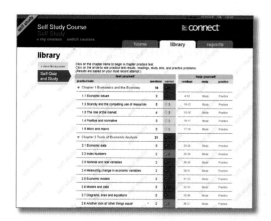

Acknowledgements

Our thanks go to the following reviewers for their comments at various stages in the text's development:

Sanghamitra Bandyopadhyay, Queen Mary University, London

Stuart Barrett, Manchester Metropolitan University

Prabir Battacharya, Heriot Watt University

Andre de Campos, University of Brighton

David Carpenter, Aston University

Carlos Carrillo Tudela, University of Essex

Simeon Coleman, Nottingham Trent University

Martina Fifekova, Hertfordshire University

Robert Fraser, University of Kent

Tim Hinks, University of the West of England

Peter Jackson, University of Leicester

David Kraithman, University of Hertfordshire

Lu Liu, Bath Spa University

Douglas McCulloch, University of Ulster

Bibhas Saha, University of East Anglia

Neelu Seetaram, Bournemouth University

Kent Springdal, Kingston University

Jean-Marc Trouille, University of Bradford

Pamela Whisker, University of Plymouth

Our thanks go to Abhijit Sharma, who created and accuracy checked a huge range of resources to accompany this text. From creating new graphing questions to revising technical worksheets and developing questions for Connect and the Online Learning Centre, Abhijit has worked tirelessly to help us provide a comprehensive and invaluable resource package.

We would also like to thank Nigel Grimwade for his hard work on all the case studies, vignettes and weblinks; and Davide Consoli for his diligence in creating PowerPoints, animated graphs and lecture outlines.

Thanks to Natalie Jacobs, Kiera Jamison and Rebecca Birtwistle from the editorial team at McGraw-Hill. Also thanks to the copy-editor, proofreader and everyone who has spent time producing this book.

About the Authors

David Begg is Professor of Economics at Imperial College Business School. He has been an adviser to the Bank of England, HM Treasury, the IMF and the European Commission. He is a fellow of the Royal Society of Edinburgh, a fellow of the City and Guilds of London Institute and a non-executive director of Imperial Innovations, which invests in technology start-ups from Imperial, Cambridge, Oxford and UCL.

Damian Ward is Associate Dean in the Faculty of Business and Law at Leeds Metropolitan University. He has experience of teaching undergraduate and MBA students, including executive management programmes for leading global organizations. His research interests focus on the application of economic theory to the workings of the financial services industry. He regularly appears on television and radio providing economic commentary and has acted as an adviser to the UK Financial Services Authority.

Economics for Business

Fourth Edition

SECTION

1

Introduction

Section contents

1   Economics for business   4

Economics for business

Chapter contents

Economics for business at a glance   5

1.1 What is economics?   5

1.2 Why study economics for business?   11

1.3 Business data application: understanding the main economic
         resources within major economies   14

1.4 Appendix: the economist's approach   17

Summary   25

Learning checklist   26

Questions   26

Exercises   27

Learning outcomes

By the end of this chapter you should understand:

Economic theory

LO1 Economics is the study of how society resolves the problem of scarcity

LO2 The concept of opportunity cost

LO3 The difference between microeconomics and macroeconomics

LO4 The difference between market and planned economies

Business application

LO5 How firms operate within microeconomic and macroeconomic environments

LO6 The main economic resources within major economies

At a glance   Economics for business

The issue

What is economics and how does economics relate to business?

The understanding

Economics seeks to understand the functioning of marketplaces. Microeconomics examines consumers, firms and workers within markets, seeking to understand why prices change for particular products, what influences the costs of firms and, in particular, what will influence a firm's level of profitability. Macroeconomics examines the whole economy as one very large market. Macroeconomics seeks to address how the government might manage the entire economy to deliver stable economic growth, including current topics of managing debt and implementing austerity packages. The basic economic concepts will be introduced to you through the development of the production possibility frontier and an initial discussion of markets.

The usefulness

Firms operate within an economic environment. The revenue they receive from selling a product is determined within a market. Furthermore, the costs that the firm has to pay for its labour, raw materials and equipment are also priced within markets. Microeconomics addresses the various market influences that impact upon a firm's revenues and costs. Macroeconomics addresses the economy-level issues which similarly affect a firm's revenues and costs. Understanding, reacting to and possibly even controlling micro- and macroeconomic influences on the firm are crucial business skills.

 ## 1.1   What is economics?

Think about everything you would like to own, or consume. Table 1.1 contains a list of material items as examples, but it could equally contain items such as a healthy life and peace in the world.

Now list the resources that might contribute to paying for these desirable items; Table 1.2 shows ours.

You will be quick to note that the wish list is significantly longer than the resources list and there will be a significant gap between the expense required by the wish list and the likely yield of the resources list.

Table 1.1   Wish list

Big house	Luxury restaurant meals
Luxury car	Designer clothes
Top of the range smartphone	Membership of a fitness club
Holiday in an exotic location	A case (or two) of fine wine
Designer shoes	Large flat-screen television
Carbon-frame cycle	Games console
HD camcorder	Tickets to the Monaco Grand Prix

So, we have a problem: we have a wish list that is very long and a resources list that is very short. What will we spend our resources on and what will we decide to leave in the shops? This problem is economics, one which recognizes the difference between **infinite wants** and **finite resources**.

We as individuals would all like to consume more of everything; bigger houses, bigger cars. But we only have finite resources with which to meet all our wants.[1] Firms also have infinite wants. They would like to be operating in more countries, selling larger product ranges. But firms are limited by their access to shareholders' funds and good

Infinite wants are the limitless desires to consume goods and services.

Finite resources are the limited amount of resources that enable the production and purchase of goods and services.

---

[1] This is true at least at one point in time. In the future, capital could be expanded by firms investing in additional capital.

Table 1.2   Resources list

Salary	Royalties from book
Consulting fees	Generous friends

Factors of production are resources needed to make goods and services: land, labour, capital and enterprise.

labour. Governments too have infinite wants, providing more health care and better education, but are limited by their access to tax receipts.

Factors of production

Economists start their analysis by focusing on the entire economy and noting that there are a variety of wants from individuals, firms and governments, and only a limited number of resources, or **factors of production**, which economists group into four categories: land, labour, capital and enterprise.

Land is where raw materials come from: oil, gas, base metals and other minerals. Some economies have enormous access to such resources and build entire economies around resource extraction. These would include Saudi Arabia and oil; Australia and iron, copper and coal; and Qatar and gas. Over time, new extraction technologies make previously inaccessible resources available for exploitation (see Box 1.1).

Labour is the ability of individuals to work. Populous economies such as India and China have workforces that run into hundreds of millions. This provides these economies with the huge potential to generate enormous amounts of economic activity and wealth. In modern developed economies in Europe, labour forces are much smaller, but they are more highly educated and skilled. This enables many high-valued goods and services, such as aeronautics and banking, to be produced. Whereas India and China create value through the volume of workers, Europe achieves wealth creation through the quality of workers.

Capital is production machinery, computers, office space or retail shops. Again, in many modern economies access to productive capital is good. Many banking and retail companies have good access to information technology (IT) infrastructure. In economies like Dubai there has been a massive expansion of commercial and residential construction, providing much needed offices and homes. In China, the government is spending huge sums of money improving and expanding road, rail and energy infrastructure.

Enterprise is the final factor of production that brings land, labour and capital together and organizes them into business units that produce goods and services with the objective of making a profit. Shareholders are perhaps the simplest form of enterprise. Shareholders provide companies with financial backing that enables risk taking and the pursuit of profits.

In spotting new market opportunities entrepreneurs are often innovators and risk-takers, committing resources to commercial projects that may flourish or, alternatively, perish. Proven entrepreneurs might include Richard Branson of Virgin, Bill Gates of Microsoft and, in Box 1.2, Steve Jobs of Apple. Perhaps an important feature of very successful entrepreneurs

Box 1.1

Huge gas find

Cuadrilla Resources believes there are 200 trillion cubic feet of 'shale' gas in the Bowland basin, which could result in a Lancashire gas boom creating 5600 jobs at peak production. Shale is a type of onshore gas common in the US, which is extracted by blasting apart rock in a process called fracking. More testing is needed, but the estimates suggest Britain could have more shale gas than Poland, which has been considered Europe's biggest holder of probable reserves.

Executive director Dennis Carlton said initial results show a basin five to 10 times thicker than America's Marcellus shale. Discoveries of shale have in recent years transformed the US gas production industry.

Adapted from 'Cuadrilla Resources' huge gas find in Blackpool could create 5,600 jobs', by Rowena Mason, *The Telegraph*, 22 September 2011. © Telegraph Media Group Limited 2011.

Box 1.2

Steve Jobs and Apple

Steve Jobs, Apple Inc.'s co-founder and former CEO who died Wednesday after a long battle with pancreatic cancer, created a series of seminal electronics products, reinvented several industries, and built Apple into a $350 billion (£226 billion) juggernaut.

Jobs was famous for keeping an iron grip on every step of the product development process, from conception to execution. The Macintosh, the iPod, the iPhone and the iPad all shine with his distinct design sensibility. Apple has plenty of new products in the pipeline, and there should be few bumps in the short term. But it's not clear if Jobs' brilliance – both as a product visionary and a super-salesman – was ultimately transferable.

Jobs is counted among the greatest CEOs in history, mentioned in the same breath as Henry Ford and other historical giants of corporate America. One of his most unique achievements was vaulting Apple to world leadership not just once, but twice. After co-founding the company with Steve Wozniak in 1976 and giving the world the Apple II and the Macintosh, he was famously pushed out in a clash with his hand-picked CEO, John Sculley. When Jobs returned in 1997 the floundering company's survival was in doubt, but he proceeded to radically transform an ageing computer-maker and take it in a new, and wildly successful, direction. There are few examples in any field of such a brilliant second act.

Along the way, Jobs in 1986 also bought Pixar, which was then little more than an experiment in digital animation technology. The company ultimately became a juggernaut of its own, and when it was acquired by Disney in 2006, Jobs became the largest shareholder of the entertainment giant. Again, there are few examples of a CEO turning a side project into a world-class innovator and business success story.

Jobs' few critics say the Macintosh was mostly borrowed technology, and beyond that all Apple gave the world was a sleek cellphone and an improved music-player. But many people – in the tech world and beyond – believe his impact on society and culture was monumental. He prompted millions to embrace digital technology, online media and mobile communications in ways they never did before.

Adapted from 'Q&A – What happens to Apple after Jobs?' by Edwin Chan, *Reuters Online*, 6 October 2011.

is their drive, motivation and ability to stamp their own personality on a company. Entrepreneurs can bring far more to a company than simply risk-bearing capacity. They can bring management skill, vision and purpose and strategic direction. When they retreat from running companies, as with Apple, then question marks over the future success of the company can be raised.

Production possibility frontier

The **production possibility frontier** is an important illustrative tool because it can be used to highlight crucial economic concepts. These are:

> Production possibility frontier shows the maximum number of products that can be produced by an economy with a given amount of resources.

- Finite resources
- Opportunity costs
- Macroeconomics and microeconomics
- Planned, market and mixed economies

We will discuss each in turn.

Finite resources

Figure 1.1 shows the production possibility frontier for an imaginary economy that produces only two goods, pizza and beer, and highlights the constraint created by access to only a finite amount of resources. With a fixed quantity of resources an infinite amount of beer, or pizzas,

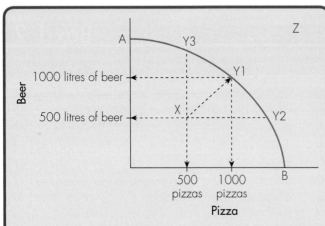

The production possibility frontier shows the maximum amounts of beer and pizza that can be produced with a fixed amount of resources. At Y1, 1000 litres of beer and 1000 pizzas can be produced. At Y3, more beer can be produced but some pizza production has to be sacrificed, while at Y2, beer can be sacrificed in order to produce more pizzas. Z cannot be achieved with current resource levels and X represents unemployment, with production of beer and pizzas below the optimal levels attainable on the frontier, such as Y1, Y2 and Y3.

Figure 1.1   Production possibility frontier

cannot be produced. If all resources were allocated to the production of beer, then we would be at point A on the diagram, with a maximum amount of beer being produced and no pizzas. But if all resources were allocated to pizzas, then we would be at point B, with a maximum number of pizzas being produced and no beer. The curve between points A and B indicates all the maximum combinations of beer and pizza that can be produced. The frontier shows what it is possible to produce with a limited amount of resources.

Operating on the frontier is optimal; all finite resources are employed. Operating at a point such as Z is currently impossible. The economy does not have the resources to produce at Z. Operating at X is inefficient, because some resources must be unemployed. More output could be produced by employing all factors of production and moving towards the frontier.

Opportunity costs

If pizza production is reduced in order to make more beer, then the **opportunity cost** consists of the benefits that could have been received from the pizzas that have not been made. Opportunity costs give the production possibility frontier a negative slope; simply, more pizzas must mean less beer. Reading this book now has an opportunity cost. You could be watching television. Recalling that the economic problem is one of infinite wants and finite resources, ideally you will try to make your opportunity cost as low as possible. With your limited resources you will try to maximize your gains from consumption. This way you are sacrificing the least amount of benefit.

> Opportunity costs are the benefits forgone from the next best alternative.
>
> Macroeconomics is the study of how the entire economy works.
>
> Microeconomics is the study of how individuals make economic decisions within an economy.

Macroeconomics and microeconomics

By focusing on points X, Y and Z in Figure 1.1, we can draw your attention to two important distinctions in economics: (i) the study of **macroeconomics** and (ii) the study of **microeconomics**.

Maximizing gains

If the benefit of reading this book to you can be estimated at £1 per hour and the benefit of watching television can be estimated at £0.50 per hour, then the opportunity cost of reading this book, rather than watching television, is £0.50, the benefit you have given up. In contrast, if you watched television, then the opportunity cost would be £1 – the benefit forgone from not reading this book. Given the ratio of these benefits, you can minimize your opportunity cost by reading this book. If we add in an option to

reflect the true student lifestyle, a night out with your friends might be worth £5 per hour to you. Staying in and reading this book would then represent an opportunity cost of £5 per hour, while going out and not reading the book would only represent an opportunity cost of £1 per hour, the benefits forgone by not reading this book. In terms of opportunity cost, it is cheaper to go out with your friends than to stay in and read this book. If you fail this module, at least you can understand why.

Points X and Z represent mainly macroeconomic problems. At point X, the economy is not operating at its optimal level; we said point X was likely to be associated with unemployment. This occurs during a recession. Part of macroeconomics is understanding what creates a recession and how to remedy a recession. Governments and the central bank adjust interest rates, taxation and government spending to try to move the economy from point X towards point Y. Point Z is also a macroeconomic issue. The economy cannot achieve point Z now, but in the future the economy could grow and eventually attain point Z. How do we develop policies to move the economy over the long term to point Z? This question has been the recent focus of economic policy-makers, with the focus placed upon the issue of 'sustainable economic growth'.

Microeconomics places the focus of analysis on the behaviour of individuals, firms or consumers. Rather than looking at the economy as a whole, it attempts to understand why consumers prefer particular products. How will changes in income or prices influence consumption patterns? In relation to firms, microeconomists are interested in the motives for supplying products. Do firms wish to maximize sales, profits or market share? What factors influence costs and how can firms manage costs? What determines the level of competition in a market and how can firms compete against each other?

By focusing on individual consumers, firms and the interaction between the two, the economist is particularly interested in the functioning of markets. This particular aspect of economics can be highlighted by examining movements along the production possibility frontier. Point Y1 on the frontier has been described as being efficient. But points Y2 and Y3 are also on the frontier and are, therefore, equally efficient. At Y1, the economy produces a balanced mix of pizza and beer. At Y2, the economy specializes more in pizza and, at Y3, the economy specializes more in beer production. How will the economy decide among operating at Y1, Y2 and Y3? The answer lies in understanding resource allocation mechanisms.

Planned, market and mixed economies

In a **planned economy**, the government plans whether the economy should operate at point Y1 or another point. Historically, these systems were common in the former Soviet Bloc and China, and are still in use in Cuba and North Korea.

In a planned economy, the government sets an economic plan, typically for the next five years. Within the economic plan are decisions about which industries to support and how much output each industry should produce. This could include a plan for car production, house building and the expansion of travel infrastructure, including rail, roads and air. The economic plan may also go so far as to set prices for goods, services and wages.

In planned economies, the government is the major owner of the factors of production, and in the case of Cuba around 76 per cent of the entire workforce is employed by the government.

In a **market economy**, private individuals own the majority of economic factors of production. Market economies have two important groups: consumers that buy products and firms that sell products. Consumers buy products because they seek the benefits associated with the consumption of the products. For example, you eat food because it stops you feeling hungry; you drive a car because it helps you to travel between various locations. Similarly, firms sell products in order to make a profit.

In the marketplace information is exchanged between consumers and firms. This information relates to the prices at which consumers are willing to buy products and, similarly, the prices at which firms are willing to sell. For any particular product you will have a maximum price at which you are willing to buy. The more desirable you find the product, the greater will be your maximum price. In contrast, firms will have a minimum price at which they are willing to sell. The easier, or cheaper, it is to make the good, the lower this minimum price will be. If the minimum price at which firms are willing to sell is less than consumers'

> In a planned economy, the government decides how resources are allocated to the production of particular products.
>
> In a market economy, the government plays no role in allocating resources. Instead, markets allocate resources to the production of various products.

maximum willingness to pay, then the potential for a market in the good exists. Firms can make the product in the clear expectation of making a profit.

Firms are likely to move their productive resources – land, labour, capital and enterprise – to the markets that present the greatest opportunities for profit. Given our discussion above, profits will vary with the willingness of consumers to pay and the costs incurred by firms. If consumers are willing to pay higher prices, or production costs fall, then profits will increase. Increasing profits will lead firms to move resources into the market. In contrast, as consumers reduce their willingness to buy a product, or if firms' costs increase, profits will fall and firms will look to reallocate their resources into more profitable markets.

Box 1.4

Pizza and beer

In our pizza and beer example, let us consider the following: we are at point Y1 on Figure 1.1 and suddenly scientists show that beer is very good for your health. Following this news, we would expect consumers to buy more beer. As beer increases in popularity, beer producers are able to sell for a higher price and make greater profits. As consumers allocate more of their income to beer, pizza producers begin to lose sales and profits. Over time, pizza makers would recognize that consumers have reduced their consumption of pizzas. In response, pizza producers would begin to close down their operations and move their resources into the popular beer market. The economy moves from Y1 to Y3 in the figure.

Comparing command and market economies

Market economies rely on a very quick and efficient communication of information that occurs through prices. Firms ordinarily set a price that indicates their willingness to sell. Consumers communicate their willingness to buy by purchasing the product at the given price. The problem of what should be produced and what should not be produced is solved by the price system.

The command (or planned) economy, in setting production levels for various goods and services, requires similar market-based information regarding the costs of production and the consumption requirements of consumers. But how would you go about setting food, clothing, drink, transport and education output levels for an economy? You might conduct a questionnaire survey asking consumers to rank the different products by level of importance. But this has a number of problems. It is costly, the respondents might not represent the views of all consumers and it might not be timely with the questionnaire only being carried out every couple of years. The collection of information required for effective planning is very complicated and costly within a command economy, especially when compared with the simple and efficient exchange of information in the market economy through the pricing system. It is of little surprise that, in recent years, planned economies have become less popular.

> In a mixed economy, the government and the private sector jointly solve economic problems.
>
> Gross domestic product (GDP) is a measure of overall economic activity within an economy. (See Chapters 9 and 10 for more details.)

In reality, many economies function as an amalgam of planned and market economies – a **mixed economy**.

For example, within many modern economies the sale of groceries is a purely market solution, with private firms deciding what they will offer to consumers within their own supermarkets. The provision of public health care is an example of the government deciding what health-care treatments will be offered to the population.

A means of measuring the planned side of the economy is to examine the size of government expenditure as a percentage of **gross domestic product (GDP)**. Government expenditure can include spending on infrastructure such as roads, health care, education, defence and social contributions such as unemployment benefits.

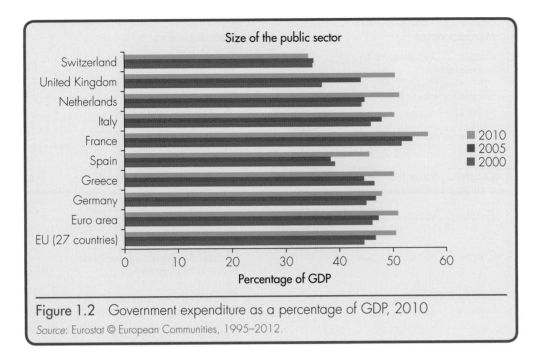

Figure 1.2　Government expenditure as a percentage of GDP, 2010
Source: Eurostat © European Communities, 1995–2012.

Figure 1.2 illustrates the size of the planned or public sector for a number of European economies. For most economies, the size of the planned economy is large. Even in Switzerland, with the smallest government sector, it still represents almost 34 per cent of GDP.

In summary, economics studies how individuals, firms, governments and economies deal with the problem of infinite wants and finite resources. Microeconomics examines the economic issues faced by individuals and firms, while macroeconomics studies the workings and performance of the entire economy. We will now indicate why an understanding of economics can provide an essential understanding for business.

1.2　Why study economics for business?

Business and management draw upon a number of different disciplines, including, but not limited to, accounting and finance, human resource management, operations management, marketing, law, statistics and economics. Each discipline has a particular focus and set of issues that it specializes in understanding.

The economist's analysis of business begins with a simple assumption: firms are in business to make profits for their owners. Moreover, firms are in business to maximize profits, or make the highest amount of profit possible.

The assumption that firms are profit-maximizers is clearly a simplification. Firms represent a collection of workers, managers, shareholders, consumers and perhaps individuals living within the locality of the firm's operations. Each of these groups may have a different interest within the firm. For example, shareholders may seek greater profit, but workers and managers may seek increased wages. These conflicts generate complexity within the organizational environment of firms. Economists try to simplify the complex nature of reality. Therefore, rather than attempt an understanding of all the complex interrelationships within a firm, economists simply assume that the firm is in business to maximize profits.

Economists are not arguing that the complex interrelationships between the various interest groups within a firm are not important. However, economists are assuming that, without profits, firms would find it difficult to survive financially. Therefore, while subjects such as

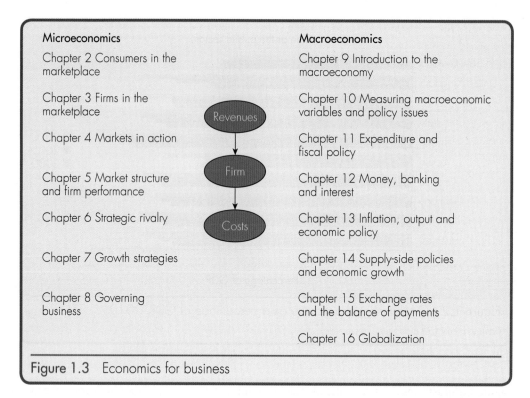

Microeconomics

Chapter 2 Consumers in the marketplace

Chapter 3 Firms in the marketplace

Chapter 4 Markets in action

Chapter 5 Market structure and firm performance

Chapter 6 Strategic rivalry

Chapter 7 Growth strategies

Chapter 8 Governing business

Macroeconomics

Chapter 9 Introduction to the macroeconomy

Chapter 10 Measuring macroeconomic variables and policy issues

Chapter 11 Expenditure and fiscal policy

Chapter 12 Money, banking and interest

Chapter 13 Inflation, output and economic policy

Chapter 14 Supply-side policies and economic growth

Chapter 15 Exchange rates and the balance of payments

Chapter 16 Globalization

Figure 1.3   Economics for business

human resource management, organization theory and corporate social responsibility focus upon how the firm might manage the conflicting relationships between the competing interest groups of shareholders, workers and wider society, business economists have focused upon an understanding of firms' profits.

Firms, as profit-making organizations, can be viewed as a combination of revenue-based cash flows going in, and cost-based cash flows going out. Within this view of firms, economics for business can be simplified to an analysis of the economic influences that enhance revenues and reduce costs, thereby increasing firm-level financial performance or, more directly, profit.

In Figure 1.3, the firm is positioned between its revenue and its costs. In placing the firm in the middle of the diagram, it is also recognized that the firm operates within microeconomic and macroeconomic environments. The micro and macro environments are covered in detail by the various chapters within this book but importantly, and perhaps simplistically, each chapter adds to an understanding of how the firm can improve its revenue and/or cost position. Broad areas of interest and importance are now discussed.

Markets and competition

The particular focus of economics is on the functioning of markets. Markets are important for firms in a number of ways. First, a marketplace is where a firm will sell its product and, therefore, generate revenue. Second, a firm's inputs – land, labour, capital and enterprise – are all purchased through markets and, therefore, markets influence a firm's level of costs. The level of competition varies across markets: some are highly competitive; others are not. Throughout life, if you wish to be a winner, it is easier to achieve success when the competition is weak; and business is no different. In highly competitive business environments prices will fall, while in low competitive environments price competition will be less severe. If interested in enhancing revenues, it is important to understand how to recognize issues likely to promote competition and influences that will enable competition to be managed and controlled. It is also important to understand how a firm can change its mode of operations in order to improve its competitive advantage. Growth by acquisition of a rival clearly reduces competition, but growth by the purchase of a raw material supplier into the industry also places your rivals at a disadvantage, because you then own what your rivals need. Good business people understand how to manage and exploit competitive opportunities.

Government intervention

Governments can also intervene in markets. Society, or government, does not view excessive pollution of the environment as desirable. Some pollution may be an unavoidable consequence of beneficial production. In order to manage pollution the government can attempt to influence the commercial activities of firms. This usually involves increased taxes for firms that pollute, and subsidies, or grants, for firms that attempt to operate in a more environmentally friendly manner. Therefore, the government can seek to influence firms' costs and revenues, boosting them when the firm operates in the interest of society, and reducing profits when the firm operates against the public interest. Firms need to be able to understand when their activities are likely to attract the attention of government, or pressure groups, and what policies could be imposed upon them.

Globalization

Finally, firms do not operate within singular markets; rather, they function within massive macroeconomic systems. Traditionally, such systems have been the national economy but, more recently, firms have begun to operate within an increasingly global environment. Therefore, in order for firms to be successful they need to understand how macroeconomic events and global change will impact on their current and future operations.

National economies have a tendency to move from economic booms into economic recessions. If a firm's sales, and therefore revenues, are determined by the state of the macroeconomy, then it is important for the firm to understand why an economy might move from a position of economic prosperity to one of economic recession. Similarly, during a recession firms struggle to sell all of their output. Price discounts can make products and inputs – such as labour, raw materials and capital equipment – cheaper, thereby reducing a firm's costs.

While understanding the state of the macroeconomy is important, it is also beneficial to have an understanding of how the government might try to manage the economy. How will changes in taxation affect consumers, firms and the health of the economy? How will interest rate changes influence inflation and the state of the economy? These are common governmental policy decisions with important implications for business.

Moreover, within the global economy matters of international trade, exchange rates, European monetary union and the increasing globalization of business all impact upon the operations and competitive position of business. Operating internationally may enable a firm to source cheaper production or access new markets and revenue streams. However, equally, international firms can access UK markets, leading to an increase in competition for UK domestic producers. Successful companies will not only recognize these issues but, more importantly, they will also understand how these issues relate to themselves and business generally. From this, strategies will be developed and firms will attempt to manage their competitive environment.

In order to develop your understanding of these issues, this book is separated into a number of parts that build on each other. In Section II you will be introduced to the workings of marketplaces. Section III will develop an understanding of competition in markets, followed by an overview of firm governance by shareholders and government. This will conclude the microeconomic section of the book. Macroeconomics is split into two obvious parts: macroeconomics in the domestic economy and macroeconomics in the global economy. At the domestic level, you will be introduced to how the macroeconomy works, the factors leading to the level of economic activity and the options available to a government trying to control the economy. At the global level, you will be provided with an understanding of international trade and the workings of exchange rates. This will lead to the important issue of European monetary union. Finally, an assessment of globalization and the implications for business will be provided.

In order to highlight the relevance of economics to business, each chapter begins with a business problem. Theory relevant to an understanding of the problem is then developed. Each chapter closes with two applications of the theory to further highlight the relevance of the theory to business and management. In this way, economic theory is clearly sandwiched between real-world business issues and practices, highlighting for you that economics, where appropriate, is a subject to be applied in the understanding of business problems.

Business data application: understanding the main economic resources within major economies

Economists love data. This love of data comes from the potential to illustrate trends and movements in important economic variables. Throughout this book, and at the end of every chapter, we will suggest to you where business people can find useful economic data and how it can be interpreted using the economic frameworks developed in each chapter. The purpose of such an approach is to emphasize the applicability of economics to business problems and to help students solve business problems, once they graduate, by indicating where to find useful economic data. We begin in this chapter by highlighting some key trends in factor resources for a selection of important economic regions.

We have identified economic resources as land, labour, capital and enterprise. Such resources represent the economic fabric of a region and can help determine the attractiveness of a particular location to business. Therefore, understanding where to find data on the resources of an economy, and assessing the quantity and quality of those resources, can be an important business skill.

One provider of economic data, which covers resources, is the World Bank (www.worldbank.org). Identifying key measures of economic resources is not as easy as simply saying there is land, labour, capital and enterprise. These four headings are nothing more than broad categories. Under each category it is possible to list a number of important indicators of resource availability. For example, under land we might ask how much land in an economy is allocated to agricultural, urban and commercial purposes. Under labour, the size of the population and then the percentage of the population participating in employment may give an indication of the amount of labour resource, while statistics on the number of individuals gaining a university-level education may indicate the economy's access to skilled and productive labour. Under capital, there would be interest in commercial, public and household infrastructure. Asking how many individuals have access to the Internet, how much power consumption occurs in the economy, how many roads are paved and how many international flights the nation's airports support, are all ways of addressing the capital endowment of the economy. Finally, in assessing enterprise we can assess the extent to which well-functioning stock markets and banking sectors are developed, providing an indication of the economy's ability to provide financial support to business.

The list of measures can be extensive and in Figures 1.4a and 1.4b we present data on a selected number of resource measures for three major economic areas: North America, the European Union and China. Note that the World Bank has not tracked all of the measures for the same amount of time. Some resource measures have become more interesting to measure and easier to collate during recent times, therefore the time periods for each of the measures do not always coincide.

Looking at the percentage of land used for agriculture in the top left of Figure 1.4a, we can see modest declines for North America and the European Union. Agriculture is often viewed

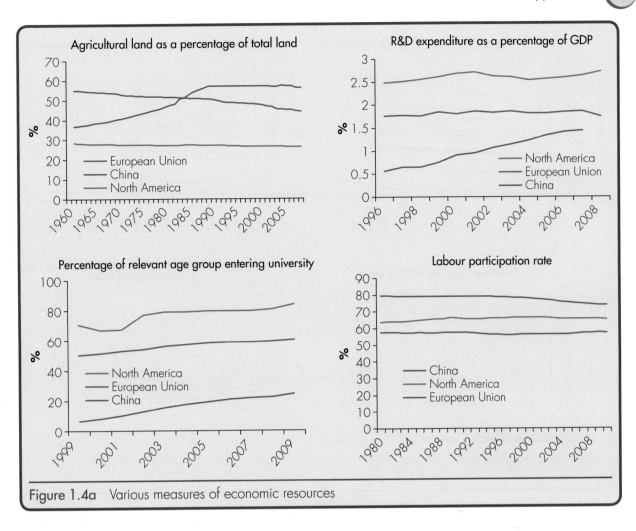

Figure 1.4a   Various measures of economic resources

as a low value-adding activity within an economy and as such does not generate lots of economic wealth. As economies become more industrialized and perhaps even more knowledge based, then we expect to see a move away from land being used for agriculture. That said, the upward movement in land used for agriculture in China is likely to reflect the fast-growing population and the need to expand food production. The move towards more knowledge-based economies can be seen in the top right of Figure 1.4a, with an increase in research and development (R&D) expenditure for all three areas, most notably China, highlighting the importance of scientific knowledge as an economic resource.

In terms of labour, the bottom half of Figure 1.4a shows that China has the highest percentage of those in the working age group in employment, the so-called labour participation rate. This pattern may reflect China's industrial reliance on labour to generate economic growth, whereas in North America and the European Union there is a greater use of non-labour resource, e.g. capital machinery in the production process. The quality of labour in terms of advance cognitive skills can be measured by the number of individuals entering university level education. For all three areas, the trend has been upwards, but China lags behind the European Union and North America.

In Figure 1.4b we provide evidence on some additional resources. Electrical power consumption per capita provides some evidence of the power-producing capacity of the economy; it may also provide some indication of the assets and resources within an economy that are power hungry, including computers, server centres, retail centres, train travel, metal production, such as aluminium, and into the future, electrically powered cars. Power consumption in North America is huge. In contrast China's power consumption per capita is much smaller.

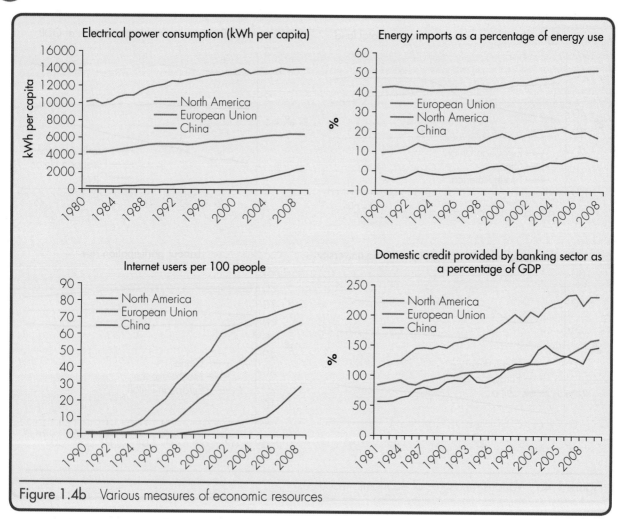

Figure 1.4b   Various measures of economic resources

Energy imports as a percentage of total energy use provide some measure of the economy's ability to meet internal energy demands from domestic oil, gas and coal reserves. North America is very reliant on energy resources from other economies, while China in some years has actually managed to export more energy than it uses itself.

Technology and the availability of information are important economic resources. Access to the Internet has become an important means of enabling consumers to find products and for firms to find consumers. The proportion of the population using the Internet has exploded during the last decade, most notably in North America and the European Union.

Finally, the provision of financial credit to enable firms to grow is important and for our three areas we have witnessed a huge increase in the ability of the banking sector to provide financing. For all of the areas, domestic credit provided by banks is greater than the value of annual economic output, known as GDP. In the case of North America, the figure is double that of GDP. The extent to which bank credit can grow and facilitate economic growth will undoubtedly fall following the financial crises of recent years.

By examining a small number of resources we can draw useful, though admittedly broad, insights for business. In particular, China is still relatively committed to agriculture, it has an economy which is heavily dependent upon labour and at present it is not very energy intensive. In contrast, the European Union and to a greater degree North America are less dependent upon labour, but that labour is more educated. Science, in terms of research and development, is an important activity; the use of technology within the economy, as evidenced by Internet use is strong; and power consumption is high. These factors would tend to suggest that China as an economic location currently facilitates economic activities which require lots of labour, such as assembly work. North America and the European Union are regions which provide more knowledge-intensive products and more energy-intensive production and consumption. Some of these ideas we will discuss in more detail in Chapter 16 when we explore the global nature of business.

We now encourage you to visit the statistical area of the World Bank website and explore other data measures for other economies. The web address is http://data.worldbank.org.

Appendix: the economist's approach

Economics as a subject has a number of characteristics associated with it and, to aid your learning, it is worth pointing them out to you.

Language

The economist makes use of terms and phrases that are particular and peculiar to economics. For example, from the above discussion economics is the study of why you cannot have everything. But the economist talks about infinite wants, finite resources, opportunity costs and production possibility frontiers. Using the economic terminology will help you. Economists use particular terminology because it helps them to understand each other when communicating ideas. Succinct terms, such as opportunity cost, once understood, convey complex ideas quickly to anyone else who understands the phrase.

Abstract models

Economists think about the world in terms of **models** or **theories**.

Economists recognize that the world is extremely complicated and, therefore, prefer to make models using simplifying assumptions. The complexity of the real world is stripped out in favour of a simple analysis of the central, or essential, issues. As an example, consider Box 1.5, where we discuss how an economist might approach how David Beckham bends free kicks.

> Models or theories are frameworks for organizing how we think about an economic problem.

Normative and positive economics

A **positive economics** question and a **normative economics** statement will help to clarify the differences:

Positive question: What level of production will maximize the firm's profits?
Normative statement: Firms should maximize profits.

The positive question seeks to address a technical point – can economics identify the output level where firms will make the largest profit? The normative statement, in contrast, seeks to assert the opinion that profit maximization is best – it is making a value judgement. In the case of the positive question, economists can make a response with theory consisting of a set of accepted rational arguments that provide a technical answer to the question. However, in respect of the normative statement, economists can only reply with similar, or alternative, value statements: for example, firms should not focus entirely on profit maximization; I believe they should also consider the needs of wider stakeholders such as workers, the environment, suppliers and customers.

> Positive economics studies objective or scientific explanations of how the economy works.
>
> Normative economics offers recommendations based on personal value judgements.

This is an important distinction. Positive economics is the technical and objective pursuit of economic understanding. As a subject it seeks to provide answers to questions and propose solutions to problems. Normative economics is different in that it does not seek to answer questions; rather, it seeks to assert and represent particular beliefs – which are difficult, if not impossible, to provide positive answers to.

Box 1.5

Professor Juninho

In modelling Juninho's ability to bend free kicks, economists would strip out the complex issues, such as natural talent, good practice and high-pressure championship experience, and take the simplifying assumption that Juninho behaves like a professor of physics. Juninho must behave like a highly accomplished physicist because he can clearly calculate all the angles and force needed to bend a free kick and score a goal.

In reality, Juninho probably has no more understanding of physics than many of us. So, to say that Juninho behaves like a physicist seems peculiar. However, the important point is that the theory *predicts*; it need not *explain*. The theory does not *explain* why Juninho can bend free kicks and score goals with such accuracy. But it does *predict* that Juninho will score spectacular goals if he behaves like a world-class physicist. This is because a leading physicist, indeed any physicist, could use the Newtonian laws of motion to work out the perfect angle and trajectory for the football to travel in a spectacular arc into the back of the net. But why should economists wish to develop strange

abstract assumptions about reality, leading to theories that predict, as opposed to theories that can explain?

The answer to this question is that economists try to keep things simple and extract only the important points for analysis. The world is very complex, so what we try to do as economists is to simplify things to the important points. Juninho is probably a football player because of some natural talent, a good deal of practice, championship experience and perhaps some poorer opponents. All these would explain why Juninho can score great goals. But to keep things simple we will assume he behaves like a leading physicist. If theoretically true, then Juninho will also be an amazing free-kick specialist. Therefore, the predictive approach is a theoretical short cut that enables economists to simplify the complex nature of reality. So, whenever you come across a theory in this book that is not a true reflection of reality, do not worry. We economists are happy in our little fantasy world where people like Juninho, David Beckham, Zico and Diego Maradonna all double up as Einstein.

Economics is not peculiar in exhibiting a tension between objective and subjective approaches to reason. In art, the positive approach may centre on a technical understanding of various media. But the use of these media, the choice of images to create and how to interpret them are all normative, value laden and subjective.

Diagrams

Quickly flick through all the pages of this book. How many diagrams did you see? Economists like diagrams. For the economist, diagrams are an effective way of communicating complex ideas. In order to develop your understanding of economics, you will need to develop your competence in this area, as it is almost impossible to manage without them – which is disappointing for any of you who detest them with a passion.

A positive relationship exists between two variables if the values for both variables increase and decrease together.

A negative relationship exists between two variables if the value for one variable increases (decreases) as the value of the other variable decreases (increases).

As a brief reminder, diagrams, at least as we will be using them, provide a visual indication of the relationship between two variables. For example, consider a fridge and an oven. Neither is currently switched on. When we do switch them on we are interested in seeing how the temperature inside the oven and the fridge changes the longer each appliance is on. This is not rocket science: the fridge will get colder and the oven hotter. A maths teacher would say that there is a **positive relationship** between time and temperature in the cooker.

In our example of the oven, as time increases – 1 minute, 2 minutes, etc. – the temperature of the oven also increases. Our two variables, time and temperature, increase together.

In contrast, the maths teacher would say that there is a **negative relationship** between time and temperature in the fridge.

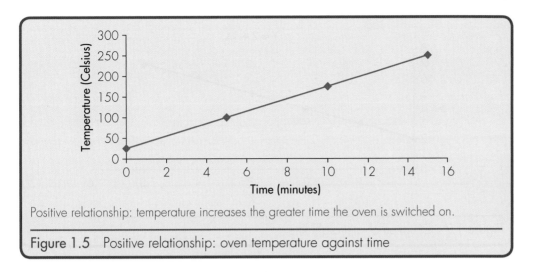

Positive relationship: temperature increases the greater time the oven is switched on.

Figure 1.5 Positive relationship: oven temperature against time

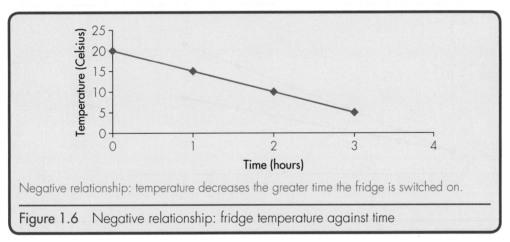

Negative relationship: temperature decreases the greater time the fridge is switched on.

Figure 1.6 Negative relationship: fridge temperature against time

In our example of the fridge, as time increases, the temperature of the fridge decreases. Figure 1.5 is a diagram showing the positive relationship between time and temperature within the oven, while Figure 1.6 is a diagram of the negative relationship between time and the temperature inside the fridge.

We will be doing nothing more complicated than this. We might reasonably argue that, as prices increase, consumers will buy less; we therefore expect to see a negative relationship between the price of a product and the amount of the product purchased by consumers. Similarly, in the case of a positive relationship we might argue that consumer expenditure increases as income levels rise. Essentially the diagrams are a simple visual illustration of the relationship between two variables. The more you try to understand them and gain confidence in using them, the easier economics becomes.

Equations of lines

We can also describe relationships between variables using equations. If there is a linear relationship between two variables, then we can use the general **equation of a straight line** to describe the relationship. The general linear relationship states that $Y = a + bX$, where a is the intercept and b is the gradient of the line. The intercept is the value of Y when X is zero. The gradient is the steepness of the line.

> Equation of a straight line is $Y = a + bX$

In Figure 1.7, the two axes are Y and X and the equation of the straight line describing the relationship between Y and X is $Y = 2 + 1X$; that is, a = 2 and b = 1. So, when X is zero, Y = 2; and for every one-unit increase in X, then Y also increases by 1. So if X is 4, Y must be $2 + 4 = 6$.

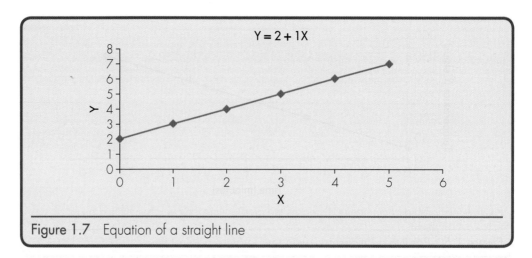

Figure 1.7   Equation of a straight line

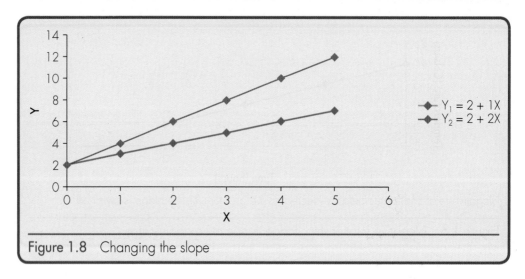

Figure 1.8   Changing the slope

In Figure 1.8, we have altered the equation to make the gradient twice as steep. The relationship between Y and X is now $Y_2 = 2 + 2X$. So, when X = 4, then Y = 2 + (2 × 4) = 10. If we changed the intercept to, say, 4, then the line for Y_2 would move up the Y axis and start from Y = 4, and not Y = 2.

If we require a negative relationship, then we simply change the sign of the gradient to minus. So Y = 10 − 2X. This is illustrated in Figure 1.9. When X = 0, then Y = 10. When X = 3, then Y = 10 − (3 × 2) = 4.

> A quadratic is generally specified as $Y = a + bX + cX^2$

We may also need to consider a non-linear relationship, such as a **quadratic**. A quadratic is generally specified as $Y = a + bX + cX^2$. In Figure 1.10, we have plotted two quadratic relationships, one of the form $Y = 20 − 6X + X^2$, which creates a U-shaped relationship. Then, by simply changing the signs on b and c, we can create $Y = 25 + 6X − X^2$, which creates an n-shaped relationship. (We changed a, the intercept, to generate vertical distance between the two lines.)

Gradients and turning points

The **gradient** measures the slope or steepness of a line. One method of measuring the gradient of a line is to calculate the ratio $\Delta Y/\Delta X$, where the symbol Δ means change.

> The gradient is a measure of the slope of a line.

The values for ΔY and ΔX can be calculated by drawing a triangle against the slope of a line. If we examine the slopes in Figure 1.8, for Y_2 over the range X = 3 to X = 4, then $\Delta X = 1$. At the same time, Y increases from 8 to 10, so $\Delta Y = 2$. So the gradient = 2/1 = 2.

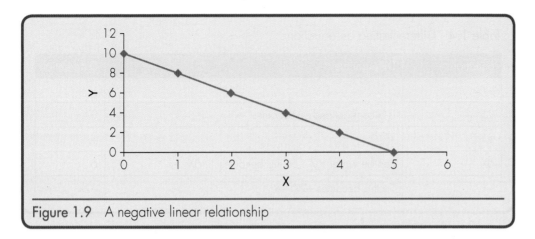

Figure 1.9   A negative linear relationship

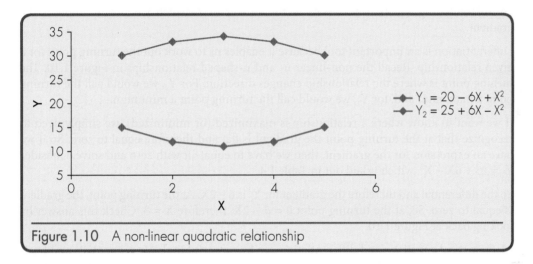

Figure 1.10   A non-linear quadratic relationship

Recall that the general equation of a straight line is $Y = a + bX$, where b is the gradient. From Y_2, we can see that $b = 2$, which corresponds with our measure based on Figure 1.8.

There is also another means of gaining a measure of the gradient. This involves the use of a simple mathematical function called **differentiation**. Differentiation involves a very simple rule: the differential of X^n is nX^{n-1} (and all constants become zeros); so the differential of X^3 is $3X^2$.

> Differentiation is a means of understanding the gradient.

Importantly, if you differentiate any mathematical equation, then you will always be left with the gradient. For example, consider the linear equation $Y_2 = 2 + 2X$, which is laid out in Table 1.3 and then differentiated.

Table 1.3   An example of differentiation

Equation	Differentiate	Differential
$Y_2 =$		
2	is a constant and so becomes $\rightarrow$	0
+	+	+
2X	can be written $2X^1$. So this becomes $1*2X^0 \rightarrow$	2

Table 1.4   Differentiating an equation

Equation	Differentiate	Differential
$Y_2 =$		
25	is a constant and so becomes $\rightarrow$	0
+	+	+
6X	can be written $6X^1$. So this becomes $1*6X^0 \rightarrow$	6
$-X^2$	So this becomes $-2X^1 \rightarrow$	$-2X$

So differentiating equation Y_2 results in the answer of 2, which we already know is the gradient.

Differentiation is an important tool because it enables us to work out the turning point for a given relationship. Recall the non-linear u- and n-shaped relationships in Figure 1.10. The turning point is where the relationship changes direction. For Y_2, we would call the turning point a maximum and, for Y_1, we would call the turning point a minimum.

If we want to know where a relationship is maximized (or minimized), we simply need to recognize that at the turning point the gradient is flat and therefore equal to zero. So if we have an expression for the gradient, then we have to equate it with zero and solve. Consider $Y_2 = 25 + 6X - X^2$, which is laid out in Table 1.4.

So the differential and therefore the gradient for Y_2 is $6 - 2X$. At the turning point, the gradient is equal to zero. So, at the turning point $0 = 6 - 2X$, therefore $X = 3$. Check this answer by looking back at Figure 1.10.

Mathematical equations and differentiation can be powerful tools for economists and business analysts. If we wish to know the price that maximizes revenues, then we need to find a mathematical equation which describes the relationship between prices and revenues. We then simply differentiate, set to zero and solve to find the best price to maximize revenues. Equally, if we want to discover the level of production that leads to minimum costs per unit, then we need a mathematical equation which links production and costs, differentiate, set to zero and solve to find the ideal level of production.

Economic data

Economists make use of data to examine relationships between variables. Data can be categorized into **time series data** and **cross-sectional data**.

Time series data are the measurements of one variable at different points in time.

Cross-sectional data are the measurements of one variable at the same point in time across different individuals.

Panel data combines cross-sectional and time series data.

For example, the price of a cinema ticket recorded for each year between 1990 and 2010 is an example of one variable measured at various points in time. The time period between each observation is usually fixed. So, in the case of cinema tickets, the variable, price, is measured once every year. However, time series can be measured in a variety of periods – yearly, monthly, daily, hourly or by the minute. The price of shares on the London stock market is measured in all of these formats.

The profits of individual companies in the supermarket industry in 2010 would be an example of cross-sectional data, with profits of different companies being measured at the same point in time.

Rather than measure the profits of individual supermarkets in 2008, we could also measure individual companies' profits in 2009, 2010, 2011 and so on. This way, we are combining cross-sections and time, thus providing us with **panel data**.

Using data

In using data economists employ a number of simple mathematical techniques, including calculations of percentages and the use of index numbers. Both are simple to understand, but a refresher may help your understanding.

In order to measure the change in a variable, we can use **percentages**. We can use Table 1.5 to understand how big a particular percentage change is.

> Percentage measures the change in a variable as a fraction of 100.

Table 1.5 Percentage changes

Percentage	Size of change	
10	10% = 10/100 = 1/10	The variable has increased by one-tenth of its original value
25	25% = 25/100 = 1/4	The variable has increased by one-quarter of its original value
50	50% = 50/100 = 1/2	The variable has increased by one-half of its original value
100	100% = 100/100 = 1	The variable has increased by the same amount as its original value; it has doubled in size
200	200% = 200/100 = 2	The variable has increased by twice its original value; it has tripled in size
500	500% = 500/100 = 5	The variable has increased by five times its original size

Since a percentage measures the rate of change in a variable, we need both the variable's original and new value.

We calculate the percentage as the absolute change divided by the original number, then multiplied by 100:

$$\frac{(\text{New value} - \text{Original value})}{\text{Original value}} \times 100$$

For example, the share price of Company A was £2.00 in 2010 and £3.00 in 2011. The percentage change is therefore:

$$\frac{(£3.00 - £2.00)}{£2.00} \times 100 = 50\%$$

Index numbers

As an example of the use of **index numbers**, take the data series in Table 1.6, which measures the price of a pint of beer.

> Index numbers are used to transform a data series into a series with a base value of 100.

The price of beer is in pounds sterling. To convert this data series into a unit-less series with a base value of 100, we first need to select the base year. In Table 1.6, we have selected 2009 as the base year. In order to generate the index, we simply take the price of beer in any year, divide by the base year value and times by 100. So, in 2009, we have (£2.40/£2.40 × 100 = 100. In 2010, we have (£2.60/£2.40) × 100 = 108.

A sensible question to ask is why do we use index numbers? There are a number of reasons. The first is to recognize that, since we have a base value of 100, it is very easy to calculate the percentage change in the variable over time. From Table 1.6 we can readily see that between 2009 and 2012 beer increases in price by 25 per cent.

The second reason is that index numbers facilitate averaging. Assume we are interested in how prices across the economy are rising. If an index was created not only for beer prices but

Table 1.6　Index numbers

Year	Price of beer	Index
2009	£2.40	100
2010	£2.60	108
2011	£2.90	121
2012	£3.00	125

also for car prices, cigarettes and in fact all products that are commonly sold, then an average of all the indices would enable an assessment of average price rises in the UK.

The Retail Price Index does exactly this. It is an average of many individual product price indices. The average is weighted by the importance of the product within the average household's consumption. For example, since housing costs represent a major element of household consumption, the house price index receives a higher weight in the Retail Price Index than the price index for sweets and confectionery. The FTSE 100 is another example of an index and combines as an average the prices of all shares in the FTSE 100. The value of the index increases (decreases) if, on average, share prices in the FTSE 100 increase (decrease).

In summary, index numbers are used to create data series that are unitless. They have a base year of 100 and can be used to calculate percentage changes from the base year with ease. By virtue of having a common base year value of 100, index numbers can also be used to create averages from many different indices, such as price level indices or stock market indices.

Methods of averaging in economics

Economists tend to use two different types of averages: the arithmetic and geometric means. The arithmetic mean is the more familiar one and simply adds up all the observed values for a variable and then divides by n, the number of observations. The geometric average calculates the product of all the observations and then calculates the nth root. See Table 1.7 for examples.

In the first example, we have two observations, both of which are equal to two. So the arithmetic mean is 2. The geometric mean is also 2. We have used this simple example so that both means can be worked out easily and without the aid of a calculator. However, you should not be fooled into thinking that the two means will always be the same. In the second example, we use three observations, all of which are different. This time, the arithmetic mean is larger than the geometric mean.

An important question to ask is, why use two different ways to calculate the mean? The answer is because economists are often interested in rates of growth. How fast is the economy growing? How slowly have prices increased? What rate of return is an investment generating? When measuring growth, the use of arithmetic means would create a compounding problem. For example, if the value of a share was £100 and then increased by 5 per cent in year one and 15 per cent in year two, then the arithmetic average rate of return would be 10 per cent. This would suggest that the value of the share at the end of year two is $£100 \times 1.1 = £110$; and then $£110 \times 1.1 = £1.21$. But if we use the actual growth rates, 5 and 15 per cent, we get $£100 \times 1.05 = £105$; and then $£105 \times 1.15 = £120.75$. The arithmetic mean therefore generates an error. This is simple to understand because we are dealing in percentages. Five per cent of £100 and 15 per cent of £105 are not comparable, because the base values (£100 and £105) are not the same. The geometric mean solves this problem.

Table 1.7　Arithmetic and geometric means

Observations	Arithmetic mean	Geometric mean
2, 2	$(2 + 2)/2 = 2$	$(2 \times 2)^{1/2} = 2$
2, 3, 4	$(2 + 3 + 4)/3 = 3$	$(2 \times 3 \times 4)^{1/3} = 2.88$

Summary

1. Economics assumes that everybody would like to consume more of everything, but we only have a limited amount of resources with which to facilitate such consumption.

2. Economic factor resources are split into four categories: land, labour, capital and enterprise.

3. The production possibility frontier is used by economists to provide an illustration of finite resources. The production possibility frontier shows the maximum total output that can be produced using the limited amount of factor inputs. As more of one good is produced, less of the remaining good can be produced.

4. Opportunity cost is measured as the benefits forgone from the next best alternative.

5. Operating on the frontier represents full employment and is defined as productively efficient. Operating inside the frontier is inefficient as the output of both goods can be increased by making an efficient utilization of the underemployed factor resources. Operating outside the frontier is currently impossible. However, over time the economy may become more productively efficient, producing more output for a given level of input, or the economy may gain access to additional factor inputs, also enabling output to increase.

6. Macroeconomics is an examination of the economy as a whole and, therefore, considers issues such as the level of economic activity, the level of prices, unemployment, economic growth, and international trade and exchange rates.

7. Microeconomics focuses upon the economic decision making of individuals and firms. Microeconomics examines how individual markets function and how firms compete with one another.

8. Where on the frontier an economy operates, producing more beer than pizza, or vice versa, depends upon the resource allocation mechanism. In command economies, the government plans how much of each good to produce. In market economies, the interaction of consumers and firms through the pricing system of the market directs resources away from non-profitable markets and towards profitable ones.

9. Measures of various economic resources for different economies are available from a variety of sources. One global resource is the World Bank dataset.

10. Economics has a language and terminology; this aids communication of ideas and should be mastered.

11. Economics uses abstract models. In reality, the world is very complex. In economics, simplifying assumptions are deployed in order to make the world simple. As a consequence, an explanation of reality is often sacrificed for prediction.

12. Positive economics seeks to address objective questions with theory. Normative economics seeks to assert value judgements on what is preferable economic behaviour.

13. Economists place an emphasis on diagrams when explaining ideas and theories. A positive relationship exists between two variables if both variables increase together. A negative relationship between two variables exists when, as one variable increases, the other decreases.

14. Economic data can be time series, cross-sectional or a combination of the two (panel data). Time series data are the measurements of one variable at various points in time. Cross-sectional data are the measurements of one variable at the same point in time, but across a number of firms or individuals.

15. A percentage measures the change in a variable as a fraction of 100. You can calculate a percentage change as (New value − Original value)/Original value × 100.

16. An index converts a variable into a unitless data series with a base year of 100. This is achieved by dividing each value by the base year value and then multiplying by 100.

17. Index numbers can be combined to create averages. Common examples are the retail price index and the FTSE 100. Changes in the individual price indices then lead to changes in the average indices.

Learning checklist

You should now be able to:

- Explain the economic problem of scarcity
- Understand the concept of opportunity cost
- Explain the difference between microeconomics and macroeconomics
- Highlight the differences between market and planned economies
- Explain why an understanding of economics is important for business
- Source data on different measures of economic resource for different economies

Questions   connect

1. Explain the concept of opportunity cost.

2. List goods, or services, that compete for your income. Similarly, list activities that compete for your time. In deciding what you will spend your income on and how you will allocate your time, do you minimize your opportunity costs?

3. Consider whether it is ever possible to solve the problem of scarcity.

4. An economy produces two goods, Ferraris and Ray-Ban sunglasses. Using a production possibility frontier, assess what must happen to the production of Ferraris if the production of Ray-Ban sunglasses decreases.

5. The same Ferrari and Ray-Ban economy receives an influx of migrant workers. What do you think will happen to the production possibility frontier for this economy?

EASY

6. How does the production possibility frontier illustrate the concept of opportunity cost?

7. Why does the law of diminishing returns require the production possibility frontier to be curved rather than a straight line?

8. Explain the resource allocation mechanism within a market economy and also a planned economy.

9. Using examples, highlight why your own economy is probably best described as a mixed economy.

10. State whether the following relate to macroeconomics or to microeconomics.
(a) During the last 12 months average car prices have fallen; (b) inflation for the past 12 months has been 3.5 per cent; (c) strong sales in the housing market have prevented the Bank of England from reducing interest rates.

11. Is the labour market a microeconomic or macroeconomic topic?

12. Why does business need to understand the functioning of markets?

13. Why does business need to understand the functioning of the economy?

Questions 14 and 15 relate to material within the appendix.

14. Which of the following is positive and which is normative? (a) It is in the long-term interest of the UK to be a member of the euro. (b) Will entry into the euro reduce UK inflation?

15. Using the data listed in Table 1.8, plot house prices on the Y axis and time on the X axis. Is there a positive or a negative relationship between time and house prices? Convert the data series on house prices into an index using 2005 as the base year.

Calculate the percentage increase in house prices for each year.

Table 1.8

Year	Average price of a house
2005	£100 000
2006	£120 000
2007	£155 000
2008	£190 000
2009	£170 000
2010	£150 000

DIFFICULT

Exercises

1. True or false?

   (a) Economics is about human behaviour and so cannot be a science.

   (b) An expansion of the economy's productive capacity would be reflected in an outward movement of the production possibility frontier.

   (c) China is an example of a command economy in which private markets play no part.

   (d) When you make a choice there will always be an opportunity cost.

   (e) 'Firms should operate in the interests of their wider stakeholders' is an example of a normative economic statement.

   (f) Economists assume that business operates in a purely economic environment.

2. In Figure 1.11:

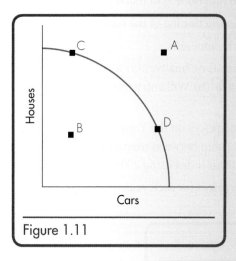

Figure 1.11

(a) Which combination of goods can be produced, with surplus resources being unemployed?

(b) Which combination of goods would represent full employment, with resources mainly allocated to the production of houses?

(c) Which combination of goods cannot currently be achieved?

(d) Which combination of goods represents full employment, with resources mainly allocated to the production of cars?

(e) How might the level of output identified in (c) be achieved in the future?

(f) Can you envisage circumstances under which the production possibility frontier could move to the left?

SECTION

2

Understanding markets

Section contents

2 Consumers in the marketplace 32

3 Firms in the marketplace 58

4 Markets in action 84

Consumers in
the marketplace

Chapter contents

Demand theory at a glance		33
2.1	Business problem: what is the best price?	33
2.2	Introducing demand curves	34
2.3	Factors influencing demand	35
2.4	Measuring the responsiveness of demand	40
2.5	Income and cross-price elasticity	44
2.6	Business application: pricing strategies i – exploiting elasticities	45
2.7	Business application: pricing strategies ii – extracting consumer surplus	49
2.8	Business data applications	52
Summary		54
Learning checklist		55
Questions		55
Exercises		56

Learning outcomes

By the end of this chapter you should understand:

Economic theory

LO1   Demand curves

LO2   Factors leading to a change in demand

LO3   The price elasticity of demand

LO4   Cross-price and income elasticity

Business application

LO5   How measures of elasticity can lead to improved management of total revenue

LO6   How an appreciation of consumer surplus can lead to enhanced pricing strategies

LO7   How market research data can be understood using demand-based ideas

At a glance Demand theory

The issue

Setting the price for a product is crucial for the product's and a company's success. But what is the best price for a particular product?

The understanding

As a product becomes more expensive, consumers will begin to demand less. In some markets, consumers will be very sensitive to a change in price. In others, they may not react at all. This reaction is measured using elasticity. An examination of demand theory and the concept of elasticity will develop these ideas more fully.

The usefulness

If the price of the product can be made to rise at a quicker rate than the decline in demand, then total revenue will rise. Therefore, by understanding how consumers respond to price changes we can optimize the price charged.

Business problem: what is the best price?

What is the best price? The best price is determined by the firm's objectives. The following provides a common list of objectives for a firm:

1 Maximize the amount of profit made by the firm

2 Maximize the market share for the firm's product

3 Maximize the firm's total revenues

These are all commercial objectives. Firms could also adopt non-commercial objectives, such as reducing environmental impact or being a socially responsible employer. But, for the purpose of this chapter, we will concentrate on the three objectives listed above. It is generally not possible for a firm to choose more than one of these objectives. For example, in order to maximize market share, a firm might reasonably be expected to reduce its prices in order to attract more customers. But, by dropping its prices, the firm could be sacrificing profit. Therefore, we will assume that a firm seeks to maximize one of our three objectives[1] and the best price can be defined as the one that enables the firm to meet its preferred objective.

How are prices set? Take the case of supermarkets. When walking around a supermarket have you, as a consumer, ever set the price for a product? The answer is probably no. Now compare the case of supermarkets with buying a house, or a car. When we purchase a house or a car we might make an opening offer to the vendor as part of a negotiation over the price. At the supermarket, by contrast, we would never consider negotiating over a trolley full of shopping; nor would we negotiate in many other types of shop, such as a clothing retailer. Admittedly, we may have an indirect effect on prices by refusing to buy a product that we consider too expensive, but in the main it appears that supermarkets, retailers and perhaps even the producers of the products are controlling the prices that we have to pay.

As business students, it is important to recognize the position of product suppliers. This is because control is essential when seeking to set the best price and achieve the firm's objectives. But herein lies the business problem: what is the best price? To illustrate the problem, consider the following: very high sales can be generated with low prices, while very high prices will tend to generate low sales. But which option is preferable? As an example, we can show that these alternative scenarios can be similar. If a low price of £5 generates ten sales,

---

[1] We will examine the objectives of a firm more fully in Chapters 5 and 7.

then total revenue is £50; if a high price of £10 generates only five sales, then total revenue is also £50. Given that these options are identical, a businessperson would really like to know if there is a pricing option of around £8, selling to eight customers, making a total revenue of £64.

Whether £8 is the best price, or indeed whether £8.25 is even better, is a difficult question to address. When a national supermarket chain is selling beer, soap powder or even oven chips by the hundreds of thousands, a small change in the price can generate huge changes in total revenue. By the end of this chapter you will understand how you assist the supermarkets in finding the best price. Every time you pass through the till at the supermarket, scanner data are stored and matched with promotional offers such as 'buy one get one free'. This is then modelled and used to address strategic price changes.

It is clearly important to recognize that firms will price items relative to their cost structures. If a firm wishes to make a profit, then the price must be greater than costs. If the firm wishes to maximize market share, while not making a loss, then the price cannot fall below the cost of making the product. While recognizing the importance of costs, in this chapter we will simply focus on the interaction between pricing and consumers' willingness to buy a particular product. In Chapters 3, 4 and 5 we will develop a fuller understanding of pricing decisions by recognizing both firms' cost structures and consumers' willingness to purchase. In this chapter, we begin this analysis by developing a clear understanding of demand theory.

Introducing demand curves

The demand curve illustrates the relationship between price and quantity demanded of a particular product.

In attempting to understand consumer behaviour, economists use a very simple construct known as the **demand curve**.

Figure 2.1 is an example of a demand curve, where the line Q_D represents quantity demanded. The slope of the demand curve Q_D is negative. This simply depicts the rather obvious argument that, as prices fall, more of a product will be demanded by consumers. Using our previous example, at a price of £10 the demand curve indicates that consumers across the market are willing to demand five units in total. But if the company dropped the price to £5, then it might expect to sell ten units.

The negative relationship between price and quantity demanded is often exploited by businesses. For example, Figure 2.1 could be an example of a 'buy one get one free' offer. Firms use such offers because they are sometimes reluctant to reduce the price of their product. This is because overt price reductions could lead to a retaliatory price war from rivals. Lower prices may also provide a signal to the market that the product is of an inferior quality. A 'buy one get one free' offer allows the published price to stay the same, but the effective price for consumers is halved. Under such an offer, consumers are more willing to demand the product and, not surprisingly, companies use such promotions to boost sales and gain market share.

Furthermore, we all like end-of-season sales at our favourite clothing retailers. But sales simply represent an attempt by the retailer to shift stock that we, as consumers, would not buy at the higher price and are, therefore, another example of the demand curve in action.

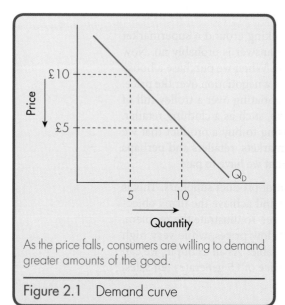

As the price falls, consumers are willing to demand greater amounts of the good.

Figure 2.1   Demand curve

In Box 2.1 we have a business example of price cutting by Nintendo to attract demand. The price cut did increase demand, the sales of the handheld games console were the highest recorded for such devices, but ultimately revenues

3DS price cut by almost a third as Nintendo reports loss

Mere months after its launch, Nintendo is dropping the price of its 3DS handheld console by almost a third to counter disappointing sales figures. Coming less than five months after the innovative glasses-free 3D handheld console's launch, this swift response to disappointing sales figures is unprecedented for Nintendo.

Currently, the machine has a recommended retail price of £269.99, which retailers have already eroded to a street price of £199.99 with a game bundled in. But from 12 August, presuming that retailers resist the urge to increase their margins on the 3DS, we can anticipate a new RRP of around £170 – equating to a street price of between £130 and £140.

In the past, Nintendo has tended to leave the price of its handheld consoles constant until they are replaced by new variants (which was the case with the original DS, released in March 2005 and superseded by the DS Lite in late 2006).

Even the 3DS's predecessor, the DSi (the last of the DS variants), was on sale for 18 months before its price was cut. In mitigation, the 3DS had the highest launch price of any handheld Nintendo console, but the swiftness of the price cut will lead to questions as to whether it should have been priced so highly in the first place, especially during a global economic slump.

Announcing the price cut, Nintendo said: 'So that we will be able to create momentum for Nintendo 3DS and accelerate its market penetration toward the year-end sales season, when the line-up for the applicable software shall be enriched, the company has decided to make this markdown.'

Adapted from an article by Steve Boxer in *The Guardian*, 28 July 2011. © Guardian News & Media Ltd 2011.

were harmed and Nintendo later announced a sharp fall in profits. Balancing price and trade volumes is crucial for overall financial performance and is something we will return to in section 2.6.

(2.3) Factors influencing demand

It is also possible to consider movements in the demand line itself. Assume that we have 100 customers and we ask them about their willingness to demand at various prices. We could use the data collected to draw a demand line. If we then had 200 customers and we surveyed them about their willingness to pay, where we would we be likely to draw the demand line? Equally, where would we draw the demand line if we only had 50 customers to survey? The answer to these questions is fairly easy. Because the x-axis is the quantity demanded, then an increase in the number of customers will lead to more demand at all prices and so the demand line moves to the right in the direction of the x-axis; see Q_{D1} in Figure 2.2. Similarly, if we have fewer customers, then less will be demanded at each price and so the demand line will move to the left in the direction of the x-axis; see Q_{D2} in Figure 2.2.

There are a number of other circumstances which will lead to an increase or decrease in the number of customers, or an increase or decrease in the amount of units demanded by customers. These circumstances are listed overleaf and each will be discussed in detail.

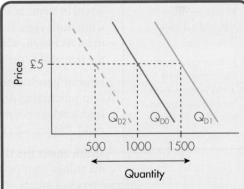

Demand shifts to the left following: (i) a reduction/increase in the price of a substitute/complement product; (ii) a reduction/increase in income if the good is normal/inferior; or (iii) a fall in consumers' preferences for the product. Demand shifts to the right following: (i) an increase/reduction in the price of a substitute/complement product; (ii) an increase/reduction in income if the good is normal/inferior; or (iii) an improvement in consumers' preferences for the product.

Figure 2.2 Movements in demand

1 Price of substitutes and complements

2 Consumer income

3 Tastes and preferences

4 Price expectations

Price of substitutes and complements

Substitutes are competing products in the same marketplace, seeking to gain customers from their rivals. So, if French wine producers decided to reduce the price of their wine, they would hope to gain some of the Australian wine producers' customers. As a result, the Australians sell less wine for the same price. This is depicted in Figure 2.2, with the demand curve for Australian wine moving in to the left to Q_{D2} and Australian wine consumption decreasing from 1000 to 500 units at a constant price of £5 per bottle. Clearly, the opposite will also be true. If the French increased their prices, then they might expect to lose customers to the Australians. This would be depicted as a rightward shift in the demand curve, from Q_{D0} to Q_{D1}.

Complements are products that are demanded together. For example, if you buy a car, then you will have to buy petrol. This, therefore, means that the demand for the two products is related. If cars become cheaper, then more cars will be demanded. As a consequence, more petrol will also be demanded. If Figure 2.2 represents demand for petrol, then a reduction in the price of cars will lead to increased demand for cars. This increased demand for cars will lead to a higher demand for petrol. The demand curve for petrol will shift to the right from Q_{D0} to Q_{D1}, with more petrol being demanded at the existing price of £5 per gallon.

> Substitutes are rival products; for example, a BMW car is a substitute for a Mercedes, or a bottle of wine from France is a substitute for a bottle from Australia.
>
> Complements are products that are purchased jointly. Beer and kebabs would be a youthful and modern example; another would be cars and petrol.

Consumer income

In understanding the effect of income on demand, we need to distinguish between **normal goods** and **inferior goods**.

If we consider Australian wine to be a normal good, as income increases we buy more. Then, in terms of Figure 2.2, when income increases, the demand curve for Australian wine shifts right to Q_{D1} and more is demanded at every possible price. However, during a recession, when incomes are likely to fall, consumers will cut back on wine and the demand curve shifts left to Q_{D2}.

Inferior goods tend to be those characterized as cheaper brands – products that we stop purchasing once our income rises and we move to more normal types of goods. Inferior does not necessarily mean that the product has a lower quality than a normal good. Rather, we consume less when incomes fall and vice versa.

> Normal goods are demanded more when consumer income increases and less when income falls.
>
> Inferior goods are demanded more when income levels fall and demanded less when income levels rise.

Think about the things you buy at the supermarket as a poor indebted student and the things your parents buy as significant income earners. You will tend to be buying inferior types of goods, such as supermarkets' own-label items. Your parents will be buying normal types of goods, such as branded lines in bread, alcohol and frozen foods. In terms of Figure 2.2, as income rises, the demand curve for an inferior good would shift left to Q_{D2}. When income falls, the demand curve for an inferior good would shift right to Q_{D1}. In brief, the behaviour of the demand curve for normal goods is opposite to that of inferior goods.

In Box 2.2 the provision of free wi-fi access in Starbucks to entice additional coffee drinkers is discussed.

Tastes and preferences

Tastes and preferences reflect consumers' attitudes towards particular products. Over time, these tastes and preferences are likely to change. Fashion is an obvious example: what might be popular this year will be out of fashion next year. Technological development might

Box 2.2

A new revenue drip for Starbucks

On a recent visit to a Starbucks near my office, I asked about the signs of ongoing construction inside the store. Why not close for renovation? The baristas explained the outlet was far too busy to shutter. This is Seattle, after all, and I can walk to five other chain and independent stores within seconds. The renovation is now complete. The store has replaced carpet with tile and made room for a long communal table in the middle. My Starbucks is begging me to stay a while.

I now know what I'm expected to stay for. Starbucks launched its Digital Network on 20 October. While in the café, using the free in-store wi-fi, customers now gain digital access to content they'd otherwise have to pay for. The *Wall Street Journal* opens up full access to its $103-per-year website, and the *New York Times* provides its $240-per-year Web app reader for free. Kids' entertainment giant Nickelodeon lets the rugrats in to the paid Nick Jr Boost, a subscription that costs about $100 per year. Apple will give away free music and videos. All these offers seem designed to fill the store with happy, stationary readers.

Starbucks and other coffee shops typically have their busiest times between 5 a.m. and 9 a.m.; the rest of the day is relatively calm. Filling the store during those periods, even with seat squatters, can enhance revenue. Giving such surfers free content with enticements to purchase subscriptions and media items could turn into a constant drip of incremental revenue.

Adapted from an article in *The Economist*, 20 October 2010.
© The Economist Newspaper Limited, London 2010.

be another. Mobile phones capable of sending images and connecting to the Internet are becoming increasingly popular. We can survive quite well without such technology but, through advertising, companies try to influence our tastes and preferences for such advanced capabilities.

In order to represent a positive improvement in tastes and preference for a product, in Figure 2.2 the demand curve would shift right to Q_{D1}, with more products being sold at any given price, while a reduction in consumer backing for a product would lead to a leftward shift in the demand curve, with less being sold at any given price. For example, in recent times flat-screen, high-definition televisions have begun to replace cathode-ray televisions, reflecting changed tastes and preferences for flat-screen technologies and, therefore, lower demand for cathode-ray televisions at all prices.

The role of advertising

Advertising can play at least one of two roles in demand theory. First, it provides consumers with information about products. Advertising informs consumers that new products have arrived on the market, that a product has new features, or that a product is being offered at a lower price. In this way, advertising plays a very valuable informational role for firms and for consumers. Demand for products increases simply because consumers are informed about the nature and availability of the product. Therefore, when advertising plays an informational role, the demand curve for the product shifts out to Q_{D1} as more consumers become informed about the existence of the product.

There is, however, another role for advertising. If adverts are simply about informing consumers about the existence of products, why are they played repeatedly over very long periods of time? Moreover, why do product suppliers hire well-known celebrities to appear in their adverts? How many adverts do you see on the television, or in the press, that provide information about the product's characteristics, price or availability? Advertising is also about trying to change consumers' tastes and preferences. We all know that mobile phones are capable of sending pictures and video, so why would we be interested in knowing that celebrities use such technology? We all know that a Swiss watch looks good and can keep reasonable time, so why would we be interested in knowing which celebrities wear such watches? One possible answer is that the product provider is not simply selling a product. Instead, they are selling you a desirable lifestyle. We do buy technologically advanced mobile phones because they are useful; but we also buy such phones because we believe that they say something positive about who we are. By emphasizing these less tangible aspects of a product, it is possible to build additional differentiation into the product. Two mobile phones might provide the same functions, but only one is used by a world-class footballer. Accordingly, advertising is not simply about informing consumers about what they *can* buy; it is also about informing them about what they *should* buy. Whether advertising is providing information, or developing consumers' tastes and preferences, the overriding aim is to shift the demand curve from Q_{D0} to Q_{D1}, while at the same time shifting the competitors' demand curves from Q_{D0} to Q_{D2}.

Price expectations

If you expect prices to fall in the future, then it may be wise to wait and delay your purchase. For example, recently launched computers, televisions and DVD systems are often sold in the market at premium prices. Within three to six months, newer models are brought out and the old versions are then sold at lower prices. If you do not have a taste or preference for cutting-edge technology, you can cut back on consumption today in the expectation that prices will fall in the future. In terms of our demand curves, if we expect prices to fall in the future, then demand today will be reduced, shifting back to Q_{D2}. But the demand curve for three to six months' time will shift right to Q_{D1}.

> Price expectations are beliefs about how prices in the future will differ from prices today: will they rise or fall?
>
> The law of demand states that, *ceteris paribus*, as the price of a product falls, more will be demanded.
>
> *Ceteris paribus* means all other things being equal.

Opposite **price expectations** can also be true. It is possible to believe that in the future prices will rise. Property may be more expensive in the future, share prices might increase or oil will be more expensive in six months' time. Therefore, if you expect prices to rise in the future, you are likely to bring your consumption forward and purchase now. In terms of our demand curves, your demand for now shifts out to Q_{D1}, but your demand in the future shifts back to Q_{D2}.

We now understand that the demand for a product is influenced by (i) its own price, (ii) the price of substitutes and complements, (iii) the level of consumer income, (iv) consumers' tastes and preferences, and (v) price expectations. We are now in a position to introduce the **law of demand**, which states that, *ceteris paribus*, as the price of a product falls more will be demanded. The law is saying that if (i) through to (v) stay the same, i.e. 'ceteris paribus', then price and demand are negatively ralated.

Do higher prices attract higher demand?

The negative relationship between price and quantity demanded can cause students and business managers problems. For example, designer clothes and perfumes would not be purchased if they were cheap. So, does a positive relationship exist between price and willingness to demand luxury items? While it remains an appealing idea, the answer to this question is still no, since all products have a negative demand curve. This is because even when you are very rich you still have a budget constraint.

Assume you are fortunate to have an annual expense account of £500 000. Your designer clothes cost £300 000 per year, champagne is another £100 000 and the private jet another £100 000. If your favourite designer suddenly increases their prices by £50 000, you are faced with a choice. If you continue to buy the same quantity of clothes, they will now cost £350 000, and you will have to cut back on the champagne and the jet. Alternatively, you could cut back on your clothes and maintain the same amount of champagne and the private jet. However, most probably you will reduce some of your demand for designer clothes, perhaps buying fewer clothes at the higher price of £325 000, as opposed to the £350 000 it would cost to buy the same quantity as last year. The extra £25 000 might come from reducing your flights and the amount of champagne that you drink.

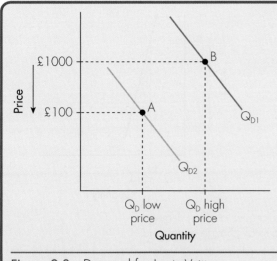

Q_{D1} and Q_{D2} are the demand curves for Louis Vuitton bags. Under Q_{D1}, stores are not allowed to sell Louis Vuitton bags at discount prices, while under Q_{D2} they are able to sell them at discounted prices. Consumers with a taste and preference for expensive and exclusive bags are willing to buy bags at £1000. But once discounting by stores makes Louis Vuitton bags become cheap and not exclusive, consumers are less willing to buy bags. Demand shifts from Q_{D1} to Q_{D2} and fewer bags are purchased. The reason we sometimes think there is a positive relationship between price and willingness to demand is because we only focus on points A and B. If we joined up these two points, we would see a positive relationship between price and quantity demanded. But this is a mistake, as we really need to focus on the shifts in the demand curves reflecting a change in tastes and preferences.

Figure 2.3   Demand for Louis Vuitton

It is important to understand, from the example above, that higher prices for one product limit how much money you can spend on *all* goods and services that you like to consume. The demand curve for designer clothes should have a negative slope, because you will decrease the quantity of clothes purchased in order to retain consumption of the champagne and jet travel.

Therefore, for luxury items, how do we explain the positive relationship between price and quantity demanded? Some consumers prefer products that have an element of exclusivity. A high price not only ensures exclusivity, but also signals that the product is special. A low price would not create the same image. Therefore, the high price attracts particular consumers into the market. This leads to the demand curve shifting out to the right in Figure 2.2 and means that the positive relationship between price and quantity is associated with a change in tastes and preferences. As such, the positive relationship of price and demand is best described as a shift of the demand curve, rather than a movement along the curve.

These points are picked up in Figure 2.3, with product providers such as Louis Vuitton keen to avoid their product being sold at discount prices. The high price of the product and the distribution of the product through licensed clothing retailers is deliberately managed in a way to promote the product's high-quality image. Consumers' tastes and preferences have been developed by Louis Vuitton to the extent that consumers expect Louis Vuitton bags to be expensive and more exclusive than cheaper alternatives. Louis Vuitton will be concerned to protect the high-price image of its product, fearful that a low price would have a detrimental effect on consumers' tastes and preferences. The demand curve for Louis Vuitton will shift to the left, reducing the number of bags sold.

In Figure 2.3, Q_{D1} represents the demand for Louis Vuitton handbags among consumers who have a strong taste and preference for expensive and exclusive bags. At a price of £1000, demand is Q_D. Q_{D2} is the demand for Louis Vuitton among consumers who do not have a strong taste and preference for expensive and exclusive bags. We can see that, at a price of £1000, none of these consumers will buy – the line from £1000 does not touch Q_{D2}. However, at a discounted price of £100, consumers represented by Q_{D2} are willing to buy Louis Vuitton. The demand curves Q_{D1} and Q_{D2} both have a negative slope. However, if we were to focus mistakenly on points A and B, and draw a line connecting the two points, then we might be led to believe that increases in price lead to increases in demand. This would be a mistake, because it is the differing tastes and preferences for cheap and exclusive brands that lead to the shift between the two points A and B.

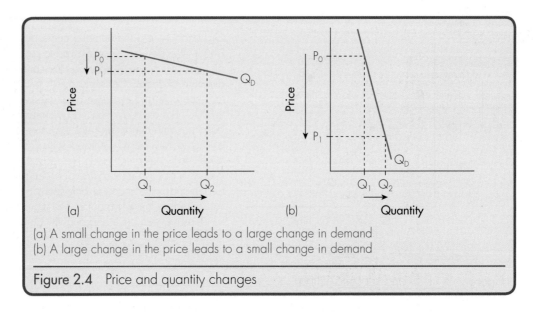

(a) A small change in the price leads to a large change in demand
(b) A large change in the price leads to a small change in demand

Figure 2.4　Price and quantity changes

2.4　Measuring the responsiveness of demand

You have been introduced to the demand curve and the factors that cause demand to shift. However, for the business person it is not enough to know that the demand for a product is determined by (i) its own price, (ii) the price of substitutes and complements, (iii) the level of consumer income, (iv) consumers' tastes and preferences, and (v) expectations regarding future prices. As a person in the marketplace making real pricing decisions, the business person needs to know the impact of price changes on the quantity demanded.

> Elasticity is a measure of the responsiveness of demand to a change in price.

Figure 2.4 provides an illustration of **elasticity**. In Figure 2.4a, a small change in the price leads to a much bigger change in the quantity demanded. But in Figure 2.4b, a very large change in the price leads to a small change in the quantity demanded. So, we might say that in Figure 2.4a demand is responsive to a change in price, while in Figure 2.4b demand is not very responsive to a change in price.

Businesses use elasticity ideas to formulate competitive strategies, including pricing decisions, promotional decisions and product placement decisions relative to rivals. Understanding what your consumers want and how price sensitive they are requires data and Box 2.3 highlights that consumers are willing to provide valuable personal data both by survey and indirectly through online forums and social networks.

Determinants of elasticity

The elasticity of a product is determined by a number of factors:

1　Number of substitutes
2　Time
3　Definition of the market

Substitutes

As the number of substitutes increases, the more elastic will be demand. For example, if a product has no substitutes and the supplier decides to increase its prices, then consumers cannot switch to a cheaper alternative. Therefore, when the price increases for this product, demand will only fall by a small amount. In contrast, when a product has a very large number of substitutes, its price elasticity will be very high. If the price of the product increases, consumers will very quickly switch to the cheaper alternatives. Cigarettes – and, more importantly, nicotine as an

Box 2.3

Survey data and price sensitivity

Welcome to the era of the candid consumer. From their food allergies to home addresses, shoppers around the world are becoming increasingly willing to share more personal information with their favourite merchants, as they look for a more personalized and efficient shopping experience, an IBM survey of more than 28 000 people in 15 countries showed.

That is good news for retailers on both sides of the Atlantic as they look for ways to target the right demographic of shoppers with new products.

While consumers around the world still have reservations about sharing financial details such as how much they earn, they are less worried about divulging other private information. For instance, about three-quarters of the people surveyed were willing to dish out details about their media usage such as the television shows they watch, while 73 per cent of the group were fine with disclosing demographic information such as their ethnicity. About 61 per cent of people were comfortable sharing their names and addresses with retailers, while about 59 per cent of those surveyed said they were OK with disclosing lifestyle-related information such as whether they owned more than one car, or had moved into a new home, or had a child recently.

Shoppers also want information from merchants delivered through channels relevant to them. For example, fewer shoppers rely on email to find out about new products. Meanwhile, 85 per cent of consumers believe social networks will save them time, IBM's Puleri said. Retailers should pay more attention to 'noise on the wire' to understand better how their brands are perceived by the public, she went on. For example, discussions around some brands focus predominantly on price, availability, where to purchase, etc., indicating that these brands are highly price-sensitive. On the other hand, discussions around other brands are focused on terms such as 'self-improvement' and style, indicating that these brands are less price-sensitive.

With these insights, retailers selling brands with more price sensitivity should focus their marketing around promotions and sales, while the others could adopt a different approach, according to public.

Adapted from an article by Dhanya Skariachan on *Reuters Online*, 'More shoppers open to giving personal info – survey', 16 January 2012.

addictive drug – have few, if any, substitutes. Therefore, if the price of cigarettes increases, then few smokers will quit cigarettes. Alternatively, in the market for mobile telecommunications, with many competing suppliers, if one provider reduces its prices, then there will be a rapid change in demand, with consumers switching to the cheapest provider.

Time

Time is also important, as it is likely to influence the development and introduction of substitutes. Initially, new products or markets will only have a small number of substitutes. Only if these products are successful will new entrants come into the market and begin to compete. Therefore, in the early periods of a new market, demand is likely to be inelastic, but in the long term, as more products enter the market, demand is likely to become more elastic. For example, the launch of alcoholic drinks for the youth market, mixing alcoholic drinks with soft drinks, started with a small number of product offerings. As sales in the market have grown, the number of competing products has also increased.

Market definition

Market definitions are also important when measuring elasticity. The demand for beer is relatively unresponsive to a change in price. As the price of beer increases, consumers still continue to buy beer, because they perhaps view wine as a poor alternative. In contrast, the demand for a particular brand of beer is likely to be price responsive. This is because all the separate beer brands are competitive substitutes. So, if one brand becomes more expensive, it is likely that drinkers will switch to the cheaper alternatives.

Measuring elasticity

Mathematically, economists can measure elasticity, or the responsiveness of demand to a change in price, using the following formulae.

Formulae for elasticity

$$\varepsilon = \frac{\text{Percentage change in quantity demanded}}{\text{Percentage change in price}} \qquad (2.1)$$

$$\frac{\text{Change in quantity demanded}}{\text{Change in price}} \times \frac{\text{Price}}{\text{Quantity demanded}} \qquad (2.2)$$

The value of ε for elasticity will lie between zero and infinity $(0 < \varepsilon < \infty)$.[2] Since this is a very large number range, so economists break the range down into regions that they can describe and utilize. Using the first formula, each of these regions is described in Table 2.1.

We will begin with an easy example. If the price of cigarettes increased by 10 per cent, how many smokers would cut back on the number of cigarettes smoked? Many smokers would continue smoking. In an extreme situation, a 10 per cent change in the price of cigarettes could lead to no change in the quantity demanded. (In reality this would not happen, but the example provides a reasonable description of a theoretical extreme.)

> **Inelastic demand** is where elasticity ε < 1, or a change in the price will lead to a proportionately smaller change in the quantity demanded.

In economic terms, demand is said to be perfectly **inelastic** when ε = 0; that is, demand does not respond to a change in price. This is detailed in the first row of Table 2.1.

Clearly, *perfectly inelastic demand* is an extreme situation. So, in the second row of Table 2.1, we consider the situation where a 10 per cent change in the price leads to a 5 per cent change in demand.

The demand for Coca-Cola may well be inelastic. If Coke increased its prices by 10 per cent we might expect it to lose a small, rather than large, number of customers. So, demand is not very responsive to a change in price.

Table 2.1 Important elasticity measures

	Percentage change in price	Percentage change in demand	Numerical calculations	Elasticity value	Description
1	10	0	$\frac{0}{10} = 0$	ε = 0	Perfectly inelastic
2	10	5	$\frac{5}{10} = \frac{1}{2}$	ε < 1	Inelastic demand
3	10	10	$\frac{10}{10} = 1$	ε = 1	Unit elasticity
4	10	20		ε > 1	Elastic demand
5	10	Infinitely large		ε = ∞	Perfectly elastic

---

[2] You will shortly understand that elasticity must lie between zero and minus infinity. This is because if we increase prices, then quantity demanded will decrease. So a negative change in demand will be divided by a positive change in the price. So the elasticity measure will always be negative. Economists ignore the negative sign and simply look at the numerical value for elasticity.

In row 3, we have the situation where a 10 per cent change in the price leads to a 10 per cent change in the quantity demanded – **unit elasticity**.

In row 4, we consider the situation where a 10 per cent change in the price leads to a much bigger change in quantity demanded, in this case 20 per cent, resulting in **elastic demand**.

Consider the price of mobile phone contracts; nearly all competing networks offer very similar menus and prices. One of the reasons for this is because demand is reasonably elastic. If one company raised its prices, then over time many of its subscribers would switch to another network. Therefore, similar prices are offered because each network recognizes that demand is responsive to price differences.

Finally, in row 5, we consider **perfectly elastic demand**. In this case, the change in price is 10 per cent and, in response, demand changes by a very large amount. The London financial markets come close to a situation of perfectly elastic demand. If the market price of shares in Shell is £10, then you can sell all of your holdings at £10. But if you offered to sell at £10.01, you would not sell a single share, as potential buyers would move to the many other sellers offering to sell at £10.

> Unit elasticity is when $\varepsilon = 1$, or demand is equally responsive to a change in price.
>
> Elastic demand is where $\varepsilon > 1$, or demand is responsive to a change in price.
>
> Perfectly elastic demand exists when $\varepsilon = \infty$. In other words, demand is very responsive to a change in price.

Elasticity and the slope of the demand curve

We mentioned above that the slope of the demand curve is only an indication of how elastic demand is. In fact, we can now show that the elasticity of demand changes all the way along a particular demand curve. We will do this by using the second formula for elasticity (see Figure 2.5).

During a basic maths course you will have been told that, to measure the slope of a line, you need to draw a triangle next to the line. The slope, or gradient, of the line is then the change in the vertical distance divided by the change in the horizontal distance. In our case, the gradient is the change in price (the vertical) divided by the change in quantity demanded (the horizontal). For our second formula we need the 'inverse' of the slope; that is, we need the change in quantity demanded (horizontal) divided by the change in price (vertical). But what we can say is that the slope of the line is constant, so the inverse of the slope is also constant. We have measured the slope and the inverse in the middle of the line and it is equal to 10/10 = 1. In fact, in our example, because the slope is constant, it does not matter where we measure the slope – it is always 10/10 = 1. descuptive

We can now calculate the elasticity of demand at two special points, A and B. At A, the demand line just touches the vertical axis. The price is so high that demand is zero. At B, the demand line just touches the horizontal axis. The price is zero and demand is very high. Using our second formula for elasticity, at A the elasticity is:

$$(10/10) \times (\text{price}/0) = \text{infinity} = \infty$$

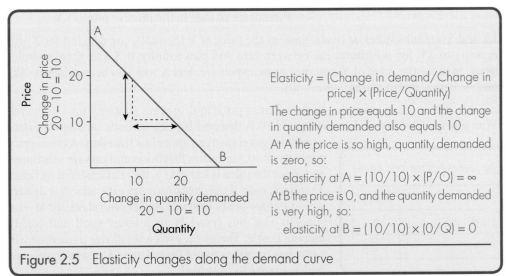

Elasticity = (Change in demand/Change in price) × (Price/Quantity)

The change in price equals 10 and the change in quantity demanded also equals 10

At A the price is so high, quantity demanded is zero, so:

elasticity at A = (10/10) × (P/O) = ∞

At B the price is O, and the quantity demanded is very high, so:

elasticity at B = (10/10) × (0/Q) = 0

Figure 2.5 Elasticity changes along the demand curve

Because at A the demand is zero, the elasticity of demand must be infinite. We know that this means that demand is perfectly elastic.

The elasticity at B is:

$$(10/10) \times (\text{quantity demanded}/0) = 0$$

Because at B the price is zero, the elasticity of demand must be zero. We know that this means that demand is perfectly inelastic.

Therefore, all the way along the demand curve the elasticity changes from being perfectly elastic to perfectly inelastic, even though the slope has remained constant. This is because the elasticity of demand is influenced by the slope of the demand line *and* by the ratio of price and quantity demanded. When the price is very high, a small reduction in the price will generate a proportionately bigger change in demand. But when the price is very low, a small change will not generate a proportionately bigger change in demand.

In simple terms, consumers react to price reductions when a product is very expensive. But they are less motivated by price reductions when a product is already very cheap. Therefore, demand is more elastic at higher prices than at lower ones.

 Income and cross-price elasticity

Before considering the application of this knowledge, it is also worth introducing you to two related measures: **income elasticity** and **cross-price elasticity**.

> Income elasticity measures the responsiveness of demand to a change in income.
>
> Cross-price elasticity measures the responsiveness of demand to a change in the price of a substitute or complement.

$$\text{Income elasticity} = Y_\varepsilon = \frac{\text{Percentage change in demand}}{\text{Percentage change in income}}$$

For normal goods, income elasticity is above zero because as consumers' income rises, say during an economic boom, more normal types of goods will be produced. If $Y_\varepsilon < 1$, the product is described as income inelastic, or demand will grow at a slower rate than income, while if $Y_\varepsilon > 1$, demand is income elastic, or demand will grow at a faster rate than income. The recent UK and US housing booms were a reflection of positive income elasticity, with consumers being more willing to spend money on property as their incomes increased within a prosperous economy.

For inferior goods, income elasticity lies between zero and minus infinity because, as incomes rise, consumers buy fewer inferior goods. This time demand is income inelastic if Y_ε lies between zero and -1, or is income elastic if Y_ε is smaller than -1, e.g. -5.

$$\text{Cross-price elasticity} = XY_\varepsilon = \frac{\text{Percentage change in demand of product X}}{\text{Percentage change in the price of product Y}}$$

If X and Y are substitutes or rivals, then, as the price of Y increases, the demand for X will increase, so XY_ε for substitutes lies between zero and plus infinity. If X and Y are complements, then, as the price of Y becomes more expensive, less X will also be purchased; XY_ε must lie between zero and minus infinity.

In Table 2.2 we have examples of price, cross-price and income elasticity for bus travel. With a price elasticity of demand equal to 0.1, demand is price inelastic. A drop in prices would not generate many more bus travellers. A cross-price elasticity of +0.3 indicates that buses and cars are substitutes and, since the value is less than 1, the relationship is inelastic. Therefore, even if cars became more expensive few drivers would opt for buses instead. The income elasticity of −2.4 suggests that bus travel is an inferior good and highly income elastic. Therefore, even a small rise in income will cause bus travellers to cut their demand for bus travel, and perhaps move to car travel.

Table 2.2   Elasticity measures for bus travel

Price elasticity	(−)0.1
Cross-price elasticity (with cars)	+0.3
Income elasticity	−2.4

Business application: pricing strategies i – exploiting elasticities

Finding the best price was this chapter's business problem. After introducing demand theory and the concept of elasticity, we are now able to return to this particular problem.

Cost-plus pricing

A rather simple approach to pricing is to simply take the costs of producing the product and add a mark-up, such as 30 per cent. This might cover some stray, unaccounted-for costs and also the required profit margin. The benefit of this approach lies in its computational simplicity, only requiring a basic idea of costs and a grasp of a desirable profit margin. It may also appear to be fair. Who would begrudge a firm asking for a 30 per cent mark-up? After all, they are taking a risk and they should be able to generate a decent financial return.

Unfortunately, while appealing, cost-plus pricing neglects almost everything we have introduced you to in this chapter. That is, it fails to take account of consumers' willingness to demand. There is no guarantee that consumers will be willing to buy your product when the mark-up is 30 per cent. Alternatively, 30 per cent may not be a sufficiently high mark-up. Consumers may exhibit a very keen preference for your product and a low elasticity of demand. While 30 per cent appears fair, you might be able to gain good sales volumes with a mark-up of 50–100 per cent. It therefore appears that we need also to consider demand theory when setting prices.

'Buy one get one free' – discounting or price experiment?

In simple terms, the need to find the best price stems from a broader need to generate revenues. At the beginning of this chapter, in the business problem example, it was suggested that, at a price of £5, we might sell ten units, making £50 of revenue. But, at a price of £8, we might sell eight units, making a total revenue of £64. This looks like a better option. But how can we be sure that moving from £5 to £8 is a good idea? We might have ended up selling only six units, making a total revenue of only £48 (see Table 2.3).

Table 2.3 Total revenue

Price	Quantity	Total revenue
£5	10	£50
£8	8	£64
£8	6	£48

Price elasticity measures the response of demand to a change in price. We face two outcomes when changing the price: demand falls to eight or six units. Falling from ten to eight units is a small response to a change in price or, in our new terminology, demand is inelastic. But when demand falls to six units, the response is much bigger and demand can be described as elastic. But what happens to total revenues? When demand is inelastic, total revenues have increased to £64. But when demand is price elastic, total revenues have fallen to £48. We can expand upon these simple ideas using Figure 2.6.

In Figure 2.6a, we have a price elastic demand curve. So, at a price of P_0, we can expect to sell Q_0 units. Therefore, **total revenue** is represented by the rectangle defined by P_0 and Q_0.

> Total revenue is price multiplied by number of units sold.

If we drop the price to P_1, then sales increase to Q_1 and total revenue is now equal to the new rectangle defined by P_1 and Q_1.

The impact of a price reduction on total revenue is the difference in size between the two rectangles. By selling at a lower price, we lose some total revenue. For example, if we were selling at £10 and now we are only asking for £8, we are losing £2 per unit. But by reducing the price we will also gain some total revenue by selling to more customers – in this example, Q_1 as opposed to Q_0 customers. Hence, when demand is price elastic, selling at a lower price

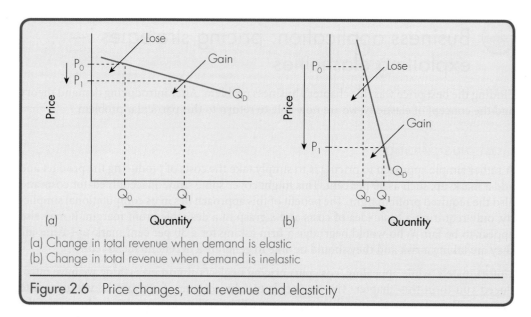

(a) Change in total revenue when demand is elastic
(b) Change in total revenue when demand is inelastic

Figure 2.6 Price changes, total revenue and elasticity

will boost total revenues. In contrast, if we examine the case of inelastic demand in Figure 2.6b, we see that reducing the price leads to a drop in total revenues.

We now have economic guidance for business. If demand is elastic, then dropping prices raises total revenues; but if demand is inelastic, prices should be increased in order to increase total revenues.

If we return to our business problem, the best price occurs when price elasticity equals 1, which is exactly in between the elastic and inelastic region. With unit elasticity, a 10 per cent increase in the price leads to a 10 per cent change in quantity demanded. Total revenue does not change; the maximum has been found.

Admittedly, firms may not always target a price elasticity equal to 1. They may not have revenue maximization as their objective. They may wish to maximize market share or profits. Changing the price involves the development of new pricing plans and the communication of price changes to retailers of the product. As a result, change can be costly and not offset by improvements in revenue. Change can also represent a risk. Competitors could react to your price changes. A reduction in your price could lead to a price war, which you may not find attractive. Furthermore, you may not fully understand the price elasticity of demand for your product. If you consider the demand for your product to be elastic, you should think about reducing your price. But if you have got it wrong and demand is inelastic, your revenues will fall, not rise. It is, therefore, important to understand how you might measure your elasticity of demand.

Elastic or inelastic?

Cigarettes were used as an example of inelastic demand and mobile phone networks as an example of elastic demand. Cigarettes have few substitutes: if all cigarettes become expensive, smokers will not switch to another type of vice, as there are few sources of nicotine. If one telephone network increases its prices, however, mobile phone users can switch to the cheaper networks. It is the level of competition for a product that influences its elasticity.

The level of competition provides an indication of how elastic demand is. However, if we wish to target unit elasticity we will need a measure of how far our current pricing is from this best price. To find the best price we need to gather data that will enable the demand curve for our product to be plotted, or mathematically modelled.

Once we have a demand curve, we can see the relationship between price and quantity and measure the elasticity of demand at various prices. Unfortunately the data required for a demand curve are difficult to find. Ideally, an experiment should occur where the price of a product is changed and the effect on demand noted, but product suppliers are not keen to change the price of the product to see what happens to the demand. Indeed, if they raise the price they are likely to lose customers to a rival brand. Recognizing this problem, market researchers can make use of promotional exercises. For example, a 'buy one get one free' offer is basically a 50 per cent discount in the market. A 'buy two get the third free' offer is a 33 per cent discount. When you buy a product at the supermarket, so-called 'scanner data' are created. Therefore, for any given period of time the supermarket knows how much soap powder was sold and what discounts were on offer. Market research companies make it their business to buy scanner data from a large selection of supermarkets across the country. They then use this to advise companies on pricing, because by using the data on sales and promotional discounts they can begin to estimate the elasticity of demand. For each price at which the product is sold, the market researchers also note down how many units of the product are sold at the tills. They then plot this as in Figure 2.7. The plot shows a negative relationship between price and quantity demanded. To smooth out this relationship the researchers then use a computer to calculate the trend line, as in Figure 2.8. The trend line is in fact the demand curve that we have been using throughout this chapter.

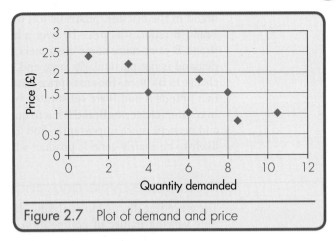

Figure 2.7 Plot of demand and price

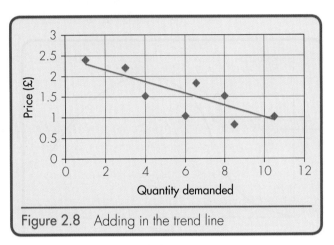

Figure 2.8 Adding in the trend line

By using mathematical techniques known as econometrics, the trend line can be analysed and manipulated to provide an estimate of the price elasticity of demand. Knowing that unit elasticity is optimal, product managers can then make an informed decision about whether to raise or lower prices. In your working life you are unlikely ever to calculate the elasticity of demand for a product, but being able to understand the concept will be very important.

Going one step further, competitors within a product category can use price promotion activities to analyse cross-price elasticity. It is then possible to understand the degree to which consumers are price sensitive between competing brands. If there is a high degree of cross-price elasticity, then price discounts maybe effective in attracting new customers whereas a low cross-price elasticity would suggest that price discounts are an ineffective and expensive means of attracting new customers. Take the data in Table 2.4 as an example. Brand A could be the leading

Table 2.4 Cross-price elasticity example

	Original demand for A	Demand for A when B reduces its price	Change in demand	Percentage change in demand	Cross-price elasticity
Brand A	256956	211572	−45384	−0.18	0.33
	Original price for B	Discount price for B	Change in price	Percentage change in price	
Brand B	£1.28	£0.60	−0.68	−0.53	

brand in the biscuits, pizzas or soft drinks category. Brand B is a much weaker competitor. Brand B reduces its price by over a half for a period of one week. The price reduction for Brand B does cause some customers to switch over from Brand A, however the change in demand is not particularly large and in percentage terms is much less than the percentage change in B's price. The cross-price elasticity is therefore calculated at 0.33, which would suggest that Brands A and B are substitutes, but many customers of Brand A are not price sensitive. In commercial terms Brand B has to question whether a price promotion is profitable, unlikely, and perhaps more importantly, how Brand A has managed to lock in customers for what is likely to be a fairly generic product within the biscuits, pizza or soft drinks category.

Product life cycle and pricing

The preceding discussion analysing elasticity and total revenue for the most part neglects the time-varying nature of competition and elasticity. When a new and innovative product emerges onto the market, it faces very few competitors. In the technology industry, BlackBerry was a leader in bringing email, Internet and telecommunications to the mobile market. But this lead was quickly chased down by Apple and its iPhone, which then faced competition from Google Android phones. In the automobile industry, Renault was the first to convert a Mégane into a Scénic and create the MPV segment of the market, but Citroën soon followed with a Picasso, Ford has a C Max and Toyota has its Verso range. Successful innovation spawns imitation and aggressive competition as the market grows.

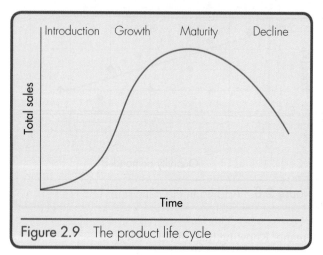

Eventually consumers will become tired of old designs and concepts. Newer models and ideas will emerge and sales will track the latest fashion. Demand for iPhone-type products and MPVs will fall, competitors will leave the market and competition will become less severe. These arguments are captured in the concept of a product life cycle, which is illustrated in Figure 2.9.

Figure 2.9 The product life cycle

Successful products go through four phases of the product life cycle: introduction, growth, maturity and decline. (Unsuccessful products never pass introduction.) At each stage of the product life cycle the number of competitors is different. This leads to differing substitutability and differing elasticities of demand for the products.

Pricing at launch

In the introduction stage, an innovative product is likely to be unique and face few, if any, competitors. For early adopters who wish to be seen with the latest technology, demand will be price inelastic. Firms could, therefore, seek to price high in order to capture the high demand from this set of consumers.

Pricing during growth

In the growth phase, companies who have witnessed the success of the innovative product also join the market. This increases competition and substitutability and increases the elasticity of demand. Recognizing the inverse relationship between price and consumers' willingness to demand, firms can seek to gain a dominant position by cutting prices in the hope of gaining market share. Under this strategy firms are trading a revenue-maximizing strategy for a sales-maximizing strategy. This could be temporary: maximizing sales and market coverage in the short run and winning the hearts and minds of customers, only to then exploit this commercial position in the long run with a strategy which maximizes revenues.

Pricing during maturity

The ferocity of competition is most acute during the mature phase of the cycle, sales are at a peak and the market can be supplied by the largest number of competitors. The potential for a high degree of price elasticity in the mature phase of the cycle provides a basic rationale for the sales-maximization strategy during the growth phase – gain market share, cut out competition or face the consequences of merciless price competition in the mature phase of the cycle. High price elasticity means little control over pricing, as competitive pressures force the price down to the lowest possible level.

Pricing during decline

In the decline phase of the market, consumers will begin to leave the market. In response, some firms will also exit, seeking better commercial opportunities elsewhere. Competition will fall and the degree of price sensitivity among consumers will diminish. Firms remaining in the market will see the elasticity of demand begin to become more inelastic, and an element of price stability, and hopefully price rises, might occur. Therefore, throughout the product life cycle the pricing strategy has to be reactive to the changing competitive nature of the market.

 # Business application: pricing strategies ii – extracting consumer surplus

Consumer surplus – the island of lost profits

Here is a true but curious thought: when you buy a product you are nearly always willing to pay *more* for it. This is the concept of **consumer surplus**.

> Consumer surplus is the difference between the price you are charged for a product and the maximum price that you would have been willing to pay.

For example, you may have been willing to pay £750 for a flight to Australia, but you manage to find a flight for £500. Your consumer surplus is £250.

Figure 2.10 illustrates the idea of consumer surplus using the demand curve. You are charged £500, but you are willing to pay £750. Indeed, in the market there may be some consumers who would be willing to pay even more than you. The entire amount of consumer surplus in the market is the area under the demand line down to the price charged of £500. This area represents the amount each consumer would be willing to pay in excess of the price charged.

Consumer surplus represents a benefit for consumers, but clearly for a firm it represents missed profits, because you were willing to pay £750 and were only charged £500. This is not good. So, as a business person, how do you discover a consumer's true willingness to pay and charge them accordingly?

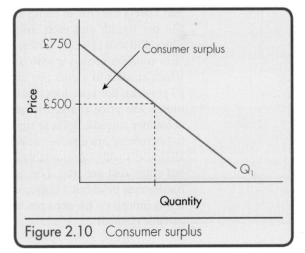

Figure 2.10   Consumer surplus

Price discrimination

In order for a firm to extract consumer surplus, it needs to undertake **price discrimination** – the act of charging different consumers different prices for the same good. For price discrimination to be successful, three conditions must exist. First, the firm must have some control over its prices: it therefore cannot face a perfectly elastic demand line. Economists refer to this as having some degree of market power in setting prices. Second, the firm must be capable of identifying different groups of consumers who are willing to pay different prices. Third, resale of the good or service must be prohibited. If it isn't, a consumer who buys at a low price can then sell to a consumer who is willing

> Price discrimination is the act of charging different prices to different consumers for an identical good or service.

to buy at a high price. The profits from price discrimination then flow to the consumer, rather than the firm. Economists identify first-, second- and third-degree price discrimination.

First-degree price discrimination

Under first-degree price discrimination, each consumer is charged exactly what they are willing to pay for the good or service. This is unlikely to work in practice because it would involve each customer freely admitting to the top price that they would be willing to pay. For example, an airline might line up all of its passengers and ask them to write on a large card the price they would be willing to pay to fly on the aircraft. The passengers would then be admitted onto the aircraft in price order. Highest first, lowest last. Those who bid too low may not fly if the aircraft is full. However, passengers might not write a truthful price and why should they? In addition, the entire process is very costly in terms of time and administration to carry out.

First-degree price discrimination is therefore seen to be difficult to carry out in practice. Instead, a seller looks for cues or signals of a consumer's willingness to pay. For example, a builder, plumber or electrician might charge for work based on the type of car parked on the drive. Car sales people are trained to look at items worn by a potential buyer, such as the watch, coat, clothes and even areas where they live. These all provide reasonable, but imperfect, signals of someone's ability to pay and perhaps willingness to pay. Finally, there is the use of auctions, where each potential buyer is forced to bid for an item. In bidding, each buyer is communicating their willingness to pay. The highest bidder wins when the price is above every other bidder's willingness to pay – that is, every other bidder has no consumer surplus. However, auctions are costly to organize, only one sale at a time occurs and there is no guarantee that bidders will attend.

Second-degree price discrimination

Under second-degree price discrimination, consumers are charged according to the number of units they buy. For example, gas, electricity and telephones tend to be offered under two-part tariffs. The first part is a fixed element to cover the cost of the infrastructure. The second part covers the cost of using additional units of electricity, gas, etc. If the fixed element is £10 per month and each unit costs £0.1, then a user of 100 units a month is charged £10 + (100 × £0.1) = £20. Taking account of the fixed element, the cost per unit is £20/100 = £0.2. Now consider someone who uses 200 units: their monthly bill is £10 + (200 × £0.1) = £30, which equates to a cost per unit of £30/200 = £0.15. The higher user gains a discount of 25 per cent. But how does this extract the consumer surplus? The listed unit cost of £0.1 per unit is the price charged to all consumers. The fixed price element is set to extract the consumer surplus. Because the consumer surplus is not constant across all consumers, the fixed element can also be varied across consumers through the provision of pricing menus. High users with a presumably high willingness to pay are offered a high fixed access price, but a low cost per unit. Low users with a presumably low willingness to pay select a low fixed access price but a high cost per unit. These pricing strategies are also used beyond the utility industry – for example, membership of gyms and golf clubs often includes a fixed and variable element.

Third-degree price discrimination

Finally, we have third-degree price discrimination where each consumer group is charged a different price. This tends to occur where firms can identify different market segments for a similar product or service. In the case of airlines, young students are fairly flexible when it comes to flying around the world. If the plane is full on Monday, they can fly on Tuesday. In fact, demand by young travellers is elastic, as different days of travel provide substitutes. A business traveller is more likely to have very specific needs. The overseas meeting will take place on a specific date and they will need to be back in the UK very quickly to attend more meetings. These travellers are less sensitive to price and so exhibit price-inelastic demand.

Therefore, rather than offering each traveller the same product at the same price, you can segment the market. Offer two different products at different prices: cheap economy tickets with no frills to the student; and expensive business-class tickets to the business person, with comfortable seats, good food and access to airport lounges.

Premium television channels use the same idea. Instead of paying one fee for all digital channels, consumers are offered a menu. The base price includes the standard assortment of channels. The sport and movie channels are additional extras. Consumers that value sport highly will pay the higher price.

This is known as de-bundling the product. If the product is composed of many different parts, in our case various television channels, the offering is not sold as one bundle; rather, it is sold as a number of separate bundles, each with an individual price.

This stripping-out of valued products from the standard range enables companies to deal with the problem of consumer surplus by targeting customers with the combination of products that they value the most.

Similar tactics are arguably employed by Apple when marketing iPhones, iPads and iPods. Within the iPod range is a selection of devices – nano, classic, etc. – and each range is further differentiated by the amount of storage capacity. Rather than sell one version of iPod to all customers at one price, Apple instead sells a range of iPods at different prices. This is an attempt by Apple to extract some of the available consumer surplus. Customers who are willing to pay a high price are those who are most likely to place the highest value on features and storage space. To access these features, such customers have to buy the most expensive iPod. Customers who just want a portable music player are likely to buy the cheapest iPod.

Apple differentiates the market further by offering iPhones and iPod Touches and iPads. If you want an iPod and a mobile phone, then the iPhone is for you. If you want all the features of an iPhone, but without a phone, then the iPod Touch or iPad is an attractive option. By meeting a variety of demand needs at various prices, Apple has become a profitable company. More importantly, by targeting a variety of segments, Apple has achieved revenue growth through the extraction of consumer surplus. The alternative route to revenue growth involves cutting prices and driving volumes. This approach can be self-defeating, requiring ever cheaper versions of the product to continually drive volume growth. By pricing high and meeting consumer needs across many segments, Apple has successfully managed a premium price strategy. Of course, this may fail if a recession cuts demand for premium goods, such as Apple's.

A summary of price discrimination is provided in Table 2.5.

Table 2.5 Key features of each type of price discrimination

Price discrimination	Key features
First degree	Each consumer is charged their maximum willingness to pay. All consumer surplus is reduced to zero. An auction would be an example. Very costly to implement in markets where there are many buyers.
Second degree	Customers pay a fixed amount and a unit amount. Often seen in utility markets such as gas and electricity. The combination of fixed and unit prices results in a price which varies across consumers according to usage. Easy to implement and enables some extraction of the consumer surplus.
Third degree	Products are differentiated according to features which are valuable to the consumer. Easy to implement if the product has multiple features and providers are skilled at product differentiation. Some consumer surplus can be extracted.

Box 2.4

Why heavier people should pay more to fly

People who weigh more should pay more to fly on planes – in the same way that people who exceed their baggage allowance must pay extra. The rationale is simple. The fuel burnt by planes depends on many things, but the most important is the weight of the aircraft. The more a plane weighs, the more fuel it must burn. If the passengers on the aircraft weigh more, the aircraft consumes more fuel and the airline's costs go up.

Between 1926 and 2008, the average weight of an Australian female adult increased from 59 kilograms to 71 kilograms and the average weight of an Australian male adult increased from 72 to 85 kilograms. These increases represent weight gains of around 0.23 per cent and 0.20 per year for women and men, respectively. Since 2000, the extra loading that an average adult passenger carries is about 2 kilograms.

So what does this increase mean for additional fuel consumption on a big, modern aircraft like the A380? On a route like Sydney to London via Singapore, it means around 3.72 extra barrels of jet fuel per flight is burnt, which at current prices costs about $472.

If the airline flies three times a day to London the cost of carrying 2 extra kilograms per person is about $1 million per year. This cost represents around 13 per cent of profit if the airline only clears $10 per passenger from the route.

Assuming that a 'weight surcharge' would be applied on a per-excess-kilogram basis for both men and women who weigh above a certain limit, the fee that would recover costs at current jet fuel prices is about 58 cents per kilogram on the Sydney to London via Singapore route.

This calculation means that if the critical weight limit is 75 kilograms and a man weighed 100 kilograms, then the surcharge would be $14.50 one-way or double this for return. Conversely, a female weighing just 50 kilos would get a 'petite' discount of $14.50 each way.

This debate may sound discriminatory, but in fact is a common feature in the modern market.

Cinemas practise price discrimination on the basis of age and employment status. Trains price discriminate on the basis of time of travel. Taxis price discriminate on the basis of the payment method customers use. Retailers price discriminate on the basis of whether a sale is in-store or over the Internet. Insurance companies price discriminate on the basis of where a car is usually parked, or the suburb in which a house is located.

In short, companies usually practise price discrimination because they think they can make more money by doing so.

Adapted from an article by Tony Webber in the
Sydney Morning Herald, 11 January 2012.

 ## 2.8 Business data applications

Companies generally turn to market research companies when seeking data on how a market is growing, developing and changing. There are many market research companies in the world and some of the leading and popular sources of market research data are listed in Table 2.6. Your university may have online access to reports published by one of these companies.

When reviewing a market, sector or product category, a market research company is likely to use many of the frameworks developed in this chapter, for example revenues, output, the changing nature of substitutes and developing needs or tastes and preferences among consumers.

Datamonitor provides data on the European soft drinks industry. The data in Table 2.7 show that total revenue stands at an enormous €44 billion. Over the

Table 2.6 Market research companies

AC Neilsen	http://www.acnielsen.com/
Datamonitor	http://www.datamonitor.com/
Euromonitor	http://www.euromonitor.com/
Ipsos-Mori	http://www.ipsos-mori.com/
Kantar	http://www.kantar.com/
Mintel	http://www.mintel.com/

Table 2.7　The European market for soft drinks

Year	Revenue €bn	Growth %	Output millions of litres	Growth %
2005	41.2		46.9	
2006	41.6	1.0	48.0	2.3
2007	42.5	2.2	49.4	2.9
2008	43.2	1.6	50.4	2.0
2009	44.0	1.9	51.3	1.8

Source: Datamonitor.

five-year period 2005–09 revenue growth was modest. This weak growth in revenues appears to have been almost entirely down to output growth, where the growth in output aligns fairly well with the growth in revenues. We might therefore conclude that prices have stayed relatively constant and demand has increased, a so-called rightward shift in demand.

Looking across Europe, Figure 2.11 illustrates the consumption of carbonated drinks by country. Germany and the UK are the largest markets, closely followed by Italy and France. The most popular line of drinks in the carbonated market are cola varieties. Cola standard and cola diet together account for over 50 per cent of the market (see Figure 2.12).

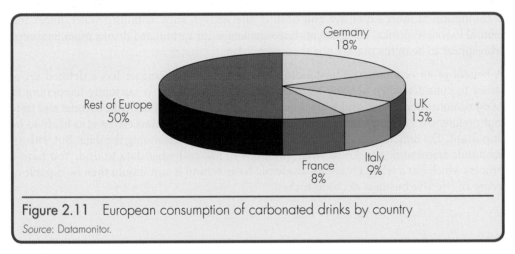

Figure 2.11　European consumption of carbonated drinks by country
Source: Datamonitor.

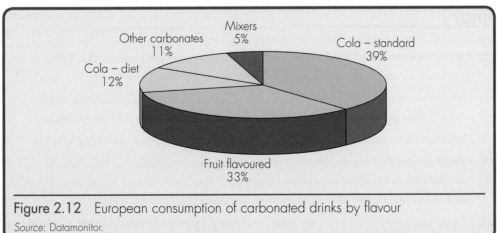

Figure 2.12　European consumption of carbonated drinks by flavour
Source: Datamonitor.

An important question for business managers is to understand where demand will grow in the future. Will Germany and the UK remain important markets and will cola still be the leading carbonated drink? These questions can be framed and addressed by beginning to think about substitutes, income and taste and preferences.

Substitutes are a complex issue when considering carbonated drinks and depend very much on a concept we introduced earlier in this chapter: what is the definition of the market? We could consider substitutes only within the cola market. We could consider substitutes within the carbonated drinks market. We could go wider and consider substitutes within the soft drinks categories, which includes tea, coffee, bottled water, sports drinks and juices. Broader still and we begin to include alcoholic beverages.

Relevance is important: which of these market definitions is most relevant to an understanding of which substitutes are attracting consumer demand? Growing tastes and preferences for healthy lifestyles, nutritious diets, international fruit flavours and natural ingredients are driving demand away from carbonated and particularly sugary drinks. Fresh juices, smoothies and botanical-flavoured drinks are all growing in importance at the expense of carbonated drinks and might help to explain the lack of growth in the mature carbonated drinks sector.

In terms of income, the leading carbonated drinks markets of Germany, the UK, Italy and France do not offer much scope for future growth. Income levels are already well developed and consumers can easily afford to purchase soft drinks. A more worrying trend can be seen in the consumption patterns by age and income levels. Market research shows that consumers of carbonated drinks are concentrated in the lower-income groups. Ageing populations and rising affluence, particularly among middle-income earners, is associated with increased consumption of more expensive and healthy alternatives, such as bottled water, juices and natural flavoured drinks. This presents huge challenges for carbonated drinks manufacturers, who appear to be in the mature phase of the market.

A benefit of an economic understanding is that a business manager has a defined set of issues to consider when seeking to understand demand. What is currently happening to sales, revenues and prices, and what impact will substitutes, complements, income and taste and preferences have on future demand? Understanding price elasticity is also likely to be important. The difficult part then becomes finding and understanding the data. But with an economic framework you know what questions to ask and what data to find. You have a process which has a relatively sound academic basis behind it and should then be capable of being an effective business decision maker.

Summary

1. A key characteristic of modern economic life is that companies set prices. With companies in such a powerful position, what is the optimal price to set for a product?

2. The demand curve shows consumers' willingness to demand a product at various prices. As the price increases, consumers are less willing to demand the product.

3. Demand is also seen to be influenced by the price of substitutes and complements.

4. Substitutes are rivals; complements are products that are purchased together. As a substitute becomes more expensive, demand for the rival product will increase. As the price of a complement rises, demand for the remaining product will fall.

5. Rising income will lead to an increase in demand for normal goods. But it will lead to a fall in demand for inferior goods.

6. The tastes and preferences of consumers change over time. As goods become popular, consumers move into the market. As products become unfashionable, consumers leave the market and demand falls.

7. Price elasticity, income elasticity and cross-price elasticity measure how much demand changes when price, income or the price of a substitute or complement changes.

8. If the percentage change in demand is greater than the percentage change in price, then demand is said to be elastic. If the percentage change in demand is less than the percentage change in price, demand is said to be inelastic.

9. Companies use the concept of elasticity when setting prices. If demand is elastic, reducing prices will lead to a rise in total revenue. When demand is inelastic, raising prices will lead to an increase in total revenue.

10. Companies measure the elasticity of demand by analysing mathematically what happens to sales when they offer promotional discounts in the market.

11. Consumer surplus is the difference between the price charged and how much a consumer would have been willing to pay. This difference represents lost profit.

12. It is possible to capture some consumer surplus by de-bundling product offerings. Consumers can be offered a base package but extras are offered at much higher prices.

Learning checklist

You should now be able to:
- Draw a demand curve for a good or service
- Understand how changes in income, the price of substitutes and complements, tastes and price expectations shift the demand curve left or right
- Explain the concept of price elasticity of demand and understand the distinction between elastic and inelastic demand
- Understand and use income and cross-price elasticity to develop pricing strategies in relation to consumer income, substitutes and complements
- Explain how total revenue can be improved by understanding how elastic demand is for a good or service
- Explain how firms can develop strategies to access consumer surplus
- Understand where to gain market data and use economic ideas to understand the important trends within the data

Questions   connect

1. Draw a demand line which illustrates the effect of a price reduction on consumers' willingness to demand.

2. Identify the main factors which can lead to a shift in demand.

3. If a consumer's willingness to demand a product is sensitive to a change in the price, then their elasticity of demand is elastic, or inelastic?

4. The price of pasta at the supermarket falls. What do you think will happen to the demand for rice?

EASY

5. Explain the difference between an inferior and a normal good.

6. How would you expect your consumption of normal and inferior goods to change over your lifetime?

7. Provide examples of your own consumption activities where your consumer surplus is high and also where it is small.

8. A successful advertising campaign has a slogan which is adopted by teenagers across your economy. Illustrate what will happen to the demand line for the product being advertised.

9. How does consumer surplus vary with elasticity? How might firms use this to their advantage?

10. Products that have low price elasticity have low prices and high volumes. Products that have high elasticity have smaller volumes and higher profit margins. Do you consider these statements to be true?

11. Assess how easy it is for firms to measure the elasticity of demand for a given good or service.

12. List five products that you think are price elastic. List five products that you think are price inelastic.

13. Is consumer surplus greater under elastic or inelastic demand?

14. How would you advise a company to go about changing the elasticity of demand for one of its products?

15. Using ideas relating to income elasticity, how would you build a portfolio or collection of products that would perform well when the economy was growing during a boom and contracting during a recession?

Exercises

1. True or false?

   (a) An increase in income will cause an increase in demand for all goods.

   (b) Two goods are complements if an increase in the price of X results in an increase in demand for Y.

   (c) Price elasticity measures the responsiveness of the quantity demanded to the change in the price.

   (d) The price elasticity is constant along the length of a demand line.

   (e) If a car costs £15 000 and a consumer is willing to pay up to £18 000, then the consumer surplus is £3000.

   (f) If a product is price inelastic, revenues will rise following an increase in the price.

2. (a) Plot the demand curve and associated total revenue curve for Table 2.8.

   - Calculate the elasticity at each price.

   - What is the change in total revenue if the firm moves from a price of £8 to £4?

   - Which price maximizes total revenue?

   - What is the elasticity when revenue is maximized?

   (b) As a result of rising income, demand increases at all prices by five units. Explain whether this good is normal or inferior.

(c) Is the new demand line more or less elastic than the original? Why do you think this should be the case?

Table 2.8

Price (£)	10	8	6	4	2
Demand	1	2	3	4	5
Total revenue					
Elasticity					

3. You have been hired by Louis Vuitton to advise the firm on its pricing strategy. Your brief is to cover each of the following:

DIFFICULT

(a) The benefit of raising its existing prices.

(b) The potential of broadening the brand's appeal through a gradual reduction in prices.

(c) The potential benefits of launching a new brand called 'Louis'. Who should this product be sold to and at what price level?

4. Using data from a market research company, produce a short report for a product category which identifies current demand patterns. In addition, identify the impact that substitutes, complements, income and taste and preferences will have on future demand patterns.

Firms in the marketplace

Chapter contents

Cost theory at a glance   59

3.1 Business problem: managing fixed and variable costs   59

3.2 The short and long run   60

3.3 The nature of productivity and costs in the short run   61

3.4 Output decisions in the short run   66

3.5 Cost inefficiency   69

3.6 The nature of productivity and costs in the long run   71

3.7 Business application: linking pricing with cost structures   75

3.8 Business application: footballers as sweaty assets   77

3.9 Business data application: wages and productivity   78

Summary   80

Learning checklist   81

Questions   81

Exercises   82

Learning outcomes

By the end of this chapter you should understand:

Economic theory

LO1   The difference between the short and the long run

LO2   The difference between variable, fixed and total costs

LO3   The concepts of marginal product and marginal costs

LO4   The law of diminishing returns

LO5   Economies of scale

LO6   The concept of minimum efficient scale

Business applications

LO7   Why low pricing and high-volume sales strategies, deployed by budget airlines, reflect high fixed costs

LO8   Why qualification for the Champions League by leading football clubs is a strategy for dealing with the high cost of owning and employing footballers

LO9   When times get tough, when to decide to quit and when to hang on for a bit

LO10 Where to find data on labour costs and productivity

At a glance Cost theory

The issue

World-class footballers cost in excess of €60 million, and the Superjumbo A380 costs $264 million. Neither are cheap. So how does a business make money when using such expensive assets?

The understanding

Such assets represent costs that do not vary with the level of output. The way to exploit such assets is to make them productive. The more games Ronaldo plays for Real Madrid, the cheaper per game he becomes. The more flights a plane flies, the cheaper per flight the plane becomes. Unfortunately, over short periods of time, volume may come up against a problem known as the 'law of diminishing returns', while in the long run firms can encounter an additional problem known as 'diseconomies of scale'. By the end of this chapter you will understand each of these problems and how costs can be managed in the short and the long run.

The usefulness

This chapter will enable you to understand why successful airlines sell their seats at low prices, why teams such as Manchester United are desperate to stay in the Champions League and why research and development (R&D)-intensive technology products need to conquer world markets.

3.1 Business problem: managing fixed and variable costs

Economists categorize costs as being fixed or variable.

Supermarket stores represent **fixed costs**. If the store attracts one shopper or 1000 shoppers per day, the cost of developing and maintaining the store is fixed. However, the number of checkout staff does change with the number of shoppers and, therefore, represents a **variable cost**. The cost of developing Apple's iPhone was a fixed cost. Development costs do not increase if more iPhones are sold. Rather, the cost of producing more iPhones increases. Universities are a vast collection of fixed costs. The cost of lecture theatres, lecturers, library resources, central administration units and computer facilities is not hugely influenced by the number of recruited students. For example, the cost of lecturing to 50 students is the same as lecturing to 250 students.

> Fixed costs are constant. They remain the same whatever the level of output.
>
> Variable costs change or vary with the amount of production.

The nature of fixed and variable costs has enormous implications for business. As an example, consider the contrasting differences between employing workers in a fast-food restaurant and professional footballers.

Workers at fast-food restaurants are perhaps paid no more than £6 per hour. The majority of employed hours are on weekends, evenings or lunch times, periods when consumer demand is highest. This is because the employment of workers at a fast-food restaurant is linked to the demand for burgers. More workers are employed at lunch times and weekends when demand, and therefore the production of burgers, is highest. As a result, the cost of employing fast-food workers is a predominantly variable cost. The wages paid rise and fall with the level of output. Ultimately, if demand for burgers drops dramatically, restaurants can generally terminate the employment of their workers by giving one month's notice.

Professional footballers can be paid £150 000 a week when they play a game. This may fall by a fraction if they are on the substitutes' bench or when they are injured. Similarly, the wage may increase with bonuses if goals are scored or after a specified number of first-team appearances. It is important to remember that the bulk of a professional footballer's wages is

The economics of very big ships

ABOARD one of the world's largest container ships, it's easy to appreciate how a T-shirt made in China can be sent to the Netherlands for just 2.5 cents. The *Eleonora Maersk* and the other seven ships in her class are among the biggest ever built: almost 400 metres long, or the length of four football pitches, and another half-pitch across. The ship can carry 7500 or so 40-foot containers, each of which can hold 70 000 T-shirts.

Maersk Lines, the world's biggest container-shipping company and owner of the *Eleonora*, is betting that, given the current economics of world trade, the only

way to go is yet bigger. In February it announced an order for 20 even larger ships with a capacity of 18 000 twenty-foot-equivalent units (TEUs), the standard measure of container size. (The *Eleonora* can carry a mere 15 000.) The new ships will cost $200 million each. Most of these vessels will be designed for the Europe–Asia run – now the world's busiest trade route. Given the rising price of fuel and fears of a renewed slowdown, many shippers think they need huge ships to turn a profit.

Adapted from an article in *The Economist*, 12 November 2011.
© The Economist Newspaper Limited, London 2011.

not linked directly to the creation of output, namely, football games. Playing games or sitting on the subs' bench only leads to relatively small changes up or down in the wages paid to the player. The cost of employing professional footballers is, therefore, a predominantly fixed cost. A club's wages bill is changed very little by the number of games played. Furthermore, because footballers' contracts are fixed for anything up to five years, if the club wishes to terminate the employment of the player two years into the contract, it would have to pay three years' worth of compensation. These employment differences between footballers and fast-food workers are crucial.

The business problem associated with employing footballers, or fixed costs, is *not* that they cost huge sums of money, but that the *nature* of the cost *does not change* with *output* and *revenues*.

If the revenues received from fans and television rights drop, clubs still have to honour their contractual obligations with their players. In contrast, fast-food restaurants can change the number of workers when demand falls. The transfer of football players between clubs is the transfer of both an asset and a liability. The buying club gains what it believes is a good player, but at the same time it also commits itself to an increase in its fixed costs.

It is important for businesses to recognize the various components of their cost structures and to differentiate between fixed and variable costs. By doing so, they can then develop business models that accommodate the financial commitment associated with fixed costs. Box 3.1 highlights how shipping companies are turning to larger and larger ships. Such assets are enormous fixed costs, as is the fuel used to move them around the world. By carrying more cargo on each journey the cost per unit falls and the ship becomes more competitive and potentially more profitable. By the end of this chapter you will understand how to manage such cost structures highlighted by our initial discussion. But in order to achieve this, you need to develop a broader understanding of cost theory.

 ## The short and long run

Short run is a period of time where one factor of production is fixed. We tend to assume that capital is fixed and labour is variable.

We will begin by considering a firm that employs two factors of production: labour in the form of workers and capital in the form of computers and office space.

If a firm needs to increase its level of output in the **short run**, it is fairly easy to employ more workers. Agencies specializing in temporary employment are able to offer suitable candidates within a day, or even an hour. In contrast, it is not as easy to expand the amount of office space. It takes time to find additional buildings, arrange the finance to purchase the buildings, and then fit out the buildings with suitable furniture and equipment. The problem also exists when trying to downsize. It is fairly easy to lay off workers, but it takes time to decommission a building and sell it to some other user. Therefore, only in the **long run** are all factors of production seen to be variable.

> Long run is a period of time when all factors of production are variable.

Given our business problem, we should not confine our thinking to capital as the only fixed factor of production. Clearly, the nature of employment can make labour fixed. Contracts signed by footballers, company chief executives and many academics are for a fixed period of time. Contracts for fast-food workers and many other types of work are open-ended, with the employer and employee given the right to terminate the relationship with, typically, one month's notice. In the latter case, the employment of labour is reasonably variable, whereas for footballers labour is fixed.

A reasonable question is, how long is the long run? The answer is, it depends. For some companies it can be very long. Airlines place orders with aircraft suppliers up to five years in advance, while an Internet company might be able to buy an additional Internet server system within a week and double its output capacity.

However, an important issue is to understand how costs behave in the short and long runs. In the next two sections we will see how in the short run costs are determined by the fixed amount of capital being exploited by more workers, while in the long run costs are influenced by varying the amount of capital.

The nature of productivity and costs in the short run

Productivity in the short run

If we are interested in knowing how the level of costs changes with the level of output, then we need to consider more than just the cost of employing labour and capital. We are also interested in understanding how the productivity of labour and capital changes. If labour becomes more productive, then output increases for any given amount of cost.

In assessing productivity, we need to distinguish between **total product** and **marginal product**.

> Total product is the total output produced by a firm's workers.
>
> Marginal product is the addition to total product after employing one more unit of factor input. In economics, marginal always means 'one more'.
>
> Task specialization occurs where the various activities of a production process are broken down into their separate components. Each worker then specializes in one particular task, becoming an expert in the task and raising overall productivity.

Consider the following. An online supplier of electrical goods has two vans for deliveries, the fixed factor of production. The firm can also employ up to 10 workers, the variable component. The total product and marginal product at each level of employment are detailed in Table 3.1. When the firm employs one worker, total product is 40 delivered items per day. This worker has to collate the orders, pick the items from the warehouse, package them for delivery, print off invoices, load the van, deliver the items and then deal with any enquiries and returned items. When the firm employs a second worker, total output increases. This second worker can utilize the additional van and may specialize in dealing with enquiries and returns. When the third worker is employed, they do not have access to a van, but they could help by specializing in collating orders, picking and packing. This again would help to raise output. The fourth worker might load vans and print invoices. The fifth worker might then help the third by specializing in picking orders from the warehouse, and so on and so on. The important point is that task specialization helps to raise productivity, as evidenced by the increasing marginal product for workers two, three and four, but thereafter diminishes. There is only so much **task specialization** that can occur without leaving a worker without a full day's work. Workers five, six and seven, and onwards, will be filling the remainder of their working day by answering emails, checking their text messages, making coffee and collecting sandwiches for lunch – activities which do not raise the total product of the firm.

Table 3.1   Total and marginal product of labour with a fixed amount of capital

Labour input (workers)	Total product (number of deliveries)	Marginal product of labour (number of deliveries)
1	40	40
2	90	50
3	145	55
4	205	60
5	255	50
6	295	40
7	325	30
8	345	20
9	355	10
10	360	5

The law of diminishing returns states that, as more of a variable factor of production, usually labour, is added to a fixed factor of production, usually capital, then at some point the returns to the variable factor will diminish.

The productivity of all the workers in our example is constrained by the number of vans the firm uses. With only two vans, there is an upper limit to how many orders can be met per day, no matter how much task specialization occurs at the warehouse.

Most working environments are characterized by a mixture of workers and capital, in various forms: lecturers and lecture theatres, office staff and computers, fast-food workers and burger grills. The relationship depicted in Figures 3.1 and 3.2 is therefore very important and economists know it as the **law of diminishing returns**.

The law of diminishing returns is highlighted by the marginal product of labour (see Figure 3.2). When we have a fixed factor of production, such as capital, and we add

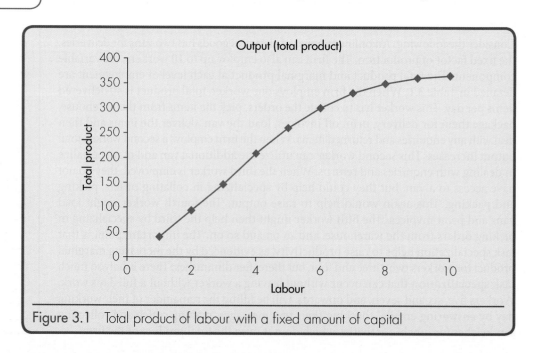

Figure 3.1   Total product of labour with a fixed amount of capital

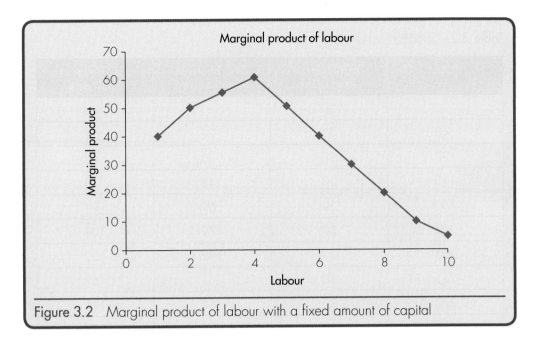

Figure 3.2   Marginal product of labour with a fixed amount of capital

workers to the production process, these workers can exploit an underutilized resource. So, the marginal product rises. When we begin to over-resource the production process with too much labour, there is no more capital to utilize. As a result, the marginal product begins to fall. This is the point at which the law of diminishing returns occurs. In our particular example, additional workers are able to exploit the vans and become more productive. But once we begin to employ more workers, and there are not enough vans, the productivity of labour must begin to fall.

Costs in the short run

Now that we have an understanding of how productivity changes, we need to begin to think about how costs behave. In the short run, we have three types of cost: variable, fixed and **total costs**.

> Total costs are simply fixed costs plus variable costs.

Variable costs change with the level of output. This was picked up when we discussed the fast-food workers. The higher the level of output, the more labour we employ and the higher the amount of variable cost.

Fixed costs do not change with the level of output. If we produce nothing, or a very large amount of output, fixed costs remain the same.

Each of these costs is listed in Table 3.2 for various levels of output, and plotted in Figure 3.3.

Fixed costs are represented as the orange line, which is horizontal. In this example, fixed costs are constant at £30. Variable costs rise, slowly; then, as output increases, they begin to rise more quickly. This simply reflects the law of diminishing returns. As additional workers become less productive, costs rise quicker than output. The total cost line in purple is simply fixed plus variable costs.

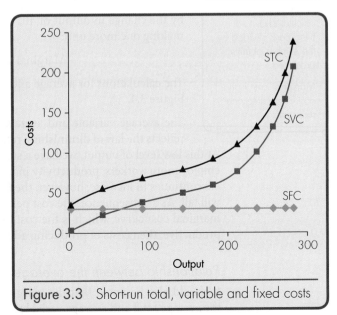

Figure 3.3   Short-run total, variable and fixed costs

Table 3.2   Short-run costs

Output	SFC (short-run fixed costs)	SVC (short-run variable costs)	STC (short-run total costs)
0	30	0	30
40	30	22	52
90	30	38	68
140	30	48	78
180	30	61	91
210	30	79	109
235	30	102	132
255	30	131	161
270	30	166	196
280	30	207	237

Average costs

> Average total cost is calculated as total cost divided by the number of units produced.
>
> Average variable cost is calculated as total variable cost divided by the number of units produced.
>
> Average fixed cost is calculated as total fixed costs divided by the number of units produced.
>
> Marginal cost is the cost of creating one more unit.

The next step is to consider how the cost per unit changes with the level of output. We measure the cost per unit using average costs (**average total cost, average variable cost** and **average fixed cost**).

In addition to the average costs, we also examine the **marginal costs**, calculated as:

$$\frac{\text{Change in total cost}}{\text{Change in output}}$$

(Since the marginal cost is the cost of producing one more unit, the change in output should be 1.)

However, firms rarely increase output by one unit and in our example output initially increases from 0 to 40 units of output: therefore, by dividing the change in total cost by the change in output of 40, we can approximate the marginal cost, or the cost of making one more unit:

$$\text{Marginal cost} = (52 - 30)/(40 - 0) = 0.55$$

The calculations for average and marginal costs are listed in Table 3.3, and plotted in Figure 3.4.

The average variable and average total cost curves are both U-shaped. This simply reflects the law of diminishing returns. Towards the left of the figure, the output is low. At this low level of output, we have a small number of workers using the fixed capital. As we employ more workers, productivity increases and costs per unit fall. As the number of workers continues to increase, however, the law of diminishing returns predicts that productivity will fall. As a consequence, the cost per unit will increase. This point is also picked up in the marginal cost curve, which is the cost of producing one more unit. As labour becomes less productive, then costs of producing additional units must rise.

Relationship between the average and the marginal

It should also be noted that the marginal cost curve cuts through the minimum points of the average total and average variable cost curves. This is because of a simple mathematical

Table 3.3 Short-run average and marginal costs

Output	SAFC (short-run average fixed costs)	SAVC (short-run average variable costs)	SATC (short-run average total costs)	SMC (short-run marginal costs)
0				
40	0.75	0.55	1.30	0.55
90	0.33	0.42	0.76	0.32
140	0.21	0.34	0.56	0.20
180	0.17	0.34	0.51	0.33
210	0.14	0.38	0.52	0.60
235	0.13	0.43	0.56	0.92
255	0.12	0.51	0.63	1.45
270	0.11	0.61	0.73	2.33
280	0.11	0.74	0.85	4.10

relationship between the marginal and the average. Assume your average examination score is 50. Your next exam is your marginal exam. If you gain a score of 70, then your average will increase. But if you gain a score of 20, your average will come down. Therefore, whenever the marginal is lower than the average, the average will move down; and whenever the marginal is higher than the average, the average will rise. Therefore, the marginal cost curve has to cut through the average cost curves at their minimum point.

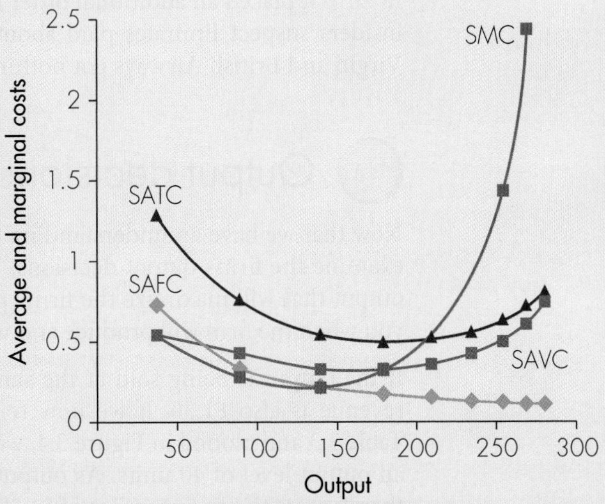

Average fixed costs

The average fixed cost curve is different. It is always falling as output increases. This reflects simple mathematics. If fixed costs are £100 and we produce 10 units, the average fixed costs are £100/10 = £10. But if we increase output to 100 units, then average fixed costs become £100/100 = £1. Accountants refer to this as 'spreading the overhead'. As fixed costs are spread over a larger level of output, the fixed costs per unit will fall.

Figure 3.4 Plotted short-run average and marginal costs

This relationship has important implications for managers. Consider the case of the Super Jumbo Airbus A380. Development costs have been estimated at €12 billion. If we assume Airbus finds two customers to buy the A380, the average fixed cost will be €12/2 billion = €6 billion. Therefore, in order for Airbus to break even, it will require its two customers to pay at least €6 billion; and then there is the cost of making the aircraft! Airbus has orders for 236 A380s, up from 100 in 2008, which helps to reduce the fixed cost per unit. But at a list price of €250 million, Airbus will have to sell many more A380s in order to recoup its variable costs of manufacturing and its fixed costs of development.

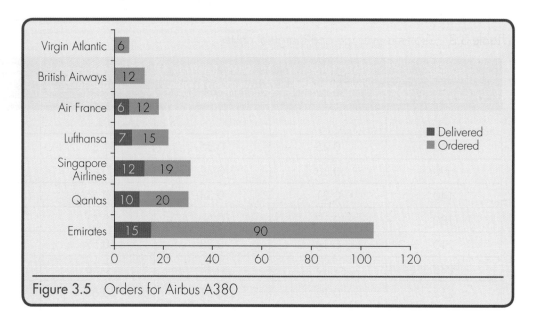

Figure 3.5 Orders for Airbus A380

The existence of large fixed costs also presents buyers with a negotiating opportunity. Firms with large fixed costs need volume. If you as a buyer can provide large volumes of sales, then you are more valuable and should use this to negotiate a larger discount. Figure 3.5 presents order data for the A380 for a number of carriers. Emirates is by far the biggest customer. In 2010 it placed an additional order for 32 A380s with a list price of €11.5 billion. Industry insiders suspect Emirates paid about half that price. You can be certain that the likes of Virgin and British Airways got nothing like that deal.

3.4 Output decisions in the short run

Now that we have an understanding of how costs behave in the short run, we can begin to examine the firm's output decisions. In Chapter 5 we will see how we can find the level of output that will maximize the firm's profits. However, at this point we merely wish to show you when the firm will produce and when it will close down.

If the output is being sold at the same price to all consumers for £1.50, then the average revenue is also £1.50. If we now re-examine the short-run average total costs, SATC in Table 3.3 and plotted in Figure 3.4, we can see that the maximum value for SATC is £1.30 at an output level of 40 units. As output grows, SATC drops to a minimum of £0.51. Clearly, therefore, at the current price of £1.50 the firm can make a profit at any output level.

Now consider two much lower prices, £0.45 and £0.30. At both prices the firm will make a loss as its minimum SATC is only £0.51, so its revenues will never be greater than its costs at either of these prices. But there is an important difference between the two scenarios. In the short run, the firm will operate and make a loss at prices of £0.45, but it will shut down and cease operating at prices of £0.30.

The understanding rests on whether or not the firm can make a positive contribution to its fixed costs. If the firm produces nothing, its fixed costs are £30 and its losses will also be £30. However, if the price is £0.45 there are output levels where the firm's average variable costs, SAVC, are less than £0.45. For example, at an output of 180 units, SAVC = £0.34. So, if the firm operates at 180 units of output, it can cover its variable cost per unit of £0.34 and have £0.45 − £0.34 = £0.11 per unit left over. Selling 180 units represents 180 × 0.11 = £19.80. The £19.80 can be used to make a contribution towards the fixed costs. So, by producing 180, the loss drops to £30 − £19.80 = £11.20, as opposed to a loss of £30 (the fixed costs) if it produced nothing.

However, when the price drops to £0.30 the firm cannot cover any of its variable costs. Therefore, if it did decide to operate, then, not being able to cover its entire wage bill, it would be adding to the losses generated by its fixed costs. Hence, the best the firm can do is to shut down and incur only the fixed-cost losses of £30.

We can now go one step further. The marginal cost is the cost of producing one more unit. If the firm can receive a price that is equal to or greater than the marginal cost, then it can break even or earn a profit on the last unit. If the firm maximizes profits, clearly it will supply an additional unit of output when the price is equal to or greater than marginal cost. If we couple this argument with the previous point, that firms will not operate below short-run average variable cost, we can show, as in Figure 3.6, that the firm's supply curve is in fact the firm's short-run marginal cost curve above short-run average variable costs.

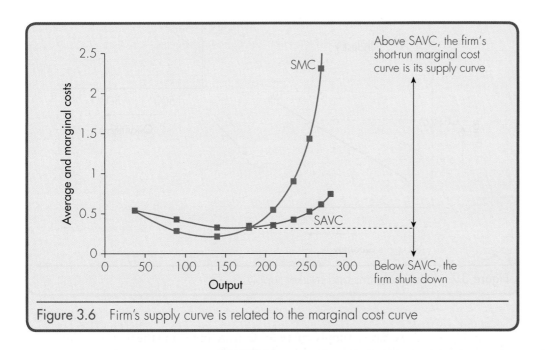

Figure 3.6   Firm's supply curve is related to the marginal cost curve

Box 3.2

Theme parks

Theme parks offering thrilling rollercoaster rides often close down during the winter. We can now offer an economic explanation for why they close. The rides are capital and represent fixed costs. The staff who operate the rides and keep the theme park clean are the variable costs. During the summer months many people are willing to go to a theme park and pay the entrance fee. The revenues generated cover the theme park's fixed and variable costs. However, in the winter, when it is cold and wet, very few people are willing to go to the theme park.

The revenues generated by the theme park would be unlikely to cover the wages it would have to pay to its staff to open the park. It is, therefore, best for the theme park to close and incur no variable costs during the winter; and simply incur its fixed costs. If the theme park decided to stay open during the winter, its losses would rise since the wage bill would not be covered by the small number of paying visitors to the park. Firms, therefore, are only willing to supply output if revenues are greater than variable costs.

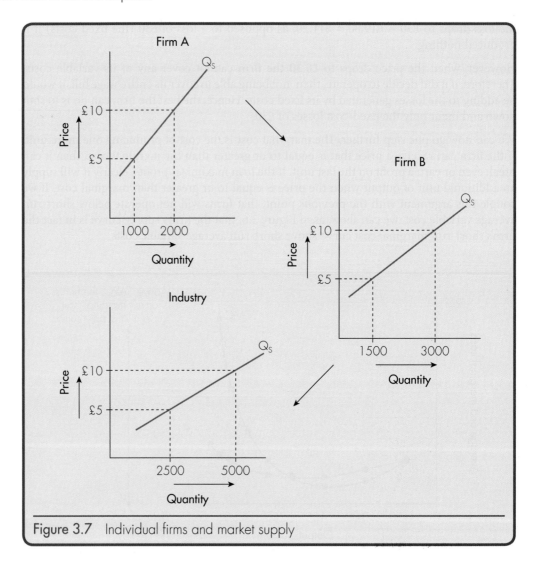

Figure 3.7 Individual firms and market supply

In Figure 3.7, we have a **supply curve** for firms A and B and the industry. Unlike the demand curve, the supply curve has a positive slope.

At each price, firm B is willing to supply more output than firm A. This is because the marginal cost at each output level is lower for firm B. At a price of £5, B is willing to supply 1500 units; A is only willing to supply 1000 units. Therefore, at all prices B is more willing to supply than A. The industry's willingness to supply is equal to the sum of A and B's willingness to supply.

Therefore, at a price of £5, the industry willingness to supply is 1000 + 1500 = 2500.

The industry supply curve in Figure 3.7 is the sum of each firm's willingness to supply at each possible price.

Just as we discussed with the demand curve, we also need to think about the factors that will lead to a shift in supply:

- If more firms enter the market, then supply must shift out to the right with more industry output being offered for sale at any given price. Conversely, if firms close down and exit the market, then the supply curve must shift in to the left, with less industry output being sold at any given price.

> The supply curve depicts a positive relationship between the price of a product and firms' willingness to supply the product.

- If the costs of labour, or other inputs, increase, profits must fall. As the potential to make profits decreases, then firms will be less willing to supply and so the supply curve will move in to the left. Conversely, if input prices fall, then the ability to make a profit increases and supply will shift out to the right.
- If a new technology is invented that enables firms to be more productive, then their costs will fall. This makes profits increase and firms are willing to supply more. The supply curve will then move out to the right.

For firms A and B, as the price increases, willingness to supply also increases. At each price, firm B is more willing to supply than firm A. For example, at £5 A is willing to supply 1000 units and B is willing to supply 1500. The industry supply is simply the sum of A and B. So, at £5 the industry's willingness to supply is 1000 + 1500 = 2500. Clearly, as more firms enter the industry, the industry's willingness to supply will increase and the industry supply curve will shift to the right. Similarly, as firms leave the industry, the willingness to supply will reduce and the industry supply curve will shift to the right.

Elasticity of supply

The **elasticity of supply** is a measure of how responsive firms' output is to a change in the price and is measured as the percentage change in supply divided by the percentage change in the price. The elasticity of supply will always be positive because of the positive relationship between price and supply. Like the price elasticity of demand, values greater than 1 are defined as elastic and values between 0 and 1 are described as inelastic. A value of 0 would be perfectly inelastic and a value of infinity would be perfectly elastic.

> Elasticity of supply is a measure of how responsive supply is to a change in price.

We can see from Figure 3.7 that firm B's willingness to supply is more price elastic than firm A. When the price rises from £5 to £10, B is willing to supply an extra 1500 units; A is only willing to supply an extra 1000 units.

The degree of supply elasticity is determined by the ability of firms to react to price changes. If firms are operating at full capacity, an increase in the price is unlikely to draw forward increased supply as firms simply cannot expand output. In contrast, if an industry has spare capacity, factories running below maximum capacity and access to additional sources of labour is relatively easy, then supply is likely to be more elastic, or responsive to an increase in the price. We will return to the importance of supply elasticity in Chapter 4 when discussing markets in more detail.

Cost inefficiency

Our discussion so far has assumed that firms are operating on the cost curve. This is troublesome, since some firms are more cost-effective than their rivals; and in addition some firms are better at raising productivity over time. In Box 3.3 the cost disadvantage of Chinese aluminium producers is highlighted and the opportunities for more cost-efficient producers, like Alcoa, are discussed.

If firms have the same productive technology, they have the same knowledge and manufacturing know-how. As such, they are assumed to share the same cost curves. However, if one firm pays more for its workers, or uses them less effectively, then this firm will operate off its cost curve, as illustrated in Figure 3.8.

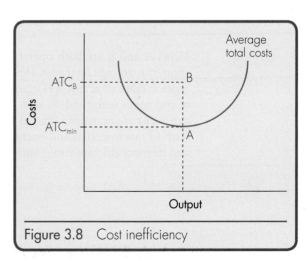

Figure 3.8   Cost inefficiency

Box 3.3

Cost inefficiencies in the Chinese aluminium industry

It has been so common for Chinese companies to be among the lowest-cost producers in an industry that it comes as something of a shock when they are not. Klaus Kleinfeld says aluminium is an example of an industry in which China has no particular cost advantage; and as a result is likely to become an increasingly significant importer in the next few years.

'When you look at the structure of the Chinese aluminium industry, it is not a very competitive industry. It's very expensive and it's not particularly clean,' Mr Kleinfeld says. 'What you're seeing here is an industry structure that doesn't really quite fit. It is very energy-intense and energy is probably the thing that China has least.' China's relative weakness could create opportunities for Alcoa, Mr Kleinfeld says at the company's modest New York offices – the largest corporate centre is in Pittsburgh.

As the largest producer and consumer of aluminium, China accounts for more than 40 per cent of global supply and demand, and its market is growing at a startling pace. Demand rose 21 per cent last year, and Alcoa expects a 17 per cent rise this year. Industrialization and urbanization are driving demand for aluminium for uses including construction, packaging, cars and aircraft. Barring a collapse in the Chinese economy, growth is likely to continue. Brook Hunt, the metals research firm owned by Wood Mackenzie, has forecast that Chinese aluminium demand will rise from 19.8 million tonnes this year to 29.8 million tonnes in 2015.

However, Mr Kleinfeld says, the Chinese industry has weaknesses. For a start, its supply of bauxite,

the raw material, is insufficient. China imports about 40 per cent of its needs, and a third of domestic production is mined underground, a high-cost means of extraction compared with the surface operations used for production in countries such as Australia and Guinea.

Of the Chinese refineries that turn bauxite into alumina, the intermediate product, 37 per cent are in the top quartile in the world for costs. They are also mostly coal-fired, causing much of the pollution that China is seeking to control. Smelting alumina to make aluminium is energy-intensive to the extent that energy typically accounts for about 40 per cent of the cost of production, putting Chinese plants at an even greater disadvantage. About 45 per cent of China's smelters are in the top cost quartile.

In the coming years, the pressure on those plants will intensify. Chinese aluminium production is still likely to grow – Brook Hunt estimates that in 2015 China will import 2 million tonnes, or only about 7 per cent of its demand.

Mr Kleinfeld says that will have significant implications for the industry. 'You will see a huge opportunity for the industry to help in renovating the Chinese aluminium industry by imports and by co-operating outside with Chinese firms.'

Firms A and B are both operating at the output level which is associated with the lowest short-run average total cost. However, only A is operating on the curve and achieving minimum average total cost ATC_{min}. B has much higher costs and this reflects a significant degree of cost inefficiency and, as such, A has a cost advantage over its rival. The reasons why this can occur are numerous, and in the case of Chinese aluminium producers relate to the high costs of raw materials and energy prices. This means that Chinese producers are at point B and its more efficient rivals, such as Alcoa, are at point A.

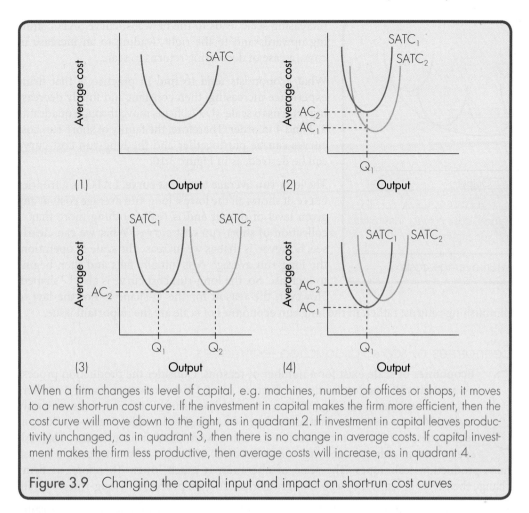

When a firm changes its level of capital, e.g. machines, number of offices or shops, it moves to a new short-run cost curve. If the investment in capital makes the firm more efficient, then the cost curve will move down to the right, as in quadrant 2. If investment in capital leaves productivity unchanged, as in quadrant 3, then there is no change in average costs. If capital investment makes the firm less productive, then average costs will increase, as in quadrant 4.

Figure 3.9   Changing the capital input and impact on short-run cost curves

3.6 The nature of productivity and costs in the long run

In the long run, both capital and labour are variable. Firms can change the number of machines or the amount of office space that they use. Therefore, the law of diminishing returns does not determine the productivity of a firm in the long run. This is simply because there is no fixed capital in the long run to constrain productivity growth. So, in the long run, productivity and costs must be driven by something else. This something else is termed **returns to scale**.

> Returns to scale simply measure the change in output for a given change in the inputs.

Increasing returns to scale exist when output grows at a faster rate than inputs. Decreasing returns exist when inputs grow at a faster rate than outputs. Constant returns to scale exist when inputs and outputs grow at the same rate.

This is not complicated. Look at Figure 3.9: in quadrant 1, we have the short-run average total cost curve, SATC, with which we are familiar. Now consider adding more capital and labour to the production process.

In so doing we have changed the scale of operation and we now have a new cost curve. In quadrant 2, we have the situation where the new cost curve $SATC_2$ moves down and to the right. The company can now produce the same level of output Q_1 for the lower average cost of AC_2. This is increasing returns to scale. As we increase inputs, outputs grow faster, so the cost per unit must fall. In quadrant 3, increasing the scale moves the cost curve $SATC_2$ to the right and leaves average costs constant, a case of constant returns to scale. In quadrant 4,

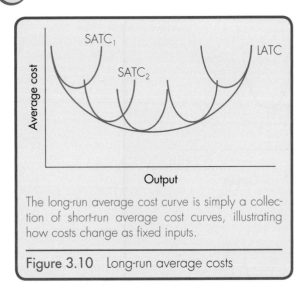

The long-run average cost curve is simply a collection of short-run average cost curves, illustrating how costs change as fixed inputs.

Figure 3.10   Long-run average costs

increasing scale leads to the new cost curve SATC$_2$ shifting upwards and to the right, leading to an increase in costs, a case of decreasing returns to scale.

What economists tend to find in practice is that firms experience increasing, then constant and finally decreasing returns to scale: that is, firms move through quadrants 2, 3 and 4 in order. Therefore, the family of short-run cost curves can be put together and the long-run cost curve can be derived, as in Figure 3.10.

The long-run average total cost curve, LATC, is a frontier curve. It shows all the lowest long-run average costs at any given level of output and is really nothing more than a collection of short-run cost curves. What we can clearly see, however, is that as we increase the scale of operation, the long-run average cost initially falls and then begins to increase. So, the long-run cost curve is also U-shaped. However, the reason for the U-shape is not the law of diminishing returns; rather, in the long run economies of scale are the important issue.

Economies of scale: production techniques

Economies of scale cause long-run average costs to fall as output increases.

Economies of scale exist for a number of reasons. Consider the production process associated with making Fords and Ferraris. At a Ford production facility, workers might be capable of making 1000 cars in a 24-hour shift. Ferrari workers may only make 1000 cars in a year. At massive levels of scale, Ford employs mass-production techniques; one person is responsible for fixing tyres, another for exhausts. This task specialization aids productivity and cuts costs. At Ferrari it is not possible to use mass-production techniques. The scale of operation is much lower. Therefore, as firms change their level of scale, they also change their production process and long-run costs fall.

Box 3.4 shows that while Samsung and Apple compete in the smartphone market, Samsung is also one of Apple's most important component suppliers. Samsung's strategy is to achieve economies of scale in component supply by offering to also supply its main rivals.

Box 3.4

How much of an iPhone is made by Samsung?

Apple doesn't make the iPhone itself. It neither manufactures the components nor assembles them into a finished product. The components come from a variety of suppliers and the assembly is done by Foxconn, a Taiwanese firm, at its plant in Shenzhen, China.

Samsung is an important supplier for Apple. It provides some of the phone's most important components: the flash memory that holds the phone's apps, music and operating software; the working memory, or DRAM; and the applications processor that makes the whole thing work. Together these account for 26 per cent of the component cost of an iPhone.

This puts Samsung in the somewhat unusual position of supplying a significant proportion of one of its main rival's products, since Samsung also makes smartphones and tablet computers of its own. Apple is one of Samsung's largest customers, and Samsung is one of Apple's biggest suppliers. This is actually part of Samsung's business model: acting as a supplier of components for others gives it the scale to produce its own products more cheaply. For its part, Apple is happy to let other firms handle component production and assembly, because that leaves it free to concentrate on its strengths: designing elegant, easy-to-use combinations of hardware, software and services.

Adapted from an article in *The Economist*, 'Apple and Samsung's symbiotic relationship', 10 August 2011. © The Economist Newspaper Limited, London 2011.

Indivisibilities

In order to operate as a commercial airline you have to buy a jumbo jet. Assume the jumbo has 400 seats and you plan to fly between Manchester and Dubai, but only manage to find 300 passengers a day. You cannot chop off the back of the plane to cut your costs! But if you increase your scale and buy a second plane and use this to fly between Dubai and Hong Kong, you might find another 100 passengers who wish to fly Manchester to Hong Kong, via Dubai. In essence, this is nothing more than spreading fixed costs. The same arguments can be made regarding professional corporate staff. A company may only need one accountant, one lawyer and one marketing executive. In a small company there are not many accounts to manage, many contracts to negotiate and sign, or many marketing campaigns to organize. However, as the scale of the company grows, the utilization of these expensive professional staff improves. The accountant manages more accounts and the lawyer oversees more contracts and, as a result, the cost per unit of output falls.

Box 3.5 highlights the construction of the world's tallest building, Burj Khalifa, Dubai. The indivisibility is land space. Once this has been purchased it can be increasingly exploited by

Box 3.5

The world's tallest building: the Burj Khalifa, Dubai

Burj Khalifa construction timeline

January 2004	Excavation started
February 2004	Piling started
March 2005	Superstructure started
June 2006	Level 50 reached
January 2007	Level 100 reached
March 2007	Level 110 reached
April 2007	Level 120 reached
May 2007	Level 130 reached
July 2007	Level 141 reached – world's tallest building
September 2007	Level 150 reached – world's tallest free-standing structure
April 2008	Level 160 reached – world's tallest man-made structure
January 2009	Completion of spire – Burj Khalifa tops out
September 2009	Exterior cladding competed
January 2010	Official launch ceremony

Construction highlights

Over 45 000 m³ (58 900 cubic yards) of concrete, weighing more than 110 000 tonnes were used to construct the concrete and steel foundation, which features 192 piles buried more than 50 metres (164 feet) deep. Burj Khalifa's construction will have used 330 000 m³ (431 600 cubic yards) of concrete and 39 000 tonnes (43 000 ST; 38 000 LT) of steel rebar, and construction will have taken 22 million man-hours.

Exterior cladding of Burj Khalifa began in May 2007 and was completed in September 2009. The vast project involved more than 380 skilled engineers and on-site technicians. At the initial stage of installation, the team progressed at the rate of about 20 to 30 panels per day and eventually achieved as many as 175 panels per day.

The tower accomplished a world record for the highest installation of an aluminium and glass façade, at a height of 512 metres. The total weight of aluminium used on Burj Khalifa is equivalent to that of five A380 aircraft and the total length of stainless steel bull nose fins is 293 times the height of the Eiffel Tower in Paris.

In November 2007, the highest reinforced concrete core walls were pumped using 80 MPa concrete from ground level; a vertical height of 601 metres, smashing the previous pumping record on a building of 470 metres on the Taipei 101, the world's second tallest tower, and the previous world record for vertical pumping of 532 metres for an extension to the Riva del Garda Hydroelectric Power Plant in 1994. The concrete pressure during pumping to this level was nearly 200 bars.

The amount of rebar used for the tower is 31 400 tonnes – laid end to end this would extend over a quarter of the way around the world.

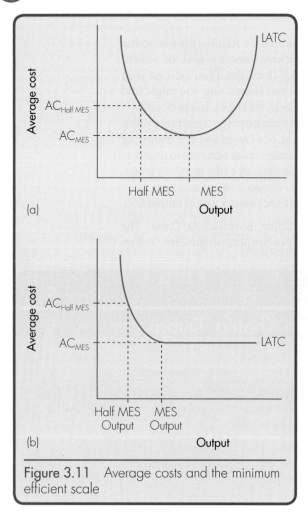

Figure 3.11   Average costs and the minimum efficient scale

building more floors. Air space is free, land space is not. Therefore, while often being monuments to engineering ingenuity and visually appealing, skyscrapers rest on the economic foundations of economies of scale. This is very true in areas of high population density and where land prices are high: New York, Shanghai, Taipei and Dubai – all places where skyscrapers are popular.

Geometric relationships

Have you ever noticed that bubbles are always round? Engineers and business managers have. Bubbles are round because they provide the biggest volume for the smallest surface area. More specifically, volume grows at a faster rate than the surface area. Volume is a measure of storage capacity. So, if we need to create a tank to brew beer, and we decide to double the volume of the tank, the material needed to cover the surface area, the sides and bottom, will not double in size. Instead, it will grow at a slower rate. Hence, it becomes proportionately cheaper to build larger tanks than it does to build smaller tanks. Look around your lecture theatre – we expect it will be big.

Diseconomies of scale

Long-run average costs will eventually begin to rise. The most obvious reason is that, as companies increase in size, they become more difficult to control and co-ordinate. More managerial input is required to run the business, and managers themselves require additional management. So, as the scale of the company increases, the average cost also increases. Excessive bureaucracy now offsets any productivity gains.

Competitive issues

Firms within a market are often of different sizes. Within the grocery industry there are some very large supermarkets and some much smaller convenience stores. Within education, there are very large universities and some smaller schools and colleges; and within fast food there are huge global chains and small local operators. An important question is how big do you have to be in order to be competitive on cost? To answer this question economists have developed the concept of **minimum efficient scale**, which is the minimum size a firm must be in order to achieve the lowest average total costs. This concept is illustrated in Figure 3.11.

> Minimum efficient scale (MES) is the output level at which long-run costs are at a minimum.

The minimum efficient scale (MES) is the size of operation with the lowest average cost. Operating with a company size only half of the MES results in higher average costs. In Figure 3.11(a) the long-run average total cost is U-shaped and has a region of economies of scale and diseconomies of scale, with constant economies of scale at the minimum point. In Figure 3.11(b) the long-run average total cost curve has economies of scale and then constant economies; that is, as a firm increases its level of output, then average costs remain constant.

In either of the cases illustrated in Figure 3.11, if a company operates at a level of scale significantly below the minimum efficient scale, then it is likely to be competing against its larger rivals at a cost disadvantage. The size of this cost disadvantage varies. In some industries, economies of scale are small and the long-run average cost curve is fairly flat across all output ranges. In other industries, economies of scale are significant. As a general rule, industries that are capital and/or brand intensive generate higher fixed costs and lead to higher minimum efficient scale. Supermarkets, universities, fast food, plus banking and car manufacturing all require large capital and/or brand investment and therefore exhibit high minimum efficient scale.

Firms that are operate at or, in the case of Figure 3.11(b), beyond the minimum efficient scale can be described as following a **cost leadership strategy**. Such a firm leads the industry on cost and this is its main competitive strength. If a firm is small and does not have a cost advantage then it may undertake a number of alternative strategies. First, it might merge with another company in the same line of business. Clearly, the new company will be bigger than the two separate parts and economies of scale can be realized. Alternatively the company can pursue a **product differentiation strategy**. Under such a strategy the company seeks to make its products different from those of the cost leader. When competing products become different, then consumers view them less as substitutes. A product with fewer perfect substitutes faces less price elastic consumers and the firm can charge a higher price and recover its higher costs.

> Under a cost leadership strategy, a firm will seek competitive advantage by reducing average costs and pursuing economies of scale.
>
> Under a product differentiation strategy, a firm will seek a competitive advantage by making its products less substitutable.

Business application: linking pricing with cost structures

Fixed costs have been a dominant feature of this chapter. Professional footballers were shown in the business problem to be fixed costs, as were larger container ships. The development of the Airbus A380 was seen as a fixed cost; and the indivisibility of a skyscraper was also seen as a fixed cost.

In every example, the fixed cost is a major component of total costs. Because an Airbus A380 without fuel weighs around 280 tons, the cost of moving the plane between two airports massively outweighs the cost of moving you and your suitcase. In fact, most airlines would let you fly between London and Sydney for as little as £30 – the same amount as many cheap flights from the UK to some European destinations. This trivial amount is again the variable cost and this time is associated with the cost of issuing tickets, handling your luggage and feeding you en route. This is nothing more than the marginal cost of carrying you between two cities. Prices above £30 are a bonus to the airline. Using this cost-based knowledge, we can now explore the commercial decisions faced by the airlines that have ordered A380s.

More than any other commercial aircraft the A380 is a fixed cost for its operators, and moving the huge airframe between airports represents the bulk of the operators' costs. Interestingly, the aircraft is certified to carry 853 passengers, yet airlines appear to be ordering seating configurations between 480 and 580, presumably filling the free space with extra leg room, bars, gyms and other in-flight leisure facilities. However, we know that volume is crucial when fixed costs are high, because additional volume helps to spread the fixed cost over additional units of output. This lowers cost per unit sold, which ultimately lowers prices. With a simple piece of economic knowledge, it is easy to envisage airlines very quickly moving towards 850 seats on A380s in the pursuit of a cost advantage over their rivals. History also provides a precedent. When the Boeing 747 was first launched, no one knew what to place inside the front end 'bubble'. Ideas of gyms and bars were discussed, before operators decided on extra seating.

Discount airlines, while not yet flying A380s, gain competitive advantage by being cost-efficient. They know how to keep variable costs down through no-frills service and they are extremely effective in dealing with their fixed costs. Load factor is reported by all discount carriers such as Ryanair and easyJet on a monthly basis. Load factor measures how good the airline is at

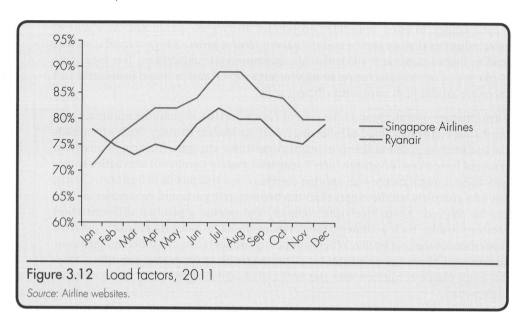

Figure 3.12 Load factors, 2011

Source: Airline websites.

selling all its available seats, and discount carriers can often achieve a load factor of 85 per cent, beating their scheduled rivals (see Figure 3.12). As suggested earlier, the aircraft is a fixed cost of many millions of pounds. But also, as a scheduled airline, the company has committed to fly between two cities on any given day. So, if it flies with no passengers, or a full plane, the airline will still incur fuel costs, staff costs and airport fees. In a sense these costs are also fixed, as they do not vary with the level of output, in this case the number of passengers carried. In the case of no-frills easyJet, the variable costs are exceptionally low as no meals are offered and all tickets are electronic. Therefore, with such high fixed costs, airlines need to utilize their assets. They have to push volume through the aircraft and fill as many seats as possible. Each passenger makes a contribution to paying the huge fixed costs. The more passengers you carry, the more likely it is that you will be able to pay all of your fixed costs. Once this is achieved, you start to make profits.

How do you drive volume through an aircraft? The simple answer is volume itself. For example, if it costs £10 000 to fly a jet between Manchester and Amsterdam and the plane carries 50 passengers, then the average fixed cost per passenger is £10 000/50 = £200. Then the company needs to charge at least £200 per passenger and this is only for a one-way ticket! But if the plane carries 150 passengers, then the average fixed cost is £10 000/150 = £67.

From demand theory we know that we can generate higher demand at lower prices. So, we can drive volume by dropping the price. In part, easyJet tries to achieve this with a twist. If you want to book a flight three months in advance the price will be very cheap. This is because easyJet has lots of seats available and it has a higher need to drive volume. Once momentum picks up in the market and the flight date approaches, it raises the price and begins to extract profits from late bookers. But, crucially, what can be observed from a business perspective is that easyJet is using a fine-tuned pricing strategy to deal with a cost-based problem.

However, we should not be fooled into thinking that in ordering A380s with only 480 seats the likes of Singapore Airlines have got it all wrong. This is because Singapore Airlines' seats are worth more money; easyJet succeeds in driving the load factor forward by sacrificing revenue. Its heavy discounts in the marketplace are used to drive sales volumes. But driving volumes through price reduction damages revenue yields, and easyJet counters this revenue strategy by also minimizing its costs. It is a no-frills airline.

So, no meals, no reissue of the ticket if you miss the flight, plus the use of unpopular airports where the landing fees are lower. In contrast, Singapore Airlines uses popular airports. It undertakes extensive brand development. It provides meals and drinks onboard. It will assist passengers who have missed their flight. In summary, Singapore Airlines provides more than simply a means of transport between two points. It also provides extras such as late checking, drinks and meals during the flight and re-routing if you miss your flight. In addition, some of the earlier adopters of the A380 such as Singapore Airlines have an ability to offer a unique travel experience and can charge a premium price. With few other operators owning an A380, at least in the early years after launch, the demand for a flight on an A380 will be price inelastic. The added extras of gyms and bars are designed to exploit this demand. However, in 10 years' time, when the world is awash with A380s, 850 seats is likely to be common; and do not be surprised if easyJet or Ryanair owns one, or two, for short hops into Europe.

Business application: footballers as sweaty assets

A common business term for making your fixed inputs work harder is 'to sweat the assets' and this is exactly what easyJet is trying to do by making its planes operate at maximum capacity. But how are Premiership football teams utilizing their very expensive football stars?

Few football clubs are looking at the huge expense of footballers as a problem that requires a pricing solution. Admittedly, pricing may play a role. Football fans are willing to pay a higher price to watch a top Premiership side than, say, a Championship one. But the real and most obvious solution for Premiership sides is to increase the volume of games played.

In Figure 3.13, we have the demand for tickets at football games. Assuming the ticket price is £50, the demand curve for Premiership games indicates how many fans will buy at £50. Total revenue from Premiership games is illustrated by rectangle A. If the team qualifies for the Champions League, then more games are played and ticket demand rises. Assuming a similar ticket price of £50, rectangle B defines the additional total revenue. In the recent past, Manchester United have been very successful in using this strategy. By focusing on qualifying for the Champions League and progressing within the competition they can literally sweat their assets, namely, the players. (Admittedly, making sports stars work harder may diminish their average performance and make them injury prone, so there could also be a variable cost to playing more games.)

However, by selling television rights to their games, replica team kits and other merchandising products, Manchester United do not rely only on the revenue streams from the turnstiles. However, once they fail to progress within the Champions League, then a financial hole appears in their business model. Players are utilized less, resulting in less television revenue and gate receipts. Moreover, the value of the brand and the worth of merchandise decreases. Exposure and utilization of the players is a critical success factor for the business model underpinning the club.

Whether the problem is easyJet's or Manchester United's, it is the same problem: one of exploiting fixed costs. Economics provides you with an ability to identify this type of problem and suggests some possible solutions. Implementing and managing the strategic solution is perhaps a more challenging problem.

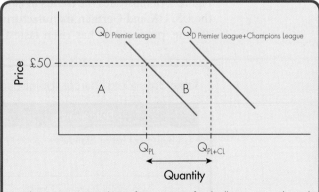

Higher output resulting from more football games played yields more total revenue. This can go to paying the large fixed costs associated with employing top-class footballers.

Figure 3.13 Demand for Premiership games and the Champions League

Business data application: wages and productivity

Finding data on firm-level costs is often very difficult. This difficulty is for a variety of reasons, including the fact that firms often view cost data as confidential. Notwithstanding this problem, economists do try to model cost curves for an industry and measure the size of any economies of scale effects. However, economists often only work with broad-level cost data made available within publically available documents, such as company's financial accounts. For example, total wages paid are often published, but this figure is a combination of workers', managers' and senior managers' earnings. The earnings of workers will vary with output. Higher output will be linked to increased overtime payments and greater use of temporary staff. Senior management pay is more likely to stay constant. Hence, the pay for one part of the labour force is variable and for another it is fixed. This inability to separate costs into fixed and variable makes much of the costs analysis within this chapter difficult to implement. In addition, any modelling of the long run cost curve requires the use of advanced statistical techniques. Such techniques are beyond the scope of this textbook, but they do bring further complexity and problems to any attempt to understand costs within a firm, or industry. Therefore, with such a number of problems, what data are both easily available and of use to business managers?

A message from this chapter is that when seeking to understand costs, it is not just wages that are of interest; the productivity of labour is also important. In the short run the law of diminishing returns highlights how labour productivity can change with output, while in the long run, economies of scale can result from higher labour productivity, for example where a firm employs mass production techniques.

Reflecting the commercial and economic importance of wages and productivity is the good availability of data on these variables. Data relating to labour costs and labour productivity are often available at a national level and are useful to firms which are seeking to understand where to gain a competitive cost base in the global marketplace. Sources of national and international data on labour costs and productivity are generally available from government statistical agencies. A number of useful sources are listed in Table 3.4.

The US Bureau of Labor Statistics provides a reasonably rich source of employment, earnings and labour productivity data across a number of economies, enabling a comparison of key trends to be assessed over many decades.

Figure 3.14 illustrates the trends in labour productivity, measured by output per hour within the US, UK and German manufacturing sectors between 1990 and 2009. Over that period of time, productivity has risen fastest in the US with an average annualized growth rate

Table 3.4 Data sources for labour productivity and costs

Data source	Link
US Bureau of Labor Statistics	http://www.bls.gov
Eurostat	http://epp.eurostat.ec.europa.eu
France, National Institute for Statistics and Economic Studies	www.insee.fr/en
Germany, Federal Statistical Office	http://www.destatis.de/en
UK, Office for National Statistics	http://www.statistics.gov.uk

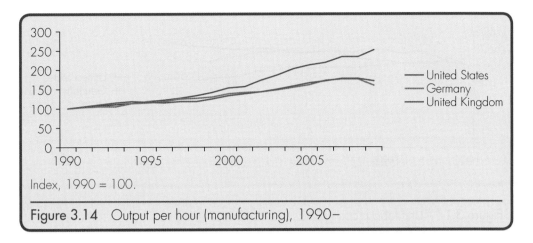

Index, 1990 = 100.

Figure 3.14 Output per hour (manufacturing), 1990–

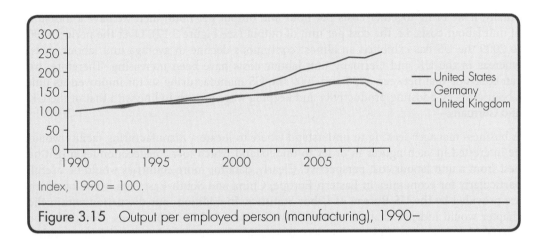

Index, 1990 = 100.

Figure 3.15 Output per employed person (manufacturing), 1990–

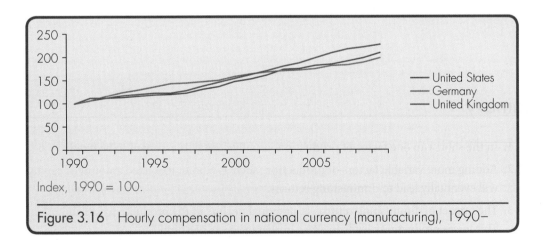

Index, 1990 = 100.

Figure 3.16 Hourly compensation in national currency (manufacturing), 1990–

of around 5 per cent, compared with approximately 3 per cent for Germany and the UK. The same pattern emerges when we use output per employee to measure productivity (see Figure 3.15).

The rise in wages, as measured by hourly compensation, has increased the most in the UK over the period (see Figure 3.16), but the difference between the three economies is much less than the different growth rates in labour productivity.

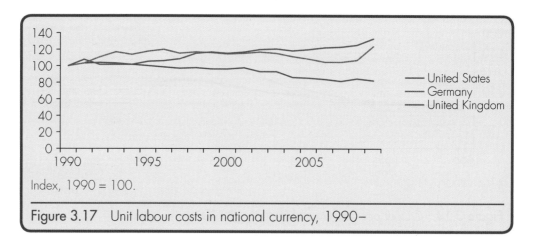

Index, 1990 = 100.

Figure 3.17   Unit labour costs in national currency, 1990–

Finally, if we bring together costs per hour and output per hour, then we have a measure of unit labour costs, i.e. the cost per unit of output (see Figure 3.17). Over the period 1990 to 2009 the US has exhibited an almost continuous decline in average unit labour costs, whereas in the UK and Germany unit labour costs have been increasing. Therefore, we can conclude that between 1990 and 2009 the US manufacturing sector improved its unit labour costs by boosting productivity and keeping wage growth in line with that of the UK and Germany.

A business manager seeking to understand where to locate a manufacturing facility would be interested in such figures in order to understand which locations/economies might be best from a unit labour cost perspective. Clearly, data for more countries would be useful, particularly for economies in Eastern Europe, China and South-East Asia, some of which are provided by the US Bureau of Labor Statistics. In addition, our discussion within the chapter would indicate that the manager, while interested in labour costs, would also be interested in the costs and productivity of capital, the mix of capital and labour within the factory and the potential to commission a large factory and gain significant economies of scale.

Summary

1. In the short run one factor of production, usually capital, is assumed to be fixed.

2. Adding more variable factors of production, such as labour, to a fixed amount of capital will eventually lead to diminishing returns.

3. The impact of diminishing returns is a gradual decline in the productivity of labour. This lower productivity leads to a rise in average costs per unit.

4. The U-shaped nature of the average total and average variable cost curves is related to the change in productivity brought about by the diminishing returns.

5. Average fixed costs are always declining, as the fixed costs are divided by higher levels of outputs.

6. Marginal cost is the cost of producing one more unit. The marginal cost curve is, in effect, a reflection of the marginal product curve for labour. As marginal product declines due to the law of diminishing returns, the marginal cost increases.

7. Supply is linked to firms' marginal cost curves at prices above average variable costs. Entry of more firms increases supply. A reduction in costs would also increase firms' willingness to supply, by boosting potential profits. The price elasticity of supply measures how responsive firms' output is to a change in the price.

8. In the long run all factors of production are variable. Costs are no longer determined by the law of diminishing returns. Instead, they are related to economies of scale.

9. Initially, as companies grow in size, they benefit from economies of scale and unit costs fall. But eventually they will grow too big and diseconomies of scale will cause average costs to rise.

10. High levels of fixed costs generally require high levels of volume.

Learning checklist

You should now be able to:

- Explain the difference between the short and long run
- Calculate and explain the difference between variable, fixed and total costs
- Explain the concepts of marginal product and marginal costs
- Explain and provide examples of the law of diminishing returns
- Understand a firm's decision to operate or shut down and develop this understanding to explain how supply is linked to marginal cost at prices above average variable cost
- Understand the factors that will cause supply to increase
- Explain the concept of price elasticity of supply and understand how the degree of elasticity is linked to firms' abilities to respond to price increases
- Understand the concept of economies of scale and explain why economies of scale may exist
- Explain the concept of minimum efficient scale and understand the importance of operating at the minimum efficient scale
- Explain, using reference to fixed costs, why budget airlines sell at low prices
- Provide economic reasons relating to costs as to why Premiership clubs wish to be in the Champions League
- Understand where data covering labour costs and productivity can be found and how such data can be used to develop an understanding unit labour costs

Questions   connect

1. Explain the difference between the short and the long run.
2. Is it sensible to consider capital, rather than labour, as a fixed factor of production?
3. How does the law of diminishing returns explain the short-run productivity of a firm?
4. What is the difference between total fixed costs, total variable costs and total costs?
5. In the short run, why do average total costs initially fall and then increase?
6. Explain why average fixed costs are always declining. What commercial strategies can be supported by falling average fixed costs?

EASY

7. What are marginal product and marginal costs?

8. Marginal costs must go through the minimum point of which other cost curves: average total costs, average variable costs or average fixed costs?

9. When should a firm shut down? Is it when prices go below average total costs, or average variable costs? Explain.

10. It is reported in the news that two firms have agreed to merge in the belief that they can generate cost savings. Which economic idea would support this belief?

11. Explain why airlines suspend some of their routes during the winter.

12. What are economies of scale and what are considered to be the main sources of economies of scale?

13. From a cost perspective, why do you think ice cream is on special offer in November, but not in July?

14. Is it ever sensible to operate at prices below average variable costs?

15. Do economies of scale offer a competitive advantage?

Exercises

1. True or false?

   (a) Specialization can lead to economies of scale.

   (b) Holding labour constant while increasing capital will lead to diminishing returns.

   (c) The long-run cost curve meets the bottom of each short-run cost curve.

   (d) Pursuit of minimum efficient scale can be a reason for merger.

   (e) A rising marginal cost is a result of diminishing returns.

   (f) Investing in brands represents a fixed cost.

2. A firm faces fixed costs of £45 and short-run variable costs (SAVC) as shown in Table 3.5.

Table 3.5   Short-run costs of production

Output	SAVC	SAFC	SATC	STC	SMC
1	17				
2	15				
3	14				
4	15				
5	19				
6	29				

   (a) Fill in the remainder of the table, where SAFC is the short-run average fixed cost; SATC is the short run average total cost; STC is the short-run total cost; and SMC is the short-run marginal cost.

(b) Plot SAVC, SAFC, SATC and SMC, checking that SMC goes through the minimum points of SAVC and SATC.

(c) The firm finds that it is always receiving orders for six units per week. Advise the firm on how to minimize its costs in the long run. Now consider Table 3.6.

Table 3.6 Short- and long-run decisions

Price	Short-run decision			Long-run decision		
	Produce at a profit	Produce at a loss	Close down	Produce at a profit	Produce at a loss	Close down
18.00						
5.00						
7.00						
13.00						
11.50						

Cost conditions are such that LAC is £12; SATC is £17 (made up of SAVC £11 and SAFC £6). In Table 3.6, tick the appropriate short- and long-run decisions at each price.

3. Your company is considering where to locate a new manufacturing facility. The options include Japan, Singapore and Taiwan. Using data on productivity and wages, present a report which highlights the main trends in unit labour costs for each of these economies and also highlights any other cost concepts which you think your senior management team need to be aware of before taking a final decision on the location of the new facility.

DIFFICULT

Markets in action

Chapter contents

Market theory at a glance   85

4.1 Business problem: picking a winner   85

4.2 Bringing demand and supply together   86

4.3 Changes in supply and demand   88

4.4 Disequilibrium analysis   91

4.5 Price floors and ceilings   92

4.6 Pooling and separating equilibria   93

4.7 Business application: marketing pop concerts – a case of avoiding
the equilibrium price   93

4.8 Business application: labour markets   95

4.9 Business data application: understanding supply and demand
in the car market   96

Summary   98

Learning checklist   98

Questions   99

Exercises   99

Learning outcomes

By the end of this chapter you should understand:

Economic theory

LO1   The concept of market equilibrium

LO2   How changes in demand and supply
lead to changes in the market equilibrium

LO3   How price elasticity influences the size
of changes in market price and output

LO4   Market shortages and surpluses as
instances of market disequilibria

LO5   The difference between pooling and
separating disequilibria

Business application

LO6   How firms can try to manage a market
shortage to boost sales – and product,
or brand – awareness

LO7   The importance of being able to
assess short- and long-run influences
on demand, supply, market output and
prices in the short and long run

LO8   The role of supply and demand in the
car market

At a glance   Market theory

The issue

The price and the amount of goods and services traded change over time. But what causes these changes in particular product markets?

The understanding

Price changes in all markets, whether it is the price of a coffee, entrance to a nightclub or the price of a DVD, stem from changes in supply and demand. Sometimes the price may change simply because demand or supply has changed. In more complex cases, demand and supply could change together. Understanding how and why supply and demand change and the implications for market prices are important business skills.

The usefulness

Markets with upward price expectations will look more attractive than markets with downward price projections. If businesses can appreciate how competing factors will influence the price for their products or of key inputs, they can begin to develop successful strategies for the firm.

(4.1) Business problem: picking a winner

How does a firm, or business person, know which product to promote and sell, and which to leave alone? Take Box 4.1 which contains an article on Samsung and the large bets it has placed on different markets over time. How has Samsung managed to be so successful in choosing the correct bets to place? The company invested in batteries, flash memory, flat screens, all of which turned out to be highly profitable. It is now planning to move into completely different markets over the next five years; how does it know or how does it assure itself that these markets will also be profitable? Samsung appears to have a skill and it is a skill which is different to its technological expertise. Samsung can make great products, but its managers are also highly skilled or gifted in spotting the right growth opportunities. Samsung's managers appear to understand markets and can spot the important characteristics that will create a market that has high volumes and good profit margins. Equally, they also appear to be able to understand when volumes are likely to fall, margins erode and it is time to exit. While technological expertise enables a business to design and build products, commercial expertise requires an understanding of markets.

The importance of understanding future prices and volumes is not just limited to business. Consider your own futures. Some of you may wish to supply yourselves as marketing executives, others as accountants and perhaps some as business economists. The wage or price at which you will be hired will depend upon how many other workers wish to supply themselves to your chosen occupation; and how many firms demand such types of workers. Greater supply will increase competition and the price or wage rate will fall, while higher demand by firms will lead to higher wages. You, therefore, have to decide if the supply of workers into your chosen profession will rise or fall, and whether or not demand will rise or fall. Predicting correctly can potentially lead to higher income levels in the future.

The discussion in this chapter will offer you an economist's understanding of the marketplace, explicitly highlighting the link between demand and supply in marketplaces and illustrating how changes in demand and supply lead to changes in the market price of a product. By the end of the chapter you will have an understanding of how markets work and, more importantly, how business managers might try to make markets work for them.

Box 4.1

The next big bet

In 2000 Samsung started making batteries for digital gadgets. Ten years later it sold more of them than any other company in the world. In 2001 it threw resources into flat-panel televisions. Within four years it was the market leader. In 2002 the firm bet heavily on 'flash' memory. The technology it delivered made the iPhone and iPad a reality.

The handsome payoffs from these ballsy bets made the South Korean company a colossus; last year its sales passed $135 billion. Now it is embarking on a similarly audacious plan to move away from electronics into technologies where it barely has a presence today. It intends to spend $20 billion over 10 years on solar panels, light-emitting diodes (LEDs) used for lighting, electric-vehicle batteries, medical devices and biotech drugs. These businesses shift Samsung away from easily substitutable gadgets towards more essential industrial goods. Just as electronics defined swathes of the twentieth century, the company believes green technology and health care will be central to the twenty-first.

The plans are an ambitious industrial power play, one that challenges some of the world's biggest companies. Success would raise Samsung to new heights. Failure could lead to the firm losing what it already has, no longer able to flourish just as a maker of commodity gadgets and components.

Samsung wants to diversify away from consumer electronics, a market that suffers from falling prices, thin margins, fast product cycles and fickle customers. Chinese rivals may do to Samsung what Samsung did to Western and Japanese firms in the past. 'The majority of our products today will be gone in ten years,' Samsung's patriarch and chairman, Lee Kun-hee, told executives in deliberately alarmist tones last January.

To survive, he said, the company must not only go into the new businesses it has identified, but open itself up to work with partners and even make acquisitions.

By 2020 Samsung's Mr Lee wants the five new business areas to provide $50 billion of revenue, and Samsung Electronics to be a $400 billion company (for all his provocations to his staff, there are still going to be a lot of flat screens and memory sold). It is a brash goal, but 10 years ago people were incredulous when Mr Lee insisted that Samsung, which then had sales of $23 billion, could be the number-one technology company, with sales of $100 billion. It claimed that crown just eight years later. 'This is why you have to believe us,' Mr Hahn, a member of Samsung's strategy team, insists.

Adapted from 'The next big bet', 1 October 2011. © The Economist Newspaper Limited, London 2011.

4.2 Bringing demand and supply together

In Chapter 2, where we examined the price set in the market, we cheated by simply focusing on the willingness to demand. In Chapter 3, when examining the short-run costs of firms, we argued that the firm's supply curve is its marginal cost curve at prices above short-run average variable cost. We are now at a point where we can bring demand and supply together.

Market equilibrium

> Market equilibrium occurs at the price where consumers' willingness to demand is exactly equal to firms' willingness to supply.

In order to understand the marketplace we bring consumers and firms together. In Figure 4.1, we have the supply and demand curve together. Where demand and supply meet is known as the **market equilibrium.**

As a more realistic example, consider buying a second-hand car. Assume the seller (supplier) offers to sell the car for £5000. You examine the car and make an offer to buy at £4000. This is not equilibrium as you and the seller are willing to buy and sell at different prices. A trade will not occur because you cannot agree on the price. But

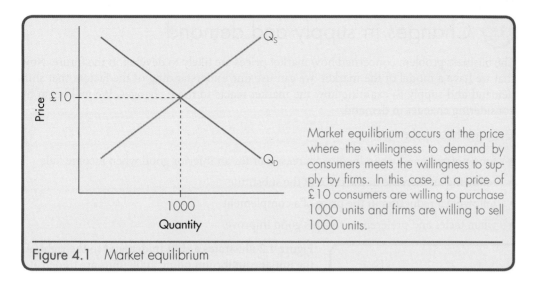

Market equilibrium occurs at the price where the willingness to demand by consumers meets the willingness to supply by firms. In this case, at a price of £10 consumers are willing to purchase 1000 units and firms are willing to sell 1000 units.

Figure 4.1 Market equilibrium

assume the seller is now willing to reduce the asking price to £4500 and you accept. This is the equilibrium – you have both agreed a price at which you are willing to buy and the owner is willing to sell. As such, a trade will occur.

Before moving on it is worth making a few comments about the equilibrium. First, we assume that the equilibrium is unique. The demand and supply curve only intersect at one point. Given the condition of *ceteris paribus*, all other things being equal, the equilibrium is a stable position as there are no forces acting to move the price away from the equilibrium. In the case of our car, both the seller and the buyer are happy to trade at the agreed price of £4500. Second, any other combinations of price and quantity that are not the equilibrium values are described as market **disequilibria**.

> In situations of disequilibria, at the current price the willingness to demand will differ from the willingness to supply.

Third, if the market is in disequilibrium, then, as with the case of our car traders, negotiations and resulting price changes will push the market towards its equilibrium position. We will explain these points as we develop your understanding of the market.

For those readers who are mathematically inclined, it is possible to think of the market equilibrium as the solution to a simultaneous equation problem. See Box 4.2 for further details.

Box 4.2

Market equilibrium as simultaneous equations

Since the demand and supply lines in Figure 4.1 are linear, they can be expressed using the equation of a straight line.

$$Q_D = a_d - b_d P$$

where a_d is the intercept and $- b_d$ is the (negative) slope of the demand line

$$Q_S = a_s + b_s P$$

where a_s is the intercept and b_s is the (positive) slope of the supply line.

In equilibrium $Q_D = Q_S$; we can therefore solve the two equations above for P.

So,

$$a_d - b_d P = a_s + b_s P$$

$$b_s P + b_d P = a_d - a_s$$

$$P = (a_d - a_s)/(b_d + b_s)$$

4.3 Changes in supply and demand

The business problem concerned how market prices are likely to develop in the future. Now that we have a model of the market, we can use our understanding of the factors that shift demand and supply to examine how the market reacts to these changes. We will begin by considering changes in demand.

Demand shifts to the right:

- for a normal good when income increases, or for an inferior good when income falls
- following an increase in the price of the substitute
- following a reduction in the price of a complement
- when tastes and preferences for this good improve.

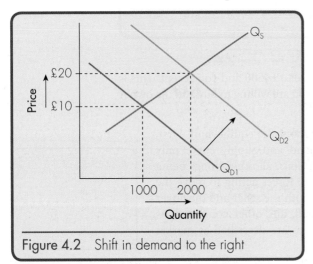

Figure 4.2   Shift in demand to the right

Figure 4.2 illustrates a shift in demand to the right. At the initial equilibrium point, 1000 units are traded at a price of £10. But as demand shifts out to the right, a new equilibrium is achieved and now 2000 units are sold at a higher price of £20.

This can be used to explain property prices when the price of loans is cheap and income is growing steadily. Loans are a complement when buying a home. If you buy a house, you buy a loan. So, cheaper loans increase both the demand for loans and the demand for houses. As income increases, then as a normal good, demand increases for homes. So, for these two reasons the demand line shifts to the right and the equilibrium price and quantity increase.

We can also bring price expectations into the analysis. If you think prices are going to rise in the future, then you will bring forward your consumption. The demand curve for consumption now, as opposed to consumption in the future, shifts to the right.

We can now explore what happens when demand shifts to the left, as in Figure 4.3. Demand shifts to the left:

- for a normal good when income falls, or for an inferior good when income rises
- following a decrease in the price of the substitute
- following an increase in the price of a complement
- when tastes and preferences for this good deteriorate.

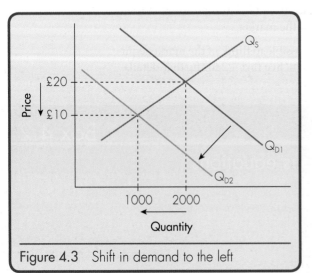

Figure 4.3   Shift in demand to the left

This time we have simply changed the diagram around. We start at an equilibrium price of £20 selling 2000 units and then demand shifts to the left. The equilibrium price falls to £10 selling only 1000 units. Fewer companies are exporting goods around the world, so there is less demand for ships. The demand line shifts to the left and the equilibrium price and quantity fall.

Now let us consider supply. Supply shifts to the right:

- if more firms enter the market
- if the cost of inputs, such as labour, becomes cheaper
- if technological developments bring about productivity gains.

In Figure 4.4, supply has shifted to the right. The equilibrium moves from a price of £20 selling 1000 units to £10 selling 2000 units. If we assume that the supply has moved to the right because more firms are competing in the market, then this outcome appears sensible.

Increased competition should lead to a drop in prices and more consumers taking up the product. The Internet is a significant technological development and it effectively cuts the costs of being a product provider. For example, rather than having to buy or lease many high-street shops, a new retailer can deal with its customers over the Internet. This significantly reduces its costs. Hence the market price, in major Internet areas such as travel, should fall. Lower prices mean lower profits and therefore economists predicted the dot.com crash with ease. We will return to Internet-based business in the business applications at the end of the chapter.

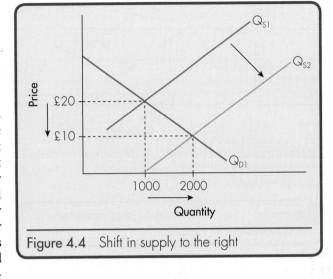

Figure 4.4   Shift in supply to the right

Let us now examine a shift in supply to the left. Supply shifts to the left:

- if firms exit the market
- if the cost of inputs, such as labour, becomes expensive.

If supply shifts to the left, as in Figure 4.5, then the equilibrium price moves from £10 selling 2000 units to £20 selling 1000 units. This might occur if one firm exited the market or took steps to reduce its capacity. Airlines sometime use this strategy. They take aircraft off unpopular routes, or swap large jumbos for smaller ones. Both tactics reduce capacity/supply on particular routes. As this happens, the cost of running the airline drops and the market price for tickets increases. The airline is then more likely to make a profit.

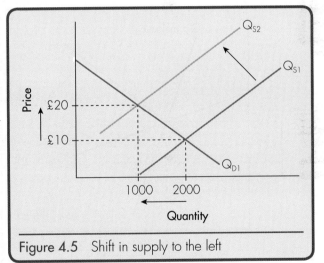

Figure 4.5   Shift in supply to the left

Elasticity and changes in the equilibrium

It is also worth noting that the elasticity of supply and demand will influence how the equilibrium changes. In Figure 4.6, we have an inelastic and an elastic supply curve and we can observe what happens to the equilibrium when we shift demand to the right.

Under inelastic supply we should expect that supply will not react strongly to a change in the price, and this is what we observe. The price rises from £10 to £30, but output only increases from 100 to 200 units. In the case of elastic supply, the increase in demand brings about a large change in output, 100 to 500 units, but only a small rise in the price, from £10 to £13.

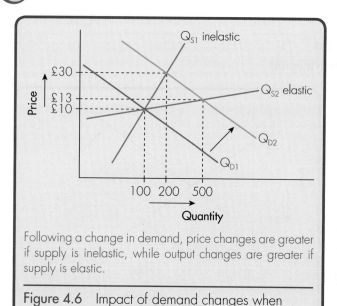

Following a change in demand, price changes are greater if supply is inelastic, while output changes are greater if supply is elastic.

Figure 4.6 Impact of demand changes when supply is elastic or inelastic

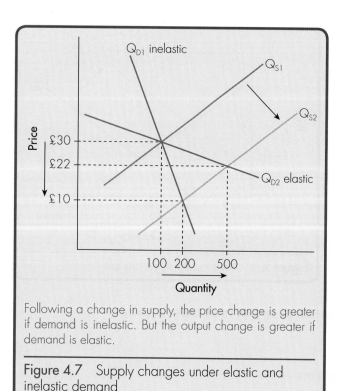

Following a change in supply, the price change is greater if demand is inelastic. But the output change is greater if demand is elastic.

Figure 4.7 Supply changes under elastic and inelastic demand

Why might supply be inelastic?

The elasticity of supply reflects the ability of the supply side of the market to react to price changes. So, if prices increase, will suppliers be willing to supply more? If supply is inelastic, then the answer to this question will be no. Inelastic supply can result from an inability to react to prices, or indeed a desire to control supply.

If the ability to supply is determined by access to fixed assets, such as office, retail or manufacturing space, then even with higher demand, it takes time for increased capacity to be built and for supply to increase. However, if during a recession, demand is low and firms are not utilizing all of their capacity, then any increase in prices is likely to result in a rapid increase in supply. Therefore, excess capacity can lead to elastic supply.

Firms, industries and professions may also actively seek to control, or at least influence, supply. Lawyers and accountants restrict supply into their professions through the need to pass professional examinations in order to act as a lawyer or an accountant. Some people comment that lawyers and accountants have a licence to print money and, in part, you now know why.

Sport is also a successful industry. Formula 1 (F1) motor racing strictly controls the number of teams in the sport and the number of races in a season. It also controls television rights for the F1 season and it can thereby limit the means by which the races are supplied to the viewing public. This is all done with the objective of running a commercially profitable sporting event. The success of Premiership football and other leagues across Europe is similarly linked to the control of supply. Television access to games is strictly controlled by governing bodies, which sell television rights en bloc to television networks. The alternative would be for each club to sell its games on an individual basis. For example, one week Manchester United might sell their game with Liverpool to one broadcaster, while the week after they could sell their game with Chelsea to another channel. Instead, the supply of games is managed. Out of a possible 400 games a season, around 60 are shown per year by a small number of television networks. By making the product scarce, or by engineering inelastic supply, the price in the television market for football games will rise.

In Figure 4.7, we consider how a change in supply affects the equilibrium when demand is elastic or inelastic. When demand is elastic, the increase in supply brings about a small change in the price, dropping from £30 to £22, with output increasing from 100 to 500 units. In the case of inelastic demand, the increase in supply generates a large drop in the price from £30 to £10, but only a small change in output from 100 to 200 units.

The clear lesson from this example is that, if faced with inelastic demand for your product, do not increase your production capacity and thereby increase supply, because the price will drop quicker than output increases and your total revenues will fall. However, if you are faced with elastic demand, do consider increasing your capacity and supplying more to the market, as output grows at a faster rate than the declining price and so total revenues will rise.

 4.4 ## Disequilibrium analysis

So far we have only considered the market to be in equilibrium, where demand equals supply. In reality, markets may never be in equilibrium; they may instead always be moving between equilibrium positions. First, let us consider a situation in which the price is higher than the equilibrium.

In Figure 4.8, the current market price of £10 is higher than the equilibrium price of £8. At a price of £10 consumers are willing to demand 1000 units, but firms are willing to supply 2000 units. This is clearly not an equilibrium position. With supply exceeding demand by 2000 − 1000 = 1000 units, the market is said to be running a surplus. In effect, firms will be left with excess stock in their warehouses. We suggested earlier that natural forces would push the market towards the equilibrium, so how might this happen?

If the firm has too much stock, then, in accounting terms, its working capital is tied up. The firm has spent money making the product and it now needs to sell the product in order to free its cash for future production. The only way to sell the excess stock is to begin discounting the price until everything is sold. The more excess stock a firm has, the bigger the discount it has to offer. You will have noticed the trick used by clothing retailers: '50% off' is written large but 'on selected ranges' is written much smaller. The goods that are discounted by 50 per cent will almost certainly be those that few, if any, people wanted at the original price. The biggest discounts are generally offered on the products where the retailer has observed the biggest difference between its willingness to supply and consumers' willingness to demand. Therefore, the biggest discounts are offered on the products where the retailer has the biggest level of unwanted stock.

Figure 4.9 illustrates the opposite situation, a market shortage. This time we have the market price of £8, which is below the market equilibrium price of £10. At £8, we can see that consumers are willing to demand 2000 units, but firms are only willing to supply 1000 units. We now have a shortage of 2000 − 1000 = 1000 units. Consumers would like to buy twice as much of the product as firms are willing to provide. Two responses are likely. Firms may recognize the high demand for their products and raise the price. Or consumers may begin to bid up the price in order to gain access to the product. If you really want to see the market in action, then watch the Internet auction sites for the most popular Christmas presents, such as game consoles, the latest mobile phones or recent film releases on Blu-ray or DVD.

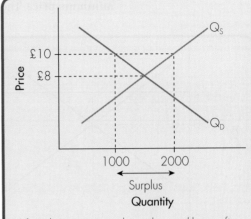

When the price is set above the equilibrium, firms are very willing to supply but consumers are not willing to demand. As a consequence, more is supplied than demanded. Firms are left with excess stock. In this case, at a market price of £10, firms supply 2000 units but consumers only demand 1000 units, leaving a surplus of 1000 units.

Figure 4.8 A market surplus

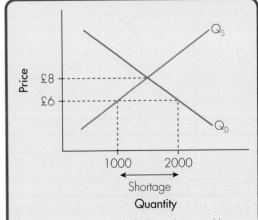

When the price is set below the equilibrium, firms are less willing to supply but consumers are very willing to demand. As a consequence, more is demanded than supplied. In this case, at a market price of £8, firms supply 1000 units but consumers demand 2000 units, leaving a shortage of 1000 units.

Figure 4.9 A market shortage

Price floors and ceilings

> A minimum price/ price floor prevents prices from falling below a set level.

Governments are sometimes interested in preventing prices from going too high or too low. For example, enormous capacity and economies of scale in the brewing and alcoholic drinks sector, plus strong competition among retailers and supermarkets have forced down the price of drinks, fuelling increased consumption of alcohol. To address the excess consumption of alcohol the government may consider imposing a **minimum price**. The minimum price then acts as a floor below which it is illegal to set a price. To be effective in reducing consumption, the minimum price must be higher than the market equilibrium price.

Figure 4.10 illustrates the impact of a minimum price. In Figure 4.10 a proposed minimum price of £2 for a bottle of wine is above the market price. A minimum price above the market equilibrium results in supply exceeding demand and a surplus of output on the market. Where might that surplus (wine) go? Firms may seek to sell the wine illegally below the minimum price. Some wine may be re-exported to other countries, which would boost supply in that country, reduce the price and fuel binge drinking in another economy. Perhaps not very good for international relations.

Some readers may consider a cheap bottle of wine to be one that costs less than £2. Others might be happy to pay £4 to £5 for what they consider to be a cheap wine. A minimum price of £2 is therefore unlikely to be above the equilibrium price for wine and would have no effect on consumption. If consumers are willing to pay £4, then the only way to reduce consumption is to make the minimum price higher, say £4.50.

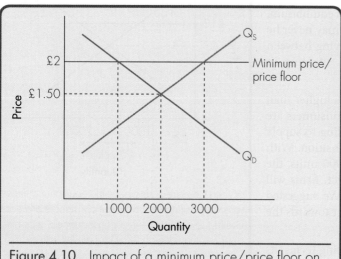

Figure 4.10 Impact of a minimum price/price floor on demand and supply

A government may also be concerned when prices, especially for important items, such as fuel and energy can become too high. In such circumstances, the government may impose **maximum prices**. A maximum price acts as a price ceiling above which it is illegal to set prices. Figure 4.11 illustrates the impact of a maximum price on the demand and supply for fuel. If the government sets a maximum price of £1 per litre of fuel, then with an equilibrium price of around £1.40, the market is likely to be in disequilibrium and be characterized by a significant shortage of supply. While households may find the fuel price attractive, the inability to find fuel, coupled with the likelihood of having fuel stolen/siphoned from your car will be extremely annoying.

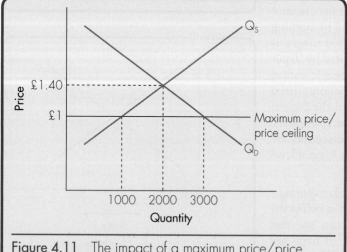

Figure 4.11 The impact of a maximum price/price ceiling on supply and demand

> A maximum price/ price ceiling prevents prices from rising above a set level.

Pooling and separating equilibria

Consider the second-hand car market and assume good-quality cars cost £5000 and bad-quality cars cost £2500. Sellers of good and bad cars specialize in each type of car. So, if you want a good car, you go to a good car seller. Under these arrangements you would be willing to pay £5000 if you wanted a good car, or £2500 if you wanted a bad car. This is a **separating equilibrium**, as each type of product is sold in a separate market.

Now consider a more realistic situation where good and bad cars are sold together. This is a **pooling equilibrium**, where the consumer finds it difficult to differentiate between good and bad products. So, unlike the separating equilibrium, both types of car are sold in the same market.

When you arrive at the dealership you are offered the following option. In a cloth bag are a number of car keys: 50 per cent open up good cars, 50 per cent open up bad cars. How much would you be willing to pay to put your hand in the bag and drive away with a car?

The statistical approach is to work out the expected value of the car. You have a 0.5 chance of gaining a good car worth £5000 and a 0.5 chance of ending up with a bad car worth £2500. The expected value is therefore $0.5 \times £5000 + 0.5 \times £2500 = £3750$.

So, all cars are sold at the pooling equilibrium price of £3750. If this permeates across the market, sellers of bad cars gain an extra £1250, while suppliers of good cars lose £1250. Over time more bad cars will come to the market and good cars will leave the market. This is known as **Gresham's Law**, where bad products drive out good products.

> A separating equilibrium is where a market splits into two clearly identifiable sub-markets with separate supply and demand.
>
> A pooling equilibrium is a market where demand and supply for good and poor products pool into one demand and one supply.
>
> Gresham's Law states that an increasing supply of bad products will drive out good products from the market.

Suppliers of good-quality cars under a pooling equilibrium are disadvantaged because they are unable to differentiate their products from the bad offerings. In order to solve this problem they need to find a way of creating a separating equilibrium. The way to achieve this is to do something that the bad suppliers would be unwilling to copy. Therefore, in the used car markets we can observe car dealerships offering cars with 100-point checks and 12-month warranties. Offering a 12-month warranty is cheap for good car sellers because the likelihood of the car breaking down is low. In contrast, the bad car suppliers are unwilling to offer warranties because the bad cars are likely to break down and, therefore, the cost of honouring the warranties would be very high.

In terms of a further example, consider the purchase of car insurance. The insurance company asks for many details before quoting you a price for car insurance. How old are you? How many years no claims bonus do you have? Where do you live? What type of car do you drive? The insurer is trying to separate the market by assessing whether you are a good or bad risk. If it did not do this, then clearly the market for insurance risks would move towards a pooling equilibrium. Every driver would be charged the same price for car insurance. However, in such a market bad drivers, with high accident or theft rates, pay less than they should, while good drivers, with low accident and theft rates, pay more than they should. Therefore, by separating the market the insurance company is able to charge the right insurance premiums for good and bad drivers.

Business application: marketing pop concerts – a case of avoiding the equilibrium price

The preceding discussion argued that markets will always find the equilibrium. So-called market forces push the market to a state where demand equals supply. This seems fairly reasonable, but how might a firm manage its market for strategic benefit? Or, can a firm control market forces? A successful business person would more than likely answer this last question with a yes.

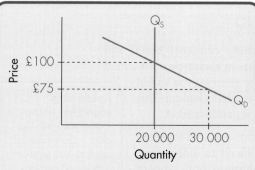

The equilibrium price of £100 clears the market with supply equalling demand. But at a discounted price of £75, a market shortage of tickets can be engineered, with demand outstripping supply. This helps to ensure an instant sell-out success for the concert.

Figure 4.12 Managing the market

Take, for example, the task of managing a pop star. Whether or not you like Madonna, she is undoubtedly a megastar. Some of her status stems from talent, but some also stems from commercial management. By way of an example, assume Madonna is going on tour to promote her new album and you are overseeing the task of pricing tickets for various venues.

An arena being used by Madonna holds 20000 people. The supply of seats at this venue is fixed at 20000, so supply is perfectly inelastic. If we plot demand and supply, then the result may look like Figure 4.12.

In equilibrium, demand equals supply. The task is to sell 20000 tickets, so your business problem becomes one of finding the price that will generate a demand of 20000. In this example, we have assumed that £100 is the price that will ensure a demand of exactly 20000.

Unfortunately, £100 as an equilibrium price is not a good outcome for Madonna. Selling all of the 20000 tickets for £100 is a huge success but, since £100 is the equilibrium price, the concert is only just a sell-out. Madonna is a megastar and, as such, the media and press expect her to sell out in a matter of hours. A price of £100 will *only just* ensure that she sells out.

However, if we set a ticket price of £75 we can engineer a ticket shortage in the market. At £75, 30000 fans are willing to buy a ticket. With only 20000 seats the concert will be a sell-out, with an additional 10000 fans still trying to find a ticket on the black market. The importance of a sell-out concert will be evidenced by the positive media attention. Column inches in the celebrity pages of the press confirming Madonna's success will help to reinforce her image as a major celebrity. In this way, Madonna's management company is sacrificing ticket revenue, but it is gaining free advertisements in the press.

Box 4.3

Madonna's 2012 tour 'on track' to be among 'top 10 of all time'

Ongoing chatter that the Madonna tour, and by extension her multi-rights deal with Live Nation, are underperforming is 'baseless', according to sales figures provided by tour producer Arthur Fogel, chairman of Live Nation Global Touring.

The precipitous drop of *MDNA* in its second week, while certainly not something an artist would want, actually has little to do with the performance of Live Nation's 10-year, $120 million multi-rights deal with Madonna. The days of tours supporting records are long gone; for some time now, touring drives record sales, not the reverse, and the Madonna touring business is more than solid.

As for the multi-rights deal, while *MDNA* is the first album under the 360, the upcoming trek is not the first

tour. That would be 'Sticky and Sweet' of 2008–09, which grossed $408 million, according to Billboard Boxscore, the third-highest gross all-time and the highest ever notched by a solo artist. Merchandising is also a component of this tour and in Madonna's case is a significant revenue producer. Finally, given that the entire deal is, at its core, performance-based and assuredly tour-driven in its concept, Madonna is delivering.

These are the facts: 76 Madonna shows at arenas and stadiums are on sale in North America and Europe combined. More than 1.4 million tickets have been sold, banking about $214 million for an average $2.7 million per show in a mix of stadiums and arenas. And the tour doesn't even begin until 29 May in Tel Aviv, first hitting America in Philadelphia on 28 August.

'This tour is completely on track to end up in the top 10 tours of all time, especially considering we haven't put South America or Australia on sale,' Fogel from promoter 360 tells Billboard.biz. 'To say this tour is not performing is so off base I don't even know what to say. When this tour is said and done, combined with "Sticky and Sweet", you're talking $750 million in gross ticket sales. That sounds pretty impressive to me.'

The price reduction in the marketplace also generates positive momentum in the market for Madonna's other products. As a successful recording artist, fans will be more willing to buy Madonna's album, calendars, T-shirts and DVDs. Furthermore, a sell-out concert this year ensures that Madonna can tour next year. However, if the tickets are mispriced and sales are slow, negative press will follow. This is only likely to slow demand for Madonna's products. Her megastar status will come under question and next year's tour will be in doubt.

Adapted from an article on Billboard by Ray Waddell, 19 April 2012.

(4.8) Business application: labour markets

Input markets

Firms not only sell into markets, they also buy inputs, such as labour and raw materials, from markets. It is therefore important to understand how these **input markets** will develop as rises in input prices will lead to increases in firms' costs.

> Input markets are where factor inputs, such as land, labour, capital or enterprise, are traded.

For example, consider the market for professional staff, bankers, lawyers and accountants. In recent years the wages offered to these individuals were very high. These high wages reflected a booming economy, where the demand for services offered by professionals in lending, property transactions and financial management were high. The demand shifted to the right, as in Figure 4.13, and wage rates increased.

Two further influences then occurred. First, the high wage rates being paid to professional staff attracted workers into the banking, legal and accounting industries, graduates entered the sector and new student recruitment at university level moved towards professional services courses. The supply of capable workers shifted to the right and wage rates softened. Then the credit crunch recession led to many firms going bust and massive cutbacks in employment.

So, when thinking now about your future employment plans, it is essential to have a view on the future path of demand and supply in your chosen career area. See Table 4.1 for details on earnings and employment for graduates by subject groupings. High wages in some sectors are likely to attract increased supply. By the time graduates leave university, the extra supply, in the absence of additional demand, will lead to falling wages. So what might appear to be an attractive career today, may not be that attractive once you enter the labour market.

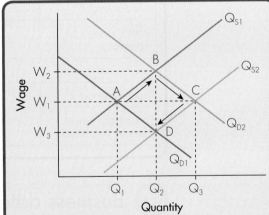

Beginning at A: demand for professional workers shifts to the right following a rise in demand for their services in a booming economy. The equilibrium moves to B and wage rates rise to W_2. Higher wages attract new additional workers into the market and supply shifts from Q_{S1} to Q_{S2}. The equilibrium is now at C and wages fall to W_1. Following the credit crunch recession, demand for professional staff shifts back to the left from Q_{D2} to Q_{D1}. The equilibrium is now at D and wages have fallen to W_3.

Figure 4.13   Input price changes over time

Table 4.1 Graduate earnings and employment, 2011

Subject	Graduate salary (£)	Non-graduate salary (£)	Straight to graduate job (%)
Dentistry	30 143	–	91
Medicine	29 146	–	91
Chemical engineering	27 151	–	48
Veterinary medicine	25 807	–	86
Economics	25 637	16 249	36
General engineering	24 937	24 246	47
Mathematics	23 160	15 807	28
Nursing	21 910	19 415	90
Computer science	21 712	16 465	43
Accounting & finance	21 551	16 157	27
Business studies	21 007	15 776	40
Education	20 890	14 164	60
Food science	20 505	15 880	48
Pharmacology & pharmacy	20 059	14 236	61
Law	18 911	14 826	17
Sports science	18 315	14 231	32
Hospitality, leisure, recreation & tourism	17 664	14 836	36

 ## Business data application: understanding supply and demand in the car market

The car market provides a useful environment in which to apply and explore our new concepts of supply and demand. Car production is undertaken by a relatively small group of major manufacturers, so the units of production, supply, can be measured by surveys. In addition, when a new car is sold then that car has to be registered, so there is data on demand/consumer purchases. The data are not perfect, because there is not sufficient detail to inform us about consumers' willingness to demand at different prices, or firms' willingness to supply, but it does provide us with a general indication of movements in the market.

Using data provided by the UK Society of Motor Manufacturers, new car registrations fell 4.5 per cent between 2010 and 2011 to 1.8 million units. However, that fall masks some other interesting patterns: the registration of diesel cars rose 5.4 per cent, petrol fell 13 per cent, alternative fuel vehicles increased 10 per cent, private purchases fell 14 per cent, and fleet and business rose by 6 per cent.

In terms of supply, the data available from the Society of Motor Manufacturers show that car production rose 6 per cent in 2011 to 1.2 million units of which 1 million units were exported, representing an increase of 18 per cent on the number exported the year previously.

What does this data on purchases and production tell us about the market for cars? Are prices likely to rise or fall, what other information would we need and how might we worry about near-term equilibrium between supply and demand, and long-term trends towards greater demand for alternative fuel vehicles?

Using the frameworks developed in this chapter we might at first sight worry that supply is outstripping demand and prices could fall, but if we dig into the numbers a little, we can see that domestic production accounts for very little of UK car supply. In 2011 1.8 million cars were purchased in the UK but only 0.2 million of cars produced in the UK were for domestic consumption. Of the cars made in the UK, 1 million are being supplied somewhere else, and 1.6 million cars purchased in the UK are being made somewhere else. Given it is costly to transport cars then the most likely source is Europe.

Data from the European Automobile Manufacturers Association show that new car registrations have changed dramatically across different countries. In Figure 4.14 we can see strong demand growth in Germany, the Netherlands and the Baltic states. This growth is offset by plummeting demand in Portugal, Spain, Greece and Ireland. However, overall, new car registrations across Europe have only fallen by a very modest 1.4 per cent.

What these patterns would tend to suggest is that managers in the automotive sector have to be good at spotting long-term emerging trends and also quickly rebalancing supply capacity to demand conditions across many different markets. For example, over time manufacturers will need to react to the growing demand for alternative fuel vehicles and protect themselves

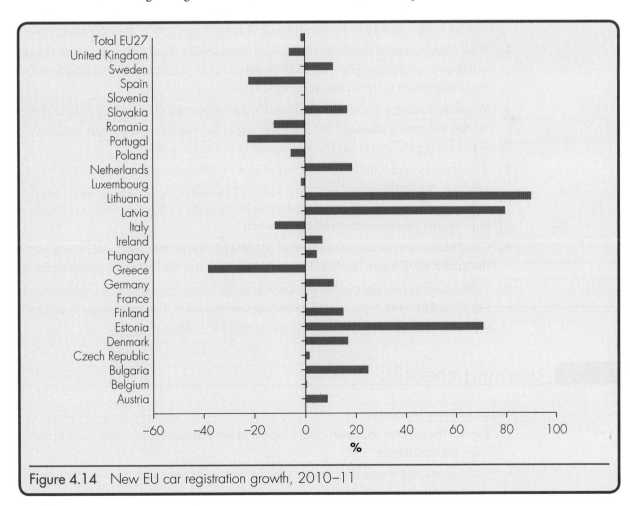

Figure 4.14   New EU car registration growth, 2010–11

from the falling demand for petrol-powered vehicles. Following these long-term trends requires investment, vision and commitment to technology and particular customer groups.

In contrast, balancing existing supply and demand on an annual, perhaps even quarter by quarter, basis requires car manufacturers to know what their supply capacity is and where demand is growing and slowing across Europe. Matching supply and demand by diverting stock and output from declining markets to growing markets will require stockholding facilities and responsive logistic and transport systems. But when €20 000 or more is locked within a motor vehicle, there is a strong incentive to know your market and know where you can find an equilibrium sale.

Summary

1. The supply curve shows a positive relationship between the market price and the willingness to supply.

2. The industry supply curve is the sum of all the individual firms' supply curves.

3. The market equilibrium occurs where the willingness to supply equals the willingness to demand.

4. The equilibrium is changed whenever demand or supply changes. If demand increases, the price will rise and more will be traded. But if supply increases, the price will drop while more will be traded. A reduction in demand leads to a reduction in prices and the amount traded, while a reduction in supply leads to higher prices and less being traded.

5. If the current price is above the equilibrium, supply will exceed demand and the market will show a surplus. Suppliers are likely to discount the price to shift excess stock and eventually return to the equilibrium price.

6. When the current price is below the equilibrium, demand will exceed supply and the market will show a shortage. The price will rise in the market as consumers seek out scarce supply and eventually the market will return to its equilibrium.

7. If consumers cannot differentiate between quality differences among competing products, the market is said to exhibit a pooling equilibrium. Providers of good-quality products will strive to create a separating equilibrium by undertaking behaviour that poor-quality providers are unwilling to match.

8. Good businesses can attempt to control or influence the market. Setting a price below the market equilibrium can help to launch a product and gain valuable market share.

9. Understanding how the market will develop in the future requires an understanding of supply and demand. Such an understanding can be used to forecast changes in product prices and input prices, all of which are essential for strategic planning.

Learning checklist

You should now be able to:

- Explain the concept of market equilibrium and use a demand and supply diagram to show the equilibrium
- Use demand and supply diagrams to analyse changes to price and quantity following changes in demand and supply

- Explain how changes in the equilibrium price and quantity are influenced by the elasticity of demand and supply
- Explain the difference between a shortage and a surplus
- Explain the difference between a pooling and a separating equilibrium
- Explain how firms can benefit from pricing below the equilibrium price
- Explain how an understanding of future trends in demand, supply and prices is of use to business

Questions   connect

1. At a price of £10, consumers are willing to demand 20 000 units and firms are willing to supply 20 000 units. Is this market in equilibrium?

2. Following an economic crisis, a number of banks collapse. What do you think happens to the supply of banking services and the price of banking services in general?

3. If income levels fall in an economy, what do you think will happen to the price of inferior goods and services?

4. As incomes in China rise, the global price of chicken and pork increases. Why?

5. An expansion of the world's shipping fleet threatens to depress the daily charter rates for ocean-going freighters. What must happen to demand in order to keep charter rates relatively constant?

6. Draw a diagram to illustrate a market surplus and a market shortage.

7. If there is a surplus amount of rental office space in a city, what do you expect to happen to rents? Use a diagram to explain your answer.

8. The elasticity of demand for electricity is relatively price inelastic. Will a change in supply have a large or a small impact on the equilibrium price and quantity?

9. What is the difference between a pooling and a separating equilibrium?

10. List three markets where pooling equilibria are a problem.

11. Why is the market for new staff characterized by the problem of adverse selection?

12. Celebrity status brings riches, but will the increase in the number of boy bands, docusoaps and reality television programmes, such as *Big Brother*, change the market price of celebrities?

13. If incomes were falling in an economy would you wish to invest in a housebuilding company?

14. Is studying for a degree a strategy for creating a separating equilibrium in the labour market?

15. Health care in the UK is free. Draw a diagram illustrating how waiting lists for hospital treatment in the UK reflect a market shortage at zero price.

EASY

INTERMEDIATE

DIFFICULT

Exercises

1. True or false?
   (a) An increase in demand for coffee will lead to a higher price at Starbucks.
   (b) The merger of two firms can lead to higher prices.

EASY

(c) The equilibrium price is always optimal for a firm.

(d) Demand and supply are said to move separately under a separating equilibrium.

(e) The adoption of clam phones by celebrities will raise the equilibrium price of clam phones.

(f) Prices above the equilibrium will create a shortage.

2. Suppose that the data in Table 4.2 represent the market demand and supply for baked beans over a range of prices.

Table 4.2   Demand and supply

Price	Quantity demanded (million tins per year)	Quantity supplied (million tins per year)
8	70	10
16	60	30
24	50	50
32	40	70
40	30	90

(a) Plot on a single diagram the demand and supply curve, remembering to label the axes appropriately.

(b) What would be the excess demand or supply if the price was set at 8p?

(c) What would be the excess demand or supply if the price was 32p?

(d) Find the equilibrium price and quantity.

(e) Suppose that, following an increase in consumers' incomes, demand for baked beans rises by 15 million tins per year at all prices. Find the new equilibrium price and quantity.

3. Consider Box 4.3:

(a) Explain the difference between a market surplus and a market shortage.

(b) Draw a demand and supply diagram which illustrates a surplus for Madonna's live performances.

(c) Is the practice of minimizing the supply of concerts by leading artists one of risk minimization or sales maximization?

SECTION

3

Competition and profitability

Section contents

5 Market structure and firm performance 104

6 Strategic rivalry 135

7 Growth strategies 164

8 Governing business 188

Market structure and firm performance

Chapter contents

Perfect competition and monopoly at a glance 105

5.1 Business problem: where can you make profits? 105

5.2 Profit maximization 106

5.3 The spectrum of market structures 111

5.4 Perfect competition 112

5.5 Monopoly 119

5.6 When is a monopoly not a monopoly? 125

5.7 Business application: 'Oops, we're in the wrong box' – the case of the airline industry 126

5.8 Business data application: understanding the forces of competition 127

Summary 132

Learning checklist 132

Questions 132

Exercises 133

Learning outcomes

By the end of this chapter you should understand:

Economic theory

LO1 Why firms maximize profits by producing an output where marginal cost equals marginal revenue

LO2 Perfect competition

LO3 The difference between normal and supernormal profits

LO4 How profit and losses lead to entry and exit

LO5 Monopoly

LO6 How barriers to entry protect supernormal profits

LO7 The key differences in profit, output and prices between perfect competition and monopoly

Business application

LO8 How a monopoly may end up competing with itself

LO9 To what extent a firm can change its competitive environment

LO10 How to use data and Porter's five forces model to assess the strength of competition in an industry

At a glance | Perfect competition and monopoly

The issue

An essential business skill is being able to understand why different market structures create differing levels of competition and, therefore, business performance, particularly in terms of profit. On this matter, economics offers some interesting insights.

The understanding

The understanding rests on how firms compete with each other. Firms can find themselves with any number of competitors. But instead of modelling every possible scenario, economists have concentrated on three: perfect competition, where there are many competitors; monopoly, where there are no competitors; and oligopoly, where there is only a very small number of competitors.

The usefulness

This chapter will provide you with an understanding of the important industrial characteristics which in part influence the level of competition and profitability that your business will generate.

5.1 Business problem: where can you make profits?

The simple answer is that you can make profits in any market where consumers are willing to pay a price that exceeds your costs. But an economist and a successful business person have a more valuable insight into this problem. They can identify markets that are more likely to make profits. They can do this because they understand the factors that determine whether the market price will be in excess of the firm's costs.

However, before we begin the theory, we will take a semi-empirical approach to this problem. Think about a business that you are familiar with and consider how profitable it is. We will take some common examples. Consider the pizza and kebab shops located near your university or accommodation. Are they profitable? We suspect that they make money. But you rarely see a local outlet growing and operating more than one or two outlets. The interiors of the shops are often basic and the decorations tend to be worn. Refurbishments occur only occasionally. So, given that the owners do not grow the business, or invest in new fixtures and fittings, it might be argued that profits are limited.

Now consider Apple, a company so large and profitable that it has cash reserves approaching $100 billion. The article in Box 5.1 suggests that Apple is hoovering cash into its bank account.

So why is it that Apple is so successful and kebab shops are not? It can be argued that Apple has been successful in managing its market and principally its competition. By managing competition effectively, Apple has grown into a successful company. In contrast, there are many kebab and pizza shops around your university. They are all competing with each other. Demand is elastic: if one shop drops its prices, students will flock to this shop. So price competition, or the threat of price competition, keeps prices low. Apple currently faces less competition, its products are distinctive and consumers value the brand. With limited substitutes, Apple faces relatively inelastic demand.

In this chapter we will present the assumption that firms are in business to maximize profits. After explaining how firms should maximize profits, we will examine how the different market structures of perfect competition and monopoly influence the amount of profits earned by a firm in each type of market structure.

Box 5.1

Apple restores US profits with enough cash to cover Greece

Apple's 116 per cent profit growth helped push its total cash to $97.6 billion – enough to cover Greece's debt payments due in the next two years, according to data compiled by Bloomberg.

Apple, the world's largest technology company, beat revenue forecasts by $7.3 billion, the most ever. The performance came during a quarter in which US unemployment averaged 8.7 per cent and about 12.7 million Americans were looking for work.

'They can probably bail out Greece,' Ian Ainsworth, a Toronto-based money manager at Mackenzie Financial Corp., said in a telephone interview. 'It just puts the power of the company in perspective with near $100 billion in cash on the balance sheet and generating that kind of free cash flow. It's hard to conceive of a company with that kind of power.'

Net income more than doubled to $13.1 billion as Apple sold 37 million iPhones and posted $46.3 billion in sales. The total ranks among the highest quarterly profits on record. Apple's earnings were about 11 times the size of Zambia's gross domestic product.

The company's almost $100 billion in cash and equivalents is larger than the combined market value of Boeing Co., Alcoa Inc. and Travelers Cos. – three of the 30 Dow Jones Industrial Average companies. That's enough money to cover Greece's €48.2 billion ($62.56 billion) due in 2012 and €27.9 billion due next year, depending on the exchange rate. The country is facing a €14.5 billion bond payment on 20 March.

For calendar year 2011, Apple's sales rose to $127.8 billion, bigger than the size of New Zealand's economy, according to data compiled by Bloomberg. More iPhones were sold each day in the quarter ending 31 December than babies were born in the world, according to data compiled by Bloomberg and the United Nations.

Apple's $97.6 billion in cash and equivalents is enough for the company to buy 2000 tons of gold at current prices, the weight of 10 blue whales.

Adapted from an article on Bloomberg Businessweek *by Whitney Kisling, 26 January 2012. Used with permission of Bloomberg L.P. © 2012. All rights reserved.*

 ## 5.2 Profit maximization

> Average revenue is the average price charged by the firm and is equal to total revenue/quantity demanded: (PQ)/Q.
>
> Marginal revenue is the change in revenue from selling one more unit.

Economists assume that firms are in business to maximize profits. This seems reasonable. As an investor, you take a risk when investing in a company and so you expect a financial return. In Chapter 7, we will challenge the assumption of profit maximization, but for now it will suffice as a reasonable assumption for the firm.

The profits of a company are determined by the degree to which revenues are greater than costs. Therefore, in order to understand both (1) the output level at which profits are maximized and (2) the amount of profit generated at the maximum, we need to understand average and marginal revenue, plus average and marginal costs. We discussed average and marginal costs in detail during Chapter 3, but we need to develop your understanding of **marginal** and **average revenues**.

Average and marginal revenues

Consider the demand data in Table 5.1. In the first two columns we have data from a demand curve; as the price increases in column 1, the quantity demanded, listed in column 2, decreases. Total revenue = price × quantity; for example, at a price of £7 demand is six units, therefore total revenue = £7 × 6 = £42. The remaining total revenue values are provided in column 3. Average revenue = (price × quantity)/quantity. Therefore, at a price of £7 we have (£7 × 6)/6 = £7. The average revenue is the same as the price. You can see this clearly by noting that the column for price and the column for average revenue in Table 5.2 are identical. If you were asked to plot the demand curve (price against quantity demanded) and then also

Table 5.1 Demand and total, average and marginal revenue

Price (£)	Quantity demanded	Total revenue (PQ)	Average revenue (PQ/Q)	Marginal revenue
12	1	12	12	
11	2	22	11	10
10	3	30	10	8
9	4	36	9	6
8	5	40	8	4
7	6	42	7	2
6	7	42	6	0
5	8	40	5	−2
4	9	36	4	−4
3	10	30	3	−6
2	11	22	2	−8
1	12	12	1	−10

Table 5.2 Monopolistic average and total revenues

Price	Quantity	Total revenue (PQ)	Average revenue (PQ/Q)	Marginal revenue
12	4	48	12	
11	5	55	11	7
10	6	60	10	5

asked to plot the average revenue line (average revenue against quantity) on the same piece of graph paper, the two lines would lie on top of each other. If you are not convinced, take the data from Table 5.1 and use a spreadsheet package such as MS Excel to create an XY scatter plot of the demand and average revenue. You will only see one line on the screen, not two.

The demand line and the average revenue line are therefore the same thing.

In the final column, we have the values for marginal revenue. Marginal revenue is the revenue received by selling one more unit. Therefore, in moving from one unit to two units (selling one more unit), our revenues have increased from 12 to 22. Marginal revenue is therefore 22 − 12 = 10. All the values for marginal revenue are plotted in Figure 5.1.

The marginal revenue line slopes down. This is because of two factors. First, marginal revenue is related to the demand curve. In order to sell one more unit, we know from Chapter 2 that we have to reduce the price of the product. Second, in reducing the price we are also reducing the price of all the previous units. Consider the following. We can sell seven units at a price of 6, or reduce the price to 5 and sell eight units. In comparing the two situations, we gain one more unit at a price of 5, but we are reducing the price from 6 to 5 on the other seven units. Therefore,

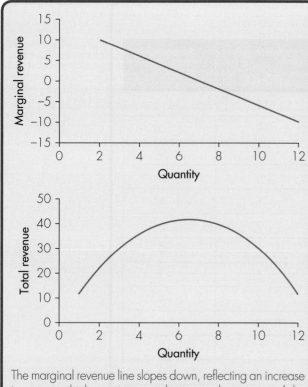

The marginal revenue line slopes down, reflecting an increase in output which requires a reduction in the price and the impact of the price reduction on the price of previous units. Total revenue is greatest when marginal revenue is zero; this is because selling one more unit neither adds to nor subtracts from the total revenue.

Figure 5.1 Marginal revenue and total revenue

the marginal revenue associated with selling one more unit is $+5 - (7 \times 1) = -2$. We can see that in order to sell one more unit we also have to accept a reduction in marginal revenue and not just the price.

Finally, in the bottom half of Figure 5.1, we have the plot of total revenue. You can see that maximum revenue occurs where marginal revenue equals zero in the top diagram. This is because a marginal revenue of 0 lies between positive and negative marginal revenue. When marginal revenue is positive, each unit adds a positive amount to total revenue. Once marginal revenue becomes negative, each additional unit reduces total revenue.

Profit maximization

We can now combine our understanding of revenue and costs to understand how firms maximize profits. Firms will maximize profits or, in other words, make the most amount of profit, when the marginal cost of the last unit of output equals the marginal revenue, or MC = MR.

It is important to note that MC = MR and profit maximization are not policy prescriptions for firms. Economists are not saying firms must behave in this way. Rather, economists have said profit maximization is a reasonable assumption to hold about the behaviour of firms; and if we do model firms as profit-maximizers, then output must be at the point where MC = MR. In Chapter 8 we will revisit the assumption of profit maximization and consider other assumptions, including growth maximizationa and revenue maximization.

> Profit maximization is the output level at which the firm generates the highest profit.
>
> Marginal profit is the profit made on the last unit and is equal to the marginal revenue minus the marginal cost.

In understanding how the economist arrives at the **profit maximization** rule of MC = MR, we need to make some assumptions. The firm does not decide to produce 10 or 20 units of output; rather, it decides if it wants to produce one unit of output. Then it decides if it wants to produce the second unit. At some point it will decide not to produce any more. So the economist is assuming that the firm is making stepped decisions.

In Table 5.3, we have added marginal cost data to the marginal revenue data discussed above. In the fourth column we have marginal revenue minus marginal cost.

The firm maximizes profits when marginal cost equals marginal revenue, i.e. MC = MR. If MC = MR, then MR − MC = 0. The firm maximizes profits when the **marginal profit** = 0. This is similar to revenue maximization in Figure 5.1. When MR > MC, the firm is making a marginal profit – each additional unit generates a positive profit and adds to overall profits. However, once MR < MC the firm is making a marginal loss – each additional unit generates a loss and therefore diminishes total profits. We can, therefore, argue that the firm will increase production if marginal revenue is greater than marginal cost, i.e. MR > MC. But the firm will reduce output if it is incurring a marginal loss, i.e. MR < MC.

Using these insights we can take our stepped approach to discover the profit-maximizing output. From Table 5.3, if the firm produced one unit of output, then the marginal profit would be 6. Since this is positive, the firm will make one unit. The firm now decides whether or not to make the second unit. The additional or marginal profit associated with making the second unit is 8. Again, since this is positive the firm will make the second unit. Likewise,

Table 5.3 Marginal revenue and marginal cost

Quantity	MR	MC	MR – MC	Output decision	Profit
1	21	15	6	Raise	6
2	19	11	8	Raise	14
3	17	8	9	Raise	23
4	15	7	8	Raise	31
5	13	8	5	Raise	36
6	11	10	1		37
7	9	12	–3	Lower	34
8	7	14	–7	Lower	27
9	5	16	–11	Lower	16
10	3	18	–15	Lower	1

the firm will decide to make units three, four, five and six, as the marginal profits are all positive. The firm will not produce beyond the sixth unit because the marginal profits are negative. For example, a loss of 3 is associated with making the seventh unit. Profits are, therefore, maximized at 6 units of output. This can be seen in the final column of Table 5.3, with profits peeking at 37 with an output of 6.

Admittedly, we stated that the firm will maximize profits when MC = MR and in our example profits appear to peak at six units of output, where marginal revenue is one unit greater than marginal cost. From an examination of the data, we might argue that MC = MR somewhere between six and seven units, let us say 6.5. Some products are easy to divide into smaller units of output, for example oil, beer and milk. A firm could decide to produce 6.5 litres of milk. But it would not be sensible to produce 6.5 cars. We can, therefore, say that MC = MR is strictly and mathematically correct, but it is not always the most practical output level for a firm to maximize profits at. If the firm produces whole units, it will stop at the highest level of output with a positive marginal profit. This way, the firm chooses a level of output that is nearest to its profit-maximizing level of output.

Figure 5.2 provides a diagrammatic illustration of profit maximization where marginal cost equals marginal revenue. Firms will increase output if marginal revenue is greater than marginal cost; and they will reduce output if marginal cost is greater than marginal revenue.

Profit maximization and differences in demand

In Chapter 3, when considering costs, we saw that marginal cost always has a positive slope, that is, all firms face diminishing returns in the short run. However, firms in different markets face

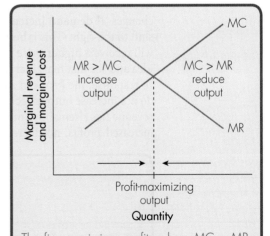

The firm maximizes profits where MC = MR. Alternatively, the firm will produce an additional unit of output if the MR is greater than the MC, because it then makes additional profit. But it will not produce any more output if the marginal revenue is less than the marginal cost because this will generate a loss on the last unit produced, leading to a reduction in overall profits.

Figure 5.2 Marginal revenue, marginal cost and profit maximization

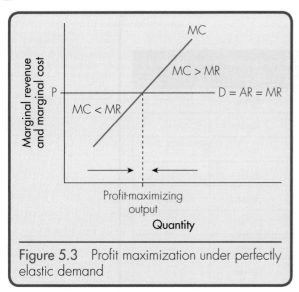

Figure 5.3 Profit maximization under perfectly elastic demand

different demand conditions and this leads to different average revenue and therefore different marginal revenue lines. However, under the assumption of profit maximization the optimal output will still occur where MC = MR.

In Figure 5.3, we consider an important and special case where demand is perfectly elastic. We explained in Chapter 2 that a perfectly elastic demand line is horizontal. Firms can sell *any* amount of output at the current price, but if they price above the market price they sell nothing, because customers are extremely price sensitive.

The consequences of a perfectly elastic demand line are that average revenue and marginal revenue are also horizontal lines. Each unit of output is sold for the same price, so the average revenue is constant (and equal to the price); and the revenue from the last unit is equal to the revenue from the previous unit. Therefore, marginal revenue is also constant and equal to the price.

Figure 5.3 follows a similar reasoning to Figure 5.2. When marginal cost is below marginal revenue, the firm can expand output and raise profits. However, once marginal cost is greater than marginal revenue, the firm should reduce output and profits will rise. The important difference between Figures 5.2 and 5.3 is the relationship between marginal cost and price. In Figure 5.3, under profit maximization MC = MR = AR = P, or in shorthand MC = P. However, in Figure 5.2, MC = MR, but MR ≠ AR (also see the columns in Table 5.1 and Figure 5.1 to remind yourself of this fact). Therefore, MC ≠ P. As we explore perfect competition and monopoly later in this chapter, the importance of this distinction will become clearer.

Changes in costs and revenues

In Figures 5.4 and 5.5 we examine what happens if either marginal revenue or marginal cost changes. If demand increases for a product, then the marginal revenue curve will similarly shift to the right. This is because when the market price increases at all output levels, the firm will receive a higher price for each additional unit of output. In Figure 5.4, we illustrate this idea and see that marginal revenue now meets marginal cost at a much higher level of output. In response, the firm can maximize profits at a much higher level of output. Therefore, firms do not increase output because prices rise; rather, they increase output because the marginal revenue has risen above marginal cost. The motive for increasing output is, therefore, one of increased profits, not increased prices. In contrast, if demand for the product fell, then the

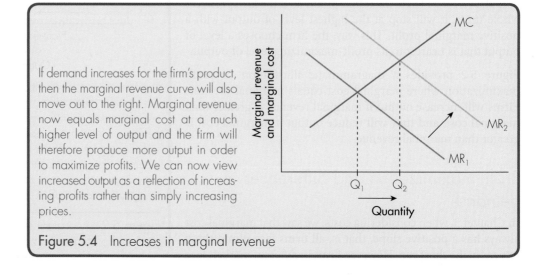

If demand increases for the firm's product, then the marginal revenue curve will also move out to the right. Marginal revenue now equals marginal cost at a much higher level of output and the firm will therefore produce more output in order to maximize profits. We can now view increased output as a reflection of increasing profits rather than simply increasing prices.

Figure 5.4 Increases in marginal revenue

marginal revenue curve would shift to the left. With lower marginal revenues, the profit-maximizing output would be reduced.

In Figure 5.5, we illustrate a reduction in marginal cost. We saw in Chapter 3 that marginal cost is influenced by the price of factor inputs such as labour and factor productivity. If labour became more productive it could produce more output and the marginal cost would fall. We see from Figure 5.5 that, if this did occur, then the marginal cost would fall below marginal revenue and the firm would increase output in order to maximize profits. Similarly, marginal cost could increase because labour wage rates increase. The marginal cost curve would then shift to the left. With higher marginal costs at all levels of output the profit-maximizing level of output would be reduced.

We have now brought together the understandings of demand and prices from Chapter 2 and cost theory from Chapter 3. Combining the two enables an understanding of how the firm will maximize its profits. Unlike in Chapter 2, where we discussed a firm's response to changes in the price of the final good or service, and in Chapter 3, where we analysed a firm's responses to cost

If a firm experiences productivity growth, then its marginal costs may fall. With lower marginal costs at all levels of output the firm will be more able to maximize profits at a higher level of output. We can now view increased output as a reflection of increasing profits rather than simply decreasing costs.

Figure 5.5 Falling marginal costs

changes, we can now see how the firm changes its output level based on an interaction of revenue and costs. In the economic sense, the firm is not concerned with prices or costs per se, but rather profit, which is a combination of the two.

Having highlighted profit as the major incentive for firms, we now need to consider how market structure will impact upon the marginal revenue and perhaps even marginal cost of a firm. By examining perfect competition and monopoly, we will see how the level of profits at the profit-maximizing output level is likely to be lower under perfect competition than under monopoly. However, before we embark upon the theory it is fairly straightforward to understand that profits will be lower in perfect competition. This can be seen from our definition that perfect competition is the market environment with the greatest amount of competition. With lots of competitors all chasing the same customers, profits have to be small. Now let us provide the theoretical, rather than commonsense, framework.

(5.3) The spectrum of market structures

> Perfect competition is a highly competitive marketplace.
>
> Monopoly is a marketplace supplied by only one competitor, so no competition exists.

We can see in Figure 5.6 that **perfect competition** and **monopoly** are extreme and opposite forms of market structure. In reality, it is difficult to find true perfectly competitive markets or even monopolies. Financial markets trading shares in companies are highly competitive, as are commodity markets trading such goods as oil, copper

Perfect competition	Imperfect competition	Oligopoly	Monopoly
Financial and commodity markets	Small service sectors, bars, restaurants	Supermarkets and banking	Microsoft and the Beckhams

Figure 5.6 Range of possible market structures

and gold. But, as we will see below, while such markets are *highly* competitive, they are not necessarily *perfectly* competitive.

Perfectly competitive signifies that competition in the market is the greatest possible. No alternative market structure can be more competitive. Similarly, Microsoft is not a perfect example of a monopoly, as its products compete with a number of smaller suppliers, such as Linux. Likewise, Angelina Jolie and Brad Pitt have a monopoly on their lifestyle, image and personalities but, in the celebrity market, they still face competition from a range of married celebrity couples.

Other types of market structure are **imperfect competition** and **oligopoly**. Imperfect competition is very competitive, but differs from perfect competition by the recognition of product differentiation. Small service sector industries tend to have the characteristics of imperfect competition. The supermarket industry and the banking industry are oligopolistic. These are clearly more common modes of **market structure** and we will analyse imperfect competition and oligopoly in more detail in Chapter 6.

We will see when we examine the alternative market structures of perfect competition and monopoly that important competitive structures are: (1) the number of competitors; (2) the number of buyers; (3) the degree of product differentiation; and (4) the level of entry and exit barriers. Further explanation of these concepts will be provided when we discuss perfect competition in detail, where we will see very clearly how the structure, or characteristics, of a market determines the level of competition and, ultimately, profitability.

> **Imperfect competition** is a highly competitive market where firms may use product differentiation.
>
> **Oligopoly** is a market that consists of a small number of large players, such as banking, supermarkets and the media.
>
> **Market structure** is the economist's general title for the major competitive structures of a particular marketplace.

Perfect competition

Perfect competition is the most competitive type of market structure. Economists assume that perfect competition is characterized by the following structure:

- Many buyers and sellers
- Firms have no market power
- Homogeneous products
- No barriers to exit or entry
- Perfect information.

These elements are explored below:

- **Buyers, sellers and market values** – the first two assumptions are related. The market has many different buyers and sellers. Because of this, no firm, or indeed buyer, has any market power. Market power is the ability to set prices. By many buyers and sellers we do not mean 10, 50 or 100 – we mean *many*! Each buyer and seller is a very small part of the market. For example, the market for shares in any FTSE-100 company might be in excess of 10 million traded shares per day. But an individual shareholder may only hold 1000 shares, which is clearly small when compared to the entire market. The individual shareholder, therefore, has little power over the market price; they simply accept the current price on the stock exchange screens.

- **Homogeneous products** – if all products are homogeneous, all firms provide identical products. Milk is an example; milk from one supermarket is the same as milk from another. Cars are heterogeneous or differentiated.

  - **No barriers to exit or entry** – in order to operate a 4G telecommunications network you require a licence from the government and a very large amount of investment. Both restrict entry into the market and, therefore, act as an **entry barrier**. Similarly, if a firm decides to leave the 4G market, then the cost associated with selling the accumulated assets, whether technical network

> **Barriers to entry** make entry into a market by new competitors difficult.

infrastructure or brand name capital, will be costly and act as a restraint on exit. Alternatively, if you wished to start selling flowers from your garden, then you only need some seeds, sunshine and water. The entry barriers into the flower market are limited. Similarly, if you decided to stop producing flowers in your garden, then you would face little if any **exit barriers** or costs. You simply pull up the flowers and lay some additional turf.

> Exit barriers make exit from a market by existing competitors difficult.

No barriers to exit or entry means that a business person can move economic resources into a market in the pursuit of profit and can also move them out. This transfer of resources is assumed to be effortless and relatively inexpensive, if not free.

- **Perfect information** – if you have a secret ingredient for your kebabs, then any competitor will be able to discover what the ingredient is. They can send in a customer and then arrange for the kebab to be analysed by a scientist or master kebab chef. So any informational advantage will be short-lived. Similarly, if a firm decided to sell at a higher price than its competitors, everyone in the marketplace would know that the price was expensive. In the stock market, all offers to sell and buy are published on the brokers' screens, hence there is **perfect information** regarding prices.

> Perfect information assumes that every buyer and every seller knows everything.

Perfect competition and the firm's demand curve

We will now see how the assumptions of perfect competition drive the outcomes of a perfectly competitive market. For example, the assumption regarding a lack of market power is illustrated in Figure 5.7.

In the marketplace many buyers and sellers come together and the market price of £10 is set. This is illustrated in the right-hand side of Figure 5.7. As the firm has no market power it simply accepts the market price.

As a **price taker**, the demand curve for a perfectly competitive firm is perfectly elastic. The firm can sell whatever quantity it likes at £10. This is illustrated on the left-hand side of Figure 5.7. While a perfectly competitive firm can sell whatever quantity it likes at the market price, this does not mean that the firm produces everything the market can bear. Rather, all firms can reasonably expect to sell their profit-maximizing level of output at the market price.

> A price taker is a firm that accepts the market price.

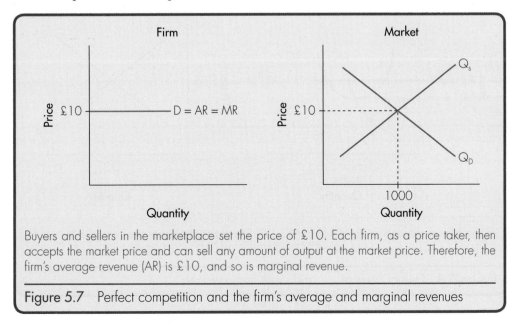

Buyers and sellers in the marketplace set the price of £10. Each firm, as a price taker, then accepts the market price and can sell any amount of output at the market price. Therefore, the firm's average revenue (AR) is £10, and so is marginal revenue.

Figure 5.7   Perfect competition and the firm's average and marginal revenues

Since the firm faces many competitors, its market share will be extremely small. When this competition is coupled with perfect information, if the firm raised its prices above the equilibrium level it would sell nothing, with customers quickly swapping to the cheaper suppliers. In contrast, because the firm can sell all that it likes at the current market price, there is no reason to sell below the market price. Taking these points together, the firm faces a perfectly elastic demand curve, because demand reacts instantly, fully and perfectly to an increase or decrease in the firm's price.

Average and marginal revenue

Marginal revenue is the revenue received by selling one more unit. In perfect competition, the firm faces a perfectly elastic, or horizontal, demand line. If it decides to sell one more unit, then it does not have to reduce its price. Therefore, if the market price is £10, the firm can sell one more unit and receive an additional £10. Unlike in our discussion of Table 5.1 and Figure 5.2, the perfectly competitive firm does not have to suffer a reduction in revenue on its previous units. Therefore, the marginal revenue line is also horizontal and equal to the average revenue line, but only in the special case of perfect competition.

Adding in costs

We can now take Figure 5.7 and add in the short-run average cost curves developed in Chapter 3 to produce Figure 5.8. In so doing, we will have average revenue and costs on the same figure as well as marginal revenue and marginal cost. We can then examine the profit-ability of the firm.

The diagram is fairly straightforward. Remember, we are assuming the firm is a profit-maximizer and we would simply like to know how much profit the firm would make. So:

- **Step 1**: The firm maximizes profits by producing the profit-maximizing level of output associated with MC = MR.
- **Step 2**: What does it cost to produce the profit-maximizing output? Simply draw the line up from the profit-maximizing output until it touches the short-run average total cost curve, SATC. So, in this case, £8 per unit.

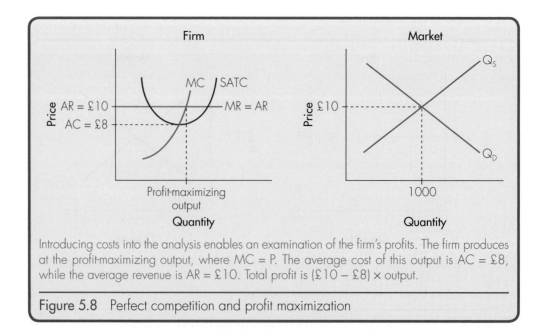

Introducing costs into the analysis enables an examination of the firm's profits. The firm produces at the profit-maximizing output, where MC = P. The average cost of this output is AC = £8, while the average revenue is AR = £10. Total profit is (£10 − £8) × output.

Figure 5.8   Perfect competition and profit maximization

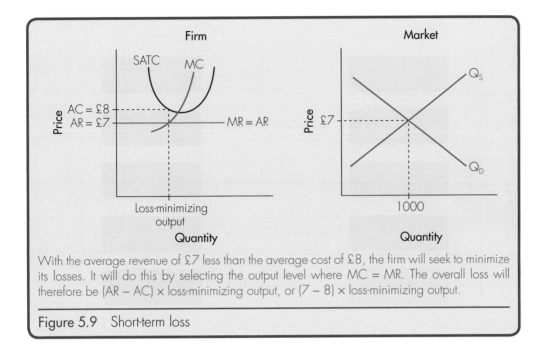

With the average revenue of £7 less than the average cost of £8, the firm will seek to minimize its losses. It will do this by selecting the output level where MC = MR. The overall loss will therefore be (AR – AC) × loss-minimizing output, or (7 – 8) × loss-minimizing output.

Figure 5.9 Short-term loss

- **Step 3**: What revenue will the firm earn by selling the profit-maximizing output? Simply draw the line up from the profit-maximizing output until it touches the average revenue line, AR. So, in this case, £10.
- **Step 4**: Profit per unit is AR minus AC, so £10 – £8 or £2 per unit.
- **Step 5**: Total profit is profit per unit times the number of units produced. Or, in our figure, the rectangle defined by AR – AC and the profit-maximizing output.

So, we can see that this particular firm is making a profit. In economic terms, it is making a 'supernormal profit'. See the next section on normal and supernormal profits.

We can also consider the situation where a firm is making a loss, and this is depicted in Figure 5.9. In comparison to Figure 5.7, we have simply reduced the market price from £10 to £7, and therefore the AR and MR to £7. At this market price, the firm's average revenue is below even the lowest point on the firm's average cost curve, so the firm cannot make a profit at any output level. The firm will now seek to minimize its losses rather than maximize its profits. It will achieve this in the same way as it maximizes its profits – that is, by selecting the output level where MR = MC. The loss generated by the firm will be equal to (AR – AC) × loss-minimizing output.

Normal and supernormal profits

Importantly, economists and accountants differ in their definition of profits. In Figure 5.10, we illustrate each of these views. An accountant calculates profits by taking total costs away from total revenues. The accountant would generally categorize raw materials, labour and depreciation as costs. Taking these costs from revenue leaves **accounting profits**.

> Accounting profits are revenues less raw material costs, wages and depreciation.

The economist also takes costs away from revenues. But the economist thinks about the costs of using economic factors of production. These, from Chapter 1, are land, labour, capital and enterprise. The first three in this list map directly onto the accountant's cost categories. For example, the cost of labour is wages. But what is the cost of our fourth factor of production, namely that of enterprise? Recall that enterprise is individuals who are risk-takers and

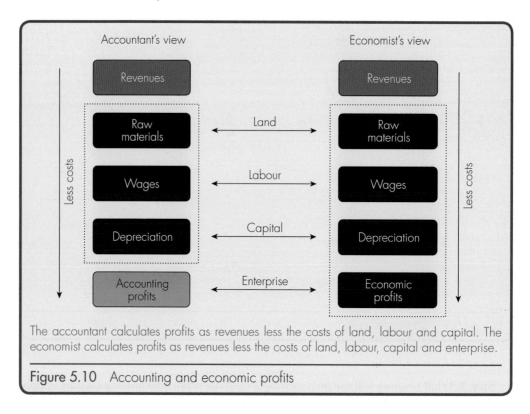

The accountant calculates profits as revenues less the costs of land, labour and capital. The economist calculates profits as revenues less the costs of land, labour, capital and enterprise.

Figure 5.10   Accounting and economic profits

> Economic profits are revenues less the costs of all factors of production.
>
> Normal economic profits are equal to the average rate of return which can be gained in the economy.
>
> Supernormal profits are financial returns greater than normal profits.

provide financial capital for companies. Entrepreneurs receive the benefits of taking financial risks. They receive profits. Therefore the economist views profits as a cost of using enterprise and we call these **economic profits**.

Economists further divide economic profits into two categories, **normal** and **supernormal**. **Normal economic profits** are the minimum rate of return required for an entrepreneur to retain their investment in a company. If the entrepreneur can gain 5 per cent by placing their money in a bank account, then this may act as a benchmark rate of normal return. We would then adjust this figure upwards for the degree of risk offered by the company. If the company was very risky, then we might say the normal rate of return for the company is 10 per cent. If the company was less risky, we might expect an entrepreneur to be seeking 7 per cent from their investment.

Anything above the normal rate of return is called **supernormal profits**; and anything less than normal profits is called a supernormal loss.

Long-run equilibrium

Having seen supernormal profits and losses in the short run, it is now time to recall the remaining assumptions regarding perfect competition. Perfect information implies that all business people outside the industry are aware of the profits to be made inside this industry. No barriers to entry imply that entry into this market is easy. Therefore, businesses know about the profitable opportunities in this market and can enter the market with ease. The consequences of increased market entry for profits are illustrated in Figure 5.11.

If we begin in market equilibrium at QS_1 and QD, the market price is £15. This sets an average revenue AR_1, which is higher than firms' short-run average costs, SATC. Firms are making supernormal profits and this attracts new entrants into the industry. The supply curve moves to QS_2, the market price falls to £10 and firms are making normal profits. There is no longer any reason to enter the market as similar risk-adjusted profits can be earned by putting money in the bank.

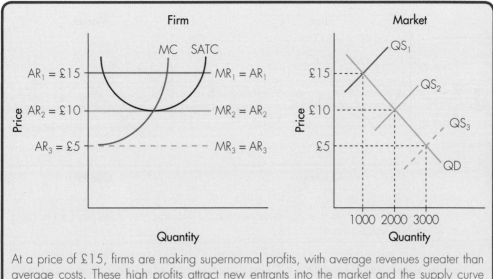

At a price of £15, firms are making supernormal profits, with average revenues greater than average costs. These high profits attract new entrants into the market and the supply curve moves from QS$_1$ to QS$_2$. The price falls until it reaches £10. At this price the average revenue and average costs are equal, the firm earns normal profits, and firms are no longer attracted into the market. At a price of £5, firms are making losses, with average revenue below average costs. These losses force some firms out of the industry. Supply moves from QS$_3$ to QS$_2$. The price rises to £10 and firms earn normal profits.

Figure 5.11   Perfect competition in the long run

We can also consider the situation where firms are making a loss. When market supply is at QS$_3$, the market price is £5 and this sets average revenue AR$_3$ less than short-run average cost, SATC. Firms are making losses and some exit the market. This leads to QS$_3$ moving towards QS$_2$. Once the market price returns to £10, the remaining firms in the industry are making normal profits and exit stops.

Clearly, entry and exit are not the only factors that will influence the market equilibrium. We can envisage a number of short-term scenarios leading to a long equilibrium. In scenario 1, the good is a normal good. Income increases and, therefore, the market demand shifts to the right. The market price increases and the firm's marginal revenue and average revenue rise relative to costs. Increased profits then attract new entry into the market. The market supply curve shifts to the right and the market equilibrium price drops until average revenues equal average costs and only normal profits are earned. These points are highlighted in Figure 5.12.

In scenario 2, following wage negotiations the cost of labour increases. The firms' marginal cost curves shift to the left and average costs rise upwards. Firms' profits decrease. Exit occurs and the market supply curve shifts to the left. As a result, the market equilibrium price increases until the average revenues earned by the firms match the higher cost level brought about by increased labour costs. Normal profits are earned and exit stops. These points are illustrated in Figure 5.13.

The review questions contain an additional scenario to test your understanding and use of the diagrams.

It is important to remember that, whether we begin with a supernormal profit or a supernormal loss, firms in perfect competition will always end up earning only normal profits in the long run. That is, firms in a perfectly competitive long-run equilibrium will be indifferent between being in business and placing their money in the bank.

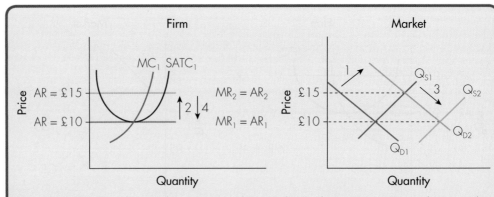

The market is in equilibrium where Q_{D1} equals Q_{S1}. The market price is £10. At this price the firm earns a normal profit, with average revenue equal to average cost at the profit-maximizing output, where $MR_1 = MC$. Then:

1. Income levels in the economy increase. The good is income normal and therefore the demand curve shifts to the right to QD_2 (consumers use the increased income to buy more of the good). The equilibrium price rises to £15.

2. The average revenue for the firm rises to £15, reflecting the increased market price. The marginal revenue also increases to £15 and the profit-maximizing output increases. Since average revenues exceed average cost, the firm is making a supernormal profit.

3. The supernormal profits attract new entrants into the market and supply shifts from Q_{S1} to Q_{S2} and the market equilibrium price falls to £10.

4. The average and marginal revenues fall to £10. The profit-maximizing output returns to its original level and the firm generates normal profits.

Figure 5.12 Changes in market demand and adjustments to long-run equilibrium

---

Productive efficiency means that the firm is operating at the minimum point on its long-run average cost curve. Moreover, in long-run equilibrium the firm is charging a price that is equal to the marginal cost. This means that the firm is also allocatively efficient. We highlighted this outcome in section 5.2 and Figure 5.3.

Allocative efficiency occurs when price equals marginal cost, or P = MC.

In the long-run equilibrium, the perfectly competitive firm is operating at the minimum point of the average cost curve. This means that the firm is **productively efficient** as it is producing at least cost.

Recall that the cost of using scarce factor resources to produce one more unit of output is the marginal cost; and the price paid by consumers reflects the value placed on the final good. If the marginal cost of making a laptop computer is £300 and consumers are willing to pay no more than £250, then there is an inefficient use of society's scarce resources. The £300 of resources, including labour, capital and raw materials, which went into the laptop are not worth £300 to consumers. If the same resources could have been used to produce the latest high-tech mobile phones and consumers were willing to pay £300 per phone, then society's scarce resources would have been allocated efficiently. The value of the phones produced is exactly equal to the value of the resources used. In summary, **allocative efficiency** occurs when price = marginal cost. We will return to these points when we compare perfect competition with monopoly.

A quick consideration of kebab shops

Now let us consider the kebab shop sector and in particular assess the kebab market against the assumptions of perfect competition. There are many (buyers) students and there are many (sellers) kebab shops. A kebab is a fairly homogeneous product – kebabs from different shops are fairly similar. Prices are listed on boards inside the shop and are usually visible from the street, so information regarding prices is near perfect. Barriers to entry are fairly limited. You need a shop, a food licence, some pitta bread and some cheap meat. All are easily available. The kebab market is not perfectly competitive, but the characteristics of the market are close to perfectly competitive. Profits are likely to be low in the

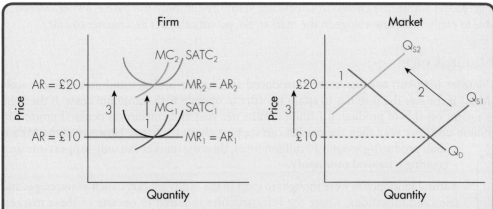

The market is in equilibrium where Q_D equals Q_{S1}. The market price is £10. At this price the firm earns a normal profit, with average revenue equal to average cost at the profit-maximizing output. Then:

1 Negotiations lead to a rise in the wages paid to the firms' labour forces. This leads to an increase in the individual firm's costs. The average and marginal costs rise to $SATC_2$ and MC_2.

2 The firms' costs are now greater than the average revenue of £10, leading to losses. Some firms exit the industry and the industry supply curve shifts to the left, to Q_{S2}.

3 The equilibrium market price rises to £20, also raising average revenue to £20. This is just enough to cover the increase in the firms' costs. Firms again generate normal profits at the profit-maximizing output.

Figure 5.13   An increase in firms' costs and adjustment to long-run equilibrium

kebab market and so it is likely to be an unattractive business proposition. Let us now see if monopoly is better.

5.5 Monopoly

In a strict sense, a monopoly is said to exist when only one firm supplies the market. In practice, the UK competition authorities define a monopoly to exist if one firm controls more than 25 per cent of the market. So, clearly, a monopoly exists if there is a dominant firm in the market with few rivals.

Monopolies tend to exist because of barriers to entry, where barriers to entry restrict the ability of potential rivals to enter the market.

Let us begin with some easy examples.

Licences

The National Lottery is a monopoly. Only one firm, currently Camelot, is licensed by the government to operate a national lottery in the UK. Licences also act as a barrier to entry on the railways. Until recently, only Eurostar was allowed to operate high-speed trains between London and Paris.

Patents

When a pharmaceutical company develops a new drug it can apply for a patent. This provides it with up to 20 years of protection from its rivals. While everyone can discover the ingredients within the cholesterol-reducing statin Zocor, only the patent owner, Merck, is able to exploit this knowledge in the market. So, patents also act as a barrier to entry.

Natural monopoly

Consider long-run average costs, introduced in Chapter 3. The minimum efficient scale (MES) is the size the firm has to attain in order to operate with minimum costs. If the MES is a plant capable of producing 1 million units per year and consumers demand around 10 million units per year, then the market can support about ten firms. However, if the MES is a plant producing around 10 million units, then the market can only support one firm – creating a **natural monopoly**.

> Natural monopoly exists if scale economies lead to only one firm in the market.

Natural monopolies were thought to exist in the utility markets, such as water, gas and telecommunications, where the infrastructure required to operate in these markets was so large that it restricted entry. For example, the scale needed to operate an effective telecommunications network in the UK was thought to be so large, because of all the cables, switches and exchanges that were required, that only one firm was capable of investing and generating a return. Two firms would double the amount of investment, but at best share the market and, therefore, the financial returns. However, when telecommunications began to move from copper wire to mobile communications, other firms could build networks much more cheaply. The barriers to entry fell and more firms now operate in the telecommunications market.

What does one firm and significant entry barriers mean for firm-level profitability?

Revenues and costs in monopoly

Just like perfect competition, we need to think about the revenues and costs generated by a monopoly. In perfect competition, MR and AR are the same. As a price-taker, if the firm sells more output it does not cause the market price to fall, so its MR and AR stay constant. In a monopoly, the situation is different. As the only supplier in the market, the monopoly faces the downward-sloping market demand curve. Therefore, if it sells more output, the price must fall. This has implications for the monopoly's AR and MR.

Consider Figure 5.14. The average revenue line, AR, is downward sloping and this follows from above. If the firm sells more output, then, under the law of demand, consumers will only demand more output at lower prices. So, as the price drops, the average price per unit must drop.

Marginal revenue is more difficult to understand. Again, consider Figure 5.14 and Table 5.2. Initially, we are selling four units at £12. Total revenue is £48 and average revenue is the price, £12. To sell one more unit, we need to drop the price to £11. This generates total revenue of £11 × 5 = £55, and the average revenue is now £11. But what has happened to marginal revenue? Two things have occurred. First, we are selling one more unit for £11 but, second, we are losing £1 per unit on the previous four units. So marginal revenue = £11 – (4 × £1) = £7. So, MR = £7, while AR = £11. Now let us drop the price to sell one more unit. Selling six units at £10 generates a total revenue of £10 × 6 = £60. The marginal revenue from selling the sixth unit is £60 – £55. So, MR = £5, while AR = £10. Going from the fifth to sixth unit changed the price from £11 to £10; in effect, we reduced the average revenue by £1. However, the marginal revenue changed from £7 to £5, a change of £2. We can therefore

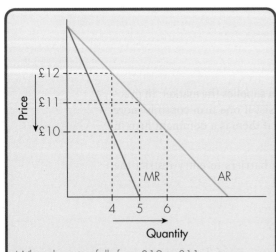

When the price falls from £12 to £11, average revenue falls. But marginal revenue falls by more. One more unit is sold for £11, but the previous four units sold at £12 are now selling for £11, resulting in lost revenue of £4. Marginal revenue is therefore + £11 – £4 = £7.

Figure 5.14 Monopoly's marginal and average revenue

see that, in selling more units, we have to accept a bigger reduction in marginal revenue than in average revenue. Reflecting this point, in monopoly, the marginal revenue line will always be steeper and below the average revenue line.

As with perfect competition, we now need to add in the firm's cost curves (see Figure 5.15).

The monopoly will also maximize profits where MC = MR. This point defines the profit-maximizing output. If we then draw the line up from Q until it touches the short-run average total cost curve (SATC), then we see that the average cost equals £10. Drawing the line further until it touches the average revenue line, we see that the output can be sold for £20 per unit, making a profit per unit of £20 − £10 = £10. Total profit is £10 per unit multiplied by the profit-maximizing output Q. This is the short-term profit-maximizing position and, because of significant entry barriers, this profit will not be competed away in the long run. So, unlike perfect competition, monopolies can expect to earn supernormal profits in both the short and long run.

Perfect competition and monopoly compared

The long-term profit position of monopoly is not the only difference and so it is worth comparing perfect competition and monopoly in more detail. In order to do this, we will assume that we have a perfectly competitive industry, with 1000 firms supplying the market. Overnight, a business person buys out all the firms and begins to act as a monopoly.

As a consequence of this transfer of ownership from 1000 people to one person, the cost structure will not change; the monopoly will simply have a cost curve that is the sum of all the 1000 individual cost curves under perfect competition. The same will apply to the marginal cost curve and this is illustrated in Figure 5.16. The customers in the market have not changed, so the demand curves or AR lines faced by the perfectly competitive industry and the monopoly are identical. The marginal revenue lines are different. Remember, in perfect competition, marginal and average revenue are the same, but in monopoly they are different. We can now use Figure 5.16 to assess the differences between perfect competition and monopoly.

In order to maximize profit, the perfectly competitive industry will set $MC_{pc} = MR_{pc}$. Its profit-maximizing output is Q_{pc} and the price it sells for is PC. The monopoly sets $MC_{mp} = MR_{mp}$ and its profit-maximizing output is Q_{mp} and the price it sells this output for is MP. It is now clear to see that, in moving from perfect competition to monopoly, the industry output drops and the price increases. Furthermore, in perfect competition the price equals the industry's marginal

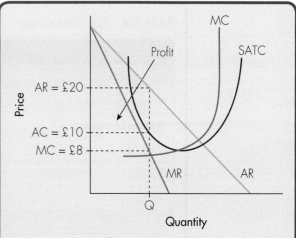
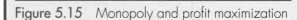

The monopoly's profits are maximized at Q, where MC = MR. The average cost of producing Q is £10; the average revenue from selling Q is £20. Total profit = (£20 − £10) × Q. Unlike perfect competition, the price of £20 charged by the monopoly is greater than the marginal cost of £8. This difference between the price and the cost of making the last unit is an indication of market power.

Figure 5.15   Monopoly and profit maximization

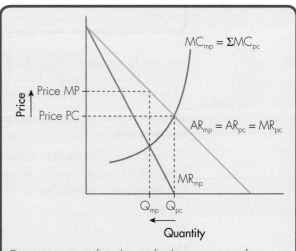

To maximize profits, the perfectly competitive firm sets $MC_{pc} = MR_{pc}$, while the monopoly sets $MC_{mp} = MR_{mp}$. When compared with monopoly, perfect competition provides more output at lower prices.

Figure 5.16   Comparing perfect competition and monopoly

Table 5.4 Key comparisons of perfect competition and monopoly

	Perfect competition	Monopoly
Assumptions:		
Number of buyers	Many	Many
Number of suppliers	Many	One
Barriers to entry and exit	None	High
Product	Homogeneous	Not considered
Information	Perfect	Not considered
Outcomes:		
Costs	Productive efficiency – average total costs minimized	Productive inefficiency – average total costs not minimized
Average revenue and marginal revenue	Average revenue = marginal revenue	Average revenue > marginal revenue
Short-run losses and profits	Supernormal	Supernormal
Long-run profits	Normal	Supernormal
Price	Allocative efficiency: price = marginal cost	Allocative inefficiency: price > marginal cost
Market power	No market power, price = marginal cost	Market power, price > marginal cost
Level of prices	Monopoly price is higher than in perfect competition unless monopoly benefits from economies of scale	
Level of output	Monopoly output is lower than in perfect competition unless monopoly benefits from economies of scale	

cost, but in monopoly the price is higher than the industry's marginal cost. This difference between price and marginal cost in monopoly is known as 'market power', which is the ability to price above the cost of the last unit made.

Table 5.4 provides a concise comparison of the key differences between perfect competition and monopoly.

The summary points within Table 5.4 are generally accepted key differences between perfect competition and monopoly. Below we discuss some important challenges to the argument that monopoly is always bad for society and the consumer.

Monopoly and economies of scale

However, the arguments put forward are weak. The idea that a monopoly would have the same cost curves as a perfectly competitive industry neglects the points made in Chapter 3 relating to economies of scale. A monopoly may be capable of reducing costs. A single company is unlikely to operate 1000 separate plants. Instead, it is more likely to rationalize the 1000 plants into a smaller number of very large plants, which can exploit economies of scale. If this is true, then the cost reduction would lead to the monopoly's marginal cost curve moving out to the right. This is shown in Figure 5.17, with the marginal cost for the monopoly shifting to the right. At all output levels, the marginal cost of the monopoly is

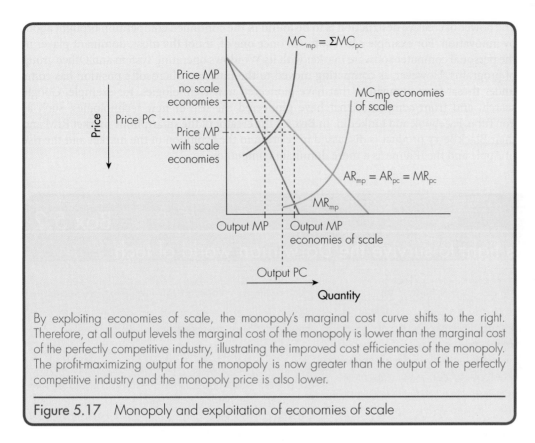

By exploiting economies of scale, the monopoly's marginal cost curve shifts to the right. Therefore, at all output levels the marginal cost of the monopoly is lower than the marginal cost of the perfectly competitive industry, illustrating the improved cost efficiencies of the monopoly. The profit-maximizing output for the monopoly is now greater than the output of the perfectly competitive industry and the monopoly price is also lower.

Figure 5.17   Monopoly and exploitation of economies of scale

now lower than the marginal cost of the perfectly competitive industry. The monopoly is now more cost-efficient than perfect competition. The profit-maximizing output for the monopoly now occurs where marginal revenue intersects the new marginal cost curve under economies of scale. Output is higher than in perfect competition and the market price is lower than in perfect competition.

Of course it also needs to be recognized that a monopoly has no incentive to improve efficiency, as it has no competition. So why should it try to exploit economies of scale? Moreover, it is also possible that the monopoly may be too large and displays diseconomies of scale. Its costs would then be greater than the perfectly competitive industry, with the marginal cost curve shifting to the left. This would lead to even higher prices and a greater reduction in output under monopoly.

Creative destruction

An alternative argument in favour of monopoly is that of **creative destruction**. Under this approach, monopolies are generally accepted as raising prices, restricting output and earning supernormal profits, which are potentially all bad. However, what should also be recognized is the benefits which stem from the supernormal profits, especially when they act as an incentive to innovate. Firms which are not monopolies can be motivated to be innovative and creative, developing new products for the market or new production techniques which provide them with a competitive advantage and destroy the entry barriers of the incumbent firms or monopoly. The innovating firm, through creative destruction, then becomes a monopoly. The firm benefits from higher profits; and society benefits from the supply of new innovative goods and services. One potential drawback with this approach is that firms have to undertake expensive **rent-seeking behaviour** and they may not always be successful. Some inventions work, others do not. So, for every monopoly brought about by innovation, there can be many failures which have used the scarce resources of the economy.

Creative destruction occurs when a new entrant out-competes incumbent companies by virtue of being innovative.

Rent-seeking behaviour is the pursuit of supernormal profits. An economic rent is a payment in excess of the minimum price at which a good or service will be supplied.

The power of creative destruction is to be found in the continued competition brought about by innovation. For example Microsoft was once one of, if not the most, dominant player in the personal computer software market with its Windows operating system and Office group of programs. However, as computing moved to the Internet, Microsoft's position has come under threat from companies that have pioneered new technologies, for example, Google search, and from companies that have pioneered the use of new technologies, such as YouTube, Facebook and LinkedIn. In Box 5.2 the creator of the smartphone market RIM and their BlackBerry product is discussed in relation to the evolution of the market and the rise of Apple and the iPhone as a more dominant competitor.

Box 5.2

BlackBerry's fight to survive the Darwinian world of tech

I am an executive, but I do not use a BlackBerry. Oh, I know such people: I see you in airports, blowsy but serious in rumpled suits, bent frowning over the little screens of your preferred smartphone, thumbs flying over its little keys. I know you are loyal to the devices. You like the reliability of BlackBerry's email service and your chief technology officer, who bought the machine for you, feels sure your communications are secure.

The October 2011 BlackBerry outage undercut RIM's remaining competitive advantage. Reliable communications were the thing that RIM did best: smartphones from other manufacturers possess more appealing features and run more software. I, too, was a loyal BlackBerry customer for many years. But I switched to Apple's iPhone two years ago.

About 70 million people – often working for companies or in fields that demand security, such as government – rely upon the BlackBerry for mobile communications. It is a business that brought RIM $20 billion in revenues last year. But sales of BlackBerry phones are slowing. According to the market research firm Gartner, BlackBerry phones accounted for about 20 per cent of new smartphone sales from April to June 2010. RIM had just 12 per cent of the smartphone market in the same period this year.

RIM, which helped establish the market for smartphones, no longer makes devices that seem very smart. The BlackBerry is a messaging machine that can also be used as a phone. Reading news, listening to music or watching videos on them is unpleasant. By contrast, iPhones and Android handsets are multimedia devices that can also be used for phone calls and messaging.

Composing an email on an iPhone's flat screen may be frustrating in comparison to typing on a BlackBerry's clever keyboard but people do not mind because they care about media more.

RIM's problems have been compounded by changes in the way businesses use technology. Individual consumers have never been the main buyers of the BlackBerry. Technology officers bought them, in much the same way they once purchased personal computers. But employees, especially younger ones, increasingly expect IT departments to support software on machines they have bought.

The business of technology is Darwinian. The reward for a successful product is a monopoly but such monopolies are short-lived because the environments where products thrive are so ephemeral. The BlackBerry was supremely adapted to the early market for smartphones, because technology officers valued reliability and security above other features. But the market for smartphones is expanding and manufacturers must now appeal first to consumers.

Until last week, people thought the BlackBerry uncool but reliable. Now they believe it is neither. RIM's device might evolve: the company could rewrite its network and it might sell new devices with all the delightful features of iPhones and Androids. But I doubt it will happen. Evolution is perilous; most products, like species, become extinct. In five years, I suspect business travellers will be crouching over Android and Apple phones and tablets rather than a BlackBerry.

Adapted from an article by Jason Pontin, 18 October 2011. From the *Financial Times* © The Financial Times Limited 2011. All rights reserved.[1]

When is a monopoly not a monopoly?

Licensing and patents are means of creating entry barriers and establishing a monopoly. Companies and individuals use licensing, patents and copyright to protect their intellectual capital, innovations and creative outputs, but to what extent do they create a monopoly?

At a simplistic level, a film studio which copyrights its latest release creates a monopoly for that one film. No one can legally copy the film and distribute it for sale, except for the studio and those companies to which it licenses the film. However, the market for films is well served with many competing films; and so, while a studio maybe a monopoly provider of its own film, it is not a monopoly provider of all films and therefore the value of the film monopoly is perhaps not that great to the studio.

Next consider an extremely successful and popular film, perhaps a film which wins a number of awards, such as an Oscar. The value of the film, its copyright and its monopoly is now greater and of considerable interest to the film studio. However, films have an inherent commercial flaw which damages their monopoly value. This flaw is most apparent in the DVD/Blu-Ray market for films. When a consumer buys a film on DVD or Blu-Ray, they receive a **durable good**. A durable good, in contrast to a **perishable good**, is one which lasts over time and does not degrade despite repeat usage. Wine is not durable, you drink it and then it is finished. Cars are not durable, you drive them and they need maintaining and repairing. Movies on a disc are durable. You watch them and can then watch them again and again and again. Durable goods create a problem for monopoly providers.

> A durable good is one in which consumption is ongoing, for example, a DVD.
>
> A perishable good is one which either decays, for example, fruit and vegetables, or is consumed quickly, for example, wine, Coca-Cola.

Consider the film studio; it launches the DVD and Blu-Ray versions of its latest blockbuster and it sets a price which maximizes its profits. Let us assume that at the profit-maximizing price half of the studio's consumers are willing to buy the film; the remaining consumers think the film is too expensive.

Importantly, because the DVD or Blu-Ray disc is a durable good, once the studio has sold the film, then it does not generate any repeat business. The only customers available to the studio are those that found the launch price too expensive. So, in order to generate further sales, the studio must attract new customers by reducing the price of the DVD and Blu-Ray discs.

Price reduction of films is often observed in practice. The film is initially released on disc at a high price and then over time the price is reduced and customers know this happens. This practice creates an acute problem for studios: if they price too high at launch, then more customers will wait for the price to fall and buy later. To protect revenues, it may therefore be better to price lower during the launch period and then not have to discount to many more customers in later periods.

The heart of the problem is that the studio as a provider of a durable good is in competition with itself over time and is therefore not a monopoly. It then becomes interesting to ask, other than reducing prices at launch, what other tactics might be used by the studio to raise profits? There are a number of tactics used, including adding in additional bonus material. But an interesting approach and one with applicability to other products is to ensure that the good or service being provided is not durable. In the case of DVDs and Blu-Rays this does not mean making discs that fall apart, break and stop working. Instead, renting the disc, rather than selling the disc converts the transaction from one of a durable good, to that of a perishable service. At the end of the rental term, the disc must be returned and cannot be shared around friends or watched again without an additional rental.

Some e-books are now being rented, particularly e-textbooks for periods of up to two years; and photocopying machines are often rented as a means of generating ongoing revenues, rather than one-off payments from buyers. Firms are clearly very adaptive and create business models to deal with many types of problems. Our task is to understand what problems exist and how economics can be used to understand why a particular tactic is being used. The problem just discussed is known within economics as the *Coase conjecture* and is something we will return to in Chapter 8 when we discuss carbon trading.

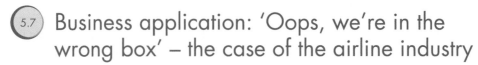

5.7 Business application: 'Oops, we're in the wrong box' – the case of the airline industry

Financial performance is essential, or, in other words, profits count. The firm's revenues and costs determine profits. If we look closely at revenues and costs, we find they are both influenced by prices. A firm's revenues are determined by the price it sells its output for and a firm's costs are determined by the price it has to pay for its labour, capital and raw materials. Price is determined by market structure – it is higher in monopoly and lower in perfect competition. We can use this to think about business structures that are optimal for business by considering the input–output matrix in Figure 5.18.

	Output market	
	Perfect competition	Monopoly
Perfect competition	A Low revenues Low costs	B High revenues Low costs
Monopoly	C Low revenues High costs	D High revenues High costs

*(Left axis label: **Input market**)*

Output markets are where firms sell products. Input markets are where firms buy their labour, raw materials and capital inputs. When selling output the firm desires a high price, so monopoly is best. But when buying inputs the firm likes to keep its costs down, so perfectly competitive markets are preferable. Therefore, from a firm's perspective the best combination is associated with box B.

Figure 5.18 Optimal mix input and output markets

Across the top, we have the market structure of the firm's output market, where it sells its product. Down the side, we have the market structure for the firm's input markets, where the firm purchases its labour, capital and raw materials. Box C could be the worst box to be in. The input markets are characterized by monopoly supply, so cost will be high, and the output markets are perfectly competitive, so revenues will be low. Box B is the best box for business. Inputs come from a perfectly competitive market, so costs are low, while output is sold in a monopoly market, so revenues will be high. Box B is where there is the greatest chance to make a profit. Box A is probably preferable to box D. In A, both markets are perfectly competitive so supernormal profits are unlikely. But how do you think box D compares with box C? In C and D, both firms face a monopoly input supplier. But firms in C have a perfectly competitive output market. This could actually make it more attractive than D. With a perfectly competitive output market the firm will make only normal profits, so the monopoly input supplier cannot afford to squeeze the perfectly competitive firms. In fact, there are no profits to squeeze; but in D, the monopoly output will create profits that the monopoly supplier can try to expropriate for itself by charging higher input prices. So D may be less attractive than C.

Rarely will a firm find itself comfortably inside box B, but it might be expected to try to move towards box B over time. For example, in box D the obvious solution is to purchase the monopoly input supplier and make it part of your company. This is known as vertical integration, and it will be discussed at length in Chapter 7. In box A, you would try to buy up your competitors or force them out of the market. This way, competition is reduced and the market moves towards monopoly.

But, for a more illuminating example, let us look at the airline industry. First, examine its key inputs: aircraft, landing rights at international airports, and pilots. There are only two major aircraft manufacturers in the world, Airbus and Boeing. The market is not perfectly competitive. Most major cities have one airport, a monopoly. Pilots are expensive and unionized. Unions are effectively a monopoly supplier of labour. So, on the input side, airlines are not in a good position. In terms of output, tickets for airlines are sold via travel agents or via the Internet. Most travellers say, 'I would like to go on this date between these two cities: who is offering the cheapest fare?' Ten options appear upon the screen and the cheapest option is generally selected. This would suggest that the market is highly competitive. This is clearly not good for the airline industry.

Solutions

With monopoly suppliers and competitive output markets, airlines are firmly located in box C. How can they deal with this situation? Airline alliances are a likely solution. In such alliances, airlines come together and in the first instance they agree to share passengers – so-called code sharing. This reduces competition in the output market and moves airlines towards box B. In addition, airlines may also swap landing rights at various airports and share the training of pilots. On the aircraft front, they can place joint orders for aircraft and, as with many products, a bulk order usually generates a substantial discount. This provides some control over input prices and again moves airlines towards box B.

A more intriguing idea is the exploitation of natural monopolies. As discussed earlier, a natural monopoly exists where scale economies lead to one supplier in the market. Often these are associated with industries which require enormous levels of infrastructure such as utilities – gas, water and electricity – but they are equally applicable in much smaller markets. Consider the level of demand for flights between two regional airports, say, Leeds in the UK and Nice in France. It is a two-hour flight and around 80 people a day wish to fly direct between the two airports. A small commercial jet might carry 120 passengers, so this route will only be supplied by one airline – a monopoly.

Now consider flying from Leeds to Singapore. Here are a couple of suggested routings: Leeds, Heathrow, and then either direct to Singapore or via Dubai, Bangkok or Kuala Lumpur; or Leeds, Amsterdam and then either direct, or via Dubai, Bangkok or Kuala Lumpur. There are many other options. Therefore, because international airlines utilize hub-and-spoke operations, the market for flights from Leeds to Singapore is a combination of many sub-markets. There is no natural monopoly on these routes. Airlines can fill planes with passengers who are travelling to multiple destinations.

What can we learn from this? Discount airlines tend to fly point-to-point between small regional airports. International carriers operate hub-and-spoke operations. Discount airlines make huge profits; international airlines do not. So are discount airlines natural monopolies? If they are, the very intriguing thought is that they could charge a lot less than they currently do.

Business data application: understanding the forces of competition

Understanding the strength of competition is one of the most important aspects of being a business manager. Markets closer in character to perfect competition will normally generate weaker levels of profit. Harvard Business School professor Michael Porter drawing on the key characteristics of perfect competition developed an often used tool within business, Porter's

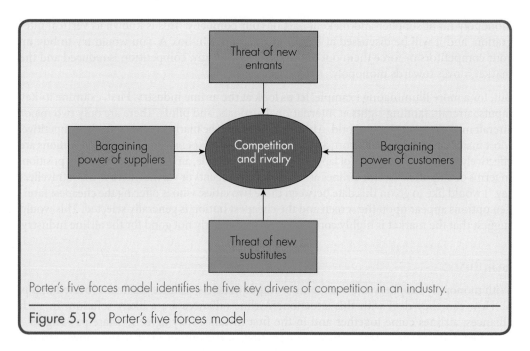

Porter's five forces model identifies the five key drivers of competition in an industry.

Figure 5.19 Porter's five forces model

five forces model of competition (see Figure 5.19). Using data to measure and quantify the level of each force of competition enables a business manager to form a view about the sources of competition, the degree of competition and ultimately the likely impact on profitability.

Around the outside of Figure 5.19 are four drivers of competition: the threat of entry, the threat from substitutes and the buying power of buyers and suppliers. These characterize an industry's initial competitive environment. The firms within the industry then have to decide how to react. The level of competition and rivalry could be high, or they may decide to collude with each other and lower competition. The intensity of each of these five competitive forces determines the overall level of competition within the industry.

Porter's five forces model is closely related to the assumptions of perfect competition. Many buyers and many sellers relates to the bargaining power of buyers and sellers. The threat of new entrants is linked to the assumption of no entry barriers. The threat from substitutes links to the assumption of homogeneous products, where the threat of substitutes is very high under perfect competition. In essence, Porter has taken the abstract assumptions of perfect competition and turned them into tangible concepts that business managers can understand and use to assess the degree of competition in their industry.

Porter's approach is very useful in enabling managers to scan and audit their business environment. The approach directs managers to assess sensible and measurable drivers of competition. Many industry reports often include a section covering competition and Porter's five forces approach is nearly always applied. We consider the market for service stations, fuel, etc. in France (Figures 5.20–5.24). The source for this data is Data Monitor 360, (2011) Service Stations in France.

We can then combine these assessments into one diagram (Figure 5.25) and summarize the strength of competition in each area.

The strength of Porter's five forces approach is in its simplicity. Important aspects of competition can be categorized around five key themes and then assessed with a reasonable degree of accuracy. The importance of economics is that, through the models of perfect competition and monopoly, it highlights to businesses the consequences for profit. If a company has a weak understanding, or lack of control over its competitive forces, then profits will plummet. In contrast, if the firm can understand and manage the forces of competition that it faces, then it has a better chance of becoming a monopoly.

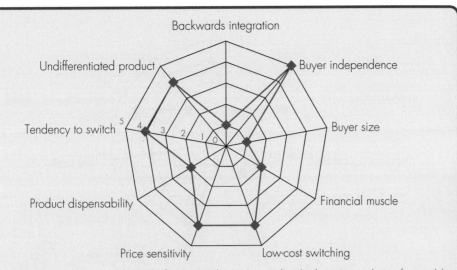

Buyers in this industry are drivers of cars and commercial vehicles. A number of possible aspects of buying power are listed around the outside of the diagram and are then rated on a scale of 0 to 5, where 5 denotes that the buying power is very strong. There is mixed evidence in support of strong buying power. Buyers are small in size, they lack financial muscle and their demand for fuel is very price inelastic. However, there are many substitutes in the market, differentiation is low and the cost of switching to alternative suppliers of fuel is low. Hence, buying power is judged as being moderately strong overall.

Figure 5.20   Buyer power in the French service station industry

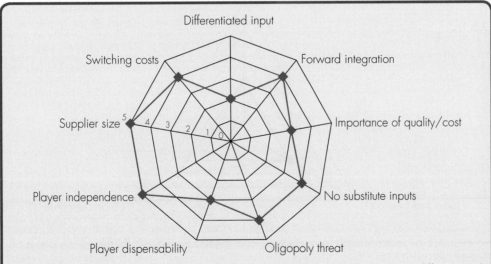

Major oil companies are the major suppliers to service stations. Fuel is not very differentiated and independent service stations and large supermarket chains can to some degree dispense with one fuel supplier and begin trading with another with improved financial terms. However, it needs to be noted that oil companies also own service stations and so have a route to market without having to sell to supermarkets and independent retailers. Oil companies have few competitors, enormous size and financial resource and therefore have strength as suppliers.

Figure 5.21   Supplier power in the French service station industry

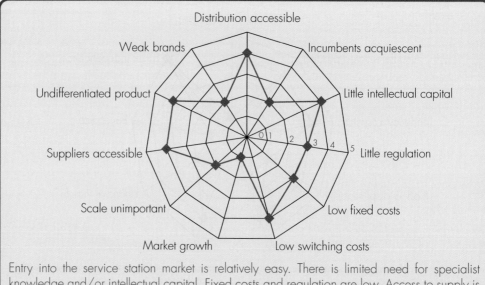

Entry into the service station market is relatively easy. There is limited need for specialist knowledge and/or intellectual capital. Fixed costs and regulation are low. Access to supply is easy and the need for a differentiated product is low. However, the market is unlikely to accommodate a new entrant, growth is low and strong incumbents are likely to resist entry. The threat of entry is therefore moderate.

Figure 5.22   The threat of new entrants in the French service station industry

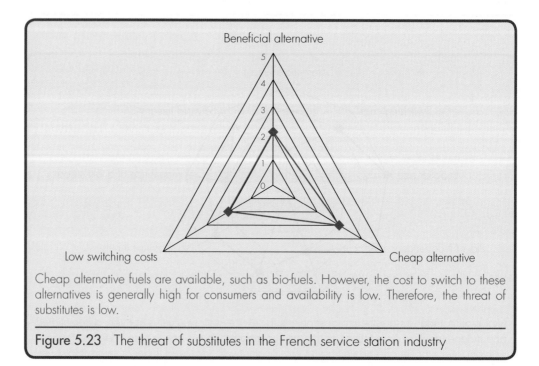

Cheap alternative fuels are available, such as bio-fuels. However, the cost to switch to these alternatives is generally high for consumers and availability is low. Therefore, the threat of substitutes is low.

Figure 5.23   The threat of substitutes in the French service station industry

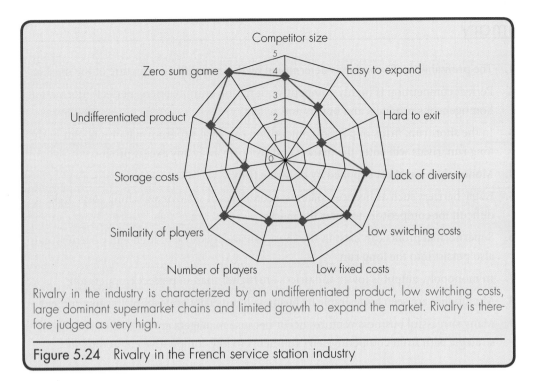

Rivalry in the industry is characterized by an undifferentiated product, low switching costs, large dominant supermarket chains and limited growth to expand the market. Rivalry is therefore judged as very high.

Figure 5.24   Rivalry in the French service station industry

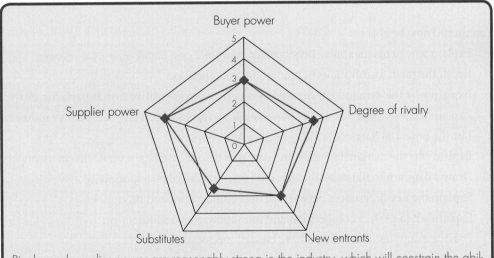

Rivalry and supplier power are reasonably strong in the industry, which will constrain the ability of firms to generate profits. However, lack of new entry, few substitutes and lack of buyer power help to strengthen profitability. The task of a manager in this sector is to understand these competitive forces, avoid rivalry and gain some control over supply. It should therefore be of no surprise that supermarkets as large retailers of fuel have been most successful in this industry. By their size they gain some negotiating power over the major fuel suppliers and equally smaller independent chains are unwilling to engage with them in direct competition.

Figure 5.25   Porter's five forces in the French service station industry

Summary

1. The profitability of a market is determined by the competitive structure of the market.
2. Perfect competition is highly competitive. It has no entry barriers, perfect information, homogeneous products and buyers and sellers.
3. In the short run, firms in perfect competition can earn supernormal profits. But in the long run, rivals will enter the market and compete away any excess profits.
4. Monopoly is a market supplied by only one firm.
5. Entry barriers such as licences, patents, economies of scale or switching costs make it difficult for competitors to enter the market.
6. Supernormal profits can exist in the short run and, because of high entry barriers, can also persist into the long run.
7. In monopoly, output is lower and prices are higher than in perfect competition.
8. Monopolies are seen as desirable by business but usually undesirable by government.
9. Many successful business ventures occur because managers are capable of steering a strategic path from competitive environments to low competitive environments.

Learning checklist

You should now be able to:

*   Explain why firms maximize profits when marginal cost equals marginal revenue
*   Recall the main assumptions behind perfect competition
*   Explain why the demand curve faced by a perfectly competitive firm is perfectly elastic
*   Explain the level of profits in the short and long run in a perfectly competitive industry
*   List the potential barriers to entry used by a monopoly
*   Explain why the marginal revenue line is steeper than the average revenue line in monopoly
*   Draw a diagram to illustrate the amount of profit earned by a monopoly
*   Explain the key differences between perfect competition and monopoly
*   Explain when perfect competition and monopoly are good for a firm
*   Provide examples of how firms have created monopolies
*   Use Porter's five forces to assess the strength of competition in an industry

Questions   connect

1. If a firm is a profit-maximizer, then marginal cost and marginal revenue must be ………….. (Fill in the blank)
2. A firm discovers that its marginal cost is less than its marginal revenue. Should it increase or decrease output?

EASY

3. Describe the key assumptions that characterize a perfectly competitive market.
4. In the short run, a firm in perfect competition finds that average revenues exceed average costs. Is this firm making a normal profit, a supernormal profit, a normal loss or a supernormal loss?

5. Taking the scenario described in question 4, what do you think will happen to supply in the long run?

6. How would you establish a benchmark for normal profits in your own economy?

7. What barriers to entry are associated with monopolies?

8. Is equilibrium in monopoly associated with allocative efficiency?

9. List markets that you think are (a) perfectly competitive and (b) monopolies.

10. Does the concept of creative destruction paint monopolies as good or bad for an economy?

11. Explain the difference between accounting profits and economic profits.

12. Draw a diagram for a perfectly competitive industry with firms earning normal profits. All firms in the industry use oil as a key input. Using your diagram, illustrate a reduction in the price of oil. Will firm-level profits increase or decrease and will market supply increase or decrease?

13. Identify the key differences between perfect competition and monopoly.

14. Assess whether Porter's five forces model of competition has greater value for business managers than the models of perfect competition and monopoly.

15. Would the lack of competition in monopoly result in the company making losses?

Exercises

1. True or false?

    (a) Price is equal to marginal revenue for a firm under perfect competition.

    (b) A firm making normal profits is said by an accountant to be breaking even.

    (c) A monopoly makes supernormal profits because it is more efficient than a perfectly competitive firm.

    (d) A perfectly competitive firm will sell at a price equal to marginal cost. A monopoly may sell at a price above marginal cost.

    (e) A patent protects a monopoly by not enabling perfect information.

    (f) In perfect competition, if price is above short-run average cost, firms will exit the market.

2. Figure 5.26 shows the short-run cost curves for a perfectly competitive firm.

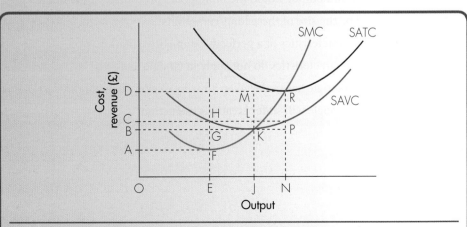

Figure 5.26   Short-run cost curves for a perfectly competitive firm

(a) What is the shutdown price for the firm?

(b) At what price would the firm just make normal profits?

(c) What area would represent total fixed cost at this price?

(d) Within what range of prices would the firm choose to operate at a loss in the short run?

(e) Identify the firm's short-run supply curve.

(f) Within what range of prices would the firm be able to make short-run supernormal profits?

A perfectly competitive industry is taken over by a monopolist who intends to run it as a multi-plant concern. Consequently, the long-run supply curve of the competitive industry (LRSS) becomes the monopolist's long-run marginal cost curve (LMC$_m$); in the short run, the SRSS curve becomes the monopolist's SMC$_m$. The position is shown in Figure 5.27.

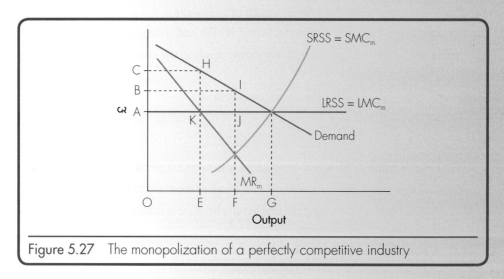

Figure 5.27 The monopolization of a perfectly competitive industry

(g) What was the equilibrium price and industry output under perfect competition?

(h) At what price and output would the monopolist choose to operate in the short run?

(i) At what price and output would the monopolist maximize profits in the long run?

(j) What would be the size of these long-run profits?

3. (a) List the key characteristics of a perfectly competitive market.

DIFFICULT

(b) Which of the characteristics do not apply to Google and why?

(c) Do you think Google has undertaken any rent-seeking behaviour?

(d) Do you think Google will suffer creative destruction?

Strategic rivalry

Chapter contents

Strategic rivalry at a glance   136

6.1   Business problem: will rivals always compete?   136

6.2   Monopolistic competition   137

6.3   Oligopoly theory: natural and strategic entry barriers   139

6.4   Oligopoly theory: competition among the big ones   142

6.5   Competition among rivals   146

6.6   Game theory   148

6.7   Game theory extensions: reaction functions   150

6.8   Business application: compete, co-operate or gain a first-mover advantage?   152

6.9   Business application: managing supply costs – anonymous auctions for supermarket contracts   153

6.10   Business data application: competition in the bus market   154

6.11   Appendix: auction theory   156

Summary   160

Learning checklist   161

Questions   161

Exercises   162

Learning outcomes

By the end of this chapter you should understand:

Economic theory

LO1   Monopolistic competition

LO2   Natural and strategic entry barriers

LO3   Oligopoly and interdependence

LO4   The kinked demand curve model

LO5   Game theory and strategic behaviour

LO6   Auction theory

Business application

LO7   Why it may be better for leading technology firms to co-operate on standards, rather than compete

LO8   Why supermarkets use blind auctions to prevent co-operation between suppliers

LO9   How an understanding of oligopolies can be used to assess competition within the market for local bus services

The issue

Firms in perfect competition earn normal economic profits. But can firms avoid direct price competition, say by product differentiation, and, if so, what are the consequences for pricing and profits? In addition, in markets where there are only a small number of large players, should firms compete or try to co-operate with each other? Co-operation leads to increased profits; competition does not.

The understanding

Many firms in highly competitive markets, such as bars, restaurants and hairdressing, differentiate themselves by location, style and range of products or services. Prices then often vary across differentiated providers, but this may not necessarily lead to supernormal profits. We will address these issues using the model of monopolistic competition.

In terms of co-operation, or competition, we will examine the concept of strategic interdependence. For example, while co-operation is likely to lead to increased profits, it is not necessarily the correct option. If you decide to be friendly and your rival is aggressive, then they will win. So, given that your rival is aggressive, it is best if you are also aggressive. This is an essential part of the understanding; optimal strategies are developed from an understanding of what your rival is going to do, not from what you would like to do. This is known as strategic interdependence. The strategy of one firm is dependent upon the likely strategy of its rivals. We will explore these ideas more fully by examining game theory.

The usefulness

An understanding of monopolistic competition provides insights into the consequences for prices and profits resulting from product positioning and differentiation, especially in service sector markets characterized by numerous small-scale providers.

An understanding of strategic interaction from the perspective of game theory is extremely powerful. Government uses game theory when designing auctions for telecommunications licences. Sporting associations and team owners use game theory and auctions when selling television rights. Car dealerships use game theory when selling second-hand cars, and so should you. Finally, supermarkets use it to reduce the price that they have to pay for own-label products by applying game theory to auctions.

 ## Business problem: will rivals always compete?

A good competitor can control their rivals. In sport, Formula 1 drivers try to achieve this from pole position and, in war, armed forces try to gain control through air supremacy. In fact any successful competitor, whether it be in sport, war, politics or business, will ordinarily have a good strategy.

An important recognition is that competition is expensive. War is hugely expensive, particularly in terms of lost lives. Ferrari's annual racing budget exceeds $200 million. Competition in business is also expensive. In monopoly, with no competition, profits are higher and more sustainable than in the highly competitive environment of perfect competition.

So, if competition is expensive, should rivals always compete? The answer depends on the expected response of your rival. Consider this old, but illuminating, true story. When the Spanish arrived in Central America in the seventeenth century they were greeted by fearsome-looking locals, sporting war paint and shaking menacing spears in the air – a clear declaration that they were willing to compete with the Spanish invaders. In response, most of us would sensibly pull up the anchor and sail away. The Spanish burnt their boats and walked onto the beach. If a fight between the Spanish and the Incas started, the Spanish had to fight or die: no boats, no escape plan. The local Incas quickly understood the Spanish soldiers' need and desire to win and retreated inland. So, by committing to a fight, the Spanish influenced the behaviour of their rivals. This is a significant point for business.

In perfect competition, the behaviour of one firm will not influence its rivals. Each firm is a price-taker and it can sell any amount of output at the market price. If the market price is £10, there is no point starting a price war and selling at £5 because you can sell everything at £10. There is said to be no **strategic interdependence**. We will also assume that there is no strategic interdependence when we discuss monopolistic competition. However, under *oligopoly*, if one firm begins a competitive move, such as starting a price war, then this will have immediate implications for its rivals. The actions of one firm are linked to the actions of its rivals. Strategic interdependence exists.

> Strategic interdependence exists when the actions of one firm will have implications for its rivals.

In developing your understanding we will begin by introducing the model of monopolistic competition. While not directly addressing the issue of strategic interdependence, it does examine the profitability of many small firms under product differentiation. As such, it provides an insight into how firms in near-perfect competition try to deal with competitive rivalry. We then develop the analysis through an examination of the characteristics of an oligopolistic market. In discussing why oligopolies exist, we will consider both natural and strategic entry barriers. Finally, we will turn our discussion to strategic responses and in so doing develop your understanding of game theory. We will then utilize the insights from game theory to understand the operation and optimal design of auctions.

6.2 Monopolistic competition

We begin with an examination of **monopolistic competition**, which for the most part is an industry much like perfect competition except for the existence of product differentiation. So, we are still assuming a large number of competitors, freedom of entry and exit, but not homogeneous products. Rather, firms produce similar goods or services which are differentiated in some way.

> Monopolistic competition is a highly competitive market where firms may use product differentiation.

There are many examples of monopolistic competition and they all must relate to differentiation in some form or other. Bars can be differentiated by location, the beers or other drinks offered for sale, type of food served, or theme, such as a cocktail or sports bar. Shops can be differentiated by distance. Local shops sell newspapers and many people will not walk more than 300 yards for a paper. They will, however, drive a number of miles to access a supermarket. Even bread, a fairly standard product, is differentiated: brown, white, soft, with seeds, with fruit, and different varieties from around the world. Even your classes are differentiated by day of the week and time of day.

Importantly, because each supplier offers a similar but not identical product, each supplier does not face a perfectly elastic (horizontal) demand line, as they would in perfect competition. Instead, the element of differentiation lowers the degree of substitutability between rival offerings – and results in each firm facing a downward-sloping demand line.

The result of this differentiation is for each small firm to have a monopoly over the differentiated version of the product or service that it provides. We, therefore, have lots of small firms offering similar but slightly different competitive offerings to consumers with varied tastes and preferences. This combination of competition and monopoly gives rise to the term 'monopolistic competition'. In Box 6.1 the move by Starbucks into 'drive-thru' outlets highlights an attempt to further differentiate Starbuck's offer and meet the needs of a particular type of coffee consumer.

Each monopolistic firm can influence its market share to some extent by changing its price relative to its rivals. By lowering drink prices a bar may attract some customers from its rivals, but it will not attract all the rivals' customers. Differentiation will lock in some customers to the more expensive provider; for example, if one bar provides beers while another specializes

Starbucks to open 200 drive-thrus for roadside caffeine fix

Starbucks announced that it will open 200 'drive-thrus' in Britain over the next five years. Car drivers will order their triple-shot frappuccinos or skinny caramel lattés by speaking into a microphone and then drive forward to pick up their coffee from a hatch – all from the seat of their car.

Drive-thrus are big business in America – two-thirds of McDonald's turnover comes from car-based diners and Starbucks has 2500 outlets, but they have had limited success in Britain. Kris Engskov, the new UK managing director of Starbucks, insisted customers had already embraced the idea. It has been experimenting with 10 roadside shops over the last three years.

'This is absolutely about customers asking for this. The drive-thru meets a customer need,' he said, pointing out that many commuters drove to work without passing a shop and parents enjoyed the ability to buy a coffee without having to park their car and take out the children from their car seats.

Mr Engskov said the new outlets were not a sign that the company was abandoning the high street, at a time when many retailers were struggling. 'We'll continue to develop there, but we need to be flexible. Coffee purchase is driven by convenience, be it a drive-thru or a kiosk, or retail.' The company suggested that 100 new shops could be opened in addition to the drive-thrus over the next five years.

Analysts said the move was proof that the high-street coffee market was becoming saturated. Neil Saunders, managing director at Conlumino, said: 'The coffee shop market competition is intense in the UK. If you educate people about drive-thru it is possible they will embrace it.'

Adapted from an article by Harry Wallop in
The Telegraph, 1 December 2011. © Telegraph Media
Group Limited 2011.

in fruit and alcoholic cocktails. Cheap prices in the beer bar will not attract drinkers who have a strong taste and preference for cocktails.

Monopolistic competition also requires an absence of economies of scale. Without the ability, or need, to exploit size and scale, a monopolistic industry will be characterized by a large number of small firms. We will see that, when we discuss oligopoly in the next section, the existence of economies of scale can lead to a small number of large players.

The demand curve for the firm depends upon the industry demand curve, the number of firms and the prices charged by these firms. A bigger industry demand, with a fixed number of firms, will result in a higher demand for each firm. An increase in the number of firms will lead to a reduced share of the market for each firm. The price of a firm, relative to its rivals, will also determine its level of demand.

In Figure 6.1, we have drawn a diagram depicting a firm's supply decision under monopolistic competition. Initially, the firm faces an average revenue line of AR_1 and marginal revenue line MR of MR_1. Under profit maximization, the firm will produce Q_1 units and sell at a price of P_1. With an average cost per unit of AC_1, the firm will make $(P_1 - AC_1) \times Q_1$ profit. These supernormal profits will attract entry into

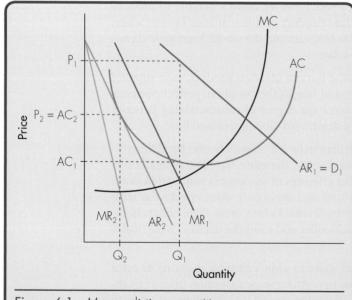

Figure 6.1   Monopolistic competition

the market. As more firms enter this market, the firm will lose market share and the demand curve for the firm will move back towards the origin. Entry stops when each firm is breaking even. This is when the new demand line, AR_2, just touches the average cost line at a tangent. The firm now makes Q_2 units at a price of P_2. Economic profits are now zero since $P_2 - AC_2 = 0$, and therefore entry into the industry stops.

Excess capacity

The monopolistic long-run equilibrium has some important features. First, the **tangency equilibrium** results in average costs being above minimum average costs. In comparison with perfect competition, long-run equilibrium in monopolistic competition does not result in firms operating at minimum average total costs. Therefore, monopolistic competition is not productively efficient. In fact, firms in monopolistic competition operate with excess capacity. They could increase output and reduce costs.

> Tangency equilibrium occurs when the firm's average revenue line just touches the firm's average total cost line.

This productive inefficiency might suggest that the excess capacity in monopolistic competition is bad for society. It may be, but it is also important to recognize that monopolistic competition delivers greater choice for consumers that have varied tastes and preferences. So, in assessing whether monopolistic competition is good or bad for society, it is necessary to consider the gains from increased choice against the costs of excess capacity and inefficient production.

Market power

In long-run equilibrium, firms in monopolistic competition have some monopoly power because price exceeds marginal cost. In perfect competition, freedom of entry and exit ensures that in long-run equilibrium price, average cost and marginal cost are equal. There is no market power in perfect competition. Firms in perfect competition are indifferent between serving a new customer and turning them away. This is because the revenue from one extra sale is equal to the cost of the sale ($P = MC$). In monopolistic competition, the revenue from one more sale is always higher than the costs ($P > MC$). Firms in monopolistic competition will always be willing to sell to one more customer. This in part may explain why firms in monopolistic competition, such as food outlets, bars and hairdressers, are willing to engage in promotional activities such as advertising as a means of drawing in extra customers.

The characteristics of monopolistic competition – product differentiation, few opportunities for economies of scale, zero economic profits, but yet some power over pricing – are those we often associate with service sector businesses, such as bars, restaurants, local grocery stores, hairdressers, estate agents and fast-food outlets. As such, the model of monopolistic competition has some merit in being able to explain the characteristics of many service sector industries. However, apart from a simple consideration of product differentiation, the model does not provide much of an insight into strategic interdependence. This is principally because monopolistic competition still assumes a large number of small players. As such, each firm is small relative to the market, and its competitive actions have only limited consequences for all of its rivals. This negligible impact results in strategic interdependence being almost entirely ignored. We will address this concern by considering oligopolies and, in particular, game theory.

Oligopoly theory: natural and strategic entry barriers

An oligopoly is a market with a small number of large players. Unlike in perfect competition, each firm has a significant share of the total market and therefore faces a downward-sloping demand curve for its product. Firms in oligopolies are price-setters as opposed to price-takers. Obvious examples of oligopolies include supermarkets, banks and the soft drinks market.

Oligopolies are often referred to as highly concentrated industries, implying that competition is concentrated in a small number of competitors. A simple measure of concentration is the

Table 6.1 Supermarket market shares

Supermarket	Percentage market share
Tesco	31
Asda	17
Sainsbury's	16
Morrisons	12
Co-operative	7

Source: Kanter (2011).

Table 6.2 Most and least concentrated UK industries

Most concentrated industries (5-firm CR > 80%)	Least concentrated industries (5-firm CR < 10%)
Sugar	Metal forging
Tobacco	Plastic pressing
Gas distribution	Furniture
Banking	Construction
Soft drinks	Structural metal products

Source: ONS

> **N-firm concentration ratio, CR,** is a measure of the industry output controlled by the industry's N largest firms.

N-firm concentration ratio, which is a measure of the total market share attributed to the N largest firms. Table 6.1 presents the market shares for the leading five UK supermarkets. The five-firm concentration ratio is 83 per cent. Table 6.2 lists the most and least concentrated industries for the UK economy.

A natural question to ask is why are some industries, such as soft drinks, highly concentrated and others, such as furniture, not? The key to the answer lies in recognizing the importance of entry barriers.

Entry barriers can exist for natural or strategic reasons.

Natural entry barriers

> **Exogenous costs of the firm** are outside its control.

The costs for a firm can be exogenously or endogenously determined. Our natural entry barriers are concerned with **exogenous costs,** so let us concentrate on them first.

The fact that exogenous costs are outside the firm's control does not mean that these costs are uncontrollable; rather, the firm does not influence the price of labour, machines, raw materials and the production technology used. For example, the price of labour is a market price determined outside the firm's control. The level of costs associated with a particular industry, as we saw with monopolies, can create an entry barrier.

In Figure 6.2, we have the long-run average cost curve LRAC and the minimum efficient scale. (We considered these in Chapter 3.) At the minimum efficient scale, MES, the average cost is

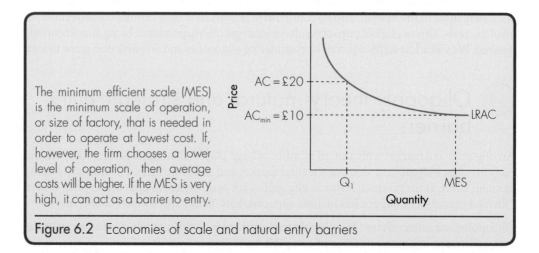

> The minimum efficient scale (MES) is the minimum scale of operation, or size of factory, that is needed in order to operate at lowest cost. If, however, the firm chooses a lower level of operation, then average costs will be higher. If the MES is very high, it can act as a barrier to entry.

Figure 6.2 Economies of scale and natural entry barriers

£10. But with a much smaller plant, Q_1, the cost per unit rises to £20. In order to enter and compete in the industry it is essential to build a plant that is at least as big as the MES. In oligopolies, the MES is large when compared to the overall market. For example, if we have 50 million customers and the MES is 10 million units per year, then we might reasonably expect 50m/10m = 5 firms in the market.

If we consider supermarkets, it is easy to see why natural barriers to entry may exist. In the case of supermarkets, the big players have in excess of 500 stores each. So the MES must be around 500 stores. This level of scale is probably essential when trying to negotiate discounts from product suppliers, optimizing marketing spend and building efficient distribution systems to move stock from suppliers to the stores. Given that the UK is a small island with around 60 million inhabitants, it is sensible that we should only see a small number of large supermarket chains. Four large players operating at 500-plus stores is all that the UK market is capable of supporting. So, it is the natural, or exogenous, cost characteristics, coupled with the market size that leads to a natural entry barrier and the creation of an oligopoly.

Strategic entry barriers

What happens if the MES is not very big when compared with the market size? Entry is easier and aids competition. Consider the case of soft drink manufacturers. If you wish to enter the soft drinks market, then you need to buy a bottling plant and a big steel factory to house it in and a warehouse; and a couple of trucks for deliveries will also help. The cost will not exceed £5 million. (It is amazing what you can learn when taking summer jobs as a student.) For many businesses £5 million is not a huge sum of money. The MES is not big and, therefore, the entry barrier into the market is limited. So, as a firm inside the market, how do you prevent entry? Easy – you change the cost characteristics of the industry and make the MES bigger, or, as the economist would say, you **endogenize** the cost function.

Coca-Cola and Pepsi are clear examples of how to achieve this strategy. The core assets for these companies are not production facilities; rather, they are brand names. A successful brand may cost £100 million or more to buy, or develop through advertising. Therefore, the entry barrier is not a £5 million factory, it is instead a £100 million brand.

> If costs are **endogenized**, the firms inside the industry have strategically influenced the level and nature of costs.
>
> A **sunk cost** is an expenditure that cannot be regained when exiting the market.

Figure 6.3 illustrates these points. $\text{LRAC}_{\text{Production}}$ is the cost curve that relates to production only. $\text{LRAC}_{\text{Production+Advertising}}$ is the cost curve when we consider production and advertising together. The MES for production is much smaller than the MES for production and advertising. Therefore, by strategically changing the cost nature of the soft drinks industry, from production based to managing brands, the dominant players can try to prevent entry.

Perhaps more important, the £100 million brand development fee is a **sunk cost**. This means that if the entrant decided to exit the market after spending £100 million on brand development, it would be unlikely to sell the asset on. The asset has no value to any other business and so the cost is sunk. In contrast, the production facility could be sold on. A soft drinks manufacturer may not buy the plant, but some other food processing company could be interested in the facility. This asset can be sold on, so its costs are not sunk. As a consequence, the need for a brand simultaneously increases the size of entry into the market and it makes it more risky as the asset cannot be sold on. The investment is lost.

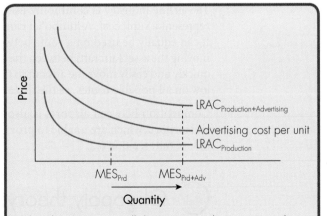

When the MES is naturally low, entry can be easy. Incumbents can change this by altering the cost characteristics of the industry. One suggestion is to move away from production and build in large investments in intangible assets such as brand names. This can substantially increase the MES and reduce entry.

Figure 6.3   Strategic entry barriers

Box 6.2

How Britain lags behind continental competitors

Heathrow is the world's busiest two-runway airport and is currently running at 98 per cent of its capacity. Not only is it limited to two runways, but the British Airports Authority (BAA) faces a restriction on how these runways are used, with Heathrow limited to 480 000 flights a year. As a result it takes very little for the airport to grind to a halt, especially during bad weather.

Heathrow's major competitors for hub traffic are in a far better position. Last October Frankfurt airport opened its fourth runway, increasing its capacity from 83 take-offs and landings an hour to potentially 126 an hour. Charles de Gaulle Airport in Paris also has four runways, while Schiphol Airport in Amsterdam now has six.

Barajas airport in Madrid also has four runways and is emerging as a major international hub, especially for traffic to South America. Elsewhere Dubai airport, which has four runways, has cemented its position as a significant aviation stopping point.

The lack of runway capacity not only means that Heathrow is more prone to delays than its competitors, but Britain is also in danger of failing to exploit the growing market in China in particular. Heathrow for example only has two routes to China, while Frankfurt serves four destinations and Amsterdam six. More alarmingly, London remains without any direct connection to 12 cities in mainland China that are predicted to be among the 25 global cities with the highest gross domestic product (GDP) in the world by 2025.

Adapted from an article by David Millward in The Telegraph, 19 January 2012. © Telegraph Media Group Limited 2012.

> A contestable market is one where firms can enter and exit a market freely.

The existence of sunk costs is important because without them markets are **contestable**. With freedom to enter and exit, contestable markets proxy perfectly competitive markets. So, even if the market has only a small number of large players, the absence of sunk costs enables potential rivals to threaten future entry. The only way to prevent entry is to make it look unattractive, with low levels of profit. So, contestable markets, even with oligopolistic structures, only produce normal economic profits.

Examples of contestable markets

The airline industry is commonly used as an example of contestability. An aircraft does not represent a sunk cost. A jumbo jet can be used on a route between Heathrow and New York. It can equally be used on a route between Heathrow and Hong Kong. There are no costs in moving the asset (aircraft) between the two routes, or any other route. Therefore, the airline can quickly and easily move the aircraft to the most profitable route. This ability should keep profits low on all possible routes, as the threat of entry by rivals is very real, with no entry barriers.

Competition between airports is also facilitated by the ability of airlines to move capacity and airports which are unable to provide airlines with future growth opportunities are likely to lose out; see Box 6.2.

6.4 Oligopoly theory: competition among the big ones

Now that we have an understanding of why oligopolies exist, it is important to understand how competition occurs between rival firms within an oligopoly. A simple fact is that firms in an oligopoly are torn between a desire to compete and the benefits of colluding. The following discussion illustrates this point.

Optimally, all firms in an oligopoly should agree to co-operate and act as one monopolist, as this generates the highest level of profits. This is known as a cartel and is illustrated in

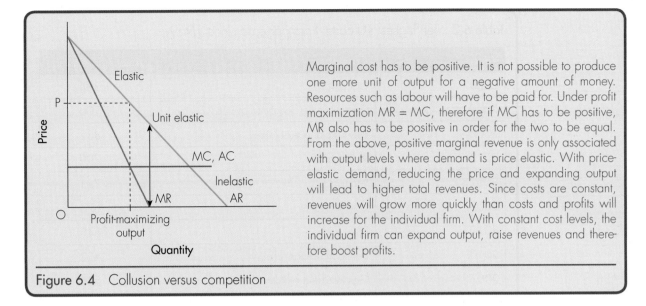

Marginal cost has to be positive. It is not possible to produce one more unit of output for a negative amount of money. Resources such as labour will have to be paid for. Under profit maximization MR = MC, therefore if MC has to be positive, MR also has to be positive in order for the two to be equal. From the above, positive marginal revenue is only associated with output levels where demand is price elastic. With price-elastic demand, reducing the price and expanding output will lead to higher total revenues. Since costs are constant, revenues will grow more quickly than costs and profits will increase for the individual firm. With constant cost levels, the individual firm can expand output, raise revenues and therefore boost profits.

Figure 6.4   Collusion versus competition

Figure 6.4. For simplicity, assume all firms face identical constant marginal and average costs. These are shown as a horizontal line in Figure 6.4. The profit-maximizing output occurs where MR = MC. This output maximizes the joint profits of all the firms in the cartel, acting as a monopoly. However, each firm will quickly recognize that it can undercut the market price and raise its own profits at the expense of its rivals. Why?

The answer rests in an understanding that a profit-maximizing monopoly will only operate in the price-elastic region of its demand curve. Marginal cost has to be positive, because it is impossible to produce an additional unit of output without incurring additional costs. Therefore, if profits are maximized when MC = MR, then, because MC is positive, MR must also be positive. If marginal revenue is positive, reducing the price to sell one more unit has made a positive contribution to total revenue. We saw in Chapter 2 that cutting prices and raising total revenue only occurs when demand is price elastic.

Therefore, a single firm within the cartel illustrated in Figure 6.4 can see that its marginal and average costs are constant. However, reducing prices will generate greater revenues because demand is price elastic. The individual firm can, therefore, earn more profit by cheating on its cartel colleagues and expanding output. Unfortunately, any member of the cartel could recognize that, being on the elastic part of the demand curve, it could also drop its own prices and raise revenues. Therefore, all rivals would respond by dropping their prices, leaving the cartel and in effect competing with each other. This is strategic interdependence in action. Should firms in oligopoly co-operate with each other and act as a monopoly, or compete with each other and start a price war?

When a cartel might work

Some basic points at this stage help in understanding when a cartel can work and when competition will prevail. Collusion is likely to fail when there is:

- a large number of firms
- product differentiation
- instability in demand and costs.

Collusion is much harder when there are many firms in the industry: co-ordination and enforcement is too complex and it is easy for firms to blame each other for cheating. If the product is not standardized, perhaps differentiated in some way, then collusion is unlikely to work. Differentiation is a means of reducing substitutability. Why agree on price fixing when

Table 6.3   Ten highest EU cartel fines per case since 1969

Year	Case name	Amount in €million
2008	Car glass	1,384
2009	Gas	1,106
2007	Elevators and escalators	832
2010	Airfreight	799
2001	Vitamins	791
2008	Candle waxes	676
2010	LCD	648
2010	Bathroom fittings	622
2007	Gas insulated switchgear	539
2007	Flat glass	487

Source: European Competition Commission Cartel Statistics.

your products are not near-substitutes? Finally, collusion benefits from stability in demand and costs. If the equilibrium is changing frequently, then the cartel has frequently to adjust its agreed prices. It is costly to co-ordinate and the variation in market conditions provides firms with the cover needed to cheat and not get caught.

Examples of price fixing include the Organization of Petroleum Exporting Countries (OPEC), which meets on a frequent basis to agree oil production levels for all member countries. By managing oil production, OPEC is seeking to influence oil supply in the world and ultimately set the world price for oil. Since this is an agreement between countries it is not illegal, although perhaps it is not desirable.

Recent commercial examples include the agreement between British Airways and Virgin to fix fuel surcharges on transatlantic flights. Sony and Hitachi were suspected of agreeing to fix the price for LCD screens used in the Nintendo DS; and in Europe both Unilever and Proctor and Gamble have been fined for fixing the price of detergents (see Box 6.3). In all these cases the number of large competitors is small, the product displays little differentiation and costs are relatively stable, all of which provide a possible mechanism for co-ordinating price increases. Table 6.3 presents further examples ranked by the size of the fine imposed by the European Union (EU) Competition Commission. Again a quick consideration of each case would suggest fairly homogeneous products and large economies of scale, leading to a small number of firms and relatively stable costs and demand.

Price fixing can have economy-wide implications and in many countries and economic regions cartels are considered an illegal activity. Within the EU, suspected cartels are investigated by the European Competition Commission, which under antitrust legislation has the power to seek penalties in the courts for up to 10 per cent of a company's global turnover. In practice big headline cases are most likely to suffer the 10 per cent penalties, while the vast majority of cases pay fines which equal less than 1 per cent of their global turnover. Any company involved in a cartel can seek immunity from prosecution under the Commission's leniency policy. The leniency policy provides protection to companies that inform on other members of the cartel and/or assist in the investigation and prosecution of a cartel. In order to gain immunity under the leniency policy, then a company must be the first to inform the Commission about the cartel. If a company is not the first to inform the Commission, then a reduction in penalties can be achieved if that company provides the Commission with evidence which reinforces its ability to prove the existence of the cartel. Again the first company to provide evidence gains most, with a possible penalty reduction of 30–50 per cent, the second company can gain a reduction of 20–30 per cent and subsequent companies up to 20 per cent. In addition to placing large fines on the companies involved in cartels, a number of countries have begun to make company directors face criminal prosecution and, where guilty, serve prison sentences.

Figure 6.5 provides data on the number of suspected cartels investigated between 2007 and 2010 by the EU Competition Commission and the number of decisions where the case was proven. While the number of investigations has been increasing the number of decisions has remained fairly constant.

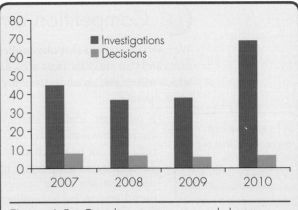

Figure 6.5   Cartel investigations and decisions
Source: EU Competition Commission, Cartel Data.

Box 6.3

Unilever and P&G fined $457 million by EU for detergent cartel

Unilever and Procter & Gamble Co. (P&G) agreed to pay €315.2 million ($457 million) in fines to end a European Union probe into price fixing of laundry detergent.

P&G, the maker of Ariel washing powder, was fined €211.2 million and Unilever will pay €104 million for agreeing with Henkel KGaA, the German maker of Persil, to fix prices of the detergent in eight countries over a three-year period, the European Commission said today in an emailed statement.

Henkel was not fined because it was the first company to supply evidence to regulators. Antitrust agencies across Europe have been investigating cosmetics and detergent manufacturers for agreements to fix or increase prices. The commission said it reduced fines on the other two companies because they co-operated in the probe and agreed to settle.

'Henkel, Procter & Gamble and Unilever engaged in their anti-competitive practices at their own initiative and at their own risk,' Joaquin Almunia, the EU's competition chief, said. Almunia said the companies agreed not to cut prices when they shrank the size of packaging for laundry detergent and then later agreed to increase prices.

Unilever spokesman Trevor Gorin said the amount it has to pay was 'within the provision made by Unilever in its 2010 results'. Procter & Gamble spokeswoman Marina Barker said it had 'previously taken an appropriate financial reserve' to cover the fine and strengthened its global compliance program.

The three companies started co-ordinating prices in 2002, the Commission said, when they put into practice an industry-wide initiative to improve environmental performance by reducing the weight of washing powder and its packaging.

The price-fixing deal covered Belgium, France, Germany, Greece, Italy, Portugal, Spain and the Netherlands, the Commission said.

In 2010, Italy fined Unilever, P&G and 13 other companies for co-ordinating price increases for cosmetics. It did not fine Henkel because it was the first to inform regulators of the cartel. German units of Unilever, Henkel and Sara Lee were fined about €37 million by the country's cartel office in February 2008 for fixing toothpaste and detergent prices.

Adapted from an article by Aoife White, Bloomberg, 13 April 2011. Used with permission of Bloomberg L.P. © 2012. All rights reserved.

Competition among rivals

We now understand that oligopolies are industries characterized by a small number of large firms and that entry barriers are a likely cause of them. We now need to develop a framework which will enable an understanding of how firms within an oligopoly will decide to compete or co-operate.

> A kinked demand curve shows that price rises will not be matched by rivals, but price reductions will be.

Economists' earliest attempts to model oligopolies involved the **kinked demand curve**, shown in Figure 6.6. The idea behind the kinked demand curve is that price rises will not be matched by rivals, but price reductions will be matched. The kinked demand curve is therefore often used to explain the pricing behaviour of competing petrol stations. Since car drivers can always drive on to the next filling station, each petrol station has a number of nearby competitors. If one station increases prices, then all others will hold prices and attract additional traffic. If a station cuts prices, then more traffic will flow to that station and competing outlets will counter the move by matching the price cut. It is only when the price of oil changes that all petrol stations move prices together.

At the price of £10, there is no point in a firm changing its prices. If it increases prices, all rivals will hold their prices; but if the firm drops prices, all rivals will also reduce their prices. Therefore, above the price of £10 demand is price elastic and below demand is inelastic, thus leading to the kinked demand curve.

The marginal revenue line is vertical at the profit-maximizing output. This is because the demand curve changes slope at this output level. The difference between the elastic and inelastic demand curves leads to a stepped change in the marginal revenue.

As a result, the demand curve has a different shape above and below the current market price:

1 If the firm raises its price, rivals will keep their prices constant. The firm will, therefore, lose customers when it raises prices. As a result, demand above the current market price is elastic.

2 In contrast, if the firm reduces its prices, all rivals will match the price reduction. The firm will not gain more demand by reducing prices. Demand below the current market price is therefore inelastic.

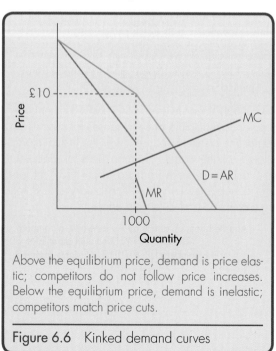

Above the equilibrium price, demand is price elastic; competitors do not follow price increases. Below the equilibrium price, demand is inelastic; competitors match price cuts.

Figure 6.6 Kinked demand curves

We will see below that economists question the theoretical merits of the kinked demand curve, but it provides a reasonable starting point for understanding some real-world examples. The pricing of petrol, or at least the reduction in petrol prices, can be explained using the kinked demand curve. Once one petrol supplier announces a price reduction, all other petrol suppliers respond with similar price reductions in order to protect their market share. We might therefore argue that demand is inelastic for price reductions. Similarly, no firm would increase prices without full knowledge that other firms would follow. This occurs in the petrol market because of the cost of oil. So price rises only occur when all firms face increased input costs and are therefore willing to increase prices together. But no firm would make a decision to be more expensive than its rivals. Furthermore, because of the vertical portion of the marginal revenue line, the change in the marginal cost of oil has to be quite large in order to deliver a change in the equilibrium price of petrol. Therefore, because of the kinked demand line, modest daily changes in oil prices are unlikely to feed into erratic daily price changes at the petrol pumps.

Box 6.4

EDF 'throws first punch' in energy price war

Experts are predicting an 'energy price war' as pressure mounts on the Big Six providers following an announcement by EDF Energy that it will slash its gas prices by 5 per cent.

The firm said the cut meant its standard dual-fuel tariff would be the cheapest on the market – but the typical cost for households is still £166 or 16 per cent higher than EDF's average bill of £1037 in September 2010.

EDF's move comes shortly after smaller companies Ovo and Co-operative Energy announced plans to cut their prices.

Consumer groups welcomed the cut, but pointed to the round of price rises last autumn. 'EDF has thrown the first punch in the energy price war to come,' said Mark Todd, director of the independent price comparison service Energyhelpline.com. 'The reduction is less than expected, but it is quicker, and for that millions of homeowners concerned about winter bills will be relieved.'

Overall, suppliers put prices up in the past 18 months by 21 per cent – or an average of £224 – adding £2.24 billion on to household energy bills. The latest cut will mean that bills of EDF Energy customers on a dual-fuel tariff will drop from £1241 to £1203.

Richard Lloyd, executive director of consumer organization Which?, said: 'This gas price cut will be welcome news for millions of consumers with already squeezed household budgets. But it follows a hike of 15 per cent last November. Now the pressure is on for the rest of the major suppliers to follow suit.' Ann Robinson, director of consumer policy at uSwitch.com, added: 'Pressure to cut prices has been mounting, and now one of Britain's biggest energy suppliers has let the cork out of the bottle.'

Adapted from an article in *The Scotsman*, 12 January 2012.

In Box 6.4 the case of energy price cuts is discussed. When EDF cut its energy prices, the almost perfect substitutability between suppliers raised the strong expectation that all other competitors would follow.

In contrast to the petrol market, Box 6.5 provides an example of how firms reacted to Netflix's decision to enter the UK market. Lovefilm, as a close competitor in the streaming market for films, immediately cut prices. BSkyB, the dominant supplier of movies but using satellite technology, retained its price position. The difference between the pricing strategy of energy suppliers and BSkyB probably reflects the degree of substitutability. Energy is very homogeneous and so the market demand is very elastic below the equilibrium price; therefore all suppliers follow price cuts. Films via satellite do not require a good broadband connection and are easily accessible. As such they are differentiated and therefore not perfect substitutes for those offered by cheaper rivals. Market demand is likely to be less elastic below the equilibrium price.

Problems with the kinked demand curve

The kinked demand model has a number of positive features. First, the demand curves for the firm are based on potential or expected responses from the firm's rivals. Hence, strategic interdependence is a feature of the model. Second, the model predicts stability in pricing. This occurs because of strategic interdependence; rivals will react to price changes in a way that makes them ineffective. Also, price stability occurs because, even when the firm's costs increase, as a result of the vertical portion of the firm's MR line the profit-maximizing output and price are unlikely to change. Only when costs change by a large amount will the intersection of marginal cost and marginal revenue move from the vertical portion of the marginal revenue line.

The major drawback associated with the kinked demand curve is that it does not explain how the stable price is arrived at in the first place. There must be a prior process that determines the price. The kinked demand curve merely explains the stability once the price is set. We therefore need an approach that understands strategic interdependence more fully.

Box 6.5

Netflix sparks price war with UK launch

US online DVD rental company Netflix launched in Britain and Ireland on Monday, taking on BSkyB's premium drama and movies offerings and prompting Amazon-owned rival Lovefilm to offer a new cut-price service.

In its first expansion outside the Americas, which the company has said will push it into a loss this year, Netflix said its prices and instant access to a broad range of online entertainment would attract new customers.

Lovefilm, which has 2 million customers in its core British market, immediately announced Lovefilm Instant – an Internet streaming-only offer to undercut Netflix – in addition to its current offer that combines streaming and DVD rental by post.

Netflix Chief Executive Reed Hastings told Reuters in an interview that BSkyB would be its main competition. 'Lovefilm is not the enemy. When you talk about big entertainment businesses, Sky Atlantic and Sky Movies are huge, and our advantage is we are much lower priced than the Sky packages, and it is all on demand – click and watch,' he said.

Co-founded by Hastings in 1997, Netflix created the US market for DVD rental by post but has suffered more recently as it shifts to lower-margin instant online delivery. Nonetheless, Hastings said Netflix had no option but to press ahead aggressively with the new delivery technology, describing DVD postal delivery as being 'a little bit like travelling by horse and buggy'.

'In the long term, Internet TV – the idea that you can click and watch anything you want – is such a powerful concept that we are investing heavily,' he said.

Netflix is offering unlimited online access to tens of thousands of hours of movies and drama for £5.99 per month in Britain and €6.99 (£5.76) in Ireland, plus a month's free trial. The new streaming-only package from Lovefilm, which said on Monday it had had a record number of subscribers signing up in the fourth quarter, will cost £4.99 per month.

BSkyB charges £20 per month for an entertainment package that includes Sky Atlantic, a US-focused drama channel launched a year ago that includes exclusive rights to HBO's back catalogue, including the popular *Game of Thrones*. Europe's biggest satellite broadcaster demands that customers sign up for contracts, and have a set-top box and connection to a Sky dish. Sky Movies costs £16 per month on top of the basic television package.

Both Netflix and Lovefilm can deliver their content via a wide range of Internet-connected devices such as games consoles, tablets and Blu-ray players as well as computers and smart televisions.

Adapted from an article by Georgina Prodhan and Matt Cowan on Reuters, 9 January 2012.

6.6 Game theory

> Game theory seeks to understand whether strategic interaction will lead to competition or co-operation between rivals.

In response to this challenge, economists have now turned to **game theory** as a means of understanding strategic interdependence. In economic jargon, a game has players who have different pay-offs associated with different strategic options. In the business sense, we could have two firms (players): they could start a price war and compete against each other or they could try to co-operate with each other (strategic options). Each combination has different profit outcomes (pay-offs) for the two firms.

The original version of game theory is known as the prisoners' dilemma, where two criminals have to decide to co-operate or compete with each other in order to win their freedom. The prisoners' dilemma is similar in style to the end game in the television show *Golden Balls*, where opposing players have to decide to steal or share, in order to win the cash prize.

The prisoners' dilemma

Two criminals, Robin Banks and Nick Scars, are arrested by the police. There is little evidence against the criminals and they face a short spell in prison if convicted. The police decide to offer each prisoner a deal. If they provide evidence against their fellow criminal, then they will go free. The dilemma facing the prisoners is illustrated in Figure 6.7.

The matrix of sentences represents the possible pay-offs to each prisoner. If they both stay silent, then they will receive a short sentence. If Nick Scars stays silent and Robin Banks provides evidence, then Nick Scars receives a long sentence and Robin Banks goes free. Sitting in separate cells, with no ability to communicate, both prisoners are most likely to provide evidence and receive medium sentences. They will cheat, or compete with each other, when it would have been in their interests to co-operate and stay silent. Just as with the game *Golden Balls*, sharing is attractive, but it is possibly outweighed by the gains of stealing – but only if the other player does not steal as well.

		Robin Banks	
		Stays silent	Betrays
Nick Scar	Stays silent	Nick Scar: short sentence Robin Banks: short sentence	Nick Scar: long sentence Robin Banks: goes free
	Betrays	Nick Scar: goes free Robin Banks: long sentence	Nick Scar: medium sentence Robin Banks: medium sentence

Figure 6.7 The prisoners' dilemma

To understand why competing, rather than co-operating, with a rival is preferable, we need to understand the importance of the Nash equilibrium.

The Nobel Laureate John Nash proved that the optimal solution for any game must result in each player making an optimal decision given the potential response of its rival. This is now known as the **Nash equilibrium**. The important point to note from the Nash equilibrium is that each firm considers what its rivals can do before deciding on its own strategy. A player does not simply decide what it wants to do. For example, Liverpool or Barcelona do not decide to run on the pitch and kick the ball in the back of the opposition's net. Clearly, this is what they want to do. Instead, they think about what their rivals will do, how they play, what formation they might use and who their opponent's key players are. Liverpool or Barcelona can then develop a football strategy based on what their rivals are going to do. The Nash equilibrium is just formalizing this obvious decision-making process by saying, 'Consider your rival's likely behaviour before you decide what you are going to do'.

		Firm A	
		Co-operate	Price war
Firm B	Co-operate	50:50	20:60
	Price war	60:20	30:30

The numbers in each box are the pay-offs to each firm (firm B is always on the left and firm A on the right). The Nash equilibrium is where both firms choose to start a price war, earning £30 million each. This is because when choosing its strategy A examines B's options: if B tries to co-operate, A's best response is to start a price war; and if B starts a price war, A's best response is again to start a price war. B will come to the same conclusion when examining its response to A.

Figure 6.8 Game theory, pay-off matrix

Now let us examine a price war game in Figure 6.8, using Nash's argument. Firm A looks at firm B and sees that B can do one of two things: co-operate or start a price war. We can begin by examining what happens if B decides to co-operate. If A then also co-operates, it will earn £50 million, but if A begins a price war, then it will earn £60 million. Firm A now thinks about B's other option, which is to start a price war. If A tries to co-operate, it will only earn £20 million, but if A also takes up the option of a price war, then it will earn £30 million. Firm A now knows that, whatever B does, it is always optimal for A to start a price war. Firm B will go through a similar decision-making process and come to the same conclusion – that whatever A does, B will start a price war. The Nash equilibrium has both firms embarking on a price war earning £30 million each.

Nash equilibrium occurs when each player does what is best for themselves, given what their rivals may do in response.

Dominant strategy is a player's best response, whatever its rival decides.

In this example, each firm's optimal decision is independent of its rival's decision. A's optimal decision is to cheat, regardless of whether B cheats or co-operates. A is known as having a **dominant strategy** and, given that our example has symmetric pay-offs for B, then B also has a dominant strategy.

When each player has a dominant strategy, the Nash equilibrium will be unique – only one cell in the pay-off matrix will provide an equilibrium solution. However, this unique equilibrium is not necessarily optimal. In the case of the prisoners' dilemma, both players would be better off if they co-operated.

Repeated games

> In a single-period game, the game is only played once. In a repeated game, the game is played a number of rounds.
>
> A credible commitment or threat has to be one that is optimal to carry out.

Starting a price war or displaying 'non-cooperative' behaviour is a general response in a **single-period game**. Therefore, as a rule, whenever you play a game once, as our rivals did in Figure 6.6, or strategically interact with someone once, then cheat. For example, consider buying a second-hand car from the classified ads. You see a car and go to meet the owner. You will say the car is not perfect and the owner will tell you that the car is fantastic. It does not matter whether the car is good or not; you are both displaying non-co-operative behaviour. You both do this because you do not expect to meet again to buy or sell cars in the future. It is a one-period game, so you both cheat. You would like the price to fall; they would like the price to rise.

The way to move from a non-co-operative Nash equilibrium to a co-operative Nash equilibrium is to play the game repeatedly and use a strategy known as 'tit-for-tat'. Under tit-for-tat, you will co-operate with your rival in the next round if they co-operated with you in the last round. If they cheated on you in the last round, you will never co-operate with them again.

In the game above, if A and B co-operate they both receive £50 million. If, in the next round, A decides to cheat and start a price war, it will earn £60 million, or £10 million more than from co-operation. But in the next rounds B will always commit to a price war, so the most A can earn is £30 million. Firm A has the choice of gaining £10 million in the next round and then losing £50 million – £30 million = £20 million for every round afterwards. Therefore, short-term gains from cheating are outweighed by the long-term losses of a repeated game.

However, in order for tit-for-tat to work, the threat to always display non-co-operative behaviour, if your rival cheated in the last round, has to be a **credible commitment**.

Recall the Spanish invaders who burnt their boats – their threat to fight the local Incas, rather than sail off to a safer shore, was very credible when they no longer had any boats!

For a business illustration, let us go back to the car example. This time consider buying a car from a dealer of one of the major manufacturers. With a second-hand car they usually provide a warranty. They do this because they value your repeat business. The dealer does not want to sell you a bad car. Instead, they would like you to feel secure in the fact that the car is good and they will fix any problems. They are not cheating; they are trying to co-operate. In fact, by offering warranties they are making a credible commitment to provide you with a trouble-free car. They are willing to do this because the potential revenue streams from your repeat business outweigh any gains from selling you a bad car at an expensive price.

Finally, we can consider the market for love. Marriage is a repeated game. If one partner cheats by seeing someone else, then divorce is a fairly robust method of never agreeing to co-operate with the cheating partner again. In the singles market, in contrast, seeking co-operation for fun with someone you find attractive could be a one-period game if you only expect to see them once. If they ask what you do, it is better to cheat. Claiming to be a catwalk model or a professional footballer are better options than admitting to being an indebted student.

In summary, strategic decisions require an understanding of the potential responses. If a firm, or individual, plays a game once, they should cheat. If they play repeatedly, then they should try to co-operate for as long as their rivals co-operate.

Game theory extensions: reaction functions

The prisoners' dilemma is a simplification and the existence of joint dominating strategies is not always assured. We therefore need to understand how interdependent firms should react

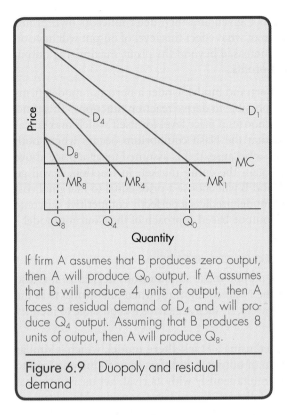

If firm A assumes that B produces zero output, then A will produce Q_0 output. If A assumes that B will produce 4 units of output, then A faces a residual demand of D_4 and will produce Q_4 output. Assuming that B produces 8 units of output, then A will produce Q_8.

Figure 6.9   Duopoly and residual demand

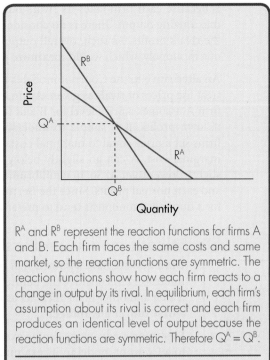

R^A and R^B represent the reaction functions for firms A and B. Each firm faces the same costs and same market, so the reaction functions are symmetric. The reaction functions show how each firm reacts to a change in output by its rival. In equilibrium, each firm's assumption about its rival is correct and each firm produces an identical level of output because the reaction functions are symmetric. Therefore $Q^A = Q^B$.

Figure 6.10   Reaction functions

to the expected behaviour of their rivals. We can achieve this by considering a market with two firms – known as a duopoly.

Assume two firms, A and B, face an industry demand D_1 and constant marginal costs MC. This situation is illustrated in Figure 6.9. Firm A must decide how much to produce based on what it expects firm B to produce. To begin the analysis, A assumes that B produces nothing. A, therefore, faces the entire industry demand D_1 and the associated MR_1. As a profit-maximizer, A selects the output Q_0, where MC is equal to MR_1. If A now assumes that B produces four units, then A faces the **residual demand** line D_4 and the associated marginal revenue line MR_4. The profit-maximizing output for A is now Q_4. We can continue allowing A to alter its assumption about B. So, if A assumes that B produces eight units, then A faces the residual demand D_8 and the marginal revenue MR_8. The profit-maximizing output for A is now Q_8.

The model depicted in Figure 6.9 is referred to as a **Cournot model**, after the French economist Augustin Cournot. Under a Cournot model, each firm treats its rival's output as a given. In our example, A assumed B's output was 0, 4 and then 8. If we continued the analysis by enabling A to consider each possible output by B, we would understand how A would react to every possible output choice available to B. This would derive the **reaction function** for A. Similarly, the analysis can be repeated in order to derive the reaction function for B.

Figure 6.10 presents the reaction functions for A and B. R^A is the reaction function for A and R^B is the reaction function for B. Both reaction functions slope down, indicating the negative relationship between the output choices made by A and B. If B decreased its output, then A would react by increasing its output. Importantly, A would increase its output by less than B's reduction. This ensures that output falls overall and that the price increases in the market. Since A is not cutting its output, it now receives a higher revenue on all its previous units.

The equilibrium output occurs where both reaction functions intersect. This is a Nash equilibrium since each firm is making an optimal decision based on what its rival is expected to do. This equilibrium is also sub-optimal, just as in the case of the prisoners' dilemma. This

Residual demand is equal to the market demand less the amount produced by the firm's rivals.

In a Cournot model, each firm treats its rival's output as a given.

A reaction function shows that a firm's profit-maximizing output varies with the output decision of its rival.

is because each firm takes its rival's output as a given and then determines its own profit-maximizing output. There is no consideration of what effect this level of output will have on the rival's profits. As such, overall output is increased beyond the profit-maximizing output of a monopoly, which would maximize joint profits.

An alternative to the Cournot model is the Bertrand model. Under a Bertrand model, firms treat the prices of rivals as given. Again, it is possible to derive reaction functions. This time, firm A assumes a price level for B and then chooses a price level for itself which maximizes its own profits. It is simple to understand that the Nash equilibrium occurs where both firms set a price equal to marginal cost. This is because, if B is assumed to set a price above marginal cost, A can go slightly below and gain the entire market. In reaction, B will go slightly lower than A. So, in equilibrium, A and B will choose a price equal to marginal cost and earn normal profits. Since the Bertrand model predicts a perfectly competitive outcome for a duopoly, economists tend to prefer the output-based approach of the Cournot model.

Stackelberg models and first-mover advantage

> First-mover advantage ensures that the firm which makes its strategic decision first gains a profitable advantage over its rivals.
>
> A Stackelberg model is similar to the output approach of Cournot, but firms do not make strategic decisions simultaneously.

Until now we have assumed that both players make simultaneous decisions. It is also interesting to consider the nature of the Nash equilibrium when one firm acts as the leader and other firms then act as followers. In such scenarios it is possible to identify a **first-mover advantage**.

First-mover advantage can be examined using a **Stackelberg model**, which is similar to a Cournot model in its examination of output, but differs in enabling one firm to make its decisions first, rather than simultaneously with its rival. Let us assume that firm A is the leader and firm B is the follower. A now has a considerable advantage over its rival. In full knowledge that B will react to A's decision, it is clear to A that the equilibrium must be located on B's reaction function. A must therefore choose an output which maximizes its own profits and is located on B's reaction function. If A goes higher than the Cournot equilibrium output, B must reduce output and this helps to support a higher price and greater profits for A.

Under a Stackelberg model, A's marginal revenue in Figure 6.9 will be higher than under Cournot. This is because A knows that B will support the market price by reducing its output Q^B in response to an increase in Q^A. A will therefore choose a higher level of profit-maximizing output. In the case of Figure 6.10, A's reaction function R^A becomes steeper and intersects R^B higher up and in equilibrium $Q^A > Q^B$, with A earning higher profits than under a Cournot equilibrium. Of course, this equilibrium is only feasible if A's output decision constitutes a sunk cost and is thereby a credible commitment to produce at Q^A. If B suspects that A has incurred no sunk costs, then it will be likely to increase output and A will follow with a cut in output. The equilibrium will then revert to the Nash–Cournot solution.

A business example may help to illustrate the complexities of the model. If a leader is planning to build a production facility, then the Stackelberg model would suggest that the leader can gain a first-mover advantage by building a bigger facility. The followers will then observe the leader's productive capacity and follow with a smaller facility. If additional profits do accrue from being first, then these can be reinvested in additional plant, R&D and new product lines. As such, first-mover advantages become persistent advantages. Of course, there are risks with first-mover advantages. Costs can be high, risks can be unknown and followers can learn from your mistakes.

 ## Business application: compete, co-operate or gain a first-mover advantage?

If we return to our game theory illustration in Figure 6.8, the most desirable box for firm A is top right, where it earns 60. However, from our discussion we know that A will never find itself in this box. In a one-period game its rival will also compete and the two firms will earn 30 each, while in a repeated game both firms will try to co-operate and earn 50 each. Earning 60 in the top right is a situation where firm A competes and B decides to be friendly. A, therefore, dominates its rival B and in so doing controls the market. So, how do you convince your rival not to compete? We now know that the answer to this question rests on gaining a first-mover advantage.

This is a problem which taxed Sony and Toshiba, who battled for supremacy in the high definition DVD market. Sony developed and launched Blu-ray, while Toshiba led the HD DVD project. The competing approaches used different recording formats and were incompatible with each other.

The race to win market share can be viewed as a game. If Toshiba and Sony had agreed to cooperate and develop the same format, then movie-makers and consumers would have been very happy. Movie-makers would have felt assured that they could sell high-definition DVDs of their films, and consumers would have been happy to purchase a high-definition DVD player and television to view the films. The market would have grown and Sony and Toshiba would have shared a higher level of overall profits. This would be the top-left box of Figure 6.8.

In contrast, if Sony and Toshiba continued competing, movie-makers did not know which format to support and consumers ran the risk of buying a machine that could only play one format of discs. The market was slow to grow, and both firms earned reduced profits. This would be the bottom-right box of Figure 6.8.

Alternatively, if one company had won enough support that it became commercially unattractive for the remaining competitor to continue, then the winning firm would have been a monopoly and earned huge profits. Depending upon which firm won, this would be the top-right or bottom-left box of Figure 6.8.

In order to try to win, Sony and Toshiba sought out and gained the support of leading film studios. At times, some film studios changed sides and the balance of power between Blu-ray and HD DVD was finely balanced. Fortunately for Sony, it possessed a strategic option which offered the chance of first-mover advantage – Playstation 3 (PS3). By building Blu-ray into the PS3, Sony accelerated the adoption of its technology into many households around the world. In contrast, Toshiba's hopes of being adopted rested on the family decision to upgrade the trusted and reliable DVD player. By going first, or quickest, into households Sony gained a commanding lead in the market. Film studios realized and switched allegiance from Toshiba to Sony. Blu-ray is now the dominant format for high definition films.

6.9 Business application: managing supply costs – anonymous auctions for supermarket contracts

We have seen that, in repeated games, firms are likely to behave co-operatively. This presents a substantial risk to supermarkets who repeatedly run auctions to provide them with products. In particular, because supermarkets are retailers, they do not ordinarily manufacture their 'own-labelled' products. Instead, they ask competing manufacturers to bid for contracts. Today, it might be next month's lemonade contract; tomorrow, it might be fish fingers or soap powder. The firm that can produce the product most cheaply wins the contract. With supermarkets coming to the market repeatedly, it is in the interest of competing manufacturers to co-operate with each other. For example, rival manufacturers of fish fingers could agree to split the market. When bidding for supermarket X's contract, company A would never undercut company B. In return, when bidding for supermarket Y's contract, B would never undercut A.

For a supermarket, this is a serious problem. The way to stop it is to prevent co-operation. Supermarkets try to achieve this by organizing blind auctions over the Internet. The fish finger contract opens for bidding at 2.00 p.m. on Wednesday and companies make bids. The web page shows the amount of it, but it does not say who made it. The bidders now find it difficult to co-operate. In fact, it is now very easy to cheat because only the supermarket knows who you are. In this example, supermarkets can see the problem of co-operation and take steps to prevent its occurrence.

There is, however, a problem with the supermarket's strategy. In generating competition among its suppliers, it runs the risk of pushing some of them out of business. Therefore, in the long run the supermarkets could end up with monopoly suppliers in their key product markets rather than competitive industries, and we saw in Chapter 5 that such a situation could be dangerous.

 ## 6.10 Business data application: competition in the bus market

In 2011 the UK Competition Commission reported on an investigation into the market for local bus services. The market was found to be highly concentrated and a number of factors led to the conclusion that there was likely to be an adverse effect on competition. We can use some key learning points from this chapter to explore and understand many of the issues raised by the Competition Commission.

First, the Competition Commission found that majority of local bus services are highly concentrated. While there are 1245 bus operators in the UK, the five-firm concentration ratio for local bus services was 69 per cent. In fact, so concentrated is the market, that only another five companies have a share of the market which exceeds 1 per cent. This highly concentrated industry reflects the impact of merger activity, where on average 14 bus-operating companies have merged per year for the past 20 years.

Figure 6.11 presents market share data for the largest operators in urban areas. For the vast majority of urban areas, the largest company has a market share which is at least 50 per cent or more. Therefore, not only is the UK market highly concentrated among five large players, but each local market is dominated by one big operator.

Profitability was also investigated. Figure 6.12 presents data on the increases in operating costs and ticket revenues. During the period under investigation costs have generally increased faster than revenues. However, further analysis indicated that profit margins are good, in particular, for the largest operators the average rate of return over five years was estimated at 13.6 per cent, almost 4 per cent higher than the estimated cost of capital.

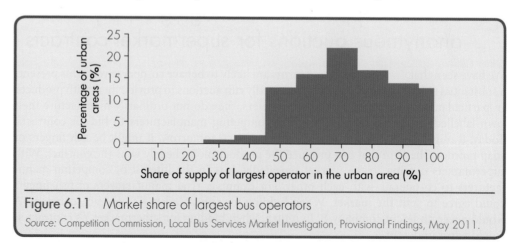

Figure 6.11 Market share of largest bus operators

Source: Competition Commission, Local Bus Services Market Investigation, Provisional Findings, May 2011.

Three types of competition were identified and examined by the Competition Commission, head-to-head, potential and new entrant. Head-to-head competition occurs between rival operators where their routes overlap in part, or as a whole. Potential competition is the threat effect from operators in other areas who may redeploy some of their buses onto routes in another area and in competition with the incumbent bus company. New entrants are bus operators who are not nearby to a local market and who may decide to expand their operations by entering new markets where there is already a competitor.

Bus operators were found to avoid head-to-head competition. Not many overlapping routes were found and where they existed

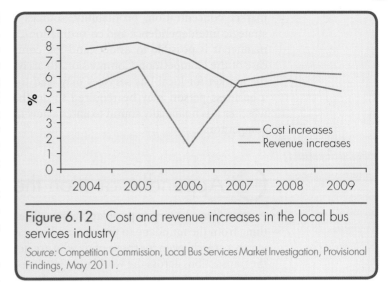

Figure 6.12 Cost and revenue increases in the local bus services industry

Source: Competition Commission, Local Bus Services Market Investigation, Provisional Findings, May 2011.

the partial overlaps were small. Historically, head-to-head competition in the local bus market has been intense and short-lived. Competition tends to be almost predatory with the incentive to remove the competition as quickly as possible. Competition is often characterized by increased frequency of service, rather than fare reductions, or improved quality. In effect, rivals seek to starve each other of passengers. Head-to-head competition tends to be unstable with services changing, operators exiting and the services changing yet again. For this reason, bus operators were found to avoid head-to-head competition.

Threats from potential competition and actual new entrant competition were also found to be limited due to entry barriers. Sunk costs were found to be significant. Bringing a route to profitability requires substantial investment in promotional activities and running services at below optimal capacity. Unlike the sale of a bus, or the transfer of q bus to an alternative route, investing in the setup and development of routes cannot be recouped once a decision to exit is taken. Therefore with significant sunk costs the threat of potential and new competition is constrained. Further entry barriers were also identified, including access to suitable depot sites and bus stations. Finally, threats of competitive retaliatory action from incumbents highlights the importance of strategic interdependence in highly concentrated markets. If incumbent bus operators are willing to compete at a loss to drive out competition, then a new entrant will be inclined to stay away from the market.

The Competition Commission did not find any significant cost economies related to scale. However, they did note that with scale comes the advantage of offering passengers network connections and attractive multi-journey tickets. A small new entrant is unlikely to have multiple routes and so cannot offer a network travel solution to multiple destinations across an urban area. Without the scale and benefits of a network, the opportunity to sell discounted multi-journey tickets is also reduced. As such, small-scale new entrants are placed at a significant disadvantage to large-scale incumbents.

The Competition Commission also explored co-ordinated effects: were the local bus service companies acting together, rather than competing? Given the small number of large competitors, the relatively homogeneous nature of bus travel and the stability in supply and demand, cartel-like behaviour could be possible. There was some evidence that bus operators in one area did not bid for new contracts against companies in other areas. However, there were also sound commercial reasons for not doing so, such as the cost of servicing the distant geographic region from a distant bus depot. Therefore, evidence in support of a co-ordination effect was deemed by the Competition Commission to be weak.

In summary, the Competition Commission when investigating the local bus services market covered a number of areas with which you should now be familiar. These areas included market concentration, profitability, sources of competition, entry barriers, sunk costs, strategic interdependence and co-ordination/cartels. By using these concepts in a structured manner it is possible to understand the competitive dynamics of the market and, in the case of the Competition Commission, to arrive at the conclusion that the characteristics of the market for local bus services may lead to an adverse effect upon competition. You as a business person may be required to do the same and, like new bus operators, decide whether it is financially sound to enter a new market which already contains large dominant competitors.

Appendix: auction theory

Auctions have become a popular pastime. The online auction site eBay offers for sale everything from the mundane to the bizarre. If you are trying to find something, eBay is generally worth a search, even for those of us who are not addicted to bidding online. Amazingly, if all the transactions across the world on eBay were added together, this auction site would be the world's fourth largest economy; and auction fever does not stop with eBay. Where home makeover shows once dominated television programme-making, auction format television shows now lead the schedules. With the likes of *Flog It*, individuals are invited to bring along heirlooms and see what they can make in an auction.

While clearly an attraction of auctions is the risky, almost gambling-based adrenalin of seeing what you have to pay to gain an item, or what you can gain by selling an item, the uncertainty is also a very important part of the experience. However, while eBay and *Flog It* might be a bit of fun, for firms auctions are serious commercial activities and, just as with eBay and the like, auctions for commercial services have grown in popularity. Supermarkets use auctions to place orders for own-label items. Sporting associations use auctions to license live television rights, and governments use them to license railway operators, mobile telecommunications and even the right to run lotteries. Fortunately, game theory can provide an understanding of optimal behaviour in auctions. Under a Nash equilibrium, each player will make an optimal bid based on what they believe their rivals will do in response.

The purpose of this section is to provide you with an understanding of auctions. It will begin by explaining the four main types of auction format and introduce the important concepts of private versus common values. With these basic blocks of knowledge in place, the discussion assesses auctions from both a buyer's and a seller's perspective. Understanding optimal bidding strategies under each auction format will enable a seller to assess the auction format that will deliver the greatest revenue; and recognizing the problem of the winner's curse will provide a cautionary note to bidders.

Auction formats

There are seen to be four auction formats: the English auction, the Dutch auction, the first-price sealed-bid auction and the second-price sealed-bid auction.

In an English auction, bids begin low and are increased incrementally until no other bidder is willing to raise the bid. Bids can either be cried out by the auctioneer, with bidders nodding, or waving their papers in acceptance, or they can be input electronically, as is the case with eBay. In a Dutch auction, prices start high and are gradually reduced until a bidder accepts the price and wins the auction. This type of auction is commonly used in Holland to sell flowers and agricultural produce. Under the first-price sealed bid auction, bidders must submit a single bid, usually in writing. Bidders have little idea what anyone else has bid, and the highest bidder wins. The second-price sealed bid is a variation on the first-price auction. Again, bids are submitted in writing, but the highest bidder pays the price of the second-highest bid.

Common versus private values

Auctions can also differ in the values held by bidders. With **private values** each bidder forms a private, probably subjective, view of the item for sale. This would be especially true with an item on eBay such as a watch, suit or an antique. Some individuals will like the item, but others will love it! Each bidder knows their own value of the item, but they do not know the value of the item to the other bidders. Furthermore, each bidder is unlikely to change their assessment of the item's value, even when they become informed of other bidders' valuations.

> **Private values** means each bidder has a private, subjective, value of an item's worth.
>
> **Common values** means the value of the item is identical for all bidders, but each bidder may form a different assessment of the item's worth.

Under common values, an item is worth exactly the same to all bidders, but no bidder is sure what the item is truly worth. For example, as part of a game you might be shown a jar filled with coins. Along with your friends, you are asked to bid for the jar; the highest bid wins the jar. Clearly, in this example the jar is worth the same to each bidder, but no one is sure how much the jar is worth (without opening it and counting the coins). Real-life commercial auctions tend to be characterized by **common values** – the rights to an oilfield, to show live football games or to run a national lottery. The commercial value of the rights is common to all bidders, but what they are truly worth is presently unknown. Significantly, under common values a bidder might be willing to change their bid once they know all the bids. For example, a comparison of bids will help to inform bidders about the accuracy of their own valuation of the item for sale. If other bidders are bidding high, then a bidder might be led to believe that they have undervalued the item.

With this basic understanding of auction formats, we can now consider which is the best auction format for a seller. If we assume that a seller wishes to maximize their revenue, we need to find the auction format which results in the highest bid. We will therefore analyse bidding behaviour in each auction format under which bidders have private values.

English auction with private values

A second-hand Swiss watch is offered for sale. You value the watch at £1000, a rival bidder values the watch at £900. What is your optimal bidding strategy? Under a Nash equilibrium, you should consider what your rival will do in response. So, if your rival bids £500, offer £501. Your rival may back out of the auction and you win at £501, saving yourself £499. Or your rival may top your bid and you are no worse off, since it cost you nothing to bid and you gained nothing. This strategy of raising the bid should continue until either your rival quits, or you reach your maximum willingness to pay. Significantly, in English auctions the winning bid will always be a fraction higher than the second-highest valuation. For this example, you will win the auction with a bid of £901.

Second-price sealed bid auction with private values

Under this auction format each bidder's dominant strategy is to submit a bid equal to their maximum willingness to pay. So, in the case of the Swiss watch, you will bid £1000 and your rival will bid £900. Since the highest bidder pays the second-highest price, you will win the auction for £900, which is almost identical to the outcome from the English auction.

To see why submitting a bid equal to your maximum willingness to pay is optimal, consider the following:

* **Lowering the bid.** If you lower your bid below your maximum willingness to pay, this will only alter the outcome if your new lower bid is less than your rival's. For example, a bid of £950 will still ensure you win the auction and pay £900. But a bid of £850 will result in you losing the auction (and your rival gaining the item for £50 less than they were willing to pay). So, in simple terms, you cannot win by lowering your bid, you can only lose.

- **Raising your bid**. If you bid £1050, this will not help you if your rival is going to bid less than £1000, your maximum willingness to pay. You will still win the auction and still pay the second price. If your rival is going to bid more than £1050, then again raising your bid has no impact. However, if your rival was to bid between £1000 and £1050, say £1030, you would now win the auction, but at a penalty. You would now have to pay £30 more than your maximum value. So, raising your bid above your maximum willingness to pay can only harm you.

So, you should not raise or lower your bid, simply submit your maximum willingness to pay.

First-price sealed bid auction with private values

Again, we are bidding for the Swiss watch and you value it at £1000. Should you submit a bid equal to your maximum willingness to pay as in the second-price sealed bid auction? To answer this question, consider Figure 6.13. The line S has a positive slope indicating that an increase in your bid raises the probability of winning the auction. If you bid your maximum willingness to pay, £1000, the expected payment on winning the auction will be equal to the areas A + B + C + D + E + F. If you lowered your bid to, say, £900, your expected payment upon winning the auction will be E + F.

The expected value (the benefit) from winning at £1000 will be A + B + C + D + E + F; exactly equal to the expected payment. The expected value (the benefit) of winning at £900 will be made up of the expected value of £900, plus the expected value of saving £100. So the expected value will be E + F + D.

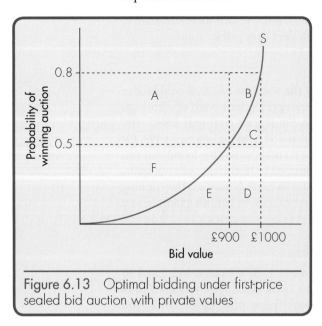

Figure 6.13 Optimal bidding under first-price sealed bid auction with private values

In the case of bidding £1000, the expected value equals the expected cost, so you break even. But when reducing your bid to £900, the expected value exceeds your expected payment by the area D. It is therefore always optimal to bid below your maximum willingness to pay. You reduce your chances of winning, but you raise your potential gains.

The question now becomes by how much should you reduce your bid below your maximum willingness to pay. The answer rests on understanding the likely behaviour of your rival bidders and recognizing the interdependence of your bids. While beyond the scope of this discussion, it can be shown in Nash equilibrium that the optimal bid is (N − 1)/N multiplied by the bidder's maximum willingness to pay, where N is the number of bidders. So, with two bidders, the bid should be a half of your maximum willingness to pay. The winning bid will turn out to be the expected value of the second-highest willingness to pay.

Dutch auction with private values

Under this type of auction, prices are called out and you bid when they have fallen to a level which is optimal for you to make a bid. In the case of our Swiss watch, you will not bid when prices are above your valuation of £1000. You will also not bid when the watch reaches the price of £1000, because you would not save yourself anything. Rather, you will let the price fall and try to maximize the difference between the price you pay and the price at which you value the item. In essence, you would be trying to maximize area D in Figure 6.13. But how far should you allow the price to fall? The answer to this question is the same as for the first-price sealed bid auction. You would consider the likely bidding behaviour of your rivals and as long as your rival had not accepted a higher price, you would bid (N − 1)/N multiplied by your maximum willingness to pay. In Nash equilibrium, the price received by the seller would again be the expected value of the second-highest willingness to pay.

The revenue equivalence theorem

This brings us to an important result. Under all auction formats, the bidder with the highest willingness to pay wins, but they always pay a price roughly equal to the second-highest valuation. So, since the auction format does not alter the amount of revenue received by the bidder, we observe **revenue equivalence** across competing auction formats.

> The revenue equivalence theorem states that under private values each auction format will generate the same level of revenue for the seller.

Auctions and common values: the problem of the winner's curse

Let us return to our jar filled with coins. The auction will be a first-price sealed bid auction. No bidder is better or worse at estimating the value of the jar of coins. Some will overestimate, others will underestimate, but on average (if the auction was repeated) all bidders would form an unbiased estimate of the jar's value. Each bidder also submits a bid which is increasing in their estimation of the jar's worth. So, the bidder with the highest valuation submits the highest bid and wins.

The problem with this type of auction for bidders is that the winner must by definition have formed an overly optimistic valuation of the jar of coins. They will therefore end up paying more for the jar than it is actually worth. So the **winner's curse** is that the winner actually loses. Knowing that the winner's curse exists will alter bidders' behaviour. If you think the jar is worth £100, you might then adjust your bid down to compensate for the risk of overestimating its worth and bid, say, £50. If all bidders are rational, they will all reduce their bids for this reason. In addition, bidders might reduce their bids further in order to maximize area D in Figure 6.13. Therefore, the problem for the seller in auctions with common values is that bidders will behave conservatively in order to avoid the winner's curse, leading to a lower sale price.

> The winner's curse is where a winning bid exceeds the true value of the sale item.

Unlike the case with private values and first-price auctions, where the optimal bid increases with the number of bidders, e.g. when $N = 2$, $(N - 1)/N = 1/2$; and when $N = 3$, $(N - 1)/N = 2/3$, under common values and a first-price sealed bid auction, optimal bids will decrease with an increase in the number of bidders. For example, if there are three bidders and you win, you have outbid only two other people. However, if there are 101 bidders, then you have outbid 100 other bidders and your estimate must have been very wrong. So, with an increase in the number of bidders, individual bidders will behave more conservatively and reduce their bids by more to avoid the winner's curse.

What can sellers do to avoid this problem? Simple: the winner's curse and conservative pricing occur because of a lack of information. If bidders had more information regarding other bidders' valuations, then they could more appropriately gauge the accuracy of their own willingness to pay. English auctions offer a solution. As bids are called out, each bidder can observe the valuation and willingness to pay by other bidders. If bids rise quickly, pessimistic bidders can revise their valuation of the item and enter the bidding. Therefore, within an English auction and common values, the incentive to be conservative is removed and the final price is higher. This perhaps helps explain why the English auction is the most commonly observed format.

Summary

1. Under monopolistic competition, there are a large number of small firms, freedom of entry and exit, few opportunities for economies of scale, and the use of product differentiation.

2. Long-run equilibrium in monopolistic competition is a tangency equilibrium, which results in zero economic profits, excess capacity, above-minimum average costs and price in excess of marginal costs.

3. Oligopolies are marketplaces with a small number of large firms, typically four or five. UK banking, supermarkets and even the media industry are good examples.

4. An important feature of oligopolistic markets is strategic interaction. If one firm makes a strategic change, all other firms react. When one UK supermarket decided to open on Sundays, all other supermarkets followed.

5. Two interesting questions occur when examining oligopolies: (i) Why do oligopolies exist? (ii) How will firms compete with each other?

6. Oligopolies can exist because of exogenous economies of scale. The natural cost structure of the industry results in only a small number of large firms meeting the minimum efficient scale.

7. Alternatively, natural scale economies might be limited and so, in order to create entry barriers, existing firms might manipulate the cost characteristics of the industry by perhaps making advertising a large component of operating costs. This creates high levels of endogenous costs and reduces entry.

8. Sunk costs cannot be recovered when exiting a market. If large costs are associated with brand development, then these will be sunk. This increases the risk of entry and so can also lead to the creation of entry barriers.

9. Without sunk costs, markets are contestable. Potential rivals can threaten to enter a market. In order to limit entry, firms within the market will reduce prices and profits to make entry less attractive. As a result, even with a small number of large firms, contestable markets will approximate to perfect competition.

10. Game theory can be used to understand strategic interaction. Games consist of players, pay-offs and decision rules.

11. A Nash equilibrium is where players make an optimal decision based on what their rivals might do. In single-period games, the Nash equilibrium requires each player to cheat or display non-co-operative behaviour. In a multi-period game with no known end, the optimal strategy is tit-for-tat, where if you co-operated in the last round, your rival should co-operate with you in the next round. If not, you should never co-operate with them again.

12. Reaction functions illustrate a firm's best response given the possible responses of its rival.

13. A Cournot game involves firms making decisions over output. A Bertrand game involves firms making decisions over prices.

14. The Nash equilibrium for a Bertrand game has both firms charging a price equal to marginal cost.

15. The Stackelberg model illustrates first-mover advantages.

16. In the repeated environment of firms bidding for supermarkets' own-label contracts, it is likely that co-operation will occur, where rivals agree not to undercut each other on price. In order to prevent this and generate competition in the auction, supermarkets run blind auctions, where it becomes difficult for rivals to co-ordinate their bids. It even enables rivals to cheat on each other behind a cloak of secrecy.

17. There are four auction formats: English auction, first-price sealed bid auction, second-price sealed bid auction and Dutch auction.

18. Under private values, the value of an item differs across bidders. Under common values, the item has the same intrinsic value to each bidder, but bidders are unsure of the true value of the item.

19. Under private values, all four auction formats enable the bidder with the highest willingness to pay to win the auction. But they only pay the second-highest price. This is known as the 'revenue equivalence theorem'.

20. Under common values, bidders face the problem of the winner's curse, where the highest willingness to pay vastly exceeds the intrinsic value of the item.

21. To avoid conservative bidding under the winner's curse, an English auction format provides bidders with clearer information on the item's true value.

Learning checklist

You should now be able to:
- Explain monopolistic competition
- Provide examples of oligopolies
- Explain the concept of strategic interdependence
- Identify natural and strategic entry barriers
- Understand the kinked demand curve model of oligopoly and provide a critical review
- Explain game theory, the concept of a Nash equilibrium and optimal strategies in single-period and repeated games
- Understand reaction functions
- Discuss the key differences between the Cournot, Bertrand and Stackelberg models
- Explain how game theory can be used to control the behaviour of rivals in auctions
- Identify the main types of auction and discuss the difference between common and private values
- Explain the revenue equivalence theorem and the winner's curse
- Examine and review Competition Commission reports on the degree of competition using economic concepts

Questions

connect

1. How do the assumptions of perfect competition and monopolistic competition differ?
2. List five industries which are likely examples of monopolistic competition.
3. How do the equilibrium conditions differ between perfect competition and monopolistic competition?

EASY

EASY

4. What are the main types of entry barrier that are likely to be associated with oligopoly?

5. Under a kinked demand line, is demand more or less elastic above and below the equilibrium price?

6. When is collusion likely to fail?

7. What is a Nash equilibrium?

8. In the single-period Prisoners' Dilemma, both prisoners confess. Is this optimal?

9. How might two strategically interdependent players be encouraged to co-operate with each other?

10. Is it possible and sensible to gain a first-mover advantage?

INTERMEDIATE

11. Monopolistic competition is sometimes criticized for displaying excess capacity. Explain why excess capacity exists in equilibrium and evaluate whether it is bad for society.

12. Do you consider it fair that whistle-blowers, who are the first to admit to being in a cartel, are immune from prosecution?

13. Assume your company is operating in a cartel, agreeing to raise prices and reduce output. If the cartel is ongoing, then the game is in effect repeated. Under what circumstances would your company cheat?

DIFFICULT

14. Electrical retailers promise to match each other's prices. Is this co-operation or competition?

15. A firm is considering whether it should be first to invest in a new market. Provide the company with your best economic advice.

Exercises

EASY

1. True or false?

   (a) A key aspect of an oligopolistic market is that firms cannot operate independently of each other.

   (b) Cartels may be workable if members enter into binding pre-commitments.

   (c) Under a kinked demand curve, demand is assumed to be price inelastic under a rise in prices.

   (d) In a one-period game, the strategy of tit-for-tat is optimal.

   (e) In a repeated game with no known end, it is always optimal to cheat.

   (f) With private values, an English auction format will raise the highest revenue for an item.

INTERMEDIATE

2. Suppose that there are two firms (X and Y) operating in a market, each of which can choose to produce either 'high' or 'low' output. Table 6.4 summarizes the range of possible outcomes of the firms' decisions in a single time period. Imagine that you are taking the decisions for firm X.

   (a) If firm Y produces 'low', what level of output would maximize your profit in this time period?

   (b) If you (X) produce 'high', what level of output would maximize profits for firm Y?

   (c) If firm Y produces 'high', what level of output would maximize your profit in this time period?

(d) Under what circumstances would you decide to produce 'low'?

(e) Suppose you enter into an agreement with firm Y that you both will produce 'low': what measures could you adopt to ensure that Y keeps to the agreement?

(f) What measures could you adopt to convince Y that you will keep to the agreement?

(g) Suppose that the profit combinations are the same as in Table 6.3, except that if both firms produce 'high' each firm makes a loss of 8. Does this affect the analysis?

Table 6.4 Firms' decisions

		Firm Y			
		Low output profits		High output profits	
Profits:		X	Y	X	Y
Firm X	Low output profits	15	15	2	20
	High output profits	20	2	8	8

3. In what ways can an understanding of game theory be used to understand the development of competition between Sony and Toshiba in the market for high-definition DVD players?

DIFFICULT

Growth strategies

CHAPTER

7

Chapter contents

Growth strategies at a glance 165

7.1 Business problem: how should companies grow? 165

7.2 Reasons for growth 167

7.3 Horizontal growth 167

7.4 Vertical growth 170

7.5 Diversified growth 177

7.6 Evidence on mergers 178

7.7 Business application: horizontal growth by merger 180

7.8 Business application: vertical growth – moving with the value 181

7.9 Business application: economies of scope 182

7.10 Business data application: trends in mergers and acquisitions 183

Summary 185

Learning checklist 186

Questions 186

Exercises 187

Learning outcomes

By the end of this chapter you should understand:

Economic theory

LO1 The difference between horizontal, vertical and diversified growth

LO2 Learning curves

LO3 Transaction costs

LO4 The hold-up problem

LO5 Economies of scope

Business applications

LO6 Why a small company within an oligopoly wished to merge with a rival

LO7 Why Madonna left her record label and joined a tour company

LO8 Why Google is branching out beyond search technology

LO9 How to recognize and understand recent patterns in merger and acquisition activity

At a glance Growth strategies

The issue

If firms are profit-maximizers, then it seems reasonable to assume that, in the longer term, increasing profits will be associated with increased size. Admittedly, in the near term some profits may have to be sacrificed in order to grow the business. Managerial time might be diverted to finding and selecting growth opportunities, rather than concentrating on generating profits from the current operations. It therefore becomes important to understand how a firm can grow, benefit from and manage the problems associated with different modes of growth.

The understanding

A firm can grow in three main ways. First it can 'do more of the same'. A car-maker might decide to make more cars. Second, a firm might reduce its trading relationships by providing its own inputs, or by organizing its own distribution and retailing. Third, a firm might begin to operate in a completely different market. These three options are, respectively, known as horizontal, vertical and diversified growth. The reasons behind each type of growth are varied, but essentially they relate to the ability to increase revenues and reduce costs. This chapter will provide an understanding of these issues.

The usefulness

An understanding of growth options is essential for understanding how a business can exploit profitable opportunities. Moreover, an understanding of growth options provides an insight into strategic behaviour and, therefore, how the firm can gain greater control over its markets and its competitors.

7.1 Business problem: how should companies grow?

Box 7.1 highlights the growth achieved by French supermarket Carrefour by investing in emerging markets. This type of growth would be classed as **organic growth**. A key question for business managers is: how fast and how sustainable is organic growth?

In a market with rapidly expanding demand, organic growth can be very sustainable. In mature markets, such as the European supermarket sector, organic growth can be slow and limited to the rate of growth of consumer spending on food and other grocery items. Also, organic growth can be reduced by competition. Strong competition can cut prices and volumes. Prices across all supermarkets fall and customers may move to the cheapest competitor. So organic growth can be good, but it also has its problems.

Not all growth has to be organic. Companies can expand their existing capacity by acquiring or combining their current assets with those of another company and/or competitor. In Box 7.1 a number of international competitors, including Walmart and Tesco, may be willing to acquire parts of Carrefour's business.

Merging two similar companies is referred to as **horizontal growth** because the company is growing its current operations. While such growth brings in more sales, it may also enable a company to achieve economies of scale and bring down operating costs.

In addition to horizontal growth it has become common for many supermarkets to move into non-food areas such as banking, electronics and clothing. This type of product line expansion would be considered diversification by an economist. **Diversification** is not a particularly easy category to define because it can include related and unrelated diversification. For example, a supermarket operating in the grocery, banking, electronics and food sectors could be viewed as having unrelated diversification, but they could equally be seen as different aspects of the retail market and therefore related.

> Organic growth is an increase in sales from the same or comparable retail space.
>
> Horizontal growth occurs when a company develops or grows activities at the same stage of the production process.
>
> Diversification is the growth of the business in a related or unrelated market.

Box 7.1

Carrefour's EM conundrum

Georges Plassat, who was appointed on Monday as the new chief executive of Carrefour, the world's second largest retailer after Walmart, will have many questions on his agenda.

Among them is what to do about emerging markets (EMs), arguably the brightest spot in the French group's business. After a decade of slow but steady decline – including five profit warnings in 18 months and three chief executives in five years – Carrefour shareholders have good reason to be grateful for these far-flung operations. But will they hang on to their jewels, or will they sell?

Emerging markets – namely Brazil, Argentina, Colombia, China, Taiwan and Indonesia – accounted for more than 27 per cent of Carrefour's sales last year. Latin America and Asia were the company's fastest growing regions – up 10.1 per cent and 5.1 per cent respectively, compared to France (+0.9 per cent) and Europe (−2.9 per cent).

With shares in Carrefour down nearly 50 per cent over the past year and little hope of a quick turnaround, the case for selling off the EM business is getting compelling.

Jaime Vazquez, analyst at Santander in Madrid, reckons that the break-up value of the company is about three times the current market capitalisation. He calculates that Carrefour's Latin American operations could be worth €10 billion–€12 billion ($14 billion–$17 billion), with Asia worth some €6 billion–€7 billion. The French business could be worth €10 billion, while the rest of Europe could be worth €8.5 billion. This amounts to as much as €37.5 billion against Carrefour's current market capitalization of €12.4 billion.

Carrefour will have no shortage of suitors. Walmart has hired advisers at UBS to examine a potential bid for Carrefour's Brazilian business. Casino, which bought Carrefour's Thai operations in late 2010, and Tesco, which also took part in the auction, would be natural candidates for Carrefour's Asian businesses.

Pressure for Carrefour to release value from the business has already prompted the group to exit part of its Asian operations and spin off Dia, its discount operations. It also looked into splitting its property assets into a separate listed unit but backtracked following opposition from some shareholders and criticism from analysts.

Plassat cannot deal with all these questions at once. But shareholders will be looking for action.

Adapted from an article by
Pan Kwan Yuk, 31 January 2012. From the *Financial Times*
© The Financial Times Limited 2012. All rights reserved.[1]

> **Vertical chain of production** encapsulates the various stages of production from the extraction of a raw material input, through the production of the product or service, to the final retailing of the product.
>
> A company is said to be **vertically integrated** if it owns consecutive stages of the vertical chain.

A company may grow in a diversified way to offset risk. Non-food sales may grow more than food sales. Equally, sales in emerging markets may grow at a faster rate, reducing a supermarket's dependence on developed economies for sales and profits.

There is also a third means of growth and this is known as vertical growth. Supermarkets are a collection of separate and sequential operations. Sourcing, producing, distributing and retailing constitute what economists refer to as separate aspects of the **vertical chain of production**.

The vertical chain is composed of all the separate commercial activities that add value to a product. For example, a supermarket may own farms and processing facilities to produce and package its own meat and vegetables. One reason for integrating all stages of production, is to seek greater control over the value chain and is described by economists as **vertical integration**. As a retailer of fresh produce, a supermarket can derive greater security and quality in relation to its supplies by growing vertically.

In order to understand why a company might wish to grow horizontally, vertically or in a diversified manner, we need to understand the benefits and problems associated with horizontal, vertical and diversified expansion.

---

[1] McGraw-Hill Education is solely responsible for providing this abridged version of the original article, and The Financial Times Limited does not accept any liability for the accuracy or quality of the abridged version.

7.2 Reasons for growth

If we begin by accepting the general proposition that firms are in business to maximize profits, then it seems reasonable to suggest that firms grow in order to improve profitability. If this is true, then, examining Figure 7.1, a firm seeking horizontal, vertical or diversified growth must be expecting to gain from increases in total revenues and/or decreases in total costs. In this way, the two curves in Figure 7.1 will move further apart from each other. As the curves move apart, both the profit-maximizing level of output and the amount of profit-maximizing profit will increase.

We will examine horizontal, vertical and diversified growth in turn.

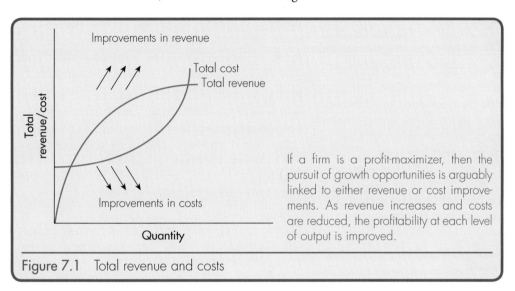

Figure 7.1 Total revenue and costs

7.3 Horizontal growth

Horizontal growth, or expansion at a singular point on the vertical chain, can occur in a number of ways.

Organic growth is associated with firms growing through internal expansion. For example, a manufacturer might build additional production facilities, such as assembly lines, or a new factory. A retailer, such as a supermarket, might build more outlets. An airline might buy more aircraft. Crucially, the firm is growing by investing in new assets, which add to its current stock of capital. As an alternative, a firm might consider growth by **acquisition** and **merger**.

In either case, the company grows by merging its activities with those of an existing operator. By going back through the theory established in previous chapters, we can now begin to analyse the benefits of horizontal growth.

> Acquisition involves one firm purchasing another firm. This might occur by mutual consent or, in the case of a hostile takeover, the managers of the acquired firm might try to resist the takeover.
>
> Merger generally involves two companies agreeing by mutual consent to merge their existing operations.

Horizontal growth and revenue

In Chapter 2 we examined the elasticity, or responsiveness, of demand to a change in price. The greater the number of substitutes, or rival products, the greater the price elasticity of demand. If demand is elastic, then a small change in the price results in a huge change in the quantity demanded. Therefore, in price-elastic markets, with lots of substitute products, we argued that there is a clear incentive for firms to engage in a price war. If one firm reduces its prices, it quickly attracts market share from its rivals. However, in response, rivals may also drop their prices and each firm will retain the same market share but selling at a lower price. If demand is price inelastic, or not responsive to a change in price, then a price reduction will not have a significant impact on demand. Moreover, total revenues will decline.

Box 7.2

British Airways' rivalry with Virgin resumes over bmi airline sale

British Airways and Virgin Atlantic have resumed their bitter, decades-old rivalry in a suitors' duel over the airline bmi.

Bmi's owner, the German national carrier Lufthansa, confirmed that takeover talks were underway with Virgin Atlantic as well as at BA's parent, International Airlines Group. 'We can confirm that we are also in talks with Virgin Atlantic,' said Lufthansa, which hopes to make a final decision on the auction winner by the end of March.

IAG had emerged as the frontrunner in November when it confirmed that it had reached 'an agreement in principle' to acquire bmi, which would take its share of slots at Heathrow from 45 per cent to 53 per cent. That brought immediate warnings from BA's arch-competitor in the UK-to-US market, Virgin Atlantic, which said a takeover could be bad for consumers by allowing its rival to raise fares on routes to and from Heathrow.

Virgin Atlantic is now hoping to capitalise on those concerns with its bid. It is offering a deal that would expect less scrutiny from officials at the European Commission, the authority responsible for competition concerns within the European Union, and therefore would be signed off more quickly.

The carrier founded by Sir Richard Branson, who co-owns the business with Singapore Airlines, controls just 3 per cent of the slots at Heathrow.

Both bidders are now conducting due diligence, amid reports that Virgin Atlantic has bid £50 million for the loss-making carrier, which reported an operating loss of €154 million (£131 million) for the first nine months of the year. Andrew Lobbenberg, analyst at Royal Bank of Scotland, said the news was 'straightforwardly adverse' for IAG, which was created this year by the merger of BA and Spain's Iberia. 'The probability of them winning bmi looks lower today and if they do win it, it seems likely it will be for a higher price than they previously might have thought,' said Lobbenberg.

BA has reportedly bid £100 million for bmi and analysts believe it might have to raise its price further in order to dissuade Lufthansa from choosing the swifter option of a Virgin Atlantic deal. One legal expert said Virgin Atlantic appeared to hold a regulatory advantage owing to its much smaller share of the Heathrow slots market, even in combination with bmi.

Julianne O'Leary, head of competition at the law firm Stephenson Harwood, said: 'From a competition perspective, the Virgin Atlantic deal does indeed appear to raise fewer issues.'

Competition over the lucrative transatlantic market has been at the heart of a series of spats between BA and Virgin Atlantic, most recently over the formation of an alliance between BA and American Airlines that allows both carriers to co-operate over fares and scheduling – anathema under conventional competition rules.

Adapted from an article by Dan Milmo in *The Guardian*, 12 December 2011. © Guardian News & Media Ltd 2011.

Therefore, the optimal response under price-inelastic demand is to raise prices in order to boost total revenues.

Reducing competition

If we now think about merger and acquisition, by definition the number of competitors in the market is reduced by one. Therefore, because merger and acquisition lead to a reduction in the number of substitutes, it is likely that the elasticity of demand is reduced. When competition is reduced, price wars are less likely and firms have more scope for increasing, rather than decreasing, prices. See Box 7.2 and the case of the take-off and landing slots and London's Heathrow airport.

If we also think about perfect competition, oligopoly and monopoly, as discussed in Chapters 5 and 6, we can reinforce the arguments made above. Under perfect competition with a large number of competitors, prices and profits are lowest. Under monopoly, prices and profits will be highest. In the case of oligopoly, consolidation in the industry can lead to greater co-operation as opposed to increased competition. As discussed in Chapter 6, it is optimal for a cartel to act as a monopoly supplier and reduce output to the market. However, it is in each firm's interest to cheat and increase output. It is easier to monitor and enforce the tacit or explicit agreement made among the members of a small cartel than of a large one. In a small cartel you only need to gain agreement among, say, two or three companies. In a large cartel you need to gain agreement among a much larger number of companies, which is difficult. Therefore, mergers and acquisitions can lead to increased co-operation and the success of cartels.

Exploiting market growth

Aside from any changes in the price elasticity of demand, horizontal growth may be undertaken in order to exploit revenue growth. Growing demand could stimulate organic growth. As more customers move into a market, the firm can exploit increased revenue opportunities by investing in more productive assets. As more passengers have been willing to fly with low-cost airlines, easyJet and Ryanair have purchased more aircraft. In recent years, coffee bars have suddenly appeared on many high streets, seeking to meet and exploit the rapid increase in customers.

In summary, the incentives from revenue and horizontal growth emanate from two main sources: first, a reduction in the number of competitors and, therefore, a fall in the price elasticity of demand, making price rises easier and price wars less likely; and second, to take advantage of customer growth opportunities in the market.

Horizontal growth and costs

The obvious reason for horizontal growth relates to costs. In Chapter 3, we discussed economies of scale at length. However, in summary, as a firm increases its scale of operation, by increasing its capital input, it generally experiences a reduction in long-run average costs. Therefore, we can argue that a firm will try to grow in order to exploit economies of scale. This is often used as a rationale for merger. When bringing two companies together, managers often talk up the potential for cost reductions by reducing and sharing managerial functions. Two companies need two chief executives; one company needs only one chief executive. Two companies need two finance, legal, marketing and human resource management (HRM) departments; one company needs only one of each. These single departments will generally be capable of operating at a size which is less than the sum of the two separate departments, achieving this through greater staff utilization. This is often referred to as **rationalization**.

> **Rationalization** is associated with cutbacks in excess resources in the pursuit of increased operational efficiencies.
>
> The **learning curve** suggests that, as cumulative output increases, average costs fall.

However, it is also possible that a firm can become too big. We saw in Chapter 3 that a very large firm can experience diseconomies of scale, where problems of control and co-ordination make the productivity of a large firm decrease, leading to a rise in long-run average costs. Therefore, it is sometimes the case that large firms decrease the scale of their operations in order to bring about cost improvements.

An alternative cost reason for horizontal expansion is the benefit to be had from the **learning curve**.

This is depicted in Figure 7.2 and shows that, as the firm produces successive units, or adds to its cumulative output, average costs fall. Importantly, the firm is considered to be in long-run equilibrium. The fall in average costs is not driven by the law of diminishing returns. Instead, as a firm produces additional output, it learns how to improve productivity. The classic example is the production of a jumbo jet. This is a massive project and requires careful planning and learning. In what order should the plane be assembled? When are the wings attached, when is the wiring completed, when can the seats be added? If wings are added too early, then there is the risk of having to remove them at a later date in order to finish another task, such as adding the fuel tanks. However, once the mistake is made and learnt, it will not be made again. So, when the next plane is built, fewer assembly mistakes will occur. The

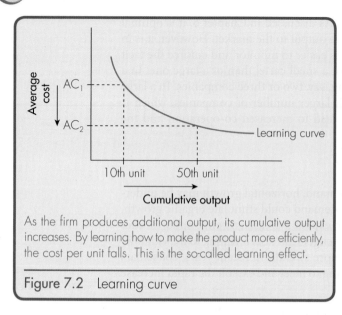

As the firm produces additional output, its cumulative output increases. By learning how to make the product more efficiently, the cost per unit falls. This is the so-called learning effect.

Figure 7.2   Learning curve

plane will be built more quickly and at a lower cost. As more planes are built, the assembly teams will learn how to carry out each assembly task more quickly and develop new operating techniques. Eventually, at high levels of cumulative output, all learning opportunities are exploited and the reduction in costs diminishes to zero. At this point the learning curve becomes flat.

A firm producing 100 units a day learns faster than a firm producing ten units a day. In recognizing this point, a firm could grow organically in order to be in a position to exploit the learning effect sooner than its rivals. Alternatively, a competitor may have already produced many units and acquired the relevant cumulative experience through learning. An attractive strategy is to merge with or acquire the existing firm, in an attempt to gain the acquired experience. However, it is debatable how easy it is to transfer experience between organizations. The experience of one company is likely to be related to the systems, producers and cultures of that company. The learning effect stems from the experiences of a group of individuals with shared memories, values and understanding. Transferring such intangible understandings and benefits effectively to another organization is likely to be problematic.

7.4 Vertical growth

Cost reasons

When a firm grows vertically, either moving up or down its vertical chain, it is attempting to integrate additional value-adding activities into its existing activities. There can be a number of reasons for doing this.

Location benefits

Integrating consecutive activities from the vertical chain can reduce production costs. For example, steel smelting plants are often located next to steel rolling plants. This reduces transport and heating costs. Extremely high temperatures are needed to produce steel. Similarly, in order to roll the steel into usable sheets, the steel has to be hot. With the plants co-owned and located next to each other, the hot steel can be transferred easily to the rolling plant. If the two activities were separate, the new hot steel would have to be cooled, transferred by road to the rolling plant, re-heated and then rolled – resulting in much higher production costs.

Industrial clusters occur when related industries co-locate in a region. Examples include Silicon Valley and electronics, Germany and automotives, London and finance.

The importance of co-location is also relevant in understanding **industrial clusters**. In particular locations similar industries cluster together in order to gain advantages, either in terms of cost, or in accessing supporting technologies and expertise. In Figure 7.3 we can see that financial services clusters are located in particular countries and indeed cities, UK (London), France (Paris), Germany (Frankfurt) and Switzerland (Zurich). Banks, insurance companies, investment companies, lawyers and accountants co-locate providing a concentrated pool of expertise which facilitates the growth of the cluster.

In the automotive sector the strongest clusters are in Germany, Czech Republic and Sweden, where there is design expertise, supply lines and assembly activities.

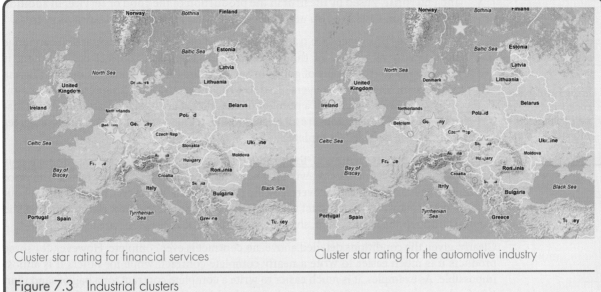

Cluster star rating for financial services

Cluster star rating for the automotive industry

Figure 7.3 Industrial clusters

Source: The European Cluster Observatory, www.clusterobservatory.eu.

Economies of scale

In contrast, when economies of scale are important, vertical disintegration may also result in cost benefits. For example, the manufacture of a product may require a particular raw material input. If the manufacturer developed its own raw material division, then, without supplying other companies, the division is likely to be operating at a very small scale. However, if a raw material supplier is able to operate independently and supply many manufacturers, it is possible that it can exploit economies of scale. If economies of scale are important in a value-adding activity, it could be better for the manufacturer to abandon its raw material division and instead buy from a larger independent company.

Problems from monopoly

While economies of scale might be important cost considerations, it is also possible that raw materials might be supplied by a monopoly, in which case the price of the raw material could be higher than under a competitive market. A simple solution to this problem is to purchase the monopoly supplier and transfer the raw material between divisions of the same company. But what price will the production division pay the raw material division? The optimal price for transferring the raw material to the production division is the marginal cost of production in the raw material division. Under such a price, allocative efficiency would hold with the price being equal to marginal cost. As an explanation, the price paid and, therefore, the value of the last unit will be exactly equal to the cost of producing the last unit. This enables the combined profits of the raw material division and the production division to be maximized. More important, if we return to an argument made in Chapter 5, the monopoly price is always greater than the marginal cost. Therefore, buying the raw material supplier and charging an internal price equal to the marginal cost has to be cheaper than the price charged by a monopoly supplier.

Transaction costs

In order to fully develop your understanding of the various cost reasons for vertical growth, we need to introduce a new cost concept. In Chapter 3, when examining costs, we only focused on production costs. These are the costs of the factor resources – land, labour, capital

> Transaction costs are the costs associated with organizing the transaction of goods or services.
>
> Under a **complete contract** all aspects of the contractual arrangement are fully specified.

and enterprise – used by the firm in the production of the good or service. In addition to production costs, we also need to consider what are known as **transaction costs**.

When goods or services are traded, the costs of organizing the transaction can range from low to very high. At the most simplistic level, if a contract or agreement is entered into for the supply of goods or services, the time of managers negotiating the contract and the cost of lawyers hired to write the contract both represent transaction costs. Economists highlight a number of factors that are likely to lead to higher transaction costs. These factors are all related to the degree to which the contract or agreement can be declared '**complete**'.

For example, the nature of the product, including its characteristics, the materials used to make it and its size, will all be described within the contract terms. The price and time of delivery will also be covered by the contract. Finally, the contract will also set out how the performance of the product supplier will be measured and how the contract will be enforced through the legal system, should the terms of the contract be breached.

Clearly, given the conditions detailed above, no contract is ever complete. However, for some products it is much easier to write a nearly complete contract, while for others it is almost impossible. As examples, it is much easier to write a complete contract for a bag of sand than it is for lecturing services. Sand comes in standard bag sizes, a limited number of ranges, such as river sand or building sand, and if a company agreed to deliver a bag you would be able to verify its arrival. Now consider writing a contract for lecturing services. For a complete contract it would be necessary to define many things, including: during which hours the lectures would be given; what textbooks should be used; what topics should be covered each week; how the module should be examined; what topics and questions should be used during the tutorials; how difficult the examination should be; how marks should be awarded; how many students are expected to pass; how tutorial staff should be managed; and much more. It is clearly very difficult to define in full all the actions a lecturer should take during the running of a module. As a consequence, universities, like many employers, use incomplete contracts. Instead of defining all possible actions, contracts resort to simple statements such as 'a lecturer will be expected to communicate and expand knowledge'.

Rather than being complete, the contract is extremely vague. A sensible interpretation of the statement is that a lecturer is expected to communicate knowledge through teaching and expand knowledge through research. But of course there are many other interpretations. For example, answering the telephone and handling student enquiries is communicating and expanding knowledge. If the university expected the lecturer to teach and research, but the lecturer decided to simply answer telephone enquiries, then the university would experience substantial transaction costs. This is because the lecturer is choosing to undertake activities that the university did not intend. Aside from the ability to reinterpret the meaning of the contract, it is also very difficult for the university to measure the lecturer's performance. For example, let us assume many students fail the module. There could be many explanations, but let us concentrate on two. First, the lecturer did not perform well and the students did not benefit from the lectures. Second, even if this is true, the lecturer could blame the poor performance on the students' lack of effort during tutorials and revision. Because the effort of the lecturer and the students is not monitored by anyone from the university, it is difficult to support either argument. This therefore creates an environment within which the lecturer could act less than professionally. Lower performance by the lecturer represents a transaction cost.

We will shortly see how firms, and in our case universities, try to deal with these problems. But, first, it is useful to provide an understanding of the general factors which lead to greater transaction costs.

Complexity

Complexity is an obvious factor. Sand is an uncomplicated product; lecturing is a very complicated product. As the product or service becomes more complex (simple), the more incomplete (complete) the contract becomes. As the contract becomes more incomplete (complete), the higher (lower) are the costs of transacting.

Uncertainty

Uncertainty also affects the ability to write a complete contract. In the case of a bag of sand, uncertainty is less of an issue. You are not going to request a different bag of sand depending upon the nature of the weather. By contrast, in the case of lecturing services a university will expect the lecturer to be adaptable in the face of future changes. New theories may enter the subject, new ways of teaching might emerge, or the quality of the students each year could change. The university cannot write a contract detailing how the lecturer should deal with these changes, but a good lecturer will be expected to deal with these problems and opportunities using their professional discretion.

So, as uncertainty increases, the ability to write a complete contract diminishes and the cost of transacting increases.

Monitoring

While complexity and uncertainty are problems associated with writing a contract, monitoring and enforcement are problems associated with managing a contractual arrangement. The more simple and certain the environment, the easier it is to monitor a contract. Again, let us compare a bag of sand with the lecturer. It is very easy to monitor whether or not a bag of sand is delivered. You can see it, you can feel it and you can weigh it. But how do you know if a lecturer has communicated and expanded knowledge? How do you measure effective communication, or teaching? A high pass rate for the module could indicate good teaching. But it could equally indicate good students, or an easy examination.

In general when the good or service is more complex and the environment is more uncertain, the ability to monitor the incomplete contract is more difficult and costly.

Enforcement

When the contract is incomplete, the enforcement of the contract, by use of the legal process, is much more difficult.

If a company does not deliver your sand, it is fairly easy to prove breach of contract and ask a court to enforce delivery. However, if you cannot effectively define or measure the activities of a lecturer, then it is almost impossible to prove breach of contract. For example, if the university says that the lecturer has not communicated knowledge effectively, it will have to find a way of measuring the lecturer's level of effective communication. Since measuring communication is very difficult, it will be almost impossible to ask a judge to enforce the contract on a lecturer. The legal system cannot be used to enforce the contract. In knowledge of the fact that a university will find it difficult to measure and enforce performance, the lecturer can use the discretion provided within the contract to teach what they like, in a fashion that they prefer and examine the topics that they would like. Some do it well, others less well. The difference is transaction costs.

Make or buy?

In the case of production costs, we argued that firms are cost-efficient when they operate with minimum average costs at the lowest point on the average cost curve. It therefore also seems sensible to argue that firms will try to minimize transaction costs. In fact, the reduction or control of transaction costs is of fundamental importance for economists, because transaction costs are the very driving force behind firms. Without transaction costs, firms would not exist.

Transaction costs can be managed through competing systems. These are the market and the hierarchy, or managerial structure, of a firm. Theoretically, the system with the lowest transaction cost will be chosen.

The hierarchy, or managerial structure, of a firm is composed of the various managerial layers, beginning with directors, then moving down to senior managers, and eventually ordinary workers.

Transaction costs and markets

For market-based transactions to have a low transaction cost, the contract has to be as complete as possible. This requires low complexity and low uncertainty. In addition, monitoring must be easy and enforcement feasible. In such situations the ability to write a contract is easy and, therefore, low cost. Furthermore, the scope of the provider to perform below expectation in the delivery of the good or service is constrained by the easy monitoring and legal enforcement of the contract. The transaction costs of operating through the market are low.

In contrast, when the product is complex and uncertainty is high, it becomes more difficult and, therefore, more costly to write a contract. In addition, as the contract becomes more incomplete, greater discretion is handed to the provider of the good or service. Monitoring of the output becomes difficult, as the output is not clearly defined by the contract. As a result, enforcement becomes impossible. Recall the lecturer communicating and expanding knowledge. The output of the lecturer is not defined. It is left to the lecturer to use their discretion when designing the syllabus and delivery of the module. The potential for very high transaction costs by operating through the market becomes very high.

Transaction costs and hierarchies

The alternative is to organize the transaction within the firm and use the hierarchy or managerial structure to organize the transaction. The problem with incomplete contractual relationships is that they provide the producer of the good or service with too much discretion. To economize on writing a complete contract the university uses the phrase 'communicate and expand knowledge'. But by using the managerial structure of the university, it is possible to minimize the resulting transaction costs. For example, when a lecturer begins employment they will ordinarily be placed on probation for perhaps three years. Removal from probation and the confirmation of employment will only follow a set of successful lectures. Before a module begins the lecturer will not generally be allowed to choose any set of topics. Rather, they will be required to work to a module descriptor, which details the topics to be taught, the nature of the assessment and the key learning outcomes of the module for the students.

At the end of the module, students are asked to evaluate the module on various criteria. This is monitoring, and over a number of years and across a range of taught modules the university can develop an understanding of how well the lecturer performs. Through annual appraisals, annual training programmes and departmental discussions, the lecturer can begin to understand peer expectations regarding the acceptable level of lecturing performance and the nature of acceptable teaching styles. Management and colleagues have the potential to condition the lecturer's discretion, by advising on what is acceptable behaviour at work. Finally, with a shared understanding of acceptable performance the university can attempt to enforce acceptable delivery of lecturing services through pay awards and promotions. Lecturers who continually provide superior services, develop new teaching methods and lead research will generally be promoted. In contrast, over time, management will also be able to see who is not performing optimally and their cases for promotion might be declined.

Essentially, in the marketplace the legal process and competition among the various suppliers are used to enforce contractual commitments and keep transaction costs low. Within firms, contractual commitments are enforced through long-term monitoring by the managerial hierarchy and the periodic pay awards and promotion associated with good performance. In this way, transaction costs are reduced.

Firms therefore exist in order to reduce transaction costs. In fact, economists often refer to firms as a **nexus of contracts**.

> Nexus of contracts is a collection of interrelated contractual relationships, where the firm represents a nexus or central point, at which all these interrelated contractual relationships are managed in the pursuit of profit.

Transaction costs and vertical growth

How can we use these insights in order to understand how and when a firm will grow or shrink along its vertical axis?

If we consider the vertical chain, the answer is simple. The firm as a nexus of contracts will grow up or down its vertical chain when it needs to reduce its transaction costs by making use of its hierarchy or managerial structure to control its transactions. Similarly, a firm will shrink, or reduce in size as a nexus of contracts, when it believes it is possible to use the market to control its transactions. Consider the following examples.

Hospitals produce health care, but we need to recognize that health care is a combination of various value-adding activities: medical treatment from doctors and nurses, plus catering and cleaning services. Traditionally, all three services were performed by employees of the hospital. More recently, catering and cleaning services have been subcontracted to independent private companies. In doing so, the hospital has not grown vertically; rather, it has reduced its vertical boundaries. This is illustrated in Figure 7.4. The dotted lines represent the boundaries of the hospital's activities. In the left half of Figure 7.4, cleaning, catering and medical treatment are all inside the dotted lines. This is how hospitals traditionally organized themselves. Staff of the hospital carried out all three activities. In the right half of Figure 7.4, we see that only medical treatment is within the dotted lines of the overall healthcare provided by a hospital. Catering and cleaning are within their own dotted lines. This signifies that private companies provide catering and cleaning. Cleaning and catering are now being provided, or transacted, through the market. Periodically, the hospital will hold a tendering process, where it in effect holds an auction for its catering or cleaning contracts. The firm willing to offer its services at the lowest cost may win the contract.

Why have cleaning and catering been moved into the market, while medical treatment has been retained inside the hospital? The answer is that, from a transactional perspective, it is cheaper to buy catering and cleaning services from the market, but it is cheaper to provide medical treatment in-house. Consider trying to write a contract for cleaning services. It is reasonably easy to write a near complete contract: each hospital ward must be cleaned twice a day, each waiting room once, and operating theatres after each operation. Now consider trying to write a complete contract for a heart surgeon. For each possible heart problem the contract would have to stipulate how the surgeon would treat the patient. This is very complex

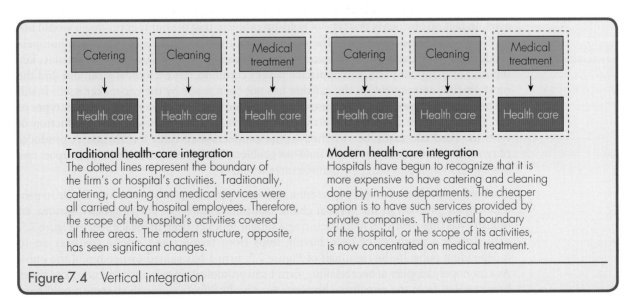

Traditional health-care integration
The dotted lines represent the boundary of the firm's or hospital's activities. Traditionally, catering, cleaning and medical services were all carried out by hospital employees. Therefore, the scope of the hospital's activities covered all three areas. The modern structure, opposite, has seen significant changes.

Modern health-care integration
Hospitals have begun to recognize that it is more expensive to have catering and cleaning done by in-house departments. The cheaper option is to have such services provided by private companies. The vertical boundary of the hospital, or the scope of its activities, is now concentrated on medical treatment.

Figure 7.4   Vertical integration

and, therefore, just as in the case of the university lecturer, it is better to leave treatment to the surgeon's discretion using an incomplete contract, where the contract might simply state that the 'surgeon will provide medical expertise in the cardiovascular department'. The hospital needs to measure the surgeon's performance against the contract. However, the performance of the surgeon can only be monitored over time by the hospital's management team. Good surgeons are promoted; poor ones are advised to move on. This long-term monitoring is best done inside the hospital's management systems, where other medical consultants can periodically provide a review of the surgeon's efforts and expertise. Such a process is very difficult if the hospital decided to contract surgeons on a short-term basis through the market.

Vertical growth: strategic considerations

> Hold-up problem is the renegotiation of contracts, and is linked to asset specificity.
>
> A specific asset has a specific use; a general asset has many uses.

An important transactional problem, not discussed above, is associated with asset specificity and the **hold-up problem**.

An aircraft can be used on a number of routes. Its use is more general than specific. A production line designed to make bumpers for a Ford Focus is a very **specific asset**, as it is very difficult to use the production line to make bumpers for any other car.

Consider the vertical chain for airlines. A new aircraft is purchased and used to fly between cities A and B. Additional value-adding inputs are landing slots at each city's airport. If the route between A and B is highly profitable, one of the airports, say B, might try to gain some of the airline's profit by increasing its landing charges. However, since the aircraft is a general asset, the airline has the option of moving the aircraft to a route between A and C (assuming this route is also profitable). The airline can use the general nature of aircraft to discipline airport B and prevent an increase in landing charges.

Now consider the producer of bumpers for a particular car. Each car model is unique and the shape of the car's bumper will be very specific. The production plant will be dedicated to producing bumpers for this one type of car. The car manufacturer could approach the bumper manufacturer and ask for a new production facility to be built for its bumpers. In return, the car manufacturer agrees a price for each bumper. We might assume that the agreed price is £100 per bumper. This price per bumper will make the investment in the new plant profitable for the bumper manufacturer. However, once the plant is up and running, the car manufacturer has a substantial incentive to renegotiate a discount price for the bumpers. Why? Because, unlike the airline company, the bumper manufacturer has a specific asset; it only makes one type of bumper. The plant cannot be used to produce bumpers for another car manufacturer, so it is dependent upon the one car maker. This is the hold-up problem.

The car manufacturer can take advantage of the bumper producer's investment in a specific asset. In fact, so obvious is this type of hold-up problem that the bumper producer would not invest in the production facility. The car producer, therefore, has to build its own bumper-producing plant. The car manufacturer grows vertically and begins to produce one of its key inputs. For many car parts, this approach is very common. Take a look at a car and find the most obvious component on the car that has not been made by the car-maker itself. It will probably be the tyres. This is because tyres are round and will fit on many different types of car. Tyres, or more correctly the plant making tyres, is a general asset. The production of tyres for Ford can easily be switched to the production of tyres for Toyota. A producer of tyres, therefore, does not face a hold-up problem, because it is not dependent upon one buying relationship. A bumper manufacturer would be.

The hold-up problem can also represent a strategic opportunity when one firm is able to gain a monopoly position in the vertical chain. Consider Figure 7.5. For simplicity, assume an industry has three firms, all manufacturing a similar product, beer. In the left half of Figure 7.5, each firm is a producer of beer, buying hops from farmers and selling the beer on to independent pubs. In the right half of Figure 7.5, firm 1 has gained ownership of the pubs. As a monopoly supplier of beer retailing, firm 1 can promote its own brands and negotiate cheap beer supplies from the remaining brewers. An equally effective growth strategy would have

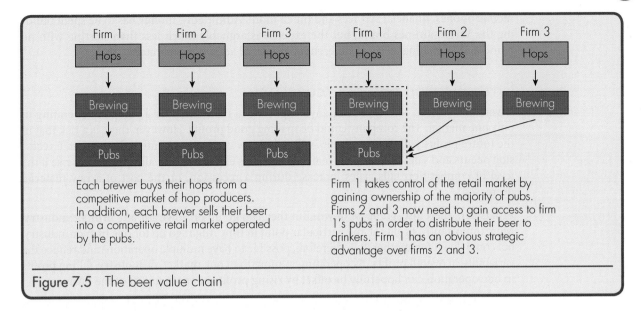

Each brewer buys their hops from a competitive market of hop producers. In addition, each brewer sells their beer into a competitive retail market operated by the pubs.

Firm 1 takes control of the retail market by gaining ownership of the majority of pubs. Firms 2 and 3 now need to gain access to firm 1's pubs in order to distribute their beer to drinkers. Firm 1 has an obvious strategic advantage over firms 2 and 3.

Figure 7.5   The beer value chain

been to gain control of the hop supply and gain a monopoly position at the top of the vertical chain. It could then sell hops to itself cheaply, but charge brewing rivals a very high price.

In summary, firms will grow vertically up or down the vertical chain if the transaction costs of operating through the market are too high. By internalizing transactions, or making the value-adding product or service inside the company, the firm will attempt to control its transaction costs more effectively. Similarly, when the transaction costs of the market are very low, a firm will seek to reduce its vertical integration and begin to seek subcontractors for some of its inputs. Buying in, rather than making the product or service, has lower transaction costs. In addition to the costs of organizing the transaction, we also need to consider the transaction costs generated by the hold-up problem. The firm will grow vertically along the vertical chain whenever it can gain strategic advantage over its rivals and whenever the market refuses to supply products for fear of the hold-up problem.

 ## Diversified growth

Diversification involves a company expanding its operations into related or unrelated markets. This can occur for a variety of reasons, but a strong cost reason centres on the concept of **economies of scope**.

If two products, A and B, are being produced, then economies of scope are sometimes expressed as:

$$\text{Cost (A)} + \text{Cost (B)} > \text{Cost (A + B)}$$

> Economies of scope are said to exist if the cost of producing two or more outputs jointly is less than the cost of producing the outputs separately.

This suggests that the cost of producing A on its own, Cost (A), plus the cost of making B on its own, Cost (B), is greater than making A and B together, Cost (A + B).

An obvious example can be found in the news-gathering services of the BBC. News on politics, business, world affairs and crime can be collected centrally. This is then drawn on by BBC News 24, BBC Evening News, Radio 1, 2, etc., and by BBC News Online. If each division operated separately, then the news would be collected many times. By centralizing news gathering, the BBC cuts down on duplication and exploits economies of scope. An alternative example can be found in the business activities of Virgin. The brand name of Virgin is very important, but just like the news gathering of the BBC, it can reduce duplication. As Virgin initially invested many millions developing its brand name for the music industry, the brand could then also be used to launch products in other markets. This has included airlines, mobile phones, financial services and much more. Admittedly, money has to be spent building the Virgin airlines brand, but the expense is arguably much less than starting with no brand and launching all these different commercial activities separately.

Diversification and risk reduction

Diversification can reduce a company's exposure to risk. Consider a company operating in only one market. The company could be making good profits. However, there is a risk that in the future profits will change. Profits will fall if new competition enters the market, a recession occurs and sales fall, or a raw material becomes expensive. Equally, profits will rise if the level of competition falls, sales increase during a recession, or the cost of a raw material decreases.

Profits can, therefore, go up or down. But they can go up or down for any firm, or industry. More importantly, profits at any particular point in time might go up for one firm or industry, but come down for another. It is, therefore, possible to have multiple operations and reduce the variability in overall profits. By operating in more than one market, or industry, falling profits in one operation can hopefully be offset by rising profits in another part of the business.

> Diversified portfolio of activities contains a mix of uncorrelated business operations.

Tesco, the leading UK supermarket chain, is a reasonable example. Operating across grocery, non-food items such as CDs, magazines and home electricals, and financial services, including insurance and banking, enables Tesco to reduce its operating risks. If grocery and non-food profits fall, it is possible that financial services profits could rise. In order for this to be true the various operations must form a **diversified portfolio** of business activities.

If two business activities are correlated, then the profit levels of each activity will move together. As such, the combined profits will still show large swings over time. For a diversified portfolio, business activities must be uncorrelated. This means the level of profits from one business activity is not related to the level of profits from another activity. The combined profits from diversified activities will now be less variable; as one operation incurs losses, another is likely to rise into profitability.

While diversification can reduce the financial risks of a company, it does not add value to the company. The problem lies in the fact that variability in profits is the risk of shareholders. If an individual shareholder wishes to diversify their risks, then they can do so at low cost. They achieve this by simply buying small amounts of shares in various different uncorrelated companies. If a Tesco shareholder is worried about future losses in the grocery business, they can buy shares in any high street bank. They do not need Tesco to create its own bank. Furthermore, the investor may already have shares in a bank. As a result of Tesco moving into the personal financial services sector, the investor's risk or exposure to the financial services sector has increased, not diminished. Therefore, diversification by a company does not add value for shareholders. So, why do companies diversify?

As we will see in Chapter 8, we need to make a distinction between shareholders and managers. On a day-to-day basis it is managers who run and control companies. Managers have a great deal of asset tied up in the company they work for. The company pays their salary and funds their pension. If the company closed, due to substantial losses, how likely is it that the manager would gain employment elsewhere? Managers, therefore, face substantial non-diversified risk from employment. Diversification is arguably more in the interests of managers than shareholders.

Evidence on mergers

In examining how mergers of all types improve firm-level performance, economists have used a variety of techniques. These techniques have included stock market studies, financial ratio analysis and case studies.

Stock market studies investigate whether shareholders from the buying firm or the acquired target firm gain most. Evidence tends to suggest that most of the stock market gains from merger accrue to shareholders of target firms. The price of target firms rises rapidly prior to merger and the stock price for the buying firm stagnates or even falls post-merger.

Financial and accounting studies examine merger activity within similar industries; banking, brewing and automobiles would be examples. Using statistical techniques, economists look for increases in revenues, reductions in costs, increased market share and improvements in operating efficiencies. The evidence is at best mixed; some firms and some industries have a greater tendency to deliver post-merger benefits. But this is not a common pattern and many firms manage to destroy value post-merger.

Case studies examine specific mergers and look for firm-specific examples of merger benefits. Again, these studies confirm the message from the stock market and financial accounting-based studies: mergers are not always a good idea.

So, if mergers are at best risky strategies – some work, some do not – then why do firms continue to engage in merger activity? A possible answer is that mergers are very much in the interests of managers. The pay of managers tends to increase more with firm size than with financial performance of the firm. Merger increases firm size and therefore can boost managers' pay. Faced with such incentives, managers may seek to convince shareholders that a merger is a good idea (see Box 7.3).

Box 7.3

Failed G4S deal is lesson in the rules of M&A engagement

There was much wailing and gnashing of teeth in the Square Mile this week after G4S was forced to abandon its £5.2 billion bid for ISS, the Danish cleaning company. Bankers immediately accused the big institutional shareholders who blocked the deal of making it impossible for chief executives to do things with their reluctance to back bold, transformational acquisitions.

But is this correct? Is it really the case that investors will not back big deals or did G4S and its advisers simply misread the mood of the market?

Certainly, it is not easy to pull off a large acquisition in the current environment. Shareholders are wary and rightly so, given a backdrop of slowing economic growth and the small matter of a eurozone sovereign debt crisis. Withdrawn European deal volumes in 2011 now stand at $131.3 billion, double last year's total and the highest since 2008 when Lehman collapsed. In the UK alone, 20 transactions worth $42.4 billion have been pulled.

It has never been easy to pull off transformational deals, for the simple reason that they often destroy more value than they create. But that does not mean it is impossible, even at times like these. However, management and their advisers must work very hard to get a deal com-

pleted. There has to be a close relationship and strong dialogue between management and investors to allay concerns and get an acquisition over the line.

This does not appear to have happened in this deal. Put simply, G4S and its chief executive, Nick Buckles, did not take shareholders with them. Although G4S briefed its 14 top investors before the deal was announced, they were given just an hour of face time with management to discuss the merits of the transaction. For a deal of this size – it was classed a reverse takeover because it was so big – this complexity (the combined group would have employed 1 million people) and risk (net debt would have risen to three times underlying earnings), that was not enough. Nowhere near enough.

And that is a pity. The idea of creating the world's biggest integrated security and facilities management group was not a bad one, but G4S had to explain in greater detail the rationale behind its shift in strategy from internally funded bolt-on acquisitions to a 'bet the ranch deal'.

Adapted from an article by Neil Hume, 5 November 2011. From the *Financial Times* © The Financial Times Limited 2011. All rights reserved.[2]

---

[2] McGraw-Hill Education is solely responsible for providing this abridged version of the original article, and The Financial Times Limited does not accept any liability for the accuracy or quality of the abridged version.

Business application: horizontal growth by merger

Economic boom or bust, the attractions of horizontal merger always seem attractive to business. When the economy is growing rapidly, firms see the option to merge as a means of exploiting growth while achieving economies of scale. During a recession, in contrast, merger and economies of scale offer valuable cost-efficiencies.

The occurrence of mergers in both good and bad economic times possibly underlines the importance of economies of scale in providing firms with a competitive advantage. Size matters, costs matter. Achieving significant scale economies often costs huge sums of money and, once you merge with a rival, then that lowers the opportunities for other competitors to follow suit and achieve similar economies of scale. So, by merging, firms can achieve a competitive advantage which other competitors may find difficult to replicate. Economies of scale provide cost savings and provide the firm with the potential to dominate.

In Box 7.4, we provide an insight into the world of network supply in the telecommunications market. Scale is highlighted as being important, but so is the basis on which that scale

Box 7.4

Two's company

Revolutions in technology bring benefits to millions, but the companies that make them happen do not always thrive. Even when demand is booming, competition to meet it can be brutal. Makers of telecommunications networks know this only too well. They perform the unseen miracles that allow ever more people to talk, work and play on ever smarter devices just about anywhere, but their rewards have been mostly meagre.

Merger and failure have thinned their ranks. In 2009 Nortel, a Canadian equipment-maker, went bankrupt. This year Motorola's wireless-network division was bought by Nokia Siemens Networks (NSN), a Finnish-German joint venture created in 2007. France's Alcatel and America's Lucent merged in 2006.

None of these mergers has brought much success. NSN has yet to make an annual profit. On 23 November it said it would shed 17 000 of its 74 000 workers. Alcatel-Lucent reported falling revenues and negative cash flow in the third quarter.

Must all struggle? All but two, it seems. 'Telecoms equipment is a scale game,' says Richard Windsor of Nomura, an investment bank. Network-builders need scale to support the hefty fixed costs of research and development. 'You can be either the cost leader or the technology leader. If you're neither of those, you're in a spot of bother.'

The technological pace is set by Ericsson, a Swedish company that scoops more than a third of global mobile-infrastructure revenues, according to Gartner, a research firm. It boasts 27 000 patents and was part of a six-firm consortium that paid $4.5 billion for a load of Nortel's patents in July. 'Anyone [designing] mobile phones or networks needs an agreement with us,' says Hans Vestberg, its boss.

The cost leader is Huawei, a Chinese firm. Its global market share went up from 4.5 per cent in 2006 to 15.6 per cent in 2010, reckons Gartner, despite the political obstacles it faces in America. (Some American politicians fret about Huawei's opaque ownership and possible military ties.)

Mr Windsor says that the companies caught in the middle lack the margins either to invest on Ericsson's scale in R&D or to fight Huawei on price. NSN was loath to compete on prices before Rajeev Suri became its boss in 2009, says Bengt Nordstrom of Northstream, a consulting firm. Its market share is down to around a sixth, even with Motorola; it inherited a quarter from its parents.

Life will get no easier for those squeezed between the Swedes and the Chinese. Ericsson's scale and technical edge are handy when, say, talking to mobile operators wanting to handle lots of data faster and without interference. And for those for whom cheap kit is paramount, Huawei will still be hard to beat.

Adapted from an article in *The Economist*, 'In an industry with a cost leader and a price leader, is there room for others?', 3 December 2011. © The Economist Newspaper Limited, London 2011.

is built. Ericsson has achieved scale by being innovative and attracting business not on cost and price, but on the quality and technological leading elements of its product offer. In contrast, Huawei has simply gained scale by cutting costs and gaining an increasing market share. Now that the market has two dominant suppliers, one offering low cost and one offering new technology, there appears to be little room for a new competitor, even if they do merge and grow with a rival.

7.8 Business application: vertical growth – moving with the value

A common feature of many business environments is *change*. Technology changes, the product on offer changes and even the tastes and preferences of consumers change. The consequence of these changes is that the value added in each stage of the vertical chain of production also changes. As costs fall, or revenues rise, then one part of the chain becomes more valuable. Similarly, as costs rise or revenues fall, then another part of the chain becomes less valuable. Predicting and understanding these trends can help enormously in developing strategies for change and ensuring greater longevity of profits.

You may, or may not, like Madonna's music. But unquestionably she is an artistic and commercial success. Madonna is an artist who is not only capable of reinventing her image and music but, as described in Box 7.5, is also very skilled at understanding business and how the market for pop stars has changed.

Box 7.5

Madonna's deal with Live Nation-Interscope worth $40 million

Madonna's new album is finished and will be released in March 2012 on Interscope Records, the label and Live Nation Entertainment announced on Thursday morning. The deal, which has been rumoured for weeks, was confirmed by sources to Billboard Wednesday.

In 2007, Live Nation signed the superstar to a 10-year deal reportedly worth $100 million that includes new studio albums, touring, merchandising, fan club/website, DVDs, music-related television and film projects and associated sponsorship agreements. This portion of the commitment is being valued at $40 million, sources tell Billboard.

The Universal Music Group-owned label will release three albums by the Material Girl. Her first single, called 'Gimme All Your Luvin', is due out the last week in January. Shortly afterwards, the film *W.E.*, which Madonna directed and co-wrote, is scheduled to hit theatres.

The as-yet-untitled album is her first in five years. Madonna had been signed to Warner Bros. since 1982.

Live Nation CEO Irving Azoff reiterated to Billboard in February that it would partner with some other entity in releasing Madonna's next album. Executives at the firm have stated repeatedly that they do not intend to enter the record business full-tilt.

'Live Nation, prior to the merger, entered into some of these all-rights deals, so there are certain artists, Madonna being one of them, that there is a recorded music strategy,' Azoff said. 'Once she gets the album recorded, we'll sit down with her and her manager Guy Oseary and figure out what's best for the record. It has to start with the music.'

Until recently, the keys to the valuable parts of the pop music value chain were a competent music artist and access to music lovers through music publishing and distribution. Publishing and distribution were commonly achieved through the creation of CDs, which were then sold in music stores. Record companies were able to insist that buyers purchase all songs on an album. As such, the publishing and distribution stages of the vertical chain were extremely valuable.

As the distribution technology moved towards electronic storage and online delivery, the value of music publishing and delivery declined. Consumers were able to download music (illegally) for free and online retailers of music began to offer downloads of tracks from albums, rather than the entire album. Such moves have led to a reduction in profits for record companies and for artists such as Madonna.

When Madonna broke her relationship with music producer Warner's and signed with tour promoter Live Nation, she was also indicating where the profits lay. We can use our understanding of competition to understand the commercial attractions of concerts. If you wish to see Madonna in concert in your nearest capital city, then the event exists once. It happens, it is over, it is gone. You cannot experience a concert as a download. You cannot download parts of the concert and you cannot access the concert for free. Madonna, in conjunction with Live Nation, is a monopoly provider of Madonna concerts.

In contrast, Madonna and Live Nation have little control over pricing and distribution of her recorded music and they need a partner to effectively front end the value chain and publish her music. By joining with Interscope, Madonna and Live Nation have decided to let someone else take the risk in the singles and album market.

Adapted from an article by Shirley Halperin on Billboard Biz, 15 December 2011.

(7.9) Business application: economies of scope

Google is everywhere and offering everything. Why? The range of services now offered by Google simply reflects economies of scope – the ability to provide services jointly at a lower cost than offering each separately. But where do these economies of scope stem from?

At the core of Google's success is a search engine which is arguably unsurpassed by any competitor. The technology advantage rests on clever computer programming and a vast bank of computers – some estimate as much as a 100 000-machine server farm. Such an asset base means it becomes technically feasible and economically cheap to launch related services, such as Gmail and Android. The more Google can exploit its massive technical advantage across products, the greater the economies of scope it can realize. As revenues and, ultimately, profits grow from its scope advantages, Google has more finance to pour back in to boost its technological advantage and remain dominant.

The growth of Amazon is also related to economies of scope. Amazon began by offering books for sale online. This was quickly expanded into music and movies. Currently, Amazon also sells toys, electronics, health and beauty and jewellery items. This all represents economies of scope. When Amazon built an Internet infrastructure to sell books and acquired a warehouse and distribution system for stocking and delivery, it made strong commercial sense to put more product ranges through the same pipe.

The examples of Amazon and Google illustrate what is perhaps related diversification. However, the economies of scope argument can also be used to explain some examples of unrelated diversification. Tesco, a UK supermarket chain, developed its business from grocery into non-food electricals, and prior to this into financial services. It simply capitalized on its huge existing customer base. With details about its customers gained from loyalty cards and online shopping, Tesco can use this marketing research data to sell not only groceries but also other products such as financial services, including personal loans and insurance. Therefore, by operating as a supermarket and as a personal financial services company, Tesco is able to reduce its costs by exploiting the customer information base across multiple activities.

While grocery and financial services are very different activities, one of the core underlying assets that ensures success in both markets is an informative customer database. This database includes information on customers' ages, marital status, income levels, home address and products generally purchased within the Tesco stores. These data can be analysed and used to target particular customer groups with specific products.

Economies of scope and control

An important issue when considering economies of scope is *control*. If we extend the economies of scope condition to Tesco, then we would have:

$$\text{Cost (Grocery)} + \text{Cost (Financial Services)} > \text{Cost (Grocery + Financial Services)}$$

An obvious reason for these economies of scope is lower production costs associated with the joint use of the Tesco customer base. But, in addition, we also need to consider transaction costs. Tesco does not have to enter the financial services market in order to exploit its customer base. Rather, it could sell its customer information to a number of third parties, including existing financial services companies. The obvious problem with such an approach is that valuable information could then find its way into the hands of Tesco's rivals in the supermarket sector. Lowering the transaction costs associated with the information's additional use, therefore, protects the value of the customer base. Tesco cannot risk selling the information in the marketplace; instead, in order to exploit the asset beyond grocery, it has to enter into the financial services sector. In this particular instance, Tesco has achieved this through an exclusive arrangement with Direct Line, a leading insurance provider.

We can also use the case of Tesco to address the issue of managerial motives for merger, as discussed in section 7.5. Managers may pursue diversification to protect their own employment, as opposed to adding value for shareholders. We even argued that, if a shareholder of Tesco was concerned about risks in the supermarket sector, they could easily diversify this risk by buying shares in a financial services company. However, we can now see that diversification will add value for shareholders if the control of the economies of scope reduces transaction costs. Tesco is a clear example of this. So too is the Virgin brand. Licensing the brand to other users would run the risk of a third party damaging the brand. (This of course does not prevent Virgin from damaging the brand via its rail operations.) However, when Virgin takes the brand into many different markets the integrity of the brand is the sole responsibility of Virgin. It retains control over the use of the brand and reduces its transaction costs.

7.10 Business data application: trends in mergers and acquisitions

Data on mergers and acquisitions provides an insight into the number of deals being undertaken, the amount of money being spent, the type of financing being used and geographic concentration of target and acquiring firms. Such data provides an indication of firms' appetite for growth, their ability to finance growth and where they see growth opportunities around the world.

Figure 7.6 illustrates the number of mergers and acquisitions undertaken on an annual basis in the UK. During the period 2001 to 2007 the number of deals exceeding £1 million rose from 500 to 875 per year. Following the financial crisis the number of deals fell to 320 per year. As an economy falters, then growth opportunities recede and firms become less willing to expand.

In addition, the financial crisis had an impact on the ability of firms to finance deals. Following the crisis, we can see in Figure 7.7 a huge switch in the use of share-based equity financing for mergers and a fall-off in the use of cash. The pattern reflected the inability of companies to access loans from the banking system. So in order to fund mergers and acquisitions companies turned to shareholder finance.

While the use of cash (sometimes borrowed from banks) has returned as a popular means of financing mergers and acquisitions, this pattern needs to be

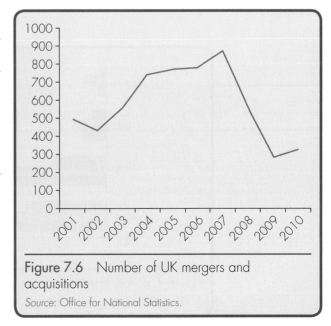

Figure 7.6 Number of UK mergers and acquisitions
Source: Office for National Statistics.

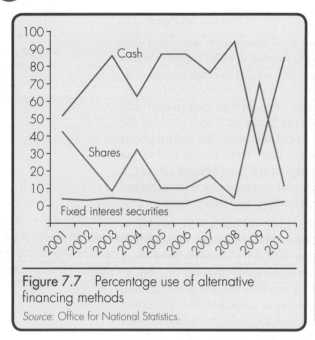

Figure 7.7 Percentage use of alternative financing methods

Source: Office for National Statistics.

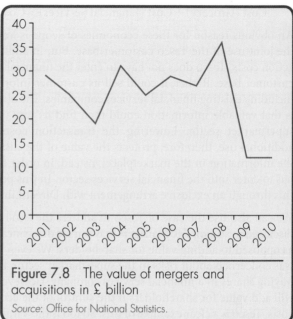

Figure 7.8 The value of mergers and acquisitions in £ billion

Source: Office for National Statistics.

seen against the backdrop of falling deal numbers and lower valuations. Looking at Figure 7.8 we can see that the value of deals has fallen from a peak of £35 billion to a level of £12 billion in 2010. This low value may indicate an unwillingness of companies to do deals, an inability to access finance, or a combination of the two.

Finally, it is worth exploring where firms undertake mergers and acquisitions, because such patterns should provide an indication of where firms see growth opportunities. Figure 7.9 illustrates key trends in the geographic pattern of mergers and acquisitions by UK firms.

Both before and after the financial crisis Europe and the USA have attracted most UK overseas merge and acquisition activity. Asia and Africa have been less important. However, while the number of deals for all regions has fallen, the impact on Europe and the USA has been greatest, with the number of deals in 2010 falling significantly below 2005 levels. The activity in Asia and Africa, while more modest, has been more resilient, which may indicate continuing robust opportunities for growth.

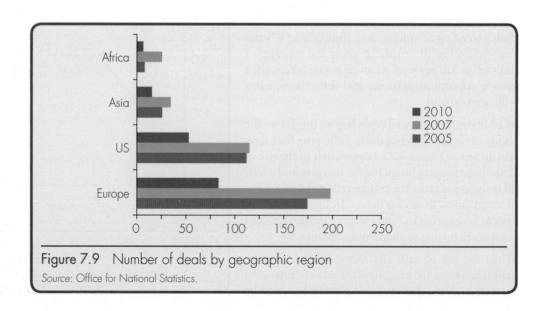

Figure 7.9 Number of deals by geographic region

Source: Office for National Statistics.

Summary

1. Horizontal growth is the expansion of a firm's activities at the same stage of the production process.

2. Vertical growth is expansion of the firm up or down the value chain, incorporating more than one stage of production.

3. Diversified growth is an expansion of the firm's activities into related and unrelated markets.

4. Growth in its various forms can be organic, where the firm grows internally by developing ties to existing operations; alternatively, growth can occur externally, where the firm either acquires, or agrees to merge with, another firm.

5. Firms can grow for a variety of reasons, but if we accept that a firm is a profit-maximizer, then growth must be linked to long-term, profit-maximizing objectives. Growth opportunities must, therefore, offer revenue enhancements or potential cost savings.

6. Horizontal growth can promote revenue enhancements by exploiting growth in the market. As the market size grows, the firm can seek to expand its operations. Moreover, the firm can seek to grow its share of the market. Greater control of the market improves the potential to set prices. If greater market share stems from merger, or acquisition of a rival, then the elasticity of demand must fall and the potential to raise prices increases.

7. Economies of scale are important motives for horizontal growth. As a company increases its scale of operation, its average costs fall. In addition, the positive effects of learning can motivate horizontal growth. As cumulative production increases, the firm begins to learn how to produce the product more efficiently. The firm learns how to reduce its costs. However, if the size of the firm is bigger, the potential to erase cumulative output more quickly also exists.

8. Vertical growth can also be motivated by considerations of production costs. Consecutive stages of the value chain could be merged if production and transaction costs have the potential to be reduced.

9. In addition to production costs, transaction costs are also a potential reason for vertical growth.

10. Transaction costs are associated with organizing the transaction of goods and services. These include the costs associated with writing, monitoring and enforcing contractual relationships. Transactions are seen to increase when complexity and uncertainty are greater, monitoring is difficult and enforcement limited. If the transaction costs associated with buying the good or service through the market increase, then a firm will attempt to minimize its transaction costs by vertically integrating and making the good or service within the firm.

11. A specific asset is designed for one use only. Without the flexibility to deploy the asset to an alternative use, a firm can be subject to the hold-up problem. Contract prices can be renegotiated and the financial value of the specific asset can fall. In order to avoid such problems, firms will tend to vertically integrate and thereby avoid market negotiations.

12. Economies of scope exist if the production of two goods jointly is less expensive than producing the two goods separately. Diversification can sometimes be understood as a process of exploiting economies of scope, i.e. where a firm uses an asset that it has developed in its current operations to exploit opportunities in another market.

13. If diversification is pursued in an attempt to create a portfolio of activities, then the firm's overall financial risk might be reduced. However, it is questionable whether such strategies add value for shareholders who may already hold a diversified portfolio of shares in many different companies. Diversification is more likely to reduce the non-diversified employment risks faced by managers.

14. Data on mergers and acquisitions provides an insight into the willingness of firms to grow, their ability to finance growth and where they prefer to grow, and where they might be considering growth opportunities around the world.

Learning checklist

You should now be able to:

- Explain the difference between horizontal, vertical and diversified growth
- Provide arguments for why firms may grow in a horizontal, vertical or diversified manner
- Explain how the learning curve links cumulative output with falling unit costs
- Understand and explain transaction costs
- Recognize the hold-up problem and explain why firms try to avoid this problem
- Explain economies of scope, provide examples and argue why firms might exploit scope economies
- Demonstrate an awareness of key patterns in recent merger and acquisition activity

Questions   connect

1. Is a merger between rivals horizontal, vertical or conglomerate growth?

2. Horizontal growth can occur for cost and revenue reasons. Explain both of these justifications for horizontal growth.

3. Formula 1 teams are banned from in-season tests to reduce costs. The learning curve says this is a bad idea. Why?

4. What is the value chain?

5. What are transaction costs and should firms be concerned about them?

 EASY

6. Your university decides to use an external catering company for the main university food outlets. What economic justifications can you provide for this decision?

7. What is the hold-up problem and how might a firm deal with this particular type of issue?

8. Explain why a range of activities can reduce risk. In order for diversification to be effective, has the correlation between activities to be high or low?

9. Why are the benefits of diversification low for shareholders?

10. What is an economy of scope and how might it lead a firm to diversify?

11. If cost advantages from cumulative production were low, would the learning curve be steep or shallow?

12. Why are horizontal mergers sometimes blocked by governments?

13. Should governments also block vertical mergers?

14. Pubs in the UK are being encouraged to take on other activities, such as those of the Post Office. On economic grounds, how would you justify such initiatives?

15. How can a firm use horizontal, vertical or diversified growth to gain a strategic advantage over its rivals?

Exercises

1. True or false?

   (a) Following a merger the price elasticity of demand should fall.

   (b) Economies of scale can be a rationale for merger.

   (c) Late delivery of supplies due to heavy traffic is an example of the hold-up problem.

   (d) An organization's total costs are production costs plus transaction costs.

   (e) Diversification reduces a firm's level of risk.

   (f) Free cash flow is cash in excess of funds required to invest in all projects with a positive net present value.

2. (a) Draw a long-run average cost curve and use it to explain the gains in scale achieved by two small firms merging.

   (b) Diversification is not about moving the firm's total cost and total revenue lines further apart; it is more concerned with reducing the volatility of earnings. Discuss.

3. Consider the following questions by referring to Box 7.3:

   (a) Explain what is meant by the term vertical integration.

   (b) How would business economists explain the location of server farms?

Governing business

Chapter contents

Governing business at a glance   189

8.1   Business problem: managing managers   189

8.2   Profit maximization and the separation of ownership from control   190

8.3   Principal–agent theory   194

8.4   Business application: stock options and the reduction of agency costs   195

8.5   Regulation of business   199

8.6   Externalities   200

8.7   Dealing with externalities   202

8.8   Merit, demerit and public goods   204

8.9   Price volatility   204

8.10 Market power and competition policy   207

8.11 Assessing government interventions   209

8.12 Business application: carbon trading   210

8.13 Business data application: impact analysis and smart metering   213

Summary   215

Learning checklist   216

Questions   216

Exercises   217

Learning outcomes

By the end of this chapter you should understand:

Economic theory

LO1   Principal–agent problems

LO2   The separation of ownership from control

LO3   Alternative theories of the firm

LO4   The concept of positive and negative externalities

LO5   The notion of market failures

LO6   The use of tax and subsidies to correct market failures

LO7   The regulation of monopoly

Business application

LO8   Why companies use stock options to reward chief executives

LO9   Why governments have introduced trading in carbon

LO10 The costs and benefits associated with smart metering of energy

At a glance Governing business

The issue

Actions taken by managers and workers are often not in the interests of their shareholders. Similarly, actions taken by firms, such as polluting the atmosphere, are often not in the interests of other stakeholders, such as wider society. Can these conflicts be resolved?

The understanding

Conflicts exist because of a misalignment of interests. Without government control, firms can pollute the environment without cost to themselves. The cost of pollution is instead picked up by society. By making the firm bear the responsibility and costs of pollution, both the firm's and society's interests are aligned. The way to achieve this is to tax the firm if it pollutes; and perhaps even provide it with subsidies if it tries to operate without pollution. More generally, one solution to the misalignment of interests is the use of financial incentives to change the behaviour of one of the parties.

The usefulness

Why do company executives receive huge bonuses via stock options? The answer is because stock options provide financial incentives for managers to act in the interests of shareholders. Can the government reduce carbon emissions by creating a market for pollution permits? We will now explore each of these issues.

Business problem: managing managers

Within all of us there is an element of Homer Simpson. The similarities at work are particularly acute, where we often have a willingness to do little but appear to be doing a great deal. Colleagues and perhaps even ourselves display a need to frequent the coffee room, the toilets or even the local pub during work hours. Such behaviour is a deviation from what our employers might consider best practice. They might consider we are employed to sit at our desks and pursue profit maximization. When such behaviour occurs, we might label it 'lazy', 'cheeky' or 'taking the Michael'. You will not be surprised to learn that economists prefer the more technical label, 'the **principal–agent problem**'.

> The principal–agent problem refers to the difficulties of a principal or owner in monitoring an agent to whom decisions have been delegated.

Principals can suffer two confounding problems when hiring agents to work for them. First, the interests of the agent and the principal may differ. For example, the principal may value hard work, while the agent may dislike hard work. Second, principals can often find it difficult to monitor the work and effort of their agents. Given the potential difference in interests and the difficulty associated with monitoring the agent, there is little reason why the agent should expend effort on the principal's behalf.

We can compare examples of a taxi driver and a manager to illuminate these arguments. In the case of the taxi driver, you may wish to be driven between two points using the shortest route. In contrast, the taxi driver may wish to take you via a much longer route, hoping to generate a higher fare. Hence, there is a difference in interest between you, as the principal, and the taxi driver, as the agent. However, since you are sitting in the taxi, you can monitor with ease the route taken by the driver. Therefore, if you know the area, and are not a tourist in a foreign land, the taxi driver will generally take you by the shortest route.

A manager of a company, the agent, may be tasked with improving the profitability of a company by the shareholders of that company, the principals. However, if the shareholders are buying and selling shares in many companies on the London stock market, they will find it difficult to monitor the manager on a daily basis. Unlike the passenger in a taxi, the shareholders cannot directly observe the behaviour of their manager. The manager could decide to sit in the office surfing the Internet, or practising their golf putting. When the profits of the company fail to increase, the shareholders will not be aware that the agent has been lazy. In fact, because of the lack of monitoring, the manager could blame the poor performance on external factors such as a lazy workforce, a bad sales manager or a fall in demand for the product.

Economists describe the manager as displaying **moral hazard**-type behaviour.

> Moral hazard occurs when someone agrees to undertake a certain set of actions but then, once a contractual arrangement has been agreed, behaves in a different manner.
>
> Agency costs reflect reductions in value to principals from using agents to undertake work on their behalf.

The manager offers to increase the profits of the company but, once hired by the shareholders, exploits the monitoring problems of shareholders and behaves in their own best interests. In contrast, the taxi driver, actively monitored by the hiring passenger, does not display moral hazard-type behaviour because the passenger will contest the higher fare.

The costs of moral hazard-type behaviour, such as inferior performance by the agent, coupled with monitoring costs, result in what are more generally termed **agency costs**.

In the case of the taxi driver, agency costs are very low. Monitoring is easy and, therefore, moral hazard-type behaviour is unlikely. In the case of the manager, agency costs are very high, because monitoring is difficult and costly, and therefore this behaviour is likely.

A natural question arises as to how principals might seek to reduce agency costs. In particular, how can shareholders motivate managers to provide higher levels of output or, as the economist would say, how can we align the interests of firms and managers so that managers act in the interests of shareholders?

The answer will be developed throughout the first part of this chapter. In the case of managers, however, modes of corporate governance are placed on the firm that provide incentives for managers to work in the interests of shareholders. At a very simple level, managers can be turned into shareholders by providing them with shares in the company. As shareholders, managers then have an interest in working hard in order to improve the performance of the company. In order to consider these ideas further, we will extend our analysis of how firms are owned and managed and examine why managers may not wish to follow the interests of shareholders. Only then can we return to the issue of how shareholders can try to motivate managers to act in their interests.

Profit maximization and the separation of ownership from control

Throughout this book we have assumed that firms are profit-maximizers. In fact, when we first introduced the idea in Chapter 5, we suggested that this was a sensible argument. We would now like to question this assumption.

In order to maximize profits firms are required to set marginal cost, MC, equal to marginal revenue, MR. Even though professional accountants are also schooled in this central idea, many are incapable of calculating MC or MR from a company's cost and revenue data. Accountants are not fools, it is just that the task of measuring and collating data on MR and MC is extremely complex, especially when the firm makes and sells multiple products. Furthermore, the firm's costs and revenues may not be very stable. Changes in raw material prices or output prices will lead to repeated changes in MC and MR. Therefore, if anything, firms can at best only approximate profit maximization. They may seek to maximize profits, but they will never be sure what the optimal level of output and profits is.

Aside from these practical problems of trying to equate MC and MR, there are strong reasons why a firm might pursue objectives other than profit maximization. Crucially, it is often the case that the individuals who manage a firm are different from the individuals who own a firm. Table 8.1 provides data on the size of shareholdings within the telecommunications company BT. With 1.1 million shareholders, it is reasonable to say that many people and investment companies own BT. BT employed just in excess of 100 000 individuals in 2011. Therefore, with 1.1 million shareholders and only 100 000 workers, it is clear that shareholders and the people who work for BT are, in the main, different individuals. Among the largest shareholders, 172 holdings are greater than 5 million shares and represent 0.02 per cent of shareholders. We can see, therefore, that the vast majority of shareholders, small and large, are not the same people who manage BT. While BT is a popular share among many individuals in the UK, the pattern of dispersed shareholdings is common among large companies and is known as the separation of ownership from control.

The **separation of ownership from control** becomes more acute when shareholders become more disperse. With 1.1 million shareholders, it is difficult for all BT shareholders to co-ordinate themselves and try to remove a poorly performing management team. Moreover, in the UK it is common for the largest shareholder to own less than 3 per cent of a company's shares. This is important because, if the largest shareholder wanted to remove a team of underperforming managers, then they would bear the full cost of this activity. This might include meetings with the managers, other large shareholders and legal advisers, and recruitment of a new management team. While bearing all these costs, the benefits of better company performance would be shared among all shareholders. Therefore, if the major shareholder has only 3 per cent, then it will only gain a 3 per cent share of the benefits of employing a new management team. All other shareholders are **free riders** on the back of the dominant shareholder.

Given the unattractive financial terms brought about by free riding and small shareholdings, even the dominant shareholder is unlikely to act against the incumbent management team.

Dispersed shareholdings, therefore, leave management teams, even bad ones, in a position where they do not have to react to shareholders' interests. So, while it might

> Separation of ownership from control exists where the shareholders, who own the company, are a different set of individuals from the managers that control the business on a day-to-day basis.
>
> Free riders are individuals, or firms, who can benefit from the actions of others without contributing to the effort made by others. They gain benefits from the actions of others for free.

Table 8.1 Analysis of BT shareholdings, 2011

Range	Number of holdings	Percentage of total	Number of shares held (millions)	Percentage of total
1–399	427 887	38.88	90	1.1
400–799	300 012	27.26	168	2.06
800–1599	215 895	19.62	241	2.96
1600–9999	150 133	13.64	448	5.49
10 000–99 999	5 253	0.47	95	1.17
100 000–999 999	615	0.05	229	2.81
1 000 000–4 999 999	309	0.02	728	8.93
5 000 000 and above	172	0.01	6152	75.48
Total	1 100 276	100.00	8151	100.00

be reasonable to argue that shareholders are profit-maximizers, managers have the scope to pursue their own objectives. But what might these objectives be?

Managerial objectives

Economists have proposed a number of alternative theories relating to the objectives that managers might pursue. The first relates to what is known as 'expense preference behaviour'. If shareholders are interested in maximizing profits, then managers are interested in maximizing their own satisfaction.

Consumption of perquisites

So, rather than work hard for the company's owners, managers would rather indulge themselves in the purchase of expensive cars, jets, lavish expense accounts that can be used to dine clients (and friends) at the most fashionable restaurants and, of course, lots of personal assistants. A clear reason for doing this is a positive recognition provided by society for success, dominance and status. In trying to meet these requirements, managers use the company's funds to finance a prestigious image makeover and lifestyle.

Managers may even spend the company's money on business projects that have little value to the shareholder but have personal value to the company's managers. Diversification, as discussed in Chapter 7, is a case in point. Companies that specialize in one product line are vulnerable to competition, or a downturn in demand. In order to protect themselves, managers may diversify and use the company's money to buy unrelated businesses. Statements of strategic change along the lines of 'yes, I know we are in waste handling, but I think we should move into leisure and purchase a cruise ship' are extreme, but sadly evident among some senior managers. However, the essential problem is that managers are using the company's and, therefore shareholders', money to diversify a risk that only managers face. If shareholders are concerned about risk in one market, they can buy shares in other companies. Hence, diversification within firms does not protect shareholders; rather, it protects managers.

Sales maximization

An alternative hypothesis recognizes that the measurement of profits can be subjective. How much will the firm decide to depreciate its assets and what provision for bad debts will it charge to the profit and loss statement this year? Given these problems, managers may prefer to maximize a more tangible measure of performance, such as sales. A common misunderstanding follows the reasoning that, if sales are increasing, then so are profits. But, as we have seen, this is not true – the law of diminishing returns and diseconomies of scale point to increases in costs as output increases. Sales maximization may, therefore, indicate that sales managers are doing a good job but, without an additional consideration of costs and ultimately profits, sales growth may not be a good indicator of overall performance.

Growth maximization

The final hypothesis is that managers will seek to maximize growth, rather than profits. It is no surprise that the pay of top directors is linked to the size of the company. The bigger the company, the greater the responsibility. What is surprising is that chief executive (the leading director of a company) pay is linked more closely to company size than it is to financial performance, such as profitability. This suggests that managers have a financial, or salary, incentive to pursue growth maximization over profit maximization. However, while seeing this rather obvious argument, there are some subtleties. If a company grows at a faster rate now, will it be in a stronger position to outperform its rivals in the future? Economies of scale can be attained more quickly, leading to a reduction in costs. In addition, as we saw in Chapters 5 and 7, increased market share brings increased power over pricing. If this is true, growth maximization now is simply a strategy for profit maximization over the long term.

Behavioural theories

Behavioural theories of the firm are based on how individuals actually behave inside firms. This is in contrast to theories such as profit maximization, which predict how individuals should behave. Important behavioural points are what goals will be set for the organization and how the targets will be set.

Goal setting

Cyert and March[1] recognized that organizations are complex environments represented by a mixture of interest groups, including shareholders, managers, workers, consumers and trade unions. Even within managers there are various sub-groups, including marketing, accounting and production. The goals of the organization, or firm, are more a reflection of these competing interests than a theoretical prediction such as profit maximization. If a marketing manager rises to the top of the organization, it is likely that marketing issues will rise to the top of the managerial decision-making agenda. Resources may flow into the marketing department and the goals of the organization may reflect marketing issues, such as the most recognized global brand or growing customer reach and market share. In contrast, if an accountant led the organization, then goals relating to sales growth, cost reduction and profitability might be set. Decision making, the development of targets and the focus of the organization are, therefore, a reflection of the coalition of interests within the organization. Whichever group has greater power, or enhanced negotiation skills, will have a greater say over the targets of the organization.

Target setting

Regardless of which goals or objectives predominate, the complexity of the environment will mean that measures and targets are difficult to set. Should sales growth be 10 per cent or 20 per cent? How do managers accommodate failure in meeting the target? In recognizing these points, Herbert Simon[2] developed the concept of **satisficing**.

> Satisficing is the attainment of acceptable levels of performance.
>
> Maximizing is the attainment of maximum levels of performance.

For example, 20 per cent annual growth in sales could be the maximum possible. But a 10 per cent growth in sales would be acceptable, especially if other firms or organizations were achieving similar results; 10 per cent represents a satisfactory level of performance. If managers negotiate a 10 per cent target growth rate, rather than a 20 per cent target, they are displaying satisficing rather than **maximizing** behaviour. Why might they do this? First, the maximum growth rate is unknown; it could be 15, 20, 25 or even 50 per cent. Second, failure to meet a target creates tension between the group setting the target and the individuals pursuing the target. Therefore, in order to avoid failure in a complex world, where the maximum is unknown, it is perhaps better to set a realistic and satisfactory target. Behavioural considerations, therefore, lead to firms and organizations setting minimum levels of performance, rather than maximum ones.

We do not have to decide which of the above alternative hypotheses are correct. Instead, we simply have to recognize that the separation of ownership from control provides managers with the incentive to pursue any of the above objectives. The problem for shareholders is the absence of direct control over managers: how might they motivate managers to behave in the interests of shareholders? The straightforward answer is to make managers shareholders. But the complex answer is to understand how difficult this might be. To understand the problem more fully, we will examine principal–agent theory.

---

[1] R.M. Cyert and J.G. March, *A Behavioral Theory of the Firm*, 2nd edn. Englewood Cliffs, NJ: Prentice Hall, 1963.

[2] H.A. Simon, *Models of Man: Social and Rational*. New York: Wiley, 1957.

8.3 Principal–agent theory

Agency costs between managers and shareholders

When a business is small the owner is also likely to be the manager. In this case, there is no agency relationship because the owner and the manager are the same person. Therefore, there can be no misalignment of interests. The owner-manager is likely to work very hard to ensure the success of the business. Furthermore, even if the owner-manager decides to pursue expense preference behaviour and spend the company's money on a top-of-the-range BMW, they are only robbing themself as the shareholder. An important consideration is that the value of the company to the owner does not change with the behaviour of the manager; simply, the financial benefits are being paid to the same person in different ways. For example, if the company generated £100 000 in profits, but the owner-manager decided to use £30 000 to buy the BMW and only receive a dividend of (£100 000 − £30 000) = £70 000, then the owner-manager has still received £100 000 from the company.

We can now consider what happens when the company grows and the owner wishes to sell half their stake in the company. The original owner will still manage the company, but the new shareholder will just be an owner, not a manager. Before buying the stake, any potential buyer will attempt to value the company. Crucially, the value of the company now depends upon the expense preference behaviour of the owner-manager. When the owner-manager buys a BMW with the company's money, the other shareholder is paying for half of the car, but gaining no benefit. For example, if the company again generates £100 000 in profits, then each shareholder should receive £50 000. But if the shareholder who also manages the company uses £30 000 of the profits to buy the BMW, then the remaining profits are only £70 000. Split two ways, each shareholder receives £35 000. The owner-manager has received a £30 000 car plus £35 000 in dividends = £65 000. The shareholder who does not run the company has received only £35 000 in dividends. Therefore, the value of a share in the company is not £50 000, but rather £35 000. Indeed, the more a manager displays expense preference behaviour, the lower the potential buyer will value the company.

> Agents run companies on behalf of shareholders (principals).

This reduction in company value from employing an **agent** to manage the company is an example of an agency cost. Agency costs are not the wages associated with employing an agent; rather, they reflect reductions in value to **principals** from using agents to undertake work on their behalf.

The agency cost in our example is £50 000 − £35 000 = £15 000. It arises because the interests of the owner-manager are different from those of the other shareholder; and because the owner-manager is not monitored on a daily basis. It is, therefore, possible to use the company's money to fund benefits for the owner-manager at the expense of the remaining owner.

Agency costs between workers and managers

> Piece rates occur when a worker is paid according to the output produced. Under hourly wage rates, workers are paid for time at work.

Agency costs occur not just between owners and managers of companies. They can also occur when managers employ workers to do work for them. For example, let us consider two employment relationships. First, a supermarket employs a shelf stacker on **piece rates**. For each tray of tinned food put on the shelf, the shelf stacker receives £0.20. Second, a supermarket employs a shelf stacker on an hourly rate of £5.

If agency problems exist because principals find it difficult to monitor the effort of their agents, then piece rates will reduce agency costs. With an hourly wage rate of £5, the shelf stacker will earn £5 for one hour's work if they fill the shelf or if they sit in the staff restaurant drinking coffee and reading the paper. However, under piece rates the worker has to provide sufficient effort to place 25 trays of tinned food on the shelf in order to earn the same £5. Under piece rates, the employer does not have to continually monitor the effort of the agent; instead, they can merely add up all the output at the end of the shift. If the agent works hard, then greater output will lead to greater pay. If they are lazy and read the newspaper, then their pay will decrease. By linking pay more directly to the effort provided, the agency costs are reduced.

We tend to see piece rates used when the output is easy to verify. For example, car sales-persons are paid a commission for selling cars. It is fairly easy to verify that a car has been sold. Packers are often paid by the number of boxes that have been filled; and bricklayers are paid by the square metre of laid bricks and not by the hour.

However, when it comes to managers and many other occupations, output is more difficult to verify. How do you measure if a manager has managed? The many activities undertaken by managers, including monitoring workers, communicating and implementing business plans, reviewing operations and making investment decisions, make it difficult to measure the total output of the manager. The outputs are numerous, varied and difficult to quantify. For example, how do you measure effective communication? However, given that we have shown that company value is reduced by increased agency costs, we need to develop a means of aligning managers' interests with those of shareholders, thereby reducing agency costs and boosting company value. How might this be achieved? We need an alternative way of reducing agency costs. In the following business application, stock options will highlight how agency costs associated with employing managers might be reduced.

 ## 8.4 Business application: stock options and the reduction of agency costs

In order to reduce agency costs, principals have to develop contracts that align agents' interests with their own. Piece rates lower agency costs by forcing the agent to work hard to receive greater pay. A more complicated example is the use of **stock options** in the financial packages offered to senior managers of leading companies.

> Stock options provide individuals with the *option* to buy shares in the future at a price agreed in the past.

For example, assume the share price today for company X is £10. A manager at X may be offered the option to purchase 1 million shares at £10 in three years' time. Assume the manager works hard, the company makes profits and over the three years the shares rise to £12. The stock option has moved into the money. The manager can take up the option and buy at £10 and then sell instantly for £12, making £2 million profit. Stock options, therefore, link managers' and shareholders' interests via the share price. But how effective are stock options as a solution to agency problems?

An examination of the key points associated with stock options will help:

1 Stock options transfer an element of shareholder risk to the manager. Under a fixed salary contract a manager will earn perhaps £30 000 per annum. The manager will earn this salary if the company performs well or not. Under a stock option, part of the fixed contract is swapped for the stock options. The manager may now be offered a basic salary of £20 000, plus stock options. When the company performs well, the manager's stock options move into the money. The manager's pay increases whenever the stock option moves into the money and the manager executes the option, that is, uses the option to buy the shares cheaply and make a profit. But when the company underperforms, the share price drops and the stock options are worthless. Therefore, performance contracts, such as stock options, swap part of the certain salary for a chance of earning a higher overall amount. This increase in risk may not be attractive to the manager and they could decide to reject the contract or work somewhere else.

2 Stock options make a manager's pay contingent upon the share price. The share price is being used as a measure of the manager's hard work. The harder the manager works, the

higher the share price climbs. But what if the share price is influenced by industry factors, such as the degree of competition, or by domestic government policy on interest rates? A manager may work very hard but, due to government policy, the share price may fall. This increases the risk being transferred to the manager. For this reason, the measure of performance should be linked closely to managerial, or worker, effort. In some cases, the measures can be very specific. Workers in telephone sales are paid a commission every time they secure a sale, while car salespersons are paid every time they sell a car. In contrast, the output measures for managers tend to be very general, based on overall profitability, or simply linked to the share price.

3 The stronger the link between worker effort and the performance measure, the stronger the incentive. This merely reflects risk again. If you work hard, but the output measure does not reflect high effort, then you receive no pay. Managers are measured by share prices and car salespersons by number of sales. We might argue that there is a stronger link between worker effort and car sales than between worker effort and share price. At a simple level, if a salesperson works hard to sell a car, then a sale may materialize. But if a manager works hard, other managers may not and, therefore, due to a lack of teamwork, the share price is unaffected. As a reflection of these arguments, what tends to be observed is that, as a percentage of their overall pay, car salespersons receive a low fixed salary component and a high performance bonus. In contrast, managers tend to receive a high fixed salary component and a lower performance bonus. Therefore, as in the case of car salespersons, when the performance measure is a more accurate measure of worker effort, the more likely it is that pay will move to performance-based, rather than fixed, salary.

4 Incentive contracts can promote a single type of behaviour. Managers with stock options face incentives to raise the company's share price. But what if shareholders are interested in more than this? Box 8.1 provides Vodafone's strategic statement.

5 Finally, a manager's behaviour and effort must be verifiable. It should not be possible for the worker or manager to influence the performance measure inappropriately. This was clearly not the case with Enron and Worldcom. With Enron, managers were able to keep liabilities off the company's balance sheet, thereby inflating its share price. Even though the company was performing badly, the managers were able to make it appear highly successful. The share price rose and stock options were cashed in. In the case of Worldcom, expenses on stationery were capitalized and moved to the balance sheet as an asset, rather than sent to the profit and loss statement as an expense. This is common practice for substantial assets such as buildings and cars, but not for stationery, which you may no longer own as you have sent it out in letters! But, again, profits were seen to rise, assets increased and the share price rose. Once again, managers cashed in on stock options.

Therefore, performance contracts can help to resolve the principal–agent problem. But only if:

- workers accept the contracts, receiving greater rewards for higher risks
- there is a link between worker effort and the performance measure
- the performance can be co-ordinated across a number of objectives
- workers cannot unduly influence the measure.

We can use these points to understand some of the concerns relating to the excessive rewards provided to managers through stock options. One of the potential reasons why executive compensation has increased so markedly is to do with risk. A guaranteed payment of £100 is better than a 50:50 chance of receiving £100 or £0. But how much money would you require in order to accept the 50:50 gamble and give up the guaranteed £100? Would you require £200, £300 or perhaps even £1000? If you asked for £1000, then you would be described as not liking risk, or as being **risk averse**, and, therefore, requiring a large reward for accepting the risk of the 50:50 gamble.

> Risk averse means disliking or avoiding risk, an alternative to being risk neutral or risk seeking.

Assume an executive is equally risk averse. For every £100 that is taken from their guaranteed salary, a potential reward of £1000 has to be offered through the stock option. So, executives can receive large financial rewards, but they receive such rewards for (it is hoped) improving shareholder value and taking personal financial risk. We can even suggest where the executive's risk stems from. Linking a large amount of executive wealth to one company's share price does not provide the executive with a diversified portfolio of investments. The bulk of the executive's wealth is linked to one asset. We saw in Chapter 7 that diversification reduces risk. Therefore, reduced diversification must increase risk and, in order to accept greater risk, executives require a higher potential reward. As a consequence, the size of executive stock options and executive remuneration contracts increases.

The alternative view of managers using stock options to camouflage large financial rewards also has some merit. Raising the executive's salary by 100 per cent is likely to attract the wrong type of attention from shareholders and the media. By contrast, raising total financial remuneration through stock market performance provides a tangible link between pay and performance that is more palatable to the public.

However, all of our discussion has been linked to shareholders offering managers contracts that are designed to align the interests of shareholders and managers. In reality, managers propose contracts to shareholders. It is then shareholders who reject or accept the proposed financial terms for the executive(s). This is generally discussed at the company's annual general meeting. Why is this a problem?

First, managers are defining pay and performance. Admittedly, this is achieved through the company's remuneration committee that supposedly consists of independent remuneration experts and non-executive directors of the company.

Non-executive directors are directors from other companies who provide independent advice to the boards on which they are non-executives. For example, Mr X may be an executive director of company Y, his main employer. But Mr X may also be a non-executive director of company Z, providing independent advice to the board.

Box 8.1

Vodafone's strategic direction

Vodafone is uniquely positioned to succeed through our scale and scope and the customer focus of all our employees. To achieve this success, we are focused on the execution of the six strategic goals that we outlined last year: delighting our customers, leveraging our scale and scope, expanding market boundaries, building the best global team, being a responsible business, and providing superior shareholder returns.

Vodafone's strategic vision is based on six approaches, of which one is shareholder returns. While each of the six approaches may seem sensible, it is difficult to envisage a performance contract which is able to

reward managers for such a complexity of targets. Recently, companies have recognized this and some have moved to multiple measures of performance, splitting performance bonus between the short term and the long term. Performance is not necessarily measured by reference to the share price – it might include sales growth compared with the firm's three leading competitors, or profit growth compared to the top 25 per cent of the FTSE 100, or profitability compared with other leading global players in the sector.

Source: Vodafone website, www.vodafone.com.

From our discussion of behavioural theories of the firm, we might suspect that the targets set by remuneration committees will be satisficing, not maximizing, targets. From the behavioural perspective, there is a fear that executives can negotiate the proposed financial rewards, arguing with the members of the remuneration committee what reasonable targets and performance rewards are, given what is occurring in other companies. Second, due to the separation of ownership from control, once the executive(s) package is proposed, the dispersed nature of the shareholdings may lead to free riding among the shareholders, making a majority vote against the executive(s) financial terms difficult.

Performance pay and the public sector

A current trend is to introduce performance pay within the public sector. Primary care doctors in the UK are paid a fixed salary plus a performance element which is linked to certain health-care indices. These include reductions in blood pressure and cholesterol for patients at high risk of heart disease. Teachers are eligible for performance-related pay linked to pupil progression and dental professionals are paid according to the number of units of dental treatment provided to patients.

The key, as with performance contracts in the private sector, is to ensure that workers can respond to the incentives and do not divert the effort of employees away from other important value-adding activities. For example, in the dental profession, the extraction of a tooth attracts the same reward as extensive root canal work. The latter is more beneficial for the patient, but the former is quicker to deliver by the dentist. In the case of teaching, excellent teachers are increasingly allocated to teach marginal students where there is the greatest scope to improve pupil progression. Improving highly capable pupils is difficult and offers fewer financial rewards for good teachers.

The concern about performance-related pay is often levelled at those who receive enormous financial gain. The article in Box 8.2 shows that much of the blame can be levelled at economists.

Box 8.2

Who came up with the model for excessive pay? No, it wasn't the bankers – it was academics

All the focus has been on bankers' bonuses, yet no one has looked at the economists who argued for rewarding bosses by giving them a bigger financial stake in their companies.

The ground rules for the system by which City bankers, Westminster MPs and ordinary taxpayers live today were set by two US economists just a couple of decades ago. In 1990, Michael Jensen and Kevin Murphy published one of the most famous papers in economics, which first appeared in the *Journal of Political Economy* and then in the *Harvard Business Review*. Its argument is well summed up by the latter's title: 'CEO incentives: it's not how much you pay, but how'.

The way to get better performance out of bosses, argued the economists, was by giving them a bigger financial stake in their company's performance.

You couldn't have asked for a better codification of bonus culture had you stuck a mortar board on Gordon Gekko's head. So popular, so influential was Jensen and Murphy's work that it opened the door to a new corporate culture: one where executives routinely scooped millions in stock options, apparently justified by top research that they were worth it.

Economists did not just fail to spot the financial crisis – they helped create it. They provided the intellectual framework and drew up the policies that helped caused the boom – and the bust.

Much of the blame for the financial crisis has fallen on regulators for being captured by the bankers, and seeing the world from their point of view. The same thing has happened to academics. An economic study found that the 150 most downloaded academic papers on executive pay arguing that bosses should get more (à la Jensen and Murphy) were 55 per cent more likely to get published in the top journals.

Maybe, but it also pays to be deluded. Think about the rewards for toeing the mainstream economic line. Publication in prestigious journals. Early professorships at top universities. The conferences, the consultancies at big banks, the speaking fees. And then: the solicitations of the press, the book contracts. On it goes.

Rob Johnson, director of the Institute of New Economic Thinking, quotes a dictum he was once given by a leading West Coast economist. 'If you got behind Wall Street,' he remembers the professor telling him, 'you went to Lake Como every summer. If you left finance alone, you took a nice vacation in California. And if you took on the bankers, you drove a second-hand car.'

Adapted from an article by Aditya Chakrabortty in *The Guardian*, 30 January 2012. © Guardian News & Media Ltd 2012.

8.5 Regulation of business

We have examined the governance of managers by shareholders. We would now like to examine the governance of firms within their marketplaces. We have already seen, in Chapter 5, that monopolies are an example of marketplaces that are not in consumers' interests, with higher prices and lower output than under perfect competition. We will now also show that, in other ways, markets can act against the interest of consumers, or even the public more generally. In representing the interests of society, governments can intervene in such markets in an attempt to improve the benefits society receives from the market. We will begin by providing an overview of the issues and some further examples.

How many times have you sat at a set of traffic lights having 'to keep it real' by listening to the loud bass tunes from the car drawn up next to you? The person playing the loud music obviously likes the artist. The unfortunate problem is that everyone within earshot of the car also has to listen. The driver sets the volume of the car stereo without considering the interests of the people they may be driving past. Effectively, the interests of the driver and those of a wider group of individuals are not aligned.

Not surprisingly, the private interests of firms and wider society also differ. Polluting the environment, rather than cleaning factory emissions, is a cheap alternative for a profit-maximizing firm. Unfortunately, society as a whole has to bear the costs of a polluted environment. This is again because the interests of society and the private firm are not aligned. The firm will choose to produce more pollutants than society finds desirable.

An important but underlying issue within this book, and many other texts on economics, is that markets are an optimal means of allocating society's scarce resources. That is why we have spent so much time looking at supply, demand, perfect competition and monopoly. How do markets work and how do firms operate within markets?

At the heart of most economists' understanding is that an economy characterized by perfectly competitive markets is **Pareto efficient**. In perfect competition firms operate at the minimum point on their long-run cost curves. Hence, they are productively efficient. Firms make the highest level of output for the lowest amount of cost. Also in perfect competition, price equals marginal cost. So, the price paid by consumers for the last unit also equals the cost of the resources used in making the last unit. Therefore, input resources are also allocated efficiently. Thus, in perfect competition the goods that consumers desire are the ones that are made and, moreover, they are made at lowest cost. Intuitively we can accept this as a good outcome, and economists go one step further and prove that it is Pareto efficient.

> Pareto efficient means that no one within an economy can be made better off without making some other people worse off. Therefore, the well-being of society is at a maximum.

However, perfect competition is rarely achieved in reality and in some cases monopoly might exist. Under monopoly, products are not necessarily produced at lowest cost and they are not priced at marginal cost. So, Pareto efficiency will not hold.

> **Market failure**
> is a term used by economists to cover all circumstances in which the market equilibrium is not efficient.

Monopoly is an example of a **market failure**, with perfect competition providing a more efficient market equilibrium. But there can be other reasons for market failure. As we will discuss in detail below, so-called externalities can lead to a difference between the interests of private individuals and society and an inefficient production or consumption of goods and services from the perspective of society. For example, the production and consumption of loud music by our car driver is not an efficient (desirable) allocation of resources from the perspective of society (passers-by). We will now discuss externalities, monopoly and the problems relating to market failure. Following this, we can begin to assess various government intervention strategies for making markets potentially more Pareto efficient – that is, strategies that make people better off without making others worse off, thereby improving the well-being of society.

 ## Externalities

> **Externalities** are the effects of consumption, or production, on third parties.
>
> **Positive externality** occurs if production, or consumption, by one group improves the well-being of third parties.
>
> **Negative externality** occurs if production, or consumption, by one group reduces the well-being of third parties.
>
> **Marginal private cost** is the cost to the individual of producing one more unit of output.
>
> **Marginal social cost** is the cost to society of producing one or more unit of output.

Externalities occur when the production, or consumption, of a good or service results in costs, or benefits, being passed on to individuals not involved in the production, or consumption. **Negative externalities** occur when costs are passed on to society, or benefits are reduced. **Positive externalities** occur when costs to society are reduced or benefits are enhanced.

A number of examples will help to explain the concepts of positive and negative externalities.

The cost to the private firm of producing a particular output is the **marginal private cost** (MPC). We have previously referred to this as the marginal cost. The MPC measures the costs to the firm of producing one more unit and includes those of raw materials, labour and machinery. We now wish to also include in the analysis the **marginal social cost** (MSC). This is the cost to society of producing one more unit. As the private firm or individual is a member of society, then the MSC must include the MPC. However, in addition it will also include the costs associated with using or exploiting public assets, such as the environment. So, the MSC could include costs of pollution. In such cases, the costs to society will always be bigger than the costs to the private firm. These points are summarized in Table 8.2.

MSC is greater than MPC

The consequences of this can be seen in Figure 8.1. The optimal level of output for society and the private firm will occur where marginal revenue equals marginal cost. If the firm is a price-taker, then equilibrium for the private firm occurs at point B, where MPC equals demand and, therefore, marginal revenue. The output level is 2000 units. However, for society, MSC equals demand and, therefore, marginal revenue at point A, with an output of 1000 units. Therefore, when the private firm creates negative cost externalities for the rest of society, the private firm will choose a level of output that is greater than that deemed desirable by society. In its simplest terms, the firm does not recognize the costs of pollution; society does. Therefore, society has a desire to reduce output and pollution; the firm does not.

Table 8.2 Marginal private and social costs

Marginal private cost	Marginal social cost
Raw materials	Raw materials
Labour costs	Labour costs
Machinery	Machinery + Environmental costs of production

MSC is less than MPC

If we reversed the arguments and the marginal social cost was lower than the marginal private cost, then society would find it desirable to produce more output than the private firm or individual deems optimal. For example, society might decide that it is optimal for all

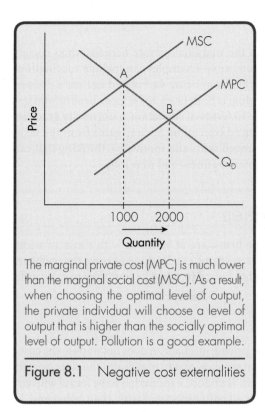

The marginal private cost (MPC) is much lower than the marginal social cost (MSC). As a result, when choosing the optimal level of output, the private individual will choose a level of output that is higher than the socially optimal level of output. Pollution is a good example.

Figure 8.1 Negative cost externalities

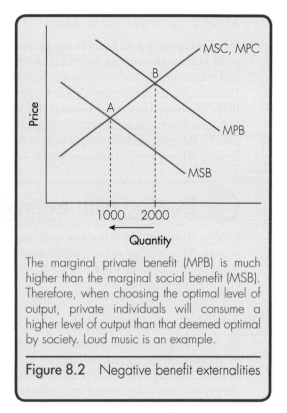

The marginal private benefit (MPB) is much higher than the marginal social benefit (MSB). Therefore, when choosing the optimal level of output, private individuals will consume a higher level of output than that deemed optimal by society. Loud music is an example.

Figure 8.2 Negative benefit externalities

individuals to gain a degree. But this requires your input in terms of time, effort and tuition fees. The costs to you are greater than to society. Hence, when deciding whether to go to university, you did not take into account society's views.

MPB is greater than MSB

The excessive car music example is a clear case of negative consumption externalities. The driver receives **marginal private benefit** (MPB) from consuming loud music. While the marginal private cost is linked to marginal cost, the marginal private benefit is linked to demand. If a consumer can place a financial value on the marginal benefit from consuming one more unit, then this value must equal the consumer's maximum willingness to pay.

The benefits for surrounding individuals are captured by the **marginal social benefit** (MSB). For simplicity, we will assume that the marginal social costs and the marginal private costs are equal. Figure 8.2 captures these points.

The optimal output of loud music for society occurs where MSC equals MSB at A, with 1000 units of output. The optimal amount of output for private individuals is where MPB equals MPC at B, with 2000 units of output. Therefore, we have 1000 too many drivers playing their music too loud. This figure would also capture the negative externalities associated with passive smoking. Private smokers gain a higher satisfaction from smoking than do non-smokers. As a result, if society is dominated by non-smokers, then smokers exhale pollutants at a level beyond what society deems desirable.

What are the business implications? If you consider advertising, the private benefits for firms are (they hope) increased sales. The benefits for consumers in society are improved information about what products are available, where they can be sourced and at what prices. If firms value higher sales more than consumers value information, firms will advertise at levels that are greater than that deemed desirable by society. If you have ever hated the adverts appearing on television, become irritated by pop-up adverts on the Internet, or been plagued by junk (e)mail, then you now understand why you were angry.

> Marginal private benefit is the benefit to the individual from consuming one more unit of output.
>
> Marginal social benefit is the benefit to society from the consumption of one more unit of output.

MSB is greater than MPB

If the marginal social benefits are greater than the marginal private benefits, then society gains more than a private individual from consumption. Examples can include vaccinations and education. An individual gains health benefits from being vaccinated against a disease. However, society gains more, because the individual is both likely to be more healthy and less likely to pass on the disease to other individuals. In terms of education, a university graduate may gain employment benefits from their advanced education. Society gains from the taxes paid by this educated person, as well as the advanced skills and innovative thinking that can be used within firms to generate profit, wealth, new business and new jobs.

(8.7) Dealing with externalities

Clearly, if the private actions of individuals, or firms, are at variance with those of wider society, there is a case for at least asking whether anything can be done to solve the problem. We will see that some solutions are fairly straightforward to describe, but they may be difficult to implement.

Taxation and subsidy

The central problem with an externality is that the pricing mechanism does not impose the costs, or benefits, on the correct individuals. If a person smokes, or a firm pollutes the river, society bears the cost of living with a polluted environment. Therefore, a means has to be found whereby the private firm or individual internalizes, or pays all costs associated with, their behaviour. In Figure 8.3, we revisit the situation where the marginal social cost is greater than the marginal private cost, the case of river pollution by a firm. Society views 1000 units of output as efficient; the firm would rather produce 2000 units of output. The problem is that marginal private costs, MPC, are different from marginal social costs, MSC. So, the obvious solution is to make MPC and MSC equal. This is achieved by taxing the firm for polluting the river, or environment. This adds to the firm's costs and, optimally, the tax will be equal to the difference between the MPC and the MSC. The imposition of the pollution tax provides firms with an incentive to cut output and move from point B to point A, thus lowering output to the socially optimum level.

Road tax for cars across a number of economies is linked to the pollution output of the car. Heavy polluters pay more road tax. This provides drivers with a clear incentive to buy cars that are more environmentally friendly, and we saw in Chapter 4 when looking at the automotive market that strong growth had been seen in the alternative fuel market.

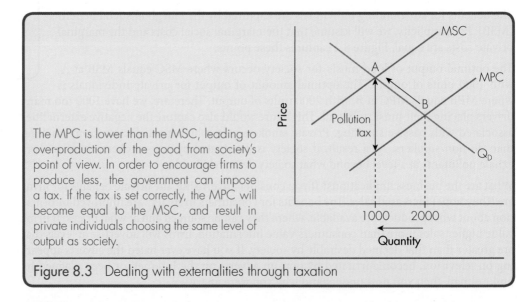

The MPC is lower than the MSC, leading to over-production of the good from society's point of view. In order to encourage firms to produce less, the government can impose a tax. If the tax is set correctly, the MPC will become equal to the MSC, and result in private individuals choosing the same level of output as society.

Figure 8.3 Dealing with externalities through taxation

Subsidies

An alternative to taxation is **subsidy**. Subsidies make consumption, or production, cheaper for the private individual. For example, home improvements which enhance energy efficiency, such as loft and wall cavity insulation, are often subsidized by government. Clearly, with a subsidy more energy-efficient home improvements will be purchased, since they are cheaper. So, subsidies will be used when governments fear

> A subsidy is a payment made to producers by government, which leads to a reduction in the market price of the product.

that the private level of output will be less than the socially optimal level of output. Consider Figure 8.4. The marginal private benefit, MPB, of an energy-efficient home is associated with lower electricity bills. The marginal social benefit, MSB, also includes the wider social benefits of a cleaner environment resulting from lower electricity generation. Hence, the MSB is greater than the MPB. In order to persuade consumers to use energy-efficient home improvements at the socially optimal level, a subsidy that is equal to the difference between MPB and MSB must be offered. This effectively reduces the price of energy-efficient home improvements and consumers buy in greater quantities.

Setting subsidies at the correct level can be difficult. Too little and consumers are unlikely to be incentivized. Too much and the cost becomes too large. Box 8.3 describes the overly attractive nature of solar panel subsidies in Germany, a problem which has occurred in other economies, such as the UK.

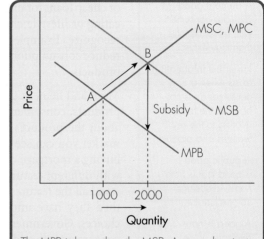

The MPB is lower than the MSB. As a result, private individuals under-consume the product. In order to increase the level of consumption, subsidies are offered to private individuals. This lowers the cost of consumption and individuals should consume more.

Figure 8.4 Dealing with externalities through subsidies

Box 8.3

German solar groups could thrive on subsidy fears

Fears Germany will cap or cut green energy subsidies is boosting demand for solar panels, and uncertainty about the shape of the measures could give the country's battered solar sector an advantage against Chinese rivals.

Installations of solar panels have boomed in Germany over the last two years due to feed-in tariffs, lavish subsidies utilities are forced to pay by the government to those who generate their own solar power. Ultimately power companies pass on the costs to their customers.

But as the burden on energy consumers soars, Berlin now wants to tighten its grip on the market and is scrambling for ideas over how best to curtail demand. Proposals range from monthly cuts in feed-in tariffs to an outright cap on subsidies.

December saw a massive installation rush and some executives and analysts are predicting a bumper first

quarter – seasonally the weakest as bad weather makes it harder to install panels on roofs – as people sign up for current schemes ahead of impending cutbacks.

Any pick-up in demand, however, will be fiercely contested. Germany, the world's largest solar market until Italy overtook it last year, has helped domestic and foreign solar companies alike to flourish as the feed-in tariffs are paid regardless of the panels' origin.

Low-cost Asian module makers now dominate the $82 billion global photovoltaic (PV) industry. Chinese companies such as Suntech, JA Solar, Yingli and Trina Solar, have all been helped by incentives in Germany, which accounted for 27 per cent of the global PV market last year.

Adapted from an article by Christoph Steitz, Reuters Online, 1 February 2011.

Merit, demerit and public goods

A merit good provides consumers with more benefits than they expect.

A demerit good provides consumers with fewer benefits than they expect.

Imperfect information exists when a consumer does not have all the facts relating to the key features of a product.

A public good is a good that is both non-rivalrous and non-excludable.

A good is non-rivalrous, if the consumption of the good does not prevent consumption by other consumers.

A good is non-excludable, if suppliers cannot restrict supply to those consumers who have paid for the good.

Economists categorize goods and services into particular groupings, including merit, demerit, public and private goods. **Merit goods** are seen by governments as providing greater benefits to consumers than consumers may recognize. Examples include education and health care and can often lead to positive externalities. Governments may support and promote the consumption of merit goods through subsidies, grants or cheap loans for university education, or communication policies promoting healthy eating or lifestyle choices. **Demerit goods** provide less benefit than consumers may recognize. Examples include smoking and drinking; and governments can seek to reduce consumption through higher taxes and restrictions on the advertising of such products.

Merit and demerit goods highlight a problem of **imperfect information**. For simple products, consumers are often capable of possessing complete (perfect) information about the product's important features. For example, if you buy fruit at the supermarket you can see if the fruit is ripe, fresh and undamaged. In contrast, if you are buying a mortgage or taking out a pension, then such products can be very complex, with different features, fees, options and penalties. When consumers do not understand all the features, or underestimate some of the risks associated with the product, then they have imperfect information and may make inappropriate consumption choices. Governments can address this problem by insisting that suppliers provide consumers with additional information. In the case of mortgages, borrowers are given key feature documents; and for alcohol and cigarettes health warnings are printed on packaging.

Public goods display two important characteristics. Such goods are non-rivalrous and non-excludable. A good or service is **non-rivalrous** if the consumption of the good or service does not reduce the amount of consumption available to all other consumers. For example, if you listen to the radio, then you do not prevent anyone else from listening, but if you consume a soft drink, then no one else can consume the drink. A good or service is **non-excludable** if the supplier cannot restrict supply to those consumers who have paid. A car company can exclude you from car ownership if you do not pay the required price for the car. A radio company cannot exclude you from listening once it sends out a radio signal. Non-rivalrous and non-excludable make the free consumption of public goods very easy for consumers, but entirely unprofitable for suppliers. Hence, companies can decide not to supply and the market may fail.

In the past, common examples of public goods have included television and radio. Supply has been by public broadcasters who have financed themselves from a government subsidy or a licence fee levied on all households. Private sector broadcasters financed themselves by showing adverts, rather than charging viewers. Now satellite and cable providers use encryption technologies to exclude viewers who have not paid for the service.

A more contemporary example of a public good is music and film. The availability of pirated music files and film for download from the Internet is both non-rivalrous and non-excludable. Without the prosecution of illegal downloaders for breaches of copyright and the closing of illegal download sites, suppliers would make less revenue, be less inclined to supply and the market could fail.

 ## Price volatility

The equilibrium prices for goods and services are not always stable. When demand and supply change, the equilibrium price of a good or service also changes. The more frequent the change in demand or supply, and the larger the change in demand or supply, the more unstable or volatile market equilibrium prices will be. These frequent and possibly large changes in equilibrium prices can make budgetary planning for households and firms very difficult; and perhaps more importantly, when prices are increasing household and firm budgets can come under pressure, leading to financial distress and hardship. In recent times we have seen large changes in fuel and food prices, as well as large increases in the price of important raw materials, such as copper, aluminum and rare earths used in smartphones.

In order to understand these prices changes it is necessary to utilize our understanding of markets developed in Chapter 4. The important factors which determine the scale of change in an equilibrium price are the amount of change in demand and supply and the price elasticity of demand and supply. Big drivers of demand changes have been the rising incomes of the emerging economies around the globe, such as China, India, Russia and Brazil. As incomes in these economies grow, there is an increase in demand for additional food stocks, increased demand for fuel and increased demand for raw materials, such as metals to enable the manufacture of cars, electronic consumables, property, roads, hospitals and factories. Developments in supply may not keep up with demand, leading to higher prices; and where supply does grow, it is often high technology and/or high risk. For example, the world's insatiable demand for fuel supports high-risk exploration for oil, such as the Deepwater Horizon rig in the Gulf of Mexico. This rig, used by BP, caught fire, sank, leaked huge amounts of oil and reduced the supply of oil to the market. The global supply of commodities can also be constrained by the desire to secure national supply. When the wheat harvest in Russia failed in 2010, the Russian government cancelled all contracts to supply wheat outside of Russia, ensuring domestic supply was protected. Such action resulted in a reduction of global supply and an increase in wheat prices, which impacted the price of bread, beer and other food items across Europe.

Inelastic demand or supply will only exacerbate any changes in demand and supply. In Figure 8.5 when supply is inelastic an increase in demand drives prices higher than when supply is elastic. Supply is likely to be inelastic when firms are unable to build additional supply, even when prices increase. New mines, new oil wells, new space for agriculture all require massive investment, which limits the development of supply.

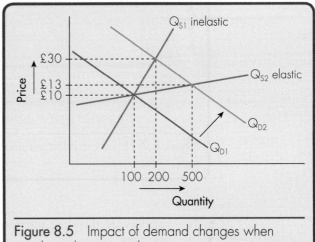

Figure 8.5 Impact of demand changes when supply is elastic or inelastic

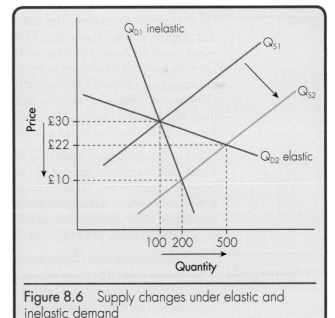

Figure 8.6 Supply changes under elastic and inelastic demand

In Figure 8.6 changes in supply move prices more when demand is inelastic. In the case of demand for stable food resources, energy and essential metals, demand is likely to be inelastic due to the lack of substitutes, hence greater changes in prices.

Price volatility is the variation in prices overtime. A price which changes by 5 per cent per month is not especially volatile when compared with a price which changes by 5 per cent, then 2 per cent, then 18 per cent, then 8 per cent. Measures of price

> Price volatility measures how prices vary over time.

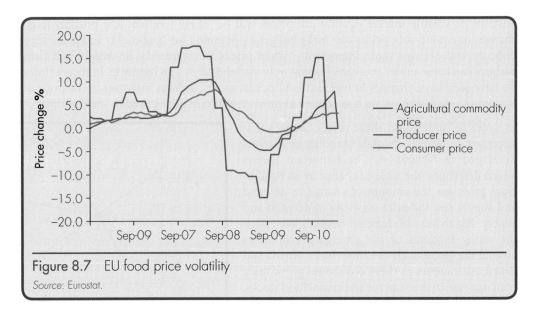

Figure 8.7   EU food price volatility

Source: Eurostat.

volatility are, therefore, often achieved by measuring the **standard deviation** of prices over time.

> Standard deviation is a measure of how much a variable differs from its average value over time.

Figure 8.7 presents data on price changes at different stages of the value chain for food (see Chapter 7). We have farm gate, or agricultural commodity, prices; producer or factory prices; and consumer or retail prices. Price changes for agricultural commodity prices show the greatest variation, while consumer prices show the least amount of variation. This difference can, in part, be explained by changes in demand and supply and price elasticities. At the commodity level, changes in demand and supply of wheat are likely to be much bigger than the changes in final demand or supply for bread. Growing incomes around the world impact the demand for wheat, while bad harvests impact the supply. At the level of bread or beer, where wheat is an ingredient, there are not huge global forces influencing demand and supply. In addition, the demand elasticity for wheat is likely to be fairly inelastic as there are few substitutes for wheat, whereas consumers can, to some degree, substitute bread as a carbohydrate for potatoes and rice.

Other forces also impact price volatility at different stages in the value chain. Producers turn wheat into bread and thereby through the baking process add value. Retailers distribute bread to shoppers and therefore add value by making access to bread easy. Since bread is comprised of wheat, baking and distribution, the price component of wheat is less important as different value elements are added in. Hence changes in wheat prices do not generate as big a variation in the price of bread.

> Menu costs are the costs associated with changing prices, which can include updating computer systems, printing new price lists, changing shelf price information.

There is also a cost associated with changing prices. Economists refer to these costs as **menu costs**. The more expensive the menu costs, the less likely a firm is to change its prices. Any gain from raising prices, for example, could be wiped out by the menu cost. There are few menu costs for wheat: buyers and sellers trade in a recognized commodity market in, say, London or Moscow, and they agree a price rather than follow a set of prices on a list. Bread, on the other hand, is sold by supermarkets and the price information is stored in computers, is listed on the shelf and maybe even advertised in newspapers. Changing the price is expensive.

Governments can try to bring some stability to the price of important staple items. Fuel has been targeted by the UK government through the fair fuel stabilizer. When crude oil rises above a certain price, then tax on the retail price of petrol and diesel will fall; and when the crude oil price falls below a certain price, then tax on the retail prices of petrol and diesel will increase. The reason why this policy may bring some stability in prices is that tax is a large part of the retail price of fuel and in addition petrol retailers are geared to, in fact experts at, changing prices quickly. You only have to see the large signs outside all petrol stations, which display the price, to see that the menu costs of changing prices are fairly simple. In contrast, while the price of the weekly shopping has also increased, the government has not sought to manage prices. There is little or no tax on most grocery items and much of the value added comes from manufacturing and retailing, not agriculture, so there is little or no scope to manage price changes in these markets.

8.10 Market power and competition policy

In Chapter 5 we compared perfect competition with monopoly and argued that under monopoly the price is higher and output is lower than under perfect competition. With the introduction of Pareto efficiency, we can now move on to show how monopoly, from the perspective of society, is not necessarily a desirable form of market structure.

In the left-hand side of Figure 8.8, we have perfect competition. The profit-maximizing level of output, Q_{pc}, is sold at a price of P_{pc}. *Consumer surplus* is the difference between the price a consumer is willing to pay and the price charged. In this case, the consumer surplus is the light blue shaded area above the market price and below the demand curve. Consumer surplus is an important measure of welfare or well-being. If you are willing to pay £50 for a product and you can buy it for £30, then you are £20 better off.

Producers also have a surplus. **Producer surplus** is the difference between the price they would be willing to sell at and the price that they do sell at. Recall Chapter 5 and the discussion of profit maximization. Under the assumption of profit maximization, a firm is willing to supply one more unit of output if the price offered is greater than

> Producer surplus is the difference between the price that a firm is willing to sell at and the price it does sell at.

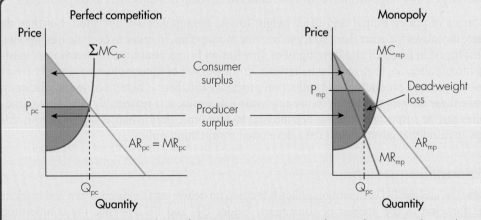

- The consumer surplus under perfect competition is greater than under monopoly simply because the price is lower under perfect competition.
- The producer surplus is greater under monopoly than under perfect competition simply because the price is higher under monopoly.
- However, the total of consumer and producer surplus is higher under perfect competition than under monopoly. This difference is known as the dead-weight loss of monopoly and represents a reduction in welfare to society. Since everyone can be made better off by moving to perfect competition, monopoly is not Pareto efficient.

Figure 8.8   Welfare costs of monopoly

or equal to marginal cost. In this way, the firm at worst breaks even on the last unit supplied. So, given our definition of producer surplus and the concept of profit maximization, the firm is willing to sell at any price which is greater than marginal cost; we now only need the price that the firm sells at in order to measure producer surplus. In Figure 8.8, producer surplus is the darker blue area below the market price and above the marginal cost curve for the industry.

The case of monopoly is shown in the right-hand side of Figure 8.8. Under monopoly, the price increases and the output shrinks. Therefore, the consumer surplus must reduce. In contrast, because the monopoly sells at a higher price, producer surplus must increase. In essence, part of the consumer surplus is being transferred to the monopoly. However, and this is the important part, if we compare the total of consumer and producer surplus under

> Dead-weight loss of monopoly is the loss of welfare to society resulting from the existence of the monopoly.

perfect competition and monopoly, we can see that the total surplus is lower under monopoly. This difference is known as the **dead-weight loss** of monopoly. It is a loss of welfare to society. Under Pareto efficiency no one can be made better off without making someone else worse off. Monopoly is clearly not Pareto efficient because if we change the market into a perfectly competitive one, then the dead-weight loss will vanish. People can be made better off without making anyone else worse off. Essentially, more products are sold and sold at a lower price.

Dead-weight loss may not be the only detrimental aspect of monopoly. Many companies will spend resources trying to attain monopoly status.

Rent-seeking activities are the allocation of resources to non-socially optimal ends and they also need to be added on to the dead-weight losses. However, following the ideas of an economist called Schumpeter, monopolies have enjoyed the academic protection of a concept known as 'creative destruction'.

For example, Microsoft is a global monopoly supplier of operating systems. If one innovator manages to invent a new and commercially successful way of operating computers, then Microsoft's position could be under threat. The potential to take over Microsoft's dominant position acts as a huge incentive for innovators to develop new products and approaches.

In terms of prices, output and dead-weight losses, monopolies are not good, but they do create incentives for other firms to try to become monopolies. In order to become monopolies, firms invest in research and development. Innovation brings about the destruction of existing monopolies. So, rent-seeking behaviour, or the pursuit of monopoly, may actually create innovation, new products, new production processes and, hence, better economic efficiency. While these debates can be left to the academic economist, it is reasonably clear that monopolies can be suspected of being detrimental to economic performance, and it is with this view in mind that governments have developed competition policy.

Competition policy

In the UK and the EU competition policy is focused on delivering fair competition and markets that function in the interest of consumers. Under UK and EU systems, the competition bodies are interested in removing cartels, preventing the abuse of dominant market positions by large companies and overseeing the merger and acquisition of companies which may lead to dominant positions. The EU also concerns itself with the competitive impact of state aid to national industries.

> The Competition Commission investigates whether a monopoly, or a potential monopoly, significantly affects competition.

Within the EU, the home country normally takes the lead on competition policy, but will pass matters of concern to the EU Competition Commission if there is a significant EU element to the case, for example if a cartel includes companies from a number of EU states, or a merger will create a dominant firm within the EU market.

In the case of the UK, the Director General of Fair Trading supervises company behaviour and when necessary will refer individual companies to the UK **Competition Commission** for investigation. Companies can be referred if they are suspected of being involved in a cartel, are abusing a dominant position, for example by using predatory pricing, or in the case of a merger, the new combined firm will own more than 25 per cent of the market and/or the firm being acquired has turnover in excess of £70 million.

The focus of a UK Competition Commission inquiry is to establish whether there is a serious threat to competition. Should the Competition Commission establish that competition is under threat, then it has wide powers to make and enforce remedies.

If a UK merger or breach of competition has a European dimension, then it can be examined by the European Commission for Competition. If the merged companies have a global turn-over which exceeds €5 billion and turnover within the EU exceeds €250 million, then the EU Commission will investigate the merger. This investigation will occur even if the merging companies are not headquartered within the EU. The EU also evaluates mergers in terms of whether they will reduce competition. The EU has taken a fairly robust approach to situations which have reduced or threaten to reduce competition. Under the law, a company can be fined up to 10 per cent of its global turnover. In the case of Microsoft, which refused to follow EU restrictions imposed on its software, a fine of €899 million was imposed. In the case of Intel, which was accused of abusing a dominant position, a fine of €1.06 billion was imposed.

Assessing government interventions

Government interventions to correct market failures can be costly and may not always be effective. In this section we examine how to evaluate government intervention and how to recognize some of the factors which are important in determining the effectiveness of policy interventions.

Government interventions are generally evaluated by a process known as **impact analysis** which seeks to understand the impact of a policy change by undertaking **cost–benefit analysis**. Under cost–benefit analysis all of the costs associated with an intervention are subtracted from all of the benefits. Different interventions, including no intervention, can then be compared by reference to the net monetary benefit of each intervention. Cost–benefit analysis is a very complicated process since it is not easy to identify all costs and benefits, measuring all costs and benefits in monetary amounts may not be accurate, and even identifying who bears a cost and who gains a benefit may be debatable. Moreover, if time is also important, say the intervention lasts over many years, then it is also necessary to estimate how costs and benefits will develop over time and then apply an appropriate **discount factor or rate** (see Chapter 12, section 12.7). Choosing an appropriate discount factor can be very difficult when interventions are long lived.

As an example of some of the difficulties, consider subsidies for the development of nuclear power stations. Who benefits from lower carbon emissions into the environ-ment, what are the benefits of lower carbon emissions and can these benefits be measured in monetary amounts? When considering the costs, decommissioning a nuclear plant and managing the waste become important. Since nuclear waste remains a problem for hundreds if not thousands of years, then at what rate do you discount the costs of dealing with the waste at say 100 years, 200 years and so on? It is fairly easy to discount a five-year project by simply taking the expected interest rate for the economy. But the interest rate might apply over an extremely long time horizon, such as 100 years.

In order for government policy to be effective, governments require a clear understanding of the problem. But just as consumers can suffer from imperfect information, so can govern-ments. An example would be cost–benefit analysis. Since much of a cost–benefit analysis is an estimate, then a government may choose a solution which looks good on paper, but in reality the costs may dramatically outweigh the costs. To some extent, this can tackled by conducting cost–benefit analysis before and after implementation of the policy. Government

> **Impact analysis** is a means of understanding the impact of a policy change on individuals and/or an economy.
>
> **Cost–benefit analysis** provides a monetary evaluation of a government intervention.
>
> **Discount factor (or rate)** provides a measure of the time value of money. If £100 saved for one year earns 2 per cent interest, at the end of year you will have £102. Equally, a cost of £102 in a year's time is worth £100 today.

agencies can also suffer from **regulatory capture**. A monopoly or group of dominant firms may be supervised by a regulator to ensure that prices are set at fair competitive levels rather than monopoly levels. The regulator will often need data from the regulated firms in order to set prices for the industry. The regulator is therefore reliant on those firms that it seeks to control. The regulated firms can then seek to influence (capture) the regulator and provide limited costing data and exaggerated investment demands in order to convince the regulator that prices need to rise higher for the firms to remain financially viable.

Finally, it is important to recognize the implications of second best solutions. Under a **first best solution** all market failures across the economy are removed and society's welfare is maximized. A first best solution would see all industries as perfectly competitive and maximizing economic efficiency. A **second best solution** is the best outcome that can be achieved when at least one market failure somewhere in the economy cannot be corrected. For example, it may be infeasible to convert a monopoly into a perfectly competitive industry. The second best solution for the economy is not necessarily to leave all the other industries as perfectly competitive. The second best solution for the economy often requires other distortions or market failures to be introduced into the economy by the government.

> Regulatory capture occurs when the regulated firms have some control or influence over the regulator.
>
> In a first best solution the economy has no market failures.
>
> A second best solution is the best outcome for an economy when at least one market failure cannot be corrected.

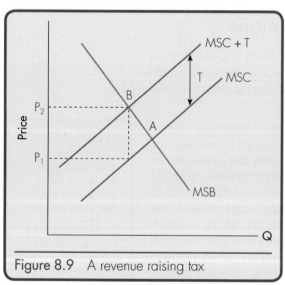

Figure 8.9 A revenue raising tax

For example, if it is necessary to tax luxury cars to provide monetary support for the poor, then the tax will drive a wedge between the equilibrium marginal social cost and marginal social benefit for luxury cars. This is illustrated in Figure 8.9. Without the tax the marginal social benefit (MSB) and the marginal social cost (MSC) are in equilibrium at A. Adding a tax T, raises society's supply line to MSC+T and the equilibrium now occurs at B. Under the imposition of a tax, the marginal social benefit of luxury cars (P_2) exceeds the marginal social cost (P_1) and as such represents a market failure. If financial support for the poor is essential and the tax cannot be removed, then a second best solution for the economy may require additional market failures by the imposition of taxes in other markets. As such, government policy in one area can have additional knock-on effects in order to achieve the second best outcome.

Business application: carbon trading

Carbon dioxide, a greenhouse gas, is a by-product of burning fossil fuels such as oil and coal. Modern industrial economies consume vast amounts of energy on a daily basis and that energy is provided by burning fossil fuels. Oil and coal are used to generate electricity and are used to propel cars, lorries and aircraft. As a greenhouse gas, carbon dioxide is a pollutant. Unfortunately, the creation of carbon dioxide is an example of a negative externality. The marginal private cost of producing electricity does not reflect the full marginal social cost, which also includes the effects of pollution on the environment.

Environmental and growth economists examine the rising production of greenhouse gases using an environmentally adapted Kuznets curve.[3] The environmental Kuznets curve shows

---

[3] Kuznets's original analysis showed an n-shaped relationship between income inequality and GDP per capita. In the early stages of economic development, income growth is seen to flow to those individuals who own capital (and so are already affluent). In later stages of development, the provision of education to everyone enables non-capital owners to share in economic growth and so income inequalities fall.

an n-shaped relationship between the production of green-house gases and GDP per capita. This relationship is depicted in Figure 8.10. As an economy grows and GDP per capita rises, then a greater use of fossil fuel production results in the rising production of detrimental greenhouse gases. Once an economy reaches a certain size and affluence, then there is likely to be sufficient wealth and technical expertise to address the use of fossil fuels and the generation of greenhouse gases. Financial resource and engineering expertise can be allocated to the production of hybrid fuel cars and wind turbine generation of electricity. Therefore, in advanced high GDP per capita economies the production of greenhouse gases begins to decline.

The environmental Kuznets curve provides a useful framework for examining the rise in pollution around the world. Fast-growing economies, such as China and India, have rapidly increased GDP per capita and as a consequence have significantly added to the global production of greenhouse gases. It is arguably unreasonable to ask these economies to avoid the use of fossil fuels and make greater use of environmentally friendly energy production. In particular, the developed economies of the world made ample use of fossil fuel technology throughout their own development, so why should China and India be expected to take a more expensive route to full economic development?

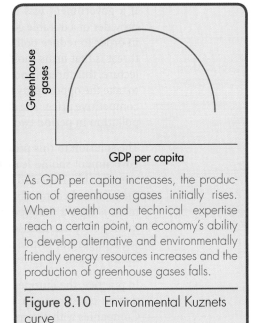

As GDP per capita increases, the production of greenhouse gases initially rises. When wealth and technical expertise reach a certain point, an economy's ability to develop alternative and environmentally friendly energy resources increases and the production of greenhouse gases falls.

Figure 8.10   Environmental Kuznets curve

However, the Kuznets curve indicates that some of the additional greenhouse gases from developing economies can be balanced by a reduction in pollution from highly developed economies. Unfortunately, the statistical evidence relating to the environmental Kuznets curve suggests that even the USA, the world's largest economy, has not yet reached its peak.

In order to address the rise in greenhouse gases around the world various governments have implemented schemes which aim to reduce carbon dioxide emissions. Two broad schemes are available. The first is the sale of licences to pollute; the second is permits to emit pollutants. In the former case, firms pay a fee for the right to pollute. If the fee is high enough, some firms may decide it is cheaper not to pollute. In the second system, governments issue permits which enable a given amount of pollution. This quantity-based system guarantees a direct impact on the amount of pollution, but the cost to polluters is unknown and determined by the market price for permits. Within Europe a cap-and-trade system has been adopted. This is a market for permits to emit and is a quantity-based system. The purpose of the scheme is two-fold. First, the scheme provides governments with a credible commitment to limit the number of permits. Second, the scheme provides benefits to firms that cut emissions and a penalty to those that do not. In understanding the need to credibly commit to a fixed number of permits, we will examine the **Coase conjecture**. We then move on to an examination of how the traded permit scheme provides financial incentives to limit pollution.

The Coase conjecture argues that a monopoly provider of a durable good will sell at the perfectly competitive price.

Ronald Coase put forward the argument that a monopoly supplier of a durable good would have no monopoly pricing power and would sell all units of output at the perfectly competitive price. Consider a monopoly that can set prices for its durable good in two periods. In the first period, it will set a high price and sell to consumers who are desperate for the product today. In the second period, the monopoly has to set a price for all customers who decided to wait in period one. The monopoly clearly has an incentive to expand output and sell for a lower price in period two. If consumers correctly anticipate the monopoly's incentive to cut prices in period two and the good is durable, then more consumers will wait for period two. This then provides a greater incentive for the monopoly to mop up the residual demand in period two with yet more output and lower prices. In fact, it will be optimal for a monopoly to sell at the perfectly competitive price in all periods.

If a government was to sell licences to pollute, then it could be considered a monopoly provider of a durable good. The government could sell licences in period one and claim that, in order to reduce pollution, the number of licences in period two will be less. The implicit threat is that firms should buy their licences today. Unfortunately, following the Coase conjecture, this threat is not a credible commitment. Polluting firms will expect the government to take the opportunity to raise revenues by selling more licences in period two at close to the competitive price. The clear incentive for firms is to wait for the cheaper licences and expand pollution in period two.

The solution to this problem is for the government not to sell durable licences. Instead, the government should lease licences for a given period. Through leasing, the licences become non-durable. In period one, a firm buys its requirement of licences. At the end of period one, the licences become obsolete and the firm is required to buy more in period two. The government is now a monopoly supplier of consumable goods in each period. It can charge the monopoly price and so faces no incentive to expand the output of permits in each subsequent period. With a credible commitment to a fixed or falling number of permits in each future period, the government is better placed to reduce pollution.

In practice, the European system for controlling carbon emissions involves governments setting an emissions cap. Permits to pollute equal to the cap are then allocated to industries. Companies with a surplus of permits trade with those that have a shortage. In essence, there is a market in pollution permits. But importantly, the size of this market is credibly limited by the governments' decision to lease permits for one year. If a firm wishes to pollute more, then it must pay for extra permits. And paying is the crucial aspect. Through the market, paying for the right to pollute increases the marginal private cost faced by polluting firms. As such, it should reduce the equilibrium level of pollution. In essence, the requirement to pay for the right to pollute is nothing more than a tax on excessive polluters. At the same time, clean producers are in effect subsidized by being able to sell their surplus permits at a profit, concepts which we discussed in section 8.7.

An important feature of this solution is that it generates an opportunity cost. Polluters are faced with a trade-off. They can either buy more credits to meet their level of pollution, or they can decide to invest in new technology which is more environmentally friendly. The market for carbon permits provides firms with an alternative option and price. As permit prices rise, then it is hoped that the attractiveness of investment in cleaner technology will increase, helping to reduce long-term pollution levels. Of course, the price of permits may just as easily fall. There is a concern that too many permits were allocated during the launch phase of the carbon trading system in Europe. This resulted in a significant price fall for each permit to pollute with 1 ton of carbon. Governments now have this under control. Each year the supply of permits will be reduced. Our understanding of markets assures us that a reduction in supply will lead to an increase in the equilibrium price. But, of course, a recession reduces the demand for goods, which reduces the demand for energy and the demand for permits.

It should also be recognized that there are problems with a system which penalizes polluters. In a global economy there is the risk that environmental policies in Europe place heavy users of fossil fuels at a cost disadvantage relative to rivals in China, where there is no environmental tax for producing greenhouse gases. In fact, much of this risk is minimal when we consider the overall economy. Services are the major engine of economic activity and are light users of energy. Even in manufacturing, estimates indicate that energy costs represent less than 1 per cent of making cars and furniture. Heavy users of fossil fuels, such as electricity generators, do not compete internationally and so much of the cost increase from carbon permits is passed on to domestic customers.

A number of other contentious issues are now being tackled. A tax is being levied on international flights into Europe and variable tax for the type of fuel burnt and the emissions caused is also under review, see Box 8.4.

Box 8.4

Greening the skies

As of 1 January, American, Chinese and all the world's airlines are being billed for the carbon emissions of their flights into and out of the European Union. About time, too: airlines contribute 2–3 per cent of global emissions, yet they were hitherto free to pollute. The European initiative, which brings airlines into the EU's existing cap-and-trade regime, the Emissions Trading Scheme (ETS), is a modest corrective. The hope is that it will speed the creation of a long-promised, more ambitious successor, governing all the world's airspace.

Foreign airlines, needless to say, are unhappy. So are their governments. Because flights into the EU have been included in their entirety, not just the portion within European airspace, they detect an infringement of their sovereignty.

Offended governments might also complain to the UN's International Civil Aviation Organisation. Having threatened 'appropriate action' if the EU went ahead with its plan, America may even be considering a retaliatory measure, such as a tariff on European carriers. But that is unlikely. In fact, given that airlines will initially be given most of their tradable ETS permits, and that the European carbon price is at a record low, the airlines may even make money from the scheme.

A second controversy concerns an EU plan to reduce the carbon intensity of transport fuel. Under proposed new rules for this scheme, different sources of crude oil would be given weightings to reflect how much they pollute. To meet the EU's target – a 6 per cent reduction in carbon intensity by 2020 – filthier-than-average sorts of fuel, such as diesel derived from coal or petrol from shale oil or Canadian tar sands, would need mixing with cleaner sorts, like biofuels.

This upset Canada, and firms such as Shell and BP which have invested heavily in Alberta's sludgy natural bitumen. They do not deny that getting oil from tar sands is a dirty business. The EU says it creates 23 per cent more emissions than the average source; Shell says 5–15 per cent. Yet they argue that the proposals would punish Canada for being upfront about this, with less transparent polluters, such as Nigeria, which flares lots of natural gas from its oil production, liable to evade the EU's censure. Fans of the weightings admit they are not perfect, but argue that, as in the case of airlines and the ETS, it is better to make the best possible start than to delay action indefinitely.

Adapted from an article in *The Economist*, 'The EU annoys airlines, energy companies and Canada', 7 January 2012. © The Economist Newspaper Limited, London 2012.

8.13 Business data application: impact analysis and smart metering

Government departments at both national and supranational level are good sources of impact analysis and cost–benefit analysis reports and data. All proposed policy changes are now routinely examined and assessed for the ability to deliver net benefits to society.

Smart meters are an interesting example of a government policy which seeks to tackle a possible market failure, which may achieve positive externalities and has been impact assessed using cost–benefit analysis.

Currently electricity and gas consumption within most homes and businesses is recorded using simple technologies. The meters in current use do not enable end-users to monitor usage minute by minute, enable energy suppliers to record usage and bill remotely, or make it possible for energy suppliers to control and activate household appliances during periods of non-peak consumption.

The benefits from smart metering could be enormous. With the provision of real-time consumption information within the home, households can identify and reduce excess consumption by perhaps unplugging devices in standby mode. Suppliers can reduce visits to properties and reduce staffing levels in customer support centres; and finally being able

---

Box 8.5

Smart meters predicted to save UK households £23 a year by 2020

The government is planning for 53 million smart meters to be installed in 30 million homes and businesses, starting in 2014 and finishing in 2019. The roll-out – the most comprehensive yet planned in any country – is likely to enable households to save £23 on their annual energy bills by 2020, the government has estimated, up from its previous estimate of £14 in savings.

Chris Huhne, the Secretary of State for energy and climate change, stressed the potential benefits of the plan, which is one of the most visible aspects of the government's low-carbon strategy, as the meters will be in every home. He said: 'Smart meters are a key part of giving us all more control over how we use energy at home and at work, helping us to cut out waste and save money. In combination with our plans to reform the electricity market and introduce the green deal [project to insulate homes], the roll-out of smart meters will help us keep the lights on while

reducing emissions and getting the best possible deal for the consumer.'

Today's announcement is expected to kick off a frenzy of activity among smart meter technology companies, utilities and communications businesses as they jockey for position in pressing for the adoption of their competing ideas on how smart meters should work. During this phase, companies are expected to build and test trial systems, get customer feedback and demonstrate how they can ensure energy savings.

Charles Hendry, Energy Minister, said: 'Smart meters will enable us to modernize the electricity system over the coming years and create the smart grids we will need to bring new low carbon energy sources online, and handle much higher demand for electricity as we progressively electrify transport and heating.'

Adapted from an article in *The Guardian*, 30 March 2011.
© Guardian News & Media Ltd 2011.

---

remotely to operate washing machines, refrigerators and charge points for motor vehicles during low-peak demand, energy suppliers can smooth demand and operating expenses.

The technology to support smart metering already exists and for gas and electricity metering would cost around £130 per property. However, adoption of smart metering may be limited due to an inability to achieve interoperability, which is the primary reason for a government roll-out. Interoperability occurs when different systems, devices and technologies can communicate with each other. If energy suppliers install different smart meters, there is a risk that when one household switches energy supplier their meters will also need to be changed in order to interface with the new supplier's system. Such a scenario adds cost and limits the payback to the energy supplier from smart metering and may result in a very limited roll-out to households. If the government wishes to see large-scale adoption of smart metering, then it needs to address the failure. By ruling on what communication technologies and standards can be used in smart meters, the government can create an interoperable system. An interoperable system that can be used and exploited by all users, suppliers and consumers will generate greater usage and therefore wider network-driven positive externalities. But is it worth paying for? Impact assessment and cost–benefit analysis now becomes useful.

Costs of installing and operating the system of smart meters have been estimated at £6.29 billion by the government. Network communication costs are estimated at £2.11 billion. Information technology cost of £1 billion and other costs including setup, disposal and marketing are estimated at £1.33 billion, bringing total costs to £10.75 billion.

Benefits to consumers, mostly made up of energy savings, are estimated at £4.64 billion. Benefits to suppliers total £8.57 billion, including avoided site visits of £3.18 billion and reduced enquiries and customer overheads of £1.24 billion. Improved network benefits of

£780 million, reduced generation benefits of £774 million and a reduced carbon permit bill of £1.1 billion lead to a total benefits package of £15.83 billion, meaning the net benefit to the economy of smart metering is in the region of £5 billion.

It should be clear from the estimated benefits that suppliers gain the most from smart metering. But if suppliers were to invest and install smart meters, then the flow of financial benefits to suppliers would only last while the household was a customer. The flow of costs and benefits has been calculated over a 20-year period and it is therefore extremely likely that the household would change energy supplier during that time. Switching supplier limits the value of the smart meter energy suppliers, so the government is arguably right to be concerned that despite the benefits, energy suppliers will not invest in smart meters. However, if the government uses its powers to set communication standards to achieve interoperability, the entire industry will benefit from all households having smart meters, regardless of which company first installed the meters.

In reviewing the UK government's impact assessment of smart metering, we can see how obvious costs and benefits have been identified and then estimated. The estimation is based on reasonably sound evidence. For example, suppliers are asked to supply costs of activities such as meter reading. Reports and studies of energy reduction following the installation of smart meters are read and reviewed. But the estimated net benefit of £5 billion may still require some additional refinement. Will costs escalate? What factors might cause installation to be higher? Will the technology become cheaper over time? In terms of benefits, do smart meters reduce consumption and if the large benefits are to be found in fewer site visits and lower customer enquiries, how confident are we that these benefits will be realised? All of these issues can be addressed by careful consideration and further investigation of the financial data and perhaps with the use of statistical techniques for finding a range of likely costs and benefits, rather than single estimates of costs and benefits.

Summary

1. It is debatable whether firms are profit-maximizers. Measuring marginal revenue and marginal cost can be difficult in practice.

2. The owners of modern corporations are often very different from the managers. This is known as separation of ownership from control.

3. If shareholders are unable to control managers, the potential exists for managers to pursue their own objectives. Various objectives have been put forward by economists, including the consumption of perquisites, growth maximization and sales maximization.

4. Managers can be incentivized to work in the interests of shareholders by also making them shareholders. This is commonly achieved through the use of stock options.

5. Financial incentives such as stock options are only useful if four criteria are met:
    - managers are not overly risk averse
    - there is a link between manager effort and measured performance
    - performance is not focused on single activities to the detriment of other key activities or tasks
    - managers cannot falsely manipulate the performance measure, such as the share price.

6. Pareto efficiency occurs when no one can be made better off without making someone else worse off.

7. Externalities exist when the costs or benefits from consumption or production are not borne entirely by the person undertaking the production or consumption.

8. The existence of externalities leads to a difference between the socially optimal level of output and the private optimal level of output.

9. The optimal level of output can be targeted by the introduction of taxes and subsidies.

10. Monopoly can result in a dead-weight loss, or lower welfare for society, when compared with perfect competition.

11. Competition policy in the UK provides a pragmatic solution to the problems presented by monopolies.

12. The Coase conjecture argues that monopoly providers of durable goods are incapable of exploiting their monopoly power.

13. An impact assessment seeks to understand and measure the cost and benefits of a new policy.

Learning checklist

You should now be able to:

- Explain the difference between a principal and an agent
- Highlight the nature of the principal–agent problem
- Explain what is meant by the separation of ownership from control
- Provide a discussion of alternative theories of profit maximization
- Explain the concepts of positive and negative externalities, and provide examples
- Explain what is meant by the term 'market failure'
- Provide an explanation and evaluation of how taxes and subsidies can be used to correct market failures
- Discuss how competition legislation functions in the UK
- Explain how stock options align the interests of managers and shareholders
- Provide an economic evaluation of carbon pollution permits
- Review and evaluate an impact assessment

Questions

1. Is profit maximization a reasonable assumption of firm behaviour?

2. Why might managers prefer to maximize sales or firm size?

3. A firm with managers and shareholders has separation of ownership from control. Why is this a potential problem for shareholders?

4. List examples where managers have been found to indulge in the consumption of perquisites.

5. What is a principal and what is an agent? Provide examples.

6. Why might performance contracts better align the interests of principals and agents? Again, provide examples.

7. Is it always possible to use performance contracts to discipline agents?

8. How do the marginal social cost and the marginal social benefit differ from marginal cost and marginal benefit?

9. List four negative externalities and four positive externalities.

10. How might taxes and subsidies be used to combat externalities?

11. If the marginal social cost of production exceeds the marginal private cost, then the price of production to firms is too low. Is this true and what is the solution?

12. Will a management buyout of a company increase, or decrease, agency costs?

13. Draw a diagram of MSB and MPB of train travel in rural and semi-rural areas. Illustrate how a subsidy might improve usage of train travel.

14. Assess the benefits of paying managers with capital rather than with income.

15. Assess the likely factors that will limit the ability of carbon trading to reduce global emissions of carbon dioxide.

EASY

INTERMEDIATE

DIFFICULT

Exercises

1. True or false?

   (a) Worker absence is highest on Mondays. This is an example of agency costs.

   (b) Risk-averse workers need to be compensated with higher rates of contingent pay.

   (c) Managers are said to suffer from shareholders' free-riding on their hard work.

   (d) The marginal social benefit of education is likely to exceed the marginal private benefit.

   (e) A negative externality can occur when the marginal private cost is less than the marginal social cost.

   (f) Subsidizing the marginal private cost of polluters will help to reduce the amount of pollution.

2. Figure 8.11 shows the market for a good in which there is a negative production externality such that marginal social cost (MSC) is above marginal private cost (MPC). The MSB represents the marginal social benefit derived from consumption of the good.

EASY

INTERMEDIATE

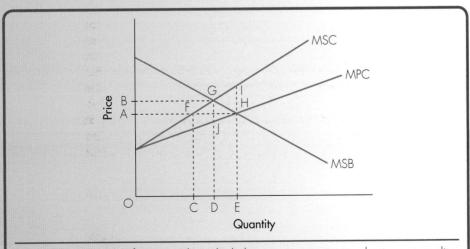

Figure 8.11   Market for a good in which there is a negative production externality

    (a)   If this market is unregulated, what quantity of this good will be produced?

    (b)   What is the socially efficient quantity?

    (c)   What is the amount of the dead-weight loss to society if the free market quantity is produced?

    (d)   What level of tax on the good would ensure that the socially efficient quantity is produced?

    (e)   Suggest an example of a situation in which this analysis might be relevant.

3.   When considering these questions, refer to Box 8.4:

    (a)   Assuming a higher demand for coal increases demand for permits, draw a demand and supply diagram which illustrates the increase in price of permits.

    (b)   Draw a demand-and-supply diagram which illustrates the argument that the higher price of permits reflects a shortage of supply.

    (c)   Evaluate how effective carbon trading will be in reducing carbon emissions.

SECTION

4

Domestic macroeconomics

Section contents

9 Introduction to the macroeconomy   222

10 Measuring macroeconomic variables and policy issues   247

11 Expenditure and fiscal policy   274

12 Money, banking and interest   299

13 Inflation, output and economic policy   328

14 Supply-side policies and economic growth   351

Introduction to the macroeconomy

Chapter contents

Macroeconomics at a glance   223

9.1 Business problem: business cycles and economic uncertainty   223

9.2 Macroeconomic issues   224

9.3 The circular flow of income   227

9.4 National income determination and business cycles   230

9.5 Business application: predicting the business cycle   235

9.6 Business application: profiting from recession   238

9.7 Business data application: finding and understanding data on key components of aggregate demand   240

Summary   243

Learning checklist   244

Questions   244

Exercises   245

Learning outcomes

By the end of this chapter you should understand:

Economic theory

LO1   The key concepts of GDP, inflation, unemployment and the balance of payments

LO2   The concept of the business cycle

LO3   The circular flow of income

LO4   Leakages and injections

LO5   Aggregate demand and aggregate supply

LO6   How changes in aggregate demand and supply lead to changes in equilibrium GDP and inflation

Business application

LO7   How to optimize investment decisions by understanding the business cycle

LO8   How to use income elasticities to profit during a recession

LO9   How to find, interpret and use data on the important components of aggregate demand

At a glance | Macroeconomics

The issue

The business cycle, consisting of moderate economic activity, fast or booming economic growth and recessions, drives changes in the consumption levels of consumers and firms. Predicting the business cycle and positioning the firm for changes in economic activity are crucial for financial success.

The understanding

In simple terms, we can understand changes in macroeconomic activity as resulting from changes in overall demand and supply in the economy. In an economic boom, overall demand or supply in the economy can be rising, while in a recession, overall demand or supply can be falling. Therefore, predicting the business cycle rests on predicting economy-level demand and supply.

The usefulness

In order to survive, firms have to be financially successful in booms as well as recessions. By anticipating when the economy is likely to peak, or bottom out, firms can plan their investments in new products, new production facilities or new retail outlets. They can also change their product offerings to reflect different consumer preferences during booms and recessions.

9.1 Business problem: business cycles and economic uncertainty

In the first eight chapters of this book we have concentrated on topics that fall under microeconomics, including markets, competition and profits. Chapter 1 also highlighted macroeconomics as the other major area of economic study, which includes topics such as inflation, growth rates, government spending and taxation, interest rates and exchange rates. The second half of the book will now concentrate on these topics.

Understanding the macroeconomic environment is of crucial importance to business. Just like private individuals, business also needs to take financial decisions. An individual might decide to buy a house, while a firm might decide to buy a new production facility.

Consider buying a house: two significant issues need addressing. How much should you offer for the house and how much can you afford to borrow?

When valuing the house you will need to consider whether the market price will fall in the near future, perhaps during a recession. Similarly, when thinking about how much you can borrow, you need to think about how much you will earn in the future. Will you be made unemployed during a recession? Furthermore, will an increase in interest rates make mortgage repayments impossible for you to meet?

A business deciding whether to spend many millions of pounds on a new production facility will go through the same process. What is the plant worth? How much can the business afford to borrow? Will a new facility be needed if consumer demand falls during a recession? Will changes in interest rates make the investment unprofitable?

Therefore, just like individuals, firms need to think very carefully when committing themselves to investment projects, because the *business cycle* will affect the success of the investment.

Box 9.1 highlights the strength of business confidence in Germany. Improvements in domestic spending as well as export growth are helping to make Germans feel increasingly confident about future prospects for the German economy. However, we also need to be

German business confidence remains bullish

German business confidence has brightened for a third consecutive month, adding to evidence that growth may already be resuming in Europe's largest economy. The Munich-based Ifo Institute said its closely watched business climate index rose from 107.3 in December to 108.3 this month – the highest since August.

Although German companies had become slightly gloomier about current conditions, expectations about the next six months improved markedly. The latest readings suggest Germany could avoid a recession and supported the German Bundesbank's view that, after a bleak winter, its economy will rebound later this year. On Tuesday, the International Monetary Fund slashed its forecast for German growth this year from 1.3 per cent to 0.3 per cent and said it expected 1.5 per cent growth in 2013.

But Jens Weidmann, Bundesbank president, said the IMF was being too pessimistic.

The Bundesbank expects 0.6 per cent growth this year and 1.8 per cent in 2013 – a respectable pace for one of Europe's most advanced economies with an ageing population. Last year, Germany's economy grew by 3 per cent – twice as fast as the eurozone overall and the USA.

German growth is being supported increasingly by domestic demand, helped by steady falls in unemployment to the lowest levels since reunification in 1990, which has helped reduce the impact of the eurozone debt crisis on economic confidence. The country's exporters were also helped in January by a weak euro.

Adapted from an article by Ralph Atkins, 25 January 2012. From the *Financial Times* © The Financial Times Limited 2012. All rights reserved.[1]

mindful that Germany sells many products to economies within the EU that are struggling and Germany itself also needs to cut its government sector spending.

> GDP, gross domestic product, is a measure of the total output produced by an economy in a given year.
>
> Inflation is the rate of change in the average price level. Inflation of 2 per cent indicates that prices have risen by 2 per cent during the previous 12 months.
>
> Unemployment is the number of individuals seeking work that do not currently have a job.
>
> Trade deficit is the difference between exported and imported goods and services.

Clearly, an understanding of how the economy works and how it is likely to develop in the short, medium and long term is of crucial importance. Firms that make bad decisions will suffer financially. Firms that understand the macroeconomy and plan expansion and consolidation of the business at the right times are more likely to prosper.

In this chapter we will provide an overview of recent macroeconomic activity. In addition, we will provide a basic understanding of how the business cycle occurs, introducing the circular flow of income and then developing our application of the demand and supply framework used in the microeconomic section of this book. This will then provide the basis for an assessment of government economic policy in later chapters.

9.2 Macroeconomic issues

Key macroeconomic outputs

Macroeconomics studies the workings of the entire economy. In Figure 9.1, we have charted four key macroeconomic issues: **GDP, inflation, unemployment** and the **trade deficit**.

It can be argued that Figure 9.1 represents the key measures of an economy: growth in GDP, or the improvement in economic activity; price stability via inflation; unemployment and success in trade overseas. For an economy to be functioning well, each of these outputs needs to be controlled and managed, with governments targeting higher economic growth, improved price stability, low unemployment and growing, but balanced, international trade.

---

[1] McGraw-Hill Education is solely responsible for providing this abridged version of the original article, and The Financial Times Limited does not accept any liability for the accuracy or quality of the abridged version.

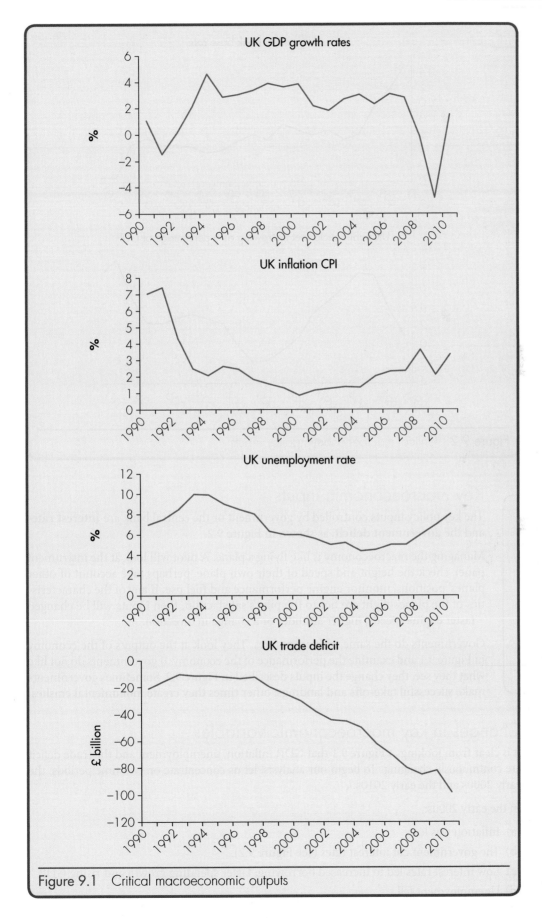

Figure 9.1   Critical macroeconomic outputs

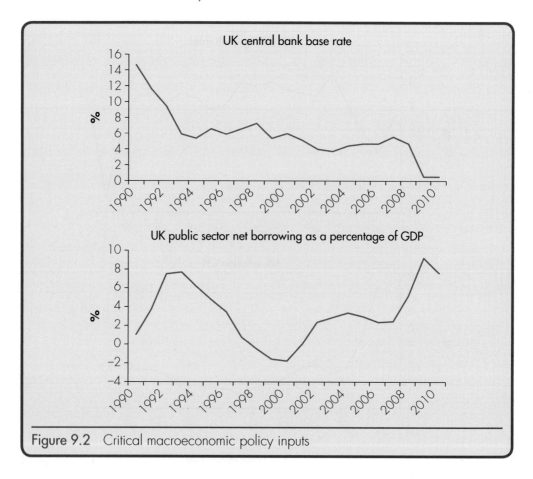

Figure 9.2   Critical macroeconomic policy inputs

Key macroeconomic inputs

The key policy inputs controlled by government or the central bank are **interest rates** and the **government deficit**, as shown in Figure 9.2.

Managing the macroeconomy is like flying a plane. A pilot will look at the instrument panel, check the height and speed of their own plane, perhaps take account of other planes' positions, monitor engine performance and fuel use. If any of the characteristics of the plane's flight are not to the pilot's satisfaction, then inputs will be changed – faster engine speeds, higher altitudes or a change in direction.

Governments do the same with economies. They look at the outputs of the economy in Figure 9.1 and examine the performance of the economy. If governments do not like what they see, they change the inputs described in Figure 9.2. Sometimes governments make successful take-offs and landings; other times they create monumental crashes.

> Interest rates are the price of money and are set by the central bank.
>
> Government deficit is the difference between government spending and tax receipts. Just as students run up overdrafts, spending more than they earn, so too does the government.

Changes in key macroeconomic variables

It is clear from looking at Figure 9.1 that GDP, inflation, unemployment and the trade deficit are continuously changing. To begin our analysis, let us concentrate on two time periods: the early 2000s and the early 2010s.

In the early 2000s:

(a) Inflation was low.

(b) The government cut interest rates (see Figure 9.2).

(c) Low interest rates led to increased borrowing, faster spending growth and rising GDP.

(d) Unemployment fell.

(e) Taxation was cut, government spending increased and the budget deficit grew.

(f) The current account went into a large deficit, with imports exceeding exports.

In the early 2010s:

(a) Inflation was high.

(b) Interest rates were low because growth was weak.

(c) Unemployment was rising.

(d) The government deficit was large and tax increases and spending cuts were being implemented.

(e) The current account was still in deficit.

Observations and comments

1 The economic conditions of the early 2010s, with weak GDP, rising unemployment and inflation, were disastrous when compared with the low-inflation, fast-growing economy of the early 2000s.

2 Given such problems, how does a government set and prioritize its objectives? Is low inflation more important than high GDP? Is unemployment acceptable? Should the government manage its deficit and should the current account be in surplus? In Chapter 10 we will return to this question and provide a review of how each key macroeconomic variable is measured, provide a review of the issues associated with each variable and, more important, the objectives generally set by government for each key macroeconomic variable.

3 Finally, why are GDP, inflation, unemployment, the current account, interest rates and government deficits all linked?

In the remainder of this chapter we will introduce the circular flow of income as a means of describing some of the linkages between the macroeconomic variables. We will then develop this analysis by adapting our supply and demand framework utilized in the microeconomic section of this book. By the end of this chapter you will be able to answer question 3. As we progress through Chapters 11, 12 and 13, you will develop your understanding of how governments can use different policies to manage the links within the macroeconomy.

The circular flow of income

In contrast to microeconomics, which examined product-specific markets such as those for pizzas or cars, macroeconomics focuses upon the workings of the whole economy. In order to begin our understanding of the macroeconomy, we will introduce the **circular flow of income** as a descriptive framework of macroeconomic activity. Figure 9.3 provides an illustration of the circular flow of income.

> Circular flow of income shows the flow of inputs, outputs and payments between households and firms within an economy.

Within the framework of the circular flow of income, households are assumed to own the factors of production – land, labour, capital and enterprise. As producers of goods and services, firms need to use the factors of production owned by the households. Firms will clearly provide households with a financial reward for using the factors of production. In the case of labour, the financial reward is wages. Households will then use the money they have earned from firms to buy the finished goods and services, thus returning cash to the firms. A virtuous circle or, in our terminology, a circular flow of income is seen to exist.

The inner loop captures the flow of resources between the two sectors. For example, resources such as labour flow to firms from households, and then goods and services flow from firms

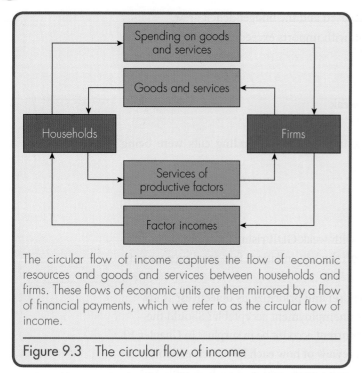

The circular flow of income captures the flow of economic resources and goods and services between households and firms. These flows of economic units are then mirrored by a flow of financial payments, which we refer to as the circular flow of income.

Figure 9.3 The circular flow of income

back to households. The outer loop captures the corresponding financial flows between the two sectors. Firms pay households wages for supplying labour resources. In return, households use their income to purchase the goods and services sold by the firms.

The circular flow of income captures the essential essence of macroeconomic activity. The economy is seen as nothing more than a revolving flow of goods, production resources and financial payments. The faster the flow, the higher the level of economic output.

The level of income activity within an economy is measured as gross domestic product.

Leakages and injections

The economy described in Figure 9.3 contains only firms and households, which produce goods and spend income on goods and services. We can begin to broaden the circular flow to take account of saving by households, investment by firms, government spending and taxation, and international trade.

In order to account for these additional items we need to understand how **leakages** and **injections** fit into the circular flow of income.

Savings and investments

Rather than spend all income on goods and services, households could save a proportion of their income. Because income is being taken from the circular flow of income and saved, it represents a leakage. But an important question relates to where these savings go. If the money is placed on deposit at the bank, then the bank will try to lend the money for profit. Borrowers are likely to be firms seeking to invest in equipment, or needing to fund overdrafts. If firms invest in capital equipment, then they are buying goods and services from other firms. As a result, investment is spending in the economy that does not come from the income earned by households. As such, investments represent an injection of financial resource and spending, by firms, into the circular flow. In equilibrium, savings will equal investments. This is because banks will set an interest rate where the supply of funds from savers equals the demand for funds by investing firms.

Leakage from the circular flow is income not spent on goods and services within the economy. Leakages can be savings, taxation and imports.

Injection into the circular flow is additional spending on goods and services that does not come from the income earned by households in the inner loop. Injections can be investment, government spending and exports.

Taxes and government spending

Government taxes the earnings of individuals and companies. Tax payments represent a leakage from the circular flow of income as they reduce the ability of households to spend on goods and services. However, the government also undertakes a number of activities that inject financial resources back into the economy. Governments buy hospitals and schools. They employ nurses and teachers. They also pay social benefits to the needy. All of which are injections.

Exports and imports

Finally, some consumption by households will be on goods made in other economies. If you buy a German car, then this represents a leakage from the UK circular flow of income, as it

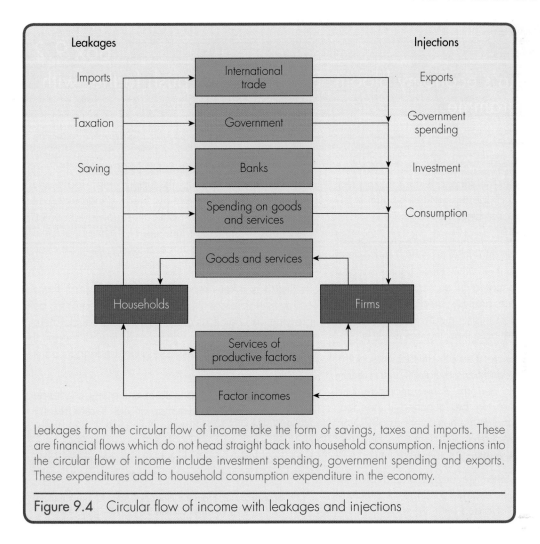

Leakages from the circular flow of income take the form of savings, taxes and imports. These are financial flows which do not head straight back into household consumption. Injections into the circular flow of income include investment spending, government spending and exports. These expenditures add to household consumption expenditure in the economy.

Figure 9.4   Circular flow of income with leakages and injections

is income spent in another economy. However, an injection will occur if a German spends money on a British car, as this represents an export.

The various leakages and injections are illustrated in Figure 9.4, which simply extends the circular flow of income. On the left of Figure 9.4, savings, taxation and imports leak from the income households could spend on consumption. On the right of Figure 9.4, investments, government spending and exports inject spending into the circular flow of income.

Total expenditure

Total expenditure is simply all the separate sources of spending within the economy. That is, consumption by households, investment by firms and public spending by government. Net exports adjust for expenditure on exports and imports by consumers, firms and government. Being able to identify the individual components of total expenditure is particularly important because it provides an understanding of which expenditures lead to an increase (or decrease) in economic activity. If consumption, investment, government spending or net exports increase, then total expenditure increases, and potentially the flow of goods and services in the inner loop also increases to match the increased demand in the economy. Similarly, if total expenditure is reduced, the flow of goods and services in the inner loop falls due to decreasing demand. We will now use these ideas to develop our understanding of changes in economic activity over time and the idea of a macroeconomic equilibrium.

Total expenditure is equal to consumption, plus investment, plus government spending, plus net exports (exports minus imports).

Box 9.2

Letting China's economy bloom: Beijing should push further with reform programme

China's economy faces two sets of problems this year. The first is the continued weakness of exports, owing to the slowdown in Europe which is China's main trading partner. The second is the faltering real estate market. New property starts fell by almost 20 per cent year on year in December alone.

The optimists prefer to look at the overall figures, which show the economy growing at 8.9 per cent in the fourth quarter. In their view, these figures suggest that Beijing is succeeding in orchestrating the 'soft landing' which some analysts predicted would be impossible. The pessimists, meanwhile, prefer to emphasize how unreliable these figures really are.

But this debate, while heated, misses the point. Whatever external conditions dictate, China's economy will be made to perform. A new monetary and fiscal stimulus is likely to be launched if needed. While this may not match the heroic efforts of 2009, it would be a bazooka of sufficient size and fire-power to buy the government some more time.

Whether or not a Sino-style bazooka is deployed, China can no longer escape a range of structural reforms which it has avoided over the years.

Top of the list are measures to rebalance aggregate demand, shifting the economy away from investment and exports towards domestic consumption. Beijing also needs to shake up its supply side. Too many firms are kept in business by overly generous credit lines, while other, less politically connected, enterprises pay too much for their credit. The debt of local governments is also a source of worry, as is the overall stability of the financial system.

Beijing has taken important steps to address these policy weaknesses. Consumption appears to be growing as a slice of gross domestic product. There have been attempts to deepen Shanghai's capital markets to make businesses less dependent on bank lending.

Keeping up the pace of reform is the key challenge for China this year, whether or not it reaches for another stimulus package. In this sense, China faces a similar challenge to stagnant Europe. Without structural economic reform, both regions are doomed to fall short of their true growth potential.

The circular flow of income underpins the review of the Chinese economy in Box 9.2. Areas of concern relate to the over-reliance on exports to drive economic activity; the possibility of government spending and relaxed monetary policy to boost spending; and the growing importance of consumption expenditure.

(9.4) National income determination and business cycles

When examining individual markets in the microeconomic section of this book, we focused on the demand and supply curve for the product. Since in macroeconomics we are examining the whole economy, we need a demand and supply curve for the whole economy.

Aggregate demand is the total demand in an economy.

Total expenditure representing consumption, plus investment, plus government spending, plus net exports is in fact **aggregate demand**. In microeconomics, we argued that the demand for a product is negatively related to its price. As prices increase, less is demanded. We could also draw an aggregate demand curve showing a negative relationship between the average level of prices in the economy and the level of aggregate demand. However, we are going to make a subtle, but important

---

[2] McGraw-Hill Education is solely responsible for providing this abridged version of the original article, and The Financial Times Limited does not accept any liability for the accuracy or quality of the abridged version.

change. We will analyse the relationship between aggregate demand and the *change* in the **price level**.

Where aggregate demand is calculated by adding up all demand changes in the economy, the price level is calculated by adding all price changes together. We will see in more detail in Chapter 10 how governments measure overall price changes. But, in simple terms, a basket of commonly purchased goods and services is defined. In the UK, this basket exceeds 600 items and includes the cost of food, fuel and clothing items. Price changes for each item are collated on a monthly basis and from this data changes in the average price level are calculated.

The benefit of looking at the relationship between aggregate demand and inflation is that control of inflation has become a key aspect of modern macroeconomic policy. Therefore, by using inflation, rather than the level of prices, we are bringing inflation to the centre of our economic models.

> Price level is the average change in the price of goods and services in an economy. The *change* in the average price level is a measure of inflation, where 5 per cent inflation means that prices on average have changed, i.e. increased, by 5 per cent.

Aggregate demand and inflation

Fortunately, the relationship between aggregate demand and inflation is also negative. If we assume that the central bank is tasked with keeping inflation at 2.5 per cent, as it is in the UK, then we know from experience that the higher the rate of inflation, the higher the central bank has to raise interest rates in order to stem inflation (and vice versa: if inflation falls, then the central bank has to cut interest rates in order to avoid deflation). As interest rates increase, consumers and firms are less willing to borrow in order to fund the purchase of goods and services. Therefore, aggregate demand falls. These points are picked up in Figure 9.5.

From the circular flow of income we have argued that aggregate demand is composed of consumption, investment, government spending and net exports. An increase in any of these types of expenditure will lead to an increase in aggregate demand. In Figure 9.6, we illustrate this idea by assuming that government spending has increased from G_1 to G_2. We could equally have assumed that consumption, investment or net exports had increased. The consequences of the increase in government spending are for the aggregate demand curve to shift from AD_1 to AD_2, with higher levels of economic output being demanded at all inflation levels.

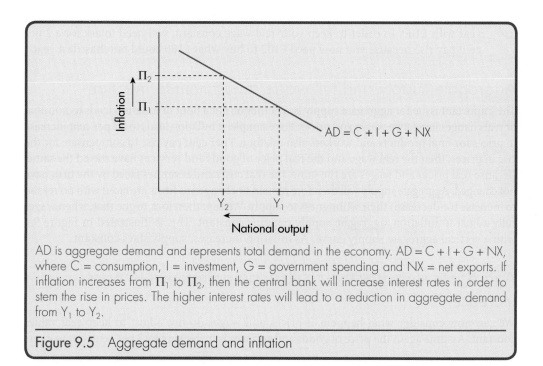

AD is aggregate demand and represents total demand in the economy. $AD = C + I + G + NX$, where C = consumption, I = investment, G = government spending and NX = net exports. If inflation increases from Π_1 to Π_2, then the central bank will increase interest rates in order to stem the rise in prices. The higher interest rates will lead to a reduction in aggregate demand from Y_1 to Y_2.

Figure 9.5 Aggregate demand and inflation

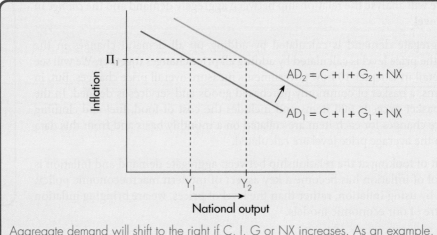

Aggregate demand will shift to the right if C, I, G or NX increases. As an example, we have simply assumed that government spending has increased from G_1 to G_2. Aggregate demand, therefore, shifts from AD_1 to AD_2. As this happens, the willingness to demand output at an inflation rate of Π_1 rises from Y_1 to Y_2. In Figure 9.10, we show how changes in aggregate demand lead to changes in equilibrium GDP and inflation.

Figure 9.6 Aggregate demand, inflation and increased government spending

Aggregate supply and inflation

In Chapters 3 and 5 we saw that, as profit-maximizers, firms will supply output if the market price is equal to, or greater than, marginal cost. Therefore, an increase in the price will bring about an increase in supply from an individual firm. But, at the macro level, how will **aggregate supply** react to a change in inflation?

We need to make a distinction between **real** and **nominal** values. Assume you are earning £100 a day and inflation is 2 per cent per year. At the end of one year your *nominal* wage will still be £100 per day. But your *real* wage will only be £98. The real wage is the nominal wage adjusted for the rate of inflation. You are receiving £100 in cash, but due to inflation it can now only buy 98 per cent of what you could buy last year with £100. In order to keep your real wage constant, you need to ask for a 2 per cent pay rise because you now need £102 to buy what £100 could purchase last year.

> **Aggregate supply** is the total supply in an economy.
>
> **Real** prices and wages are adjusted for inflation.
>
> **Nominal** prices and wages are not adjusted for inflation.

Aggregate supply and full wage adjustment to inflation

The important issue for aggregate supply is whether or not a bout of inflation leads to nominal or real changes in relative wages and prices. For example, if inflation leads to a 3 per cent increase in prices for final products and workers also ask for a 3 per cent pay rise to compensate for the rise in prices, then the real wage and the real price of goods and services have stayed the same. Because real prices and wages are the same, the real costs and revenues faced by the firm have not changed. Aggregate supply will therefore remain unchanged as firms are faced with no reason to increase (or decrease) their willingness to supply. We can, therefore, argue that, when wages fully adjust to inflation, aggregate supply remains constant. This is illustrated in Figure 9.7 with a vertical aggregate supply curve. As inflation increases, supply stays constant.

Aggregate supply without full wage adjustment to price increases

We can now consider what happens if prices and wages do not adjust to keep real values constant. Assume again the price of goods and services is increasing by 3 per cent, but workers

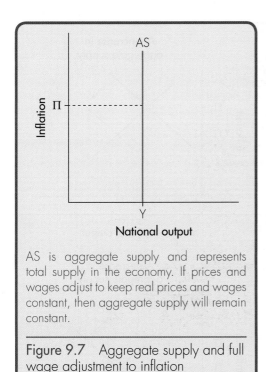

AS is aggregate supply and represents total supply in the economy. If prices and wages adjust to keep real prices and wages constant, then aggregate supply will remain constant.

Figure 9.7 Aggregate supply and full wage adjustment to inflation

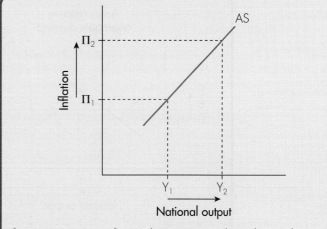

If prices increase faster than wages, then the real wage decreases. This represents a real cost reduction for firms. If firms are profit maximizers, then a reduction in the real marginal cost will motivate firms to increase output. Therefore, a reduction in the real wage leads to an increase in aggregate supply.

Figure 9.8 Aggregate supply without full wage adjustment to price increases

only manage to negotiate a 2 per cent increase in wages. The real cost of employing labour has now reduced by 1 per cent. Firms are experiencing a reduction in their real costs of production. If firms are profit-maximizers, then, as we saw in Chapter 5, a reduction in marginal cost leads to an increase in the profit-maximizing output of the firm (see section 5.2). Therefore, with a reduction in the real wage rate, firms will now be willing to increase supply and overall aggregate supply increases as inflation increases. Therefore, when wages do not fully adjust to price changes, a positive relationship between inflation and aggregate supply can exist. This is shown in Figure 9.8.

At this stage, we can perhaps go one step further and suggest that Figure 9.8 represents the short run, while Figure 9.7 represents the long run. In the short run, workers may not accurately guess the inflation rate. In our example, workers agreed a 2 per cent rise in wages, when inflation turned out to be 3 per cent. In the long run, workers will try to rectify this reduction in real wages and so, over time, real wages will fully adjust to the inflation rate and real wages will remain constant. Therefore, in the short run firms might benefit from a reduction in the real wage and boost supply. But in the long run, real wages will remain constant and so will aggregate supply.

Macroeconomic equilibrium

In Figure 9.9, we have brought aggregate demand and supply together for the whole economy. We have assumed that wages do not fully adjust to inflation and, therefore, aggregate supply is not perfectly inelastic.

Equilibrium for the entire economy occurs where aggregate demand and aggregate supply intersect. From this we can then

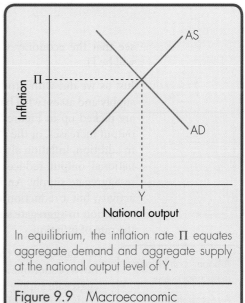

In equilibrium, the inflation rate Π equates aggregate demand and aggregate supply at the national output level of Y.

Figure 9.9 Macroeconomic equilibrium

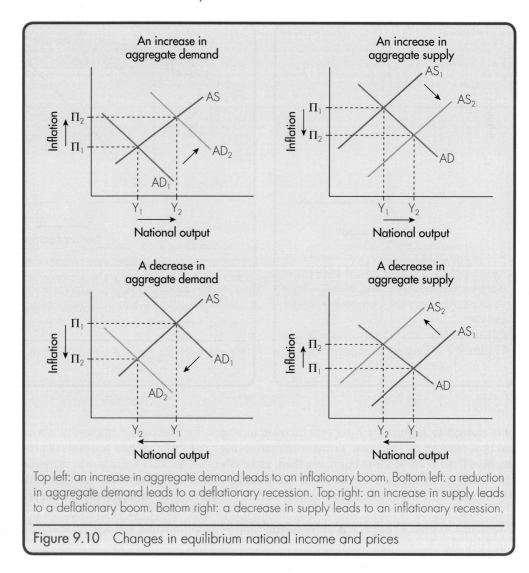

Top left: an increase in aggregate demand leads to an inflationary boom. Bottom left: a reduction in aggregate demand leads to a deflationary recession. Top right: an increase in supply leads to a deflationary boom. Bottom right: a decrease in supply leads to an inflationary recession.

Figure 9.10   Changes in equilibrium national income and prices

see that the economy will produce an output of Y in Figure 9.9; and the inflation rate will be Π.

Just as we did with product markets, we can also begin to change aggregate demand and supply and assess what happens to the equilibrium output and inflation. The following points are picked up in Figure 9.10. In the top left, if aggregate demand increases, then national output increases, or the amount of goods and services traded in the economy increases. But, in addition, inflation also increases. In the bottom left, if aggregate demand decreases, then national output reduces and inflation falls. In the top right, we can examine changes in aggregate supply. An increase in aggregate supply will lead to an increase in economic activity, but a reduction in the inflation rate. The bottom right of Figure 9.10 shows that a reduction in aggregate supply will lead to a reduction in national output and an increase in the rate of inflation.

A boom is an increase in national output.

A recession is a reduction in national output.

We can now say that an increase in aggregate demand leads to an inflationary **boom**. But a reduction in aggregate demand leads to a deflationary **recession**. An increase in aggregate supply leads to a deflationary boom, while a reduction in aggregate supply leads to an inflationary recession.

In section 9.5 we use these ideas to show how a firm might try to predict the business cycle.

9.5 Business application: predicting the business cycle

While the business cycle is outside the control of individual firms, strategies for dealing with the cycle are not. An important step for firms is to predict the business cycle and this is no easy task. Even skilled economists sitting on central banks' monetary panels disagree about how fast an economy is growing and how high interest rates should be set. Alongside predicting the growth of the economy, firms also need to time their strategies to perfection. Examine Figure 9.11.

There is no commercial value in being told that the economy is at point A, in an economic boom. By the time the firm has made investments in new products, production facilities, distribution or retail outlets, the economy will have moved into recession at point B. The business skill lies in making an educated guess at point C that in the near future the economy will be at point A. Then investments can be put in place to exploit the economic boom in a more timely fashion. Indeed, when the economy is at point A, the firm should begin to plan for the recession at point B.

In Box 9.3, the Bank of England agents around the country have been talking to businesses and asking them to score sales, investments and exports. From this survey data a summary of the conditions faced by businesses today, as well as the expected nature of conditions in the future, can be obtained.

But how do you spot an economic boom or recession before they happen? What factors enable businesses to respond by drawing meaningful and reasonably accurate conclusions about the future state of the economy? We focus on two insights from our understanding of the economy and business experience.

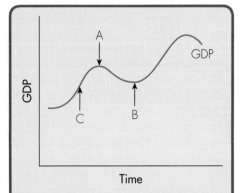

As the economy moves through the business cycle firms need to plan and manage their capital investments. There is little point in beginning to invest when the economy is booming, as at point A, because by the time the extra capital is in place, the economy will have moved on to B, a period of recession. Therefore, the smart businessperson has to judge when the economy is at C and likely to move to A in the future.

Figure 9.11   The business cycle

Economic insights

The aggregate demand and supply framework suggests that, in order to understand the business cycle, it is useful to be able to address how much demand and supply are changing in the economy. For example, in order to understand aggregate demand it is essential to have a grasp of how fast consumption, investment, government spending and net exports are changing. In particular, it is important to know if any of these expenditures are increasing or decreasing. If aggregate demand is increasing, the economy is likely to grow; however, if aggregate demand is falling, the economy is likely to move towards recession.

Aggregate supply is, in part, influenced by the costs faced by firms. When important input prices such as oil increase, firms will be less willing to supply and aggregate supply will fall. In contrast, when new technologies become available, which lower the costs of supplying goods and services, firms will be more willing to supply and aggregate supply will increase. The Internet was seen as a technology capable of improving firms' costs and helping to develop the supply of goods and services. When aggregate supply is rising, the economy is likely to grow. However, when aggregate supply is falling, the economy is likely to move into recession.

Government agencies, statistical offices, central banks and trade bodies all provide commentary and opinion on the likely development of the economy over the short and medium term. In the main these reports are based on projections for aggregate demand and supply. However, you do not have to be a skilled economist to understand the development of the economy.

Box 9.3

Business outlook: demand

Consumption

The rate of growth of consumer spending remained weak (Figure 9.12). And discounting in the run-up to Christmas had started earlier, and been deeper, than last year. Despite some fillip from bargain hunters, however, the squeeze on households' real disposable income continued to depress the overall volume of consumption and cause shifts in the pattern of spending. Value goods and services continued to outperform mid-range ones, for instance. And rising prices for essential services, such as transport and housing, had reduced the amount left over for spending on leisure activities. Many contacts expressed concerns about the possibility of a sharp fall in the volume of consumption in the first quarter, compared with a year earlier.

Business investment

Investment intentions continued to weaken, but still pointed to an increase in capital spending over the coming year (Figure 9.13), with plans usually strongest among exporters.

Heightened uncertainty had caused some investment to be put on hold, or scaled back, with a greater focus on the preservation of cash flow, particularly among smaller firms. And there had been fewer reports of plans to increase capacity, as past projects came to fruition. But many contacts continued to invest in raising efficiency, lowering energy use, waste reduction and regulatory compliance. Spending was also still being supported by some large infrastructure projects in transportation and the energy and utilities sectors, although some major schemes would go into abeyance for several months around the time of the Olympics.

Exports

Goods exports continued to grow at a fairly steady pace, but had slowed somewhat. The increase in exports reflected rising demand in emerging economies and a shift in the orientation of both established exporters and newly exporting firms towards these growth markets. Businesses supplying the aerospace, automotive and energy sectors were among those seeing the most resilient demand, while high commodity

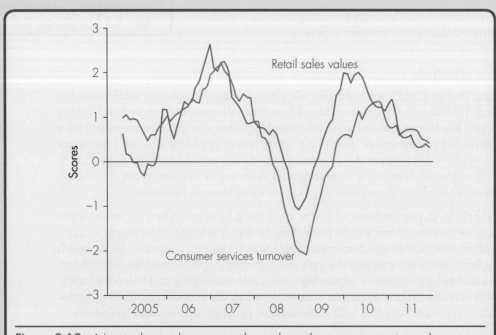

Figure 9.12 Nominal spending on retail goods and consumer services: three months on the same period a year earlier

Source: Agents' Summary of Business Conditions, Bank of England, January 2012.

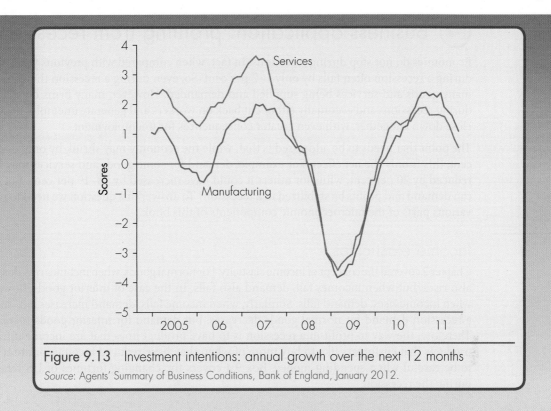

Figure 9.13   Investment intentions: annual growth over the next 12 months

Source: Agents' Summary of Business Conditions, Bank of England, January 2012.

prices had encouraged an increase in mineral extraction in large areas of the developing world, increasing the demand for exports of construction plant. A number of exporters remained optimistic about their ability to continue to expand their share of the market in emerging economies, despite slowing growth in some of these countries. Meanwhile, activity in the euro area had softened, particularly among those countries most affected by concerns over sovereign debt.

Adapted from the Agents' Summary of Business Conditions, Bank of England, January 2012.

Business experience

Experience probably counts for a great deal. If you know how the market works and have experience of working in the market for a number of years, you will have seen it move through its cycles. You will have a feeling for when it is going to boom and also a feeling for when it is time to cut back and await the recession. This experience, or 'feeling', is likely to come from an assessment of the more measurable lead indicators. Markets do not generally switch from boom to bust. Rather, they gradually grow into a boom and then slowly decline into a recession. During the growth phase enquiries from customers will increase; and then these will begin to materialize into orders and sales. You may also find that customers switch to you not because of price, but because you can promise to deliver on time. This would indicate that rivals are also becoming busy. So, as sales and profit margins begin to improve, plans for expansion should follow.

Once expansion across the industry begins, you need to have an eye on when the market begins to soften, with falling prices and excess supply of goods and services. If demand in the economy either shrinks or grows at a slower rate than supply, then prices will fall and margins will shrink. So, if you think the expansion by your own company, and also that of your rivals, is too great for the likely growth rate in demand by consumers, then you need to think about readdressing your growth options for the future. Cutting costs and reining in excess output become key in order to compete.

Business application: profiting from recession

Economies do not stop during recessions. In fact, when compared with previous years, GDP during a recession often falls by only 1–2 per cent. So, even during a recession there are still many goods and services being supplied and demanded. However, many firms do struggle during recessions and eventually either cut back on workers and generate unemployment, or close down altogether, with even greater consequences for unemployment.

The point that needs to be addressed is that, while the economy may shrink by only 1–2 per cent, this is only the net effect. For example, demand for some goods and services may have reduced by 20 per cent, while for others it could have increased by 18–19 per cent. But how can demand and profits be stabilized in a recession? To answer this question we need to recall various parts of the microeconomic components of this book.

Income elasticities

Chapter 2 covered the concept of income elasticity. For normal goods, when incomes rise, demand also rises, but when incomes fall, demand also falls. In the case of inferior goods, however, when income rises, demand falls. Similarly, when income falls, demand increases. So, during a recession demand for normal goods decreases, but demand for inferior goods increases. Therefore, the way to profit in a recession is to have product lines that are income inferior, products that customers like to buy more of when they have reduced incomes or are trying to be careful when spending money. Box 9.4 covers the changing fortunes of US retailers during the recession.

Pricing

Having products at the right price points in the market and even the ability to lower prices to gain market share are also useful tactics in a recession. Some of the big winners during the recession have been related to the food sector. Manufacturers of value lines for the supermarkets have seen enormous growth as customers look to trade down and save on grocery expenditure.

Price discounts are also an obvious promotional tool and, if customers are price elastic, then additional revenue may be gained. However, the risk of a price war is also high and this may result in all competitors charging less and no additional customers. A means of avoiding this problem is for a company to have a side range of products that can be endlessly recycled through promotional offers, such as in ready meals, soft drinks and beer. Note how the same brands keep appearing as multi-pack offers. The niche, high-quality items in these product categories cannot be promoted using special offers without risk of associating the brand with low-value, low-price alternatives. Reverting to high prices after the recession will then be difficult.

Managing costs

A lack of fixed costs is essential for profitable performances during a recession. From Chapter 3, we know that high fixed costs require high volumes. Unfortunately, high volumes are difficult to find during a recession. It is therefore essential to have a cost base which is driven by variable costs, not fixed ones. Luxury hotels, with many frills, including swimming pools, bars, restaurants, tennis courts and concierge services, often located in expensive city centres, are nothing but a huge collection of fixed costs. Not surprisingly, luxury hotel chains do not perform well during recessions and frequent customers, such as business travellers, can often negotiate good discounts from such hotels during a lean economic period.

Retailers also have high fixed costs in terms of rent for their retail space. This has led to many such companies facing financial collapse. The other fixed cost which many companies face is debt. Financial repayments have to be kept up in good times and bad. If the company faces a fall in sales, then cash flows into the company dry up. But this does not alter its fixed cost payments, including debt commitments.

Box 9.4

Profiting from recession

Retailers in America are getting ready to lay out their wares in the hope that the annual post-Thanksgiving stampede by shoppers will be bigger and better than ever before. But for some, it will not be. Normally the big day is 'Black Friday', so named because the day after the holiday is when retailers supposedly move into the black and become profitable.

American consumers have not bounced back since the massive wealth destruction of the financial crisis. According to research by Nomura, a stockbroker, American household assets shrank by $13 trillion in 2008 and have regained only a fraction of their losses in 2009 and 2010. Recent declines in the housing markets as well as the equity market's gyrations are eating away at what had been won back. Moreover, the high price of petrol, large numbers of unemployed, food inflation and uncertainty over taxes are weighing heavily on low-income Americans.

Not surprisingly, then, most shoppers are single-mindedly focused on low prices. The 'off-price sector' that exploded during the financial crisis continues to thrive. According to Accenture, low-end retailers such as Family Dollar and Dollar General saw average revenue grow by 19 per cent in total over the past three years and delivered a 78 per cent return to shareholders. Dollar General is now the largest retailer in America by store count, and is adding 600 shops a year. By contrast, retailers catering to the squeezed middle classes, such as JC Penney, Kohl's and Sears, grew by only 6 per cent in the same period and delivered a negative 5 per cent return to shareholders. Shares in Best Buy are worth barely half what they were a year ago, and the firm has abruptly scaled back its international-expansion plans, offloading its stake in Carphone Warehouse in Britain. Shares in Dollar General, however, are trading near an all-time high.

The decline in Americans' buying power has redefined the meaning of low price. Walmart used to be considered the leader in what it calls everyday low pricing, but the Bentonville-based behemoth has underperformed the broad market in the past two years. Walmart is now investing in massive price cuts that are eating away at the firm's profitability. It also reintroduced so-called layaways, which allow customers to pay for a product in instalments while Walmart holds on to it until the full payment.

There is another type of retailer, besides online ones, bound to end up with smiles on their faces. These are the high-end shops with luxury goods. As American society is bifurcating into a small, wealthy elite and a growing number of low-income households, fancy shops such as Tiffany, Saks Fifth Avenue and Nordstrom are doing well. Victoria's Secret, a lingerie shop, and the American business of Coach, a maker of handbags and accessories, recently reported strong results.

Adapted from an article in *The Economist*, ''Tis the season to be frugal', 19 November 2011. © The Economist Newspaper Limited, London 2011.

Diversification

Diversification through a portfolio of business activities was shown in Chapter 7 to reduce business risk. Car manufacturers such as Ford are renowned for this. In addition to the Ford cars, they also make Jaguars, Land Rovers, Mazdas and Aston Martins. A more extreme example is the fact that Fiat Unos are made by the same firm that makes Ferraris! The reason is that, throughout the business cycle, demand for one product in the portfolio will rise. Ferraris and Jaguars sell well during a boom, Fiat Unos and Fords sell better during a recession. Supermarkets are even more skilled at mixing the portfolio. Stores in the affluent London districts of Chelsea and Mayfair will stock different products from stores located in inner-city Manchester. But during a recession and boom, each store will fine-tune its product offering. In a boom, the Manchester store will allocate more shelf space to branded items and reduce its offering of value own-label products. Then, during a recession, the store will switch back to higher value items.

Clearly, firms operating within a changing macroeconomic environment need to be able to prosper during both boom and recession. Success is critically dependent upon being able to sell products during booms and recessions and being able to read the business cycle. They must plan ahead and be better placed than rivals to exploit the ever-changing environment.

 ## Business data application: finding and understanding data on key components of aggregate demand

The circular flow of income identifies four key areas of spending within an economy: household consumption, corporate investment, government spending and net exports. Understanding these four areas, in terms of how large they are and how fast they have grown, enables economists and business people to take a view on the current health of the economy and likely areas of spending that will promote future growth in spending and the economy. Economic institutions such as central banks, government economic agencies and international organizations, such as the International Monetary Fund (IMF) and the Organisation for Economic Co-operation and Development (OECD) provide data and opinion on each of the four key areas of spending. As part of a business planning process, data from these economic bodies can be extremely helpful in enabling managers to form a view about the risks and opportunities within various macroeconomic environments.

In Table 9.1 we present summary statements from the OECD about the likely growth potential for a number of economies. The OECD does not always use the same terminology as we have used in this book, so you will have to think about some of the statements. For example, the fiscal retrenchment referred to for Greece is a reduction in government spending (plus an increase in taxation); and external demand relates to exports.

Table 9.1   OECD summary forecasts for various economies

France	A modest recovery is under way, but the recession will leave lasting traces. Real GDP is projected to grow by over 2 per cent in both 2011 and 2012, led by business investment and exports. The unemployment rate is set to decline slightly towards 9 per cent by the end of 2012
Germany	The export-led recovery is continuing, with domestic demand, notably business investment and private consumption, increasingly contributing to growth. Employment continues to rise and, coupled with wage increases, should support private consumption growth over the next couple of years
Greece	The economy is suffering a serious recession in the context of the sizeable, but vital, fiscal retrenchment. A return to sustained positive growth is projected for 2012 as external demand strengthens, competitiveness improves and the far-reaching structural reforms implemented in response to the fiscal crisis start to take hold
Japan	The 11 March 2011 Great East Japan Earthquake triggered the country's worst disaster of the post-war era. The immediate impact has been to reduce output, although this is likely to be reversed by a strong recovery in the second half of 2011 led by reconstruction efforts
Korea	After slowing during 2010, growth picked up in early 2011, driven by the acceleration in world trade
UK	The recovery paused in end-2010 and growth is projected to remain weak in 2011, despite rising exports and business investment, but to pick up in 2012. Above-target inflation, driven by tax increases and commodity prices, and needed fiscal consolidation, will hold back private consumption and public spending during 2011–12
USA	The adverse effects of the crisis are still being felt, particularly in the form of still-high unemployment. Output growth should gain speed and the unemployment rate should continue to decline through 2012 though the pace of expansion will be limited by household deleveraging and initial steps at fiscal consolidation

Table 9.2 OECD percentage growth forecasts

	Consumption			Government spending			Investment			Net exports		
	2010	2011	2012	2010	2011	2012	2010	2011	2012	2010	2011	2012
France	1.3	1.5	1.9	1.2	0.5	0.1	−1.1	4.0	4.6	0.1	−0.5	0.0
Germany	0.4	1.3	1.4	2.3	1.5	1.0	5.7	6.3	4.0	1.2	1.5	0.8
Greece	−4.5	−5.4	0.2	−6.5	−7.1	−4.3	−16.5	−10.3	0.3	2.3	4.8	1.5
Japan	1.8	−1.3	1.6	2.3	2.6	0.4	−0.2	0.0	6.5	1.8	−0.2	−0.1
Korea	4.1	3.5	3.6	3.0	4.0	4.0	7.0	−0.4	5.9	−0.6	1.9	0.3
UK	0.6	0.2	1.2	0.8	0.2	−0.7	3.0	1.7	4.2	−0.1	0.9	0.6
USA	1.7	2.9	2.9	0.9	−0.6	0.2	3.3	4.2	8.0	−0.4	0.1	−0.3

The OECD's forecasts for consumption, investment, government spending and net exports are presented in Table 9.2; and it is possible to link the comments in Table 9.1 to the forecasts in Table 9.2. In the case of France, the OECD believes that investment growth will be a key driver of demand; and we can see from Table 9.2 that investment spending is forecast to grow the greatest during the forecast period. See if you can link other comments in Table 9.1 with the forecasts in Table 9.2.

More detailed data for an individual economy is normally made available by institutions within that economy. In the UK, the Office for National Statistics (ONS), the Office for Budgetary Responsibility (OBR) and the Bank of England (BoE) all provide data on the UK economy and the four key components of aggregate demand. The data is generally very accessible, available online and pre-graphed, providing firms and managers with easy access to important macroeconomic intelligence.

Figure 9.14 provides more detailed data which makes it possible to consider where demand within the UK economy is likely to be heading. The first chart presents household consumption data going back almost 40 years and, not surprisingly, every time the economy suffers a recession, then household consumption falls. With a slower economy, new job formation slows, unemployment increases, overtime payments fall and even wages can be cut. Households receive less income on average and may save more to protect themselves from the consequences of future unemployment. All these factors lead to a reduction in household spending.

Levels of investment spending by firms can be measured, as can intentions to invest; and because firms generally invest large sums of money, investment decisions and investment plans can take a long time, so the intention to invest is also important. Surveys by the government and by industry bodies, such as the Confederation of British Industry, gather information on the willingness, or intention, of firms to invest. We can see from the data that while investment bounced back, after a large fall in 2008, it looks likely to fall again in 2011 and 2012.

The government borrowing chart is quite detailed, but try to focus on the key trends. Borrowing will fall. In order to borrow less the government must have stronger finances, which means lower spending and higher tax.

Finally, UK exports, like those of other economies, are highly dependent upon the strength of key trading partners. The final chart provides measures of global output growth. While global output grew from 2009 onwards, the latest trend is down, spreading concerns of a double recession.

A quick interpretation of the four charts is that none of the main areas of demand is likely to demonstrate strong growth in the near future, which together means low growth for

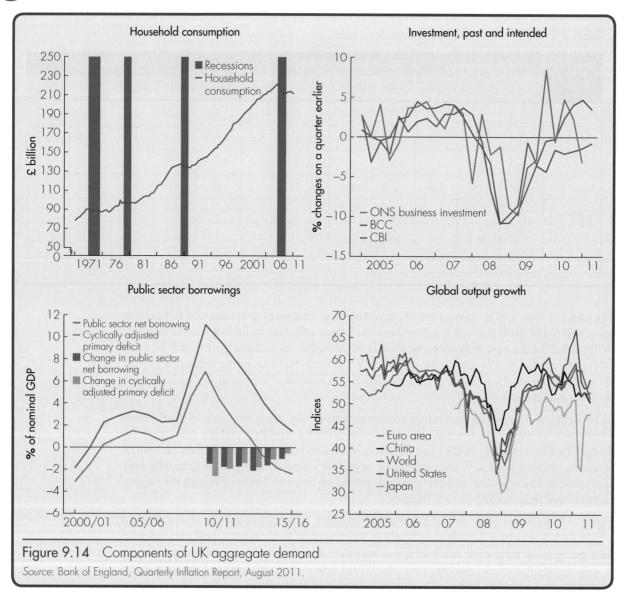

Figure 9.14 Components of UK aggregate demand

Source: Bank of England, Quarterly Inflation Report, August 2011.

aggregate demand and therefore little scope for demand-led growth of GDP. The sensible conclusion to draw is that the UK economy will not grow quickly and there are few places for UK companies to concentrate their activities. For example, focusing on household spending through retail products does not look promising. The business-to-business sector, selling capital equipment to other companies, looks unappetizing. Specializing in the support of government services, such as health and education, looks bleak with the cutbacks in government spending, and trying to compete overseas does not look especially appealing.

Your understanding of macroeconomics is at an early stage, yet the circular flow of income provides you with a simple and insightful framework. So simple and useful is the circular flow of income that professional economists working for the leading economic institutions also use it to frame their study of the world's economies. With your new knowledge you can improve your understanding of the economy by using the research insights provided by leading economic forecasters. In so doing, your ability to interpret the economy and improve your business planning decisions will grow.

Summary

1. Macroeconomics is the study of economic activity at the aggregate level, examining the entire economy rather than just single markets.

2. The circular flow of income is a representation of how an economy works. Households own all factors of production and firms hire these factors to produce goods and services. Firms pay households for using input resources and households in return purchase the goods and services.

3. The level of demand for goods and services is conditioned by the level of injections into and leakages from the circular flow of income. Savings, taxation and imports all represent leakages, while investment, government spending and exports all represent injections.

4. The whole economy can be viewed as a collection of the many small markets that go into making an economy. Therefore, rather than thinking about demand we now talk about aggregate demand and similarly aggregate supply as opposed to simply supply.

5. Aggregate demand has a negative relationship with inflation. As inflation increases, the central bank increases interest rates, resulting in a reduction in aggregate demand.

6. Aggregate supply will have a positive relationship with inflation, if real wages do not adjust fully to rises in prices. However, if real wages adjust fully to inflation, then aggregate supply will be perfectly inelastic.

7. Gross domestic product, or GDP, is a measure of economic output of an economy.

8. Inflation is a measure of price changes. The quicker prices rise, the higher the rate of inflation.

9. In part, the business cycle can be explained by changes in aggregate demand and aggregate supply. As demand increases, the economy grows and inflation increases. As demand falls, the economy slows and inflation falls. If, in contrast, supply increases, then the economy grows and inflation decreases. However, if supply shrinks, the economy shrinks and inflation increases.

10. The business cycle is a description of the tendency for economies to move from economic boom into economic recession and vice versa.

11. The rate of inflation tends to change throughout the business cycle, but this is a reflection of changes in aggregate demand and supply. An increase in aggregate demand will tend to generate an inflationary boom, while an increase in aggregate supply will tend to generate a deflationary boom. Conversely, a reduction in aggregate demand will generate a deflationary recession, while a reduction in aggregate supply will generate an inflationary recession.

12. Predicting the business cycle is not an exact science. Economists and business people will only ever know when an economy has hit its peak after the event, perhaps up to 12 months after. And the same is true of recessions. It is, therefore, crucial to plan and implement investment decisions in advance of any detrimental macroeconomic changes. How to achieve this is challenging. Some people use their experience – how did the economy behave in the past? What can I learn from other economies? What are the experts saying? And do I believe them?

13. An interesting question, or fallacy, surrounds the fact that GDP only falls by a small amount (1–2 per cent) during a recession and yet many businesses suffer severe financial hardship. Why is that? In part, recessions have different impacts in different product markets. Falling consumer incomes will cut demand for normal goods, but raise demand for inferior goods. This provides an opportunity to create a mixed portfolio of products for the business cycle. Supermarkets do this through greater use of own-brand items during recessions, while many car manufacturers produce both high- and low-value cars.

14. Data relating to the four key components of aggregate demand are often provided by important economic bodies such as central banks. Accessing data on consumption, investment, government spending and net exports can help a business to understand its macroeconomic environment and support effective business planning.

Learning checklist

You should now be able to:

- Discuss the key topics of GDP, inflation, unemployment and the balance of payments
- Explain what is meant by the term business cycle
- Provide a discussion of the circular flow of income, highlighting the various relationships between firms, households, government and international economies
- Explain the difference between leakages and injections
- Explain the determinants of aggregate demand
- Discuss whether or not aggregate supply will be perfectly inelastic
- Explain how changes in aggregate demand and supply can explain the business cycle

Questions   connect

1. What are the key macroeconomic variables for an economy? How have these variables changed in your economy over the last five years?

2. What key macroeconomic variables can a government or central bank control? How have these changed for your economy during the last five years?

3. Draw a circular flow of income for an economy that has a government sector and is open to international trade.

4. Identify the leakages, injections and components of aggregate expenditure in your circular flow diagram.

5. Explain why there is a negative relationship between inflation and aggregate demand.

EASY

6. Consumer and business confidence are increasing. Illustrate the likely consequence of these changes on aggregate demand.

7. Explain why in the long run aggregate supply is perfectly inelastic, but in the short run it is elastic.

8. Would an increase in aggregate demand generate an inflationary or deflationary boom? Would a reduction in aggregate supply generate an inflationary recession or a deflationary boom?

9. Explain what is meant by the term a lead indicator.

10. How does an understanding of income elasticity enable a firm to manage the consequences of the business cycle?

11. In the long run can GDP grow through an increase in aggregate demand, aggregate supply or both?

INTERMEDIATE

12. In an economy, if aggregate demand increases while aggregate supply stays constant, what happens to GDP and inflation?

13. An economy benefits from an influx of additional workers. Using the circular flow of income, assess how these additional workers will impact upon the output of the economy. How will the extra workers influence aggregate supply?

14. Identify the key business variables a company could monitor in order to understand whether the economy is heading towards a boom or a recession.

DIFFICULT

15. The economy has been growing for 12 months and sales are increasing, but margins, the difference between revenues and costs, are beginning to fall. Is now a good time to invest in additional production capacity?

Exercises

1. True or false?

EASY

   (a) Savings provide an injection into the circular flow of income.

   (b) Total expenditure in an economy is equal to consumption, investment, government spending and exports.

   (c) Under complete wage adjustment aggregate supply is unresponsive to a change in inflation.

   (d) Higher inflation will lead central banks to increase interest rates. This explains a negative relationship between inflation and aggregate demand.

   (e) The main injections into the circular flow of income are investment and government spending.

   (f) Diversifying macroeconomic risk through normal and inferior products is beneficial for shareholders.

2. Table 9.3 presents consumer price indices (CPIs) for the UK, USA and Spain.

INTERMEDIATE

   (a) Calculate the annual inflation rate for each of the countries.

   (b) Plot your three inflation series on a diagram against time.

Table 9.3 Consumer prices

	UK		USA		Spain	
	Consumer price index	Inflation rate (%)	Consumer price index	Inflation rate (%)	Consumer price index	Inflation rate (%)
1999	71.7		77.6		68.2	
2000	77.3		81.4		72.9	
2001	84.6		85.7		77.7	
2002	89.6		89.4		82.4	
2003	92.9		92.1		87.2	
2004	94.4		94.8		91.2	
2005	96.7		97.3		95.5	
2006	100.0		100.0		100.0	
2007	102.4		102.9		103.6	
2008	105.7		105.3		105.6	
2009	109.3		107.0		107.5	

(c)　By what percentage did prices increase in each country over the whole period – i.e. between 1999 and 2009?

(d)　Which economy has experienced most stability of the inflation rate?

(e)　Which economy saw the greatest deceleration in the rate of inflation between 2001 and 2004?

Table 9.4 presents some data relating to national output (real GDP) of the same three economies over a similar period, expressed as index numbers.

(f)　Calculate the annual growth rate for each of the countries.

(g)　Plot your three growth series on a diagram against time.

(h)　By what percentage did output increase in each country over the whole period?

(i)　To what extent did growth follow a similar pattern over time in these three countries?

Table 9.4　National production

	UK		USA		Spain	
	GDP index	Growth rate (%)	GDP index	Growth rate (%)	GDP index	Growth rate (%)
1999	91.4		86.7		86.0	
2000	93.4		89.7		90.2	
2001	93.7		90.8		93.6	
2002	91.9		89.9		95.7	
2003	91.4		92.3		96.3	
2004	93.3		94.5		95.2	
2005	97.3		97.8		97.4	
2006	100.0		100.0		100.0	
2007	102.6		103.4		102.4	
2008	106.2		107.5		106.0	
2009	108.5		111.7		110.1	

3.　Refer to Box 9.1 when considering the following questions:

(a)　Calculate the percentage increase in the index of the Ifo institute.

(b)　What evidence is there within the article to support that consumption, investment, government spending and net exports are increasing?

Measuring macroeconomic variables and policy issues

Chapter contents

Measurement and policy issues at a glance		248
10.1	Business problem: what are the macroeconomic policy issues?	248
10.2	GDP: measurement and policy	249
10.3	Inflation: measurement and policy	255
10.4	Unemployment	260
10.5	Balance of payments	262
10.6	Macroeconomic policies	263
10.7	Business application: international competitiveness and the macroeconomy	264
10.8	Business policy: inflation targeting?	266
10.9	Business data application: accuracy of economic data measurements	269
Summary		270
Learning checklist		271
Questions		271
Exercises		272

Learning outcomes

By the end of this chapter you should understand:

Economic theory

LO1 How to measure GDP using the income, expenditure and value-added approaches

LO2 How to measure inflation using index numbers

LO3 The potential causes of inflation

LO4 The costs of inflation

LO5 The reasons behind inflation targeting

LO6 Frictional, structural, demand deficient and classical as various types of unemployment

LO7 The Phillips curve

LO8 Balance of payments problems

Business application

LO9 The importance of manufacturing competitiveness to the economy; and equally the importance of economic policy for manufacturing competitiveness

LO10 How inflation targeting might impact the business environment

LO11 How to recognize and appreciate the accuracy of economic data measures

At a glance | Measurement and policy issues

The issue

How are various macroeconomic variables measured? In addition, why is managing GDP, inflation, unemployment and the balance of payments important? What are the issues and trade-offs associated with targeting each aspect of the macro economy?

The understanding

Higher and stable GDP is associated with economic prosperity and enhanced economic growth. Higher GDP may lead to higher incomes for consumers and could facilitate investment by firms and government. High inflation may lead to economic instability and increased costs for the economy. Lower inflation might facilitate economic stability and investment planning by firms, leading to higher rates of economic growth. Unemployment reflects an underutilized resource, but labour market concerns are now switching towards productivity. The balance of payments reflects a country's trading position with the rest of the world. Just like individuals, an economy has to be concerned about running a long-term deficit. It is important to recognize that a government may not be capable of targeting all macroeconomic variables; for example, higher GDP may lead to higher inflation.

The usefulness

As businesses operate within macroeconomic environments it is essential that business people are capable of deciphering the policy messages and changes instituted by governments. How will decisions regarding the management of inflation and long-term growth impact on the economy and the firm?

 ## Business problem: what are the macroeconomic policy issues?

Macroeconomic risks are wide ranging and vary across different parts of the global economy. Since companies operate within macroeconomic environments, managers need to be capable of understanding the key macroeconomic policy issues pursued by governments. Box 10.1 reports the views of the head of the UK central bank. During this speech, the head of the bank is trying to provide a review of the economy, highlighting the important issues and problems underlying the steps taken so far. The bank is seeking to provide stability and leadership. But for it to be successful in providing direction to the economy, it is necessary for those listening, especially in business, to understand the issues being raised and addressed by the central bank.

Read Box 10.1 and you will unfortunately recognize that these macroeconomic issues are important but difficult to grasp. The purpose of the chapter is to begin to provide you with an understanding of the important macroeconomic issues. We will then develop your understanding of policy responses in later chapters.

Interest rate policy and the Bank of England

The Bank of England has the task of keeping inflation in the UK at 2 per cent on average. In pursuing this target, the Bank of England is empowered to alter interest rates. What does this mean for business?

1   If firms borrow money to invest in capital, will interest rates be higher or lower when controlled by the central bank?

2   Will the central bank be capable of meeting the 2 per cent target?

Box 10.1

Inflation report

The prospects for the UK economy have worsened. Global demand slowed. And concerns about the solvency of several euro-area governments intensified, increasing strains in banking and some sovereign funding markets. Household and business confidence fell, both at home and abroad. These factors, along with the fiscal consolidation and squeeze on households' real incomes, are likely to weigh heavily on UK growth in the near term. Thereafter, the recovery should gain traction, supported by continued monetary stimulus and a gentle recovery in real incomes. Implementation of a credible and effective policy response in the euro area would help to reduce uncertainty and so support UK growth, but its absence poses the single biggest risk to the domestic recovery.

Consumer Price Index (CPI) inflation rose to 5.2 per cent in September. Inflation is likely to fall back sharply through 2012 as the contributions of value-added tax (VAT), energy and import prices decline, and downward pressure from slack in the labour market persists. But how far and how fast inflation will fall are uncertain. Under the assumption that Bank Rate moves in line with market interest rates and the size of the asset purchase programme remains at £275 billion, inflation is judged more likely to be below than above the 2 per cent target at the forecast horizon.

Adapted from the Bank of England, November 2011 Inflation Report.

3 Moreover, will targeting inflation have any implications for the business cycle, the growth of GDP and perhaps even the exchange rate?
4 Will central bank management of interest rates and inflation aid entry into the euro?

10.2 GDP: measurement and policy

The aggregate demand and supply framework developed in Chapter 9 highlighted the importance of GDP and inflation. As aggregate demand or supply changed, the equilibrium level of GDP and inflation changed accordingly. We will begin by analysing GDP.

Variations in GDP over time

Figure 10.1 plots GDP growth for the UK over the period 1990 to 2010. GDP is an estimate of the amount of economic activity in an economy and is produced by the Office for National

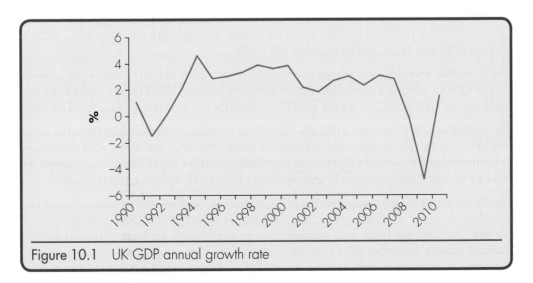

Figure 10.1   UK GDP annual growth rate

> The business cycle
> describes the
> tendency of an
> economy to move
> from economic boom
> to economic recession
> and then back into
> boom to repeat the
> cycle.

Statistics. Since 1990, UK GDP has grown at various rates between −5.0 per cent and 4.25 per cent per annum. Trend growth in the UK is around 2.5 per cent per annum. Whenever growth is below 2.5 per cent, the economy is experiencing slowing economic growth. Persistent slow growth can constitute a recession. Whenever GDP growth is above 2.5 per cent, the economy is heading towards economic boom. The variation between recession and boom is known as the **business cycle**. In fact, Figure 10.1 is a picture of the business cycle, where the economy moves through a series of booms and recessions.

Measuring economic output

By examining the circular flow of income, in Chapter 9, we saw three potential ways of measuring output. We can measure (i) the net value of goods and services produced by firms, (ii) the value of household earnings, or (iii) the value of spending on goods and services. We are simply measuring the flow at different points; each is equally applicable and will provide a similar figure to the rest.

However, the net value of goods and services approach needs to avoid the problem of double counting.

We can examine the manufacture of a car as an example. A car contains many different parts to be assembled and then sold to a customer through a dealership. Consider paint as one component. Assume the raw materials for car paint are £100; the car-paint producer mixes the materials, packages them and sends them to the car maker at a price of £200. This mixing, packaging and distribution represents £200 − £100 = £100 of value added. The car maker uses many different inputs, including paint, exhausts and engines. All the inputs cost £10 000. But the car is sold to the dealership for £12 000, so the value added from designing and assembling a car is £12 000 − £10 000 = £2000. The dealer polishes the car, shows it in a clean showroom environment, provides test drives and sells the car for £13 000. So, the value added of the dealership is £13 000 − £12 000 = £1000. If we add up all the **value added** in the economy, or we use statisticians to estimate total value added, then we have an estimate of total economic activity, or GDP.

> Value added is net
> output, after
> deducting goods and
> services used up
> during the production
> process.

Unfortunately, there are two more complications which need to be considered when measuring economic output. The first recognizes that not all factors of production are domestically owned and profits from the use of these resources will flow to another country. For example, the Japanese car manufacturer Toyota owns production facilities in Turkey and the UK. The flows of profits, interest and dividends from these assets are known as property incomes; and the balance of flows for any particular country is known as net property income. Therefore, Toyota's profits in the UK (and Turkey) will be added to the Japanese economy's gross national product (GNP). Likewise, overseas profits for large British companies, such as Vodafone, BP and Tesco, will be added to UK GNP.

The (i) output and (iii) expenditure methods will not add to the (ii) incomes measure of output without making a correction for net property income. We therefore make a distinction between GDP and GNP, which is GDP adjusted for net property income from abroad.

The second issue is to recognize that the creation of economic output results from the use of productive capital. This is such items as plant, machinery, buildings and shops, all of which need to be maintained, repaired or replaced as they wear out. These expenditures come under the heading of depreciation. Subtracting depreciation from GDP leads to national income.

Finally, all prices are quoted as market price, which can be distorted by indirect taxes and subsidies. In order to measure economic output we would prefer price measures which are not distorted by taxes and subsidies: these are known as basic prices. Adjusting national income at market prices for the distortion of taxes and subsidies leaves us with the figure of national income at basic prices. Figure 10.2 provides an illustration of all of these adjustments.

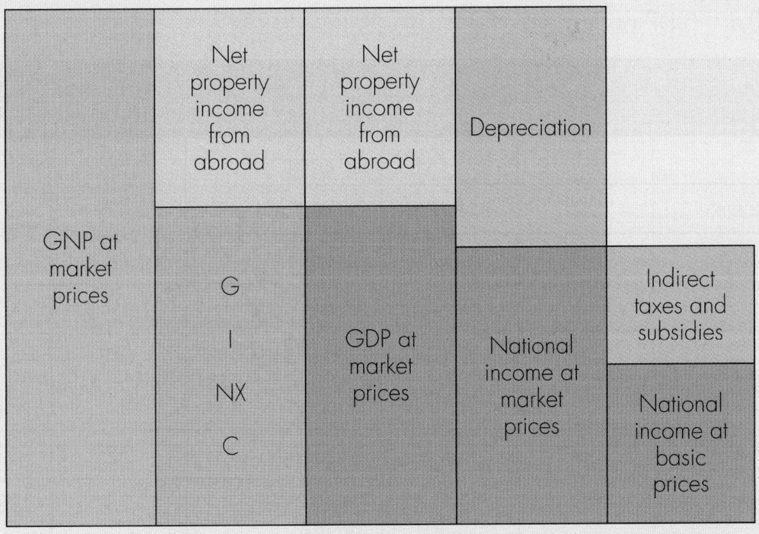

Measuring economic activity requires a number of considerations. Take the market value of what is produced in the domestic economy. Then add in the value of what is produced by operations owned in other economies. Then add depreciation to recognize the cost of using capital and an adjustment for subsidies and taxes, to arrive at national income at basic prices.

Figure 10.2 National income accounting

GDP policy issues

Is higher GDP preferable? Broadly speaking, yes. Higher GDP means more goods and services are being produced. Households' economic resources are being used more fully by firms and, as a result, financial payments to households rise. The level of income within an economy is often measured as **GDP per capita**.

Table 10.1 shows the level of GDP per capita for 30 leading countries in the world. All values have been converted into US dollars. These figures suggest that average income per person in the UK is around $12 500 lower than in the USA.

However, higher GDP per capita can mask a number of problematic features of an economy. One common concern is the distribution of income within an economy. Often within economies, even very developed economies within the EU, there is an unequal distribution of income. Typically those earning most see the fastest increase in future incomes. As such, the rich become richer and the poor become relatively poorer.

An additional concern is the cost incurred in generating higher levels of GDP per capita. These concerns are often focused upon damage to the environment, but it is equally possible to raise social concerns. See Figure 10.3, which highlights the different working hours typically endured by workers in a number of leading European economies. France, Denmark and Sweden have strong peaks at 36–40 hours per week. The UK has a moderate peak at this level, but then the distribution continues strongly towards 50+ hours per week. It should also be noted that the UK, when compared with the other economies, has a relatively high number of people working in the part-time range of hours. The UK works its full-time workers extremely hard and it is also very keen to have a large number of part-time workers. We describe the UK as having a very high **participation rate**. But at what cost? What else could these people be doing? Enjoying leisure, spending time with the family, staying away from stress counsellors?

> GDP per capita is the GDP for the economy divided by the population of the economy. GDP per capita provides a measure of average income per person.

> Participation rate is the percentage of people of working age who are in employment.

Table 10.1   GDP per capita

Country	Rank	GDP per capita ($)	Country	Rank	GDP per capita ($)
Qatar	1	179 000	Gibraltar	16	43 000
Liechtenstein	2	141 000	Switzerland	17	42 600
Luxembourg	3	83 000	Australia	18	41 000
Bermuda	4	69 900	Austria	19	40 400
Jersey	5	57 000	Netherlands	20	40 300
Norway	6	55 000	Canada	21	39 400
Singapore	7	52 900	Sweden	22	39 100
Brunei	8	52 000	British Virgin Islands	23	38 500
United Arab Emirates	9	49 600	Iceland	24	38 300
Kuwait	10	48 900	Belgium	25	37 800
United States	11	47 200	Ireland	26	37 300
Andorra	12	46 700	Denmark	27	36 300
Hong Kong	13	45 900	San Marino	28	36 200
Guernsey	14	44 600	Finland	29	35 400
Cayman Islands	15	43 800	United Kingdom	30	34 800

Source: CIA Factbook.

Sustainable economic growth

These distributional elements aside, a broad consensus is that high levels of GDP and growth in GDP are desirable. A common reason for promoting economic growth is employment. If households are buying firms' products, then firms will be using households' labour. However, when a recession occurs, households buy less, firms produce less and, as a consequence, firms employ fewer workers. As we will see later, unemployment and employment are, therefore, linked to the business cycle and economic growth.

Economies with higher levels of GDP are better able to invest in the economy's infrastructure, such as schools, hospitals and roads. This is because higher levels of GDP are likely to lead to higher incomes for workers. This in turn will result in increased taxes being paid to the government. Higher tax receipts enable the government to invest in important assets, such as schools, teachers, nurses, motorways and rail networks. Road and rail improvements help businesses to move products around, while better education and health services enable individuals to be more productive over their lifetime.

A combination of rising profits and better educational systems in a growing economy can facilitate improved levels of, and success in, research and development. Innovation can aid the development of new products that improve the lifestyle of individuals in the economy. Or innovation can bring about new and cheaper ways of making products. The Internet is a good example of both. It has changed how people can access many types of information and it has reduced the cost of providing consumers with banking and retail services.

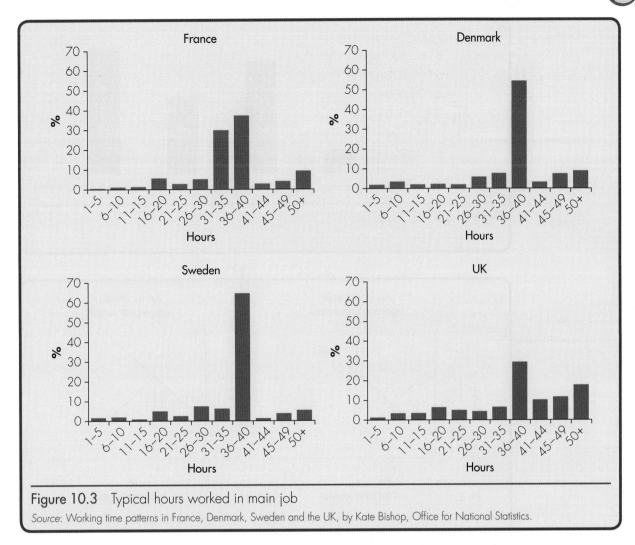

Figure 10.3 Typical hours worked in main job

Source: Working time patterns in France, Denmark, Sweden and the UK, by Kate Bishop, Office for National Statistics.

Of course, economic growth should not be regarded as costless. We have already seen that growth can come through longer working times, leading to a reduction in leisure and family time. The other major consideration is that of the environment. As economies grow, and they grow at a faster rate, they consume more resources. Energy consumption rises with economic growth. More affluent consumers buy more cars. Increased affluence also brings greater consumption of energy-hungry appliances, such as televisions, refrigerators and air-conditioning. As a consequence, economic growth drives power consumption, which leads to higher levels of CO_2.

In Figure 10.4 data on CO_2 per capita is shown for a number of economies. The USA, perhaps the most developed economy in the world, has the highest CO_2 emissions per capita. China, one of the world's fastest growing economies, has the lowest emissions per capita. But this figure is biased by China's enormous population. If we consider CO_2 emissions in Figure 10.5, we can see that China already produces more pollution than the USA. If China's economy continues

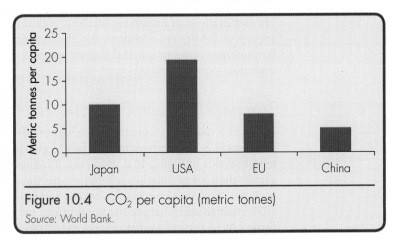

Figure 10.4 CO_2 per capita (metric tonnes)

Source: World Bank.

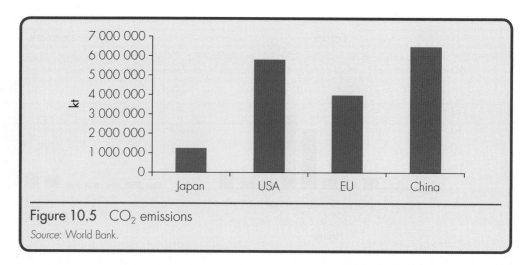

Figure 10.5 CO_2 emissions

Source: World Bank.

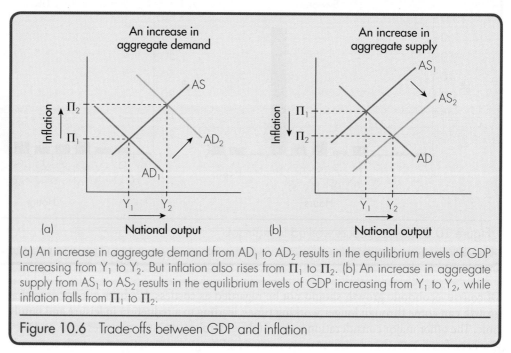

(a) An increase in aggregate demand from AD_1 to AD_2 results in the equilibrium levels of GDP increasing from Y_1 to Y_2. But inflation also rises from Π_1 to Π_2. (b) An increase in aggregate supply from AS_1 to AS_2 results in the equilibrium levels of GDP increasing from Y_1 to Y_2, while inflation falls from Π_1 to Π_2.

Figure 10.6 Trade-offs between GDP and inflation

to grow, and CO_2 per capita matches that of the USA, then the amount of overall pollution from China will be huge.

The implications of increasing levels of pollution from all economies have important consequences for the environment, the climate and public health. How economies grow and how energy consumption and cleaner energy creation aid economic growth are becoming important policy agendas.

Trade-off between GDP and inflation

However, a cautionary note regarding higher GDP has to be made. If higher GDP stems from an increase in aggregate demand, then higher inflation will follow. This is depicted on the left-hand side of Figure 10.6. However, if higher GDP stems from an increase in aggregate supply, then lower inflation will follow; see the right-hand side of Figure 10.6. Therefore, if economic growth is important, a crucial and basic question to ask is, how are higher levels of GDP attained and what are the implications for inflation? We will now explore these issues further by considering inflation and, more important, the targeting of inflation.

Inflation: measurement and policy

Variations in inflation over time

In Figure 10.7, we have a graph of inflation in the UK. The government and the Bank of England have a target inflation rate of 2.0 per cent; however, in recent times inflation has been as high as 5 per cent. Back in 1979, inflation hit 25 per cent but, more important, look at the early 1990s in Figure 10.7, the same years as were associated with recession in Figure 10.1. The UK experienced an inflationary recession. But in 2008 the **rate of inflation** dropped, so we then experienced a deflationary recession, which then turned inflationary.

Demand pull and cost push inflation

Inflation can increase if aggregate demand increases, or if aggregate supply decreases. Economists use this distinction to talk about **demand pull** and **cost push inflation**.

> **Rate of inflation** is a measure of how fast prices are rising.
>
> **Demand pull inflation** occurs when a rise in aggregate demand leads to an increase in overall prices.
>
> **Cost push inflation** occurs when a reduction in supply leads to an increase in overall prices.

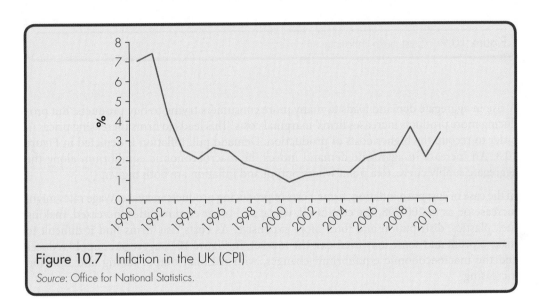

Figure 10.7 Inflation in the UK (CPI)

Source: Office for National Statistics.

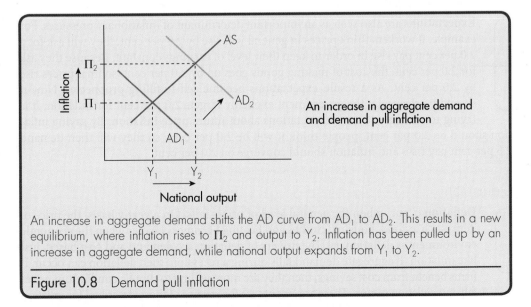

An increase in aggregate demand and demand pull inflation

An increase in aggregate demand shifts the AD curve from AD_1 to AD_2. This results in a new equilibrium, where inflation rises to Π_2 and output to Y_2. Inflation has been pulled up by an increase in aggregate demand, while national output expands from Y_1 to Y_2.

Figure 10.8 Demand pull inflation

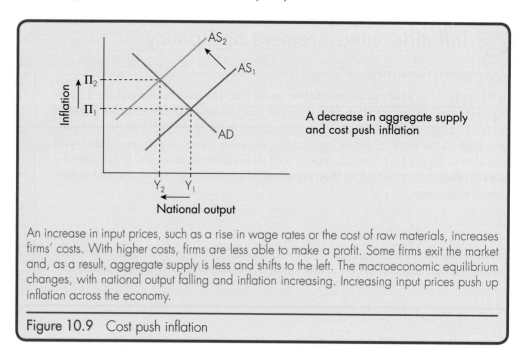

An increase in input prices, such as a rise in wage rates or the cost of raw materials, increases firms' costs. With higher costs, firms are less able to make a profit. Some firms exit the market and, as a result, aggregate supply is less and shifts to the left. The macroeconomic equilibrium changes, with national output falling and inflation increasing. Increasing input prices push up inflation across the economy.

Figure 10.9 Cost push inflation

A rise in aggregate demand leads to many more consumers trying to buy products. But producing more products increases firms' marginal costs. This leads to firms increasing prices in order to recoup the higher costs of production. Demand pull inflation is depicted in Figure 10.8. An increase in aggregate demand moves the macroeconomic equilibrium along the aggregate supply curve, to a point where output and inflation are both higher.

In the case of cost push inflation, firms' costs of producing products increase. Wage rates might increase or, as in 2007/08, the cost of oil, wheat and other commodities increased, making fuel, plastics, distribution and food more expensive. As costs rise, firms find it difficult to make a profit and some may even exit the market. In Figure 10.9, aggregate supply reduces and the macroeconomic equilibrium changes, with national output falling and inflation increasing.

Inflationary expectations

> Expectations are beliefs held by firms, workers and consumers about the future level of prices.

Expectations are also seen as an important determinant of inflationary pressures. For example, if workers think prices in general will rise by 2.0 per cent, they will ask for a 2.0 per cent pay rise in order to keep their level of earnings constant. Because they ask for 2.0 per cent, the cost of making goods goes up by 2.0 per cent, so final prices rise by 2.0 per cent. As a result, expectations become self-fulfilling prophecies. Now it should be clear why the government explicitly targets 2.0 per cent for inflation. It is trying to manage society's expectations about future price inflation. By saying inflation should be 2.0 per cent, people think it will be 2.0 per cent, so they will then demand 2.5 per cent pay rises and inflation should converge on 2.0 per cent.

Deflation

> Deflation is a fall in prices, usually on a yearly basis.

Deflation occurs when the general level of prices falls. On a yearly basis, the price of items such as food, housing, clothes and heating becomes cheaper when the economic environment is deflationary. The drivers of deflation are demand and cost based, just like inflation. If aggregate demand falls during a recession, then deflation can occur. If firms benefit from cost savings, then they are more willing to supply; equilibrium prices fall and deflation occurs. These arguments are the reverse of those described for inflation in Figures 10.8 and 10.9. For demand-based deflation, aggregate demand in Figure 10.8 moves from AD_2 to AD_1; and for supply-based deflation in Figure 10.9, AS_2 moves to AS_1.

The credit crunch created a significant recession and a demand-led deflationary period. The expansion of the Chinese economy and the export of manufactured items around the world increased supply and led to deflation in the price of manufactured goods.

Measuring inflation

To measure the rate of inflation governments use what are known as price indices. To do this, the government asks a sample of households across the UK to record all the products that they consume in a given period. From these data, government statisticians build what is known as a common basket of goods and services bought by the average UK household. This basket will include bread, milk, tobacco, petrol, mortgage repayments, insurance, cinema tickets, restaurant meals, train fares and so on.

Each good or service is assigned a weight. So, if mortgage repayments represent 50 per cent of individuals' monthly outgoings, then they will represent 50 per cent of the basket. If bread only represents 2 per cent of monthly outgoings, then bread will only fill 2 per cent of the basket. The prices of all these goods and services are then monitored on a monthly basis. A report of price changes within the basket is provided in Box 10.2 from the Office for National Statistics.

Box 10.2

Changes to CPI and RPI shopping baskets

Smartphones as well as the 'apps' that run on them have been added to the updated basket of goods and services used by ONS to calculate UK inflation rates. Phone applications are replacing mobile phone downloads, such as ringtones and wallpaper.

Also reflecting new trends, the updated basket includes dating agency fees for the first time. This is because, with the spread of the Internet, online dating sites are becoming an increasingly common way for people to find a partner.

Commenting, ONS statistician Phil Gooding said: 'Many of these new items show the way technology is changing our lives. Powerful smartphones and the applications that run on them have become essential for many when communicating or seeking information. Likewise, increasing numbers of people now seek a partner via Internet dating sites.'

In addition, television prices will now be collected differently, with the price of televisions bigger than 32 inches being measured separately. This is being introduced to reflect a change in the television market, with many households now setting up 'home cinema' systems.

Sparkling wines are also being added due to their increased consumption, showing that despite difficult economic times, people still want to enjoy themselves.

As new legislation is coming into force this year restricting the sale of cigarettes, vending machine cigarettes are now being removed from the basket.

Also going is the pork shoulder, which is being replaced by oven-ready joints, as people move further towards more ready-prepared foods.

Adapted from the Office for National Statistics (ONS), March 2011.

Source: www.statistics.gov.uk

Index and base years

The **price index** has a base year, where the value of the index, or the basket of goods and services, is set at 100 (see Chapter 1 for a reminder). Inflation is a measure of how quickly prices are rising and it measures the difference between the price level last year and the price level this year. As such, inflation is measured as:

Inflation = (Index in current year − Index in previous year)/Index in previous year

> The price index can be used to deflate current prices into constant prices, where constant prices are prices expressed in the base year.

Box 10.3

CPI down to 4.2 per cent, RPI down to 4.8 per cent

CPI annual inflation stands at 4.2 per cent in December 2011, down from 4.8 per cent in November. The CPI stands at 121.7 in December 2011 based on 2005 = 100.

The largest downward pressures to the change in CPI annual inflation between November and December came from petrol, gas and clothing. The only large upward pressure to the change in CPI annual inflation between November and December came from landline and mobile phone charges.

Retail Price Index (RPI) annual inflation stands at 4.8 per cent in December, down from 5.2 per cent in

November. The largest downward pressures to the change in RPI annual inflation between November and December 2011 came from petrol, oil and other fuels, gas, and clothing and footwear. Partially offsetting these were upward pressures from car insurance and telephone charges. The RPI stands at 239.4 in December 2011 based on January 1987 = 100.

Adapted from the Office for National Statistics,
January 2012.
Source: www.statistics.gov.uk

Table 10.2 Price index and inflation

Year	Price index	Inflation	Nominal salary	Real salary
2008	100		£20 000	£20 000
2009	102	(102 – 100)/100 = 2.0%	£20 000	£19 608
2010	105	(105 – 102)/102 = 2.9%	£20 000	£19 048
2011	110	(110 – 105)/105 = 4.8%	£20 000	£18 182
2012	113	(113 – 110)/110 = 2.7%	£20 000	£17 699

In Table 10.2, the price index has been set at 100 for the year 2008, and it rises to 113 by the year 2012. Using the formula above, the inflation rate in 2009 was 2 per cent, while in 2011 it was 4.8 per cent.

Price deflators

For example, suppose in 2012 you earned £20 000 and that by 2016 your boss had refused to give you a pay rise and you still only earned £20 000. We can calculate your real wage in each year by using the price index to convert your salary into year 2012 prices as follows:

$$\text{Real salary} = (\text{Nominal salary}) \times (100/\text{Price index})$$

So, a nominal salary of £20 000 in 2016 is a real salary of only £20 000 × (100/113) = £17 699. In other words, £20 000 has lost £2301 in value since 2012. This has wider implications: whenever prices are compared over time, whether for houses, cars, wages or wine, they need to be adjusted for inflation and converted into constant prices. Price indices provide a means of achieving this.

Costs of inflation

In recent decades governments around the world have begun to set inflation targets. This is because inflation can be costly. But this cost should not be confused with goods and services becoming more expensive.

For example: 'When I was a lad, a bag of chips cost 5p; now they cost £1.25.' But chips are not 20 times more expensive now than they were 30 years ago. This is because incomes have also risen by the same amount. So, we will only think inflation makes things more expensive if we suffer from **inflation illusion**. However, if we do suffer from inflation illusion, then we may cut back on consumption, believing the product to be too expensive. If enough people reduce consumption, then a recession may occur.

> Inflation illusion is a confusion of nominal and real changes.

Even without inflation illusion, inflation can still be costly. If prices are rising quickly, retailers will be constantly changing their prices. Shelf labels will have to be changed at supermarkets and price lists will have to be changed by other types of sellers. These are known as *menu costs* and the more rapidly prices rise, the more often prices have to be changed. So, inflation can create additional costs.

Fiscal drag

Let us assume inflation is fully expected and full adjustment occurs. Price rises of 10 per cent are matched by wage increases of 10 per cent. There are no initial cutbacks in consumption by buyers and, therefore, no recessionary consequences. But what if the government does not adjust its tax policy?

> Fiscal drag occurs when tax-free income allowances grow at a slower rate than earnings. This reduces the real value of tax-free allowances, leading to high real tax receipts.

In 2012/13, the UK government allowed individuals to earn £8105 before having to pay tax. If incomes rose by 10 per cent and the government did not lift the tax allowance by 10 per cent, then individuals would start paying more real tax. Therefore, this time, even with fully anticipated inflation, inflexibility by the government creates an inflationary cost known as **fiscal drag**.

Assets and liabilities

If mortgage interest rates are 5 per cent and inflation is 2.5 per cent, then the real interest rate is 5 − 2.5 = 2.5 per cent. Viewed this way, the lender is not making 5 per cent profits out of its customers. Rather, it is gaining 2.5 per cent to cover the rise in inflation and then it is gaining 2.5 per cent as its profit. If lenders and borrowers expect 2.5 per cent inflation, then the real cost of funds is 2.5 per cent. But what happens if expectations are wrong and inflation suddenly rises to 10 per cent? The real interest rate would become 5 − 10 = −5 per cent. Lenders are now losing 5 per cent a year and borrowers are gaining 5 per cent a year. There is a transfer of wealth from lenders to borrowers.

Borrowers tend to be young people starting out in life, buying a home and raising a family. Lenders tend to be older people who have raised their family and paid off the mortgage and are now saving with banks and building societies. Therefore, a surprise rise in the inflation rate transfers wealth from old people to young people. This influences the spending patterns of old people in a negative way and young people in a positive way. An obvious cost is the need for product suppliers to react to these consumption changes and develop different product lines to meet the main spenders in the economy. Therefore, inflation can create costs through structural change.

The fear of deflation

Falling prices might sound like a good idea. Unfortunately it is not good when the fall in prices for goods and services also impacts wages. If goods and services fall in price, then the value of labour also falls and firms will seek to pay lower wages and/or employ fewer workers.

You may consider that such changes leave workers no worse off. They earn less, but goods and services cost less, so they can still afford to buy the same things as last year. True, as long as some important prices or financial commitments are not fixed. Mortgages are important financial commitments which are relatively fixed. If you borrowed £100 000 last year and deflation results in a 5 per cent loss in earnings, then your mortgage increases in real terms to £105 000. Over a number of years, deflation can make your mortgage unaffordable.

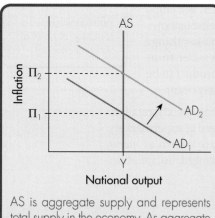

AS is aggregate supply and represents total supply in the economy. As aggregate demand increases from AD₁ to AD₂, national output remains constant at Y, but inflation rises from Π₁ to Π₂.

Figure 10.10 Aggregate demand and inelastic aggregate supply

Frictional unemployment refers to individuals who have quit one job and are currently searching for another job. As such, frictional unemployment is temporary.

Cyclical unemployment is related to the business cycle and is sometimes also referred to as demand-deficient unemployment. Cyclical unemployment reflects workers who have lost jobs due to the adversities of the business cycle.

Structural unemployment occurs when an industry moves into decline. The structurally unemployed find it difficult to gain employment in new industries because of what is known as a mismatch of skills.

Classical unemployment refers to workers who have priced themselves out of a job.

If deflation also erodes asset values, let us say property prices fall, then the difference between house prices and mortgage balances deteriorates. At worst, households can be left with negative equity, where the value of the house is less than the outstanding balance of the mortgage.

Why target inflation?

The answer to this question is very simple. If aggregate supply is perfectly inelastic and aggregate demand increases, there will be no increase in output; the only impact will be higher inflation. This is illustrated in Figure 10.10. Whenever aggregate demand shifts to the right, the government, or central bank, will pursue policies to shift aggregate demand back to the left and, therefore, keep inflation constant. The economy can now only grow if the aggregate supply curve shifts to the left.

The crucial issue is whether price stability from inflation targeting enables aggregate supply to expand and shift to the right. The belief is that inflation targeting reduces uncertainty in the economy, making investment decisions easier for firms. Volatile inflation rates lead to booms and busts within the economy, as governments try to bring inflation under control. The variations of the business cycle can make investment unprofitable. Therefore, if investment in capital increases the productive capacity of the economy and ultimately the level of aggregate supply, inflation targeting could be highly desirable. We will revisit these arguments during our discussion of fiscal, monetary and supply side policies in Chapters 11, 12 and 13.

Unemployment

Managing GDP and inflation have been at the fore of economic policy. As a result, unemployment was less important. This was to be expected as throughout the late 1990s and into the new millennium unemployment fell to almost negligible levels. As the credit crisis placed the brakes on the global economy, unemployment rose and governments have began to refocus on the issues and problems associated with unemployment. See Figure 10.11.

Economists identify four categories of unemployment: **frictional, cyclical, structural** and **classical**. Frictional unemployment is of little concern. The frictionally unemployed are between jobs. They have voluntarily quit one job and are searching for a new opportunity. Cyclical unemployment is a concern when an economy enters a recession. There is insufficient demand for all goods and services to keep all workers in employment. Factories and offices are reduced in size and workers are made redundant. The role of government is to help to bolster demand in the economy and reduce the impact of recession.

In the case of structural unemployment, an entire industry can go into decline. In the 1980s, Europe lost many jobs in traditional heavy industries such as shipbuilding, steel making and the extraction of fuels, such as coal. More recently, the financial crisis has damaged the strength of the financial system and, arguably, the industry will be more regulated, less diverse and less likely to be a dominant economic sector. So bankers and financiers will be in less demand in the future.

The problem faced by government is not one of trying to create additional demand, but how to transfer the skills of bankers and financiers to other sectors of the economy. This is not easy. Financial services workers (perhaps do not) understand financial matters; such individuals are not skilled in manufacturing, leisure services or tourism. Retraining the unemployed and bringing jobs into regions hit by structural unemployment are the difficult but key tasks.

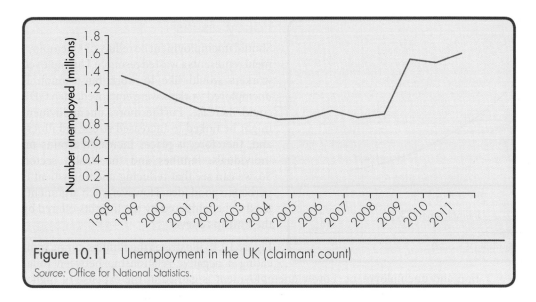

Figure 10.11 Unemployment in the UK (claimant count)

Source: Office for National Statistics.

Measuring unemployment

The government measures unemployment on a monthly basis. Over time, the measure, or definition, of unemployment has changed many times. However, the UK government has used the International Labour Organization's (ILO's) definition of unemployment for a number of years.

The ILO definition of unemployment is a count of jobless people who want to work, are available to work and are actively seeking employment. The ILO measure is used internationally, so a benefit of the measure is that it enables comparisons between countries to be made and it is also consistent over time.

An alternative measure used in the UK is the **claimant count**. The claimant count is generally lower than the ILO measure of unemployment because some individuals may be willing to work but are unable to register for the jobseeker's allowance.

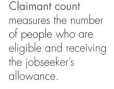

Claimant count measures the number of people who are eligible and receiving the jobseeker's allowance.

Reflecting the separate categories of unemployment, such as frictional and structural, the measures are generally broken down into region, age and time in unemployment. This provides an assessment of where unemployment is highest, which perhaps relates to industries, thereby identifying structural unemployment. Unemployment in high-age groups could reflect skill mismatch between older workers and newer industries, while time in unemployment may reflect the difference between frictional unemployment and other types of unemployment, such as classical unemployment (Figure 10.12).

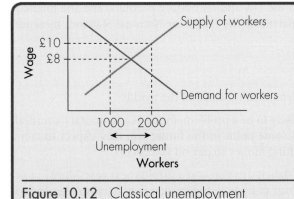

At the equilibrium wage rate of £8 per hour, the supply of workers is equal to the demand for workers. The market clears, with all workers who want to work finding employment. Unemployment is zero. If workers, or unions, are successful in raising the wage rate to £10 per hour, then the supply of workers increases as more individuals are willing to work once the wage rate increases. But, in contrast, firms are less willing to demand the more expensive workers. So, with the wage rate above the equilibrium a surplus exists, with 1000 workers unemployed.

Figure 10.12 Classical unemployment

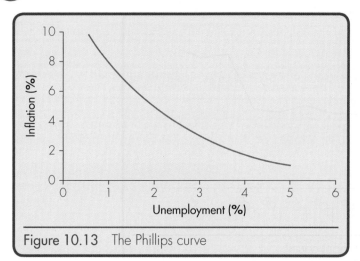

Figure 10.13   The Phillips curve

The **Phillips curve** shows that lower unemployment is associated with higher inflation. Simply, lower unemployment has to be traded for higher inflation.

Policy issues

Should unemployment be reduced? Unemployment represents a wasted resource. Unemployed workers would like to work but cannot. If unemployed workers were employed, then GDP could increase. Furthermore, unemployment might be linked to increased stress and illness and, therefore, it places increased strains on individuals, families and the health sector. So, we can see that reducing unemployment is perhaps a good idea. However, such arguments need to be tempered by the insights offered by the **Phillips curve**.

Figure 10.13 illustrates the Phillips curve, indicating a negative relationship between inflation and unemployment. Lower unemployment is gained at the expense of higher inflation. The simple explanation behind this relationship is that unemployment can be solved by creating more demand in the economy for goods and services and, ultimately, this will lead to an increase in the demand for workers. However, increased demand may also lead to higher inflation. So governments can solve high unemployment but must suffer higher inflation. In Chapter 13, we will go one step further and argue that, by increasing demand, governments only generate higher inflation and unemployment remains high.

(10.5) Balance of payments

We will cover the balance of payments in detail in Chapter 15 but, essentially, the balance of payments represents a country's net position in relation to the rest of the world. Consider your own position. You might provide a service to a company and receive a wage in return. You may then buy products and pay cash in return. If the value of the goods that you buy is greater than the value of work you provide to an employer, then your wage will be less than your spending. On a net basis, the cash flows into your bank account will be less than the cash flows out, and you may need an overdraft. In reverse, if you spend less than you receive as a wage, then the cash into your account will be greater than the cash out, and you will begin to save.

The balance of payments measures these flows for an economy, rather than for a person. For example, if the UK is buying, or importing, more goods and services than it is exporting overseas, then the UK will have to transfer financial resource from the UK to overseas. In contrast, if the UK is exporting more than it is importing, then financial resource to pay for the exports will flow into the UK. Reflecting these points, the balance of payments measures the flow of goods and services between the UK and its trading partners, and the financial flows between the UK and its trading partners. The Office for National Statistics measures these flows for the government.

Policy issues

Is it bad to run a balance of payments deficit with the rest of the world?

In the short run, a one-off deficit is unlikely to be a problem, much as a temporary overdraft is unlikely to be a problem for you. At some point in the future you may expect to run a surplus by working extra hours and earning money to pay off your debts.

Similarly, a country may expect to run a deficit this year and a surplus next year. More important, why has the deficit occurred? In your case, as a student you may have an overdraft or student loan because you are investing in your future productivity as a worker. Similarly, a country may be running an external deficit with its overseas partners because it is purchasing high-productivity capital items, which will improve the country's productivity in the future.

In the long run, the real concern arises when the deficit represents a structural, as opposed to a temporary, problem. For example, you may not be a highly valuable worker and you may be earning a low wage, but you do have very expensive tastes. As a result, you will run a deficit, spending more on goods and services than you earn in income. Similarly, if a country produces low-quality output but demands high-quality and expensive products from overseas, then it will run a deficit. The way for you to solve your debt problems is either to stop spending or to improve your value as a worker and gain a higher wage. Similarly, a country has to improve the type, quality and cost of the products that it sells to the rest of the world. In essence, by becoming more internationally competitive a country may be able to generate the finances that it requires to fund its expenditure on expensive imports.

How a country improves its international competitiveness may present another trade-off for the government. Reducing aggregate demand will result in lower inflation and more internationally competitive prices. But lowering aggregate demand may also lead to a recession. Perhaps the best option is to once again return to managing aggregate supply, introducing policies that lead to an increase in aggregate supply and a reduction in the rate of inflation, coupled with an expansion of GDP.

Macroeconomic policies

The discussion has highlighted how changes in aggregate demand and aggregate supply lead to changes in GDP and inflation. Changes in these variables may ultimately lead to changes in unemployment and the balance of payments. We have also discussed the policy issues associated with GDP, inflation, unemployment and the balance of payments, arguing why governments are interested in managing each of these macroeconomic variables. Higher GDP can improve income levels across the economy, while low and stable inflation may provide a preferable investment environment for firms. The clear question is, how do governments control aggregate demand and aggregate supply and thereby manage the economy?

The answer to these questions will be discussed at length in Chapters 11, 12 and 14. However, as an introduction we can identify demand- and supply-side policies:

- Demand-side policies influence aggregate demand.
- Fiscal policy is the use of government spending and taxation to influence the level of aggregate demand in the economy.
- Monetary policy is the use of interest rates, as well as the supply of money to the financial sector, with the aim of influencing the level of demand in the economy.

Demand-side policies

In Chapter 11, we will see how the government can use fiscal policy to change the level of spending in an economy. In Chapter 12, we will develop an understanding of the banking system and explain how changes in the base rate by central banks are transmitted through the banking system to the wider economy and affect consumption and investment spending.

Supply-side policies

Given that we have seen that aggregate supply can be vertical, or perfectly price inelastic, then aggregate supply defines the equilibrium level of GDP for the economy. In the long run, growth in GDP and lower inflation can only occur with an increase in aggregate supply. Therefore, sustainable economic growth, low inflation and even international competitiveness are crucially linked to developments in aggregate supply.

How aggregate supply can be managed by government and the implications of **supply-side policies** for business will be discussed in Chapter 14.

> Supply-side policies influence aggregate supply.

10.7 Business application: international competitiveness and the macroeconomy

Achieving higher rates of economic growth, producing more highly paid jobs and generating additional exports are not all about increasing aggregate demand within an economy. The make-up of industries can be equally important. Which industries and sectors are likely to offer opportunities for growth in the future; which will decline? In contrast to many of its European counterparts the UK has seen its manufacturing base decline towards 10 per cent of GDP. At the same time, services, especially those that are in finance, accounting and legal practice, have grown enormously. London and the South East economy of the UK are heavily dependent upon these sectors. Of course, when these sectors become embroiled in a credit crisis, then companies and jobs are lost. A natural question is to ask if the UK economy needs to be more balanced in terms of the industries that prosper within its economy. Government support for other strong employers and exporters may offer ways of providing sustainability and longevity in future GDP and employment growth rates.

Manufacturing competitiveness, GDP growth and inflation

Manufacturing can be a source of economic growth. Manufacturers of products often compete in global markets. By competing overseas, manufacturers can face increased competition from international rivals. In order to compete and survive, manufacturers can face enormous incentives to improve productivity and the quality of their products.

Investing in workers' skills and new capital technology can improve productivity. Investing in product innovation can improve the quality of the product to end-users. Spillover effects into the rest of the economy may occur if high-skilled workers move to alternative employers, taking their enhanced skills with them. Moreover, workers' experience of using advanced capital equipment may enable other firms to consider purchasing such equipment. Finally, if manufacturers make machines for other companies to use, product innovation may result in improved productivity for end-users. Therefore, manufacturing competitiveness may not only drive economic growth but, through productivity gains and cost improvements, it may also enhance aggregate supply and aid the management of inflation.

Manufacturing competitiveness and the balance of payments

The balance of payments records the trading position with the rest of the world. As manufacturing declines, consumers have to import goods, which previously they would have purchased from domestic producers. Relying on imports is not a major problem. The issue is, how do we finance the purchase of imports?

In the case of the UK, the rise of the service-based economy and service-based exports, such as insurance and banking, has helped to fund the importation of goods. But since manufacturing exports are worth around five times more than exported services, the UK will have to export more services than it would have to export goods. A significant problem is that services do not export easily. Leisure centres, restaurants, cinemas, legal and accounting services and even hairdressing are not easy to export. Box 10.4 offers an opposing view.

Manufacturing competitiveness and employment

Skills required for the manufacture of steel, cars, industrial equipment, domestic appliances, chemicals and jet fighter aircraft are fairly specific to the industry. If one of these manufacturing sectors declines, then the potential for structural unemployment is immense. Even if service sector employers were to consider locating in areas of high unemployment, the mismatch of skills between unemployed manufacturing workers and the needs of service sector providers is likely to be significant. Manufacturing competitiveness may, therefore, be important to the economy, if only to prevent costly structural change.

Box 10.4

The British economy's best-kept secret

Law seems to be defying wider economic trends: according to the latest official figures, turnover has grown by about 10 per cent in the past five years. Two of the world's top five firms are based in London, and last year alone the number of solicitors swelled by 3.5 per cent. Law is a thriving export industry, with foreign earnings accounting for about 25 per cent of the total.

Talk of rebalancing the economy away from harmful, ethereal financial services and back to honest manufacturing tends to overlook a large, thriving business sector that falls roughly between the two. Taken together, professional services (lawyers, accountants, architects and so on) and business services (anything from IT and call centres to security, training and catering) are worth 17 per cent of the economy. That compares with 11 per cent each for manufacturing and retailing, and 10 per cent for financial services. They generate huge foreign sales, too. In 2009 the Treasury estimated that professional services alone accounted for half of Britain's annual services exports. Britain was the clear European leader in this respect.

Lawyers, accountants, management consultants and other professional services are drawn to London partly for the same reasons financial services firms cluster there – the global ubiquity of English and a time zone midway between the rich old world and emerging Asia. Partly, they are attracted to those financial services outfits, which create business for them. Earlier this month Aon, an American insurance company, said it was moving its head office to London from Chicago. Its main reason was to be closer to its growing number of clients in Asia, but London's range of professional services was part of the attraction.

The less glamorous business services sector is a child of the 1980s. 'The Thatcher era got it going,' says Mark Fox, who runs the Business Services Association. The then prime minister's drive to contract out public-sector tasks to the private sector laid the foundations for firms taking over such services as school and hospital meals, buildings maintenance and even staff training. One leading outsource firm, Capita, still depends largely on the British public sector. But others have moved into new areas and international markets.

Serco, for example, runs private prisons in Britain as well as the Dubai metro and American military field hospitals. Balfour Beatty became known as a construction firm but now calls itself an infrastructure company, investing in transport systems and providing professional and support services in many markets including America, Hong Kong and the Middle East. G4S's activities range from delivering cash to banks to creating security systems for buildings and fire protection systems for America's space agency, NASA. Many of these firms benefit from long experience of public–private partnerships, which were pioneered in Britain (and often have a poor reputation there) but have spread to other countries. Professionals, versed in the complex contracts these partnerships often involve, follow in their wake. In Budapest, Kiev or Moscow you will come across London lawyers who have seen it all before.

Adapted from an article in *The Economist*, 28 January 2012.
© The Economist Newspaper Limited, London 2012.

Not all economists would agree with the points listed above. Some may think that the points made are valid, but that they overstate the case for manufacturing competitiveness. If manufacturing has declined, then there must be something inherently wrong about the location of manufacturing sectors in economies such as Italy or the UK. It could be that there are resources in South East Asia which are more appropriate for a manufacturing base – more abundant labour, better logistics networks, better financing options. It could be that European firms need to migrate to alternative parts of the value chain where they retain a competitive advantage. For example, Italians may have lost competitiveness in shoe manufacture, but they are still perhaps the best shoe designers. The critical success factors for the macroeconomy are adaptation, flexibility and migration to the next commercial opportunity.

Understanding policy

Regardless of how important manufacturing competitiveness is to the economy, it is clear that a case can be built for manufacturing having beneficial consequences for GDP, inflation, employment and the balance of payments or, more important, all of the macroeconomic objectives. But how will policy impact on manufacturing?

If manufacturing is a catalyst for economic growth through innovation and investment, low inflation and economic stability are essential for aiding manufacturers to invest. By keeping inflation low and stable, a government is endeavouring to create a stable environment within which firms feel the risks associated with investing are lower. With stable growth in GDP, the risk of an investment in new machinery being devalued by a recession is reduced.

In terms of aiding skill development, the government can invest heavily in higher education, channelling increasing numbers of students into undergraduate programmes, especially those linked to engineering and science. But this does not always alleviate skills shortages. For every university graduate, the economy loses one important, but less skilled, worker, such as a lorry driver, plumber, builder or mechanic.

Business policy: inflation targeting?

The European Central Bank and the Bank of England follow inflation-targeting policies, as do Australia, Brazil, Canada, Sweden and South Africa. In contrast, the US Federal Reserve has traditionally considered both inflation and GDP when setting interest rates. Given the importance of inflation targeting, especially within Europe, then it is useful to understand the implications for business of a policy environment characterized by inflation targeting.

What is inflation targeting?

The central bank publicizes a target goal for the inflation rate. It then steers monetary policy to try to hit the target inflation rate, raising rates to curb inflation and lowering rates to juice up growth and raise inflation. Targets differ across economies. In the UK, the inflation target is 2 per cent on average for CPI. For members of the eurozone, the inflation target is CPI less than or equal to 2 per cent.

Figure 10.14 illustrates the level of CPI from 1991 through to 2011 in the eurozone. European monetary union (EMU) began in 1999 and the inflation target of 2 per cent CPI was set. It is clear from the chart that, from 1999, CPI was allowed to rise to 2 per cent and then moved

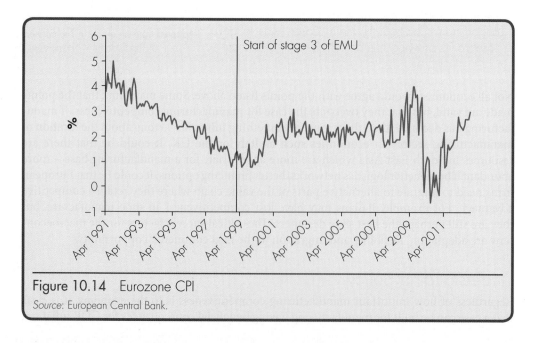

Figure 10.14 Eurozone CPI

Source: European Central Bank.

close to the 2 per cent level. This was very different from the pattern in the 1990s, when inflation targeting was less important.

Of course, it should also be noted that from 2008 onwards CPI moved markedly away from target. Initially, the oil, commodity and food price spikes of early 2008 pushed up inflation; and then, following the credit crisis, inflation fell very quickly during the recession. Therefore, despite the ECB's best efforts to target 2 per cent inflation, in times of extreme economic events targeting can be very difficult.

Why conduct inflation targeting?

The central issue is macroeconomic stability. This is a more general concern than simply low inflation fanaticism. Macroeconomic stability can encompass stability in prices and in economic activity, namely GDP. Under inflation targeting, stability in pricing is seen as essential for stability in economic activity. In fact, as we develop your understanding of macroeconomic policies, we will show you, in Chapter 13, that targeting inflation can be the same as targeting GDP. So, since it is easy to measure inflation quickly and accurately, but difficult to measure GDP quickly and accurately, then following an inflation target offers a reasonably sound and pragmatic policy for managing the economy. But why should inflation targeting lead to stability in GDP? The answer to this question requires an understanding of how macroeconomic events trigger behavioural changes in microeconomic actors, such as firms and consumers.

Inflation targeting: firms and consumers

The implications for business can be subtle but important. Within a regime of inflation targeting, there is little variation in the inflation rate. This improves price transparency. With stable inflation, it is easier for consumers to recognize changes in the relative prices of competing products and not confuse them for changes in all prices, i.e. inflation. Improved price transparency helps to drive competition. Stronger competition can drive down prices, promote innovation and generate economic growth.

Stable inflation also leads to small and infrequent changes in interest rates. The head of the Bank of England has suggested that his role is to be as boring as possible (indicating that, if inflation is kept under control, there will be little need for large or even unexpected changes in interest rates to bring about stability in inflation). Such boring stability will shape the decisions and behaviour of consumers and firms. Wage bargaining and investment decisions will be carried out within a context of reasonable certainty of future price levels. With reduced risk and improved decision making, a greater willingness to spend and invest should occur. As such, stability in economic activity is assured by a background of stable prices. Therefore, the implications for business are that tomorrow should be very much like today. In effect, no surprises and therefore boring. But boring has its virtues. When investing a huge sum of money in a project, which may reach fruition in three to five years' time, a lack of surprises can be very comforting. Macroeconomic stability now can lead to greater and more valuable productive capacity in the future.

Expectations

A target rate of inflation is very important for setting inflationary expectations among consumers, workers and firms. If the central bank maintains inflation at the target level, then it will be seen as credible by workers, consumers and firms. This credibility is enormously valuable when managing the economy. The individuals who set prices and ultimately determine inflation within an economy are consumers, workers and firms, as they represent the demand and supply side of product and labour markets. If workers expect inflation to rise to 5 per cent, then they will ask for 5 per cent pay rises and, if firms agree, then they will raise prices by 5 per cent. Inflation is then 5 per cent. But if the central bank is good at managing inflation, then wage and price increases should be in line with the inflation target for the entire economy. The central bank has to do very little to achieve its inflation target. In fact, if the bank is required to change rates, then it may only have to change rates by a small amount to achieve its desired goal. Monetary policy is boring and economic life is simple when inflationary expectations are in line with the central bank's inflation target. This again helps to bring stability to firms' macroeconomic environment.

Deflation

An inflation target also has merit if there is a concern over deflation. A concern over falling prices might seem a little bizarre, but it can be extremely troublesome for an economy. At one level consumers may refrain from expenditure on large ticket items if they think prices will fall in the future. But this cut in demand will lead to more price cuts and yet more waiting by consumers. A deflationary spiral can be disastrous for prices and GDP.

Deflation can also work against interest rate policies. When prices fall, profits and wages are also likely to fall. Reductions in workers' incomes and firms' earnings reduce their ability to service debt. Therefore, even if the central bank cuts interest rates, the real affordability of debt increases. Inflation targeting may help to avoid this problem by setting an expectation that the central bank is committed to inflation. If firms and workers believe this, then the horrors of deflation may be avoided. It should therefore be of no surprise that the US Federal Reserve has begun to consider the use of inflation targeting.

Box 10.5

In historic shift, Fed sets inflation target

The US Federal Reserve took the historic step on Wednesday of setting an inflation target, of 2 per cent, a victory for Chairman Ben Bernanke that brings the Fed in line with many of the world's other major central banks.

The inflation target is at the high end of what was traditionally seen as an informal target range of roughly 1.7 per cent to 2 per cent and caps Bernanke's crusade to improve communications at what for years had been purposefully opaque and secretive deliberations at the Fed.

The target aims to make the central bank more effective at controlling growth. 'Communicating this

inflation goal clearly to the public helps keep longer-term inflation expectations firmly anchored, thereby fostering price stability and moderate long-term interest rates and enhancing the committee's ability to promote maximum employment in the face of significant economic disturbances,' the Fed said.

The statement was released simultaneously with another first for the Fed: published charts of individual policy makers' projections for the appropriate path of the benchmark federal funds rate.

Adapted from an article by Jonathan Spicer on Reuters, 26 January 2012.

Problems with inflation targeting

Inflation targeting is not always capable of accommodating problems associated with cost push inflation. Through 2007 and into 2008, oil, commodities and food prices increased enormously. The cost of oil doubled. A cost push inflation reduces aggregate supply. This leads to falling GDP and higher inflation – a so-called inflationary contraction; recall Chapter 9 and Figure 9.10. In order to return inflation to target, the central bank would need to increase interest rates and cause GDP to fall even further. Combating cost push inflation would lead to an even greater recession.

A solution to this problem is to have some flexibility in the inflation target. In the UK, the target is for CPI to be 2 per cent *on average*. If cost push inflation is only temporary, then a rise in inflation to 4 per cent is undesirable, but can be accommodated on the presumption that in the near future inflation will move back down to trend.

The implications for business are important. Interest rates, wages, inflation and international competitiveness could all be more variable in the short run, while GDP should be more stable. On one level this policy is only beneficial to business if stability in GDP is of greater value than stability in inflation and interest rates. On another level, the acceptance of economic surprises and non-boring economic policy may represent a more realistic view of the macroeconomic environment within which a company operates.

Business data application: accuracy of economic data measurements

In this chapter we have highlighted a number of important macroeconomic variables, explained why they are important and how they are measured. In Chapter 9 we also indicated where useful macroeconomic data can be found. An important question to ask is how accurate the measurement of key macroeconomic data is, because if business decisions are being made on the basis on macroeconomic data, then more accurate data are preferable.

Data providers have to trade timeliness against accuracy. Economic decision makers and businesses like to have estimates of variables, such as GDP and inflation, as early as possible, in order to inform decision making. But early estimates are not always accurate because they rely on a limited amount of data. However, over time, as more data become available, the initial estimate of GDP can be revised and become more accurate.

Many government statistical agencies are able to provide a first estimate of quarterly GDP within one month of the end of the quarter. At this stage, the statisticians will be using early survey returns from companies which have been asked to provide data on sales, production and stock levels, among other things. As more companies fill out and send in their data, then a second estimate (first revision) can be made within two months of the end of the quarter; and the third estimate (second revision) can be made within three months of the end of the quarter. However, even at that stage the statisticians have access to less than 50 per cent of the entire data which will eventually become available and enable them to make the most accurate

estimate of GDP. All the relevant data may not become available until 12 months after the end of the quarter and even then the statisticians may revisit their estimates and use new numerical techniques, which will alter early estimates.

The important point is that macroeconomic data are nearly always subject to revision and this fact adds an additional layer of complexity to the problem of trying to provide an interpretation of the macroeconomic environment for businesses. While this complexity exists, there does seem to be a pattern to the revisions. In the case of GDP in the UK, the revisions are nearly always positive. Early estimates of GDP appear to underestimate. In Figure 10.15 the most recent estimate of GDP tends to be at the top of the range of past estimates. This finding would suggest that early estimates of GDP tend to

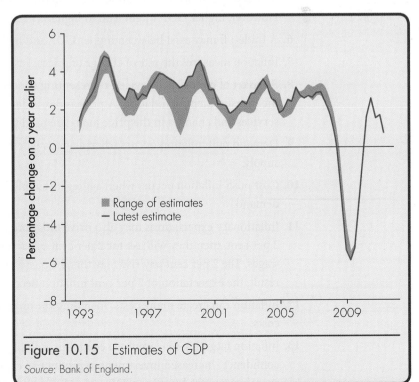

Figure 10.15 Estimates of GDP
Source: Bank of England.

underestimate. Such patterns may not always persist in the future and in some years the early forecasts could be accurate. What a business person needs to remember is that estimates are just that, an attempt to provide an informed guess as to the size of important macroeconomic variables. That means that good business managers have to question, judge and critically evaluate the accuracy of the data. Does the estimate appear out of line with previous measures of GDP? Is an estimate of high or low GDP out of line with data on other parts of the economy? For example, if exports are growing fast and GDP is said to be slowing, then why is there a difference? Sometimes the answers to these questions can be found within articles published in the business sections of newspapers. As a business manager you have to know which macroeconomic issues should concern you and where you can gain data and intelligent consideration and review of that data, in order to plan your business operations.

Summary

1. GDP is a measure of economic output.

2. The circular flow of income indicates that GDP can be measured using the income, expenditure and value-added approaches.

3. To avoid double counting, the value-added approach measures the incremental amount of value added at each stage of the production process.

4. GDP is compared across economies using GDP per capita. However, such a measure may hide an unequal distribution of income among the population.

5. Higher and stable levels of GDP are desirable policy objectives. Economic stability enables firms to invest in new capital equipment, leading to improved productivity and economic growth. Higher levels of GDP can, through tax receipts, enable governments to invest in important economic infrastructure, such as education and transport. However, higher GDP might lead to higher inflation.

6. A trade-off may exist between higher GDP and higher inflation.

7. Inflation measures the rate of change of prices. Faster price rises result in higher inflation.

8. A basket of goods and services, representing commonly purchased products, is used in the measurement of inflation. A price index is developed from the basket of goods and services and changes in the price index are used to measure inflation.

9. Demand pull inflation occurs when aggregate demand increases relative to aggregate supply.

10. Cost push inflation occurs when aggregate supply increases relative to aggregate demand.

11. Inflationary expectations may also drive inflation. If workers expect prices to rise by 2 per cent, then they will ask for 2 per cent pay rises in order to maintain constant real wages. The 2 per cent pay rise may then be passed on in higher product prices and, as a result, the expectation of 2 per cent inflation becomes reality.

12. Inflation can create many costs, including the erosion of debt and increasing menu costs.

13. Inflation targeting may improve economic stability and business investment confidence. Increased investment in productive capital may improve the economy's aggregate supply, boosting GDP and reducing inflation.

14. Targeting increases in aggregate supply avoids the trade-off associated with aggregate demand, with higher demand increasing GDP and inflation.

15. Unemployment is categorized as frictional, structural, cyclical or classical.

16. The Phillips curve suggests a negative trade-off between inflation and unemployment. However, this relationship may only exist in the short run. When real wages fully adjust to inflationary changes, then unemployment will not vary with the inflation rate.

17. Following the shift towards improving aggregate supply, government policy has moved away from unemployment and more towards labour productivity.

18. A balance of payments deficit is problematic if it is persistent and reflects a country's lack of international competitiveness.

19. Early estimates of important macroeconomic variables are nearly always subject to revision. More data become available over time and estimates of GDP, inflation etc are revised.

Learning checklist

You should now be able to:

- Explain how to measure GDP using the income, expenditure and value-added approaches
- Explain how inflation is measured using a basket of goods and services and index numbers
- Explain the main drivers of inflation
- Discuss the main costs of inflation and reasons behind inflation targeting
- List and explain the main types of unemployment
- Explain the potential trade-off between inflation and unemployment
- Explain whether a balance of payments deficit is a problem
- Explain the relevance of economic policy considerations for business

Questions   connect

1. Why is growth in GDP important?
2. Evaluate whether higher GDP per capita is always desirable.
3. Identify and explain the three main methods for measuring GDP.
4. What is inflation and how is it measured in your economy?
5. Explain why governments and central banks avoid high inflation and deflation.
6. What are the three main drivers of inflation?
7. As China continues to grow, demand for raw materials, food, shipping and energy will all increase. Will China's growth generate cost push or demand pull inflation in your economy?
8. Assess the key trends within unemployment data for your economy over the last five years. Use the economic unemployment categories to identify the patterns within your unemployment data.

EASY

9. During the credit crisis and global recession many bankers lost their jobs. Is this demand-deficient or structural unemployment?

10. Explain the relationship suggested by the Phillips curve. How might governments exploit this relationship?

11. If workers automatically adjusted their wage demands to keep their real wages constant, would the Phillips curve relationship still hold?

12. In Table 10.1 Qatar has the highest GDP per capita in the world. Is Qatar a good place to start a business?

13. The inflation forecast for next year is 3 per cent. Workers are asking for a 5 per cent pay rise. Should the firm agree to the 5 per cent rise?

14. Unemployment represents a pool of underutilized resource. Should firms relocate to areas of high unemployment?

15. Should a firm be concerned about an economy with a chronic balance of payments problem?

Exercises

1. True or false?

(a) GDP per capita is a measure of economic prosperity.

(b) High growth rates in GDP per capita can be accompanied by high inflation.

(c) Nominal wages are adjusted for inflation, real wages are not.

(d) A mismatch of skills generally results from cyclical unemployment.

(e) The Phillips curve suggests a negative relationship between inflation and GDP.

(f) A trade deficit is acceptable in the short run, but is troublesome in the long run.

2. Plot the data in Table 10.3, placing inflation on the Y axis and unemployment on the X axis.

Table 10.3 Inflation and unemployment rates

	Inflation rate	Unemployment rate
1997	2.0	8.8
1998	2.6	7.8
1999	2.5	7.1
2000	1.8	5.3
2001	1.6	4.5
2002	1.3	4.2
2003	0.8	3.7
2004	1.2	3.3
2005	1.3	3.2
2006	1.4	3.2
2007	1.3	2.9

(a)   Is there evidence in support of a Phillips curve relationship?

(b)   What is the long-run Phillips curve?

(c)   At what level of unemployment would you propose drawing the long-run Phillips curve?

3. Consider the data and figures in section 10.2. These include Table 10.1 and Figures 10.3, 10.4 and 10.5. Evaluate whether higher GDP per capita is good or bad for society.

Expenditure and fiscal policy

11

Chapter contents

Economic stability and demand side policies at a glance   275
11.1 Business problem: who's spending and where?   275
11.2 Consumption, investment expenditure and the business cycle   277
11.3 Fiscal policy   281
11.4 Government's approach to managing fiscal policy   283
11.5 Foreign trade and aggregate demand   288
11.6 Business application: debt funding and crowding out   290
11.7 Business application: taxation or government spending?   292
11.8 Business data application: understanding the fiscal position and the implications for business   293
Summary   295
Learning checklist   296
Questions   296
Exercises   297

Learning outcomes

By the end of this chapter you should understand:

Economic theory

LO1 The Keynesian Cross approach to modelling equilibrium output

LO2 The fiscal multiplier

LO3 The balanced budget

LO4 Problems associated with using fiscal policy

Business application

LO5 Debt funding and crowding out

LO6 Taxation or government spending?

LO7 Reducing government deficits and the implications for business

At a glance Economic stability and demand side policies

The issue

Both the current level of economic activity and future growth in economic activity are important for business. The government has a number of policies that it can use to control current economic activity. Understanding how these policies influence the economy and business is of enormous importance to firms operating both within their domestic markets and overseas.

The understanding

Economic activity rises and falls with the business cycle. During recessions the government may try to raise economic activity, while during economic booms the government may try to reduce economic activity. Acting through the demand side of the economy, the government can influence economic activity through fiscal and monetary policy. These will be discussed at length but, essentially, by altering interest rates, government spending or taxation, the government can try to influence the level of demand in an economy – for example, raising demand during a recession and lowering demand during a boom.

The usefulness

As the government alters domestic macroeconomic policy, it is essential for business to understand how the economy will react. Some policies, if implemented incorrectly, can have a destabilizing effect on the economy. For planning purposes, it may be important to understand what type of policies will be deployed in the future. In recent times, interest rates have been very important policy tools. But, as interest rates fall to historic lows, the scope for further cuts becomes limited. Therefore, what might replace interest rate policy and how will firms need to react?

(11.1) Business problem: who's spending and where?

Rising GDP should be associated with increased expenditure by consumers. More jobs and higher wages facilitate consumption. In turn, greater consumption drives sales and fuels profits. If only it were so simple. We know from the circular flow of income in Chapter 9 that consumption is only one element of total expenditure. In addition, we have spending by firms, which is classified as investment. We have government spending on education, health and public infrastructure; and we have international trade, where exports represent expenditure in the economy and imports represent expenditure in overseas economies. In Box 11.1, each of these components is highlighted for China; exports are still key, government spending has been important and domestic consumption and private investment still need developing.

Different firms and industrial sectors will have differing exposure to consumers, investment, government spending and international trade. Therefore, the manner in which the economy grows has varying implications across industrial sectors. For example, retailers will benefit from an increase in consumption expenditure. In contrast, construction companies are more likely to benefit directly from growth in GDP, which is fuelled by firms investing in offices and factories, as well as government wishing to build hospitals and schools. Companies and economies, such as China, are heavily reliant on external demand. This means such economies are more likely to be affected by changes in consumption across other countries, such as Europe following its struggles with the debt crisis.

While the drivers of aggregate demand appear to be multifaceted, they are still related. Returning to the circular flow of income: total expenditure occurs with firms, which

Box 11.1

Exports still driving growth

Exports will remain a major force in helping China maintain economic growth by creating jobs and stimulating domestic consumption, despite decelerating growth in overseas shipments and a gloomy outlook, said the Ministry of Commerce.

Zhang Ji, director-general of the ministry's Department of Mechanical, Electronic and High-tech Industry, said that the nation would aim for 'continuity and stability' in its policies for the processing trades, which remain a significant part of China's foreign trade. Processing trade involves taking imported parts, components and packaging materials, assembling them and re-exporting the finished product.

Although export growth declined in the second half of 2011 and prospects for the coming months are not positive, the 'significance of China's foreign trade (in advancing the economy) will be prominent, probably in the next two to three decades or even longer,' said Zhang.

The International Monetary Fund said in a report on Monday that China's economic expansion could slow to 8.25 per cent this year, from the previously projected 9 per cent, should Europe's debt crisis worsen. Exports would be a significant drag on growth in the coming two years, the fund said.

'We all know that investment, exports and domestic consumption are the three pillars of China's economic expansion, but what if we merely depend on investment and domestic consumption? Do you think we could still bet on another round of large-scale government investment after the 4-trillion-yuan ($634 billion) stimulus package was wrapped up?' Zhang said.

'Foreign trade could for a long time still guarantee jobs and growing individual disposable income, which would translate into domestic consumption.'

Adapted from an article by Ding Qingfen and Li Jiabao in China Daily, *8 February 2012.*

then pay wages to workers. These wages can then fuel consumption, or leak from the circular flow of income, in savings (to meet investments), in taxes (to meet government spending) and in imports. Therefore a rise in investment can lead to a future rise in employment, wages and, eventually, consumption. Or an increase in investment expenditure can facilitate more investment, or more government spending. It is clear that there is a complexity of intertwined relationships at the macroeconomic level, which the firm needs to appreciate.

It is essential that business people are able to disentangle the macroeconomic environment in order to understand the business opportunities and commercial threats that it poses. When will demand increase in the economy and will it impact your sector? Moreover, what factors will help to drive the various categories of expenditure? Box 11.1 alludes to the role of exports and external consumer confidence in determining economic activity. But then it can be asked, what determines consumer confidence? Employment prospects and sales might be two key drivers, which are clearly linked back to the level of economic activity, or the ever-revolving circular flow of income.

What governments have come to recognize is that stability is preferable. Volatility leads to uncertainty, and uncertainty reduces both consumer and business confidence. An increased probability of losing your job in the next 12 months will reduce your willingness to borrow and/or spend. Equally, governments have come to recognize that they can make a meaningful attempt at managing the economy. In the case of China, this has involved a massive cash injection of spending into the economy by the government. Similar policies were pursued in Europe and the USA. Business people need to be aware of how such policies feed into the circular flow of income and activate changes in consumption, investment, government spending and net exports. Equally business people need to understand what happens to an economy when governments can no longer afford to borrow and spend. This chapter seeks to achieve this by developing your understanding of fiscal policy.

11.2 Consumption, investment expenditure and the business cycle

In Chapter 9, we introduced the aggregate demand and aggregate supply approach to understanding the **equilibrium** output of an economy, i.e. where **planned aggregate expenditure** is equal to the actual output of firms, and the price level. The approach enables a clear and insightful link to be made between microeconomic and macro-economic theory.

It is unfortunate that the aggregate demand and aggregate supply approach ensures that the economy is always in equilibrium. As such, there can be no unemployment. All workers that desire a job will be employed.

This is not ideal given that we observe unemployment most of the time. We can adapt the aggregate demand and supply framework, but a useful approach is to instead introduce the Keynesian Cross as a model of equilibrium output. Under the Keynesian Cross approach, there is an assumption that prices are constant; as a result, inflation is not considered within the approach. Put simply, what firms produce is exactly equal to what consumers are planning to buy. Figure 11.1 illustrates this idea with the 45° line.

We use the 45° line because it cuts the angle 90° in half. Therefore, when we draw across a planned level of expenditure equal to 100, the actual level of output will also be 100. As a consequence, the 45° line shows all the possible equilibrium points. However, the essential question is, what will be the level of planned expenditure?

> Equilibrium is generally defined as the situation where planned aggregate expenditure is equal to the actual output of firms.
>
> Planned aggregate expenditure is the total amount of spending on goods and services within the economy that is planned by purchasers.

Planned expenditure

For simplicity, we will assume that we have a **closed economy** with no government sector. The only groups spending within the economy under such a scenario are consumers and firms (we have no government and no exports). Planned expenditure of aggregate demand can be expressed as:

$$PE = AD = C + I$$

where PE = planned expenditure, AD = aggregate demand, C = consumption and I = investment.

> A closed economy does not trade with the rest of the world. An open economy does trade with the rest of the world.
>
> Autonomous consumption does not change if income changes.
>
> Autonomous expenditure is not influenced by the level of income.

Consumption

The level of consumption undertaken by private individuals is assumed by economists to be related to two factors: (i) a basic need to consume, and (ii) the level of personal income. The basic need to consume is the level of consumption undertaken by an individual when their income is zero. It is the basic level of consumption that is required in order to survive. It is more often referred to as **autonomous consumption**, which is linked to **autonomous expenditure**.

As income increases, individuals will begin to consume more goods and services. But they may not spend all of their income on consumption. A small portion could be saved: 100 of income could result in 80 of consumption and 20 of saving. Economists link income with consumption and saving using the concepts of **marginal propensity to consume (MPC)** and **marginal propensity to save (MPS)**.

The MPC is a measure of how much additional consumption will result from an increase in income. The MPC lies between zero and one. So, if the MPC = 0.8, then for every extra £100 of income, consumers will raise consumption by £80.

Similarly, the MPS is a measure of how much additional saving will result from an increase in income. Again, the MPS lies between zero and one. So, if the MPS = 0.2, then an increase in income of £100 will lead to an extra £20 of savings.

> The marginal propensity to consume (MPC) is the extra consumption generated by one unit of extra income.
>
> The marginal propensity to save (MPS) is the extra saving generated by one unit of extra income.

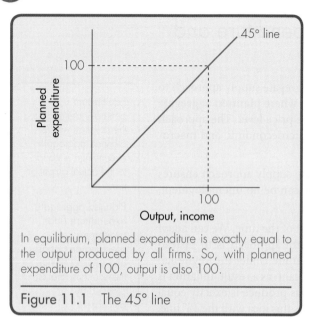

In equilibrium, planned expenditure is exactly equal to the output produced by all firms. So, with planned expenditure of 100, output is also 100.

Figure 11.1 The 45° line

Given that individuals can either consume or save, the MPC + MPS = 1.

So, if we assume that autonomous consumption is 7 and the MPC is 0.8, then we can say that:

$$C = 7 + 0.8Y$$

where Y = personal disposable income and C = consumption.

This is nothing more than the equation of a straight line, and it is drawn in Figure 11.2. Consumption has two components. A fixed amount, in this case 7, plus an amount that is determined by income, in this case $0.8 \times 100 = 80$.

When income is zero, consumption is 7. This is the intercept. The slope of the consumption line is equal to the MPC and in this case is 0.8. So, if income is 100, we can now say that consumption will be $7 + 0.8 \times 100 = 7 + 80 = 87$.

Before we move on to look at investment, it is also useful to think about what determines the marginal propensity to consume (and the marginal propensity to save). A key driver of the marginal propensity to consume is consumer confidence. As consumers become more confident about the stability of their income, they are more likely to spend. If the macroeconomic environment becomes more uncertain, or heads into a recession, then consumers may fear job losses and a reduction in income. Their confidence falls and their propensity to spend may decrease. Box 11.2 highlights how global businesses are being hit by a lack of consumer confidence in Europe and elsewhere.

Box 11.2

Vodafone hit by weak southern Europe

Vodafone, the world's largest mobile phone operator, missed quarterly revenue forecasts on Thursday as increasingly tough trading in Spain and Italy overshadowed solid performances in emerging markets and northern Europe.

The British-based group is the latest in a procession of companies to warn that austerity-hit consumers and businesses in southern Europe were cutting back spending. Spirits group Diageo highlighted weakness in parts of Europe on Thursday, while car brand Audi said it was relying on the United States and China for growth as Europe grapples with a sovereign debt crisis.

Vodafone, which kept its outlook for the year unchanged, said group organic service revenue from the provision of ongoing services to customers was up 0.9 per cent, compared with an analyst forecast of 1.1 per cent. The group, the first major European telco operator to report results, said revenues were hit by weaker consumer confidence in Spain, Italy and also Britain, while corporate clients had cut back on travelling in the last three months of the year.

Overall, however, the group benefited from strong growth in India and Turkey and continued demand by customers for Internet data services, prompting analysts to say that Vodafone would perform ahead of its peers.

European organic service revenue was slightly worse than expected, down 1.7 per cent as the financial squeeze on consumers in Italy, Spain and Greece pulled down better performances in the two big northern markets of Britain and Germany.

The Spanish market, which has previously been characterized by high prices for consumers, was slightly improved but still down 8.8 per cent. Italy, however, deteriorated further to be down 4.9 per cent compared with a fall of 3 per cent in the previous quarter. The company did not give a specific trading figure for Greece, but it has also been hit hard by the pressures on consumer spending.

Adapted from an article by Kate Holton on Reuters, 9 February 2012.

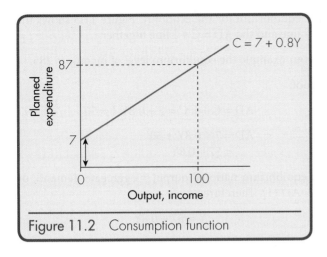

Figure 11.2 Consumption function

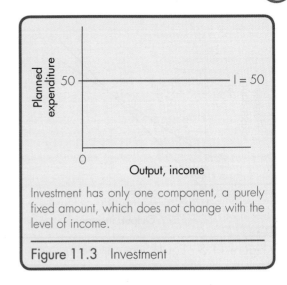

Investment has only one component, a purely fixed amount, which does not change with the level of income.

Figure 11.3 Investment

Investment

Investment is the demand for capital products by firms, plus changes to firms' inventories, or stocks.

We have seen how income determines the consumption decisions of private individuals. But what drives investment decisions? The answer to this question is highly debatable but, in general, and in simple terms, economists begin by assuming that investment decisions are based on instinct. How managers feel about the future is a major factor when deciding to invest money. If managers think the future looks good, they will be likely to invest. But if the future looks bad, they will cut back on investments. As such, investment decisions taken now are not influenced by the current level of income. For this reason, investment is also seen as autonomous. This means that, just like the 7 of consumption undertaken by consumers, firms set a base level of investment, say 50, but then there is no additional investment relating to increased income. The implications of this are shown in Figure 11.3, where the investment is set at 50 and remains constant at 50 for every level of income.

We can now add the consumption and investment together to arrive at aggregate demand or planned expenditure. This has been done in Figure 11.4, which, while looking complicated, is little more than an extension of Figure 11.2. From Figure 11.2 we have the consumption line, with 7 of consumption at zero levels of income and overall consumption of 87 when income is 100. We have then simply added in an additional 50 for investment. Aggregate demand, or planned expenditure, is now 7 + 50 = 57 at zero income, and overall planned expenditure, which is equal to consumption plus investment, 87 + 50 = 137.

We started with the 45° line and said that equilibrium occurs where planned expenditure equals actual output. From Figure 11.4 we now have an understanding of expenditure in an economy. We therefore only need to introduce the 45° line into Figure 11.4 and we can find

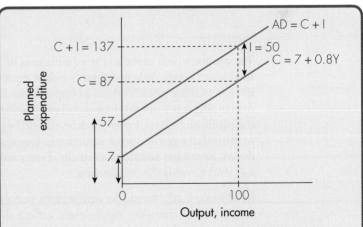

Adding investment to consumption simply increases autonomous expenditure by the increased amount of investment. In this case, investment = 50, so at all levels of income spending has increased by 50. At zero income, the level of consumption is 7; adding in investment of 50 simply means that planned expenditure = 57 when investment equals zero. Since autonomous expenditure does not change with the level of output, then, even when income = 100, the difference between consumption and investment will still be 50.

Figure 11.4 Aggregate demand: consumption plus investment

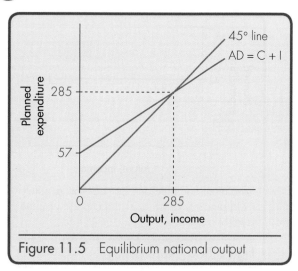

Figure 11.5 Equilibrium national output

the equilibrium for the economy. Figure 11.5 shows the 45° line and the AD = C + I line together.

In our example the equilibrium level of income is 285.

Proof:

$$AD = C + I, C = 7 + 0.8Y, I = 50$$

$$AD = 7 + 0.8Y + 50$$
$$= 57 + 0.8Y$$

In equilibrium national output = aggregate demand, or Y = AD (1). Therefore:

$$Y = 57 + 0.8Y$$

Rearranging:

$$0.2Y = 57$$

$$Y = 57/0.2 = 285$$

(Question 12 at the end of the chapter contains an additional example if you would like to test your ability to derive the equilibrium.)

Where the AD line crosses the 45° line must be the equilibrium, because this is where planned expenditure equals actual output.

At all output levels below 285, aggregate demand will be greater than national output. For example, if national output was only 200, then firms would not be producing enough output to meet the level of aggregate demand in the economy. Firms will have to meet the excess demand by using stocks held over from previous periods. Similarly, at all output levels above 285, national output will be greater than aggregate demand. For example, if national output is 300, aggregate demand will be less than the national output. As a result, firms will be left with excess stock.

Adjustment to the equilibrium

The economy will move to the equilibrium of 285 units by firms responding to changes in their stock levels. When output is below equilibrium, firms' stocks will reduce. Firms will interpret falling stock levels as an opportunity to expand production, because consumers are demanding more output than is currently being produced. In contrast, when output is above the equilibrium level, firms' stock levels will begin to increase. Rising stock levels will suggest to firms that current output is too high. Consumers are not demanding all that is being produced, hence the additions to stocks. Firms will, therefore, reduce output and the economy will shift towards the equilibrium.

In summary, adjustment to equilibrium occurs through firms reacting to changes in stock levels, where changing stock levels reflect differences between planned expenditure by consumers and actual output by firms.

> The multiplier measures the change in output following a change in autonomous expenditure (the essential or basic amount of consumption plus investment).

The multiplier

Here is a simple idea. What would happen if firms decided that the economic outlook was favourable? We might expect them to increase their levels of investment from 50 to 100. But by how much would output increase? An extra 50? The answer rests on a very important insight known as the **multiplier**.

If the multiplier is 3, an increase in investment of 50 will lead to an increase in output of 3 × 50 = 150. But what determines the size of the multiplier?

The multiplier is directly related to the marginal propensity to save. In our example, the MPS = 0.2. Consider the following. Firms buy more computers and thereby increase investment by 50. The computer manufacturers receive the 50 and for the extra output pass this on in increased wages to their workers. The workers will use this to increase consumption by 0.8 × 50 = 40 and save 10 = (0.2 × 50). So far, expenditure has now increased by the initial 50 increase in investment plus the 40 in consumption by the workers. If the computer workers spent the extra 40 at supermarkets, then income of supermarket workers increases by 40. They will spend 0.8 × 40 = 32 on consumption and save 8.

We can keep going, but even at this stage we can see that an increase of 50 in investment has led to an increase in consumption of 40 and then another 32. So, overall, the change in investment of 50 has created 50 + 40 + 32 = 122 change in expenditure and therefore national output.

This is entirely linked to the circular flow of income introduced in Chapter 9. The 50 increase in investment is an injection into the circular flow. It moves round the cycle, 10 leaks out in savings and then 40 goes around again as consumption; 8 then leaks out in savings and then 32 goes around again. Indeed, if we did keep going we would find that the initial increase of 50 would create a total change in national output of 250, or 5 × 50. Why? Because the multiplier is calculated thus:

$$\text{Multiplier} = 1/\text{MPS} = 1/(1 - \text{MPC})$$

So, if the MPS = 0.2, the multiplier = 1/0.2 = 5. So, the size of the multiplier is entirely dependent upon the MPS. The higher the MPS, the faster the initial injection leaks out of the circular flow, and so less is left to go around again.

For example, if the MPS was 0.5, then 50 would go around the circular flow and 25 would leak out as savings, with only 25 going around again as consumption. Then 12.5 would leak out, leaving only 12.5 to go around again. In total, because the multiplier is now only 1/0.5 = 2, the initial injection of 50 from investment would only result in output changing by 100.

 Fiscal policy

What is so exciting about the multiplier? For the economist, the multiplier means that small changes in autonomous expenditure can generate big changes in national income. In order to see the importance of this insight, we need to introduce the government sector.

If the government wishes to control the economy, such as moving it from a position of recession, then it only has to change autonomous expenditure by a small amount in order to generate a very large change in overall economic activity.

How might it do this? Asking firms to invest more is unlikely to be effective; firms invest because they want to, not because governments ask them to. But what about government spending? Could the government pump additional expenditure into the economy through its own projects such as health and education? We will answer this by examining **fiscal policy**.

> Fiscal policy is the government's decisions regarding taxation and spending.

We will shortly see that fiscal policy can be used to control the economy, but the implementation of effective fiscal policy may be problematic.

Government, aggregate demand and equilibrium income

In the previous section we saw how planned expenditure, or aggregate demand, is equal to consumption plus investment, AD = C + I. In introducing the government, we are

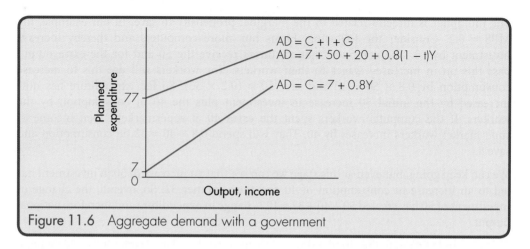

Figure 11.6 Aggregate demand with a government

creating a third source of spending within the economy. Aggregate demand is now calculated thus: AD = C + I + G, where G = government spending. Just like investment, government spending is also autonomous. It does not vary with the level of income. Governments take political spending decisions, for example how much should be spent on education and how much on roads. In the main, the level of income does not determine government spending.

In terms of our diagrammatic approach, we simply add government spending into the analysis in much the same way as we dealt with investment. Government spending as an autonomous expenditure simply raises the aggregate demand line by the amount of government spending. In Figure 11.6, we have assumed that G = 20. With no government sector, as in Figure 11.4, we saw that, when income was zero, spending equalled 57, which consisted of autonomous consumption equal to 7 and investment equal to 50. We can now add government spending equal to 20. So, aggregate demand when income equals zero is now 77.

However, we also need to address the impact of taxation. In Figure 11.4, without tax we simply argued that consumption C = 7 + 0.8Y. But if individuals are taxed, we need to reduce their income, Y, by the amount of the tax. If the tax rate = t, then after-tax income equals $(1 - t)Y$. It is this after-tax income which individuals then use for consumption, or saving. So, if the MPC = 0.8, then consumers spend 0.8 of their after-tax income. Therefore, taking account of tax we can now say that consumption is:

$$C = 7 + 0.8 (1 - t)Y$$

and not:

$$C = 7 + 0.8Y$$

The MPC determines how steep the AD line is, because it determines the link between growth in income and growth in consumption. A higher MPC will result in a steeper AD line. Tax effectively reduces the strength of the link between consumption and income, because an increase in income will be taxed before individuals can use it to increase consumption. Therefore, tax makes the AD line flatter.

Taking tax and government spending together, we can now see that the AD line with a government sector is higher because of government spending but flatter because of taxation.

What does this really tell us? The importance is in the consumption line being flatter. This means that, when taxes are applied, an increase in income has a lower impact on consumption. This is because we have opened up another avenue for leakages. By introducing the government sector, income can leak out via savings and taxes. This is significant because we have seen that the multiplier was determined by the rate of leakages and, indeed, the multiplier is now:

$$\text{Multiplier} = 1/(MPS + MPT)$$

where MPS = marginal propensity to save, and MPT = marginal propensity to tax.

So, if MPS = 0.2 and the MPT = 0.22 = the UK's basic tax rate, then the multiplier = $1/(0.2 + 0.22) = 2.38$.

When we had no government sector savings the multiplier was equal to:

$$1/MPS = 1/0.2 = 5$$

Note that introducing the government has decreased the size of the multiplier.

The balanced budget multiplier

The **balanced budget multiplier** states that an increase in government spending, plus an *equal* increase in taxes, leads to higher equilibrium output. Reducing the size of the multiplier could mean that the government might actually make itself ineffectual. For example, the government could inject 100 into the economy and then take out 100 in higher taxes. Would the multiplier then be zero? Amazingly, the answer to this question is no.

> The balanced budget multiplier states that an increase in government spending, plus an *equal* increase in taxes, leads to higher equilibrium output.

Sounds fantastic. You can put £100 in everyone's pocket, then take it out again and make everyone richer! How does this actually work? The answer requires a close examination of aggregate demand, AD = C + I + G. An increase of 100 in government spending clearly increases AD by 100. However, the effect of increasing taxes by 100 does not reduce AD by 100. This is because of the marginal propensity to consume, MPC. As the MPC is only 0.8, an increase in taxes by 100 causes income to fall by 100; the change in consumption is therefore only $0.8 \times 100 = 80$. The net effect on aggregate demand is an increase in G of 100 and a reduction in consumption of only 80. Therefore, aggregate demand increases by 20.

The obvious question to now ask is, how do governments in practice use government spending and taxation to control the equilibrium level of output?

Government's approach to managing fiscal policy

The government's spending and taxation decisions are reflected in the government deficit. The projected expenditure and revenue sources for the government are available from the so-called Red Book. For the tax year 2012–13, the revenue and expenditure figures are shown in Figure 11.7.

The largest areas of expenditure are social security, health and education. Taken together, these three areas represent more than 60 per cent of government spending. The largest sources of revenue come from personal taxation, national insurance contributions and VAT. It is perhaps surprising that revenues from corporation taxes are only £35 billion and represent a very small fraction of total government tax revenues. Government borrowing is £175 billion (£496 billion − £671 billion), the difference between government expenditure and government revenues, and represents the government's deficit.

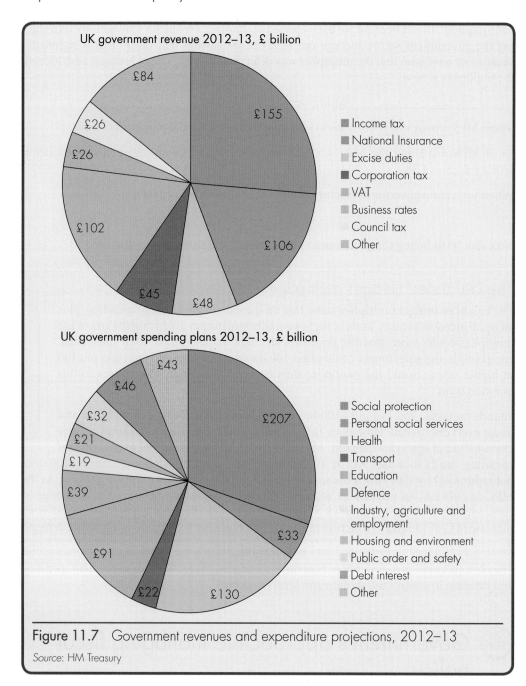

Figure 11.7   Government revenues and expenditure projections, 2012–13

Source: HM Treasury

Deficits

Government deficits as a percentage of GDP are plotted in Figure 11.8 for a number of European economies. These deficits are the annual differences between government receipts and expenditures. Government deficits tend to display a cyclical pattern. As economies have fallen into recession, or slowed in growth, tax receipts have fallen behind expenditure levels and deficits have opened up. Members of the eurozone are in normal economic times required to keep their budget deficits under 3 per cent of GDP. Because of the credit and debt crises the 3 per cent rule has been temporarily relaxed.

In Figure 11.9, the **cumulative debt** for selected European economies is shown. The cumulative debt is all current and outstanding debt. When governments borrow, just

Cumulative debt is the total outstanding government debt from borrowings over many years.

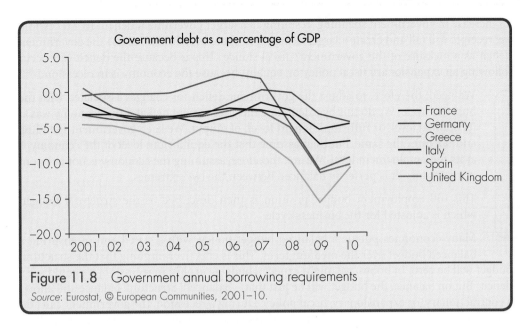

Figure 11.8 Government annual borrowing requirements

Source: Eurostat, © European Communities, 2001–10.

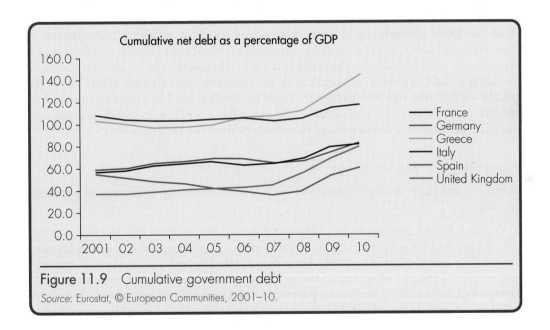

Figure 11.9 Cumulative government debt

Source: Eurostat, © European Communities, 2001–10.

like firms and households, they can arrange to borrow for many years. In some instances, governments have borrowed for up to 50 years.

We can see in Figure 11.9 that Italy and Greece have accumulated enormous amounts of debt compared to the size of their economies. While the other economies have lower levels of debt, in nearly all cases the level of debt has grown by around 20 percentage points in recent years.

Fiscal stance

Unfortunately, the continual link between the government deficit and the business cycle makes it difficult to appraise the government's **fiscal stance**. For example, an expansionary fiscal policy would ordinarily consist of a reduction in tax and

> **Fiscal stance** is the extent to which the government is using fiscal policy to increase or decrease aggregate demand in the economy.

an increase in government spending, resulting in a larger government deficit. In a recession, tax receipts will fall and create a larger deficit. It is, therefore, difficult to use the government deficit as a measure of the government's fiscal stance. This is because the deficit can occur following an expansionary fiscal policy or, equally, because the economy is in recession.

> Full employment level of the economy is a long-run equilibrium position and the economy operates on its production possibility frontier. The economy is in neither boom nor recession.

We need, therefore, to adjust the government deficit for changes associated with the business cycle. We do this by calculating the government deficit if the economy was at its optimal level, or **full employment level**, of output. We keep government spending and tax rates the same, but then assume that the equilibrium level of the economy is at its full employment level. We are, therefore, assuming the economy is not in boom or recession – it is perfectly balanced between the two extremes.

This full employment budget position is then described as the structural budget, which is adjusted for the business cycle.

Many economies pursue a balanced budget policy, with a stated aim of ensuring a balanced budget over the medium term. This is effectively arguing that the structural budget will be zero. In boom, we might expect a budget surplus; in recession, we could see a deficit. But on balance, the budget will be just that – balanced. Structural balance still allows a contractionary, or expansionary, fiscal policy. During a recession, the government can add spending into the economy through tax reductions and increases in government spending. Similarly, during an economic boom, the government can increase taxes and reduce government spending.

From the 1970s onwards, fiscal policy became less popular, reflecting the concerns of economists and politicians that an overly expansionary fiscal policy can be destabilizing for the economy. However, during the credit crisis a fiscal stimulus was an obvious means of providing a rapid expansion of spending in the economy. Governments across the world quickly realized that cuts in interest rates could be supplemented by government spending and tax cuts. Despite the immediate popularity of fiscal policy, it is still necessary to recognize the weakness which reduced its popularity from the 1970s onwards.

Fiscal policy weaknesses

Automatic stabilizers enable the economy to adjust automatically to changes in aggregate demand.

If, during a boom, income in an economy increases, tax receipts will increase, savings will increase and the government will cut back on social payments, such as unemployment benefit. This shows that the economy has automatic brakes built into the system that will help to control the rate of economic boom. Conversely, in recession, tax receipts will fall, savings will reduce and government payments will increase. This way the economy will automatically reduce the net rate of leakages and help to keep the economy moving.

Because such stabilizers work automatically, then, from a fiscal position, the economy can be placed on autopilot. There is no need for the government to overly monitor economic activity and make policy changes. It can focus its energies on other matters, such as health and education.

Fiscal policy and implementation problems

There are additional reasons for believing in the virtues of automatic stabilizers and these relate to the problems associated with actively managing fiscal policy.

Time lags

In order to actively manage fiscal policy the government needs to know when aggregate demand is falling and when it is rising. This can only be achieved with a lag. Government statisticians collect data on economic activity, but they are only able to report and, perhaps more important, confirm either a slowdown or an increase in economic activity three to six months after the event. The government then needs to consider a policy response and then introduce the response. This all takes time. Once the policy is introduced, say a cut in taxation to offset falling demand in an economy, the economy may have moved on, showing signs of economic growth. The tax stimulation is then inappropriate because it will be adding to a boom rather than assisting a recessionary problem.

Uncertainty

Assume an economy is in recession. The equilibrium level of income is £10 billion, but currently output is around £5 billion. The multiplier is 2. The economy has an output gap of £10bn − £5bn = £5bn. With a multiplier of 2, the government needs to increase aggregate demand by £2.5 billion.

Unfortunately, this example has benefited from complete certainty. We know the equilibrium level of output, the current level of output and the size of the multiplier. In practice, the government and its advisers do not know any of these values with certainty. Now let us assume that all of the factors above are estimates. We could even be generous to the government and say that it guessed the size of the multiplier and the current level of GDP accurately. But the equilibrium level of income is only £8 billion, not £10 billion. Therefore, by overestimating the optimal level of output and injecting £2.5 billion into the economy the government will push the economy straight into a boom. It simply swaps a demoralizing recession for an equally unpalatable bout of inflation.

Offsetting changes

If the government pursues an expansionary fiscal stance, it will tend to take on more debt in order to finance its spending. At some point in the future this debt has to be serviced and perhaps even repaid. In the presence of very large mountains of public debt, sensible private individuals may predict that in the future tax rates will have to rise in order to fund the current lax fiscal position of the government. In order to offset these future higher taxes, individuals might save more now. Therefore, higher government spending and reduced taxes now could generate higher levels of offsetting autonomous savings. The government's fiscal stance is effectively neutralized by the response of higher savings from the private sector. See Box 11.3 for concerns of off-setting behaviour in the UK economy.

Actively managed fiscal policy sought to manage the business cycle by adding demand during a recession and reducing demand during a boom. Due to problems of timing,

Box 11.3

Spending cuts 'should be eased'

Britain's economy will fall into recession in the first half of the year and the government needs to ease up on its tough package of spending cuts, an influential think-tank has warned. The UK economy will shrink 0.1 per cent in 2012 as cash-strapped households tighten their purse-strings and nervous businesses hold back on investment, said the National Institute of Economic and Social Research (Niesr).

Chancellor George Osborne's austerity measures are contributing to low demand in the UK, which in turn is damaging the broader economy, so a temporary

softening of his fiscal stance would give the country a much-needed boost, said Niesr.

The think-tank added: 'The UK economy currently suffers from deficient demand; the current stance of fiscal policy is contributing to this deficiency. A temporary easing of fiscal policy in the near term would boost the economy.'

uncertainty and offsetting, such policy responses have been ill-timed, misjudged and at best ineffective.

Deficits and inflation

We saw in Chapter 9 that inflation can erode the value of debt. If you borrow £100 and inflation is 10 per cent, then, in real terms, at the end of year one you will only owe £90. You, as a private individual, have very little control over the rate of inflation. But for a government the case is very different. If a government runs up a mountain of debt, the temptation to let the rate of inflation increase and erode the real value of the debt is very tempting.

This has two important implications. First, if a government is trying to manage individuals' inflationary expectations, then it needs to manage the size of the government debt. Being seen to reduce debt and fiscal deficits reduces the need to stoke up inflation. As a consequence, inflationary expectations will be lower and inflation should turn out to be lower. Second, as we see in Chapter 13, within a fixed exchange rate system such as the European single currency, harmonizing inflation across member states may aid economic convergence among those states. Therefore, as entry into the system draws nearer, the UK government needs to bring fiscal policy under control.

Crowding out

Crowding out occurs when increased government spending reduces private sector spending.

Crowding out relates back to the business problem at the beginning of this chapter. If government takes an expansionary fiscal stance, then it can achieve this by spending more public money on health, education and transport infrastructure projects. But this policy runs the risk of robbing productive resources from the private sector. For every nurse employed in a hospital, a worker is effectively removed from the private sector. This is known as crowding out, because public expenditure by government crowds out private expenditure by firms. The extent to which this occurs is debatable. When there are lots of workers without jobs, an increase in government spending will not crowd out private expenditure. Employment will rise, output will grow and income will increase. But when productive resources, such as labour, are all fully employed, then increasing public expenditure is likely to rob the private sector of its resources. Employment stays constant, at best output stays constant and so does income. An expansionary fiscal policy has no net impact on national output.

Summary

Given all of these problems, it is not surprising that economists and governments began to move away from active fiscal management of the economy. Instead, they recognized the benefits of automatic stabilizers and moved focus to monetary and supply-side policies. Fiscal policy was popular from the 1930s through to the 1970s, a period during which a global depression in the 1930s meant there was no crowding out. Economic change occurred at a more sedate and predictable pace and concerns regarding inflation were less important. All this changed in the 1980s, 1990s and 2000s. With modern economies developing with great pace and complexity, inflationary aversion was everywhere and high levels of employment ensured that crowding out was a real problem. However, following the credit crisis the effectiveness of fiscal policy has returned. This is because a prolonged recession results in little crowding out. At the same time as banks, consumers and firms become insensitive to central bank base rate changes, then fiscal policy can become more attractive than monetary policy.

Foreign trade and aggregate demand

So far in our examination of aggregate demand, we have only considered economies which do not trade with the rest of the world. While we will focus on issues of exchange rates and globalization in Chapters 15 and 16, it is worth incorporating the impact of international trade on aggregate demand.

Exports are generally expressed as X and imports as Z.

Economists generally talk about net exports, or the trade balance, which is clearly X – Z. If exports are greater than imports, the economy has a trade surplus, but if imports are greater than exports, the economy has a trade deficit.

We now need to think about incorporating X and Z into our existing analysis of aggregate demand. In fairly simple terms, exports are UK products purchased by foreign consumers; Scotch whisky produced in the UK but sold in the USA would be an example. So, exports add to UK aggregate demand. Imports work in the opposite direction. These are foreign products purchased by UK consumers; BMW cars made in Germany but bought in the UK would be an example. Therefore, aggregate demand can now be defined as AD = C + I + G + X – Z.

However, as with the introduction of the government sector, we need to address the factors that determine exports and imports. First, the level of UK income does not influence exports; instead, US consumers' willingness to purchase UK products is influenced by US income. As income rises in the US, consumers are willing to search out more expensive imports from overseas, such as Scotch whisky. Therefore, exports are autonomous, or independent, of the UK's level of income. In contrast, the level of UK income influences imports. As our income increases, we are willing to buy more expensive products from overseas.

We therefore have a marginal propensity to import (MPZ), which is the increase in income allocated to import products.

In terms of aggregate demand, exports are grouped with the other autonomous expenditures: autonomous consumption, investment and government spending. As such, exports represent a potential injection into the circular flow of income. Rising income levels in the USA, or the European Union, are likely to result in additional UK exports to these economies. Conversely, as these economies move into recession, demand for UK products will fall.

Exports add to the complexity of planning UK domestic policy because, in order to keep aggregate demand at the equilibrium level, the government has to understand the level of domestic consumption, domestic investment and how the business cycle in other economies such as Europe and the US influences UK exports. See Box 11.4.

Box 11.4

UK trade

The UK's deficit on seasonally adjusted trade in goods and services was £2.6 billion in November, compared with the deficit of £1.9 billion in October.

The deficit on seasonally adjusted trade in goods was £8.6 billion in November, compared with the deficit of £7.9 billion in October.

The surplus on seasonally adjusted trade in services was estimated at £6.1 billion in November, compared with the surplus of £6.0 billion in October.

Excluding oil and erratic items, the seasonally adjusted volume of exports was 1.7 per cent lower, and the volume of imports was 1.1 per cent higher in November, compared with October.

Export prices of goods fell by 0.4 per cent and import prices of goods fell by 0.2 per cent, compared with October.

Source: www.statistics.gov.uk

Should we be troubled by a rising trade deficit? The answer is yes because imports represent a leakage from the circular flow of income. Leakages reduce the size of the multiplier. With imports, injections leak out of the economy more quickly and, therefore, less money is left in the circular flow to go through the next cycle. In an open economy with a government sector, the multiplier is:

Open economy multiplier with government sector = 1/(MPS + MPT + MPZ)

Imports, therefore, increase the economy's leakages and in so doing can reduce the size of the multiplier.

In terms of fiscal policy, the open economy creates real practical problems for the government. For example, if the government increases government spending, then this represents an autonomous injection into the economy. With an open economy, however, there is a distinct possibility that this additional expenditure could leak out as imports, resulting in zero impact on the level of aggregate demand. For example, increased spending by the UK government on healthcare can now be used to pay for operations undertaken in French hospitals. The money spent on extending the UK's airport capacity could be spent by workers on foreign holidays.

Summary

Fiscal policy, in the main, relies on the power of the multiplier to provide the government with an effective tool for managing the economy. As the world's economies become more globally integrated, the scope of international leakages increases and the multiplier decreases in size and effectiveness. Moreover, fiscal policy requires timely and accurate information. The complexity of modern economies, including increasing globalization, makes these informational requirements difficult to attain.

 # Business application: debt funding and crowding out

Crowding out occurs when government spending absorbs economic resource that would have been used by the private sector. Increases in government spending, therefore, result in lower private sector spending. The net effect on total expenditure is zero. The government's fiscal expansion is neutralized.

Unfortunately, the problem of crowding out can be worse than this. Unless the government has enormous cash reserves, then an expansion in government spending needs to be funded by borrowings. Government debt has to increase. So who lends to governments?

The answer to this last question is varied. Lenders can include ordinary household savers, private companies, pension funds and banks. In a global financial system, lenders can also include overseas investors. So even when an economy has a very low marginal propensity to save, governments can raise huge amounts of debt by borrowing from overseas investors.

Generally, governments do not face problems when raising debt. Lenders view governments from modern developed economies as safe bets. The creditworthiness of governments is usually high. But this may not be the case when governments are seeking to increase borrowings on an unprecedented scale. In order to service debt, governments need to be capable of raising taxes. But during a recession tax receipts can fall and the ability to service enormous debts can fall. This worries individuals and companies who lend to governments. The obvious way to address these fears is to ask for a higher interest rate to cover the increased risk of lending to a heavily indebted government, something which has caused enormous problems for the likes of Greece, Ireland and Italy.

Box 11.5

Emerging borrowers face rollover risk, default threat

Scarce dollar funding and a retrenchment in bank lending will force up premiums for emerging market countries and companies refinancing debt next year, adding to strains on public finances and potentially triggering a surge in corporate defaults.

JP Morgan calculates that emerging sovereign debtors will need to find $63.6 billion to cover interest and capital debt payments in 2012 while corporates must raise $107 billion. Total issuance should be around $245 billion, the bank forecasts.

Such volumes would not usually portend difficulty – even this year, emerging bond issuance has been over $250 billion, not far off last year's record. But with markets still awaiting a solution to the eurozone's debt crisis, 2012 could be tough for entities that need to refinance debt or secure new money.

Fears are growing of a 'crowding out' effect, as many borrowers – from developed as well as emerging economies – compete for limited funds on international capital markets.

Issuers are already being forced to cough up to raise debt, with even AA/Aa2-rated Qatar recently paying a 0.4 per cent premium to an old five-year bond to raise funds. Abu Dhabi's AA-rated state energy company IPIC meanwhile paid 0.9 per cent over existing debt of lower-rated Mexican state oil firm Pemex to sell bonds last month.

For speculative-grade corporate credits, rated BB+ or lower, there may be trouble. A third of debt falling due in 2012 from emerging corporates is junk-rated. 'For those credits that can come to market, the stress is exhibited via wider spreads. The real crowding-out damage may occur with poorly rated and weakening credits in the corporate sector,' said Jeremy Brewin, a fund manager at Aviva Investors. 'Weak sovereigns can engage an IMF programme. Weak corporates cannot. That suggests default risk will increase in the high-yield space,' he added.

Such firms are already having trouble raising cash. ING Bank notes that speculative grade companies have accounted for just 10 per cent of emerging bond issuance in the last quarter of 2011 rather than 20–35 per cent that would usually be expected.

The huge volumes of eurozone and US debt maturing next year could be a further challenge, especially given the high yields currently offered by sovereigns such as Italy and Spain.

'In our view there could be a major crowding effect as emerging market issuers compete in the same credit category as developed markets, which in turn would put more pressure on funding costs,' Morgan Stanley analysts warned in a note.

Adapted from an article by Sujata Rao, Reuters, 16 December 2011.

If the price of debt rises for governments, then the price of debt also rises for the private sector. This is a simple substitution effect. If the private sector is not willing to borrow at the same prices as governments are willing to pay, then lenders will simply lend to governments only. As a consequence, there is an alternative crowding out effect. Increases in government borrowings can push up the price of debt for private sector borrowers. An increase in the price of funds reduces the demand for debt by the private sector. If debt consumption falls, then so does household consumption and company investment.

This type of financial crowding out is a current concern and the fall in sterling and the sell-off of government debt instruments, such as gilts, highlight how planned increases in UK government debt may result in higher borrowing costs for the private sector. Firms and households ordinarily do not appreciate the implications of capital flows into and out of an economy but, at times of high government borrowing, such flows become crucial in determining the price of public and private sector debt.

Business application: taxation or government spending?

A fiscal stimulus can occur through increased government spending or a reduction in tax. Both approaches increase total expenditure. Government spending directly alters the amount of expenditure, while tax cuts boost disposable income, which then leads to an increase in consumption. If government spending and tax both increase total expenditure, should the form of fiscal stimulus matter to business? The answer is yes, and it matters on a number levels, including how quickly the additional expenditure hits the economy and where the expenditure is channelled.

Timing

Governments are very good at announcing huge increases in expenditure. In our terminology, this is planned expenditure. This is very different from actual expenditure. Governments are not being disingenuous. Rather, it takes time to highlight projects, design them, contract for them and begin to spend the money. Unless there are many infrastructure projects in the pipeline, then it can take many years to develop such a pipeline. Meanwhile, the economy does not receive its much needed injection of spending.

In contrast, cuts in direct taxes, such as income tax, and cuts in indirect taxes, such as those on goods and services, create an immediate change in consumers' income. Tax cuts, therefore, have the potential to provide an almost instantaneous flow of additional spending into the economy.

Channels of spending

Governments spend on projects which they find attractive. This spending tends to be focused on education, health care and transport. Infrastructure projects in these areas are popular: new buildings, roads, railways and airports. Huge flows of money are channelled to the construction industry. Other sectors do not receive direct spending. Of course, some industries receive subsidies, loans and capital injections. In many economies, this has involved flows of money into banks and in the USA and Germany has also included cash injections into the automotive industry. But is this spending effective, efficient and valued by taxpayers?

If fiscal policy involves tax cuts, then consumers can spend money in the markets they find most desirable. If an individual does not like flying, then the value of a government-funded airport expansion is limited. But if that individual receives a tax cut, then they can spend their additional income on a holiday within the economy.

This debate goes to the heart of market-based economies. In Chapter 1, we introduced the production possibility frontier and highlighted two approaches to the allocation of economic resources: planned economies and market-based economies. Markets are generally accepted as the most effective means of solving the problem of infinite wants and finite resources. Why, during a recession, should we sacrifice this view and suddenly believe that governments are better placed to decide where spending should occur?

One response is that consumers may not react to tax cuts. They may instead save the additional income, or run down existing debts. In addition, in an economy that has a high propensity to import, then tax cuts are unlikely to fuel an increase in domestic demand. So for these reasons the government spending may be preferable because it ensures that spending occurs and that it occurs within the economy.

Firms need to be aware of these differences between government spending and tax cuts. An understanding of the differences enables an understanding of the likely time it will take to stimulate the economy and which sectors will be winners and losers.

We term this planned expenditure through disposable income and then through consumption. Should it matter to business how the stimulus occurs?

 ## 11.8 Business data application: understanding the fiscal position and the implications for business

Much has been written about the levels of government indebtedness across Europe and around the world. In this section, we highlight where useful data can be found, draw attention to some of the key trends with government debt statistics for France, Germany, Greece and the UK, and explore some important implications for the economy and for business, as governments struggle to bring their borrowings under control.

In terms of finding data, there are a number of economic institutions and organizations that provide data on a range of macroeconomic variables, including public sector/government debt. Such organizations include in-country government statistical departments, such as the UK's Office for National Statistics, the World Bank, the International Monetary Fund, Eurostat in the EU and the Organisation for Economic Co-operation and Development.

The scale and indeed the rapid rise in government debts can be seen in the expansion of annual deficit financing (see Figure 11.10) and the growth in total outstanding debt (see Figure 11.11). In nearly all four economies, the start of the credit crisis in 2008 and the onset of the global recession marks a swift deterioration in the state of government finances. In the specific case of Greece, a need to fund an annual 5 per cent deficit in 2007 quickly became a 16 per cent financial black hole by 2010. As annual deficit financing grew and governments needed to borrow more and more, then outstanding debt as a percentage of GDP also began to rise. Following a steady reduction in outstanding debt to about 33 per cent of GDP in 2002, the UK suddenly found itself with borrowings equal to more than 60 per cent of GDP by 2010. France underwent a similar experience to that of the UK, while Greece managed to raise its outstanding government debt from 80 per cent to 130 per cent of GDP.

While the recent global recession has played a role in the growth of government debt, it is not the only reason, nor indeed, perhaps, the most important reason. If we look at Figure 11.12, which illustrates GDP growth rates for our chosen economies, we can see that for all these economies, GDP growth rates were reasonably high from 2002 onwards; and yet government annual deficits from 2002 onwards were growing (see Figure 11.10). Governments were

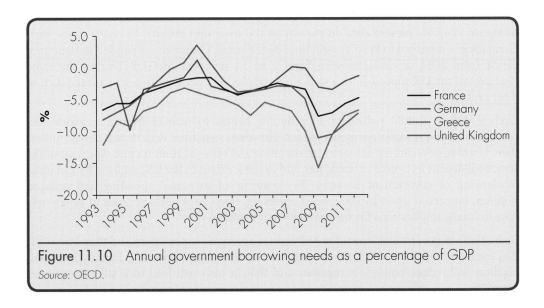

Figure 11.10 Annual government borrowing needs as a percentage of GDP

Source: OECD.

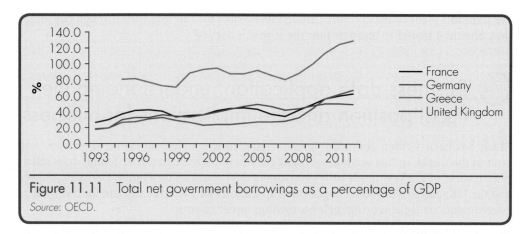

Figure 11.11   Total net government borrowings as a percentage of GDP
Source: OECD.

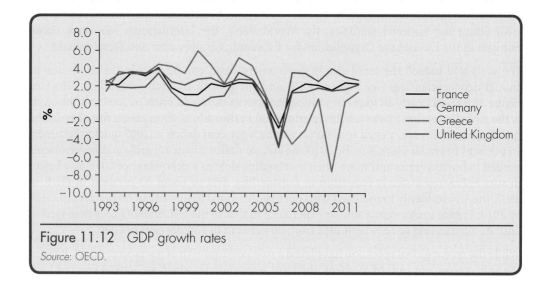

Figure 11.12   GDP growth rates
Source: OECD.

using the period of high stable growth rates to support additional borrowings. If government borrowings increase during a period of economic growth, then the expansion of government debt is structural not cyclical.

In Figure 11.13 we present data on the size of the structural deficits. In recent times, only Germany has managed to keep its structural deficit small. Greece has expanded its structural deficit from 2002 onwards, moving from 2 to 14 per cent of GDP. During the same time period the UK moved from a structural surplus of 1 per cent to a structural deficit of 6 per cent.

Cyclical deficits should reduce as an economy begins to recover from a recession, tax revenues rise and transfer payments reduce. However, structural deficits will persist, unless there is strong government action to cut spending and raise taxation further. The scale of the structural deficits in Greece in particular, and to some extent in the UK, requires a substantial rebalancing of government finances. The patterns of increased spending and reduced taxation, embarked upon in 2002, need reversing. Such large-scale reversal of policy will have dramatic implications for the economy and business.

Reductions in government spending will reduce aggregate expenditure and therefore GDP. Any fiscal multiplier effect will only serve to amplify the reduction in GDP. Equally, increased taxation will reduce household incomes and that in turn will lead to a fall in consumer spending.

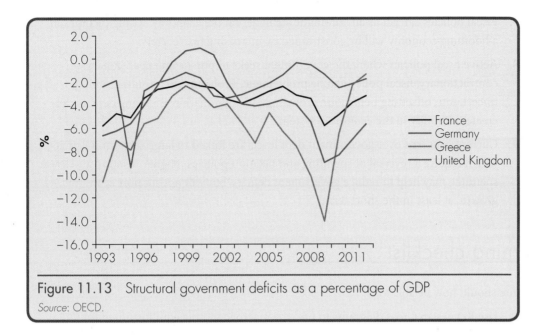

Figure 11.13 Structural government deficits as a percentage of GDP
Source: OECD.

An understanding of basic macroeconomic concepts, especially concepts linked to fiscal policy and government debt, enables business managers to have a stronger appreciation of how the business environment and the broader economy are linked to deficit reduction policies. Importantly, a significant amount of government deficits is structural and not cyclical, meaning that governments cannot rely on a growing economy to correct high fiscal deficits. Austerity plans aimed at reducing government spending and raising tax are necessary; and such policies will act as a drag on overall economic output.

Summary

1. The use of government spending and taxation to affect aggregate demand are examples of fiscal policy.

2. Aggregate demand is composed of consumption, investment, government spending and net exports.

3. In equilibrium, planned expenditure equals planned output. In the Keynesian Cross, the equilibrium is characterized by the 45° line.

4. Expenditure which does not change with the level of income is known as autonomous expenditure. Increases in autonomous expenditure lead to higher equilibrium levels of output.

5. The marginal propensity to consume (MPC) measures the increase in consumption from an increase in income. The marginal propensity to save (MPS) measures the increase in savings from an increase in income.

6. If a £100 million increase in autonomous expenditure leads to a £500 million increase in GDP, then the fiscal multiplier is 5. The multiplier is dependent upon the rate of leakage from the circular flow of income. In a closed economy, the multiplier is equal to 1/MPS. But in an open economy with a government sector, the multiplier is reduced by the marginal propensity to tax (MPT) and the marginal propensity to import (MPZ) and so equals 1/(MPS + MPT + MPZ).

7. Fiscal policies can act as an automatic stabilizer on the economy. Rising incomes in a booming economy will be constrained by increasing tax receipts.

8. Active fiscal policies where the government seeks to pursue an expansionary, or contractionary, fiscal policy can be problematic. Problems surrounding timing, uncertainty, offsetting behaviour, crowding out and inflation-inducing deficits can create instability in the economic system.

9. Current concerns over government debt levels are linked to large structural deficits, which require a reversal of spending and taxation policies. Higher taxation and lower spending may help to reduce government deficits, but will not support economic growth, at least in the short term

Learning checklist

You should now be able to:

- Use Keynesian Cross diagrams to find the macroeconomic equilibrium output
- Calculate the size of the fiscal multiplier
- Explain why the multiplier might assist fiscal policy
- Assess the government's fiscal stance
- Explain the potential problems associated with using fiscal policy

Questions

1. Identify the main components of total expenditure.

2. Explain why the 45° line represents the equilibrium in a Keynesian Cross diagram.

3. What is an autonomous expenditure? Use a suitable diagram to illustrate the effect on the economy of an increase in autonomous expenditures.

4. Explain how the consumption function links consumer spending and current income. Do you think this is a reasonable explanation of consumer spending?

5. What is the fiscal multiplier? What determines the size of the multiplier? How does the multiplier differ between closed and open economies?

EASY

6. During the last five years what are the key trends in the government deficit for your own economy?

7. Explain how you would assess the size of the government deficit to determine whether the government was using fiscal policy to expand or contract the economy.

8. Explain what is meant by the term 'balanced budget multiplier'.

9. Consider the four key components of aggregate expenditure: consumption, investment, government spending and net exports. Is your economy dominated by domestic private spending, domestic public spending or external demand?

10. What problems are associated with the implementation of fiscal policy?

11. Recall Chapters 9 and 10. Which key macroeconomic variable is missing from the Keynesian Cross approach? Is this a major drawback of the Keynesian Cross approach?

12. In a closed economy with no government sector consumption, $C = 20 + 0.8Y$, investment $I = 40$. What is the equilibrium level of income Y?

13. When examining fiscal policy, should business be more interested in taxation policy or government spending?

14. An economy requires a fiscal stimulus. How effective will this stimulus be if the economy has a high marginal propensity to import?

15. The marginal propensity to save in China is extremely high, in excess of 30 per cent. Google and find out why.

Exercises

1. True or false?

    (a) In equilibrium, planned expenditure will equal planned output.

    (b) The fiscal multiplier is equal to 1/MPC.

    (c) The following are autonomous expenditures: investment, government spending and net exports.

    (d) Credit offered by banks is backed by cash deposits.

    (e) Keynesians believe that inflation is a monetary problem.

    (f) If aggregate supply is perfectly inelastic, a reduction in interest rates will lead to higher inflation.

2. Table 11.1 shows some data on consumption and income (output). Planned investment is autonomous, and occurs at the rate of $60 billion per period.

    (a) Calculate savings and aggregate demand at each level of income.

    (b) For each level of output, work out the unplanned change in inventory holdings and the rate of actual investment.

    (c) If, in a particular period, income turned out to be $100 billion, how would you expect producers to react?

    (d) If, in a particular period, income turned out to be $350 billion, how would you expect producers to react?

    (e) What is the equilibrium level of income?

    (f) What is the marginal propensity to consume?

    (g) If investment increased by $15 billion, what would be the change in equilibrium income?

    (h) Use graph paper to plot the consumption function and aggregate demand schedule.

    (i) Add on the 45° line and confirm that equilibrium occurs at the same point suggested by your answer to 2(e) above.

    (j) Show the effect on equilibrium of an increase in investment of $15 billion.

Table 11.1   Income and consumption

Income (output)	Planned consumption	Planned investment	Savings	Aggregate demand	Unplanned inventory change	Actual investment
50	35					
100	70					
150	105					
200	140					
250	175					
300	210					
350	245					
400	280					

3. (a) Using a Keynesian Cross diagram, illustrate how an increase in exports would alter the equilibrium output for an economy. What evidence is there that your economy is currently benefiting from an export boom?

   (b) What evidence is there that at present consumption and investment expenditure are rising in your economy?

   (c) Explain the variety of ways through which an increase in interest rates by the central bank would impact your economy.

Money, banking and interest

CHAPTER 12

Chapter contents

Money, banking and interest at a glance | 300
12.1 Business problem: understanding how the monetary environment influences the commercial environment | 300
12.2 What is money? | 301
12.3 The banking system | 302
12.4 Regulation | 305
12.5 Credit creation and the money supply | 309
12.6 The demand for money | 311
12.7 Money market equilibrium | 312
12.8 Monetary policy | 315
12.9 Business application: monetary policy and investment | 319
12.10 Business application: the importance of banking to the economy | 321
12.11 Business data application: financial markets and the impact of quantitative easing | 322
Summary | 325
Learning checklist | 325
Questions | 326
Exercises | 326

Learning outcomes

By the end of this chapter you should understand:

Economic theory

LO1 The key features of money
LO2 The nature and economic importance of banking
LO3 Regulation
LO4 The credit-creation process
LO5 Broad and narrow measures of money
LO6 The transaction, precautionary and speculative motives for holding money
LO7 Money market equilibrium issues
LO8 Monetary policy

Business application

LO9 Financial stability and businesses' desire for investment
LO10 The importance of banking to the economy
LO11 The impact of quantitative easing on key financial markets and the broader economy

At a glance Money, banking and interest

The issue

Money is a key feature of economic activity. What are the key features of money, what is the purpose of the banking system and how is it that interest rates can be used to influence GDP and inflation?

The understanding

Money enables buyers and sellers to trade and is referred to as a medium of exchange. Banks are important because they channel liquidity from savers who have too much cash to borrowers who have a shortage of cash. The interest rate is the equilibrium price of money. By varying the interest rate, a central bank alters the cost of borrowing. Since borrowing can facilitate household consumption and firm-level investment, changing interest rates can change the level of demand in an economy.

The usefulness

Understanding how the money and banking markets work is extremely important. First, it enables an understanding of how interest rate changes are transmitted into the wider economy. This has important implications for the level of consumption and investment demand. Second, banking is such an important component of modern economies that it is essential to understand the role of banking within an economy and appreciate its ability to support economic growth and also damage economic stability when there is a banking crisis.

 12.1 Business problem: understanding how the monetary environment influences the commercial environment

Such is the importance of monetary policy that interest rate changes in the USA, the eurozone and the UK are dealt with as major news events. But why is interest rate policy such a significant part of economic policy? The answer to this question is complex and involves an understanding of money, banking and money market equilibrium.

Money is a key characteristic of most economic transactions. Goods and services are nearly always priced in monetary terms. A pizza is £5, or £7. You never see pizza priced in bottles of Coca-Cola, or any other good or service. Money is a common price and, just as importantly, money is commonly accepted as payment for goods and services and is equally accepted as payment for work. While a key feature of economic activity, money is not economic activity. The conversion of economic inputs – land, labour, capital and enterprise – into goods and services is economic activity. But money is the means of facilitating economic transactions; as such, money is the lubricant of the economic system. To understand the level of economic activity and the level of consumption and investment demand is, in part, to understand how much monetary grease is in the system.

Understanding how much money exists within the economic system is not straightforward. Notes and coins are an obvious example of money, but so too are the electronic digits of money in your bank accounts. While the Bank of England is responsible for printing additional amounts of money, the retail banks are capable of multiplying electronic credits of money. If a company pays in £1 million, then the bank may lend out £0.9 million in loans. The money supply has just increased by £0.9 million. The company thinks it has £1 million of money and the borrowers think they also have £0.9 million of money.

Expansion of the money supply by banks represents the provision of liquidity. Channelling money from savers, who have excess cash for their current transaction needs, to borrowers, who are short of cash, given their current transaction needs, is a very beneficial economic activity. But the rate at which this occurs can be problematic. Too much credit expansion, and consumption and investment demand can grow too quickly, leading to inflation. Too little credit expansion, such as during the credit crisis, and economic growth will slow.

In setting base rates for the economy, central banks attempt to set the rate of credit expansion within an economy. Base rates determine the money market rates for money. If the central bank raises the base rate, then the price of monetary funds increases. With a fixed demand for money, the central bank must reduce the money supply in order to raise the interest rate. By mopping up excess liquidity, through higher rates of interest, the central bank limits the ability of retail banks to expand credit for consumption and investment. Likewise, if the bank reduces interest rates, then money supply needs to be increased, which enables the retail banks to expand credit to borrowers.

Understanding the intricacies of the money and banking markets and the role of the central bank provides a deeper insight into how changes in the base rates can impact on the level of consumption, investment and overall economic activity. Furthermore, understanding the economic importance of banking in providing credit and liquidity also opens up an understanding of the financial risks undertaken by banks. When banks collapse or face a loss of confidence, there can be a loss of confidence and withdrawal of liquidity from the economy. Banking regulation and an understanding of the importance of banking to the economy are also key issues to understand.

We will now develop your understanding of these issues by considering the role of money, the economic importance of banking, the regulation of banking, the credit-creation process, the demand for money, money market equilibrium and monetary policies.

What is money?

Money facilitates exchange. Consider an economy with no money, generally referred to as a **barter economy**, where goods are swapped for other goods.

We are specialist economic textbook authors. That is what we produce. You might flip burgers or drive a taxi. This book could be worth 30 burgers or one taxi ride to the airport. We do not like burgers, but we do fly, so we need a taxi. But will the taxi driver want our economics textbook in return for a trip to the airport, and if the burger flipper wants our book, do we want 30 burgers in return?

You can see the problem: without money a so-called **double coincidence of wants** is required in order to exchange goods.

As textbook authors we need to find people who want our book, and are offering goods we want in exchange. Money solves this problem. We can pay the taxi driver £30 cash and they can then use that money to buy goods which they desire, such as food, petrol or coffee; they do not have to accept the textbook.

A central role of money is that it is recognized and accepted as a medium of exchange. Workers will accept money in exchange for their labour. Shop owners will accept money in exchange for their goods and services. As a medium of exchange, money is extremely efficient because it cuts down on the need for a double coincidence of wants.

Money also has other functions. It is generally seen to be a **unit of account**.

All prices are expressed in monetary terms. A BMW is £20 000, not 100 cows. In the USA the unit of account is dollars and in the eurozone it is euros. Goods and services are expressed in a common unit, which is monetary based. This again enables efficient transactions by facilitating comparisons and transparency in pricing. A common unit of account, or price,

> In a barter economy, there is no money, and individuals trade by exchanging different goods and services.
>
> A double coincidence of wants occurs when two people trade goods and services without money. The first individual demands the good offered by the second individual, and vice versa.
>
> Unit of account is the unit in which prices are quoted.

enables buyers and sellers to understand the value of the current market price and whether or not a transaction is profitable or loss-making.

> A store of value is something that can be used to make future purchases, e.g. money.
>
> **Fiat money** is notes and coins guaranteed by the government rather than by gold deposits.

Money should also be a **store of value**. For example, milk is not a good store of value because it deteriorates quickly and goes bad. Money, as metal coins and paper banknotes, does not perish. Money earned today can be saved and used next week or next month to facilitate a future transaction. However, money is not a perfect store of value. Money as cash earns zero interest and its value is eroded by inflation. Other assets, such as houses, gold and interest-bearing accounts can all serve as stores of value.

However, money is the predominant medium of exchange in most economies. Today money takes the form of **fiat money**. Before fiat money, governments backed money with gold. The holder of a note could approach the central bank and demand that their note be exchanged for an equivalent value of gold. Money is no longer backed by gold, but is instead guaranteed by the government or central bank. Fiat money has a number of beneficial aspects associated with it. It is legally recognized as a medium of exchange and is culturally accepted as such. People are willing to exchange goods for money. Paper notes and coins are cheap to make (see the mass-production techniques employed by the Royal Mint in Box 12.1). A £10 note does not require £10 of resource in order to make it. In contrast, a £10 gold nugget would represent £10 of resource. Government-backed money economizes on scarce resources. But here is the problem: because a £10 note can be produced for less than £10, forgers can make a profit. Therefore, forgery has to be outlawed and the law enforced.

Box 12.1

Making money: rolling in it!

The Royal Mint boasts some of the most advanced coining machinery in the world. In the foundry, strips of metal are drawn from large electric furnaces, reduced to the required thickness in a tandem rolling mill and transferred to large blanking presses where coin blanks can be punched out at the rate of 10 000 per minute. The blanks are softened and cleaned in the Annealing and Pickling Plant before the final process in the Coining Press Room. Here, the blanks are fed into coining presses where the obverse and reverse designs, as well as the milling on the edge, are stamped simultaneously onto the blank. The Royal Mint's latest presses can each strike more than 600 coins per minute, making it impossible for the human eye to separate the individual pieces as they pass through the press.

Source: Royal Mint, www.royalmint.com.

12.3 The banking system

> A **central bank** acts as a banker to the commercial bank, taking deposits and, in extreme circumstances, making loans.
>
> A **retail bank** lends to non-banks, including households and non-bank firms.

The banking system consists of the central bank, retail banks and wholesale banks. The **central bank** issues money into the economy through the banking system and the money markets more generally. The central bank acts as banker to the retail and wholesale banks. If a retail bank has spare cash, then it can safely deposit this money at the central bank. Likewise, in extreme circumstances, if a commercial bank cannot gain funds from any other lender, then the central bank may act as the lender of last resort and provide a loan to the commercial bank.

A **retail bank** takes deposits from retail customers, borrows from other banks and the money markets and raises funds from shareholders. Taken together, all these funds are then loaned out to retail borrowers or invested in financial instruments or deposited at the central bank.

Table 12.1   Balance sheet of UK banks, December 2011

Assets		Liabilities	
In foreign currency			
Securities	1693	Currency, deposits and money market instruments	4133
Loans	2758	Foreign currency capital	310
Total foreign currency assets	4451	Total foreign currency liabilities	4443
In sterling			
Securities	2699	Currency, deposits and money market instruments	3106
Loans	957	Sterling capital	558
Total sterling assets	3656	Total sterling liabilities	3664
Total	8107	Total	8107

Source: Bank of England, *Bankstats*.

Wholesale banks take very large cash deposits and broker very large loans, both for banks and other commercial companies. Wholesale banks are sometimes referred to as investment banks. Such banks tend to locate in financial hubs such as London and New York, where they can raise money on the wholesale financial markets and bring large lenders together to lend in syndicate to large commercial borrowers.

The banking system is just one part of the broader financial system. Other major financial companies include insurance companies, building societies, hedge funds and pension funds. At root, most financial companies are involved in **financial inter-mediation**, which involves raising funds from individuals with excess cash, and then lending to or investing the cash in companies or individuals who are short of funds.

The balance sheet for all UK banks in Table 12.1 highlights the banking function of financial intermediation. A balance sheet is a financial statement of a company's assets and liabilities and each side must balance against the other. So, assets = liabilities.

On the liabilities side, banks raise money from shareholders. This money is referred to as capital. Banks also raise funds from depositors and by borrowing in the money markets from other banks or financial companies, such as pension funds.

On the asset side, banks make loans to households and firms. They may also place some funds in financial securities, such as government or company bonds. Or they may simply place money on deposit at the central bank.

Deposits at banks are classified as sight and time deposits. **Sight deposits** are current accounts. Customers can access their cash instantly. **Time deposits** require the customer to give the bank notice before withdrawing funds.

The central problem for most banks is that they borrow short and lend long. Money raised from depositors, especially in sight deposits, may be run down over a month as a household pays its bills. But the bank may lend to mortgage customers for 25 years. If a deposit holder requires cash quickly, then the bank cannot ask the borrower to pay quicker. This is why the bank holds some funds in securities. These funds earn a low rate of interest, but they provide the bank with instant access to cash. This is referred to as liquidity and the bank needs to trade increased liquidity against increased

Wholesale banks take large deposits and are involved in brokering very large loans to companies.

Financial intermediation involves channelling cash from savers to borrowers.

Sight deposits provide customers with instant access to cash.

Time deposits require the customer to give the bank notice before withdrawing cash.

profits. More cash on loan means higher profits, but less liquidity. More cash in securities means higher liquidity, but lower profits.

In examining Table 12.1 further, it is important to note that the capital of UK banks is small when compared with the amount of funds generated from currency, deposits and money markets. This means that the majority of loans funded by UK banks are paid for by savers, and other lenders to the bank. Shareholders provide banks with very limited funds. This is the essence of financial intermediation, where cash from savers is channelled to borrowers. It also means that, when loans turn bad and are not repaid, banks come under enormous financial stress. Shareholders' funds can be very quickly wiped out by losses on the loan book, after which the inability to repay depositors becomes a real issue.

Such risks have resulted in governments guaranteeing deposits within banks. In addition, many governments around the world have injected billions of capital into banks to ensure their financial viability. But given that companies in other sectors are often allowed to collapse, why would a government be keen to support banking? To answer this question, we need to understand the economic importance of banking.

The economic importance of banking

Banking is now central to money. While notes and coins exist, the vast majority of money is electronic and within bank accounts. In fact, bank deposits are a medium of exchange because they are accepted as payment by sellers of goods and services.

The economic importance of banking cannot be understated. Aside from being a large component of GDP and a massive source of employment within an economy, the services that banking offers are essential to a well-functioning economy. These services can be broken down into four key areas: liquidity, risk pooling, risk selection and monitoring, and risk pricing. We will consider each of these in turn.

Liquidity

> Liquidity is the speed, price and ease of access to money.

The primary role of banks is to provide **liquidity** to the economy. Banks raise money from deposit holders. These account holders may be private households or companies who wish to place their money in a safe and accessible form. If you place your money in the bank, then you have a surplus of liquidity – you do not need so much cash. Similarly, there are also households and businesses who have a shortage of liquidity. This group can raise their liquidity by borrowing from the bank; that is, borrowing raises their access to cash. So, by channelling cash from savers to borrowers banks provide much needed liquidity to the economy.

> Government bonds are a near-cash equivalent and therefore liquid. A government pays the holder of bonds a rate of interest in return for funding the government's debt.
>
> Collateralized debt obligation is a bond. The holder of the bond is paid a rate of interest in return for funding a debt.

However, a problem faced by banks is that they tend to borrow short and lend long. Savers and, more particularly, current account holders, tend to need quick and easy access to their cash. Borrowers, in contrast, tend to repay loans over many years. In ensuring liquidity for borrowers, banks have to carefully manage the cash flows received and repaid to savers. Banks take special care to ensure that they themselves have a mixture of assets which are almost liquid and can, therefore, be converted into cash at short notice. Gold and **government bonds** are often readily bought by other investors. So with an active market and many buyers, gold and government bonds can be easily sold and converted into cash. The problem for banks is that near-liquid assets earn low rates of interest. Banks are therefore required to trade the benefits of liquidity against lower financial returns.

Prior to the global credit crisis of 2008, banks attempted to increase the interest earned on liquid assets and invested some of their cash in bonds that were linked to other banks' stocks of mortgages. These bonds were called **collateralized debt obligations** (CDOs) and paid a higher rate of interest than government bonds. However, as the sub-prime mortgage market in the USA collapsed, CDOs fell in value. Other banks were unwilling to buy, or take a CDO as collateral against a loan. When banks are unwilling to trade assets with each other, then there is a restriction on liquidity in the interbank market and this became known as the **credit crunch**.

> A credit crunch is a lack of liquidity between banks.

Risk pooling

Ordinary savers could provide liquidity to borrowers. However, with limited funds, the average saver may be able to fund only one borrower or even only a small part of their need for cash. This will leave the individual saver very exposed to the risk of default by the borrower. In contrast, by pooling savers' funds, banks have access to a larger share of funds and are therefore able to fund a larger pool of risks. By choosing a varied and non-correlated set of risks, banks can use risk pooling to derive benefits from diversification. (See Chapter 7 for a reminder of diversification economies.) If one borrower defaults, then the bank is left with a bad debt. But the profitable proceeds from lending to the rest of the pool are usually sufficient to outweigh this cost. Because of the benefits to be gained from diversification, banks are able to take on greater lending risks than an individual saver. As a result, projects or transactions that would not be funded by individuals are funded by banks. Therefore, risk pooling by banks enables the economy to grow.

Risk selection and monitoring

Banks employ individuals who are experts in understanding financial risks. Bank managers are trained to assess and evaluate the merits of lending to individuals and companies. This expertise and skill enables banks to select risks more effectively than ordinary individuals with surplus savings to invest. As a result, with a well-functioning banking sector, investment options with a greater probability of financial success should be selected. If this occurs, then there should be less waste of financial resources across the economy.

Banks are also skilled at monitoring loans made to companies. Banks are able to understand when a company is in financial difficulty and when it is right to put a company into liquidation and seek repayment of the original loan. Ordinary savers are less likely to be able to understand a company's financial statement or evaluate its chances of survival in a turbulent trading environment. As a result, banks are an efficient and effective means of selecting and monitoring risk.

Risk pricing

As experts in financial risk, banks are able to provide a good assessment of risk and therefore the price for taking on such risk. The more risky the project, the higher the interest rate on the loan. Banks can also access the pool of resources held by rival banks. This enables large and risky projects to be funded, but with the financial risk shared among many banks. Finally, banks reduce the cost of borrowing. In raising financial resources from one bank, a borrower cuts down on the costs of transacting with many small savers. Therefore banks are both a cost-efficient means of distributing loans and an effective mechanism for pricing the risk associated with lending.

 ## Regulation

Banks are institutions which take financial risks with depositors' money. While traditionally banks have been seen as very safe, recent events associated with the credit crisis have shown that banks around the world are still vulnerable to collapse. In fact, banks represent an important risk known as **contagion**. Because banks can also lend to each other, if one bank collapses, then it defaults on its loans with other banks. This weakens the other banks, which can then also collapse. Contagion leads to a domino effect, with one bank toppling more banks. It should be of little surprise to know that

> Contagion occurs when the collapse of one bank leads to the collapse of more banks.

banks are regulated. The form of regulation can vary across economies, but the main objectives of **regulation** are often to ensure financial stability and economy-wide confidence in the banking sector.

Historical review of regulation

The regulation of banks has changed greatly over the years. This is a reflection of changing political and economic concerns. Some of the biggest changes in financial regulation occurred during the 1980s, but were linked to events in the 1970s.

In the late 1960s, economies around the world operated **fixed exchange rate** regimes under the **Bretton Woods** agreement. We will consider such systems in more detail in Chapter 15. But, in brief, a fixed exchange rate regime fixes the rate of conversion between currencies. There is no daily movement in the exchange rate for a currency. Such systems often require controls on the movement of currency between economies. As an example, British holidaymakers in the 1960s could take no more than £50 with them out of the country.

From 1971, the fixed exchange rate systems were abandoned by leading economies. This also meant that currency controls could be abandoned. This allowed tourists and, more importantly, banks to move currency around the world. Banks could lend and invest money where it was possible to make the highest rate of return. The globalization of financial services had begun.

The challenge for economies was how to embrace the opportunities offered by free currency movements. The UK decided that it wished to become a global financial services centre and in order to compete on a global scale, deregulation of the financial sector was deemed necessary.

Under the political leadership of Margaret Thatcher, the City of London financial system underwent Big Bang deregulation in 1986. This allowed financial companies to operate in a broader range of products and services. This increased competition between companies who had previously been investment banks or retail banks. It also enabled these banks to enter other markets, such as stockbroking. Perhaps most importantly, foreign companies could set up operations in the UK.

These changes were followed by changes in the regulations placed on **mutual** deposit-taking institutions such as building societies. The UK government allowed such companies to operate more like banks, raising money in wholesale markets, and offering current accounts, personal loans and credit cards. Similarly, insurance companies were able to set up banking divisions, and banks were able to set up insurance divisions.

In 1993, the EU opened up competition further. Until that date, banks and insurance companies had to have a licence from the government of each EU country that it operated in. Following 1993, a bank or insurance company only had to be licensed in one EU country for it to be able to operate in all EU member countries. Cross-border competition began to increase.

Deregulation over the years can be argued to have achieved two simple outcomes: first, an ability for financial companies to take greater risks in a broader range of product markets; second, a need to take bigger risks because increased competition was a threat to profitability. The consequences can be seen in large part in the credit crisis and the willingness of banks to take on increased financial risk and place the stability of the entire financial system in danger.

Types of regulation

The regulation of banks and other financial institutions, including insurance companies, is often referred to as prudential regulation. Prudence is a careful and cautious approach to operating financial institutions, which aims to avoid reckless lending or investments which may undermine the stability of the regulated bank. There are various aspects to prudential regulation.

> Regulation is the use of rules and laws to limit, control and monitor the activities of banks.
>
> Fixed exchange rates have a fixed rate of conversion between currencies.
>
> The Bretton Woods agreement of 1944 provided a plan for managing foreign exchange rates.

> A mutual is a financial organization that is owned by its customers. This contrasts with a bank, which is owned by shareholders.

Capital adequacy

Banks in most economies are subject to capital adequacy ratios. The use of capital adequacy ratios stems from internationally agreed standards known as **Basel III**. A **capital adequacy ratio** measures the value of a bank's capital to its risk-weighted portfolio of assets. A bank's capital includes the equity invested by shareholders, retained profits and provisions for any expected losses. Assets are loans and investments. These assets are weighted according to risk. So, if loans to companies are more risky than loans to governments, then the value of the company loans will be increased by the size of the weight.

The capital adequacy ratio measures the extent to which assets within the bank are backed by shareholders' funds. If assets in the bank grow at a faster rate than shareholders' funds, then the asset growth must have come from funds provided by deposit holders and providers of debt to the bank. Therefore, capital adequacy ratios provide a guide as to who is exposed to the bank's risk of default. If governments wish to see greater protection for deposit holders, then they can insist on a greater capital adequacy ratio and shareholders have to provide greater equity to the bank. Capital adequacy is therefore a measure of bank safety. The more capital backing a bank, the bigger loss its shareholders can suffer, before losses spread to deposit holders and providers of debt.

> Basel III provides an internationally agreed set of conditions for the minimum financial strength of a bank. The conditions relate to how the risks of a bank must be assessed and how much cash and reserves a bank must hold to protect itself against large losses from the risks that it faces.
>
> Capital adequacy ratio is a measure of how much capital a bank needs to protect itself from a large loss on the investments or loans that it has made.

Minimum reserve requirements

An alternative approach to bank regulation is the use of minimum reserve requirements. Such regulation stipulates the ratio of deposits that must be held in reserves in liquid or near-liquid form. Regulation through reserve requirements seeks to ensure that deposit holders have free and open access to funds. In contrast to capital adequacy ratios, minimum reserve requirements emphasize liquidity over safety.

Box 12.2 highlights the extent to which capital needs to be strengthened by European banks and some of the possible and controversial means of demonstrating capital strength.

Box 12.2

Capital questions linger in Europe

European regulators said the Continent's banks are well on their way to replenishing their capital cushions, but concerns persist that the lenders aren't taking sufficiently drastic actions to fortify themselves.

The European Banking Authority last December ordered 31 banks to come up with a total of nearly €115 billion ($152.5 billion) of new capital by June, an effort to defuse fears about the solvency of the European banking sector. The EBA said Thursday that banks collectively have submitted plans to more than cover the shortfall.

The authority and national regulators are starting the process of sifting through the banks' proposals, a process that is scheduled to wrap up by next month. The EBA and national regulators have the power to reject plans they deem inadequate. The pan-European agency plans to pay especially close attention to

banks that are relying on robust anticipated profits in the first half of this year to bridge their capital shortfalls, according to a person familiar with the matter.

Most of the new capital that banks plan to drum up comes from socking away profits, cancelling cash dividends and converting certain debt securities into equity, according to the EBA. Dozens of European banks have announced such manoeuvres in recent months.

Far fewer have announced the sorts of measures, such as selling large quantities of new shares or ditching major business lines, that would quickly erase concerns about their health. One of the few exceptions is Italy's UniCredit SpA, which last month sold €7.5 billion of shares through a so-called rights offering.

Some analysts worry that banks are meeting the EBA's requirements without major capital-raising initiatives. 'The mood of denial with respect to raising capital at French and German banks does not help the overall sector, in our view, and contributes to a painful credit crunch,' analysts at Mediobanca Securities wrote Thursday.

About 16 per cent of the capital banks said they would come up with stems from adjustments to the way they calculate 'risk-weighted assets', the EBA said. By reducing the risk classifications on certain assets, which serve as the denominator of the most widely used capital ratios, banks can reduce the capital requirements associated with them.

Wide discrepancies between how different banks calculate the risk weightings on similar assets have fuelled concerns among some bankers, regulators and investors that certain banks are using artificially low risk weightings to inflate their capital ratios.

The EBA, at its board meeting in London this week, established a new task force to look into the issue and to come up with guidance for bank supervisors about how to reduce the inconsistencies among risk-weightings used by different banks.

Activity-based regulation

Banking regulation can also be activity based. This can limit the services banks offer and the sectors within which they operate. Following the Wall Street Crash in 1929, banks in the USA were prevented from also running insurance operations. Similar rules were also implemented in the UK and Europe. Banks often found it difficult to take over rivals and expand into new, profitable areas. However, during the last 20 years many economies have followed a policy of financial deregulation. This has enabled banks and insurance companies to move into each other's sectors. Further deregulation has enabled many banks to raise additional funds through wholesale money markets. While this raises liquidity when money markets are operating well, it also exposes banks to severe liquidity problems when the markets dry up, as in the credit crunch.

Risk-based regulation and monitoring

Banks and other financial institutions are in frequent discussions with the regulator. Monthly statutory returns provide the regulator with an ongoing picture of the institutions' financial positions and the likely risks going forward. The UK Financial Services Authority feeds this information into its risk-based regulation model. Firms are judged on risk and impact. A large bank, with low risks, still produces a high impact if it collapses and so will be monitored closely. A small company with a higher risk of collapse will be allocated less oversight, because the impact of collapse on the economy is likely to be less.

Regulators also monitor companies based on firm risk and thematic risk. Firm risks are specific to the firm, for example a firm may have a low capital adequacy ratio. In contrast, thematic risks cut across firms within the same sector. A bank may be heavily exposed to the mortgage market. Instability in this bank may then lead to a loss of confidence in other mortgage lenders. Firm and thematic risks therefore require different solutions. Firm risks require specific action within a specific firm, whereas thematic risks require co-ordinated solutions across a range of regulated companies.

When regulation fails

By the very nature of risk, it is inevitable that some financial companies will collapse at some point. However, it is the nature of the risk and the collapse that will determine the authorities' responses.

In the early 1990s, one of the UK's most venerable banks, Barings, collapsed after one of its traders ran up £800 million in losses on the Asian commodity markets. In order to protect depositors, the bank was sold to a rival for £1. (The rival also picked up the £800 million in losses!) The losses on the Asian commodity markets were a specific risk generated by a rogue trader named Nick Leeson. So the sale of the bank was a specific solution to a specific risk.

During the credit crunch many banks around the world faced collapse. In most instances, these banks have been acquired by rivals, have received enormous capital injections from their governments and have been given greater access to liquidity through credit lines offered by central banks. The credit crunch was a thematic risk, in that all banks faced limited access to liquidity and faced a loss of confidence among deposit holders and shareholders. Such risks are also referred to as **systemic risks,** or contagion, as they pose a risk to the entire financial system. If one bank collapses, then since all banks are exposed to the same thematic risk, the fear and panic will spread to other banks, leading to further damage of the banking system.

> Systemic risk is a risk which can damage the entire financial system.
>
> The central bank is a lender of last resort if a bank cannot raise funds from any other lender.

If the risk is systemic, then banks have generally relied on the central bank to act as the **lender of last resort**. If a bank is in distress and cannot raise funds from any other lenders, then the central bank may act as the lender of last resort in order to save the distressed bank and to prevent panic from spreading to other banks.

Risks of moral hazard

Moral hazard occurs when someone changes their behaviour because they are insulated from risk. For example, a car driver may become a more risky driver once they have fully comprehensive insurance.

Similarly, a central bank's acting as the lender of last resort is not without moral hazard type problems. In particular, bailing out any bank that finds itself in difficulties can provide banks with incentives to take reckless decisions. The availability of emergency funds from the central bank effectively insures banks and their shareholders against the risks they take in lending. To combat this problem, the UK government used two approaches during the credit crisis. The central bank provided liquidity as the lender of last resort. In addition, the government injected capital into the banks by becoming a shareholder. However, it became a shareholder on very favourable terms, terms which penalized those existing shareholders who had enabled the banks to take excessive risks.

Credit creation and the money supply

Importantly, banks are able to boost liquidity to borrowers by recognizing that not all depositors will withdraw their money at the same time. This enables banks to grow the amount of available money by a process known as **credit creation**.

> Credit creation is the process of turning existing bank deposits into credit facilities for borrowers. The process can result in an increase in the money supply.

Consider a business with which many of you will be familiar – clubbing. You go to the club and pay for drinks. In the morning, the manager of the club pays the previous evening's takings into the bank – let us say £1000. When your hangover subsides, you realize that the really good night out was extremely expensive. You go to the bank and join the queue for an increase in your overdraft.

The bank is sitting on £1000 from the club and assumes that only £100 will be paid out in the near future as wages. The bank thinks it can safely lend out the remaining £900 in overdrafts. You and your fellow borrowers take the £900 and head straight back to the club for another big night out. In the morning, the club manager returns to the bank and pays in the £900. The bank manager awaits your call for another advance on your overdraft.

The banks are playing a very clever trick: the club manager thinks he has £1000 in the bank. But then the bank also lets you and your fellow borrowers think you have an additional £900 in the bank by lending part of the club's money to you. When you spend this drinking and enjoying yourself, the club manager pays the next night's takings into the bank, and he now thinks he has £1900 in the bank. We can, therefore, see that an initial £1000 in notes and coins was converted into another £900 of money, via overdrafts. This is then paid back into the bank and the process occurs again. Just as we have a fiscal multiplier, we can now observe banks, through credit creation, developing what is known as a money multiplier.

We clearly have to make a distinction between how much *money* people think exists and how much *cash* actually exists.

> **Monetary base**, or the stock of high-powered money, is the quantity of notes and coins held by private individuals or held by the banking system.

The amount of money, or the money supply, is the **monetary base** plus deposits at the bank. We will see shortly that this definition can be broadened, but it clearly includes the amount of cash in circulation and the amount people think they have in the bank.

The money multiplier is, therefore, the ratio of the money supply to the monetary base.

Size of the money multiplier

The size of the money multiplier is determined by two factors: (i) the willingness of individuals to deposit money in the bank, rather than keeping it in their pockets; and (ii) the level of reserves held by the banks. For example, the credit-creation process will become greater as more individuals provide banks with cash. So, as people switch from holding money in their pockets to storing it at the bank, the more banks can create credit. Second, if banks reduce reserves from 10 per cent to 5 per cent of deposits, then more credit can be created; for example, for every £100 paid in, the banks can lend out an additional £5 by reducing reserves from 10 per cent to 5 per cent.

So, if cash deposits and reserve levels are central to the process of credit creation, what influences each of these important factors? The level of reserves is directly influenced by regulation. Governments, or central banks, may insist that banks keep a minimum level of reserves in order to meet deposit holders' cash withdrawals. This merely reflects an interest by governments to avoid bankruptcy among the banking sector. Clearly, banks also wish to avoid bankruptcy and many will use treasury management teams to build complex models capable of predicting cash flows into and out of the bank on a daily basis. The more confident the bank is that cash flows in will exceed cash flows out, the more they will be willing to lend. The less predictable these cash flows become, the more dangerous it becomes to lower reserves and lend more money.

The willingness to hold cash on deposit, rather than in your pocket, has in recent times been influenced by technological change in the financial services industry. Many firms will pay salaries and wages only into bank accounts. Wages are rarely paid in cash any more. Loans, mortgages and mobile phone contracts will only be offered if direct debits can be set up on your bank account. Utility suppliers – gas, electricity and water – will offer discounts if monthly direct debits are set up. Couple all these changes with the popularity of credit cards, and the overall requirement for cash in your pocket, rather than at the bank, has significantly reduced. As a consequence, more cash is in the banking sector and banks using treasury management are becoming more adept at modelling its flows and taking opportunities to create credit.

> **Narrow measures of money** are notes and coins held in and outside of the private banking sector.
>
> **M4** takes notes and coins and adds retail and wholesale banking deposits. M4 is, therefore, a broad measure of money.

Measures of money

We saw above that measuring the money supply requires a distinction between cash and money on deposit. The government has used this distinction to develop a number of money measures ranging from **narrow measures of money**, previously known as M0 which covers notes and coins, to **M4**, which is a broad measure of money.

Table 12.2 Narrow and broad UK money (£ billion), 2011

	Reserve balances	£164
Narrow measure of money	Notes and coins	£53
+	Retail deposits	£1211
+	Wholesale deposits	£826
=	M4	£2090

Source: Bank of England.

Look at Table 12.2: notes and coins is £53 billion. Adding in retail and wholesale deposit accounts takes the broader measure of money, M4, to £2090 billion. Therefore, cash is a very small part of the money supply.

Reserve balances are cash held at the central bank by commercial banks. Such cash is not in circulation and is now defined as being outside of the money supply. However, it should be noted that in 2008 reserve balances stood at £7 billion. The massive increase to £164 billion by 2011 is a reflection of quantitative easing and the desire of commercial banks to place money on deposit with the central bank, rather than lend to customers.

The demand for money

The previous discussion provides an understanding of money supply. However, before we begin to consider how the government might effectively control the money supply, we also need to consider the demand for money.

Do not confuse a demand for more money with a demand for additional income. We all want more income, but may not want more money. For example, if you receive £1000 in income, the question is, how much of this £1000 will you hold in money and how much in other financial securities such as bonds or equities?

Economists identify three motives for holding money: the **transaction motive**, the **precautionary motive** and the **asset motive**.

The transaction motive

We hold money because we have to pay for goods and services at various points after we receive income payments. Consider the following scenarios: (a) you are paid on Friday and carry out all your shopping on Friday; and (b) you are paid on Friday and shop each day for food, clothes, fuel, etc. Under scenario (a), your payments and receipts of money are perfectly synchronized; under (b), they are not. Therefore, you need to hold more money in scenario (b) than in (a).

As the value of our transactions increases and as the degree of synchronization between receipts and payments deteriorates, the greater becomes the transactional motive for holding cash. Moreover, we need to state that demand is for real money balances, where the demand is adjusted for inflation. So, if inflation doubles, the nominal value of our receipts and payments will also double, and we will have to hold double nominal money balances, but in real terms our demand for money will remain constant.

> The **transaction motive** for holding money recognizes that money payments and money receipts are not perfectly synchronized.
>
> The **precautionary motive** for holding money reflects the unpredictability of transactions and the need to hold liquid funds in order to meet these payments.
>
> Under the **asset motive**, individuals hold money as part of a diversified asset portfolio. Some wealth is held in equities, some in bonds, a portion in property and some in money.

The precautionary motive

We also hold money because we are unsure when transactions will occur. For example, we might hold some money against emergencies, such as the car developing a fault and needing repairing; or we might have spare cash in order to take advantage of special offers in the shops as and when they occur.

As uncertainty increases, the precautionary motive for money will also increase. In addition, as income increases, the value of potential transactions also increases. For example, someone who owns a Ferrari needs to hold more money to fix a fault with the Ferrari than someone who owns a Mini (assuming each are equally reliable).

The asset motive

Individuals hold money as part of a diversified portfolio of assets. Equities are risky assets, with values going down as well as up. Bonds are financial instruments, where a firm offers to make specified repayments in the future to the bond holder. The risk is that the firm will default on the payments. Money is a low-risk asset. Aside from the exchange rate, the value of money is only affected in real terms by the inflation rate.

Clearly, the more wealth is held in cash, the more an individual is forgoing the potential higher returns from holding other financial assets such as bonds. Indeed, bonds pay a rate of return, or interest. We can argue that the higher the rate of interest on bonds, the higher the opportunity cost of holding real money balances. Therefore, as the interest rate increases, individuals will demand fewer real money balances.

We can now use these ideas to understand how the demand for money varies with prices, income, interest and risk. In Figure 12.1, individuals will hold real money balances up to the point where the marginal benefit of cash is equal to the marginal cost. The cost of holding cash is equal to the interest forgone on a bond. So the marginal cost of money is constant, and represented by the horizontal line in Figure 12.1. The marginal benefit of money is considered for a given level of real income. The benefits of cash are downward sloping because additional cash has greater value when we have less of it. With a high income and low cash balances, we have to be careful to match payments and receipts, we have to avoid risk and reduce our precautionary needs for cash and we have limited scope for investing our scarce cash. As our real cash balances increase, then our cash requirements are more in balance with our income level and the value of additional cash falls.

In equilibrium, our real holdings of money will be determined by the intersection of the marginal benefits and marginal costs of holding cash. In Figure 12.1, this is L_1. If interest rates increase, then the marginal cost of holding cash will increase and individuals will hold less cash, L_2. Similarly, if interest rates fall, then the opportunity cost of holding cash falls and individuals' holdings of money will increase.

If real incomes increase, then the marginal benefits of holding cash at any interest rate increase and so the marginal benefit line moves to the right and the new equilibrium level of real money balances becomes L_3 in Figure 12.1.

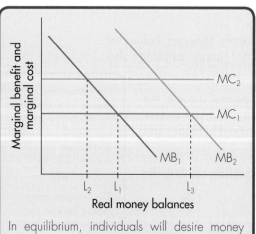

In equilibrium, individuals will desire money balances up to the amount where the marginal benefit and marginal cost of holding money are equal. If the marginal cost of holding money increases, then the desire to hold money will fall. Equally, if the marginal benefit of holding money increases, then the desire for money will increase.

Figure 12.1 Desire for real money balances

Money market equilibrium

Now that we understand the demand and supply of money, we can think about the money market equilibrium. Figure 12.2 shows the demand for real money balances, LL_1, and the supply of money, L_1. The demand for real money balances is negatively related to the rate of interest. This is easy to understand if we look back at Figure 12.1. If we increase the marginal cost of holding money (the interest rate), then fewer real money balances are held.

The supply of money is perfectly inelastic. As the interest rate, or price of money, increases, then the supply of money remains unchanged. This, as we will see shortly, is because the government (or central bank) adds to or reduces the money supply as it sees fit. Its decision is not influenced by the interest rate.

As interest rates on bonds increase, individuals find holding money too expensive and reduce their holdings of real money balances. At the equilibrium A, the demand for real money balances is equal to the money supply at an interest rate of r_0.

We can consider a change to the demand for real money balances. If income increased, or uncertainty increased, then either the transaction motive or the precautionary motive for holding money would increase. In both instances, the demand for real money balances would shift out to the right, at LL_2. If money supply remains unchanged, the equilibrium moves to B and the interest rate rises to r_1.

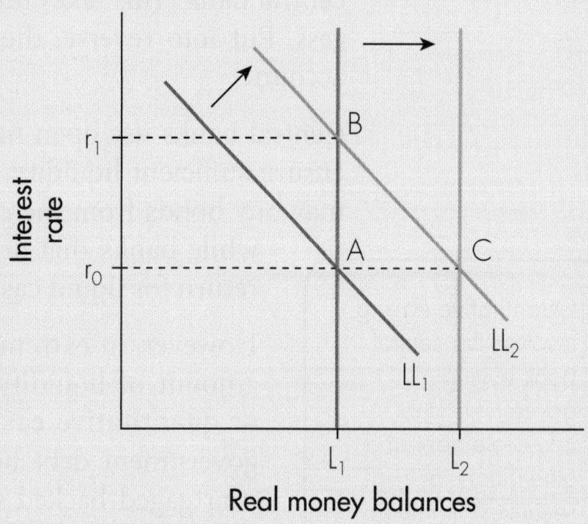

If the central bank increased the money supply from L_1 to L_2, by printing more banknotes, then the supply of money would

Money demand LL is interest responsive, reflecting a trade-off between holding non-interest-bearing money and alternative interest-generating assets such as bonds. Money supply, L, is perfectly interest inelastic. In equilibrium, money demand equals money supply. An increase in money demand will lead to a higher equilibrium interest rate, while an increase in money supply will lead to a lower equilibrium interest rate.

Figure 12.2   Money market equilibrium

move out to the right. At the higher level of money demand, LL_2, the equilibrium moves to C and the interest rate returns to r_0. Clearly, if the central bank reduced the amount of money in the economy, then the interest rate would increase.

Controlling the money supply

We know that the money supply is composed of cash in circulation plus money on deposit at the banks. In attempting to control the money supply, it is clear that the central bank has two options open to it: (1) it could regulate the credit-creation process undertaken within banks or (2) it could control the amount of notes and coins in circulation.

Managing the credit-creation process requires regulation of the minimum reserve requirements run by banks. If a bank only holds 5 per cent of its deposits in reserve, then it can create far more credit than if it is required to hold, say, 10 per cent of its deposits on reserve. So, increasing the minimum reserve requirements of a bank can help to reduce the credit-creation process and thereby limit growth in the money supply. However, banks may not like minimum reserve requirements. Holding cash on reserve can be wasteful when the cash might be profitability loaned out to a borrower. In addition, global market banks can bypass minimum reserve requirements by using a country with the lowest reserve requirements as their base.

The second method for controlling the money supply is to print more money. Ben Bernanke, the head of the US Federal Reserve, has referred to this approach as the helicopter option. Fly above a major city and drop freshly printed notes. Everyone is then free to collect and spend the new money, which eventually will end up in the banks, whereupon the credit-creation process will further expand the money supply.

A more sophisticated means of managing the monetary base is to use **open market operations**. The central bank might sell bonds in the marketplace. If a bank bought such a bond, it would write a cheque and transfer money from its account to the

Open market operations occur when the central bank buys and sells financial assets in return for money.

central bank. This takes funds out of the banking system and limits the credit-creation process. Put into reverse, the central bank could buy bonds and place money in the bank's account.

Central banks use open market operations on a daily basis and the primary purpose is to ensure sufficient liquidity within the banking system. Banks that have too much liquidity may buy bonds from the central bank and increase their reserves held at the central bank, while banks that are short of liquidity may sell bonds back to the central bank in return for liquid cash.

However, in extreme cases, the central bank may wish to dramatically increase the amount of liquidity within the banking sector and it will then consider a policy of **quantitative easing**. Under quantitative easing, the central bank will purchase government debt bonds, corporate debt bonds and other financial assets, such as mortgaged-backed securities and even equities. In return, the sellers of these assets, often banks, receive cash. This then improves the banks' liquidity. Credit creation and lending can increase.

Quantitative easing was used in Japan between 2001 and 2005. During the credit crisis it was also used by central banks such as the US Federal Reserve and the UK's Bank of England.

There are problems with quantitative easing. First, if a bank sells an asset to the central bank, then it may not use the additional cash. Instead, the bank may leave the cash on reserve at the central bank. It would be likely to do this if it felt that the economic environment was so bad that to lend out the money would offer an unacceptably high level of risk.

Second, it is necessary to recognize a difference between quantitative easing and **qualitative easing**. Under quantitative easing, the quality of the central bank's balance sheet stays roughly equal. High quality bonds are swapped for cash. Under qualitative easing, the quality of the central bank's balance sheet deteriorates. Cash is swapped for poor quality assets. In this way, quantitative easing can present problems of moral hazard. Banks wishing to offload high risk, poor quality assets can swap them at the central bank for cash. These poor quality assets then appear on the central bank's balance sheet. To avoid this problem, central banks offer to buy assets at a substantial discount. This is referred to as a **haircut**.

> Quantitative easing involves the central bank buying government debt, corporate debt and other financial securities. In return, cash is provided to the vendors of these assets.
>
> Under **qualitative easing**, the central bank swaps high quality assets for poorer quality assets.
>
> A haircut is the discount required by the buyer of a risky asset. An asset valued at £100 and bought for £80 is said to have suffered a 20 per cent haircut. The haircut will hopefully insure the buyer against any future losses in value of the asset.

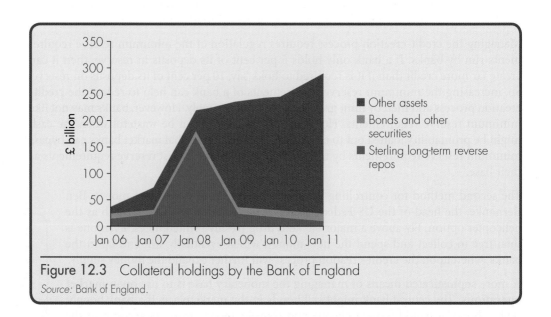

Figure 12.3   Collateral holdings by the Bank of England

Source: Bank of England.

Figure 12.3 illustrates the changing composition of the Bank of England's holdings of collateral before and after the beginning of the credit crisis. It is clear that from late 2008 onwards, the Bank of England massively expanded its purchase of assets. In the initial phase on and around 2008, the Bank purchased government bonds and mortgage-backed securities. These purchases of assets are captured in sterling long-term reverse repos and bonds and other securities. Once the Bank was enabled to undertake quantitative easing it effectively created money and began an enormous purchase of financial assets which are listed under 'other'. In total these assets totalled close to £250 billion by the end of 2011.

Controlling the interest rate

The alternative to controlling the money supply is the use of interest rates. Under such a policy, interest rates are declared and then however much money is demanded at the official base rate is how much money is supplied to the market. The central bank is effectively fixing the interest rate for the money market, and then managing the money supply through open market operations to ensure that the market price for money is the same as the central bank's declared rate of interest.

Control of interest rates can have additional benefits. Where demand for money is particularly unstable, it is best to set interest rates rather than money supply. For example, if the money supply is managed, then changes in money demand will lead to instability in interest rates. If the interest rate is set, however, changes in money demand simply lead to instability in money supply. If control of the economy operates more through interest rates than through money supply, it is of no surprise that policy has shifted from managing money supply to managing interest rates.

 ## Monetary policy

Governments and central banks across the world attempt to use money markets and the banking sector to influence overall levels of economic activity. They seek to achieve this through the setting of interest rates. So, it is not that central banks wish to bring about equilibrium in money markets when setting interest rates; rather, they believe that changes in the interest rate can be transmitted into the real economy and thereby have implications for inflation and economic activity. How this occurs is complex and can take many months, if not years, to work.

Monetary transmission

In simplistic terms, interest rates affect consumers' willingness to consume and firms' willingness to borrow for investment. How changes in the base rate feed through into changes in economic output and inflation is referred to as the **transmission mechanism**.

> The transmission mechanism is the channel through which monetary policy impacts economic output and prices.

Figure 12.4 provides the European Central Bank's schematic representation of the transmission mechanism. This figure links changes in the official bank base rate through to changes in the economy's price level.

The transmission mechanism is clearly complex. Changes in the central bank's base rate feed through into changes in retail bank and money market rates for loans. These changes impact the amount of credit in the economy, the price of other assets, such as shares, bonds and property, and can even alter the exchange rate. Changes in the base rate also help to manage expectations. As the central bank changes rates, it demonstrates its commitment to fighting inflation. This commitment has an impact on price and wage setting.

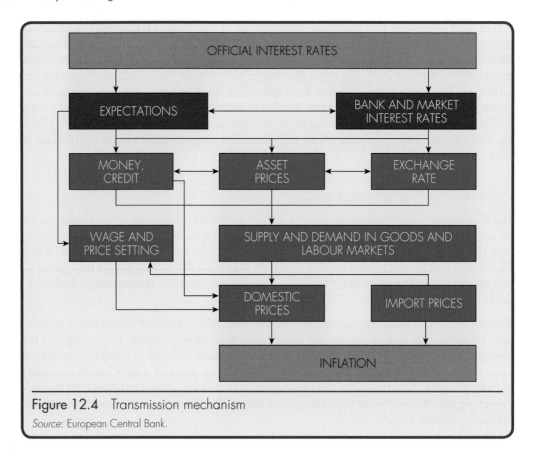

Figure 12.4 Transmission mechanism
Source: European Central Bank.

However, at the core of the transmission mechanism is how firms and consumers adjust their spending decisions in the light of rate changes. This drives changes in the demand for goods and services. Consumers borrow for consumption and firms borrow for investment, both of which are important components of aggregate demand. Changes in aggregate demand feed through into changes in equilibrium GDP and inflation; see Chapter 9 and Figure 9.10. In order to develop your understanding further, we will now concentrate on consumption and investment behaviour within the transmission mechanism.

Consumption

The Keynesian view of consumption, presented in Chapter 11, suggests that consumption is directly related to current income. As income increases, then, through the marginal propensity to consume, consumption will also increase. The link between interest rates and consumption must therefore act through income.

A simple example from Chapter 11 is that consumers' belief in a cut in interest rates will boost investment demand. Through the multiplier, this boost in autonomous investment will then lead to higher GDP. Higher GDP will, in turn, lead to higher income for consumers and therefore higher consumption.

Interest rates can also impact directly on household consumption. Interest is the price of money. If interest rates fall, then in real terms consumers are better off. They can now purchase more credit for the same amount of expenditure (interest). So, as interest rates fall, real income rises and so does consumption.

> Net present value is the discounted value of a future cash flow.

Falling interest rates also raise today's value of future income. If you expect to earn £30 000 per annum in five years' time, what is it worth today? Or in economic terminology, what is the **net present value** of £30 000?

Think of the problem in reverse. If interest rates are 5 per cent, how much money must I place in the bank today in order to have £30 000 in five years' time? The answer is £23 505. So, £30 000 in five years' time is worth £23 505 today. If interest rates fall, then more has to be saved today in order to have £30 000 in the future. So falling interest rates raise the net present value of future income streams. So, if you are thinking of borrowing over the long term, falling interest rates raise your long-term income, which enables you to borrow more to spend.

An alternative view is the **permanent income hypothesis**, put forward by Milton Friedman. This model asserts that consumption is determined by expectations of life-time earnings, rather than current income. So, two students working at Starbucks, earning the same wage, will only consume the same amount if they both expect to have the same lifetime earnings. In contrast, if one is expecting to be a doctor and the other a teacher, then the medical student will consume more now, knowing that they are effectively borrowing from future higher income.

> The permanent income hypothesis states that consumption is determined by lifetime earnings and not current income.

Under the permanent income hypothesis, changes in consumption are only achieved by changes in lifetime earnings. Temporary changes in earnings are unlikely to affect consumption. So, a minor and temporary reduction in interest rates will not change lifetime earnings and so will not alter consumption. However, if the economy moves to a period of sustained and historically low interest rates, then consumers may come to readjust their expectations of lifetime earnings. During the late 1990s and 2000s, low interest rates were a major economic theme. At the same time, incomes, consumption and borrowings grew enormously.

Another key feature of the period was a rapid growth in property prices. This is asset price inflation and can increase households' lifetime wealth. Again, if households think the change is permanent they will adjust their borrowing and consumption behaviour. One year's growth in property prices is temporary. Ten years' suggests a permanent change. Coupled with low interest rates, households began to borrow heavily to fuel consumption. Following the credit crunch and the fall in property prices, households may now consider if their lifetime earnings and wealth are falling.

Investment activity

A firm's willingness to invest is determined by cost–benefit analysis. The benefits can be measured as the financial returns from investing in a new product, office or production facility. The main costs are the funds required to invest and the cost of such funds (interest). Other costs might include disruption costs. Clearly, the rate of interest is the direct cost of investing and will determine the firm's willingness to borrow and spend.

However, interest can also have an additional role to play in the appraisal of an investment project. Consider a project which will generate financial benefits for each of the next five years. A way of evaluating a project is to calculate its net present value – what value are the project's benefits (less costs) today? The method of net present value enables projects of differing lengths, say three and five years, to be compared.

If the project generates a benefit of £10 million in year five, we can work out what that value is today. We simply have to work out how much money we would need to put in the bank today in order to have £10 million in five years' time. So, if interest rates are 5 per cent, then we would need to put £7.8 million in the bank today; or, £10 million in five years' time is worth £7.8 million today. Clearly, as the interest rate increases, we can place less in the bank to achieve the £10 million in year five; or, as the interest rate increases, £10 million in year five is worth less to us today.

The discussion above indicates that interest rates affect investment decisions in two ways. First, higher rates of interest drive up the cost of borrowing and so reduce investment. Second, higher rates of interest make the value of future financial benefits smaller in today's terms; that is, higher interest rates provide a bigger discount to future cash flows and so

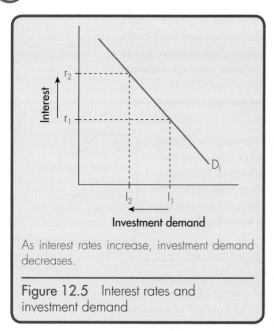

As interest rates increase, investment demand decreases.

Figure 12.5 Interest rates and investment demand

reduce investment. Taken together, both these mechanisms result in a negative relationship between the rate of interest and the willingness to borrow and invest. See Figure 12.5.

In practice, the Bank of England's monetary committee works on the assumption that interest rate changes take one year to affect economic output and two years to affect prices. These are rules of thumb reflecting more practical considerations of economic adjustment, rather than hard precise rules predicted by economic theories.

The time lag for economic output could reflect pre-committed expenditures. You may book the family summer holiday in January. But between January and the summer, interest rates may rise. Because you are pre-committed to spending the money, the interest rate rise is unlikely to alter your expenditure, or overall aggregate demand, but it may curb the amount of expenditure you pre-commit to next year's summer holiday. The same may be true of house purchases and investment in production or retail facilities by firms, where an interest rate change takes place between the decision to spend and the actual point when the transaction takes place. The transactions will still take place because the parties are committed to the sale process. It is only in the longer term that the volume of sales and the amount of investment will reflect the new higher interest rates. In a similar manner, a fall in interest rates is unlikely to lead to an immediate increase in additional expenditure because the expenditure for the coming year has already been planned out and committed. It is only next year that you may upgrade your holiday expenditure, while within firms with strict budgetary control and annual planning cycles, additional expenditure will not occur for another 12 months.

The two-year time lag for inflation is likely to reflect the prevalence of annual wage negotiations and the evolution of inflationary expectations. For example, if interest rates are increased to fend off higher inflation, it is not clear how this policy will alter inflationary expectations. In the short term, the higher interest rate may have little impact, with consumers and firms wondering about the credibility of the monetary authorities to fight inflation. Only if rates are kept high for a period of six to 12 months will inflationary expectations change. Once these changes in expectations are made, they will not impact wages and prices until wage negotiations take place. These tend to be conducted annually. So, given that interest rates take a year to affect output, the ability to change prices and wages to the new equilibrium output level may take up to one year longer.

The problem with such long time lags is that some other problem may hit the economy in the intervening period – for example, war, terrorist attack, avian flu, stock market crash or oil price increase. All of these are very real, immediate and significant threats to economic stability.

Central bank independence

A final consideration is the independence of monetary policy from political motives. A fear with fiscal policy is that governments will face incentives, particularly near to elections, to alter taxation and spending for electoral gain rather than for economic stability. The same can be true for monetary policy, except it is easier to place monetary policy with a non-government agency, such as the central bank. In the USA, the Federal Reserve is charged with setting interest rates to deliver stable economic growth and fight inflation. In the UK, the Bank of England is charged with using monetary policy to bring about financial stability and inflation rates of 2 per cent on average. In the eurozone, the European Central Bank is required to use monetary policy to achieve an inflation rate of less than 2 per cent.

Providing central banks with an inflation target reduces the political incentive to change rates. In addition, as non-political bodies, central banks may be seen as more credible bodies for fighting inflation. This should help to bring inflationary expectations into line with the inflation target. However, the appointment of key monetary decision makers, at most central banks, is a government decision. So, decisions may still be taken in the light of political patronage.

Business application: monetary policy and investment

Investment and business confidence

Debt is a complementary good for firms seeking to invest. Just as car users need to buy petrol, firms when investing in new capacity often need to purchase loans. If the interest rate falls, loans become cheaper. However, the cost of the loan is not the only factor that influences a firm's decision to invest. The interest rate reflects a cost of investing, but what about the benefits? If an economy is in recession, consumption of goods and services is falling. If a firm cannot sell the output generated by new investments, the benefits of investing are very low. A recession is, therefore, likely to reduce business confidence. If businesses are not confident about being able to sell products, or make a profit because of recession, they are likely to delay investment decisions. Reductions in interest rates are unlikely to boost investment rates.

Box 12.3 highlights the improving but different levels of business confidence across the German economy. Manufacturers appear most confident and are operating above average capacity. Construction as a sector is also feeling more confident, however, retailing is not as optimistic as it was in previous months.

Small monthly changes in confidence are unlikely to impact long-term investment decision making. It is more likely that consistent improvements in confidence over time, which lead to realized improvements in sales and profits, will generate an increased willingness to borrow and invest.

Investment under low inflation and low interest rates

A more fundamental question surrounds the recent desire for low inflation and low interest rates. What are the effects of low inflation on the economy and, in particular, on business? Constantly low inflation should bring increased stability. Businesses seeking to invest millions over many years will be assured by increased price stability. Predictions regarding costs and revenues are much easier to make and firms face less uncertainty when assessing investment risks. If low inflation reduces uncertainty, active monetary policy, leading to low inflation, may boost investment because of stability issues rather than because of cheaper borrowing.

Alternatively, low inflation may reduce the need, or desire, to invest. High wage inflation increases a firm's production costs. In order to recover these cost increases, firms may seek to raise the final price for their products. In such a scenario, firms have a clear incentive to swap increasingly expensive workers for capital equipment. But in recent times price inflation has been low. Wage demands have reflected the new lower rates of inflation and, as a result, firms have potentially less need to deal with an expensive workforce by investing in machinery.

It is, therefore, very clear that monetary policy and the pursuit of low inflation have many varied implications for business. Interest rates may influence investment simply by changing the cost of borrowing. However, the impact of interest rates on economic activity, business confidence and especially consumer spending and export growth may play a greater role in investment decisions. Finally, the use of monetary policy in targeting low inflation and economic stability may influence investments in different ways. Increased stability may make firms more willing to invest simply because it is easier to assess the relative costs and revenues from investment. However, without rising inflation and a consequential rise in labour costs, the need or desire to substitute capital for workers will be diminished.

Box 12.3

Ifo business climate continues to rise

The Ifo Business Climate for trade and industry in Germany improved for the third time in succession in January (Figure 12.6). Although companies assess the current business situation as less favourable than in December, their business expectations have brightened considerably.

The business climate improved in *manufacturing*. Manufacturers see their current business situation as slightly improved and their business outlook as clearly more favourable than in the previous month. Export expectations and personnel planning are also somewhat more positive once again. Capacity utilization in manufacturing is currently slightly lower than in autumn 2011. However, use of equipment and machinery remains above average.

In *retailing* the business climate index fell. The business situation here is no longer as favourable as it was in December. Moreover, retailers are more sceptical about their short-term business outlook. In *wholesaling* the business climate deteriorated slightly. The wholesalers surveyed continue to assess their current business situation as very positive, but less favourable than last month. Their business expectations are once again slightly more confident.

The business climate in *construction* improved for the third month in succession. The current business situation, however, is no longer as favourable as in the previous month. The constructors surveyed are nevertheless significantly more confident about their six-month business outlook.

Adapted from 'Ifo Business Climate Report' by the Ifo Institute, Munich, January 2012.

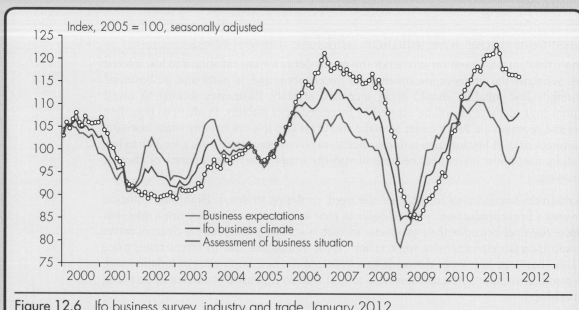

Figure 12.6 Ifo business survey, industry and trade, January 2012

Source: Ifo Institute, 2012.

Business application: the importance of banking to the economy

Should banking be the engine of economic growth, or the lubricant of the economic system? Section 12.3 emphasized the importance of banking in providing the economy with liquidity and risk management services. As such, banking plays the role of a lubricator within the economic system. When companies or households wish to undertake economic transactions using debt, then banks channel funds from savers to borrowers. Banking, therefore, plays a facilitating role within the economy.

During the past 20 years banks have benefited from repeated rounds of deregulation. Banks in many countries around the world are now able to offer a wider range of products, including credit cards, personal unsecured loans, pensions, insurance and a variety of personal investment products. This is sometimes referred to as 'bancassurance' – a conjunction of banking and insurance.

Deregulation has also enabled banks to operate internationally, not only in the products and services that they offer, but also in sourcing financial funds from depositors, debt holders and shareholders. As an example, traditional mortgage lenders raised money from savers and then loaned this money in the form of mortgages. More recently, companies in the USA and Europe have raised funds on wholesale money markets and then loaned this money in the form of mortgages. The mortgage loans have then been bundled up and sold on to investors. The notion of a bank providing mortgages by channelling savings to borrowers was almost redundant.

Deregulation has also enabled technical innovations, both in how money is managed and in the financial instruments that are available to banks and other institutions. Banks are not simply involved in savings and loans. They are just as involved in credit derivative markets, commodity markets, interest rate swap markets and currency markets. Where there is a financial risk and where there is a need for liquidity, then deregulation has enabled banks to expand their operations and profit.

Banks and financial services in general have grown to be important, significant and perhaps the largest component of growth within modern economies. Around financial hubs, such as London, Frankfurt, New York, Hong Kong and Singapore, the wealth from financial services companies has spilled out into residential property, the growing development of nearby leisure facilities and growing traffic through nearby airports and rail stations. Financial services has driven wealth within its own sector and within the wider related economy.

As financial services has become the engine of economic growth, it has arguably required greater deregulation and a greater ability to take increased risks in order to achieve yet higher rates of return. With an almost unblemished record at achieving growth without a loss of financial stability, governments were willing to see the complexity and innovativeness of financial services continue.

When this complexity resulted in the credit crunch and the collapse of many major banks, governments were required to bail out the financial system. These bailouts came with conditions. Governments became shareholders, required increased lending to households and small businesses, and required directors to sacrifice performance-related pay bonuses. The clear risk is that governments direct banks to meet political and social objectives; they do not necessarily direct banks to meet commercial objectives. Why should banks lend their new capital to households and small businesses? Does this offer the highest risk-adjusted rate of return? Will highly skilled managers stay at banks that cannot offer them performance-related pay? If not, will part-nationalized banking systems become less efficient, less effective, less profitable and less important to economic growth?

In the medium term, governments may take the view that owning banks is not necessary and may sell their stakes. Or they may take the view that owning banks ensures a degree of control and financial stability which is necessary for stable economic progress. If so, then governments will need to think about where they can gain new drivers of growth. This may herald a renaissance in the manufacturing sector, where companies generate jobs, accrue export earnings and in the main do not take risks with households' savings or with pension funds.

Business data application: financial markets and the impact of quantitative easing

In reaction to the worsening credit crisis and slowing of national economies a number of central banks operated a policy of quantitative easing. Between March 2009 and January 2010 the Bank of England purchased £200 billion of financial assets; and then in October 2011 began purchasing another £75 billion. The US Federal Reserve purchased $600 billion of financial assets between November 2008 and June 2010. Then from November 2010 to June 2011 the Federal Reserve purchased another $600 billion of financial assets in what was dubbed QE2. The European Central Bank has embarked upon less quantitative easing purchasing around €60 billion of financial assets. As central banks continue to examine ways of supporting economic activity within their economies, it is important for businesses to be able to understand the extent to which quantitative easing has altered interest rates within an economy and affected various sources of business financing. It is also important to understand the impact of quantitative easing on the key macroeconomic policy variables of inflation and GDP. For financial analysts working in the major financial markets of the world, central bank research reports offer important insights into the use and impact of quantitative easing.

In reviewing the consequences of quantitative easing in the UK, the Bank of England published a report in its 2011 Q3 Quarterly Bulletin. The report describes the approach taken by the Bank of England in undertaking quantitative easing, identifies how quantitative easing can drive changes in inflation and GDP, and assesses the evidence as to whether quantitative easing has led to changes in inflation and GDP.

The report identifies important channels for how quantitative easing can affect inflation and GDP. The first is via policy signalling. Investors, businesses and consumers form expectations about the future rate of inflation. In order to prevent inflation expectations falling below the Bank's 2 per cent medium term target rate for inflation, the Bank needs a powerful signal of its intent to hit the 2 per cent inflation. Large scale quantitative easing represents a significant policy commitment by the Bank to achieve the target; and so simply by its actions, the Bank signals to investors, businesses and consumers that inflationary expectations should be anchored at 2 per cent.

The second area, and according to the Bank of England the most important, is portfolio balance effects. When the Bank purchases assets, the sellers of financial assets are left with increased holdings of cash. This additional cash is then used to rebalance investment portfolios with an increased purchase of other financial assets, including bonds and shares. This increased demand for financial assets raises asset prices, which lowers the yield or interest rate of the asset. The lowering of yields makes financing cheaper and this boosts commercial and household borrowing, leading to higher spending.

The Bank of England's asset purchase scheme was designed to work on the portfolio balance effect. In the main, the scheme purchased medium to long-term financial assets held by insurance companies and pension funds. These companies would then be expected to return to the financial markets and purchase other assets including corporate bonds and equities. As a consequence the yields on these assets would fall and help to reduce the financing cost for commercial enterprise.

Figure 12.7 presents data on the change in holdings of government debt (gilts). The holdings of gilts by the non-bank private sector (of which the largest part is insurance and pension companies), increased, but not dramatically, following the implementation of the asset purchase scheme. The biggest changes in holdings of gilts were among non-residents, commercial

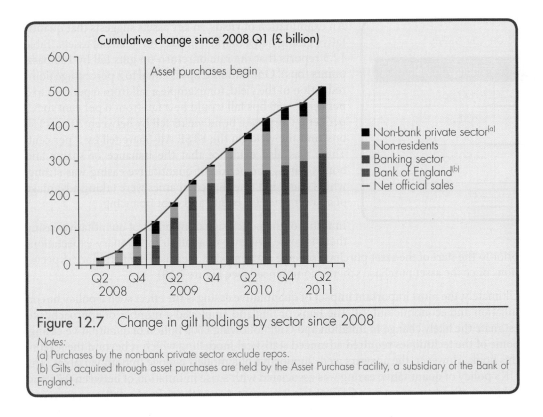

Figure 12.7 Change in gilt holdings by sector since 2008

Notes:
(a) Purchases by the non-bank private sector exclude repos.
(b) Gilts acquired through asset purchases are held by the Asset Purchase Facility, a subsidiary of the Bank of England.

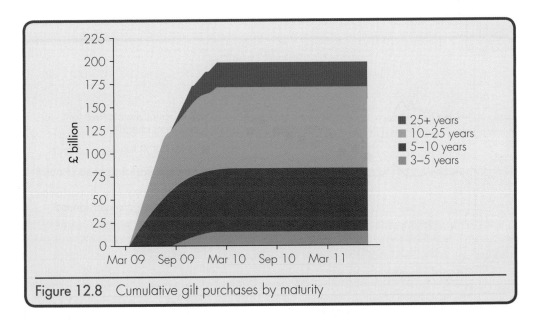

Figure 12.8 Cumulative gilt purchases by maturity

banks and the Bank of England. These data would suggest that the impact of the assets purchase scheme was to reduce the relative importance and size of the non-bank private sector as an owner of gilts.

Data in Figure 12.8 show that the vast majority of the assets purchased by the Bank of England were medium to long-term gilts. If the non-bank private sector had a desire to continue holding medium and long-term investment assets, the money from selling gilts was likely to find its way into the corporate bond and equity markets.

Table 12.3	Yields on key assets
Asset	**Change in yield**
Gilts	−100 bps
Corporate bonds investment grade	−70 bps
Corporate bonds high yield	−150 bps
FTSE All-Share	−3%

An examination of yields on key assets suggests that quantitative easing had a marked impact on financial assets. Table 12.3 reports that the rate of return on gilts fell by 100 basis points (bps). One hundred bps is equal to a percentage point reduction in the yield, for example a fall from 6 per cent to 5 per cent. A 50 bps fall would be a fall from 6 per cent to 5.5 per cent. Corporate bond yields fell by between 70 and 150 bps; and the yield on the FTSE All-Share fell by 3 per cent. There was also evidence that the issuance of shares and bonds during the period of quantitative easing was strong, which could indicate that companies were taking advantage of a lower price for equity and debt financing.

In terms of the policy signalling effect of quantitative easing there is some evidence of a fall in inflationary expectations prior to the start of the asset purchase scheme and a modest increase in inflationary expectations once the asset purchase scheme commenced (see Figure 12.9).

Ultimately, the most important impact of quantitative easing is the effect such a policy has on inflation and economic output. The Bank of England employed a number of approaches to estimate the likely change in inflation and GDP following £600 billion of quantitative easing. Some of the techniques required advanced statistical modelling which is beyond the level of this book. However, the answers were supportive of a modest change in both variables. The UK's policy of quantitative easing was associated with a rise in inflation of between 0.75 and 1.5 per cent and an increase in GDP of 1.5–2 per cent. Given the risks of a deflationary recession, the evidence suggests that quantitative easing helped the UK to avoid both deflation and a marked slowdown in GDP.

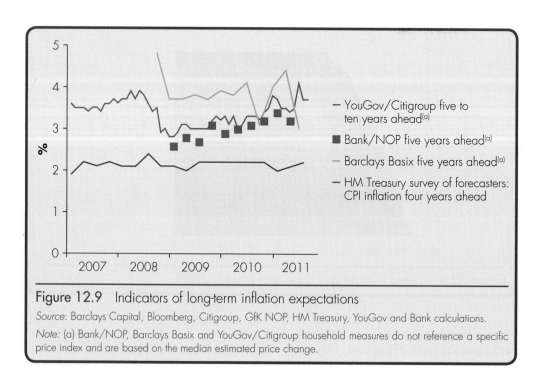

Figure 12.9 Indicators of long-term inflation expectations

Source: Barclays Capital, Bloomberg, Citigroup, GfK NOP, HM Treasury, YouGov and Bank calculations.

Note: (a) Bank/NOP, Barclays Basix and YouGov/Citigroup household measures do not reference a specific price index and are based on the median estimated price change.

Summary

1. Monetary policy is the use of interest rates, or money supply, to control aggregate demand.

2. Money has a number of characteristics. It has to be a store of value, a unit of account and accepted as a medium of exchange.

3. The banking system provides the economy with liquidity by channelling funds from savers to borrowers.

4. The banking system also reduces the cost of borrowing, improves monitoring and risk selection and reduces the transaction costs associated with matching savers and borrowers.

5. The objective of banking regulation is to bring financial stability to the economy.

6. Capital adequacy regulates banks by ensuring they have sufficient equity backing. This type of regulation focuses on the financial strength of the bank.

7. Minimum reserve requirements state the level of cash of near-liquid assets the bank must hold. This type of regulation focuses on the bank's liquidity.

8. Activity-based regulation limits banks' commercial activities to certain product ranges and sectors of the financial services industry.

9. The money supply is composed not only of notes and coins, but also deposits within the banking system. The narrow and broad measures of money, M0 and M4, attempt to take account of these differences.

10. Credit creation occurs when the banks create additional money supply by lending out money on deposit. This increases the money supply.

11. There are three motives for holding money: the transaction, precautionary and asset motives.

12. Increases in income lead to an increase in demand for real money balances and reflect the transaction and precautionary motives for holding money. The speculative motive reflects how changes in the interest rate lead to changes in demand for money.

13. In money market equilibrium, the demand for money equals the money supply.

14. Governments or central banks now seek to set the interest rate and then provide sufficient money supply in order to make the market clear.

15. It is the transmission of changes in the base rate to the economy that influences aggregate demand.

Learning checklist

You should now be able to:

- Explain the key features of money
- Understand the different types of banking and financial institutions
- Understand the structure of banks' balance sheets
- Identify the economic importance of banking

- Understand the main methods of bank regulation
- Provide an explanation of how banks create credit
- Explain why we use both broad and narrow measures of money
- Explain the three motives for holding money
- Discuss money market equilibrium using a suitable diagram
- Understand monetary policy and the transmission mechanism
- Understand and evaluate the evidence in relation to the success of quantitative easing
- Explain how business activities are influenced by changes in interest rates
- Assess the merits of a deregulated financial services industry

Questions   connect

1. Identify and explain the main features of money.
2. What are the main economic benefits to be gained from a (well-run) banking system?
3. Identify the important risks that banking regulation seeks to manage.
4. Are banks regulated by liquidity or capital adequacy? Is this a problem?
5. Identify and explain the main motives for holding money.
6. If incomes increase in an economy, how would this change the demand for real money balances?
7. Using a broad definition, what are the main components of the money supply?
8. What is the money multiplier and what factors determine the size of this multiplier?
9. The central bank cuts interest rates. How will this change in interest rate alter individuals' demand for cash?
10. What is quantitative easing and how do open market operations enable a policy of quantitative easing to be implemented?
11. Explain why a consideration of net present value may be a useful aid for managers making investment expenditure decisions.
12. Identify the key stages of the monetary transmission mechanism and what factors may prevent it from working.
13. Why might central bank independence and inflation targeting go together?
14. Why is central bank control of interest rates a control on over-exuberant fiscal policy? Is such a situation beneficial for business?
15. Do you consider income or wealth to determine the level of consumption?

EASY

INTERMEDIATE

DIFFICULT

Exercises

1. Which of the following would lead to an increase in the transaction demand for money?
   (a) An increase in prices.
   (b) An increase in real GDP.
   (c) A period of greater economic uncertainty.
   (d) A rise in interest rates.

EASY

2. A retail bank has a policy of holding cash reserves equal to 10 per cent of deposits.

   (a) If a customer deposits £1000, how much lending can the bank create? How would this lending change if cash reserves were less than 10 per cent?

   (b) How might a recession, or a banking crisis, alter a bank's willingness to hold reserves?

3. Consider Box 12.2:

   (a) 'The money markets are the plumbing of the economic system'. Explain.

   (b) Use a demand and supply diagram to illustrate the rise in the interbank interest rate.

   (c) How is the interbank market functioning today? What policies have helped to improve the interbank market?

Inflation, output and economic policy

CHAPTER 13

Chapter contents

Inflation, output and economic policy at a glance   329

13.1   Business problem: following a severe economic crisis, how does an economy return to equilibrium?   329

13.2   Short- and long-run macroeconomic equilibrium   331

13.3   Employment, inflation and output   333

13.4   Inflation, aggregate demand and supply   336

13.5   Short- and long-run equilibrium   337

13.6   Monetary policy rules   339

13.7   Adjustment speed   340

13.8   Business application: understanding the interest rate path   343

13.9   Business application: recognizing the importance of real business cycles   344

13.10   Business data application: understanding the formation of inflationary expectations   345

Summary   347

Learning checklist   348

Questions   348

Exercises   349

Learning outcomes

By the end of this chapter you should understand:

Economic theory

LO1   The short- and long-run Phillips curve

LO2   The macroeconomic demand schedule

LO3   Short- and long-run aggregate supply

LO4   The impact on macroeconomic equilibrium following shocks to demand and supply

LO5   Possible monetary policy responses to short-run disequilibria

LO6   The Taylor rule

LO7   Differing views on the speed of adjustment to long-run equilibrium

Business application

LO8   The interest rate path

LO9   The importance of real business cycles

LO10   Inflationary expectations in the long and short run

At a glance   Inflation, output and economic policy

The issue

Economic management is focused on inflation targeting and GDP. In macroeconomic equilibrium, how are inflation and GDP determined and how can government and central banks implement policies that enable inflation and GDP to be on target?

The understanding

Macroeconomic equilibrium is seen to be a reflection of equilibrium in important markets such as goods and labour. Prices and wages determine the value of employment to both workers and firms. Understanding how inflation alters real wages enables an appreciation of firms' willingness to supply output in the short term. Reactions to inflationary pressures in the longer term determine the rate of progression to long-run equilibrium.

The usefulness

Understanding the likely economic trajectory for an economy can provide businesses with a competitive edge and a greater degree of certainty. Understanding the drivers of supply- and/or demand-side shocks and being able to evaluate central bank changes in interest rates can provide businesses with a clearer understanding of the macroeconomic environment and provide a robust basis from which to build strategy and planning.

13.1 Business problem: following a severe economic crisis, how does an economy return to equilibrium?

Economies across the globe have faced enormous challenges following the banking crisis and the sovereign debt crisis. Economic activity has slowed dramatically, unemployment has increased and household earnings have declined. Governments are having to increase taxation and reduce spending, and central banks have deployed significant amounts of quantitative easing. Given the turmoil in many economies, businesses are keen to know how and when economies will move back to what might considered normality?

In addressing this question of macroeconomic adjustment, economists have come to recognize that an understanding of the macroeconomic environment must be built on microeconomic foundations. After all, the macroeconomy is nothing more than a vast collection of microeconomic decisions bundled up in an enormous assortment of markets. Therefore, the equilibrium price of goods and services, and just as important the wages paid to workers and the price of debt, are likely to have a major impact on the scale of economic activity at the macroeconomic level.

In Chapter 3, when examining the productivity of firms, we focused on two factor inputs used by firms: labour and capital. These two inputs have associated costs: wages for labour and debt repayments associated with borrowed finances used for capital investment. We also know from Chapter 10, when we examined inflation in detail, that we need to consider how inflation drives a wedge between nominal and real prices. Therefore, over time, wage and debt agreements priced in nominal values will have very different real values in the future. Inflation will reduce real values; deflation will increase real values. This feature of inflation has enormous implications for businesses that are seeking to plan long-term financial cash flows and repayment schedules.

Let us begin by looking at labour. Firms employ workers for the value they can add to profits. If wage growth is less than inflation, then workers actually become cheaper to hire and their value increases. Discrepancies between inflation and wage growth provide firms with an incentive to expand economic output. In contrast, when inflation falls behind wage growth, then workers become more expensive and firms reduce employment and output. Clearly, an understanding of how inflation and wages impact on output is crucial for companies wishing to understand the future path of the economy.

Earnings growth and inflation

Figure 13.1 provides data from the UK economy on earnings growth and inflation. Up until 2008 earnings growth exceeded inflation. This trend led to rising real earnings but can only be sustained in the long run if workers become more productive, generate more output per hour worked and so generate extra revenues to fund their higher earnings.

In the long run, prices and wages have no impact on the level of employment, economic output and therefore GDP. In the long run, the economy operates on its production possibility frontier. Every worker who desires a job is employed. This is because, in the long run, wage growth is in line with inflation. In the short run, however, unexpected changes in inflation impact the budgeted revenues and costs of firms. A worsening profit position results in output reductions, while an improving profit position results in increased outputs.

Short-run variations in output, caused by unexpected rates of inflation, are likely to be temporary. Firms and workers will form new expectations of future inflation and adjust prices and wages accordingly. New budgets will be planned and employment and output adjusted. The more rapidly and accurately prices and wages adjust to long-term levels, the more quickly the economy will return to the production possibility frontier.

Therefore, understanding the adjustment process is crucial to understanding the future path of the economy. In fact, by being closer to the adjustment process, businesses probably have a greater understanding of the correction process than economists. Factors that impede or facilitate changes in prices and wages are familiar to business. Wage negotiations with workers and unions can be difficult, contested and protracted. Similarly, the ability to change prices is constrained by competition and the actual cost of updating price lists and informing retailers. The less resistance to price and wage changes, the swifter an economy will return to equilibrium.

Changes in the real price of debt have similar implications for economic activity. As inflation rises, then the real value of debt falls. Firms (and consumers) who have debt repayment commitments find that the real value of debt falls (assuming incomes rise in line with inflation). Conversely, deflation raises the real value of debt. Incomes fall in line with the drop in prices for goods and services and the affordability of previously acquired debt rises.

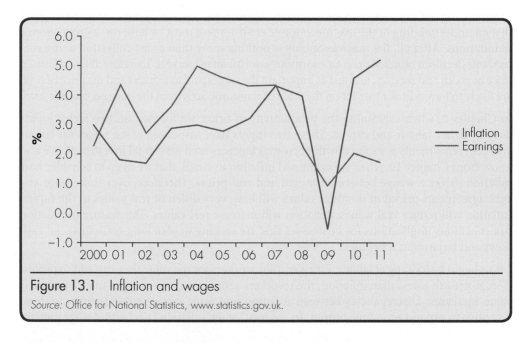

Figure 13.1　Inflation and wages

Source: Office for National Statistics, www.statistics.gov.uk.

It should therefore be clear that price, wage and debt adjustments are enormously important to the functioning of the economy, both in the short term and in enabling an economy to return to its long-run equilibrium on the production possibility frontier.

The sections within this chapter will provide you with an understanding of the relationship between inflation and employment in the short and long run. This will be developed into an understanding of the macroeconomic equilibrium in the short and long run. This will provide a clear link between the microeconomics goods and labour market and the broader macroeconomy. The analysis will then be extended to provide you with an understanding of how the economy reacts to demand- and supply-side shocks. A consideration of monetary policy and inflation targeting will then be offered, followed by a review of different economists' perceptions of how quickly the economy will adjust to long-run equilibrium.

Short- and long-run macroeconomic equilibrium

In Chapters 11 and 12, we presented the economic ideas behind fiscal and monetary policy. These previous chapters showed *how* demand side policies work. The aim of this chapter is to show more clearly the circumstances *when* these policies will be used by policy-makers.

If an economy is in long-run equilibrium, then the level of GDP is that associated with a point on the economy's production possibility frontier (recall the discussion in Chapter 1). All land, labour, capital and enterprise that are willing to be supplied are employed within firms in the pursuit of profit. The economy is said to be at its **full employment** level. At the full employment level, an economy is producing at its **potential GDP**. Therefore, if an economy is in long-run equilibrium, there is little need to correct a recession by providing a boost to spending. Similarly, there is little need to slow the economy by increasing taxes or interest rates. In simple and clear terms, because long-run equilibrium results in full employment, fiscal and monetary policy should be neutral, neither increasing nor reducing aggregate demand.

In the short run, by contrast, an economy can be shown to be in equilibrium but the level of GDP can differ from potential GDP. Short-run equilibrium GDP is referred to as **actual GDP**. When the short run and the long run coincide, then actual and potential GDP are equivalent. However, when actual GDP is greater than potential GDP, the economy is in a boom; when actual GDP is less than potential GDP, the economy is in a recession. The difference between potential and actual GDP is referred to as the **output gap**. Only when an output gap exists is there any need for fiscal, or monetary, policy to be active rather than neutral. As such, active fiscal, or monetary, policy seeks to close the economy's output gap.

> In full employment, all factors of production that wish to be employed are employed.
>
> Potential GDP is any point on the production possibility frontier.
>
> Actual GDP is short-run equilibrium GDP.
>
> The output gap is the difference between actual and potential GDP.

Figure 13.2 charts the output gap for a number of European economies. When the economy is strong, the output gap is positive; when the economy is weak, the output gap is negative. While all economies suffered a negative output gap after 2008, Greece has suffered most. Box 13.1 discusses Italy's likely return to recession and yet another output gap.

The following sections of this chapter will examine these issues in more detail. In particular, it is important to understand how differences in short- and long-run aggregate supply lead to different short- and long-run equilibrium levels of GDP. To develop this understanding, it is necessary to understand the short- and long-run equilibrium markets for labour. Moreover, in order to understand the adjustment from actual to potential levels of GDP, it is necessary to form an opinion about the rate of adjustment following the implementation of active fiscal, or monetary, policy. As will become evident, some economic schools of thought believe fiscal policy is more effective than monetary policy in closing the output gap. Each of these areas of concern will be discussed in turn, but we will start with the labour market and show how long-run equilibrium in the market for jobs leads to an understanding of long-run aggregate supply and potential GDP.

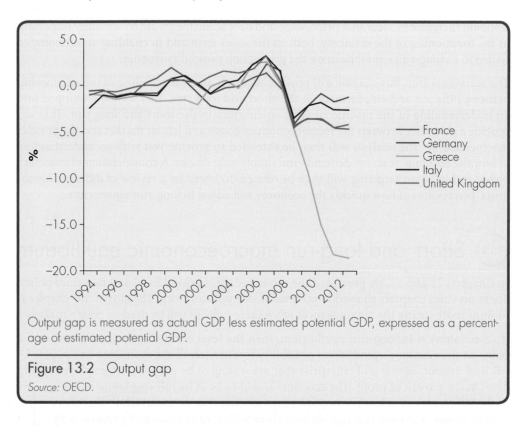

Output gap is measured as actual GDP less estimated potential GDP, expressed as a percentage of estimated potential GDP.

Figure 13.2   Output gap

Source: OECD.

Box 13.1

Italy seen in recession as GDP contraction deepens in Q4

Italy's economic slump is expected to have deepened in the fourth quarter of 2011, tipping the eurozone's third-largest economy into a recession that is expected to last well into this year.

Gross domestic product probably shrank 0.5 per cent in the fourth quarter from the previous three months, according to the median forecast of a Reuters poll of 34 economists.

That would mark a deterioration from a 0.2 per cent decline in GDP in the third quarter, and herald a recession, which is officially defined as two consecutive quarters of falling economic output.

Weak consumer demand, investments and exports and a 2.1 per cent slump in industrial output over the fourth quarter all point to an accelerated decline in economic activity as Italy suffered the effects of the eurozone debt crisis, which has weakened confidence, and as global demand slowed.

Analysts said they expected the recession to continue at the start of 2012, though possibly at a slower pace following a robust monthly rise in industrial production in December.

'There are real factors arising from the government's fiscal tightening and from the financial crisis . . . that will keep Italy in recession in the first two quarters of 2012 ahead of a gradual recovery in the second half,' said Paolo Mameli from Intesa Sanpaolo.

Mario Monti's government passed an austerity plan in December which includes tax hikes, public spending cuts and pension reform, that is set to weigh on growth in the short term.

Adapted from an article on Reuters, 13 February 2012 (reporting by Giulio Piovaccari, writing by Catherine Hornby, editing by Susan Fenton).

13.3 Employment, inflation and output

The **Phillips curve** was developed by Professor Phillips from the London School of Economics in 1958 after observing inflation and unemployment in the UK. 'Observe' is the crucial word, because the initial theoretical reasons for a Phillips curve relationship between unemployment and inflation were weak.

The Phillips curve, as illustrated in Figure 13.3, seemed very attractive. This was because it showed a clear trade-off between unemployment and inflation. The government merely had to decide which, of inflation and unemployment, it disliked more. If the government disliked unemployment, then it had to suffer higher inflation. The problem of the Phillips curve being simply an observation became a serious concern in the 1970s when the relationship broke down. As unemployment increased, so did inflation. Governments no longer witnessed a trade-off between inflation and unemployment.

If a trade-off between inflation and unemployment ever existed, then it did so in the short run. This is because, in the long run, the economy operates on its production possibility frontier at the full employment level. Therefore, in the long run, GDP is fixed; and as a consequence unemployment must also be fixed. Whatever the level of inflation, there can be no trade-off with unemployment in the long run.

Consider Figure 13.4, which includes both a short- and long-run Phillips curve. The short-run Phillips curve depicts the trade-off between inflation and unemployment, while the long-run Phillips curve shows the fixed long-run level of unemployment.

In the long run GDP is fixed at a maximum or potential GDP; the economy is on its production possibility frontier. Even though the economy is at potential GDP there is still a small amount of unemployment; these are people just in between jobs. They are searching for the right job, perhaps waiting a little while for the right job to come along. When they find the right job, someone else in another part of the economy might decide that they do not like their job and will resign. So we have a constant sized pool of unemployed workers who are in effect in the process of moving between jobs. We call this the **natural rate of unemployment** and it is fixed. In Figure 13.4, the natural rate of unemployment is fixed at 3.0 per cent. It does not matter what the rate of inflation is, unemployment is constant in the long run. In addition, in long-run equilibrium, the economy is also positioned on its short-run Phillips curve, SPC$_1$, where it intersects the long-run Phillips curve. Therefore, unemployment

> The **Phillips curve** shows that lower unemployment is associated with higher inflation. Simply, lower unemployment has to be traded for higher inflation.
>
> **Natural rate of unemployment** is the level of unemployment when the economy is operating at potential GDP.

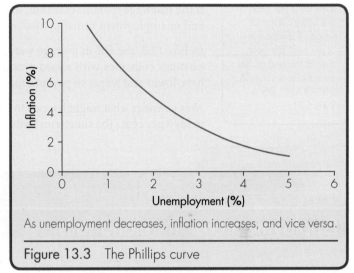

As unemployment decreases, inflation increases, and vice versa.

Figure 13.3   The Phillips curve

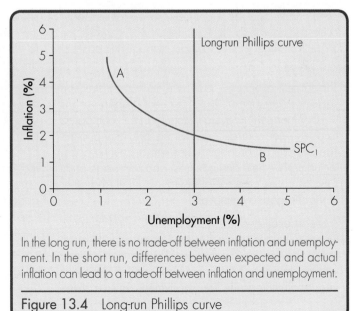

In the long run, there is no trade-off between inflation and unemployment. In the short run, differences between expected and actual inflation can lead to a trade-off between inflation and unemployment.

Figure 13.4   Long-run Phillips curve

is 3.0 per cent and inflation is 2.0 per cent in the long run. This is consistent with a central bank inflation target of 2.0 per cent.

Now consider a positive shock to the level of demand in the economy. This increase in demand will raise GDP and therefore cut unemployment. The economy moves along SPC_1 to A. As unemployment is cut, inflation rises above the target rate, to 4 per cent. The central bank now increases interest rates to bring inflation back to target. The level of economic activity slows and the economy moves back along the SPC_1 into long-run equilibrium, where unemployment is constant and inflation is 2 per cent.

> Real wages are earnings adjusted for inflation.
>
> Nominal wages are earnings unadjusted for inflation. If a worker earns £30 000 per year, this is their nominal wage. If inflation is 5 per cent per year, then at the end of the year the real wage is £30 000/1.05 = £28 571.

A reduction in demand would move the economy along SPC_1 to point B, with higher unemployment and lower inflation. The central bank would now cut interest rates, enabling the economy to grow. As jobs are created, the economy moves along SPC_1 back into long-run equilibrium.

In the long run, unemployment is constant because the **real wage** is constant. The real wage is equal to the **nominal wage** divided by inflation, often written as W/P. So, a wage rise of 2 per cent when inflation is also 2 per cent results in a constant real wage. If the real wage remains constant, then the cost incentive to hire or fire workers is zero and unemployment remains constant.

In Box 13.2, the fall in average weekly earnings in Ireland is discussed. If this fall in earnings coincides with raised productivity, and/or higher inflation, then firms may have lower real wages to pay and may be able to boost employment.

Now consider what might happen to unemployment if inflationary expectations change to say 3 per cent. The short-run Phillips curve will move up, as in Figure 13.5. However,

Box 13.2

Employment cost in Ireland falls

The cost of employing a person in Ireland fell by more than 2 per cent last quarter, according to EU statistics agency Eurostat. Only Greece (–6.8 per cent) and Ireland (–2.2 per cent) saw a fall in labour costs per hour in the first quarter of 2011, while the 27 EU member states saw an average increase of 2.6 per cent.

The largest drop in wages was in the construction sector, which saw an 11.6 per cent drop in wages – 10.9 per cent in overall labour costs – compared to a 1.1 per cent decrease in the previous quarter. The overall cost of labour takes into account wages, including overtime and bonuses, and non-wage costs such as pay-related social insurance (PRSI) and other taxes charged to employers.

A report published last week by the Central Statistics Office in Ireland, using the same data as the Eurostat study, showed the average weekly earnings for individuals dropped 3.6 per cent last quarter, despite a very small increase in hourly payment. This was due to the average number of hours worked by employees falling from 31.8 hours a week to 30.6 – an annual decrease in paid hours of 1 per cent. The same report showed that average weekly earnings in the construction sector fell by 10.9 per cent last year, to €18.74 an hour. The average hourly payment for an Irish person across all sectors, including overtime and bonus payments, is now €22.08.

A spokesman for Ibec, the employers' organization, said international competitiveness was the important factor that would lead to increased employment and consumer spending. Ireland's productivity has increased recently, he said, in line with reduced costs, putting the country in a strong position. 'This is good news,' he said. 'We are increasing our output. Greece aren't. While they're bringing down costs, they're not increasing their productivity.'

Adapted from an article by David Molloy in the *Irish Times*, 20 June 2011.

the long-run equilibrium level of unemployment and GDP will remain constant. Only long-run inflation will rise to 3 per cent. Why? The answer is simple: because inflationary expectations have risen to 3 per cent, firms and workers will now negotiate nominal wage increases of 3 per cent. As a result, real wages will remain constant and, therefore, so will unemployment and GDP. So even with a change in inflationary expectations, unemployment and GDP still remain at their constant long-run values.

The same is true in a period of deflation, where a fall in inflationary expectations would result in the short-run Phillips curve moving down from SPC_1 to SPC_3. Long-run equilibrium unemployment will remain constant, but inflation will be lower.

The key point to understand is that, in the long run, there is no trade-off between inflation and unemployment.

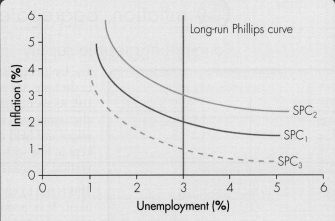

If inflationary expectations increase to 3 per cent, then the short-run Phillips curve moves up. The new long-run equilibrium is 3 per cent unemployment and 3 per cent inflation. In reverse, a fall in inflationary expectations would see the short-run Phillips curve move down from SPC_1 to SPC_3.

Figure 13.5   Expectations-augmented Phillips curve

Insights from the Phillips curve

The Phillips curve analysis provides two important insights, which we can develop further.

1 **Importance of the short run and long run.** The analysis has shown that we need to consider the short and the long run. Importantly, because labour and wages are a main input and cost for a firm, then any variation in wages results in a change in a firm's willingness to supply. Therefore, the Phillips curve analysis highlights the need to understand both short- and long-run aggregate supply within the economy.

2 **The importance of the speed of adjustment.** We need to be concerned about the speed of adjustment from the short to the long run. If a reduction in demand moves an economy to point B in Figure 13.4, then unemployment increases and inflation falls. If firms and workers are able to cut prices and wages quickly, then the economy will rapidly return to its long-run equilibrium. Cutting prices is possible, but cutting wages is rarely seen as acceptable by workers. An increase in demand moves the economy to A, so firms and workers need to increase prices and wages in order to ensure that real wages remain constant. Raising wages makes workers happy, but funding a pay rise by raising prices is not seen as that attractive by consumers or competitive by firms. In addition, prices and wages are often negotiated and set for 12 months. Therefore, for a variety of reasons, sluggish wage and price adjustments limit the scope for rapid adjustment to the long-run macroeconomic equilibrium.

Rapid adjustment in prices and wages suggests that an economy needs little active fiscal or monetary policy, while sluggish adjustments provide the possibility for fiscal or monetary intervention to move the economy more swiftly towards its equilibrium.

In order to develop your understanding of these issues, we will develop the short- and long-run Phillips curve ideas into short- and long-run aggregate supply schedules. From this, we can then examine macroeconomic equilibrium using aggregate demand and supply frameworks and consider likely responses to demand- and supply-side shocks to the economy. We can then consider the competing views on the need and scale of intervention, which relate to perceived views on the economy's speed of adjustment.

Inflation, aggregate demand and supply

Long-run aggregate supply

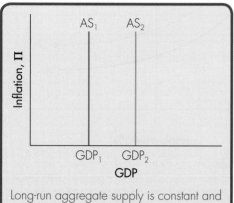

Long-run aggregate supply is constant and represents the full employment level of the economy. Any change in long-run supply must reflect real changes in economic factor inputs, technology or productivity.

Figure 13.6 Long-run aggregate supply

The long-run Phillips curve shows that unemployment is constant in the long run and, therefore, the economy operates at full potential. As such, GDP is constant and any changes in inflation do not alter employment, or GDP. This is because, in the long run, real wages are held constant through nominal wage increases being kept in line with inflation. Long-run aggregate supply is therefore vertical, or inflation inelastic, as illustrated in Figure 13.6.

This is not to say that the full employment level of GDP is entirely fixed. It is possible for an economy to attract more economic resources. A rising birth rate, an inflow of migrant workers or the discovery of oil and gas are all examples of increased economic endowments, which would result in the long-run aggregate supply schedule moving to AS_2 in Figure 13.6. Equally, if a new technology reduced the costs of economic transactions, such as Google's ability to provide low-cost information, especially on prices, then less time/resource is needed for shopping and more time is available for labour. With more labour time, the economy can grow to GDP_2. Finally, a rise in productivity, such as that brought about by more workers engaging in university education, can also lead to an increase in the full employment level of the economy.

Short-run aggregate supply

In the short run, there is no guarantee that real wages remain constant. This is because, for most jobs, nominal wages are fixed in advance, for anything from one to three years. Therefore, nominal wage adjustment is not instantaneously linked to inflation. As such, the economy does not have to be at the full employment level in the short run.

Wage bargaining is extremely expensive and involves many hours of negotiation between managers, unions and workers. These costs can be magnified when disagreements lead to strikes. Therefore, companies prefer to limit negotiations to once per year.

Workers may even benefit from inflexible wage agreements. During a boom, workers' pay may not rise quickly. But this can be compensated in a recession by pay not falling. Workers are therefore willing to sacrifice short-term constant real wages for short-term nominal wage guarantees.

For these reasons, it is necessary to examine the short-run equilibrium of the economy, where real wages are not held constant. If nominal wages are held constant and the rate of inflation rises, then real wages fall and employment increases. Recall Figure 13.4 and the movement along SPC_1 to A. We now have to incorporate these ideas into an understanding of short-run aggregate supply. Figure 13.7 helps to develop this understanding.

Figure 13.7 illustrates a long-run aggregate supply line, AS_1, and two short-run aggregate supply lines, SAS_1 and SAS_2. Each short-run aggregate supply line is drawn for a given rate of nominal wage growth. So, if workers and firms have agreed a wage increase of 5 per cent, then we might assume that the economy is on SAS_1. If they have agreed a nominal wage increase of 2 per cent, then they can assume the economy is on SAS_2.

Let us begin in long-run equilibrium, with output at GDP_1 and inflation at π_1. Workers and firms have agreed nominal wage growth of π_1, which therefore places them on SAS_1. If inflation turns out to be π_1, then real wages are held constant and the economy remains in long-run equilibrium. If inflation turns out to be higher than π_1, say π_3, then real wages will fall and the price of goods and services rises faster than expected. This provides firms with

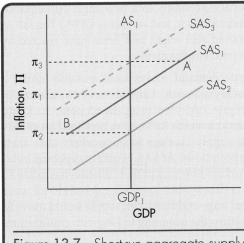

The economy is in long-run equilibrium, with an inflation rate of π_1 and output of GDP$_1$. On SAS$_1$, nominal wage growth is agreed to be π_1. Inflation higher than π_1 reduces real wages and enables firms to raise output. The economy moves to A. Inflation less than π_1 raises real wages and forces firms to reduce output. The economy moves to B. If π_2 becomes the expected rate of inflation and the agreed rate of nominal wage increases, then the economy will move to SAS$_2$ and return to long-run equilibrium. Points A and B correspond with points A and B in Figure 13.4.

Figure 13.7 Short-run aggregate supply

an incentive to hire more workers and raise short-run output. The economy moves along SAS$_1$ to point A. Inflation and GDP rise.

If inflation falls back to π_1, then the economy moves back to long-run equilibrium, where SAS$_1$ intersects AS$_1$. If inflation remains above π_1, then firms and workers are likely to negotiate higher nominal wage growth of π_3 and we would need to draw a new short-run aggregate supply line, SAS$_3$, which is higher than SAS$_1$. If inflation is less than π_1, real wages rise. This makes employment more expensive, and firms reduce employment and output. The economy moves along SAS$_1$ to point B, where inflation and output fall.

If the economy remains at B for a significant period of time, then firms and workers may come to expect that the long-term inflation rate for the economy has fallen to π_2. If they then agree nominal wage rate increases of π_2, the economy moves to SAS$_2$, and back into long-run equilibrium.

Aggregate Demand

Finally we need to provide a brief recap on aggregate demand, which was covered in Chapter 9. Aggregate demand is all demand in the economy and from our exploration of the circular flow of income total expenditure in an economy is equal to the sum of consumption, investment, government spending and net exports.

The relationship between inflation and demand is negative when a central bank has an inflation target. For example, if inflation moves above target, the central bank can raise interest rates; this will reduce consumption, investment and even exports, if the exchange rate also changes. When inflation is below target, then the central bank will reduce interest rates, leading to stronger demand through higher consumption, investment and net exports. Therefore, through interest rates, there is a negative relationship between inflation and aggregate demand. This concept is illustrated in Figure 13.8.

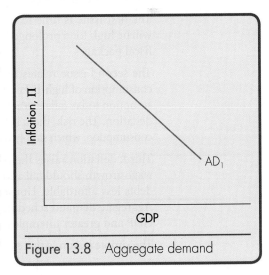

Figure 13.8 Aggregate demand

 Short- and long-run equilibrium

We can now integrate aggregate demand and long- and short-run supply.

Consider Figure 13.9; the economy is in both short- and long-run equilibrium, with an output of GDP$_1$ and an inflation rate of π_1. Then follows a drop in consumer and business confidence. Consumption and investment fall and aggregate demand moves from AD$_1$ to AD$_2$. The fall in

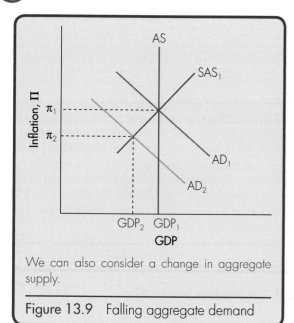

We can also consider a change in aggregate supply.

Figure 13.9   Falling aggregate demand

demand moves the economy to a new short-run equilibrium, where inflation is π_2 and output is GDP$_2$. The fall in inflation has raised real wages and firms have reacted by cutting output (and employment).

Unless aggregate demand moves back, possibly under a monetary or fiscal expansion, then only a rightward move in short-run aggregate supply will bring the economy back into long-run equilibrium on the AS line. We explained previously that short-run supply changes when workers alter their inflationary expectations. At SAS$_1$ workers expected inflation of π_1, if workers now accept that inflation has fallen to a level even lower than π_2, then lower wage demands will result in a slowing real wage and short-run supply would move to the right and return the economy to long-run equilibrium.

A recent example: deflation and the credit crisis

The credit crisis of 2008 led to a fall in consumption and investment. However, at the time inflation was above target in many economies, so the fall in demand helped economies move back towards their target inflation rate. Governments and central banks welcomed the reduction in inflation, but were concerned about a long-run adjustment which also included a significant recession at GDP$_2$, and deflation well below π_2.

Swift reductions in interest rates and planned increases in government expenditure represented a combined monetary and fiscal expansion. The intention of these policies was to rapidly increase aggregate demand, thus enabling the economy to return to long-run equilibrium quickly and not go through a prolonged adjustment of prices, wages, supply and output.

Why avoid deflation?

The first issue is time to adjust. If full employment takes many years, then unemployment will be high for a prolonged period of time. It is then better to act quickly with monetary and fiscal packages.

The second issue relates to the impact of deflation on consumption. If consumers postpone consumption of high-ticket items in the expectation of cheaper prices in the future, then consumption today falls further. This generates a bigger recession, more unemployment and more deflation. The risk, then, is that further deflation motivates households to withhold yet more consumption, which simply repeats the cycle and exacerbates the overall macroeconomic problem.

Third, deflation raises the real value of debt. If prices fall, then the value of labour falls and wage growth should fall and perhaps even become negative. This makes previously incurred debts less affordable. Households transfer earnings from consumption to debt repayment. Aggregate demand schedule shifts to the left and we observe more deflation, a larger fall in GDP and greater unemployment.

The simple lesson is that falling prices are not necessarily a good thing.

A temporary supply shock

Figure 13.10 illustrates the effect of a temporary supply shock. The economy begins in long-run equilibrium at the target rate of inflation. An increase in oil and commodity prices moves the short-run aggregate supply schedule to SAS$_2$. The short-run macroeconomic equilibrium now consists of higher inflation and lower GDP. The central bank now needs to decide whether it wishes to prioritize inflation or GDP. In the UK the Bank of England witnessed inflation rates of 5 per cent, or 3 percentage points above target. The Bank had the option of increasing interest rates, reducing aggregate demand and bringing inflation back to target at π_1. But such a move would have reduced GDP further and moved the economy a greater distance from potential GDP and long-run equilibrium. The Bank took the view that oil and commodity prices were a temporary problem and short-run supply would return to SAS_1 over one to two years.

(13.6) Monetary policy rules

How does a central bank decide to react to a rise in inflation: ignore the rise, or focus more on GDP instead of inflation? Central banks address these issues by deciding if the problem is demand- or supply-side orientated.

If inflation moves away from target because demand has increased or decreased, then the central bank simply needs to offset the change using interest rates. So if aggregate demand increases(decreases) and causes higher(lower) inflation, the bank should increase(decrease) interest rates and reduce(increase) demand. Inflation and GDP will return to target levels.

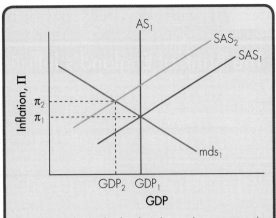

A temporary supply shock reduces short-run supply to SAS_2. This moves the economy away from its long-run equilibrium of GDP_1 and π_1. Inflation rises to π_2 and GDP falls to GDP_2. The central bank can accommodate this shock and boost demand and GDP, but will suffer even higher inflation.

Figure 13.10 A temporary supply shock

The worry for a central bank is when it operates an inflation target and faces a temporary supply-side shock; see Figure 13.11. By holding strictly to the inflation target of π_1, the central bank must alter aggregate demand to offset any inflationary impact from temporary supply-side shocks. If we begin in long-run equilibrium and short-run supply moves from SAS_1 to SAS_2, then in order to keep inflation at the target rate of π_1, aggregate demand has to be reduced and move the economy to A. This creates a recession, with output at GDP_2. If short-run aggregate supply moves to SAS_3, then, in order to keep inflation at π_1, aggregate demand has to be increased and the economy moves to B with output at GDP_3.

Inflation targeting in the face of supply shocks generates volatility in GDP and stability in prices.

Reflecting these difficulties, central banks are pragmatic in their approach to managing the economy and tend to follow what is known as a **Taylor rule**. The Taylor rule can be represented by the following equation:

$$i = \pi + i^* + a(\pi - \pi^*) + b(GDP - GDP^*)$$

where π is the rate of inflation, π^* is the target rate of inflation, GDP is actual GDP, GDP^* is potential GDP and i^* is the real interest rate; a and $b > 0$. The more the central bank is concerned about inflation deviating from the target rate, the larger a, and the more interest rates will change. Similarly, the higher the value for b, the more concerned the central bank is with variations in GDP and the more rates will change to bring about long-run equilibrium and potential GDP.

The Bank of England's overview of the economy from its November 2011 inflation report is provided in Box 13.3. Read both paragraphs carefully. Paragraph one discusses the extent to which GDP will be away from target, while paragraph two (column two) discusses how far inflation will be from target.

The Taylor rule links interest rate changes to short-term deviations in both inflation and output from long-term equilibrium values.

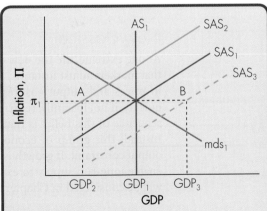

Under a strict inflation target, any temporary supply shock will invoke a change in interest rates and restoration of inflation to π_1. However, output will be volatile.

Figure 13.11 Inflation targeting and supply shocks

Box 13.3

The Bank of England's inflation report

The prospects for the UK economy have worsened. Global demand slowed. And concerns about the solvency of several euro-area governments intensified, increasing strains in banking and some sovereign funding markets. Household and business confidence fell, both at home and abroad. These factors, along with the fiscal consolidation and squeeze on households' real incomes, are likely to weigh heavily on UK growth in the near term. Thereafter, the recovery should gain traction, supported by continued monetary stimulus and a gentle recovery in real incomes. Implementation of a credible and effective policy response in the euro area would help to reduce uncertainty and so support UK growth, but its absence poses the single biggest risk to the domestic recovery.

CPI inflation rose to 5.2 per cent in September. Inflation is likely to fall back sharply through 2012 as the contributions of VAT, energy and import prices decline, and downward pressure from slack in the labour market persists. But how far and how fast inflation will fall are uncertain. Under the assumption that Bank Rate moves in line with market interest rates and the size of the asset purchase programme remains at £275 billion, inflation is judged more likely to be below than above the 2 per cent target at the forecast horizon.

Source: Bank of England, Inflation Report, November 2011.

Adjustment speed

We have considered the short- and long-run equilibrium outcomes for the economy. Throughout this analysis, there has been an assumption that the economy does not adjust to the long-run equilibrium with any degree of speed. If it did, there would be no need for fiscal or monetary intervention.

The speed with which wages and prices do adjust is debated within economics. Beliefs regarding adjustment speeds and policy responses highlight differing philosophical traditions within economics. While it is not our intention to train you as economists, a business person can benefit from some understanding of the competing macroeconomic perspectives.

New classical

At one extreme, are the new classical economists. This group of economists hold the belief that markets adjust instantly, leading to a clearing equilibrium. This full and rapid flexibility in prices and output ensures that, following any demand or supply shock, the economy quickly, if not instantly, returns to its long-run, full employment level of output. A clear consequence of this belief is that there is no need for fiscal or monetary policy interventions. Instead, this group of economists focus on long-run aggregate supply as the economy's output constraint. If growth is desirable, then policy-makers need to focus on policies which enable long-run supply to expand in a stable and consistent manner. Such growth policies will be considered in Chapter 14.

Gradual monetarist

The next group of economists are the gradual monetarists, who believe that markets adjust quickly but not instantaneously. For gradual monetarists, the long-run equilibrium can be attained in a relatively short time period, such as a year or two. Competitive product markets lead to flexibility in pricing. Free and open labour markets ensure a quick transition to new nominal wage growth rates. Firms and workers quickly, but not perfectly, arrive at new expectations of future price levels and so the adjustment of short-run aggregate supply is reasonably quick. Over a period of one to two years, the economy returns to potential GDP. Since the economy returns quickly to potential GDP, gradual monetarists also accept that supply side policies are important for long-term growth.

Active fiscal and monetary policy are frowned upon by gradual monetarists. If the economy can correct itself within an acceptable timeframe, there is no need for intervention. In fact, any policy stimulus is likely to lead to an over-correction of the economy. As the economy itself adjusts, the policy response will simply multiply the effects. This could drive the economy into a deeper recession, or lead to higher inflation.

The best monetary response stems from the quantity theory of money, which states that $MV = PY$, where M is the money supply, V is the velocity of circulation, P is the price level and Y is real GDP. If PY is nominal GDP and is equal to £10 billion, and M = 1 billion, then the velocity of circulation is 10, i.e. cash must go through everybody's pockets 10 times in order to facilitate £10 billion of economic transactions. Gradual monetarists believe that Y is constant, as depicted by a vertical long-run aggregate supply schedule. They also believe that V is a constant. This means that there is a direct relationship between M and P: inflation is driven by growth in the money supply. If you wish to control inflation, then adopt a *gradual* change in the money supply.

Moderate Keynesian

Moderate Keynesians take the view that the economy will eventually return to its long-run equilibrium, but the adjustment will not necessarily be quick. Moderate Keynesians believe that prices, wages and inflationary expectations are slow to adjust. Without flexibility in prices and wages, short-run aggregate supply will not adjust quickly either. Due to this slow adjustment, there is significant benefit to be gained from active fiscal and monetary policies. These demand side policies quickly alter macroeconomic demand and enable the economy to return to potential GDP. Once in long-run equilibrium, moderate Keynesians accept that potential GDP places a constraint on the economy and supply side policies are key to improved long-term growth.

Extreme Keynesian

Finally, we turn to extreme Keynesians, who take the opposite view to that held by new classical economists. Extreme Keynesians are extremely concerned that prices and wages are sticky. For a variety of reasons, including the cost of changing prices and the effect of unions on controlling wage rates, adjustment of short-run aggregate supply is sluggish. The attainment of potential GDP may not be achieved for many years. Economies can move into recession and then remain there, turning the economic episode into a depression. Governments therefore have an enormous duty to push spending into the economy. Extreme Keynesians believe that fiscal policy is better able to do this than monetary policy. Extreme Keynesians do not accept the quantity theory of money and question whether V and Y are constant, therefore any expansion of the money supply is unlikely to be inflationary. For extreme Keynesians, the core concern is output.

None of these competing views of thought is incorrect. Neither are they correct. This is because the speed of adjustment to potential GDP is not constant. Rather, adjustment speeds vary according to the nature and scale of shocks which impact the economy. For example, when change is small and gradual, the monetarists are more likely to be correct. This is because, when change is small and gradual, firms and workers can easily change their expectations regarding prices. It is easy for these important economic actors to understand what is happening and adjust their behaviour accordingly. Expectations are broadly correct and short-run aggregate supply moves quickly, leading to a rapid restoration of potential GDP.

Now consider the credit crisis, an event described by leading economists as 'unprecedented'; apparently, 'it is difficult to exaggerate the scale of events witnessed in financial markets'.

Such is the extreme nature of the credit crisis that not even economists can begin to understand what has occurred and what the impact will be on prices and output. There can be little doubt that consumers and firms will struggle to adapt their expectations rapidly and accurately. Hence the risk to output in the near term is huge. The Keynesians can claim to have a more accurate view of the world at this point in history. Not surprisingly, governments provided economies with enormous fiscal injections, while at the same time central banks cut interest rates.

However, the debate still continues and in extreme circumstances it is often practical, rather than ideological, considerations that take precedence. The UK economy, like many others needs a boost in demand. How that happens is perhaps a secondary concern, see Box 13.4.

Box 13.4

The UK economy needs a shower of money in the high street

It works like this. You get De La Rue to print £14 billion of banknotes, roughly the amount extracted from high-street spending in extra VAT this year. You send a fleet of vans to transfer the money to regional airports. You load it into squadrons of RAF helicopters and, in full view of television cameras, scatter it over shopping streets the length and breadth of the land. The notes are designed to disintegrate within six months and those finding them must spend them fast on goods and services.

'Helicopter money', once a satirical monetarist metaphor, suffers only one serious objection as a cure for a nation suffering from collapsed demand. It is vulgar and undignified. It seems tacky, populist, messy, a smart-alec suggestion not fit for consideration by ministers, bankers or economists.

Helicopter money is precisely what the government has for three years been dropping into bank vaults, to the tune of some £850 billion in cash, loans and guarantees. Ministers pleaded with bankers to lend it on to firms in the high street, but the banks preferred to keep it for themselves, to cover their gambling debts and bonuses. Dropping the stuff from helicopters is more effective since it does what it says on the tin: it instantly unleashes demand. It is an emergency blood transfusion straight into the veins of the economy, through high-street tills, job recruitment, restocking, warehouses and order books.

Recent antics in the global credit market have strengthened Osborne's case for budgetary austerity. But this leaves the government hopelessly adrift on growth – and by all accounts panicking. Policy is not working.

Past promises of a return to expansion, lower unemployment and less borrowing are as dust. Ministers argue that 'world events', notably in the eurozone, have wrecked confidence and blown trade off course, and that excuse has force. But it does not excuse the ham-fisted efforts to stir private sector growth. Railways, roads, housing estates and factories deliver no demand in the short term. The patient needs blood now, not in five or 10 years' time.

Meanwhile the billions spent on quantitative easing 'to boost the economy' have done no such thing. The money has simply vanished. With each round of easing, Osborne and the industry secretary, Vince Cable, have stood at the dispatch box and said it would channel money to small firms through their control of the part-nationalized banks. Yet lending to private businesses is at an all-time low. There has been no new borrowing.

As long as credit rating agencies rule the world, Osborne is right to avoid adding to his deficit. But helicopter money bypasses credit ratings, indeed both the credit agencies and the IMF favour demand stimulus just now. The government is hurling cash at banks. The only possible objection to more direct action is snobbery. The government seems in awe of bankers and will do anything to appease them. If it really wants to revive demand by printing money, it must choose between a bank and a helicopter. Choose the helicopter.

The use of fiscal policy to fine-tune the business cycle went out of fashion around 30 years ago. But when skittish banks and investors are turning away from funding private spending, there is a strong case for a more active fiscal policy to prop up demand. However, fiscal policy has its limits. A run of big budget deficits increases the risk that a government will default or repay its debts only by forcing its central banks to print money, thus creating inflation. If public debt spirals upwards as the economy stagnates, investors will worry that future taxpayers will be unable to shoulder the burden.

13.8 Business application: understanding the interest rate path

For businesses, it is crucial to understand the future path of interest rates. This is because businesses borrow to fund investment and so changes in the interest rate alter the cost of investing.

Companies also use debt to leverage their financial returns. Leverage is a very important financial concept. The use of debt by companies enables higher returns to shareholders. Consider the following. A company has £1 million of shareholders' cash to invest. A project is offering a 10 per cent rate of return, so after one year, the shareholders' funds will have grown to £1.1 million. Alternatively, the company could approach a bank and use its £1 million of equity to raise £9 million of debt. The company now has £10 million to invest. After one year and a 10 per cent rate of return, the investment is worth £11 million. So shareholder equity is now £2 million (£11 million less £9 million of debt). Not surprisingly, managers and shareholders like to use debt to enable companies to grow faster. Leverage is also known as gearing because, like a car, the more debt, the higher the gear, the faster the car and company run.

Debt is, therefore, a very attractive complement to equity financing. Of course, it comes at a cost – the rate of interest – and we should factor this into our calculations. The £2 million of equity at the end of year two should be reduced by the amount of interest that is paid. In fact, because the benefits of leverage come with high levels of debt to equity, the cash flow needed to fund interest repayments can be considerable. Therefore, interest rates matter to companies, not only because of investments but also because of the financial engineering that leverage brings to a company's finances. Understanding the future track for interest rates is crucial for appraising investment decisions and managing cash flows.

The Taylor rule enables business managers to achieve a broad understanding of where interest rates are likely to go in the future. A greater divergence between actual inflation and target inflation will lead to a change in rates. Equally, a departure of actual GDP from potential GDP will lead to an interest rate response. Data published by central banks can be used to assess the difference between actual and target values for GDP and inflation.

In Figure 13.12, fan charts for inflation and GDP from the Bank of England are presented. The darker lines within the fan charts represent the Bank's view of the most probable path for inflation and GDP. The fainter lines, which fan out over time, are less likely possibilities. The UK inflation target is 2 per cent and potential GDP has been growing at around 2.5 per cent per annum. The inflation fan chart suggests that the Bank will cut interest rates in order to avoid deflation and bring inflation back towards target. A consideration of the GDP fan charts indicates that the Bank thinks GDP will fall below target for most of 2011–12. This output gap will direct the Bank to retain low interest rates to enable the economy to return to potential GDP.

Further out, the Bank's forecast becomes less accurate, or certain. However, two trends are discernible from the fan charts. Inflation is expected to fall below target even by 2012 and GDP is expected to rise through to 2014. So, we can expect loose monetary policy until 2012–13. If inflation then returns to target and the economy grows, we may see a rise in interest rates to return monetary policy to a more long-term neutral position. If inflation remains below target, lax monetary policy may continue.

344

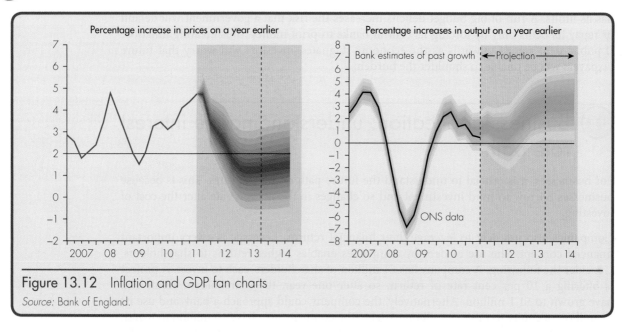

Figure 13.12 Inflation and GDP fan charts

Source: Bank of England.

13.9 Business application: recognizing the importance of real business cycles

In this chapter we have considered the short- and long-run macroeconomic equilibrium. We would like to recap on two fairly simple ideas and then pose a question.

First idea: we introduced the concept of long-run aggregate supply. In the long run the supply of the economy is fixed. The level of GDP associated with the long run is called potential GDP. Over time, the potential of the economy to produce output might increase and long-run aggregate supply would shift to the right.

Second idea: we introduced the concept of the output gap, which is the difference between actual and potential GDP. In the long run the economy operates at its potential. But in the short run, the level of actual GDP can be less than potential GDP. This output gap might be associated with slower economic growth, or even a recession.

Question: Is it safe to presume that potential GDP, long-run aggregate supply, always moves to the right, i.e. potential GDP gradually increases over time? Under what circumstances might potential GDP reduce and what might this mean in terms of understanding broad macroeconomic issues? Consider Figure 13.13.

In Figure 13.13 we have long-run aggregate supply AS_1 associated with potential GDP_1. The economy moves to a short-run equilibrium, which results in actual GDP_A. The output gap is equal to $GDP_1 - GDP_A$. The cause of the output gap stems from a financial crisis, which has destroyed banks and made remaining banks weaker and less able to lend. The banking sector is therefore less able to support the supply side of the economy, because the provision of loans and other financing facilities is less. This weaker banking sector means that the supply potential of the economy is less and long-run aggregate supply moves

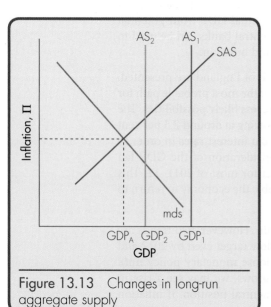

Figure 13.13 Changes in long-run aggregate supply

left from AS₁ to AS₂. The output gap is now much smaller. However, we need to recognize that we are also observing a change in real potential and this is referred to as a **real business cycle** effect.

> Real business cycle results from changes in potential GDP.

The implications of real business cycles are very important. Consider a government deficit which is equal to 10 per cent of GDP. Six per cent is structural and 4 per cent is cyclical. That 4 per cent is generated by the output gap $GDP_1 - GDP_A$. Reducing the structural deficit of 6 per cent requires a set of austerity measures which cut government spending and increase tax, all of which will impact the economy and reduce company profits. Following the reduction in potential GDP to GDP_2, the output gap falls. The cyclical part of the budget deficit decreases to 2 per cent and the structural deficit expands to 8 per cent. More austerity measures are needed which may lead to even larger cuts in company profits.

It is a job for professional economists to consider changes in real long-run supply and then worry about a government's ability to reduce a fiscal deficit. However, effective managers need to understand their environment and recognize a threat when it is discussed in the business press. Business managers who follow a line of argument being put forward by a professional economist, such as a change in potential GDP, can then consider the implications and risk to profits, plan effectively and steer the company through troubled times.

Business data application: understanding the formation of inflationary expectations

If growth in wages and prices is fundamental to the macroeconomic equilibrium, then it must be important for business to understand and respond to changing inflationary expectations. If, for example, workers believe that inflation will rise faster in the future, then they will seek to achieve higher pay awards. Firms need to form their own inflationary expectations. Do they share the same expectations as their workers and do they believe they have the potential to pass on higher wages to customers, through higher prices? Without the ability to generate additional revenue, then the real cost of labour climbs and firms become less willing to supply.

Central banks track inflationary expectations through various surveys. These surveys provide data on inflationary expectations among households, firms and economic forecasters. The surveys try to measure inflationary expectations over different time periods, including the short, medium and long terms. In Figure 13.14 we present inflationary expectations from over 2000 professional economic forecasters who respond to the European Central Bank (ECB) survey.

The data within Figure 13.14 suggest that inflationary expectations are formed in different ways over different time horizons. Near-term, one-year inflationary expectations are much more volatile than long-term five-year inflationary expectations. So what drives these differences? The answer to this question is not precise, but requires a number of factors to be recognized.

First, central banks have come to recognize that inflation targets are a powerful tool for controlling inflationary expectations, but only if the central bank is credible in achieving the inflation target. If, on average, the central bank brings inflation to the target level, then workers, firms and professional economists can confidently form expectations of future price stability. In addition, repeated requests from government for workers, especially in the public sector, to undertake pay restraint and accept pay rises in line with inflation also help. Costs rise in line with inflation and inflationary expectations remain subdued.

However, individuals are exposed to a variety of markets, and over time track price changes. For more than 10 years, an influx of cheap imports from China and South East Asia has helped to form low inflationary expectations. The cost of computers, mobile phones, televisions and cars has fallen in real terms. This trend of falling prices helps to anchor low long-term inflationary expectations.

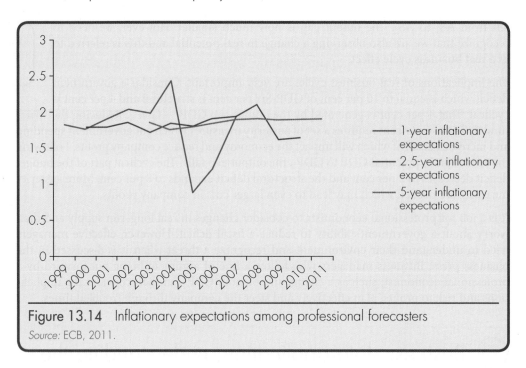

Figure 13.14 Inflationary expectations among professional forecasters
Source: ECB, 2011.

However, in more recent times, the prices of food and energy have risen enormously. Individuals recognize these significant shifts and appear to increase their near-term inflationary expectations.

Therefore, in seeking to understand the likely level of inflation in the future we need to establish which future time frame we are interested in. Over longer planning horizons, perhaps those used for large scale financial investment decisions, the key question for business is to establish if the central bank target inflation rate is acting as an inflationary anchor. Figure 13.14 provides some evidence that over a five-year planning horizon, professional economists expect the ECB to deliver the 2 per cent target rate for inflation. If a central bank has persistently failed to deliver the target rate, then long-term inflationary expectations might differ from the target rate.

In the short to medium term, inflationary expectations appear to be driven more by current events, such as commodity, fuel and food prices. Inflationary expectations can therefore be much more volatile in the short and medium-term.

The difference in inflationary expectations over time can generate problems. If as households and firms we all held firm to the view that, over the long term, inflation will be on target, then changes in wages and prices would be easy to plan and accommodate. Adjustment to long-run equilibrium could be fairly rapid. The unfortunate fact is that near-term concerns about inflation seem to play a bigger role in economic decision making and with inflationary expectations veering away from target rates there is a greater desire among firms and workers to change wages and prices more aggressively. This drive for change creates conflict and rigidities in the adjustment process to full long-run equilibrium.

Summary

1. In long-run equilibrium, the economy operates at its full employment level.

2. The full employment level of an economy is the same as potential GDP.

3. In the short run, economic output is actual GDP.

4. The difference between actual and potential GDP is known as the output gap.

5. The Phillips curve shows a negative statistical relationship between the rate of inflation and the rate of unemployment.

6. In the long run, equilibrium unemployment is fixed. Therefore, there can be no relationship between unemployment and inflation. The long-run Phillips curve is vertical.

7. Any movement along the short-run Phillips curve represents a temporary change in real wage rates. In the long run, real wages are held constant.

8. If inflationary expectations change, then the short-run Phillips curve will move. Expectations of higher inflation will result in the short-run Phillips curve moving up.

9. The speed of adjustment from the short to the long run is determined by the flexibility of wages and prices.

10. The macroeconomic demand schedule shows a negative relationship between inflation and the demand for output.

11. Long-run aggregate supply is fixed at potential GDP.

12. Short-run aggregate supply is determined by nominal wage growth.

13. If inflation differs from nominal wage growth, then real wages change and in the short run firms move along their short-run aggregate supply line.

14. In the short-run equilibrium, actual GDP can differ from potential GDP. But as workers and firms adjust wages to the new level of inflation, the economy adjusts to the long-run equilibrium of potential GDP.

15. Permanent supply side shocks can be accommodated by a reduction in the long-run interest rate.

16. Temporary supply side shocks may reduce GDP, but if they are offset with additional demand, then inflation is likely to rise.

17. The management of demand shocks brings stability to prices and output.

18. A Taylor rule suggests that a central bank sets interest rates according to the departure of inflation rates from target and also GDP from target.

19. Different groups of economists hold differing views about the flexibility of prices and wages, and the speed with which the economy will return to long-run equilibrium.

20. New classical economists think adjustment is instantaneous. Extreme Keynesians believe adjustment is very slow. Gradual monetarists think adjustment takes a couple of years and think monetary policy should enable a gradual expansion of the money supply. Moderate Keynesian economists think the economy will eventually return to long-run equilibrium, but a strong dose of fiscal and monetary policy will help in the short run.

Learning checklist

You should now be able to:

- Explain the relationship described by the Phillips curve
- Understand the key differences between the short- and long-run Phillips curves
- Link the short- and long-run Phillips curves and short- and long-run aggregate supplies
- Identify the short- and long-run macroeconomic equilibria
- Explain the adjustment to long-run equilibrium
- Assess monetary policy responses to demand and supply shocks in the economy
- Understand the different views among economists regarding the speed of adjustment to long-run equilibrium

Questions   connect

1. Explain why, when unemployment increases, inflation may decrease. Use a suitable diagram to illustrate this relationship.

2. Use numerical examples to explain the difference between nominal and real wages. How have nominal and real wages developed in your economy over the past five years?

3. If real wages are held constant, what is the relationship between unemployment and inflation in the long run?

4. If real wages are constant in the long run, is it still possible to observe a negative relationship between inflation and unemployment?

5. The central bank has an inflation target. Inflation rises above the target. What will happen next to interest rates and aggregate demand?

6. Explain why aggregate supply is inelastic in the long run and elastic in the short run.

7. The central bank follows an inflation target and the economy benefits from an improvement in productivity. What will happen to interest rates?

8. Can a central bank with an inflation target fight cost-push inflation?

9. Using a suitable diagram, illustrate why central banks are keen to avoid the potential black hole of a deflationary spiral.

10. What is the Taylor rule? How might business use the Taylor rule to forecast future interest rates?

11. Assume that you are a new classical economist. What are your recommendations for monetary policy? How do these differ from an extreme Keynesian's? Are these two views relevant to modern economies?

12. Use a diagram to illustrate how a monetary response to a loss of consumer confidence stabilizes inflation and GDP.

13. If nominal wages increase faster than the rate of inflation, under what circumstances can employment remain constant?

14. What do you consider to be the key benefits of inflation targeting?

15. Access data from your national statistical office on the rate of unemployment and the inflation rate. Plot the data, using a package such as Excel, and establish whether you can see a short-run Phillips curve relationship.

Exercises

1. Which of the following has caused the move from SPC$_1$ to SPC$_2$ in Figure 13.15?

    (a) A rise in the full employment rate.

    (b) An increase in nominal wages.

    (c) An increased expectation of higher unemployment.

    (d) An increased expectation of higher inflation.

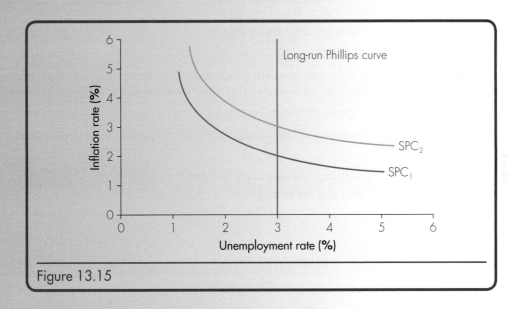

Figure 13.15

2. This exercise examines monetary and fiscal policy using the MDS and the aggregate supply schedule. Figure 13.16 shows two macroeconomic demand schedules (MDS$_a$ and MDS$_b$) and the aggregate supply schedule (AS). First, we consider the effects of monetary policy in the classical model – specifically, an increase in nominal money supply.

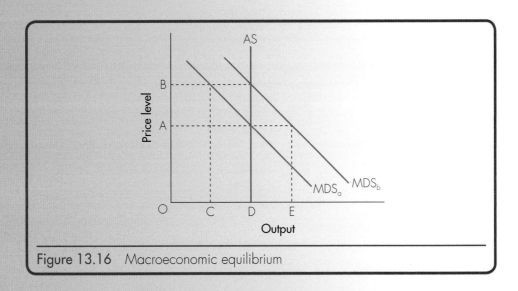

Figure 13.16   Macroeconomic equilibrium

(a) Identify the 'before' and 'after' MDS.

(b) What was the original equilibrium price and output?

(c) What is equilibrium price and output after the policy is implemented?

Next, consider fiscal policy – again in the classical model. Suppose there is a reduction in government expenditure:

(d) Identify the 'before' and 'after' MDS.

(e) What was the original equilibrium price and output?

(f) What is the equilibrium price and output after the policy is implemented? The Keynesian model is characterized by sluggish adjustment. Consider the period *after* the policy but *before* adjustment begins.

(g) Identify price and output.

(h) The MDS represents points at which goods and money markets are in equilibrium. In the position you have identified in (g), adjustment has still to take place – so, in what sense is the goods market in 'equilibrium'?

DIFFICULT

3. (a) Why is an understanding of inflationary expectations important for the economy and business?

(b) How are inflationary expectations likely to differ between students, households with young children and the retired?

(c) Will higher inflationary expectations always feed into future higher inflation?

Supply-side policies and economic growth

Chapter contents

Supply-side policies and economic growth at a glance		352
14.1	Business problem: assessing economic growth	352
14.2	Growth and aggregate supply	354
14.3	Neoclassical growth theory	358
14.4	Endogenous growth theory	359
14.5	Supply-side policies	360
14.6	Business application: how does innovation promote business?	364
14.7	Business application: the BRIC economies	365
14.8	Business data application: digging behind gross capital formation	367
Summary		368
Learning checklist		369
Questions		369
Exercises		370

Learning outcomes

By the end of this chapter you should understand:

Economic theory

LO1 How economic growth is linked to growth in long-run aggregate supply

LO2 The neoclassical model of economic growth

LO3 The convergence hypothesis

LO4 The endogenous growth model

LO5 The types of policies used to develop economic growth

Business application

LO6 Whether firms should produce or consume innovation

LO7 BRIC economies and the opportunities for business growth

LO8 The role of gross capital formation within economic growth

At a glance Supply-side policies and economic growth

The issues

Different economies grow at different rates. How do economies grow and how can governments involve business in developing economic growth?

The understanding

Economic growth can be linked to the development of long-run aggregate supply. The output potential of an economy is fixed if aggregate supply is perfectly inelastic. Changes in aggregate demand only alter the inflation rate. Therefore, in order to make the economy grow, it is essential to increase the level of aggregate supply. At a simplistic level, improving aggregate supply can be achieved by either increasing the availability of factor inputs, such as labour, or by increasing the productivity of factor inputs, so that more output can be produced with more input. However, a more interesting question relates to how fast an economy can grow. Neoclassical theory argues that growth will converge across economies to a common rate. Endogenous growth theory counters this view, suggesting that governments can develop policies which will enable the economy to grow at a faster rate.

The usefulness

The growth rate of an economy has important implications for business. First, sales and revenue growth will, in part, be related to economic growth. Second, government policies designed to improve productivity within an economy may aid a firm to reduce its costs.

14.1 Business problem: assessing economic growth

> Economic growth is measured as the percentage change in GDP per year.

The **economic growth** rates for various European Union (EU) economies and the USA are presented in Figure 14.1. Growth rates have varied by economy and over time. All economies slowed between 2001 and 2002, reflecting the impact of the terrorist events of 9/11 on the global economy. After 2002, most economies grew until the arrival of the credit crisis in late 2008. Then, all major economies slowed and headed for recession. Over the period and across economies, average growth seems to have been around 2 per cent per annum.

The importance of growth rates becomes more apparent over time. For example, assume that we have an economy and the level of GDP is 100. The economy now grows at four hypothetical growth rates, 1, 2.5, 4 and 10 per cent. The amount of GDP in each year, for each growth rate, is tabulated in Table 14.1.

The amount of GDP in year 10 is vastly different depending upon the growth rate of the economy, varying from 110 under a growth rate of 1 per cent, to 259 under a growth rate of 10 per cent. Therefore, over time the growth rate of an economy has enormous implications for the generation of individuals' incomes and the potential for companies to grow. As a consequence, governments, workers and firms are extremely interested in the projected growth rates for an economy.

For example, through a simple examination of the circular flow of income, economic growth is associated with growth in the flow of income between households and firms. More products are produced, more income is paid to workers/households and more products are sold. As a result, the faster an economy grows, the faster incomes rise and sales increase. While this makes economic growth an attractive opportunity for business, an additional consideration also has to be examined.

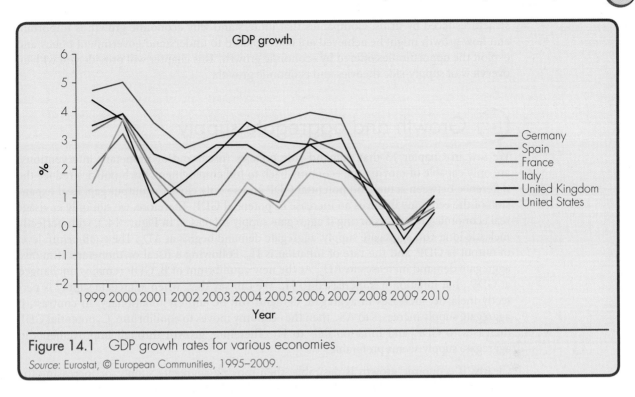

Figure 14.1   GDP growth rates for various economies

Source: Eurostat, © European Communities, 1995–2009.

Table 14.1   Impact of different growth rates

Year	Growth rate			
	1%	2.5%	4%	10%
0	100	100	100	100
1	101	103	104	110
2	102	105	108	121
3	103	108	112	133
4	104	110	117	146
5	105	113	122	161
6	106	116	127	177
7	107	119	132	195
8	108	122	137	214
9	109	125	142	236
10	110	128	148	259

In the main, governments try to make the economy grow through developments in aggregate supply, providing firms with the ability, or incentive, to supply more output. Firms will supply more if the marginal costs of production fall. Policies designed to reduce companies' costs and, moreover, boost productivity are central to developing aggregate supply and economic growth. This means that economic growth and the development of sales is not the only benefit for firms. Policies designed to aid economic growth may also aid the cost structures faced by firms. Companies that understand why economic growth is important and how growth might be achieved are better placed to understand government policy and exploit the opportunities offered by economic growth. This chapter will provide you with an overview of supply-side theories and economic growth.

14.2 Growth and aggregate supply

We saw in Chapter 13 that demand-side policies (fiscal and/or monetary interventions) are only capable of moving the economy back to full employment. Such policies reduce the difference between actual and potential GDP and so only close the output gap. Real expansion of the economy involves an increase in potential GDP. Therefore, we can only envisage real economic growth occurring if aggregate supply increases. In Figure 14.2, with perfectly inelastic long-run aggregate supply, aggregate demand begins at AD_1. The equilibrium level of output is GDP_1 and the rate of inflation is Π_0. Following a fiscal or monetary stimulus, aggregate demand increases to AD_2. At the new equilibrium of B, GDP remains unchanged at GDP_1, but inflation has increased to Π_1. We can say that, when aggregate supply is perfectly inelastic, increases in aggregate demand will be entirely inflationary. In contrast, if aggregate supply increases to AS_2, then the economy moves to equilibrium, C, potential GDP increases to GDP_2 and inflation falls to Π_2. Therefore, growth through improvements in aggregate supply seems preferable.

Clearly, if economic growth is desirable, then moving aggregate supply, or increasing the potential productive output of the economy, is key. Increasing productive potential is not easy, but there are generally three avenues for economic growth: more factor inputs, greater productivity and innovation. We will examine each in turn.

More factor inputs

In Chapter 1, we introduced the production possibility frontier and showed how the level of output for an economy is constrained by the level of factor inputs (land, labour, capital and enterprise). As the economy gains more economic factor inputs, then its productive potential increases. This is the same as the long-run aggregate supply moving to the right and potential GDP increasing.

For a number of economies, economic growth has occurred through an increase in factor inputs. In the case of China, recent economic growth has been enabled by a transfer of workers within the economy. Individuals who were previously involved in self-subsistence agriculture

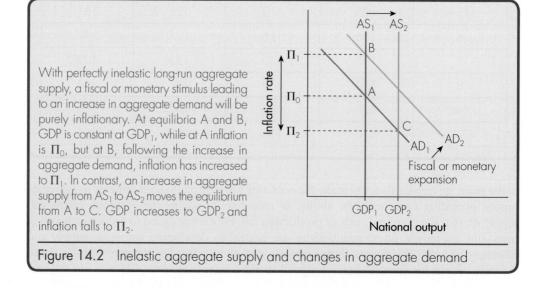

With perfectly inelastic long-run aggregate supply, a fiscal or monetary stimulus leading to an increase in aggregate demand will be purely inflationary. At equilibria A and B, GDP is constant at GDP_1, while at A inflation is Π_0, but at B, following the increase in aggregate demand, inflation has increased to Π_1. In contrast, an increase in aggregate supply from AS_1 to AS_2 moves the equilibrium from A to C. GDP increases to GDP_2 and inflation falls to Π_2.

Figure 14.2 Inelastic aggregate supply and changes in aggregate demand

Box 14.1

China faces dwindling labour supply

Lin Chang Jie is battling to save a family business making towels, cushions and robes in the eastern Chinese city of Ningbo as a dwindling supply of workers forces him to pay higher wages.

'I have to find a new way,' says Lin, 29, who is turning his Dejin Textile Co. into an online fashion retailer to cut costs and keep the business from closing. 'Wages are going up, up, up. If we don't like somebody's work we can't say anything, in case they leave.'

China's three-decade-old, one-child policy will accelerate declines in the workforce, forcing companies to upgrade to higher-value products in the way Japan did in the 1960s and 1970s. China may have as little as five years to make the transition to avoid a slump in economic growth.

The pool of 15- to 24-year-olds, a mainstay for factories making cheap clothes, toys and electronic products, will fall by almost 62 million people to a total of 164 million in the 15 years through 2025, United Nations projections show. The demographic shift is a result of the one-child policy implemented in 1979.

Products such as clothes, shoes and furniture that the General Administration of Customs does not classify as 'high-tech', accounted for about 68 per cent of China's exports last year, or $1.09 trillion, little changed from the 71 per cent share in 2005, when they were worth $544 billion, the agency's figures show. Exports account for more than a fifth of China's gross domestic product. High-tech industries include aerospace and aviation, medical instruments, software, computers and telecommunications.

'The low-end manufacturing industry is tough and will be getting tougher day by day as both labour and land costs are rising,' says Xu Hui, 39, the owner of Wenzhou Dazhan Photoelectricity Co. in Zhejiang province, south of Shanghai. She's switched to making LEDs and solar parts after starting off in the 1990s manufacturing sunglasses that sold for a dollar or two. 'Either you go for high-tech, high value-added industry or you just perish.'

(growing food for themselves and their family) have migrated to the industrialized cities and taken employment in factories. If the output per hour worked in a factory is greater in volume and, more importantly, in value than the output per hour worked as a farmer, then GDP increases. The problem for China, as discussed in Box 14.1, is how to deal with a likely fall in labour supply.

Greater productivity

If it is not possible to gain more factor inputs, then economic growth can be achieved by producing more output with the same level of factor inputs. In simple terms, economic factors such as labour must produce more output per day, and thereby become more productive.

This avenue of growth is very important for many developed economies. Unlike economies such as India and China, many EU economies are already fully developed. The transition and transfer of workers from agriculture to manufacturing and services occurred two centuries ago. The main avenue for growth is therefore through productivity improvements.

A key measure of productivity is GDP per hour worked. This is a useful measure of productivity because, by working in standard units of GDP and time, it enables a comparison across economies. In addition, and perhaps more importantly, from Chapter 9 we know that GDP is a measure of value added – in the hour worked, how much more value does the worker add to the final output? This enables a comparison across economies which produce very different goods and services. It also focuses upon income generation per hour.

Over the last 50 years, there has been a fairly consistent productivity gap between the UK and the USA. In comparison, France has managed to close its gap with the USA (see Figure 14.3).

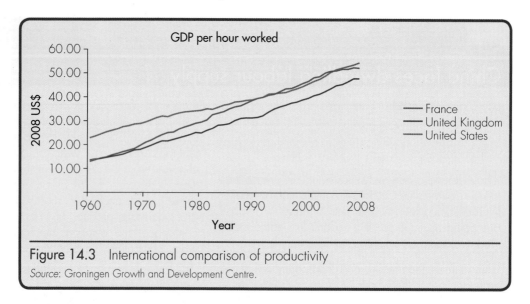

Figure 14.3 International comparison of productivity
Source: Groningen Growth and Development Centre.

If the UK could close the productivity gap, then either GDP and economic prosperity would rise or the UK workforce could earn the current level of income for fewer hours worked. Productivity growth is therefore very appealing.

We argued in Chapter 3, when examining the cost curves of individual firms, that the marginal cost curve (above average variable cost) is the firm's supply curve. Therefore, at the macroeconomic level, aggregate supply must be the sum of all firms' marginal cost curves (above average variable cost).

The firm is only willing to supply more output at any given price if its marginal costs decrease. Figure 14.4 provides details of the UK's GDP per capita gap with other developed economies and then breaks this gap into two sources, labour utilization and productivity. For example, the gap between UK and French GDP per capita is very small. But the means of producing

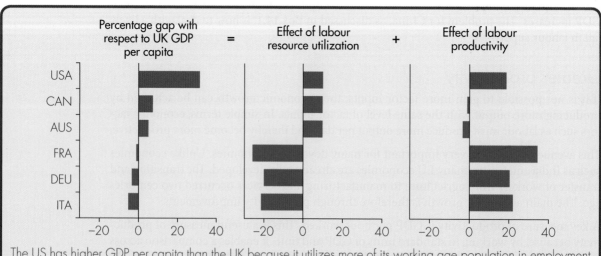

The US has higher GDP per capita than the UK because it utilizes more of its working age population in employment and on average each worker is more productive. France is similar to the UK in terms of GDP per capita and it achieves this by using fewer workers, but these workers are more productive than those used in the UK.

Figure 14.4 The UK productivity gap and sources of income difference
Source: OECD.

this level of GDP per capita are very different. The utilization rate of French labour is 25 per cent less than in the UK, but this is offset by French workers being 30 per cent more productive than their UK rivals. If the UK could raise its labour productivity, then at the same utilization rate, GDP per capita would accelerate beyond that of France and perhaps some of the other countries in the table.

Innovation

If we look back in history, we can identify a number of important inventions which have had an enormous impact on economic activity. Examples include the invention of the steam engine, the development of the railways, the introduction of electricity and telecommunications, the creation of the motor car, the growth of commercial aviation and more latterly the beginning of the Internet.

Improvements in travel, such as the railway, aviation and container ships, aid the movement of goods and services around the globe. This improves access to resources, lowers costs and boosts economic activity. The same arguments can be applied to telecommunications and the Internet. Products which were previously sold in shops are now sold online from massive distribution warehouses. This frees up retail units and labour, which can be employed in other parts of the economy, leading to more economic growth.

Clearly, a key driver of technological change is research and development (R&D). As new ideas, new knowledge and new techniques are discovered in science, engineering and medicine, innovation and technological change may result. However, again across economies there are marked differences in how research and development are funded, as well as who the main providers of R&D activities are. If we examine Figure 14.5, it can be seen that, when compared with France and the UK, the USA takes a much larger share of its R&D funds from industry. In addition, universities and government undertake much less R&D activity in the USA. Taken together, the two charts indicate that R&D in the USA is far more concentrated in the industrial sector of the economy.

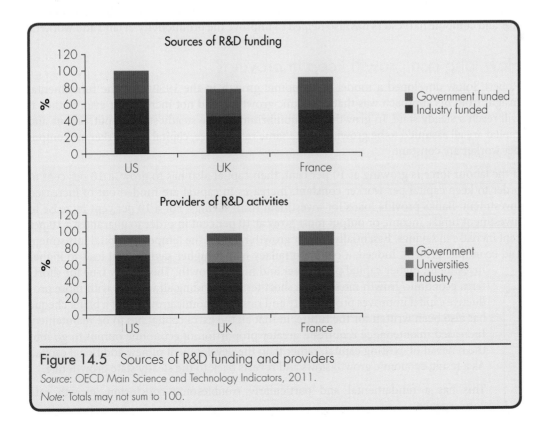

Figure 14.5 Sources of R&D funding and providers

Source: OECD Main Science and Technology Indicators, 2011.

Note: Totals may not sum to 100.

The question to ask is, does a concentration of R&D activities in the industrial sector have any implications for economic growth? A strong suspicion has to be that, when knowledge and new ideas are created in the industrial sector, then the resulting innovations have a far greater prospect of being commercialized. Therefore, R&D which is industrial and commercial in conception and creation may lead to far greater impacts on long-term economic growth.

In order to understand how we can model growth, we will next consider economic models of growth.

(14.3) Neoclassical growth theory

Assume we have a simple model where the economy's output is determined by three things: (i) technical progress, (ii) capital, and (iii) labour. There are simple but appealing features of this approach. If we allow the number of workers to increase (our population grows) but keep capital constant, then, from Chapter 3, we know that the economy will run up against the law of diminishing returns. Extra workers will not continue to improve the rate of productivity. Indeed, marginal productivity might become negative, driving down total productivity. This problem was first recognized by Thomas Malthus in 1798, who predicted that, with a fixed supply of land, adding additional workers to the land would result in slower growth of food output than growth rates in population. Essentially, diminishing returns would ensure that at some point the population would outgrow its supply of food and begin to starve. (Reflecting this point, economics is still known as the dismal science, which for professional members of the subject is less worrying than the term 'Armageddon'.)

Clearly, in the developed world we have not starved. So, the law of diminishing returns has been held back. This has been achieved by either (a) improving technical progress in agriculture, or (b) the employment of more capital. We can see evidence of each. Technical progress has developed with improved knowledge of fertilizers, insecticides and herbicides, improved irrigation systems and, more controversially, genetic modifications. Capital in the form of tractors and combine harvesters has also helped to improve the productivity of land and workers.

How long can growth keep improving?

Robert Solow developed a model of economic growth in the 1950s and the fundamental insight from his approach was that economic growth would not increase for ever. Rather, it will reach a steady state. In growth rate equilibrium, or the steady state output, labour and capital are all assumed to be growing at the same rate. Hence, capital per worker and output per worker are constant.

If the labour force is growing at 10 per cent, then capital also has to grow at 10 per cent in order to keep capital per worker constant. Increases in capital are funded out of increased investment. Banks provide loans for investment from savings. For a 10 per cent increase in investment funds, income or output must grow at 10 per cent in order to guarantee a 10 per cent increase in savings. Essentially, labour growth rates set the tempo for capital investment and economic growth. Indeed, a common fallacy is that higher savings will lead to higher investment, higher capital per worker and higher growth. This is only true for short-term economic growth rates. In the short term, providing all workers with more productive capital improves productivity and raises economic growth; but a blank cheque has also been written for the future, in that all the extra capital has to be maintained. Increased maintenance requires a greater proportion of economic output to go into the renewal of existing capital, rather than the development of new additional capital. As a result, economic growth slows and reverts back to the steady state growth rate.

The **convergence** hypothesis states that poor countries grow more quickly than average, but rich countries grow more slowly than average.

This has a fundamental and particularly troublesome conclusion: growth rate **convergence**.

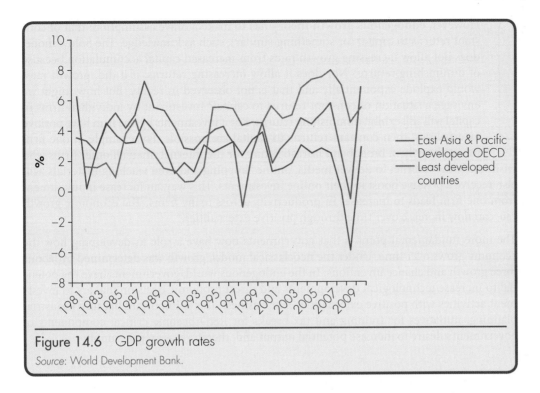

Figure 14.6 GDP growth rates
Source: World Development Bank.

If a country has a low ratio of capital per worker, it does not take much output to renew existing capital. Therefore, more resource can be put into the production of additional capital per worker. However, if capital per worker is high, then more effort is put into renewing existing capital and less resource is available for creating additional capital per worker. Therefore, economic growth rates in modern economies will fall, while growth rates in developing economies will grow. We, however, see little evidence of either. On average, the world's richest and most developed economies exhibit persistent and comparable growth rates to the world's poorest developing economies. However, emerging economies in East Asia and the Pacific have managed to consistently grow at a pace which exceeds that of the developed economies (see Figure 14.6).

14.4 Endogenous growth theory

The neoclassical model is problematic: convergence is not observed and growth is determined either by labour force growth or, at best, by developments in technology. However, neoclassical economists see even developments in technology as being exogenous, or determined outside the model.

For neoclassical economists, growth is determined by technological development, but technological development is not affected by economic growth.

For example, technological development occurs with mad professors staggering out of their labs, the air filled with fumes and the word 'eureka' being proclaimed. These dotty individuals who stumble across new insights of economic importance, such as plastic, computers, nuclear power and the Internet, find such knowledge by chance. None of these discoveries is based within economics. Clearly nuclear physics, biology and chemistry are different subjects, but surely within an economy, government and the economic system can provide structures, incentives and institutions that foster and promote technological development. Leaving such a beneficial activity to chance, in the hands of dotty individuals, is not good policy.

> Endogenous growth theory considers models in which the steady state growth rate can be affected by economic behaviour and policy.

However, **endogenous growth theory** has to make a brave assumption: that of constant returns to capital (or something similar), such as knowledge. The Solow model does not allow increasing growth rates from increased capital accumulation because of diminishing returns. Nor does it allow increasing returns; if it did, growth rates would explode exponentially and that is not observed in reality. But how might we envisage a situation of constant returns to capital? Investment by individual firms in capital will still exhibit diminishing returns. But if investments by one firm have positive externalities, then constant returns to capital are possible. For example, if one firm invests heavily in broadband infrastructure for the Internet, then all other firms who wish to use the Internet to deliver media, online shopping and even teaching materials, will also receive a positive boost to their online investments. This way, an increase in investment from one firm leads to increases in productivity across many firms. The economic growth rate can now increase over time through positive externalities.

The more fundamental point is that governments now have a role in developing how the economy grows over time. Under the neoclassical model, growth was determined by labour force growth and chance inventions. In the endogenous world, governments have the potential to increase technological developments and direct economic decision makers to investment activities with positive externalities. For business, this is important because industrial planning, initiatives for training and tax breaks for R&D become critical components of government's desire to increase potential output and, therefore, aggregate supply.

Supply-side policies

Education markets and long-term growth

Governments around the world are keen to widen participation in higher education. Universities have been tasked with taking in students from poor and deprived areas. Such a policy is political and economic. Bringing a broader and larger number of individuals into higher education widens the skill base of the workforce. This has positive externalities. With higher cognitive skills among the workforce, more advanced productive capital can be employed by firms. This is not about employing more machines per worker, it is about utilizing more productively advanced machines per worker. In addition, a university education enables people to learn for themselves and think critically. If people can learn for themselves, then they might react better to change. So, when new ways of operating come along, firms adapt more quickly and exploit new ideas more readily. Also, by thinking critically, managers can develop new means of operation more rapidly. In this way, education is at the core of technological improvement. The higher the income level of the economy, the greater scope the economy has for funding educational improvements. More education, the greater the rate of technological development, both within university labs and in the workplace.

An important point is to establish the optimal mix of skills for an economy. It is perhaps not desirable to allocate resources to the provision of a university education for all workers. Figure 14.7 provides a comparison of skill levels for many developed economies.

The UK's (GBR) problem is not in the provision of university education. If anything, the UK has one of the workforces with the highest percentage of graduates. Rather, the UK's problem is its large percentage of low-skilled workers. Where it would be more desirable to transfer these workers to the upper secondary and tertiary level of skills, those UK individuals who do not enter university are not receiving the same skills training as they do in countries such as Germany and France. It appears, therefore, that the UK has many educated managers, but an under-skilled set of workers. This can be very problematic. If managers wish to pursue innovative products or employ advanced production techniques, then workers are ill-equipped to respond. They simply do not have the skill base to exploit advanced technologies. The argument may be a generalization, but the points for government are

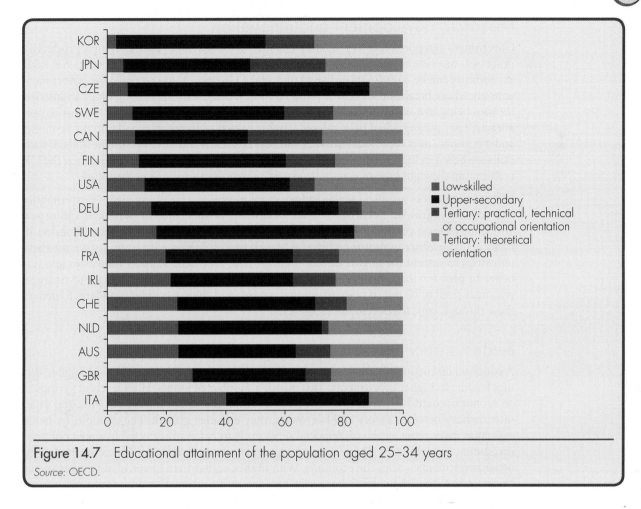

Figure 14.7 Educational attainment of the population aged 25–34 years

Source: OECD.

simple. Higher education in the UK is doing well. Attention now needs to be paid to the development of skills within those individuals who choose not to attend university. Moreover, these individuals and their employers need to be provided with incentives to engage in skills development.

Labour markets and long-term growth

For managers to be capable of exploiting innovative ways of operating, or taking advantage of new capital machinery, labour markets have to be accommodating. The existence of strong trade unions and legislation that either limits redundancies or raises redundancy payments will constrain the ability of firms to exploit new developments. Trade unions will seek to protect their members' interests and perhaps block changes that result in redundancies. Therefore, throughout the 1980s there was a strong impetus from government to reduce the power of trade unions and make it easier for firms to make workers redundant. Two things have happened. First, trade unions have begun to work with, rather than against, companies, developing greater collaborative relationships seeking, for example, to help businesses improve productivity by raising workers' awareness of inefficient practices and perhaps even supporting the development of skills and education within the current workforce. Second, the rise of the stakeholder perspective argues that firms are a collection of interest groups, including consumers, workers, managers, shareholders and government and each needs to work with and recognize the needs of others. Therefore, cultural change and regulatory change in the labour market free up the rapid redeployment of economic resource and can improve labour efficiency and economic growth.

Research, development and innovation

Government can play a role in providing incentives to undertake research in new productive processes, or even encourage the exploitation of existing knowledge. Tax breaks for R&D expenditure can be a useful incentive to undertake research. More recently, the government announced tax breaks on directors' remuneration packages for high-technology industries, the idea being that in order to attract the most able individuals from around the world, very attractive pay packages had to be offered. Highly valued skills are attracted into the economy and it is hoped, over time, local workers will observe, learn and develop similar skills. If such skills are based in high-technology industries, which will flourish in the future, then the UK is attracting the right type of economic expertise in order to survive in the future.

Industrial networks are also seen as an important means of developing positive externalities and economic growth. Local regions are beginning to specialize in particular industries: Yorkshire in food production, Cambridgeshire in technological development, London in finance, Oxfordshire in motor racing and Manchester in higher education. Again, for these industries to sustain the engine of economic growth, they need support industries and it is better to plan for these than hope that they appear. Managers need training and financial resources need to be put in place to aid investment, and the government can help to deliver these through regional development agencies.

Financial services

A common discussion of growth theories relates to savings and investment, with higher savings leading to higher investments. This misses a number of points. High levels of savings in an economy could be lent to firms overseas. Further, the financial services industry, as an intermediary between savers and borrowers, may enhance growth. For example, by being experts in investment appraisal, financial services firms can more effectively screen out poor investment opportunities. Therefore, development in the financial services sector can lead to better investments within the economy. With higher, rather than lower, quality investments being undertaken, the capital stock can become more productive and economic growth should improve. Moreover, the existence of insurance can protect firms from the financial consequences of risks, such as fire, earthquake, etc. Therefore, insurance can be seen as necessary for expensive capital accumulation. Without it firms would be less willing to invest, leading to a reduction in growth rates.

Much of this thinking drove large-scale deregulation of the financial services industry, especially in economies such as the USA and the UK. In order to play a strong role in supporting broader industries, financial services needs to be free to grow into new markets, invent new products and spread liquidity throughout the economy. So-called light touch regulation was put in place, which monitored the industry but rarely became involved in questioning the commercial or strategic decisions taken by many financial institutions. In the wake of the credit crisis, it has become clear that financial institutions are indeed enormously important to the functioning of the wider economy and that the need to protect the financial industry from collapse is crucial. How governments in the future manage to promote this crucial sector for growth within a tighter regulatory framework will be a formidable challenge.

Other policies

Tax cuts

In the 1980s, the UK and US governments reduced personal taxation rates, arguing that such policies provided incentives for individuals to work longer and raise productive output. However, most evidence tends to suggest that many individuals recognized that, with the tax cut, they could actually reduce the hours they worked and still earn the same amount of income as they did under the higher tax rates. A possible explanation for this behaviour is that individuals valued leisure time more than they did income. Therefore, following the tax cuts, individuals decided that, rather than seek higher income levels, they would retain the current income level and instead opt for more time spent with family and friends enjoying various leisure activities.

Governments have also used tax incentives to boost company profits and release cash for investment in research and development or training. Such tax rates are aimed at boosting the firm's access to new knowledge, to be innovative and to employ high skilled labour. Over time, seeking out new thinking, new science and new ways of operating should boost output and lead to higher tax revenues in the future.

Privatization

Privatization was also popular in the 1980s and 1990s. Previously, water, telephone, gas, electricity, rail and airlines were all supplied by government companies. Most nationalized industries acted as monopolies and were deemed to be inefficient through lack of competition. Furthermore, any increase in investment by nationalized industries had to be funded by the taxpayer. Such a system limited funds because the government had competing projects such as health and education to invest in. It was also not clear how financial performance would be ensured. Privatized companies can access the world's major finance markets and raise significant sums of money. Furthermore, unlike the government, private investors would be keen to ensure that the privatized industries operated at a profit and similarly only invested in profitable and productive assets. Therefore, as the privatized industries were and are important components of the national infrastructure, it is easy to see how increased investment and improvements in operational efficiency could have positive externalities for the rest of the economy – particularly if productivity improvements occurred in communications and transport. Reflecting these arguments, the governments privatized these nationalized industries and enabled new companies to compete in these markets.

The growth of competition has been slow to develop. In the case of telecommunications, economies of scale created an effective entry barrier. However, as technology changed and mobile communications became more popular, new companies found it easier to enter the market. In terms of utilities, we can now buy gas from electricity producers and vice versa. The market appears far more competitive, at least for those customers who wish to shop around. Therefore, if competition is increasing in these markets, then prices should be falling and firms will be seeking new and innovative ways of operating. In the long term, important factor inputs for other companies, such as communication, energy and transport, all become cheaper and overall supply in the economy improves.

Private finance initiatives

In seeking to develop the opportunities for the private sector to be involved in public sector activities, numerous governments have turned to **private finance initiatives** (PFIs). Generally, PFIs involve the national or local government contracting with a private sector supplier for a public infrastructure project. Examples include buildings, hospitals, schools, roads, bridges and railways. The private sector raises funds, builds the asset and ultimately owns the asset. The government then pays an annual leasing fee for the asset. In the UK, the average cost of a PFI project to the public purse is just under £100 million and lasts for around 25 years.

> Private finance initiatives involve the private sector in financing, building and owning infrastructure projects in return for an annual leasing fee from the government.

There are a number of benefits associated with PFIs. First, the private sector is seen to be better at costing and delivering infrastructure projects. Project and budget overruns should be minimized. Commercial organizations are better at understanding and managing financial risk. They also have a clear means of selling their assets and leases in an open and private market. In contrast, it can be argued that the only benefit to government when building infrastructure projects is the ability to raise funds at a lower rate than the private sector. Governments are experts at raising money and spending. They are not experts at design, construction and running infrastructure.

While PFIs have become popular, they are not without criticism. A number of projects have experienced overruns. Some private providers have become insolvent, leaving the government to finish the project and pick up the final bill. Furthermore, while private firms may be very cost-effective when building infrastructure projects, the initial transaction costs (see Chapter 7) can be extremely high. Many projects take up to 36 months to agree a contract between the private firm and the government. Lawyers' bills are extremely expensive, as is the time of senior managers and senior civil servants.

Summary

There are clearly many possible policy prescriptions for economic growth but, broadly speaking, governments seek to develop labour productivity, capital productivity or technological progress. More fundamentally, governments are beginning to return to the idea that they can *design* an economy, which will outperform in terms of growth. The neoclassical model advises governments to sit back and wait for the economy to develop. The endogenous growth theory directs governments to think about how businesses relate to the educational system, how financial services relate to the development of business and how the labour market reacts to the needs of business. Economic policy has moved to an understanding of how to enhance the whole economic system by thinking about how the individual parts work together and in particular how positive externalities can be generated throughout the economic system.

 # Business application: how does innovation promote business?

A common perception is that research and development can provide firms with a competitive advantage and we are not going to argue with this view. In fact, in Chapter 5 when we considered monopoly, we put forward the idea of creative destruction. By way of a quick reminder – through innovation, firms can overcome the entry barriers of an incumbent monopoly. As such, innovation can offer firms a competitive advantage and enable the generation of profits.

In our discussion of how innovation drives economic growth in section 14.2, we also highlighted how innovation is predominately funded and carried out by commercial enterprises in the US, suggesting a strong link between industrial R&D and overall growth in GDP. Such views also help to underpin a policy prescription for more engineering and science graduates. The future strength of an economy is seen to be dependent upon the continual creation of new ideas and technology.

Such views also drive concerns about brain drain and infringements of intellectual property rights. Government, industry and universities in developed economies invest billions in building up R&D capabilities, only to see companies in emerging economies either attract scientific talent or copy designs and technology for little cost.

Recent thinking and evidence within economics is beginning to question the significance of these concerns. Yes, innovation can provide firms with a competitive advantage, but only if consumers are also willing to be innovative and take advantage of the new technology. It is, therefore, the market-based transaction of technology which is important for firms and economic growth more generally.

At the retail level, innovation requires consumers to be adventurous in their consumption. This may require good access to credit facilities and retail environments which enable consumers to experience and sample new innovative products.

We should also recognize that firms are also consumers and buy inputs and support services from other companies. With the growing importance of outsourcing, the adoption of new

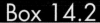

Box 14.2

New vegetable varieties offer quality and innovation

Syngenta brassica crop specialist, James Gray, believes variety breeders have got close to the top of the curve for yields, but will continue to make significant strides with quality and innovation that will improve growers' returns and increase demand through the introduction of new vegetable products.

He highlighted that new developments in conventional plant breeding technology by Syngenta, using marker and genomic assisted techniques that can select and breed-in a number of required traits simultaneously, could reduce new variety development times from the norm of 10 to 12 years, to three years or less.

Such developments will enable the company's breeders to bolster and stack disease resistance traits into new varieties, further extending the White Blister resistance already utilised in green and Savoy cabbages or Mycosphaerella Ringspot in cauliflower, he said.

It also enables breeders to work on naturally occurring beneficial traits for nutrition, taste and aroma, colour and shelf-life. 'Already we are seeing new varieties that are more uniform at harvest, so there's fewer passes through the crop to pick – requiring less labour and cost. Varieties with longer shelf life reduce

waste, whilst those that require less trimming cut down waste, reduce cost and gets product onto the shelf faster and fresher.'

But Mr Gray highlighted that while every variety produced aimed to have better agronomic traits for growers, the essential element was to enhance customer satisfaction in eating vegetables and provide improvements for the end consumer. He cited the company's new white salad cabbage, with a mild taste and crisp bite that will create an entirely new salad product line for growers.

Furthermore, a new white cabbage variety has been developed with an orange core. The colour orange can be instantly associated with elevated levels of vitamins by consumers, and gives growers a clearly differentiated product. A new Syngenta pink cabbage can give packed salads great colour and visual appeal, without the problems of bleeding and contamination experienced with red varieties. He also reported the recently introduced red Brussels sprout had received very positive feedback from retailers and consumers – even those who have hitherto shunned sprouts.

Adapted from an article in *Farming UK*, 13 February 2012.

technologies by firms in areas such as information technology from support services is generally seen as important for productivity growth and higher GDP.

If the purchase and adoption of new technology is the driver of economic growth, then an economy is as dependent on venturesome consumers and business managers as it is on scientists and engineers. Box 14.2 picks up these issues in more detail.

Business application: the BRIC economies

The BRIC economies are those of Brazil, Russia, India and China. These are seen as important economies in the future; they are growing fast and they are enormous. Other economies are also growing fast, but since they are smaller in size and population, their impact on the world economy is likely to be much less than the BRIC economies.

Growth in the BRIC economies has been impressive. For example, the growth of the Chinese economy has been one of the major economic miracles of the past 25 years. Compound growth rates approaching 10 per cent per annum over such a time period are almost unmatched by any other economy.

China's strength is built on technological expertise and an abundance of labour. Much the same can be said of India. Russia, while also technologically capable, is also reaping the benefits of vast energy resources. In a similar manner, Brazil too has access to important forestry and energy resources. With massive populations, vast natural resources and reasonable

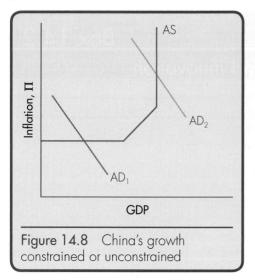

Figure 14.8 China's growth constrained or unconstrained

educational expertise, the BRIC economies can be expected to grow for many years to come. They can achieve this because they have yet to run up against the production possibility frontier. Or perhaps more accurately, the frontier and aggregate supply are constantly expanding in the BRIC economies.

When aggregate demand increases in the BRIC economies, it is met with additional aggregate supply, the economy grows and GDP rises. We are clearly considering an increase in AD_1, where aggregate supply is elastic, as in Figure 14.8. Rapid growth and low inflation go together. Only when an economy is fully developed does aggregate supply become inelastic and growth slow.

The implications of such rapid growth in the BRIC economies are enormous for business. As economies grow, the potential for growth in incomes and household consumption also increases. As incomes grow, then new consumption possibilities become a reality for the increasingly affluent households. Consider Figure 14.9, which describes car ownership in a number of economies. In the USA, 750 in every 1000 people of driving age own a car; or, put another way, nearly every person who can drive a car, owns a car. In China, only 20 in every 1000 people of driving age own a car. The scope for car consumption to expand in China and other BRIC economies is enormous. These rapidly expanding economies are very attractive when compared with the slow-growing economies of the EU and North America.

In addition, the growth of car consumption does not point to the only industry which may seek out a future in the growth of the BRIC economies. Banking, insurance, consumer electronics, computing, televisions and tourism all currently form small shares of household consumption in BRICs. Foreign companies are queuing up to cash in on the potential for economic and consumption growth to explode in the BRIC economies.

However, there should be a note of caution. The BRIC economies are still at a very different stage of economic development from other western economies. It is not simply the case that BMW can arrive in India or China and sell thousands of 5 series cars. While consumption is expanding in the auto market, the product has to be right for the level of income. This explains why domestic producers in the BRICs have sought to buy old technology for small cars from western auto companies. This enables domestic companies to build small, cheap, attractive cars at minimal cost; vehicles which the average household in a BRIC economy would feel proud to own but which have become less preferable in the developed economies of the world. So, the product has to suit the needs of the market.

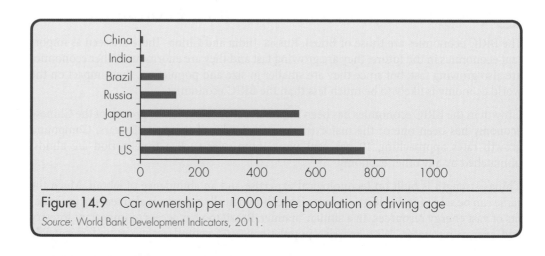

Figure 14.9 Car ownership per 1000 of the population of driving age
Source: World Bank Development Indicators, 2011.

A final and important concern for foreign companies seeking to gain from the growth of the BRICs is the share of GDP enjoyed by households. It is very interesting and exciting to see GDP increase by 10 per cent per annum. But where is this additional growth in GDP going? We know that the key units within an economy are households, firms, government and foreign consumers. Are these all growing at 10 per cent, or is a large slice of growth flowing to particular sectors of the economy? In the case of China, much of the growth has been driven by exports to the rest of the world. However, with an abundance of labour, wage rates have been kept relatively low. This has meant that the gains from export growth have flowed to firms rather than workers. This will clearly limit the expansion of consumption growth. Firms seeking to profit on the growth in China need to recognize this feature and factor it into any decision to enter the Chinese economy.

As business economists, we can now understand the majority of these issues and considerations. We are merely combining an understanding of economic growth and the circular flow of income. As you become more confident with the material of this book, then you too need to be capable of identifying the various aspects of economics which can be combined to provide you with a deeper understanding of your business environment.

 ## Business data application: digging behind gross capital formation

Is capital formation important for understanding an economy's potential to grow? The Solow growth model indicated that the rate at which an economy can add to its capital stock is constrained. Beyond a certain growth rate the economy begins to expend more effort in maintaining its asset base, rather than growing its asset base. Therefore, assessing an economy's ability to expand its asset base may give some insight into that economy's ability to continue growing at an above average rate into the future.

Businesses should be interested in an economy's growth rate potential because decisions to enter markets are often long-term commitments. A business looking at the opportunities in China is unlikely to invest just for one year to take advantage of current opportunities. It is more likely to take a long-term view and ask if China's growth rate is sustainable.

Figure 14.10 provides data on gross capital formation for China, India, Germany and the UK. Gross capital formation captures the value of additional assets created in an economy, less disposals of old assets. Gross capital formation captures the increase in private sector investment in new important assets such as buildings, factories and equipment, plus public sector investment in roads, rail, seaports, airports, schools, universities and hospitals.

Over the past 20 years the fast growing economies of China and India have exhibited strong gross capital formation. This trend tells us that much of the gains from growth are being reinvested back into the economy. In terms of the circular flow of income significant amounts of GDP are being channelled into investment expenditure. Given that this spending is creating productive assets, such as factories, telephone networks and transport infrastructure, we might form the view that strong gross capital formation aids an economy in building a strong foundation for sustainable growth. The assets being created today will support tomorrow's growth. In contrast, if much of the additional income was going into household consumption, then we might question the ability of the economy to support additional expansion.

When examining Germany and the UK, we can see a downward trend in gross capital formation. Will this lead to lower future growth? Perhaps, but it is always worth questioning and asking what are the data actually measuring and is it entirely relevant? Importantly, gross capital formation captures the value of tangible assets, things that can be seen, touched and valued. Assets that might be valuable in a manufacturing economy. But are such assets important when an economy becomes more knowledge based?

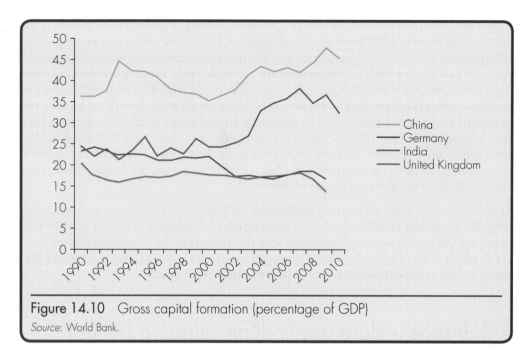

Figure 14.10 Gross capital formation (percentage of GDP)
Source: World Bank.

Knowledge-based economies generate economic output through the creation and application of ideas, not by making and doing. As developed economies, the UK in particular and Germany to a similar degree are moving into more service-based economies and away from manufacturing. Industries in finance, media, professional services and life sciences have grown in importance. Generating ideas requires science, it requires creativity and it requires innovative risk takers. Of course, generating new science, whether it be used in aerospace or the creation of new drugs, requires gross capital formation in laboratories, But the asset base has to be more than tangible assets. We therefore require an understanding of expenditure on research and development, an understanding of advanced science skills within an economy, and growth in knowledge sectors, including science, media, law, accountancy and finance.

Leading business managers grasp the basic ideas and then question, probe, dig around and question relevance. Am I understanding the situation, what else do I need to know, is the approach I am taking relevant? When you do this you can begin to operate beyond your business competitors and make more informed business decisions. As a manager you are beginning your training, you need to grasp the basics, but you also need to begin to practise the art of analysing, evaluating and reviewing ideas, concepts and data.

Summary

1. Supply-side economics is concerned with improving the potential output of the economy.

2. Economic growth can be driven by increased factor inputs, enhanced productivity and improvements in technology.

3. If it is assumed that aggregate supply is perfectly inelastic in the long run, then increasing aggregate supply is the only way of generating additional economic output without raising inflation.

4. Neoclassical growth theory asserts that diminishing returns will lead to a natural growth rate for an economy. Any increase in the natural growth rate can only stem from technological progress or an increase in the number of workers.

5. Neoclassical growth theory leads to the conclusion that all economies will converge on a common growth rate. Empirical evidence does not support this idea.

6. In response to neoclassical growth theory, endogenous growth theory asserts that diminishing returns to capital in one firm, or industry, might generate constant returns to scale across the entire economy. In essence, investments in capital by one firm, or industry, have positive externalities for the rest of the economy. Economies can now grow at different rates, rather than converge, depending upon the generation of productivity-enhancing positive externalities.

7. Under endogenous growth theory, the government has a role in facilitating growth. Developments in education, financial services, levels of R&D and freer labour markets should all lead to higher future growth rates.

Learning checklist

You should now be able to:

- Explain how economic growth is linked to growth in long-run aggregate supply
- Identify the main sources of economic growth
- Provide a review of the neoclassical model of economic growth
- Explain and evaluate the convergence hypothesis
- Explain the endogenous growth model and highlight how and why it is different from the neoclassical growth model
- Explain and evaluate the various types of policy used to develop economic growth
- Explain how and why business can be central to economic growth
- Examine data on gross capital formation and question its relevance

Questions   connect

1. Identify and explain the main sources of economic growth. What are the main sources of growth in your economy?

2. Economic growth through a higher utilization of current economic resources comes with what problems or opportunity costs?

3. Which are equivalent, the production possibility frontier and aggregate demand, or the production possibility frontier and aggregate supply?

4. Explain why GDP per hour worked is a useful measure of productivity.

5. What distinguishes the UK from France and the US in terms of R&D funding and the provision of R&D activities?

6. The Solow model of growth predicts long-run steady state growth rates. What justification can be provided for this prediction?

7. Explain the convergence hypothesis. Does the convergence hypothesis hold in reality?

EASY

EASY

8. What does the endogenous growth model assume about returns to scale? Is this assumption reasonable?

9. How do the Solow and endogenous models of growth differ in their prescriptions for the role of government in economic growth?

10. What are supply-side policies? Provide examples of current supply-side policies and assess how you would measure the success of such policies in promoting economic growth.

INTERMEDIATE

11. Is R&D important for economic growth, or is it the willingness of consumers to be innovative in their consumption that is important for economic growth?

12. Consider whether there is a simple link between more R&D and higher economic growth.

13. Does neoclassical growth theory provide an adequate understanding of economic growth? Is endogenous growth theory any better than the neoclassical approach?

DIFFICULT

14. Does it matter if growth occurs through increased utilization of resources or higher productivity of resources?

15. What are the key benefits associated with privatization and private finance initiatives?

Exercises

EASY

1. True or false?

   (a) An annual growth rate of 2 per cent per annum leads to a seven-fold increase in real output in less than a century.

   (b) Sustained growth cannot occur if production relies on a factor whose supply is largely fixed.

   (c) In the neoclassical growth theory, output, capital and labour all grow at the same rate.

   (d) Higher savings enable a higher long-run rate of growth.

   (e) Given the convergence hypothesis, we can expect all poor countries to catch up with the richer countries.

   (f) Growth may be stimulated by capital externalities: that is, higher capital in one firm increases capital productivity in other firms.

INTERMEDIATE

2. Which of the following policy suggestions are appropriate for improving economic growth in an economy?

   (a) The encouragement of R&D.

   (b) A reduction in marginal tax rates to increase labour supply.

   (c) Investment grants.

   (d) The establishment of training and education schemes to improve human capital.

   (e) An expansion of aggregate demand to increase the level of employment.

   (f) The encouragement of dissemination of new knowledge and techniques.

DIFFICULT

3. Refer to Box 14.2 when considering the following questions:

   (a) What is the difference between product innovation and consumer innovation?

   (b) For a modern economy to grow, which consumers need to be innovative, retail or wholesale?

   (c) For an economy to prosper, the supply and demand of innovation have to be in balance. Discuss.

SECTION

5

Global economics

Section contents

15 Exchange rates and the balance of payments   374

16 Globalization   399

Exchange rates and the balance of payments

Chapter contents

Exchange rates at a glance   375
15.1 Business problem: should the UK be a member of the euro?   375
15.2 Forex markets and exchange rate regimes   376
15.3 Fixed versus floating exchange rates   380
15.4 The balance of payments   382
15.5 Exchange rates and government policy   385
15.6 European monetary union   387
15.7 Business application: monetary sovereignty, exchange rate depreciation and export growth   390
15.8 Business application: hedging   391
15.9 Business data application: real exchange rates within the eurozone   393
Summary   394
Learning checklist   396
Questions   396
Exercises   397

Learning outcomes

By the end of this chapter you should understand:

Economic theory

LO1   Fixed exchange rates

LO2   Floating exchange rates

LO3   The performance differences between fixed and floating exchange rates

LO4   The balance of payments

LO5   How to evaluate fiscal and monetary policy under different exchange rate regimes

LO6   Optimal currency zones

LO7   Issues relating to European monetary union

Business application

LO8   If there is a gain to business from not being in the euro

LO9   How hedging can be used to reduce exchange rate risk and create speculative investments

LO10   How trade imbalances within the eurozone and the build-up of debt are linked to changes in the real exchange rate between member countries

At a glance Exchange rates

The issues

There are many currencies in the world. The US dollar, UK sterling and the euro are all examples of important currencies. Over time, the strength of the US dollar against UK sterling or the euro varies. When the dollar is strong, it can be exchanged for more euros than when it is weak. This generates issues for business and government. What price will businesses receive for their goods and services when they are exported overseas? Also, why is it beneficial for a number of economies to share a currency, such as the euro?

The understanding

In order to understand exchange rate movements and the potential benefits from being a member of the euro, it is necessary to understand the balance of payments, as well as floating, versus fixed, exchange rate regimes. Once this knowledge is in place, it is possible to address the effectiveness of domestic fiscal and monetary policy under the euro.

The usefulness

In part, trading overseas is determined by how internationally competitive an economy is. The euro, by fixing the exchange rate across all member economies, requires greater price flexibility within member economies. Firms need to understand these issues. Furthermore, by understanding hedging, firms can understand how exchange rate volatility can be managed.

15.1 Business problem: should the UK be a member of the euro?

There are numerous issues associated with whether or not the UK should adopt the euro, but not all of them have business implications. For example, many individuals see the pound as a symbol of 'Britishness'. The pound as a currency and the picture of the sovereign on notes and coins are seen by many as key aspects of their nationality. Indeed, this deep cultural affinity with the national currency is not a uniquely British view. Upon adopting the euro, the French held a day of national celebration and mourning as a sign of respect for the French franc.

For business the euro is not a cultural identity problem because, as many business people will tell you, 'business is no place for sentiment'. Rather, the euro has simple operational implications and profound macroeconomic consequences. Changing prices from pounds to euros and cutting back on the need for currency conversions are simple operational implications. The macroeconomic implications are far greater. Consider the following by way of a brief introduction to the issues.

Imagine boats in a harbour bobbing up and down. Each boat represents an economy: the UK, France, Germany, Spain, Italy, and so on. The waves are the business cycles. When each economy had its own currency, the boats were connected together with ropes. So, as the wave hits the first boat it is able to rise up and then fall. The next boat then moves up and down, and so on. Each boat, or each economy, has some flexibility in dealing with the business cycle. Under the common currency of the euro, Germany, France, Spain and Italy and all other members have swapped the ropes for an iron bar welded across the front of all their boats. In the face of the business cycle, the eurozone members now move together. The flexibility of the ropes has been swapped for the size and stability of a huge integrated eurozone economy. The question for the UK is whether it wishes to swap its flexible rope for a stable but relatively inflexible weld to the rest of Europe.

The answer to this problem rests on two broad areas: (i) an understanding of the trade-off between flexibility and stability; and (ii) an understanding of how strong the welds are between the different boats. This chapter will investigate these issues, highlighting how the international environment, through exchange rates and intranational economic policies, affects business.

 ## Forex markets and exchange rate regimes

> A forex market is where different currencies are traded.

Whenever you travel abroad you convert pounds sterling into euros, US dollars, etc. Since we are talking about a **forex market**, the item being traded must have a price. The price of currency is simply the rate at which it can be converted. In Table 15.1 various exchange rates for the euro are listed. For example, €1 will buy £0.8951 or 114.5150 yen.

Table 15.1   Forex rates for the euro

Currency	Rate
UK – pound	0.8380
Japan – yen	103.0152
USA – dollar	1.3188
Hong Kong – dollar	10.2253

Source: *Financial Times*, February 2012.

If these are the prices from the forex market, then the obvious question is, how does this market work? Who is demanding and selling currency?

The answer is fairly simple: individuals and firms buy and sell currencies whenever they undertake transactions with other economies. For example, whenever an import into the UK occurs, pounds have to be exchanged for another currency. Similarly, whenever an export out of the UK occurs, the foreign purchaser needs to sell their own currency in exchange for pounds. We can, therefore, think of imports as generating the supply of pounds in the market and exports as generating the demand for pounds in the market. In Figure 15.1, we have a traditional demand and supply curve for pounds.

If we begin in equilibrium with Q_S equal to Q_D, then the exchange rate is e_0, or £1 can be converted to €1.0. If exports from the UK to Europe rise, then European consumers will need to demand more UK pounds. The demand curve for pounds shifts from Q_D to Q_{D1}. The exchange rate for pounds appreciates, with £1 being converted into €1.2. If exports fall, demand shifts from Q_D to Q_{D2} and the value of the currency depreciates, with £1 being converted into only €0.8. Similarly, if UK consumers import more goods into the country, they will have to supply more pounds in exchange for euros. We could also envisage a change in supply. If the supply of pounds shifted to the right, the pound would fall in value. But if supply shifted to the left, the pound would rise in value.

Exchange rate regimes

> Under a fixed exchange rate regime, the government fixes the exchange rate between the domestic currency and another strong world currency, such as the US dollar.
>
> Under a floating exchange rate regime, the exchange rate is set purely by market forces.
>
> A dirty float occurs when the government claims that the exchange rate floats, but it is in fact managed by the government or central bank.

The exchange rate market can be characterized as operating under two extreme regimes. In a **fixed exchange rate regime**, the government sets an exchange rate and then uses the central bank to buy and sell currency to keep the market rate fixed. Under a **floating exchange rate regime**, the exchange rate is set by market forces, with holders of foreign currency demanding and selling various currencies.

A third system is known as a **dirty float**. The government claims that the currency floats but in fact, through the central bank, the currency is secretly bought and sold to achieve a target exchange rate.

We will examine the fixed and floating exchange rate regimes and then provide an analysis of their relative strengths and weaknesses.

Fixed exchange rate

In Figure 15.2, we adapt our previous figure and illustrate how a fixed exchange rate works. For simplicity, assume the government sets the exchange rate at e_0. If demand and supply meet at this rate, then the market is in equilibrium and there is no need for any market intervention. However, if, in accordance with an export boom, there is an increase in the demand for pounds, the demand curve will shift to Q_{D1}. The market would like to be in equilibrium at B, with an exchange rate of £1 equals €1.2. But the government is fixing the price at £1 equals €1.0. The government is effectively pricing below the equilibrium price and, as we saw in Chapter 4, this leads to market disequilibrium. At the fixed rate of £1 equals €1.0, the willingness to supply pounds is A, but the willingness to demand pounds is C. Therefore, in the market there is an excess demand for pounds equal to the distance A to C. The government, or the central bank, has to meet this excess demand by supplying an additional AC pounds to the market. The extra pounds are effectively swapped for US dollars, euros, etc. and are added to the central bank's foreign currency reserves.

In Figure 15.3, we can consider what happens if the demand for pounds falls to Q_{D2}. Now there will be an excess supply of pounds equal to AE. The central bank now needs to buy the excess supply of pounds. In order to buy pounds, it has to offer something other than pounds in return. When the central bank was selling pounds it will have received euros and other currencies in return. These were added to the bank's currency reserves. It now uses these reserves to buy back the pounds.

However, there is a critical problem for the central bank. It is feasible for the central bank to keep supplying additional pounds to the market because, as the central bank, it can ask for more pounds to be printed. Unfortunately, the central bank cannot commit to an indefinite purchase of the pound because, in order to do this, it has to have an infinite supply of foreign currency, such as US dollars and euros. Since the US Federal Reserve controls the supply of

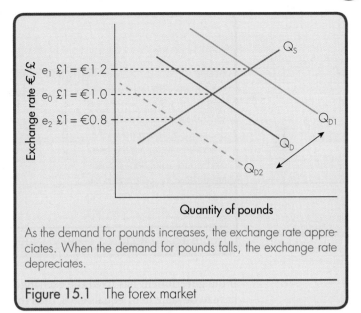

As the demand for pounds increases, the exchange rate appreciates. When the demand for pounds falls, the exchange rate depreciates.

Figure 15.1 The forex market

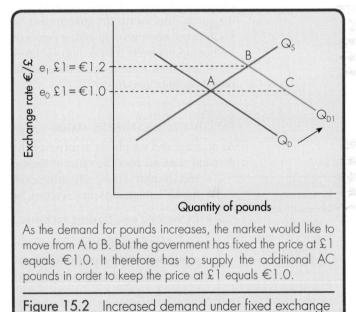

As the demand for pounds increases, the market would like to move from A to B. But the government has fixed the price at £1 equals €1.0. It therefore has to supply the additional AC pounds in order to keep the price at £1 equals €1.0.

Figure 15.2 Increased demand under fixed exchange rates

dollars and the European central bank controls the supply of euros, the Bank of England will soon run out of foreign currencies with which to buy the pound.

Devaluation

If the currency is being continually supported by the central bank, it is probably the case that the fixed exchange rate has become vastly different from the long-term market rate for the currency. The correct policy response is not to keep buying the currency. Instead, the currency should be allowed to devalue. In our example, the fixed exchange rate of £1 equals €1.0 is abandoned and the government seeks to manage the exchange rate at the new equilibrium of £1 equals €0.8.

This potential for devaluation creates a fundamental weakness within fixed exchange rates: they are open to **speculative attack**.

A speculative attack is a massive capital outflow from an economy with a fixed exchange rate.

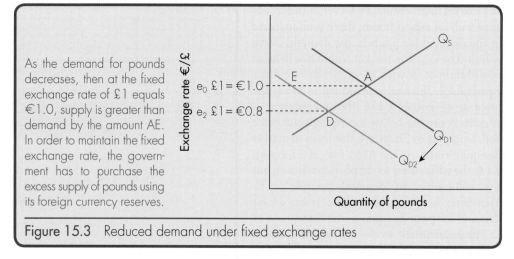

As the demand for pounds decreases, then at the fixed exchange rate of £1 equals €1.0, supply is greater than demand by the amount AE. In order to maintain the fixed exchange rate, the government has to purchase the excess supply of pounds using its foreign currency reserves.

Figure 15.3   Reduced demand under fixed exchange rates

If the government has fixed the exchange rate at £1 equals €1.0, but you think it will soon have to devalue to £1 equals €0.8, then the best thing to do is take pounds and convert them into euros: £1 million will buy you €1.0 million. If many people do this, massive capital out-flows will be observed. Note that people are cutting demand for pounds and instead demanding euros. This means the government has to offer more support to the pound at £1 equals €1.0. It will soon give up and, when it devalues to £1 equals €0.8, you can take your €1.0 million and convert it back into €1.0m/0.8m = £1.25m. So, by changing your money into euros and then waiting for a devaluation you have made £0.25 million, or a 25 per cent return on your investment.

Floating exchange rates

As demand and supply for a currency change, the equilibrium price adjusts accordingly. As demand rises, so does the value of the currency, and as demand falls, the currency depreci-ates in value. Under a **floating exchange rate** system there is no impact on the central bank's foreign currency reserves as there is no intervention in the marketplace.

In a floating exchange rate system, there is no market intervention by the government or the central bank.

Purchasing power parity requires the nominal exchange rate to adjust in order to keep the real exchange rate constant.

In the long run, floating exchange rates *should* obey **purchasing power parity**.

Consider the following example. Assume the exchange rate is £1 equals €1.5. We will also assume that a pair of designer jeans cost £50 in London and €75 in Paris. With the current exchange rate, the price of the jeans is identical in London and Paris (£50 × 1.5 = €75).

Now assume that inflation in Paris is zero, but inflation in London is 10 per cent. At the end of the year, the jeans in London have increased in price by 10 per cent and so now cost £55. The jeans in Paris have stayed the same, €75. If the exchange rate is still £1 equals €1.5, then we can save £5 by buying the jeans in Paris and importing them into the UK. Clearly £5 is not much of a saving, but if we were in business and set about buying 1000 pairs of jeans, then it might be worthwhile importing from Paris.

However, as we begin to import jeans we have to sell pounds and demand euros. As we (and everyone else) do this, the value of the euro will rise. In fact, it will rise to £1 equals €1.36. Why? Well, if we now convert the price of the jeans in Paris back to pounds, we have €75/1.36 = £55. All that happens is that the nominal exchange rate adjusts so that the price of jeans in Paris is identical to the price of jeans in London. The real exchange rate is constant and, as a result, we have purchasing power parity – it costs the same to buy goods in London as it does in Paris.

Clearly, this is an extreme illustrative example. Consumers need to be aware of the price differences between Paris and London. The price difference has to be big enough to make

Box 15.1

The Big Mac index: McCurrencies

The Economist's Big Mac index is based on the theory of purchasing power parity (PPP). If purchasing power parity holds, then using the current exchange rate, the price of a Big Mac in the USA should be equal to the price of a Big Mac in China, the UK, the EU, etc. *The Economist's* Big Mac index from January 2012, shown in Table 15.2, suggests that a number of currencies are overvalued compared with the US dollar and a number are also undervalued. The Chinese yuan would have to rise by 41 per cent in order for Big Macs to cost the same in China and the US, while the euro would have to fall by 6 per cent in order to make the Big Mac in Europe the same price as in the US.

The index was never intended to be a precise predictor of currency movements, simply a take-away guide to whether currencies are at their 'correct' long-run level. Curiously, however, burgernomics has an impressive record in predicting exchange rates: currencies that show up as overvalued often tend to weaken in later years. But you must always remember the Big Mac's limitations. Burgers cannot sensibly be traded across borders and prices are distorted by differences in taxes. In addition, it is also likely that income levels, wages and the cost of non-tradable inputs, such as rents, in different economies are likely to affect the domestic price level.

Table 15.2 The Big Mac index

	Under(−)/over(+) valuation against the dollar (%)
USA	
Australia	+18
Brazil	+35
China	−41
Euro area	+6
Russia	−40
Switzerland	+62
UK	−8

Adapted from an article in *The Economist*, 12 January 2012.
© The Economist Newspaper Limited, London 2012.

consumers interested in exploiting the price differential. Finally, the cost of moving the goods from Paris to London has to be lower than the price difference.

The Economist magazine has for a number of years used the price of a Big Mac to assess purchasing power parity. Details of this are provided in Box 15.1. While the limitations of this approach are discussed, it should be noted that the Big Mac index has been surprisingly accurate in predicting future exchange rate movements.

Exchange rates in practice

As indicated at the beginning of this section, fixed and floating exchange rate regimes are extremes. The Chinese yuan is fixed in the short term against a basket of currencies, including the US dollar, the euro, the Japanese yen and the UK pound. The euro floats against all other currencies, as does the US dollar. The UK pound is also seen as a floating currency. But the central bank and government saw the rapid depreciation of the pound in late 2008 as a way of supporting UK exports during the economic recession. While not directly entering the forex market to buy and sell pounds, comments in press interviews were clearly designed to manage the currency downwards.

A concern with the Chinese currency is that the Chinese government is seeking to undervalue the yuan. In so doing, a cheaper yuan will drive more exports and protect Chinese jobs (see Box 15.2).

Box 15.2

Fortuitous trade data give China ammunition on Yuan

The broadest measure of China's global trade surplus fell to a several-year low, providing Chinese Vice President Xi Jinping with a stark counterpoint to the long-standing US argument that the yuan is undervalued as he tours the USA next week.

China's current-account surplus for 2011 shrank to around 2.7 per cent of gross domestic product according to government data released Friday, the lowest ratio in close to a decade. It is also below the 4 per cent level which the US Treasury has suggested is a sign of an undervalued currency.

One way to measure whether a currency is undervalued is to see whether a country racks up extraordinarily high trade surpluses. In 2007, for instance, China's current-account surplus hit 10.1 per cent of GDP. Since then, with major trade partners battered by recession and China's own domestic demand strong, it has fallen every year.

Despite the shrinking global surplus, China also reported on Friday that its January trade surplus with the USA rose 32 per cent from a year ago, to $18 billion. The surplus is widely cited as evidence that relations with China costs US jobs, an argument with particular

salience during an election year with the US unemployment rate at 8.3 per cent.

Globally, China's exports shrank 0.5 per cent compared with a year ago in January, down from growth of 13.4 per cent in December. Imports fell even further, dropping 15.3 per cent, and the trade surplus rebounded to $27 billion – the highest level since July 2011. Chang Jian, China economist at Barclays Capital, cautioned that the Lunar New Year holiday was distorting the data, making it difficult to see a pattern.

Part of the reason is that the yuan looks less glaringly undervalued. It has risen 31 per cent against the dollar since June 2005, close to the 40 per cent appreciation often demanded by US lawmakers. Since June 2010, when China said it would let the yuan move more freely, it has gained 8 per cent, and factoring in inflation the rise is higher. Administration officials generally feel they have pushed China to move about as fast as it is willing to go.

Adapted from an article by Tom Orlik, 11 February 2012.
Reprinted by permission of *The Wall Street Journal*
© 2012 Dow Jones & Company, Inc. All rights reserved
worldwide. License number 2900141395774.

 ## 15.3 Fixed versus floating exchange rates

Given that both fixed and floating exchange rates are used by different governments, it should be expected that each system must have benefits and drawbacks. These are generally related to exchange rate **volatility**, **robustness** and **financial discipline**.

Volatility is a measure of variability. In the case of exchange rates, a concern over volatility is a concern over how much the exchange rate changes.

Robustness is a concern with flexibility, or the ability to accommodate change.

Financial discipline is the degree to which a government pursues stringent monetary policy and targets low inflation.

Volatility

Clearly, under a fixed exchange rate there is no volatility in the short term. The government fixes the exchange rate. In contrast, floating exchange rates are volatile. The value of the exchange rate changes on a daily and even hourly basis. A sense of the volatility is shown in Figure 15.4, illustrating the changing exchange rate between the euro and the pound sterling.

Accommodation of economic shocks

However, we also need to consider long-term volatility. In Figure 15.3, we could begin at equilibrium A under a floating exchange rate. The demand for the currency begins to shift to Q_{D2}. Over time, there is a gradual adjustment to the new equilibrium at D. The exchange rate slowly moves down and firms and consumers wishing to exchange money slowly adjust to the changing exchange price. In contrast, under a fixed exchange rate the government is committed to supporting the equilibrium at A. If

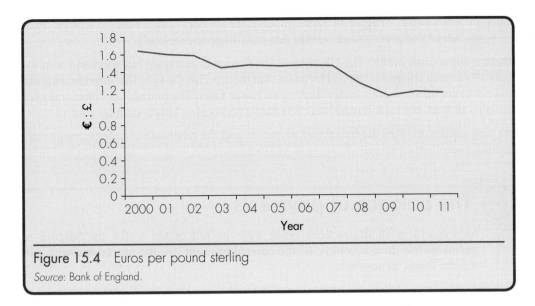

Figure 15.4 Euros per pound sterling

Source: Bank of England.

under pressure from a speculative attack the government decides to stop supporting the currency and allows it to devalue to the equilibrium at D, then there is a sudden and dramatic change in the exchange price. Such changes can be more dangerous than gradual adjustment. Indeed, currency devaluations often lead to volatility in the rest of the financial markets, such as stock markets.

So, from the perspective of business, floating exchange rates create short-term uncertainty due to their volatility, but they provide gradual adjustment in the long run, which may be preferable to dramatic one-off changes offered by fixed exchange rates.

Consider our example of the boats in the harbour. The boats connected by ropes are the economies with floating exchange rates. They are flexible and able to accommodate environmental changes. In the case of the boat, this was the rise and fall of the waves. We witnessed above, when examining purchasing power parity, that environmental change might exist in the form of inflationary differences between economies. If the UK inflation rate is 3 per cent and the euro rate is 2 per cent, then it becomes attractive for UK consumers to buy euro products rather than UK products. As they do this, they sell pounds and demand euros. The value of the pound will fall, reflecting the inflationary differences between the UK and the eurozone. When full adjustment has occurred, euro products cost the same as UK products.

Under fixed exchange rates there is no scope for exchange rate adjustment; purchasing power parity may not hold. Instead, UK companies become increasingly uncompetitive against euro companies. Imports increase, demand for domestic UK-produced goods falls, and the UK moves into recession. The recession will be expected to reduce inflation within the UK.

Therefore, under a fixed exchange rate, purchasing power parity is gained through changes in domestic prices rather than exchange rate changes.

Financial discipline

As we have seen above, floating exchange rates can accommodate inflationary differences between economies. This has led to some individuals taking the view that floating exchange rates do not provide monetary discipline. Therefore, governments under floating exchange rates have little incentive to control inflation. In contrast, fixed exchange rates, by their inherent inflexibility, struggle to accommodate inflationary differences. Therefore, fixed exchange rates force governments to take financial discipline seriously.

There is some truth in this. The UK entered the European exchange rate mechanism in the early 1990s in an attempt to control inflation. But there is also the view that governments can and do target inflation even under floating exchange rates. The pound, US dollar and even the euro all float, but each central bank is tasked with keeping inflation under control.

We now need to explain the balance of payments and the relationship with exchange rates and macroeconomic policy.

The balance of payments

> The balance of payments records all transactions between a country and the rest of the world.
>
> The current account is a record of all goods and services traded with the rest of the world.
>
> The capital account records, among other things, net contributions made to the EU.
>
> The financial account records net purchases and sales of foreign assets. (This was previously known as the capital account.)

As a record of all transactions made with the rest of the world, the **balance of payments** has three accounts: (i) the **current account**, (ii) the **capital account**, and (iii) the **financial account**.

Current account

The current account measures imports and exports and can be further divided into visible and invisible trade. Visible trade is the export and import of tangible or visible goods. Exporting a car is clearly an example of visible trade. Invisible trade captures intangible services. A London-based business consultant working for a German client is an example of an invisible export. Added together, visible and invisible trade make the trade account. After adjusting for net transfer payments, such as interest and profits on foreign assets, we get to the current account. Figure 15.5 illustrates the trade account for the UK. It is clearly evident that the UK imports more goods than it exports. But this is partially offset by the net export of services to the rest of the world. This pattern reflects the decline of manufacturing over the last 20 years in the UK and the growth of sectors such as financial services in London, as well as travel services and telecommunications services.

Capital account

Payments by the UK towards the Common Agricultural Policy and other EU contributions are collated under the capital account, as are payments from the EU to the UK

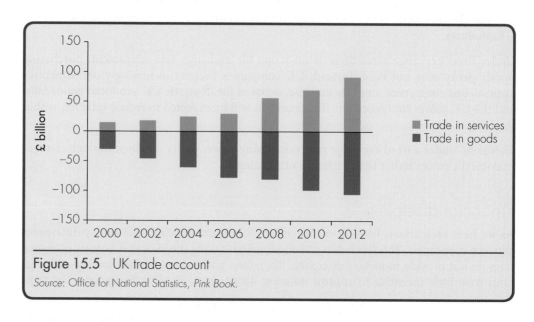

Figure 15.5 UK trade account
Source: Office for National Statistics, *Pink Book*.

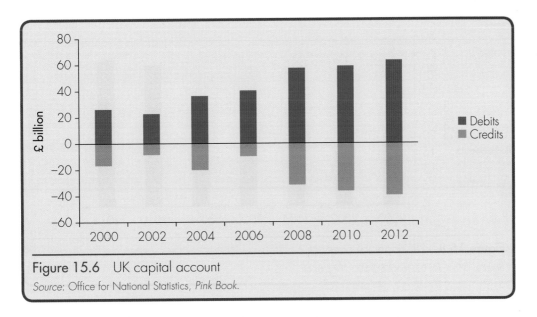

Figure 15.6 UK capital account
Source: Office for National Statistics, *Pink Book*.

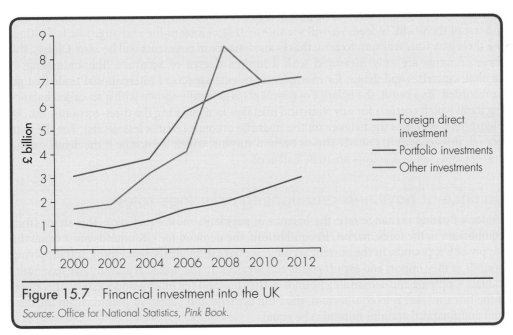

Figure 15.7 Financial investment into the UK
Source: Office for National Statistics, *Pink Book*.

for social and infrastructure development projects. Figure 15.6 shows that, throughout the last decade, the UK has been a net payer, with debits exceeding credits.

Financial account

The financial account captures all investments into an economy by foreign individuals and companies. It also captures all investments made outside an economy by its companies and private individuals. There are three broad types of investment activity. The first is direct investment, where for example a foreign company may buy a rival within another country; equally, the foreign company may build its own offices or factory inside another economy. The second is termed portfolio investment, which involves the purchase of shares and bonds in another country. Third are other investments, including loans between banks which operate internationally. In Figure 15.7, the three types of investment into the UK (the credits) are shown.

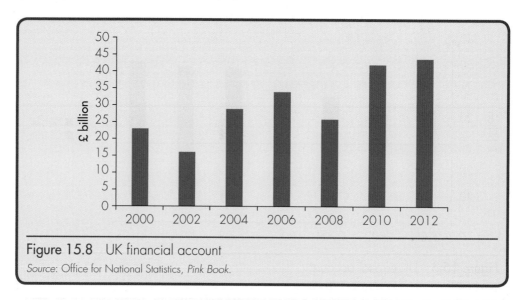

Figure 15.8 UK financial account

Source: Office for National Statistics, *Pink Book.*

In summary, the current, capital and financial accounts seek to record all transactions, whether they be goods, services or purely finance, which take place between a country and the rest of the world. Indeed, we will see shortly that as long as the exchange rate is floating, the three accounts will sum to zero; that is, the balance of payments will be zero. Clearly, the three accounts are only measured with a limited degree of accuracy. The smuggling of alcohol, cigarettes and drugs, for example, represents aspects of international trade that go unrecorded. As a result, the balance of payments is generally shown with a so-called balancing item, which corrects for any statistical mistakes in measuring the three accounts. But, in Figure 15.8, we show the balance on the financial account (credits less debits). For the data period, this account has nearly always been in surplus, which it must be if the debits on the current and capital accounts are to be balanced.

Balance of payments and floating exchange rates

Under a floating exchange rate, the balance of payments must equal zero. This stems from equilibrium in the forex market. In equilibrium, the demand for UK pounds must equal the supply of UK pounds. In the current account, we have individuals demanding and supplying pounds as they import and export goods and services. In the financial account, we have individuals supplying and demanding pounds as they buy and sell international assets. Therefore, if the forex market is in equilibrium, then the demand and supply of pounds from the current and financial account must also be equal.

Balance of payments and fixed exchange rates

Under a fixed exchange rate, the situation is vastly different. We saw that point C in Figure 15.2 and E in Figure 15.3 were points of disequilibria in the forex market. At point C in Figure 15.2, the demand for pounds is greater than the supply of pounds at the exchange rate of e_0. We can explain this excess demand for pounds by reference to the current and financial accounts. For example, if UK exports are greater than imports, foreign consumers demanding pounds to pay for the exports will outweigh UK consumers supplying pounds to pay for imports. If UK investors do not wish to buy foreign assets at the existing exchange rate, then the supply of pounds will be less than the demand. In contrast, if we consider point E in Figure 15.3, the supply of pounds at the fixed exchange rate of e_0 led to an excess supply of pounds. We can, again, explain this excess supply of pounds by reference to the current and financial accounts. For example, if UK imports are greater than exports, then the supply of pounds will increase. But if foreign investors are not willing to buy British assets at the exchange rate of e_1, then the demand for pounds will be less than the supply.

Table 15.3 UK balance of payments, 2009 and 2010

	2009 (£bn)	2010 (£bn)
1 Current account	−20.3	−36.7
2 Capital account	3.6	3.7
3 Financial account	24.8	41.5
4 Net errors and omissions	−8.1	−8.5
Balance of payments (1 + 2 + 3 + 4)	0	0

Source: Office for National Statistics

Therefore, under a fixed exchange rate, the balance of payments will not necessarily be zero.

In order to make the balance of payments zero, we have to incorporate the concept of **official financing**.

> Official financing is the extent of government intervention in the forex markets.

We know that, in order to keep the exchange rate at its fixed level, the government must buy up the excess supply of pounds. This is called official financing and is added into the balance of payments as the final balancing item. It represents the extent to which the government has changed its foreign currency reserves by either buying up the excess supply of pounds or, alternatively, adding to its reserves by selling pounds in the forex market.

If we examine Table 15.3, we can see the actual values for each of the three accounts during 2009 and 2010. It is clear that the balancing item, or net errors and omissions, for both years is very large. It might be worth checking the figure in the future to see if the government revises its estimates of the three accounts. Information on the trade of goods and services or assets might have been recorded slowly, with correct figures not becoming known for some time. As a result, the figures provided by the government are only an initial estimate.

Exchange rates and government policy

We can now begin to consider the effectiveness of fiscal and monetary policy under fixed and floating exchange rate regimes. While this is theoretically interesting, it also has practical implications. The UK currently operates a floating exchange rate regime. If it were to enter the euro, then the exchange rate with all euro members would be fixed for ever. Before we consider fiscal and monetary effectiveness, we need to understand two further points: (a) the real exchange rate, and (b) perfect capital mobility.

Real exchange rate

International competitiveness depends upon the real and not the nominal exchange rate.

$$\textbf{Real exchange rate} = (\text{€/£ exchange rate}) \times (\text{£ price of UK goods/€ price of eurozone goods})$$

> Real exchange rate is the relative price of domestic and foreign goods measured in a common currency.

If the nominal exchange rate appreciated, then UK goods would become more expensive than European goods. European consumers would have to change more euros into pounds in order to buy UK goods. If the price of European goods rose faster than the price of UK goods, because inflation was higher in Europe than in the UK, then the UK would become more competitive. So, even if the nominal exchange rate stays constant, but inflation is 10 per cent in Europe and only 5 per cent in the UK, the real exchange rate will appreciate by 5 per cent.

In summary, international competitiveness is influenced by the nominal exchange rate and the relative price level between the two countries.

Perfect capital mobility

> Under perfect capital mobility, expected returns on all assets around the world will be zero. If interest rates are 5 per cent higher in New York than in London, then, in order to compensate, the exchange rate will rise by 5 per cent, making dollars more expensive to buy. Therefore, the expected rates of return in London and New York are then identical. Or, in economic terminology, interest parity holds.

The following describes **perfect capital mobility**.

If you had £1000 to invest in a savings account, you might visit a finance site on the Internet and ask for a ranking of savings rates offered by leading banks and building societies. If you are not concerned about when you get access to the money, you might sensibly choose the bank offering the highest rate.

Now we will assume that you are richer and have £1 million to invest. It is now worth thinking beyond the UK: what interest rates are being offered by banks in the UK, the USA, Germany or Japan? If the rates in New York are 10 per cent, but only 5 per cent in all other countries, then you can double your interest by moving your money to New York.

Or can you? A slight problem exists. In order to invest in the USA you need to sell your pounds and demand dollars. As more dollars are demanded, the price or exchange rate must appreciate. At the extreme, if financial capital is free to move around the world, then interest parity must hold and there is no incentive to move your money.

Fiscal and monetary policy under fixed exchange rates

Monetary policy

If interest parity holds, then movement in the exchange rate will offset any differential in interest rates between countries. However, this all assumes that exchange rates are floating. What happens when the exchange rate is fixed? Any difference in the interest rate between the two countries will now represent a guaranteed profit. As a result, financial capital will flow to the country with the highest interest rate.

The only way to stop capital flows putting pressure on the exchange rate is to set a single interest rate for both countries. This is a loss of monetary independence for at least one of the countries.

Fiscal policy

If we begin by backtracking to Chapter 11, in a closed economy, if the government increases aggregate demand through a fiscal stimulus, then a central bank with an inflation target will increase interest rates and cut aggregate demand in order to keep inflation under control. But under a fixed exchange rate, there is a loss of monetary independence. The central bank seeks interest parity and so cannot change the interest rate from that set by its international trading partners. Therefore, any increase in fiscal policy will not be constrained by a tightening of monetary policy.

Fiscal policy is, therefore, seen as being more powerful under fixed exchange rates.

We can even go one step further and examine what would happen if the central bank tries to increase interest rates. Because interest parity does not hold, financial capital will flow into the economy. There will be an excess demand for the currency in the forex market. The central bank is committed to printing more money in order to meet the excess demand. But an increase in the supply of money leads to a reduction in the equilibrium price of money. The price of money is the interest rate. So, an initial increase in the interest rate leads to a future reduction in the interest rate. Monetary policy is ineffective.

Why enter into a fixed exchange rate?

Aside from the stability offered by a fixed exchange rate, a very powerful benefit can be found in the real exchange rate, which is a measure of international competitiveness. The government is only fixing the nominal exchange rate. International competitiveness can be achieved by improving the real exchange rate. This is achieved by keeping the inflation rate in the economy at, or below, the inflation rates of its key trading partners. If inflation in the UK averages 2.5 per cent but its international competitors are suffering 5 per cent inflation, then each year the UK becomes 2.5 per cent cheaper.

As such, fixed exchange rates can have a strong disciplinary effect on domestic inflation. This disciplinary effect can exist in a number of forms. First, individuals under the economic consequences of a fixed exchange rate have lower inflationary expectations.

Second, if inflation rises at a faster rate in the UK, then UK goods become less competitive. Exports fall, aggregate demand falls and employment falls. Wages and prices in the UK fall, inflation is reduced and UK goods become competitive again.

Fiscal and monetary policy under floating exchange rates

Monetary policy

We will now see that monetary policy is more powerful under floating exchange rates and fiscal policy is less effective. If we begin with monetary policy, a reduction of interest rates will boost internal demand. Individuals will consume more and companies will raise investment levels. Furthermore, if interest parity holds, then a reduction in the interest rate must be offset by a reduction in the exchange rate. This reduction in the exchange rate leads to an improvement in the level of international competitiveness. Products are now cheaper for foreign consumers and so exports will rise.

Monetary policy under floating exchange rates is reinforced. A reduction in interest rates stimulates domestic and international demand for domestic goods and services.

Fiscal policy

If the government introduces a fiscal stimulus, then aggregate demand will increase and so will inflation. In order to control the inflation, the central bank will raise interest rates. In order to ensure interest parity, the exchange rate must also rise. Goods and services now cost more abroad. The rising exchange rate has reduced the international competitiveness of the economy. Exports fall and the initial fiscal stimulus provided by the government is offset by falling external demand.

Under floating exchange rates, fiscal policy is neutralized by rising interest rates, a rising currency and falling exports.

We can use the ideas developed within this section to examine European monetary union.

European monetary union

In the case of European **monetary union**, conversion rates for French francs into euros, German marks into euros, Italian lire into euros, etc. were agreed and then carried out.

On 1 January 2002, everyone in the eurozone only had euros to spend. At the same time, management of national currencies by national central banks stopped and the European Central Bank began managing the euro and setting one interest rate for the whole of the eurozone. We can understand this because we know that fixed exchange rates lead to a loss of monetary independence. But what are the major implications of euro membership for the UK and for businesses generally across the EU?

> Monetary union is the permanent fixing of exchange rates between member countries.

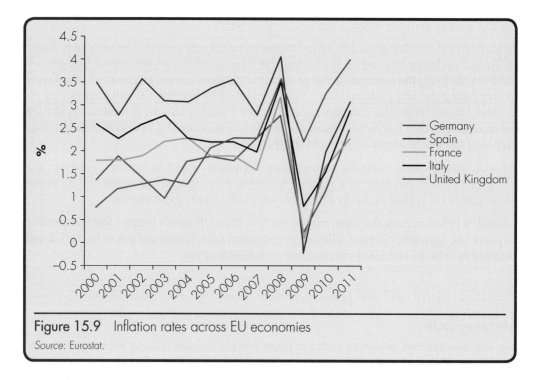

Figure 15.9   Inflation rates across EU economies

Source: Eurostat.

Starting with the simple, but less than obvious, the nominal exchange rate between each of the member states is fixed at 1 euro for 1 euro. The more serious issue is the real exchange rate and international competitiveness. Remember the real interest rate is the nominal exchange rate adjusted for the relative price level between countries. So, even though everyone in the eurozone has fixed the nominal exchange rate, differences in inflation rates will lead to changes in the real exchange rate and international competitiveness. We can examine Figure 15.9. Over the period 2000 to 2008, Spain consistently had a higher level of inflation than many other EU economies. It may be that Spain had a lower overall price level to start with and so Spain's prices have been catching up with the rest of Europe. Regardless, the price competitiveness of Spain has fallen.

If we now start to think through the points, we can begin to see a fundamental issue for the euro. A single interest rate is set by the ECB for the entire eurozone. So, the ECB could not help Spain by raising interest rates without penalizing Germany, which had low inflation. Fiscal policy is more powerful under a fixed exchange rate, so the Spanish government could decide to create a recession in Spain in order to reduce inflationary pressures and improve international competitiveness. But if Spain is pushed into a recession, when the rest of the eurozone is growing, Spain's business cycle will no longer be synchronized with all other members and the one-size-fits-all interest rate policy from the ECB will not help Spain.

Maastricht criteria and the stability pact

It is, therefore, of no surprise that strict conditions were placed on potential members of the euro, through the so-called Maastricht criteria. These conditions have now been imposed as continuing conditions as part of the stability pact. In summary, the criteria seek to create macroeconomic harmonization between the member states and ensure continuing harmonization.

Before entry, potential adopters of the euro had to have low inflation and low interest rates. In the previous two years, no devaluation of the national currency was allowed. This prevented countries from seeking any early real exchange rate advantage. Furthermore, on the fiscal side, government budget deficits were to be around 3 per cent of GDP and overall debt to GDP ratio should be 60 per cent. These rules were also imposed in an attempt to control fiscal stances and prevent a build-up of inflationary pressures within member countries. The stability pact of 1997 was a further agreement that the Maastricht criteria would continue to operate even after entry.

Optimal currency zones

The Maastricht criteria and the stability pact were and are attempts to keep all member economies moving together. But a more theoretical set of conditions for the success of a currency zone, such as the euro, were put forward by Robert Mundell in the 1960s.

Mundell began to think about the factors that would lead to an **optimal currency zone**.

Three criteria were put forward as important for the success of a currency zone.

> An optimal currency zone is a group of countries better off with a common currency than keeping separate currencies.

1. Trade integration

The first is the degree of trade between member countries of the currency zone. Trade integrates economies. However, perhaps more importantly, highly integrated economies have the most to gain from a temporary devaluation of their currency against their partners' currency. A single currency is basically a credible commitment to co-operate, rather than starting an international price war through exchange rate adjustments.

2. Similarities in industrial sectors

The second criterion concerns how the economies will deal with macroeconomic shocks. The more similar the industrial structure across all the member countries, the more likely they are to stay synchronized. For example, if all members have similar industries, an external shock, such as a rise in the oil price, or in the case of Europe, a recession in the USA leading to a reduction in export growth, will lead to similar effects in all economies. No one country will suffer more than another. In contrast, if only one member country was very reliant on oil, or the USA, then that economy would go into recession, while all the other countries would remain unaffected.

3. Flexibility and mobility

If all else fails, then there is the final safety net criterion. Factor resources such as labour and capital should display mobility and price flexibility. If an economy suffers a specific shock and goes into recession, then the quicker domestic prices adjust, the more rapid is the adjustment to international competitiveness. Furthermore, the more willing a factor resource, such as labour, is to move throughout the currency zone to find employment, the less important is the need for specific national governments to deal with domestic problems. The single monetary policy of the central bank will suffice.

Clearly, if a country is not integrated through trade, industry or factor resource transfers, the greater the need for it to keep its own currency and its own monetary independence.

Is Europe an optimal currency zone?

In terms of Europe, the evidence tends to suggest that the eurozone is integrated to a degree, and so could represent a successful currency zone. But perhaps the more important issue is one of continuing integration and stability brought about by the euro. The longer the euro succeeds as a common currency, the more closely integrated the member economies will become. The euro promotes price transparency – goods priced in Germany, for example, can be compared directly with goods priced anywhere else in the eurozone. First, this promotes trade, which is the first criterion for an optimal currency zone. Second, currency stability and transparency make cross-border investments more certain. In the absence of currency exchange rate risks, companies will be more willing to operate in other member states. The structural or industrial mix of each economy will, therefore, merge; this is the second criterion. Third, price transparency promotes competition and, therefore, an increased need or willingness for workers, employers and producers to keep prices under control and pursue international competitiveness; this is the third criterion.

Business application: monetary sovereignty, exchange rate depreciation and export growth

We began this chapter by raising the issue of whether or not the UK should become a member of the eurozone. We can now return to that question and begin a stronger assessment of the effects on business of staying out of the euro.

There are some simple advantages to UK businesses of adopting the euro. Trade with other member states is less complex. Price transparency is assured by common pricing and financial risks associated with currency movements are reduced. These potential benefits are undoubtedly important and some business and policy leaders would prefer to see the UK enter the eurozone for these reasons.

The counter-argument is one that considers the impact of adopting the euro on the UK's macroeconomic environment, a consideration which is now brought to the fore by the recessionary impact of the credit crisis.

Adopting the euro would require significant changes to the way the UK economy is managed. The UK, like the EU, seeks to follow a fairly strict fiscal policy rule, where, in normal economic conditions (not a severe credit crisis), government deficits must not exceed 3 per cent of GDP. So adopting the euro would not change this policy. However, the UK would have to abandon its monetary sovereignty. Interest rate decisions would instead be passed to the European Central Bank, which sets rates for the benefit of the entire eurozone.

We are back to our example of boats in the harbour. The economic shock and subsequent recession caused by the credit crisis can be dealt with by the Bank of England in a manner which is of greatest benefit to the UK economy. In effect, by retaining monetary sovereignty and setting its own monetary policy, the UK can rise and fall in the turbulent waves independent of its main trading partners.

The main potential benefit of an independent monetary policy for the UK is the ability for the pound to fall in value against the economy's main trading partners. As interest rates are cut, the pound falls and UK exports become cheaper. If foreign consumers are enticed by cheaper prices, then aggregate demand in the UK can increase through higher international demand.

The retention of monetary policy provides UK policy-makers with flexibility and it is this that we are trading against the known benefits of price transparency and minimal exchange rate risk associated with being a member of the euro. These points are discussed in more detail in Box 15.3.

Many of these arguments do require some reflection before it is possible to recognize if the retention of monetary sovereignty is good for UK business.

First, will a fall in the value of the pound drive export growth? As we have seen in this chapter, the UK is not a major exporter of goods. Instead, its strength lies in services, especially financial services, where there is less demand following the credit crisis. Moreover, how price sensitive are consumers of UK exports? If their demand is inelastic, then even a major fall in the value of the pound will not significantly alter the level of UK exports. A related concern is that many of the UK's main trading partners are major economies in the EU and so they are also in recession. An ability to cut the value of the pound will not have much effect on export growth if, due to an income effect, many buyers of exports cut back.

Box 15.3

Bank of England's £50 billion QE puts Britain in 'better position than Germany'

Ratings agency Fitch gave its seal of approval to the Bank of England's decision to inject fresh stimulus into the economy, saying it put the UK in a better budgetary position than both France and Germany.

The ratings agency highlighted the limited ability of individual eurozone countries to act – because they are part of a monetary union – by pointing out that Britain's economy benefited from its independence.

In December Christian Noyer, head of the French Central Bank, and François Baroin, the French Finance Minister, launched an astonishing attack saying that Britain should be stripped of its AAA rating before France because it has a higher deficit. Standard & Poor's subsequently stripped France of its top tier rating.

Fitch said: 'The UK's deficit is larger than both France and Germany; however the maturity profile of the debt means that the UK's borrowing requirement in 2012 is less than that of France.

'If the Bank of England's asset purchase scheme is taken into account the UK's 2012 borrowing needs are below that of Germany. The programme under-scores the monetary and financing flexibility enjoyed by the UK sovereign.'

Adapted from an article by Angela Monaghan in The Telegraph, 10 February 2012. © Telegraph Media Group Limited 2012.

The other consideration to note is that monetary sovereignty focuses upon the benefits to be gained from having independent control over the nominal exchange rate. While adjusting the real exchange rate through lower rates of inflation is not easy, it is still a policy option open to economies within the eurozone seeking to gain international competitiveness.

Business application: hedging

The value of currencies changes every minute. Over a month, or indeed a year, the value of a currency can change enormously. This represents an exchange rate risk to exporters and importers and, as discussed in Box 15.4, companies are worried about their exposure to the Euro and the need to find hedging strategies.

To provide a numerical example, a UK company might agree to buy steel from a French company over the next year. The price of the steel is agreed and fixed at the beginning of the contract in euros, say €1000 per ton. If, at the beginning of the contract, €1 is worth £0.66, the company is paying £666 per ton. However, if over the year the euro becomes stronger and is worth £0.80, then the price of the steel increases to £800 per ton. The euro price of the steel has not changed, but the change in the exchange rate makes the steel more expensive in pounds. So how do you protect yourself against such risks? The answer is you **hedge**.

> Hedging is the transfer of a risky asset for a non-risky asset.

In the forex market there is ample opportunity to hedge. In Table 15.4, we have the various forward exchange rates for the pound against the US dollar. The exchange rate is known as the spot price. This is the exchange rate now, i.e. the exchange rate that you might get 'on the spot'. The next set of columns list the forward prices. These are the exchange rates at which people are willing to sell a currency at one month, three months or one year into the future. The spot price is $1.5791 per £1; but the one-year forward price is $1.5736 per £1, or 0.35 per cent less. This difference reflects expectations about how the currency will move over the next year and is a reward for taking the risk of agreeing to sell at an agreed price in the future.

Box 15.4

Global firms sharpen currency hedging on euro concern

International firms are spending more time at the highest levels discussing how to hedge currency risk, particularly euro-denominated earnings and transactions, in readiness for a worst case scenario of a eurozone break-up.

Companies are scrutinizing the inbuilt protections in their hedge contracts and robustness of the settlement process if the euro were to collapse, bankers and executives said in interviews leading up to and during the World Economic Forum in Davos.

'Any CFO or any CEO of a company today, much like in the late 70s, is spending more time thinking about alternate outcomes,' said Vasant Prabhu, chief financial officer of US hotel operator Starwood Hotels & Resorts Worldwide Inc. 'And currencies clearly are an element of that right now.'

The implied volatility on 1-year euro/dollar contracts, a guide to future price direction in the spot currency market, has come down from the highs of October/November. But companies remain worried about future swings and the impact on earnings and acquisitions.

Firms are increasingly turning to tools such as currency options – which give them the right but not the obligation to buy or sell a currency at a particular exchange rate – to protect against extreme volatility. They are also trying to maximize ways of naturally hedging their exposure by trying to match assets and liabilities in a particular currency.

Tech giant Hewlett-Packard, for example, has added the possibility of a country exiting the euro and currency volatility due to the European debt crisis to the list of disclosures about risks to its business. HP gets about 65 per cent of its sales from countries outside the United States.

'In the event that one or more European countries were to replace the euro with another currency, HP sales into such countries, or into Europe generally, would likely be adversely affected until stable exchange rates are established,' HP said in a filing with the US Securities and Exchange Commission last month.

Switzerland-based Adecco Group, which provides HR services such as temporary staffing and permanent placement, gets most of its business in Europe, but also has as much as 20 per cent coming from the United States and 7 per cent from Japan.

Chief Financial Officer Dominik De Daniel said the company provides services in the same currency as its clients and has short-term – weekly or monthly – billing cycles, which hedge its currency risks automatically.

Hotel operator Starwood typically hedges about half of its euro exposure – its second-largest after the US dollar – at a fixed level through tools such as forward contracts, which allow the company to buy the currency at a specific price.

'It really does a great job of reducing the volatility without us really speculating,' Prabhu said. 'We do not view ourselves as currency experts. We do not view ourselves as currency speculators.'

Adapted from an article by Paritosh Bansal on Reuters,
25 January 2012.

Table 15.4 Spot and forward exchange rates for pound sterling

Currency	Spot price	One month	One year	% change
US dollar	1.5791	1.5788	1.5736	0.35

Source: Bank of England, February 2012.

Our steel importer can now hedge its exchange rate risk. Rather than face the risk of the pound falling against the euro, it can agree in the financial markets a rate for the next month, the month after, and even for one year into the future. Its future payments then become less risky; it has hedged the currency risk.

Speculation

We have argued that businesses might seek to reduce risk by hedging exchange rate movements. It is also the business of some individuals and companies to make money out of hedging. They do this by speculating that the forward price is wrong. For example, if the one-month forward price for converting pounds into US dollars is £1 = $1.5, but you think that in one month the spot price will fall to £1 = $1, then you can potentially make a very large profit.

Consider the following scenarios. A company goes to the bank and borrows £1 million. It then converts this into US dollars at the spot price of £1 = $1.5. The company now has $1.5 million. Assume that the one-month forward price for converting pounds into dollars is also £1 = $1.5 and the company also buys the forward rate.

What happens if the forward rate is correct?

If the forward rate is correct, then the spot price at the end of the month is also £1 = $1.5. The company can enter into the following (and profitless exercise): change its $1.5 million into £1 million and use the forward contract to change its £1 million into $1.5 million. It is no better off.

What happens if the forward rate is wrong?

If, after one month, the spot price has fallen to £1 = $1, then the company can take its $1.5 million and convert it into £1.5 million. It can then pay off its £1 million loan and it still has £0.5 million left. It then uses the forward contract to further increase its investment returns by converting the remaining £0.5 million into $0.75 million. It started owing £1 million and ended up with $0.75 million cash in the bank! Before you go out and borrow lots of money and try this strategy for yourself, remember it is high risk. The spot price could just as easily move in the other direction and then you would end up owing more than you initially borrowed.

 ## Business data application: real exchange rates within the eurozone

The eurozone is a common currency area. Each member state has the same currency. Or using a slightly more conceptual approach we might argue that one Italian euro is equal to one German euro which is equal to one Spanish euro and so on. In this mode of thinking, the member countries of the eurozone have a fixed exchange rate agreement with each other. However, this agreement only creates a fix in the nominal exchange rate. There is still scope for changes in the real exchange when wages, costs and prices change at different rates across member countries. If Italian wage rates rise faster than German wage rates, then Italian products become more expensive and German products become relatively cheaper. Italians lose business in Europe and Germans win. To avoid this winners and losers scenario, it was envisaged that members of the euro would converge and keep inflation, prices and wages comparable across member countries. Figure 15.10 suggests the case was otherwise.

During the period 1999 to 2010 the real exchange rate for member countries such as Italy, Spain, Greece and France has become more expensive. In contrast, the real exchange rate for Germany has become weaker. Not surprisingly, Italy, Spain, Greece and France have seen weaker export growth, while Germany has seen strong export growth relative to the eurozone average.

As we now know from our discussion of the balance of payments, a trade imbalance will be associated with counter flow of capital. As Germany builds up surplus finance, it asks itself where can this cash be invested? The debtor nations of the world, such as Italy, Spain, Greece and France (plus others), say thank you very much. Debt builds, repayments become a concern and debt crisis emerges.

394

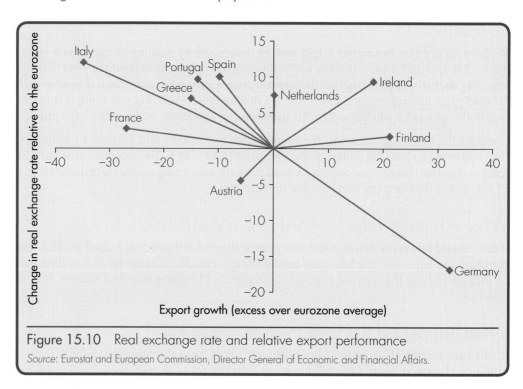

Figure 15.10 Real exchange rate and relative export performance

Source: Eurostat and European Commission, Director General of Economic and Financial Affairs.

You can see that the economic problems that Europe finds itself in are rooted within simple misalignments within the euro system. It is also not fair to say that the problems lie with the Mediterranean group of economies, because an imbalanced system has two parts. Germany must also play its role in reducing its trade surplus.

Europe's economic problems are some of the most troubling economic issues of a generation or more. You are approaching the end of your introductory module in economics and through one diagram and the application of your economic understanding you can begin to understand the causes, problems and issues that need to be addressed if the eurozone is to resolve its current plight. That is a quite a journey from where we began in Chapter 1.

Summary

1. The foreign exchange market is where currencies are traded.

2. Under a floating exchange rate, the value of the currency reflects changes in the supply and demand of the currency. When demand increases, the currency appreciates in value; when demand falls, the currency falls in value.

3. Under purchasing power parity, the price of goods in one economy is the same as the price of goods in another economy when converted into the same currency.

4. In the long run, a floating exchange rate will adjust to ensure purchasing power parity holds.

5. Under a fixed exchange rate regime, the government commits to managing the value of a currency at a set price. If the market shows signs of wishing to move above the fixed price, the government supplies more currency to the market. In contrast, if the market shows signs of wishing to move below the set price, the government supports the currency by increasing demand for the currency.

6. Fixed exchange rates do not ensure purchasing power parity and in the long run the prospect of devaluation can lead to speculative attack.

7. Most major currencies – such as the pound, the US dollar and the euro – float. Some minor economies fix their exchange rate to the dollar; Argentina is an example.

8. When considering the virtues of fixed and floating exchange rates, it is sensible to consider volatility, robustness and financial discipline.

9. Floating exchange rates are more volatile than fixed exchange rates. But the prospect of speculative attacks and devaluations can make fixed rates a source of wider economic uncertainty and volatility.

10. Floating exchange rates allow economies to adapt to external changes such as inflationary differences. Fixed exchange rates require economies to be highly integrated as they cannot accommodate change within the fixed rate.

11. Because fixed exchange rates are inflexible, they are seen as promoting financial discipline and the pursuit of low inflation.

12. The balance of payments records the transactions undertaken by a country with the rest of the world. It has three main accounts: the current account, the capital account and the financial account. The current account measures the trade of goods and services. The capital account measures the flow of transfer payments, such as UK government payments to the EU Commission. The financial account measures the investment flows.

13. Under a floating exchange rate, the balance of payments balances. The equilibrium market price of the currency means that the demand and supply of the currency that stems from the transactions recorded in the current, capital and financial accounts must balance. Under a fixed exchange rate, equilibrium in the forex market is only achieved by the government intervening. Therefore, for the balance of payments to balance, the level of intervention has to be included. This is called official financing, and it simply measures the use of the foreign currency reserves.

14. Monetary policy is more powerful than fiscal policy under a floating exchange rate system. Fiscal policy is more powerful than monetary policy under a fixed exchange rate system.

15. European monetary union is a fixed exchange rate system between all member countries: 1 euro in Germany is worth 1 euro in Italy. However, the euro floats against all other national currencies, such as the pound and the US dollar.

16. The success of the euro depends upon whether its member economies represent an optimal currency zone. For such a zone to exist, trade between members has to be high, the economies need to respond to external economic shocks in a similar way, and price flexibility or factor mobility has to be high. In essence, economies have to be either highly integrated and synchronized or capable of quickly adapting to differences through price changes.

17. The eurozone is reasonably integrated and as the system progresses it is likely to become more synchronized. The use of a single interest rate policy from the European Central Bank and the control of fiscal expenditure through the criteria set down in the stability pact should force economies to cut internal levels of inflation and synchronize their business cycles.

18. By fixing the nominal exchange rate between member economies of the euro, international competitiveness is strongly linked to the cost and productivity of factor inputs. Eurozone economies with low labour costs and high productivity growth rates should attract increased attention from businesses seeking to enhance their cost-effectiveness.

19. Currency markets and the volatility within them represent business opportunities for speculators. Firms that do not like risk will try to hedge currency risk by purchasing forward rates, which guarantee the exchange rate in one month, three months or one year. Speculators, in contrast, will seek to buy forward when they expect the forward and spot rates to be different.

20. Trade and financial imbalances will occur within the euro if real exchange rates change over time.

Learning checklist

You should now be able to:

- Explain how fixed exchange rates work
- Evaluate fixed versus floating exchange rates
- Explain the power of fiscal and monetary policy under fixed and floating exchange rate regimes
- Explain the features of an optimal currency zone
- Understand the importance of China's saving rate in the development of macroeconomic conditions around the world
- Explain hedging and how firms might use hedging within forex markets
- Understand why changes in the real exchange rate between members of the eurozone have led to trade imbalances

Questions

connect

1. What are fixed and floating exchange rate systems?

2. Use a diagram to illustrate how a fixed exchange rate can be maintained when the foreign exchange market price is moving above and also below the fixed priced.

3. What is a devaluation, and why might a speculative attack foretell a devaluation?

4. The price of computers in countries A and B is identical in year 1. Throughout year 2, inflation is higher in country B. What do you expect to happen to the exchange rate between countries A and B throughout year 2?

EASY

5. What is the real exchange rate and why is it better than the nominal exchange rate at measuring international competitiveness?

6. Explain the concept of perfect capital mobility.

7. How does perfect capital mobility limit monetary policy under a fixed exchange rate regime?

8. What is an optimal currency zone? Do you consider the EU to be one?

9. Identify and explain the main accounts within the balance of payments.

10. If a country is running a trade deficit with the rest of the world, which account is in deficit?

11. Assess whether it is a problem to run a trade deficit or a trade surplus.

12. Explain how a company can manage the financial risk associated with exchange rate volatility.

13. A country has a current account surplus of £6 billion, but a financial account deficit of £4 billion:

    (a) Is the rate system fixed or floating?

    (b) Is its balance of payments in deficit or surplus?

    (c) Are its foreign exchange reserves rising or falling?

    (d) Is the central bank buying or selling domestic currency?

    Explain.

INTERMEDIATE

14. Under fixed and floating exchange rates, which type of policy is most effective, fiscal or monetary? Why does the eurozone have one interest rate, set by the European Central Bank?

15. Should the UK be a member of the euro?

DIFFICULT

Exercises

1. True or false?

   (a) The US dollar is a floating currency.

   (b) The Chinese yuan is a managed float.

   (c) A rise in the real exchange rate reduces the competitiveness of the domestic economy.

   (d) After converting into euros, the price of Chanel perfume in Singapore is the same as in Schiphol airport; this is an example of purchasing power parity.

   (e) If the current account is in surplus and the balance of payments is not zero, then a floating exchange rate regime is in existence.

   (f) Monetary policy is more effective under a floating exchange rate.

EASY

2. Figure 15.11 shows the position in the foreign exchange market: DD is the demand schedule for sterling and SS the supply schedule. Assume a two-country world (the UK and the eurozone):

   (a) Explain briefly how the two schedules arise.

   (b) Identify the exchange rate that would prevail under a clean float. What would be the state of the overall balance of payments at this exchange rate?

   (c) Suppose the exchange rate were set at OA under a fixed exchange rate regime. What intervention would be required by the central bank? What would be the state of the balance of payments?

   (d) Suppose the exchange rate was set at OC. Identify the situation of the balance of payments and the necessary central bank intervention.

   (e) If the authorities wished to maintain the exchange rate at OC in the long run, what sorts of measures would be required?

INTERMEDIATE

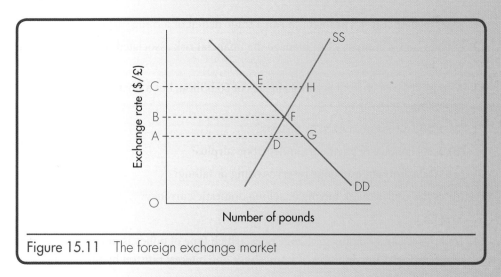

Figure 15.11   The foreign exchange market

3. Refer to Box 15.4 when considering the following questions:

   (a)   What is hedging and how might firms benefit from it?

   (b)   Explain what is meant by 'over-hedging'.

   (c)   If Mattel buys in Chinese yuan and sells in US dollars, what currency risks has it faced recently?

Globalization

Chapter contents

Globalization at a glance   400

16.1 Business problem: how do we take advantage of
the global economy?   400

16.2 Why is the global economy developing?   401

16.3 A closer look at the EU   409

16.4 To what extent are markets becoming global?   413

16.5 Business application: globalization – exploiting comparative
advantage   420

16.6 Business application: sources of international competitiveness   421

16.7 Business data application: understanding the scope for low-carbon
technologies in a global economy   423

Summary   426

Learning checklist   427

Questions   427

Exercises   428

Learning outcomes

By the end of this chapter you should understand:

Economic theory

LO1	The cultural, political and economic drivers of globalization
LO2	The concept of comparative advantage
LO3	The use of tariffs and quotas
LO4	How to assess the rise in international trade
LO5	The reasons behind the rise and fall in foreign direct investment

Business application

LO6	The impediments to an exploitation of comparative advantage
LO7	The sources of international competitiveness in the IT sector
LO8	The potential for low-carbon technologies in a global economy

The issues

The world economy is becoming increasingly integrated, with more and more products being sold across national boundaries and firms operating in more than one economy. The issues for business are numerous, but include: why is globalization happening; what opportunities does it present; and what threats might develop from globalization?

The understanding

The increase in cross-border trade and the number of firms operating in more than one country can be related to a number of issues. In recent times, barriers to international trade, such as tariffs, have fallen. The World Trade Organization has played an important role, but so has the development of trade blocs, such as the EU. Falling transportation costs and developments in communications technology have also made international trade and international operations more feasible. But this only explains why trade is easier. Why trade occurs is related to an important economic concept known as 'comparative advantage'.

The usefulness

In understanding why globalization is occurring and where it is occurring, business can begin to understand where opportunities in the global economy exist for the enhancement of costs and revenues. Similarly, as globalization is a double-edged sword, an understanding of the implications of globalization will help to highlight where threats of increased competition are likely to come from in a global economy.

 ## 16.1 Business problem: how do we take advantage of the global economy?

The world has changed. As little as 20 years ago, taking a holiday in Spain was common, but taking a holiday in the Caribbean, the Far East or even Australia was something very different. Now backpacking around the world by students, and the retired, is reasonably common. Given this trend in travel, it is of no surprise that one airline alliance decided to call itself 'One World'. Perhaps part of the mystique associated with international travel was the inaccessibility of the traveller. Communications back home generally took the form of a postcard, which invariably arrived home after the traveller. In recent years, improvements in the integration of telecommunications networks have allowed mobile phones to work almost anywhere. Text messages, video messages and voice calls mean that someone on holiday in Thailand is just as accessible as someone on the other side of town.

World travellers and international telecommunications are not the only changing features of the world. Once you are abroad, there are now many commonalities. For example, have you ever been abroad and failed to find a McDonald's or a Starbucks? This relentless march of global brands has its benefits. You can walk into a McDonald's anywhere and know what you are going to receive. The brand provides comfort and certainty in its continued deliverance of a Big Mac and fries. But the power of the global brand can be felt just as much at home as it can overseas. Take a quick look at yourself. Is there a Nokia phone in your pocket, a pair of Nike trainers on your feet and a pair of Levis on your bum? There is a reasonable chance that you have one of these, or at least something similar.

What does all this mean for business? Globalization provides opportunities and threats for business. The willingness of consumers in faraway markets to consume international products, such as Big Macs, provides opportunities for McDonald's to grow. But at the same time, by operating overseas, McDonald's gains potential access to cheaper labour, raw materials and finance. In contrast, noodle shops in Hong Kong and fish and chip shops in the UK now face international competition from the likes of McDonald's. The fast-food market is a clear and tangible example of globalization and increased competition. But the influences of globalization are far-reaching. Speak to almost any business person and they will recognize the importance of globalization. Read any business paper or magazine and you will find an article on globalization. Businesses are actively seeking out cost advantages by using the global market to source labour, finance or raw materials. They are then using these advantages to increase the presence of their brands around the world.

In this chapter we will examine the economic rationale behind globalization and highlight some of its main drivers in recent times. An examination of global products and operations, and global labour and financial markets, will provide an understanding of this important trend in the modern business environment.

Why is the global economy developing?

There are many potential drivers of globalization, ranging from the economic, through the political to the cultural. In this section, we will examine each in turn in an attempt to provide a working knowledge of globalization and the future developments for business.

Culture

The process of globalization must to some extent be facilitated by a convergence of cultures. For example, St Patrick's Day is a celebration of the patron saint of Ireland. Yet the day itself is now celebrated by many other nationalities the world over. Admittedly, many of the Irish have at some point emigrated to other parts of the world, but this does not explain the extent to which other cultures are willing to assume the St Patrick's Day celebrations.

Anthony Giddens, a leading sociological writer on globalization, has argued that globalization is the cultural suspension of space and time. If space is a cultural reference point for geography and national identity, the willingness of many other cultures to celebrate St Patrick's Day surely reflects a suspension of cultural space. Individuals from the UK, Australia and the USA, in celebrating the Irish patron saint's day, are suspending, in part, their cultural attachment to their own national culture.

If national cultural identity was important in the past, what is leading to a suspension of time and space under globalization? Some of the answers to this question lack any firm empirical support, but they do seem plausible.

Travel

Increased international travel promotes an acceptance of other cultures. Travel facilitates experimentation with different types of food, language and customs. The old adage of 'when in Rome act like a Roman' can be an enlightening and enjoyable experience for many travellers. When they then return home, they periodically like to consume products from these distant places.

Film and media

Hollywood and the American entertainment industry are successful industries. They produce films, television situation comedies and a variety of music that are enjoyed not only by Americans but also by many people around the world. The portrayal of American lifestyles, the types of cars driven, the use of coffee shops, the consumption of burgers, pizzas, doughnuts and soft drinks, and the belief that opportunity exists for everyone, can all be viewed and absorbed while watching such movies or television programmes. So, if viewers around the world enjoy watching American culture, then perhaps they will also enjoy partaking in, or consuming, American culture? If this is true, then American media are an important facilitator for US companies selling their brands around the globe.

Technology and communications

The ability to communicate with anyone, at any time, anywhere in the world increases the perception of a global village, as opposed to a large fragmented global system. Financial centres in Tokyo, London and New York probably helped to develop the first impressions of a continuous, integrated global financial system. In recent times, global news providers, such as the BBC, Sky and CNN, have developed formats built around the 24-hour clock, with the newsrooms moving between continents as the sun and daylight move around the world. This, in the terminology of Giddens, enables individuals to suspend time and space. A suspension of space is evident by the view that the global economy is everywhere, not somewhere. Similarly, time is a human concept, which slices up the day. But time is continuous; it has no beginning and no end. The continuous, ever-rolling nature of 24-hour news, financial centres and global business provides the opportunity for individuals, wherever they are in the world, to suspend time. It does not matter if it is midnight here, somewhere in the world it is 10.00 a.m. and, therefore, someone is making news and someone is making a profit. The global person and the global business are not constrained by time or space.

While telecommunications and the media have made the world feel smaller, transport technologies have made the movement of people and products more affordable. Jumbo jets make the transport of individuals between continents cheap, fast and reliable. Similarly, the invention of the container vessel in the 1960s, carrying many steel box containers with various cargoes, meant that one ship could exploit economies of scale, whereas previously a single exporter with a small cargo would have had to hire a small ship to transport their product around the world. Furthermore, the development of land-based infrastructure such as deep-sea ports, motorways and rail networks has helped to make the movement of goods around the world and overland much more feasible and affordable. Such have been the improvements, that estimates by the World Bank suggest that transport costs are now 80 per cent less than a century ago.

Culture and politics are facilitators of globalization. They enable firms and consumers to buy, sell and even produce on a global basis. But there has to be a motive for firms and consumers to act globally. Why do they wish to take advantage of a political freedom to act internationally and satisfy the global appetite of consumers?

Table 16.1 Output and opportunity costs

		Hours to make one unit	Opportunity cost
EU	Cars	30	6 TVs
	TVs	5	1/6 car
UK	Cars	60	10 TVs
	TVs	6	1/10 car

Economic rationales

The economic answer begins with an analysis of what is known as the **law of comparative advantage**.

The key word is *comparative*. We can highlight its importance with the following example. In Table 16.1, we have the required hours to produce one car or one television (TV). In the EU, it takes 30 hours to make a car and five hours to make a TV. The EU is more productive than the UK in the case of cars and TVs. If we had said that each economy should specialize in what it is good at, the UK would make nothing and

> The law of comparative advantage states that economies should specialize in the good that they are *comparatively* better at making.

the EU would make everything. This is not a good idea because the UK could make something and add to world output. This is why we employed the word 'comparative'.

In the last column of Table 16.1, we have the opportunity cost. In this case, the opportunity cost is how many cars (TVs) have to be given up in order to produce one more TV (car). In the case of the EU, if workers were transferred from TVs to cars, then the cost of making one more car is the loss of six extra TVs.

We can now compare the relative cost of providing cars and TVs in the EU and the UK. The EU can produce cars more cheaply than the UK. The EU only sacrifices six TVs for each extra car; the UK has to sacrifice 10 TVs. In the case of TVs, the EU has to sacrifice one-sixth of a car for each extra TV, but the UK only has to sacrifice one-tenth of a car for each extra TV. The UK can produce TVs more cheaply than the EU. We can now say that the EU has a comparative advantage in car production and the UK has a comparative advantage in TV production. Therefore, if the EU specializes in cars and the UK in TVs, total output will be greater than if both were to try to produce cars and TVs for themselves. For example, if the UK gives up six cars and produces 60 extra TVs, the EU can make the extra six cars by giving up only 36 TVs, providing a net addition of 24 TVs. Similarly, if the EU makes 10 more cars and gives up 60 TVs, the UK makes these extra TVs for the loss of only six cars, thus providing the world with four extra cars.

Terms of trade

While trade between the EU and the UK will lead to higher output, it needs to be profitable for trade to actually occur. Since the EU is comparatively better at producing cars, it will be an exporter of cars, or it will provide an international supply of cars. This is illustrated in Figure 16.1 with the upward-sloping supply curve. If the EU did not trade with the rest of the world, the price of cars (in TVs) would be 6. Once the international price of cars begins to rise above 6, the EU is willing to supply an additional amount of cars, or effectively increase its export of cars.

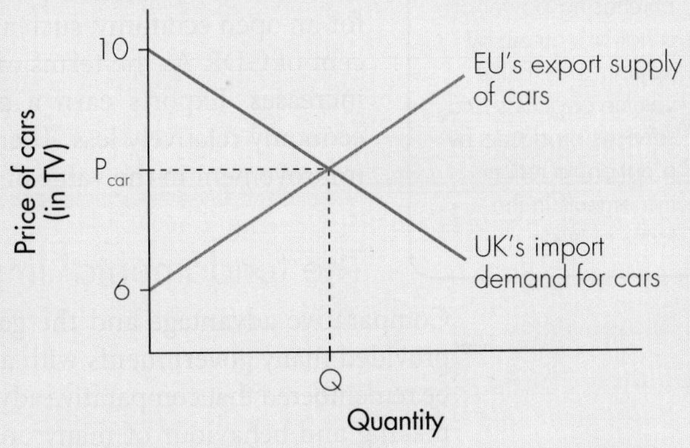

In contrast, the UK has a comparative disadvantage in the production of cars. If it did not trade with the rest of the world, the price of a car in the UK would be 10 (TVs). However, if the international price

Figure 16.1 International trade of cars expressed as the opportunity cost of making televisions

for cars is less than 10, the UK would increase its willingness to demand cars. In effect, the UK would be importing cars. Since the EU is willing to export at prices above six TVs and the UK is willing to demand at prices below 10 TVs, there must be an equilibrium international price for cars, which in Figure 16.1 is P_{car}. The actual value for P_{car} will depend upon the elasticities of supply and demand for cars in the international market.

We could draw a similar figure for TVs, but this time the UK would be exporting and the EU importing. Again, the equilibrium price for TVs would lie between the opportunity cost of TVs in the UK and the EU, at a price of P_{TV}.

A country's terms of trade measure the price ratio of exports to imports; in this case, the UK's terms of trade would be the ratio P_{TV}/P_{car}. More generally, it is a weighted average of a country's export prices to its import prices, $P_{exports}/P_{imports}$.

If a country's terms of trade improve, then the price of its exports is rising relative to the price of its imports. It has to export less in order to fund its imports. This can happen if either the exchange rate changes or the equilibrium price for exports or imports changes.

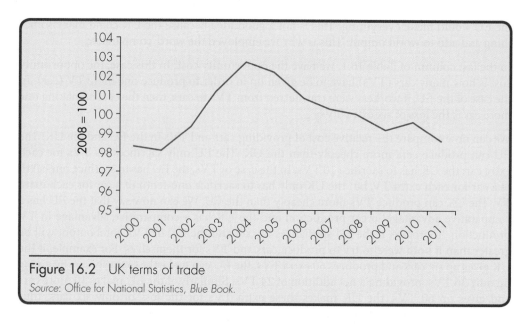

Figure 16.2   UK terms of trade

Source: Office for National Statistics, *Blue Book*.

> **Command GDP**
> describes the
> purchasing power of
> a nation's output by
> adjusting GDP (the
> volume of goods and
> services produced by
> a nation) to reflect
> movements in the
> terms of trade.

In the case of the UK, the terms of trade are illustrated in Figure 16.2. Over the period 1980 through to 2007, the terms of trade have been improving, with a steady rise in the ratio of export to import prices. This has very important economic implications for an open economy, such as the UK, where imports and exports are equal to 60 per cent of GDP. As the terms of trade improve, then the purchasing power of UK GDP increases. Exports earn a greater income for the UK and imports cost the UK economy relatively less. Therefore, an improvement in the terms of trade leads to an improvement in the value of GDP. Economists measure this using **command GDP**.

The fundamental importance of comparative advantage

Comparative advantage and the gains from trade are very powerful arguments and have provided many governments with a rationale for freer international trade. However, it must be remembered that comparative advantage is not simply an international matter. The decision-making and behaviour of many ordinary individuals conforms to comparative advantage. Families increasingly take their children to daycare centres rather than one parent leaving paid employment. Why? Because the day-care centre, when looking after many children, can exploit economies of scale which the single family cannot. The day-care centre has a comparative advantage in the care of children. With cheaper daycare, the opportunity cost of going to work is now less than the opportunity cost of staying at home and looking after the children. Similarly, why do some people specialize as decorators, doctors, academics or bank managers? Because they have a comparative advantage in their chosen vocation. Painting a wall is fairly straightforward, but in taking the time to do this, an academic, doctor or bank manager has to give up some possibly very lucrative fee-paying work or a large amount of free time. It is, therefore, more efficient to employ a decorator who is a specialist and can do the job much more quickly.

The overriding message is that comparative advantage applies to all of us. The notion of comparative advantage and international trade is nothing more than an extension of these ideas, but crucially it is being argued that factor inputs, such as labour and capital, should be employed where they have a comparative advantage. As such, we should not look at the individual, as in the case of a decorator or doctor; nor should we look at an individual economy, such as the UK. Rather, we should be looking at the global economy and seeking ways to enable resources to be allocated to their most productive ends across the globe. In this way, globalization is a natural consequence of comparative advantage. Economies do not seek to produce all the products that they need. Instead, they produce what they are comparatively good at and then trade it for products in the global economy that they are not good at making. In this way, globalization is simply like the doctor hiring a decorator to paint their house; and a decorator hiring a doctor to cure their illness. But what are the sources of comparative advantage?

Factor abundance

Think of a country and then consider what products it is famous for. Table 16.2 contains some obvious examples.

Clearly, France is famous for more than just wine, but each product listed in Table 16.2 is known to come from each of the countries. France is good at wine because it has the right land and the right climate for making the grapes ripen at just the right rate in order to concentrate the flavours required for good wine. Germany is good at cars because it has a highly skilled workforce that is required for the production of high-quality manufactured goods. Saudi Arabia has land with good oil reserves. India has lots of workers, who are required for the labour-intensive production of textiles. Australia has lots of open places required for grazing sheep. Holland, as a very flat country, is good for growing plants that do not like to be shaded from the sun by hills and valleys. Barbados, situated just above the equator, is excellent at providing year-round tropical holidays; it is also fairly good at bananas and sugar.

Economies, therefore, appear to produce goods for which they have an abundance of a key factor input.

Table 16.2 Countries and their exports

Country	Product
France	Wine
Germany	Cars
Saudi Arabia	Oil
Canada	Wheat
India	Textiles
Holland	Plants
Australia	Sheep
Barbados	Holidays

Britain does not export tropical holidays or wine. It does not have the factor inputs for such products. France and Barbados do. It is, therefore, comparatively cheap for France and Barbados to produce these types of product. The UK has an abundance of history. Castles, battlefields, the monarchy and Parliament all attract visitors. We can produce history better than most and, in exchange, France provides us with wine, India with textiles, Australia with sheep and Barbados with tropical holidays.

Comparative advantage is clearly linked to the endowment of resources within an economy.

Two-way trade

There is a key flaw with the argument that international trade is based on comparative advantage and factor abundance. Many countries trade the same product. For example, the UK sells cars to Germany in the form of Jaguars, Minis and Toyotas. Germany exports cars to the UK in the form of BMWs, VWs and Mercedes. The UK also exports more cheese than it imports. We refer to this as *intra-industry trade*.

It took economists many years to formally model and explain intra-industry trade. But finally, in 1979, the Nobel Laureate Paul Krugman developed a model of trade which recognized the importance of consumer tastes and economies of scale. Krugman's first observation was that consumers appreciate diversity. The availability of choices matters to customers with tastes for differentiated products. In such a world, markets are characterized by segments and niches. Producing exclusively for the domestic market may not enable a firm to achieve economies of scale. But if a firm has the option to trade internationally, then it can access more consumers who share a taste and preference for its particular brand. International trade, then, enables larger volumes and the attainment of minimum efficient scale. So, importantly, international trade can lead to lower-cost production and increased variety.

Trade restrictions

Despite the accepted benefits of comparative advantage, international trade has in the past been impeded by various governments around the world.

A problem with comparative advantage is that it raises economic output for the world. But this does not mean it improves economic prosperity for all individuals.

For example, in trading with the EU, if the UK decided to abandon car production and specialize in TV production, workers in the car industry would become unemployed and there is no reason to suggest that they will be happy making TVs. So, in this case, UK car-makers do not find comparative advantage particularly attractive.

However, uncompetitive industries do not have to simply roll over and die. If the industry has political influence, perhaps stemming from the number of voters that they potentially employ, then the government can be asked to provide so-called **protectionist measures**.

> Protectionist measures seek to lower the competitiveness of international rivals.

Tariffs are examples of trade protection. A tariff is a tax on imports and, therefore, raises the price of imports.

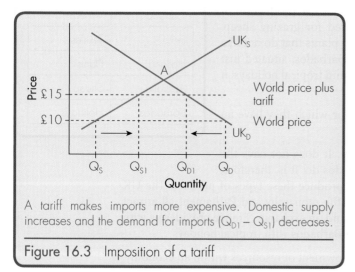

A tariff makes imports more expensive. Domestic supply increases and the demand for imports ($Q_{D1} - Q_{S1}$) decreases.

Figure 16.3 Imposition of a tariff

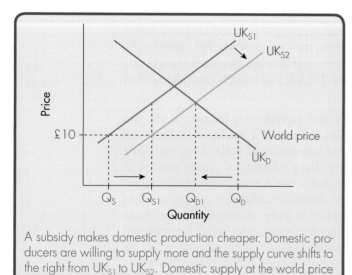

A subsidy makes domestic production cheaper. Domestic producers are willing to supply more and the supply curve shifts to the right from UK_{S1} to UK_{S2}. Domestic supply at the world price of £10 then increases from Q_S to Q_{S1}; imports ($Q_D - Q_{S1}$) shrink by the same amount.

Figure 16.4 The effect of a subsidy

For a more in-depth example of tariffs, we can examine Figure 16.3. Without imports for this good, UK supply and UK demand would form an equilibrium at A. However, the world price for this product is much lower, at £10. UK supply at £10 is only Q_S and UK demand is much greater at Q_D. This excess of UK demand over UK supply is met by imports. If the government imposes an import tariff of £5, then the world price effectively rises to £16. UK firms now raise supply from Q_S to Q_{S1}. But because the product now costs more, UK demand falls from Q_D to Q_{D1}. The level of excess demand is now much less and as a consequence the level of imports falls.

In the face of tariffs, imports fall and domestic supply increases. When tariffs are removed, international competition leads to a reduction in domestic supply and an increase in imports.

The case for tariffs is limited. They are a form of government intervention that simply supports inefficient domestic producers. Furthermore, tariffs in the main support domestic producers, and not domestic consumers. UK consumers under a tariff have to pay more for the good, via a tax to government, than they would if no tariff existed.

An alternative form of support for domestic producers could take the form of a *subsidy*. This is illustrated in Figure 16.4. A subsidy makes production cheaper for the domestic industry. The industry is more willing to supply and the supply curve shifts to the right. The domestic consumer pays the international price for the product, but a reduction in imports is brought about by the increase in domestic supply.

However, there is a question regarding how the government will fund the subsidy. Governments finance themselves principally through taxation. So increased domestic subsidies must lead to higher taxes. However, while a tariff is a tax paid by the consumer buying the product, a subsidy can be funded by taxing everyone. Funding a subsidy via increased taxation spreads the burden of supporting the domestic industry. But why should some people support an industry that they perhaps do not buy products from?

Non-tariff barriers

Governments can restrict trade in other ways.

A **quota** restricts trade by limiting the amount of a product that can be imported into a country. For example, a steel quota might limit the importation of steel to 200 million tons a year. Since quotas restrict international supply, then the price in the domestic market must increase.

> A quota has the same effect as a tariff. It makes goods more expensive for consumers and it raises the profits of inefficient domestic firms.

Those foreign firms that manage to gain part of the quota can sell inside the UK at the higher price. Under a tariff, domestic consumers pay a tax to government. Under a quota, some of the price increase leaks out of the economy to foreign firms.

Other methods include the application of standards. The EU is infamous for asserting that a banana must show a certain curve to its overall shape. The cynical view is that bananas from certain parts of the world are not 'curvy' enough. The EU can then proudly claim to reduce trade barriers on bananas. Those that are not curvy enough are not bananas, so the trade barrier still exists. Red tape required for import licences, driving on the left-hand side of the road, and an outright ban on British beef even after the BSE scare vanished – all can be viewed as means of restricting international trade.

Reasons for protecting trade

While the protection of domestic industries from international competition appears to be very contentious, a number of arguments are still put forward for creating barriers to trade.

Defence or national interest

Governments may wish to support an industry that has strategic value. Steel is very important to the UK economy and the government would not wish to see the economy dependent upon another economy for steel, the fear being that at some point in the future we manage to fall out with the steel supplier and our access to steel is terminated. But why not provide incentives for the steel producers to become more efficient, rather than pricing international competition out of the domestic market with tariffs?

Infant industry

Sometimes an industry might seek government protection. During the period of protection, the industry is expected to develop its capabilities to a level where it is able to compete internationally. But if a company is capable of making profits at some point in the future, then why does the capital market fail to provide it with funds? Is it the case, perhaps, that the industry is incapable of ever becoming internationally competitive? Domestic wages, the price of raw materials or the level of technology may mean that the industry will never catch up. Furthermore, during the five years that it might take to develop the industry, what are the international competitors going to be doing? They are unlikely to be doing nothing. Instead, they will be looking to develop their competitive advantage, through improvements in production and operating efficiency. The case for infant industries can become continual, with industries asking for extensions to the period of protection with no real hope of protection ever being withdrawn.

Way of life

The UK and perhaps even France place an economic value on the attractiveness of the countryside. If French and UK farmers are internationally uncompetitive, then, over time, they will stop farming. This *could* lead to a reduction in the management of the countryside. If true, then it might be desirable to think about protecting farmers from international competition. In so doing, trade protection also protects society from the loss of a positive externality, a well-managed countryside. This argument is sometimes used in support of the Common Agricultural Policy.

Politics

A main driver of globalization has been the merging of political and economic views on international trade. We have seen that economists are keen to promote the idea of international trade based on comparative advantage. Economists also find it hard to support trade restrictions: first, because trade restrictions prevent comparative advantage and, second, because tariffs and quotas support inefficient domestic producers at the expense of consumers, or taxpayers. Politicians have now also recognized the economic arguments against trade restrictions.

International institutions

This recognition of the importance of international trade can be traced back to the end of the Second World War, when political leaders of the time decided that stability in the world would be enhanced by greater political and economic integration. As a result, a number of supranational institutions were set up, for example the United Nations, the World Bank and the World Trade Organization (WTO, formerly known as the General Agreement on Tariffs and Trade – GATT).

The GATT, formed in 1947, was an international institution that brought countries together to negotiate reductions in tariffs. Various rounds of negotiation were held and each round lasted many years. The Tokyo Round began in 1973 and ended in 1979, with an average tariff reduction of 33 per cent. The Uruguay Round began in 1986 and ended in 1993. While this again reduced tariffs, the round also agreed the creation of the World Trade Organization. While the GATT was a place for countries to come together and discuss trade barriers and disputes, the WTO is an organization with power. Countries can now ask the WTO to rule on trade disputes and even impose fines on countries that fail to uphold international trade.

Trade blocs

A trade bloc is a region or group of countries that have agreed to remove all trade barriers among themselves.

In 1965, the Treaty of Rome led to the development of what is now known as the European Union. As an area of free trade between member nations, it can be described as a **trade bloc**.

Aside from the EU, there is also, for example, the North American Free Trade Area (NAFTA), a trade bloc promoting trade between the US, Canada and Mexico; and in South East Asia there is ASEAN, the Association of South East Asian Nations.

The importance of political institutions, such as the UN, and trade blocs, such as the EU, is that politicians increasingly recognize the economic importance of international trade and economic integration. Without international competition, domestic producers might not seek to innovate, drive down costs and keep prices low. Without access to international markets, domestic companies might not gain access to the cheapest, or most productive, factor inputs. These arguments are extremely persuasive, as evidenced by the continued success of the EU and the eagerness of other countries to join it. However, the balance of power between regional trade blocs and true internationally free trade engendered by the WTO is beginning to shift. Box 16.1 highlights how the failure to conclude the Doha round of talks may see economies retreating from globalization into regionalization.

Box 16.1

EU to look beyond Doha

British Prime Minister David Cameron called on Thursday for Europe to bypass the Doha talks on a world free trade deal in favour of seeking separate agreements with the United States, Africa and other willing parties.

Cameron's comments at the World Economic Forum in Davos break with the orthodox position of most world leaders who have for years called for a final push to conclude the complex trade negotiations, which were launched in the Qatari capital Doha in 2001. But they also reflect a growing recognition among European officials that the talks have stalled for the foreseeable future because of sticking points over proposals to cut tariffs and subsidies on goods ranging from food to chemicals.

Instead of trying to get every country to agree, Cameron said the 27-nation EU should push forward with bilateral deals. He suggested a 'coalition of the willing' – countries that wanted to do an ambitious trade deal – could forge ahead alone.

'Last year, at this very forum, world leaders called for an all-out effort to conclude the Doha round in 2011. We said it was the make-or-break year. It was. And we have to be frank about it. It didn't work,' Cameron said.

German Chancellor Angela Merkel told Davos on Wednesday that one of the pessimistic signs of the last year was the failure to conclude the Doha talks and signs of a return of protectionism. 'Because we are having such a hard time making progress with the Doha round, the EU (is) working on bilateral trade agreements with (South) Korea, which has been concluded, and working on one with Japan,' she said. 'With the United States, we have a lot of possibility to achieve a free trade zone.'

European exporters are benefiting from a 20–30 per cent fall in the value of the pound and the euro against the dollar over the past three years which should make their companies more competitive overseas.

But the efforts of big emerging economies like China and Brazil to hold down the value of their own currencies reflects the risk of a new era of protectionism, which economists warn could cripple efforts to put world growth back on its feet.

A former EU trade commissioner Peter Mandelson said that the United States and other key nations were not prepared to do the 'heavy lifting' needed to secure a Doha deal, and warned that barriers to a separate EU–US deal remained high.

'My worry about the new proposal to launch a EU–US trade agreement is that it will take years and expend a great deal of energy on what I fear will be a futile attempt to get Europe and the United States to adopt each other's regulatory practices, technical standards and the rest,' he told Reuters.

'That's not going to happen.'

Adapted from an article by Adrian Croft and Emma Thomasson, 'UK's Cameron urges EU to look beyond Doha', Reuters, 26 January 2012.

16.3 A closer look at the EU

The EU has its origins in the European Community which was established among six economies in 1957. These were West Germany, France, Italy, the Netherlands, Belgium and Luxembourg. By the 1990s, membership had expanded and included most of the economies of Western Europe. Finally, in 2004, EU enlargement added a further 10 Eastern European economies, including Poland and the Slovak Republic. The EU now comprises 27 member countries.

Table 16.3 shows that the EU in terms of GDP and population is now comparable to the USA. While China has a bigger population, economic growth has not yet caught up with the EU, the USA and Japan, but with three times as many individuals the potential to close the gap exists.

An important feature of the EU is the limited presence of internal trade barriers. Tariffs and quotas between member states have been abolished, leading to an increased movement of

Table 16.3   Comparing the EU, 2010

	EU	USA	Japan	China
GDP (US$ billions)	16 250	14 580	5500	5878
Population (millions)	502	309	127	1338

Source: World Bank.

internal free trade. The creation of the euro facilitated further the ease with which trade could occur by removing the difficulty of price comparisons and the need to convert competing currencies.

Regulatory harmonization in labour markets, tax regimes and patent systems has eased the administrative burden faced by firms wishing to operate beyond their national boundary. Furthermore, financial deregulation, principally in banking and insurance, has ensured that companies licensed to operate in one member economy are free to operate throughout the EU. The intention is to reduce domestic oligopolies and increase cross-border competition. Many of these initiatives were associated with the creation of the single European market in 1992, where the EU market was envisaged to be free of national regulations, taxes and informal practices.

Benefits of the EU

The strength of the EU economy is arguably greater and deeper than the sum of its parts. This is because the size, scope and diversity of the member states leads to increased competition, the realization of economies of scale and the improved attainment of comparative advantage.

We have already argued that increased trade enables economies to specialize in the production of goods and services in which they have a comparative advantage. This allocation of scarce resources to the production of goods with the lowest opportunity cost raises the combined output of trading partners. With 27 member economies, the opportunities for pursuing comparative advantage are enormous, especially when such economies are geographically disperse, have differing factor endowments and are at differing stages of economic development.

Furthermore, a producer who is restricted to their domestic market may face an overall market size which is smaller than the minimum efficient scale in production. Access to larger international markets, in contrast, facilitates the attainment of scale economies, leading to reduced production costs and perhaps improved pricing for consumers.

Trade creation occurs when the establishment of a trade bloc facilitates intra-member trade by reducing trade barriers.

Trade diversion occurs when the establishment of a trade bloc diverts trade from low-cost global suppliers, to higher cost member nations.

Figure 16.5 illustrates the extent to which trade occurs within the European Union, so-called intra-EU trade. All the countries in Figure 16.5 have a high amount of intra-EU trade (trade with other EU countries). The Eastern European economies (and most recent members of the European Union) are heavily reliant on EU trade while larger economies and those on the periphery of the EU, notably Germany, the UK, Italy and Ireland, are less dependent upon EU trade. That said, even the UK, which has the lowest amount of intra-EU trade, has more than 50 per cent of its trade with the EU.

The growth and importance of intra-EU trade reflects the elimination of barriers to trade between member nations. **Trade creation** is a key driver for the establishment of trade blocs. However, for trade blocs, such as the EU, there is also **trade diversion** away from non-member economies. While the EU has eliminated trade barriers between members it has maintained them against non-members. In certain areas, notably agriculture, EU members trade with each other only because trade barriers

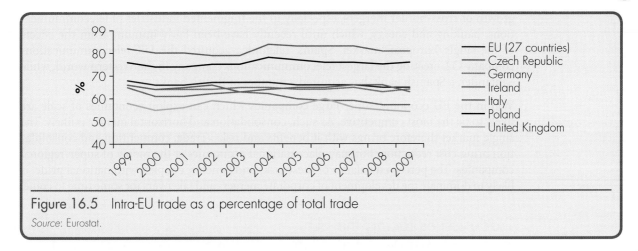

Figure 16.5 Intra-EU trade as a percentage of total trade

Source: Eurostat.

make products from non-members more expensive. Trade has been diverted from low-cost external producers, such as African economies, to less efficient EU members.

While natural scale economies may lead to the development of oligopolies in national economies, the removal of trade barriers leads to increased cross-border competition and a reduction in natural entry barriers. All of these can lead to increased levels of competition. This competition may generate lower prices, innovation in the pursuit of cost efficiencies and the development of new products. These are factors which can improve the economic performance of the EU economy.

There is evidence to support these economic arguments, at least in terms of increased consumption. Table 16.4 reports estimated gains for a number of member countries. The results indicate that smaller economies gained more than larger ones, and also that the largest gains came where the most protected industries were opened up to competition. The results reflected the consumption gains following a one-off permanent shift in aggregate supply. However, they fail to reflect any ongoing endogenous growth effect, where, for example, increased competition drives further innovation and economic growth.

A consequence of increased trade and competition has been the emerging corporate strategy of being a pan-European company. One simple manifestation of this is the swapping of Internet country designations such as www . . . co.uk, co.fr and co.de, for the more regional designation of www . . . eu. Coupled with this geographic rebranding exercise has been the

Table 16.4 Consumption gains from the single market

Range of estimates (% of GDP)	Countries
2–3	France, Germany, Italy, UK
2–5	Denmark
3–4	Netherlands, Spain
4–5	Belgium, Luxembourg
4–10	Ireland
5–16	Greece
19–20	Portugal

Source: C. Allen et al. (1998) The competition effects of the single market in Europe, *Economic Policy*, 27: 441–86.

growth of cross-border mergers, especially in the fragmented industries of telecommunications, banking and energy, which until recently have been fairly immune from the effects of the single European market. Spain's Telefonica acquired the UK telecommunications company O2, creating the largest telecommunications company in the Western world, while Santander, a Spanish bank, has acquired a number of British banks.

Within the EU economy, super-large companies which can exploit economies of scale are likely to be the most competitive. As such, consolidation and horizontal merger is likely. The single market therefore brings with it benefits and risks. Trade, competition and consolidation bring cost reduction, but may place national economies at the mercy of super-regional companies. The perceived balance of these risks and benefits, coupled with national pride, is likely to dominate the development of corporate mergers and takeovers for some time to come.

Trade issues facing the EU

The Common Agricultural Policy (CAP) was until 2003 a system of subsidies which provided price support for agricultural produce. It has now been modified to become a system of direct income payments to farmers, thereby enabling farming to survive, but not creating a direct price distortion in the market for produce. The CAP represents €40 billion of expenditure, or 40 per cent of the EU's budget. France is the biggest recipient, receiving almost €9 billion, followed by Spain with €7 billion, Germany with €6 billion and the UK with €4 billion.

The CAP is strongly defended by the French, who view the French farming sector as a key aspect of their national identity. In particular, the reputation of French gastronomy rests on its ability to grow and create fine cheese, meat, vegetables and wine. In addition, the beauty of the French countryside is arguably protected by the continued presence of farmers.

There is strong opposition to the French. In particular, the UK has questioned the wisdom of the CAP. With agriculture representing less than 2 per cent of EU GDP, why does €58 billion or close to 50 per cent of the EU budget go to support this sector? Would it be more sensible to allocate a significant portion of the EU budget to education and science, thereby building knowledge capital and generating opportunities for further economic growth?

Outside the EU, world trade negotiations have stalled on the unwillingness of the EU to remove the CAP and its agricultural trade barriers to non-member countries. However, within this situation a subtlety exists. According to the World Bank, it would be more beneficial for world trade if the EU reduced external tariffs rather than dismantled the CAP. The reason is that the CAP reduces the price of agricultural products in the EU and beyond. Removing the CAP would make it more expensive for countries in Africa, the Middle East and elsewhere to import EU agriculture. However, removing trade tariffs would make it easier for such countries to export to the EU.

The CAP is due to be revamped in 2013 and current proposals are to use the CAP to make agriculture more sustainable, with a plan to allocate 30 per cent of national agricultural budgets to environmental measures, leave 7 per cent of farmland free of crops and force farmers to diversify the crops they plant. The French currently oppose these plans as being overly restrictive.

EU enlargement

The addition of ten new members in 2004 was the single biggest expansion of the EU. Bulgaria and Romania joined in 2007, while Croatia is awaiting final approval. Turkey is still signalling its eagerness to join. Enlarged membership brings benefits as well as problems. Each new country opens up yet more markets for member countries to compete in with no trade barriers. In the case of the new accession countries, enlargement also presents an ample supply of cheap yet reasonably skilled workers, offering manufacturing companies the opportunity to relocate and exploit cost savings. This has been illustrated most obviously by the automobile industry, with the likes of Volkswagen and Ford moving European production to the new member states.

The problems brought by these new member nations reflect their transition economy status, moving from communist state planning to free market economics. Privatization programmes, poor legal infrastructure, weak bank finances, plus a need to invest heavily in transport and communications infrastructure, education and health, mean that many of these new economies face a constraint on their growth. Long-standing EU members from Western Europe have recognized the need to divert development spending into the new member states. But change will take time and will also come at the expense of development expenditure in the economies of Germany, France, the Netherlands and the UK.

Undoubtedly, the EU is a successful trade bloc and a model for others such as NAFTA and ASEAN. Its ongoing problems are small when compared with the size of its economy, the amount of cross-border trade and the degree of corporate competition. While national politicians may disagree on the way to deal with the issues presented by the EU, few would wish to sacrifice the economic power and benefits derived from being a member.

To what extent are markets becoming global?

Globalization occurs at many levels. Firms can export overseas or even operate overseas. They can exploit cheaper labour, capital or finance overseas. An examination of globalization requires an analysis of numerous issues.

Global product markets

In considering global product markets, we will concentrate on trading internationally, as opposed to operating internationally. Trading internationally is the export and import of goods and services from domestic locations to international markets – for example, BMW selling cars to other countries. McDonald's in Hong Kong is operating internationally. We will consider this later.

The growth in world exports as a percentage of world GDP has been a consistent feature of the world economy for 40 years. From 1970 exports have grown as a share of GDP from around 13 per cent to 30 per cent by 2010 (Figure 16.6).

Since exports are a component of aggregate demand and, therefore, GDP, we can now say that from the 1970s a growing proportion of world GDP was being exported. This is clear

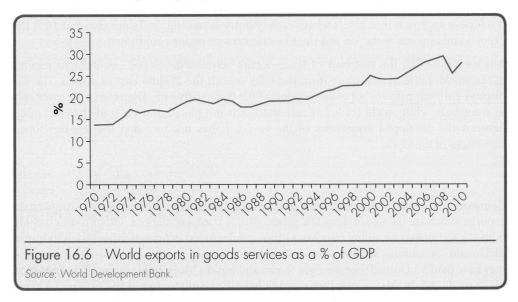

Figure 16.6 World exports in goods services as a % of GDP

Source: World Development Bank.

Table 16.5 Leading exporters and importers, 2011

Rank	Exporters	Value (US $bn)	Share (%)	Annual percentage change	Rank	Importers	Value (US $bn)	Share (%)	Annual percentage change
1	Extra-EU (27) exports	1788	15.1	17	1	Extra-EU (27) imports	1991	16.5	18
2	China	1578	13.3	31	2	United States	1969	16.4	23
3	United States	1278	10.8	21	3	China	1395	11.6	39
4	Japan	770	6.5	33	4	Japan	694	5.8	26
5	Korea, Republic of	466	3.9	28	5	Hong Kong, China	442	3.7	25
6	Hong Kong, China	401	3.4	22	6	Korea, Republic of	425	3.5	32
7	Russian Federation	400	3.4	32	7	Canada	402	3.3	22
8	Canada	388	3.3	23	8	India	327	2.7	27
9	Singapore	352	3.0	30	9	Singapore	311	2.6	26
10	Mexico	298	2.5	30	10	Mexico	311	2.6	29

Source: WTO.

evidence that the development of the GATT, the WTO and the various trade blocs, such as the EU, have been extremely successful in promoting international trade. But we still need to ask whether product markets are becoming increasingly global.

In Table 16.5, we have the world's ten biggest exporters and importers. Broadly, they are the same countries. This should not be a surprise. A country that is a significant importer needs to finance its consumption and it can achieve this by also exporting a great deal. A more productive approach is to assess where each country is trading. In Tables 16.6 and 16.7, the exports and imports of the US and the EU with various regions are shown.

It is very clear that the vast bulk of trade occurs between developed countries or regions of the world. Little, if any, trade from the USA is with the Middle East or Africa. The EU displays a similar pattern, but it also conducts little trade with Asia. Therefore, it is reasonable to argue that, while world trade has increased, it is not global. Rather, trade has increased between the developed economies of the world. It has not included the less-developed economies of the world.

Global operations

Companies have many different ways of accessing international markets. One route is via exports, which are the sale of domestic production to overseas markets. Other routes include licensing technology or selling franchises to companies based in foreign markets. For example, McDonald's restaurants are not always owned by McDonald's; instead, a local business person may have paid McDonald's for the right to run and build a McDonald's outlet in that country. McDonald's will do this because they may not have the resources to run and manage so many

Table 16.6 US trade with various regions, 2011

Exports					
Destination	Value (US $bn)	Share (%)		Annual percentage change	
	2010	2005	2010	2009	2010
World	1 278 263	100.0	100.0	−18	21
North America	413 170	36.7	32.3	−19	24
Asia	363 960	26.8	28.5	−13	28
Europe	276 278	22.7	21.6	−20	11
South and Central America	137 085	7.9	10.7	−20	27
Middle East	48 738	3.5	3.8	−19	9
Africa	28 715	1.7	2.2	−14	16
CIS	9211	0.6	0.7	−41	14
Imports					
Origin	Value (US $bn)	Share (%)		Annual percentage change	
	2010	2005	2010	2009	2010
World	1 969 184	100.0	100.0	−26	23
Asia	764 743	36.8	38.8	−19	23
North America	512 198	26.8	26.0	−27	26
Europe	359 166	20.0	18.2	−23	14
South and Central America	136 417	7.5	6.9	−32	20
Africa	87 486	3.9	4.4	−45	35
Middle East	76 925	3.8	3.9	−47	26
CIS	32 249	1.1	1.6	−37	34

Source: WTO.

restaurants across so many economies, or they may not wish to take the commercial risk. Finally, firms may also invest in foreign markets and build their own operations. This would be termed foreign direct investment.

Many leading firms around the world have operations in more than one country. *Multinational enterprises* are usually large companies with production and/or sales operations in more than one country.

The United Nations Conference for Trade and Development has developed an **index of transnationality** that seeks to measure a firm's exposure to non-domestic markets.

> The index of transnationality is an average of three ratios: foreign assets/ total assets, foreign workers/total workers, and foreign sales/ total sales for the firm.

Table 16.7 EU trade with various regions, 2011

Exports					
Destination	Value (US $bn)	Share (%)		Annual percentage change	
	2010	2005	2010	2009	2010
World	5 153 223	100.0	100.0	−22	12
Europe	3 682 611	73.5	71.5	−23	10
Asia	472 969	7.5	9.2	−13	23
North America	377 788	8.9	7.3	−23	13
CIS	162 207	2.5	3.1	−39	22
Africa	162 155	2.6	3.1	−14	10
Middle East	137 733	2.7	2.7	−18	8
South and Central America	90 112	1.3	1.7	−23	31

Imports					
Origin	Value (US $bn)	Share (%)		Annual percentage change	
	2010	2005	2010	2009	2010
World	5 356 032	100.0	100.0	−25	13
Europe	3 641 280	70.3	68.0	−23	10
Asia	747 846	12.3	14.0	−21	20
North America	264 049	5.6	4.9	−22	4
CIS	261 920	4.2	4.9	−37	27
Africa	175 552	3.1	3.3	−31	18
South and Central America	107 858	1.8	2.0	−30	19
Middle East	94 483	2.0	1.8	−39	36

Source: WTO.

Selected companies are shown in Figure 16.7. Many of us probably find it very easy to understand why Nestlé, a Swiss chocolate confectioner, is the most globally integrated company in the world.

When multinational enterprises operate overseas, they have to invest in foreign markets. This might be represented by the purchase, or building, of a production facility; alternatively, the company may decide to acquire an existing company in the foreign market and use it as the foundation for international expansion.

> Foreign direct investment (FDI) refers to the purchase of foreign assets.

As we saw with international trade, **foreign direct investment (FDI)** has exhibited rapid growth in the last 25 years. FDI as a percentage of global GDP, for various years, is shown in Figure 16.8. There was acceleration of FDI from the late 1980s, which peaked around 2000. Terrorist events and a collapse of the stock market in the early years of the millennium led to lack of financing for FDI. But as the global economy stabilized and grew, so did FDI. FDI then fell again following the financial crisis of 2008.

The distribution of FDI around the world is also very interesting. In Table 16.8 we show the main regions which receive FDI inflows. Important recipients are developing Asia, Europe and North America. Less developed regions such as Africa receive significantly less inflows of FDI, suggesting that they offer fewer benefits to international companies.

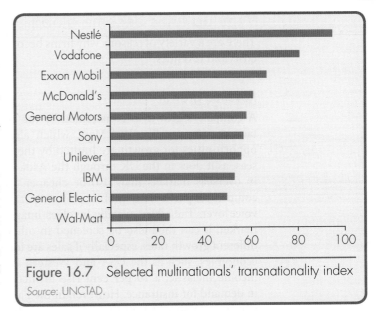

Figure 16.7 Selected multinationals' transnationality index

Source: UNCTAD.

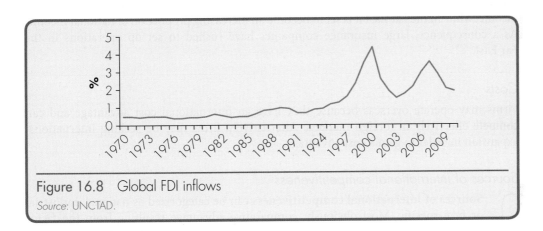

Figure 16.8 Global FDI inflows

Source: UNCTAD.

Table 16.8 Leading regions for FDI inflows (US$ billion)

	2006	2007	2008	2009	2010
Developing economies: Asia	283	339	376	308	358
European Union (EU)	582	851	488	347	305
North American Free Trade Agreement (NAFTA)	317	360	390	190	270
Developing economies: America	98	170	207	141	159
Newly industrialized Asian countries	110	132	109	91	147
Developing economies: Africa	46	63	73	60	55
Sub-Saharan Africa	27	41	52	44	40
Northern Africa excluding Sudan	20	22	21	16	15
Developed economies: Asia	9	31	35	16	4

Source: UNCTAD.

Why do firms become global?

There are a variety of reasons why firms become global, but essentially these reasons relate to costs and revenues.

Revenue growth

A company's growth is constrained by the size and growth of its domestic market. If we take a company like Wal-Mart, which already dominates the US grocery market, its opportunities for growth are limited by the size of the US market. But if it operates overseas, as it does in the UK through the Asda chain, then its sales can increase. Sales growth in overseas markets may also be cheaper. Consider the adverts of many leading global companies, particularly mobile phone operators and car makers. The advert often has no voice-over. The advert usually involves images and music, so that if it is made for the UK market, it can then also be screened in other markets too. Different economies can offer different growth rates, especially if sales are income elastic. For example, in highly developed economies, such as the USA and Western Europe, the demand for insurance products is income inelastic; a 10 per cent rise in income will generate a less than 10 per cent rise in demand for insurance. However, in the Far East insurance is income elastic; a 10 per cent rise in income will lead to a bigger than 10 per cent rise in the demand for insurance. Therefore, in the developed world insurance is set to become a smaller proportion of national income, while in the Far East it is set to become an increasing proportion of national income. As a consequence, large insurance companies have rushed to set up operations in the Far East.

Costs

Firms may operate overseas because they have an international cost advantage and can compete effectively in foreign markets. Alternatively, firms may be seeking international expansion in order to gain a cost advantage.

Sources of international competitiveness

> Sources of international competitiveness are likely to stem from the characteristics of the national economy.

Sources of international competitiveness can be categorized as national, industrial or firm-specific. Most obviously, comparative advantage resulting from the factor endowments of the economy (such as labour, raw materials or capital) can provide firms with an international competitive advantage. Operating overseas enables a firm to exploit these advantages.

Additional sources of national competitiveness may stem from macroeconomic conditions. Inflation may be falling, making prices internationally competitive. Supply side policies, such as increased levels of education and training and improved communications infrastructure, plus better functioning capital markets, may provide firms with an improved ability to operate internationally by creating the workers and capital needed to manage overseas operations, with capital markets providing the necessary finances to fund such investments.

Industrial sources of international competitiveness stem from the competitive structure of the domestic market.

In Chapters 5 and 6, we introduced perfect competition, monopoly and oligopoly as different types of market structure. The characteristics of these structures may aid international competitiveness. For example, a monopoly in the domestic market may provide a firm with the necessary financial resources to invest in an overseas operation. Similarly, if economies of scale are an important cost advantage in the domestic market, such scale economies may provide the firm with the competitive advantage to move into the international market. For example, the USA, being a very large market, enables many of its domestic suppliers to operate at the minimum efficient scale. With low costs, many of these producers can consider developing operations overseas.

Firms may have knowledge, or expertise, in any aspect of their operations, for example design, production, distribution or marketing. With a lack of national- or industrial-based advantages, **firm-specific** competences may provide a firm with an advantage over its rivals. For example, Tesco and Sainsbury's both operate in the same UK supermarket business. They have access to the same factor inputs and benefit from the same industrial structure, so why has Tesco outperformed Sainsbury's? Tesco must have some firm-specific advantage over Sainsbury's. The advantage could stem from a brand name, management know-how, logistics technology or even being able to build stores quicker and more cheaply than rival operators. Clearly, since the advantage lies within the firm, it is firm-specific. The asset may not be tangible, but it is an advantage that is specific to the firm.

> Firm-specific sources of international competitiveness stem from the characteristics of the firm's routines, knowledge and/or assets.

Economies of scope, specific assets and internationalization

This specific nature of the asset is essential for an understanding of internationalization by a firm. If, as discussed in Chapter 7 when analysing growth strategies, the firm's specific advantage generates economies of scope, internationalization provides a way of exploiting scope economies. Investment in a brand for the domestic market may present an economy of scope if the brand can also be used to enter an international market, thereby saving on the cost of developing a new brand. Research and development associated with a new product, such as a microprocessor, a drug or a plasma television, could represent an economy of scope if the product can be launched in more than one market. But should a firm exploit its own brand or new product development itself? Or, instead, sell rights to use its brand name or product development to an operator in the international market? This is the make-or-buy decision also discussed in Chapter 7. If the asset is specific, then the transaction costs of selling access to the brand or product knowledge to a third party may be very high. A hold-up problem could occur where the third party threatens to damage the brand or provide competitors with access to the product knowledge. In order to reduce the transaction costs, it is better for the firm to exploit firm-specific assets internationally within its own operations, rather than to sell access rights to other firms.

In summary, if a firm has a specific asset such as knowledge or branding which provides it with a competitive advantage, the best way to exploit that asset is to retain control. Expanding the firm's operations into international markets enables the firm-specific competitive advantage to be exploited. Transferring the asset to a third party is likely to increase transaction costs.

Accessing international competitiveness

Companies can operate overseas to exploit cheaper factor inputs, such as cheaper labour, lower raw material cost and better capital equipment. But cheap labour may not be productive labour, or it may be labour with a poor level of skills. So, the quality of labour also needs to be considered. Operating in international markets also cuts down on transportation costs. Products need not be transported around the world. Instead, they can be produced and sold in the local market.

A common concern regarding multinational enterprises has been the exploitation of workers. Wages in developing economies tend to be lower than in developed economies. Firms are tempted to move overseas in order to reduce labour costs. If developing economies are also associated with more relaxed employment laws, then the use of child labour, long working hours and limited holidays may also make such places look attractive to large multinational enterprises. However, if multinational enterprises do exploit workers, then, referring back to Tables 16.8 and 16.9, it is worth considering why FDI is more prevalent in the developed world than the developing world.

A basic observation and answer to this question would be that FDI measures investment in capital not labour. For example, a Japanese company investing in a plasma television manufacturing plant in Wales is investing in high-technology capital equipment to produce products for the developed world. A UK clothing retailer hiring workers in South East Asia to make clothes is unlikely to invest very much in capital. Foreign direct investment may, therefore, not be a good measure of the extent of global operations.

Business application: globalization – exploiting comparative advantage

Nothing is ever as easy as it sounds. The reduction in trade barriers around the world has arguably freed up world business and enabled the most competitive firms to flourish. However, a number of problems still exist. These include problems of communication and control, legal matters, access to inputs and a brand which has a global reach.

Communication and co-ordination

First, there is the matter of communication and co-ordination among suppliers, workers and customers. Language is an obvious barrier to good communication. Ordering raw material supplies for your production facility in a foreign language is fairly easy to master, especially with the aid of an interpreter. Explaining complex technical processes, however, or trying to justify recruitment procedures, marketing plans, operational procedures or financial control through budgeting will require an understanding of local culture, traditional business practice and perhaps even an awareness of local law. Therefore, communication and co-ordination of the international operation requires a great deal of specialist expertise.

Legal issues

Second, local laws may differ substantially from those of the home base. Employment law could be different, resulting in higher redundancy payments and longer periods of notice before employment can be terminated. There might be stronger trade union representation, leading to more industrial disputes. Environmental controls could be harsher, leading to cleaner but more costly production. Contract law could differ and the legal system could be ineffective at enforcing contracts. Even import restrictions might apply. For example, companies operating in the EU, but from non-EU countries, are required to source more than 70 per cent of their production inputs from within the EU.

Quality of inputs

Third, input factors can have varying quality across countries. Labour is an obvious example, with basic skills such as literacy and numeracy varying across developed and developing economies. Such skills are essential for training, developing and managing staff. Furthermore, such skills are essential for staff that are required to use machinery in the production process, particularly machinery that is computer-controlled and might require adjustments to be made to it. If the supply of staff with the appropriate level of skills is limited, then development of the local workforce may well be necessary. While enhancing skills might be seen in a favourable light by the local community, no one will be more grateful than other local firms, which in the fullness of time will be seeking to poach the international company's highly productive workers.

Image and brand

Finally, we must return to one of the key ideas laid down by Nobel Laureate Paul Krugman. Global trade needs to be understood in terms of the needs of customers. Global brands become successful because they meet the tastes and preferences of a global audience. While the products and services required by global consumers may change over time, the key services, vision and experience appear constant. See Box 16.2 for more details.

Box 16.2

Tech brands dominate top global brands list

We all want a bite out of Apple, according to a report valuing global brands out Tuesday.

The maker of the popular iPhone, iPad2, music players and computers was one of the biggest gainers in an annual marketing industry report on the top 100 global brands, jumping to No. 8 from No. 17.

'Looking at global intentions to purchase tablets, 85 per cent of people considering a tablet say they want to buy an iPad,' Frampton said. 'There isn't a single other competitor above 5 per cent.'

Coca-Cola Co. took the top spot for the 12th year in a row. The soda maker's branding strength lies in the way its brand image permeates everything from its advertising and communications to its organizational culture, Frampton said.

Overall, tech brands dominated the list. PC maker IBM was number two, mainly because of its business-to-business branding efforts. Microsoft, Google, Intel and Hewlett-Packard all also ranked in the top 10.

Interbrand ranks companies by the amount of profit they make that is attributable to the strength of their brands. It uses a formula that combines the brand's future strength and its role in creating demand, among other factors.

One of the biggest decliners was Nokia, which fell to 14th place from eighth. The Finnish cell phone maker, which once dominated the European cell phone market, has been cutting jobs and downsizing as it faces stiff smartphone competition from Apple, Research in Motion and others.

HTC, a Taiwanese cell phone maker, on the other hand, jumped onto the list at no. 98. It was the first time a Taiwanese company has made it into the top 100, Frampton said. The company makes smartphones including the HTC Evo that run on Google Inc.'s Android operating system.

Rank	Company	Brand value $m	Change %
1	Coca Cola	71 689	2
2	IBM	69 905	8
3	Microsoft	59 087	−3
4	Google	55 317	27
5	GE	42 808	0
6	McDonald's	35 932	6
7	Intel	35 217	10
8	Apple	33 492	58
9	Disney	29 018	1
10	HP	28 479	6

16.6 Business application: sources of international competitiveness

It is important for business people the world over to understand the crucial difference between competitive advantage and a sustainable competitive advantage. A competitive advantage may provide you with some short-term strength over your rivals. But if your advantage can be mimicked, then you do not have a sustainable competitive advantage.

Take a look at the back of an Apple product, such as iPhone or iPad. On the case it will say 'Designed by Apple in California. Assembled in China'. Why are these two key aspects of creating an Apple product undertaken in two very different locations?

In California, Apple can find all the key resources that it needs in order to design and develop a technologically advanced product, which is functionally consumer-friendly and is aesthetically pleasing to the eye. Skilled professional staff with technical know-how, design experience

Box 16.3

Rising Chinese labour costs

Mr Henry Tan, Chief Executive Officer and president of Luen Thai Holdings Limited, points out that in recent years China has seen its apparel exports lose some steam to Asean countries, mainly due to its rising operating costs.

In 2008 China's labour costs began to rise rapidly. In 2010, the minimum wage in 30 provinces rose by 22.8 per cent, while China's twelfth and current five-year plan (2011–15) has earmarked workers' wages increasing at 15 per cent per year over the period – effectively doubling within five years. The appreciation of the yuan, which has risen 26 per cent against the dollar since 2005, is another factor behind the rising cost of doing business in China.

A survey by the Japan External Trade Organization (JETRO) in October 2010 also shows China can no longer be considered a low labour cost country.

It found the total labour wage cost (which includes actual wage plus insurances, taxes and benefits) paid out by employers for each worker in China reached US$463 per month, compared with Thailand (US$427), India (US$342), the Philippines (US$296), Indonesia (US$259), Vietnam (US$153), Cambodia (US$125) and Bangladesh (US$85).

Likewise, China's percentage share of world clothing exports is being gnawed at by its neighbours and the decline is likely to be more rapid in the near future. In the first eight months of 2011, for example, the USA imported 1.4 per cent more clothing by volume – but saw a decline of 3.2 per cent from China while most Asean countries rose.

There's no doubt China and the Asean countries will continue to be the world's major apparel producers. But what is also likely to happen is that they will diverge to produce products at three different price levels, Mr Tan believes.

The low price products demanded by retailers such as Walmart and Kmart will be sourced from operations that pay less than US$200 per month in workers' wages. These will be in countries like Bangladesh and Cambodia.

The medium priced products for retailers like JC Penney, Macy's, Sears, Dillard's, A&F, Polo Ralph Lauren and Banana Republic will come from Vietnam, Indonesia, India and the Philippines where wages are under $400 per month.

Adapted from an article by Vicky Sung, Just Style, 'Hong Kong's changing role in the apparel industry', 10 February 2012.

and marketing skills are abundant within the technology economy in and around Silicon Valley. To try and replicate Apple's ability to add technological and design value is extremely difficult. Other companies cannot emulate the same sources of competitive advantage.

In contrast, China currently offers a cheap source of labour, which helps to keep assembly costs down. However, cheap abundant labour is highly substitutable and offers little sustainable competitive advantage. Until China begins to add value into products using resources which are difficult to replicate and copy, then it will always be at risk from a rising exchange rate and cheaper global sources of labour.

So how do you continue to reap the benefits from globalization? You must find a strategy which is sustainable; one which other locations or companies find very difficult to copy. In the absence of imitators, firms face fewer rivals and less-intense price competition. While the availability of cheap labour within a location can be copied, industrial and/or firm-level characteristics are much more differentiated. Silicon Valley has been a success for a variety of reasons, but none that relate to cheap labour.

Silicon Valley benefits from economic clustering – the co-location of supportive and competitive firms. Competition between rivals spurs innovation, while the co-location of supportive industries enables innovation. Silicon Valley may provide industry-level sources of international competitiveness by the concentration of similar companies in one area. Skilled technical and scientific workers are attracted to the area and can move between projects and companies without having to move home. Moreover, important support services such as banking and venture capital are likely to locate in the area and develop expertise in financing specialist IT innovation companies. As firms within Silicon Valley develop, firm-specific routines around developing innovation strategies and commercializing knowledge creation begin to emerge. These industrial and firm-level characteristics are much more difficult to copy and as such lead to the development of higher value-added services, where the advantage is unlikely to be competed away on price.

The challenge for a country such as India is not that difficult. It has entrepreneurial spirit, it has cash resources to invest in innovation and it has the engineering and technical skills to develop a sustainable competitive advantage. Moreover, the lessons from India are appropriate for many national economies and companies faced with global competition. The very existence of competition suggests a lack of entry barriers, substitutability and low prices. Profits, wages and economic wealth will never be generated in such industries. It is therefore important to move to less competitive positions within the value chain. We are already beginning to observe automotive companies, such as Volkswagen, locating their assembly lines in Eastern Europe where wages are lower but productivity is comparable with Western Europe. In contrast, design, engineering, product development and marketing have remained within the home economy. These are much more involved, complex tasks which are difficult to copy by low-wage economies, leading to lower competition and a higher rate of return to this section of the value chain.

After the credit crisis, the UK faces the acute problem that the economy is overly dependent on the banking and financial sector. Banking and finance generated significant wealth from activities within the UK and overseas. The UK could rebalance its economy by focusing on and developing other industries in which it excels. High-tech aeronautical engineering, fashion, music and media are prominent examples. But if these sectors fail to fill any void left by the collapse of banking, then the long-term real exchange rate for the UK pound will have to fall in order to retain some of the UK's international competitiveness. When your economic output is less valued around the world, then the price you charge and the income you earn have to fall.

So, globalization offers opportunities and threats. Working out how to maximize the opportunities and tame the threats is the art of business management, but through an understanding of micro and macro business economics you should now be prepared to meet the challenge.

Business data application: understanding the scope for low-carbon technologies in a global economy

So far we have looked at what provides companies and industries in one location with a competitive advantage that may enable them to enter international markets. It is also important that those markets have a need that can be serviced by international suppliers. In this section we look at a growing aspect of international activities, low-carbon technologies.

In Figure 16.9 we can see the rapid rise of low-carbon FDI. In 2010 low-carbon FDI represented 15 per cent of all FDI. Given the wide diversity of global commercial activities, 15 per cent for low-carbon technologies underscores the importance of the sector.

The biggest growth area within low-carbon technologies has been renewable energies. In Figure 16.10a–c we can see the source and destination for renewable technologies. Europe is a leading of source of renewable low-carbon technologies and is particularly strong in wind generation. North America and South, East and South East Asia are important destinations for these low-carbon technologies.

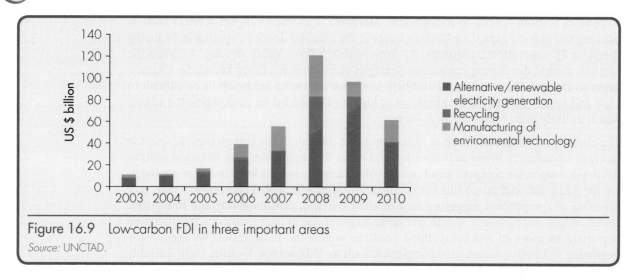

Figure 16.9 Low-carbon FDI in three important areas
Source: UNCTAD.

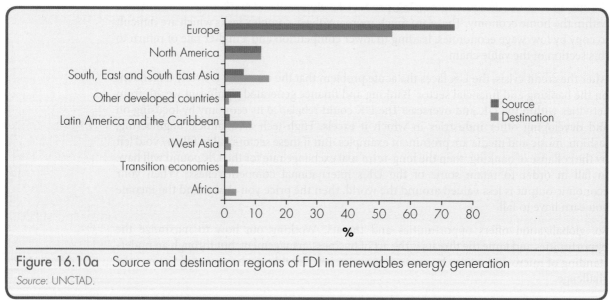

Figure 16.10a Source and destination regions of FDI in renewables energy generation
Source: UNCTAD.

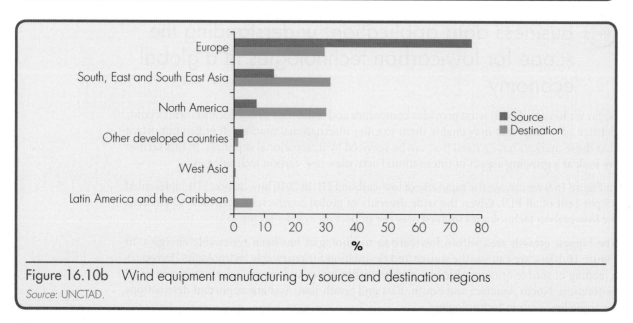

Figure 16.10b Wind equipment manufacturing by source and destination regions
Source: UNCTAD.

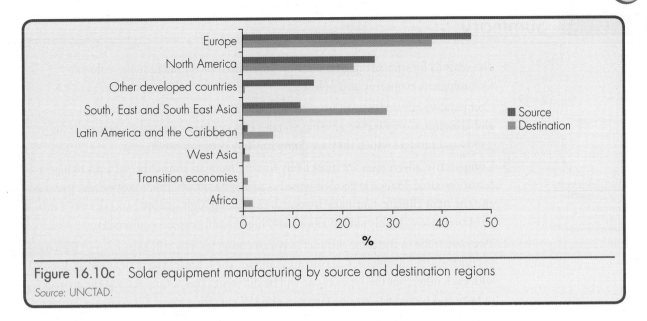

Figure 16.10c Solar equipment manufacturing by source and destination regions
Source: UNCTAD.

Foreign direct investment appears to be an important mechanism for transferring low-carbon technologies around the world and helping economies meet obligations to reduce carbon emissions. It is, therefore, interesting to know what factors support the transfer of such technologies and in particular, for companies in Europe producing low-carbon renewable energy systems, what features and characteristics of destination economies make low-carbon FDI attractive. Given the importance of low-carbon technologies to global warming, transnational organizations such as United Nations Conference on Trade and Development (UNCTAD) can be a valuable source of information.

In investigating the growth and spread of low-carbon technologies from Europe to other areas of the globe via FDI, UNCTAD has identified a number of important issues. First are source country characteristics, including limited domestic growth opportunities, high costs of labour and manufacture; coupled with financial (subsidies) and strategic (shareholder pressure) incentives to transfer low-carbon technologies overseas. Second are destination characteristics, including local government promotion of low-carbon technologies and access to wind, sun and precious metals for manufacture, plus access to local low-carbon technology clusters to benefit from knowledge, technology and the manufacturing base of the economy.

Many of the concepts behind the drivers of FDI in low-carbon technologies have been developed throughout this book. We have covered demand needs, cost considerations, growth opportunities, externalities and the role of tax and subsidies, international activities, location decisions and clusters. We have finished with an industrial sector which will be important in helping the world deal with an important environmental challenge thrown up by our many industrialized, high carbon output economies. Throughout this textbook we have introduced abstract economic theories and investigated contemporary business problem, demonstrating the importance of Economics for Business.

Summary

1. The reasons for increasing globalization are numerous but include the cultural, technological, economic and political.

2. Comparative advantage is an important economic reason behind the rise of globalization. Comparative advantage states that countries should specialize in the goods and services which they are comparatively better at producing.

3. Comparative advantages are most likely to arise from an abundance of a particular factor resource. France is good at wine because it has an abundance of productive land and the right climate. Germany is good at producing high-quality cars because it has an abundance of highly skilled labour and high-quality capital equipment.

4. Two-way trade in the same product between countries may still exist even in the face of comparative advantage. Cars are an example. The UK and Germany may trade cars with each other, but the types of car will be different. This simply reflects differences in taste and preference among German and UK car drivers and not comparative advantage in production.

5. In the past, countries have tried to protect industries from international competition by imposing trade barriers. Tariffs and quotas are common examples. Unless the industry is of strategic or defensive importance to the economy, then economists generally agree that trade restrictions are against the public interest.

6. The leading political reasons for globalization have been the acceptance of the economic importance of comparative advantage and a willingness to reduce trade barriers. The formation of trade blocs such as the EU and the work of the GATT and the WTO have been important in the process of reducing trade restrictions.

7. Following the successes of the GATT and the WTO, the trade of goods and services across national boundaries has grown faster than world GDP. This would suggest that the provision of goods and services is more globally integrated than ever before.

8. However, when examining the pattern of international trade flows, it is apparent that the vast majority of international trade occurs between a small number of developed economies. So, while trade has increased, it is questionable to what extent trade is actually global.

9. Companies operating in more than one country are known as multinational enterprises.

10. Foreign direct investment (FDI) occurs when a company invests outside its domestic base. Throughout the 1990s, FDI grew rapidly. But in recent years it has shown a marked decline.

11. Firms may begin to operate overseas for two basic reasons: (i) to increase sales, and (ii) to reduce costs.

12. However, international operations incur specific problems, such as language problems, legal issues, co-ordination problems and possible damage to the global brand. As a consequence, some multinational enterprises are beginning to reappraise their global activities, as evidenced by the falling levels of FDI.

13. The scale of global activities and the flows of international transactions are large and varied covering trade and FDI. UNCTAD has a wealth of data and reports covering the importance of the global economy.

Learning checklist

You should now be able to:

- List and explain the main drivers of globalization
- Explain comparative advantage and identify potential sources of comparative advantage
- Explain the impact of tariffs and quotas on domestic prices, firms and consumers
- Explain the reasons why trade restrictions have fallen
- Assess whether the rise in international trade is global
- Provide reasons for the growth in FDI
- Identify, collate and interpret data on trade and FDI

Questions

connect

1. Identify the various factors that have promoted the globalization of business.
2. How does comparative advantage explain international trade?
3. If the terms of trade improve for a country, then how has the price of exports changed relative to the price of imports?
4. Economies of scale and product differentiation are important for explaining what feature of international trade?
5. Identify the main types of protectionist policy.
6. If international trade has benefits for the global economy, explain why some countries still find advantages in protectionist policies.
7. What is the World Trade Organization and how important is this body for international trade?
8. What is foreign direct investment and what types of company undertake it?
9. What are the key benefits for business and consumers from membership of trade blocs such as the EU?
10. Evaluate whether the EU should remove the Common Agricultural Policy.
11. What problems do global businesses face when exploiting international business opportunities?
12. Use a diagram to explain the impact of a tariff and a quota on the domestic price of a good or service.
13. Is cheap labour a source of sustainable comparative advantage?
14. Is globalization a threat or an opportunity for business?
15. What problems might a firm face when managing global operations?

EASY

INTERMEDIATE

DIFFICULT

Exercises

1. True or false?

   (a) Comparative advantage reflects international differences in the opportunity costs of producing different goods.

   (b) The need to protect infant industries is a powerful argument in favour of protectionist measures.

   (c) The imposition of a tariff stimulates domestic demand.

   (d) The purchase of a share in Microsoft by someone who is not a citizen of the USA is an example of foreign direct investment.

   (e) Comparative advantage could stem from an abundance of factor endowments.

   (f) The increase in world merchandise trade has not been entirely global.

2. This exercise examines the gains from trade in a two-country, two-good model. To simplify matters for the time being, we assume that the two countries share a common currency; this allows us to ignore the exchange rate. The two countries are called Anywaria and Someland; the two goods are bicycles and boots. The unit labour requirements of the two goods in each country are shown in Table 16.9; we assume constant returns to scale.

   (a) Which of the countries has an absolute advantage in the production of the two commodities?

   (b) Calculate the opportunity cost of bicycles in terms of boots and of boots in terms of bicycles for each of the countries.

   (c) Which country has a comparative advantage in the production of bicycles?

Table 16.9 Production techniques	Unit labour requirements (hours per unit output)	
	Anywaria	Someland
Bicycles	60	120
Boots	30	40

Suppose there is no trade. Each of the two economies has 300 workers, who work 40 hours per week. Initially, each country devotes half of its resources to producing each of the two commodities.

   (d) Complete Table 16.10.

Table 16.10 Production of bicycles and boots, no trade case			
	Anywaria	Someland	'World' output
Bicycles			
Boots			

Trade now takes place under the following conditions: the country with a comparative advantage in boot production produces only boots. The other country produces sufficient bicycles to maintain the world 'no-trade' output, devoting the remaining resources to boot production.

(e) Complete Table 16.11 and comment on the gains from trade.

Table 16.11   Production of bicycles and boots

	Anywaria	Someland	'World' output
Bicycles			
Boots			

(f) On a single diagram, plot the production possibility frontier for each country. What aspect of your diagram is indicative of potential gains from trade?

3. Refer to Box 16.3 when considering the following questions:

DIFFICULT

(a) Identify the competitive strengths and weaknesses of China as a centre for off-shore business services.

(b) A common complaint is that 'China is stealing all our jobs'. Is this a real business and economic problem?

Glossary

Accounting profits are revenues less raw material costs, wages and depreciation.

Acquisition involves one firm purchasing another firm. This might occur by mutual consent or, in the case of a hostile takeover, the managers of the acquired firm might try to resist the takeover.

Actual GDP is short-run equilibrium GDP.

Agency costs reflect reductions in value to principals from using agents to undertake work on their behalf.

Agents run companies on behalf of shareholders (principals).

Aggregate demand is the total demand in an economy.

Aggregate supply is the total supply in an economy.

Allocative efficiency occurs when price equals marginal cost, or $P = MC$.

Asset motive, individuals hold money as part of a diversified asset portfolio. Some wealth is held in equities, some in bonds, a portion in property and some in money.

Autonomous consumption does not change if income changes.

Autonomous expenditure is not influenced by the level of income.

Average fixed cost is calculated as total fixed costs divided by the number of units produced.

Average revenue is the average price charged by the firm and is equal to total revenue/quantity demanded: (PQ)/Q.

Average total cost is calculated as total cost divided by the number of units produced.

Average variable cost is calculated as total variable cost divided by the number of units produced.

Balance of payments records all transactions between a country and the rest of the world.

Balanced budget multiplier states that an increase in government spending, plus an *equal* increase in taxes, leads to higher equilibrium output.

Barriers to entry make entry into a market by new competitors difficult.

Barter economy, there is no money, and individuals trade by exchanging different goods and services.

Basel III provides an internationally agreed set of conditions for the minimum financial strength of a bank. The conditions relate to how the risks of a bank must be assessed and how much cash and reserves a bank must hold to protect itself against large losses from the risks that it faces.

Boom is an increase in national output.

Bretton Woods agreement of 1944 provided a plan for managing foreign exchange rates.

Business cycle describes the tendency of an economy to move from economic boom to economic recession and then back into boom to repeat the cycle.

Capital account records, among other things, net contributions made to the EU.

Capital adequacy ratio is a measure of how much capital a bank needs to protect itself from a large loss on the investments or loans that it has made.

Central bank acts as a banker to the commercial bank, taking deposits and, in extreme circumstances, making loans.

Ceteris paribus means all other things being equal.

Circular flow of income shows the flow of inputs, outputs and payments between households and firms within an economy.

Claimant count measures the number of people who are eligible and receiving the jobseeker's allowance.

Classical unemployment refers to workers who have priced themselves out of a job.

Closed economy does not trade with the rest of the world. An open economy does trade with the rest of the world.

Coase conjecture argues that a monopoly provider of a durable good will sell at the perfectly competitive price.

Collateralized debt obligation is a bond. The holder of the bond is paid a rate of interest in return for funding a debt.

Command GDP is GDP (the volume of goods and services produced by a nation) adjusted to reflect movements in the terms of trade, and describes the purchasing power of a nation's output.

Common values means the value of the item is identical for all bidders, but each bidder may form a different assessment of the item's worth.

Competition Commission investigates whether a monopoly, or a potential monopoly, significantly affects competition.

Complements are products that are purchased jointly. Beer and kebabs would be a youthful and modern example; another would be cars and petrol.

Complete contract, all aspects of the contractual arrangement are fully specified.

Consumer surplus is the difference between the price you are charged for a product and the maximum price that you would have been willing to pay.

Contagion occurs when the collapse of one bank leads to the collapse of more banks.

Contestable market is one where firms can enter and exit a market freely.

Convergence hypothesis states that poor countries grow more quickly than average, but rich countries grow more slowly than average.

Cost–benefit analysis provides a monetary evaluation of a government intervention.

Cost leadership strategy, a firm will seek competitive advantage by reducing average costs and pursuing economies of scale.

Cost push inflation occurs when a reduction in supply leads to an increase in overall prices.

Cournot model, each firm treats its rival's output as a given.

Creative destruction occurs when a new entrant out-competes incumbent companies by virtue of being innovative.

Credible commitment or threat has to be one that is optimal to carry out.

Credit creation is the process of turning existing bank deposits into credit facilities for borrowers. The process can result in an increase in the money supply.

Credit crunch, a lack of liquidity between banks.

Cross-price elasticity measures the responsiveness of demand to a change in the price of a substitute or complement.

Cross-sectional data are the measurements of one variable at the same point in time across different individuals.

Crowding out occurs when increased government spending reduces private sector spending.

Cumulative debt is the total outstanding government debt from borrowings over many years.

Current account, a record of all goods and services traded with the rest of the world.

Cyclical unemployment is related to the business cycle and is sometimes also referred to as demand-deficient unemployment. Cyclical unemployment reflects workers who have lost jobs due to the adversities of the business cycle.

Dead-weight loss of monopoly is the loss of welfare to society resulting from the existence of the monopoly.

Deflation is a fall in prices, usually on a yearly basis.

Demand curve illustrates the relationship between price and quantity demanded of a particular product.

Demand pull inflation occurs when a rise in aggregate demand leads to an increase in overall prices.

Demerit good provides consumers with fewer benefits than they expect.

Differentiation is a means of understanding the gradient.

Dirty float occurs when the government claims that the exchange rate floats, but it is in fact managed by the government or central bank.

Discount factor or rate provides a measure of the time value of money. If £100 saved for one year earns 2 per cent interest, at the end of year you will have £102. Equally, a cost of £102 in a year's time is worth £100 today.

Disequilibria, at the current price the willingness to demand will differ from the willingness to supply.

Diversification is the growth of the business in a related or unrelated market.

Diversified portfolio of activities contains a mix of uncorrelated business operations.

Dominant strategy is a player's best response, whatever its rival decides.

Double coincidence of wants occurs when two people trade goods and services without money. The first individual demands the good offered by the second individual, and vice versa.

Durable good is a good in which consumption is ongoing, for example, a DVD.

Economic growth is measured as the percentage change in GDP per year.

Economic profits are revenues less the costs of all factors of production.

Economies of scale cause long-run average costs to fall as output increases.

Economies of scope are said to exist if the cost of producing two or more outputs jointly is less than the cost of producing the outputs separately.

Elastic demand is where $\varepsilon > 1$, or demand is responsive to a change in price.

Elasticity is a measure of the responsiveness of demand to a change in price.

Elasticity of supply is a measure of how responsive supply is to a change in price.

Endogenized costs, the firms inside the industry have strategically influenced the level and nature of costs.

Endogenous growth theory considers models in which the steady state growth rate can be affected by economic behaviour and policy.

Entry barriers represent an obstacle to a firm's ability to enter an industry.

Equation of a straight line is $Y = a + bX$.

Equilibrium is generally defined as the situation where planned aggregate expenditure is equal to the actual output of firms.

Exit barriers make exit from a market by existing competitors difficult.

Exogenous costs of the firm are outside its control.

Expectations are beliefs held by firms, workers and consumers about the future level of prices.

Externalities are the effects of consumption, or production, on third parties.

Factors of production are resources needed to make goods and services: land, labour, capital and enterprise.

Fiat money is notes and coins guaranteed by the government rather than by gold deposits.

Financial account records net purchases and sales of foreign assets. (This was previously known as the capital account.)

Financial discipline is the degree to which a government pursues stringent monetary policy and targets low inflation.

Financial intermediation involves channelling cash from savers to borrowers.

Finite resources are the limited amount of resources that enable the production and purchase of goods and services.

Firm-specific sources of international competitiveness stem from the characteristics of the firm's routines, knowledge and/or assets.

First best solution, the economy has no market failures.

First-mover advantage ensures that the firm which makes its strategic decision first gains a profitable advantage over its rivals.

Fiscal drag occurs when tax-free income allowances grow at a slower rate than earnings. This reduces the real value of tax-free allowances, leading to high real tax receipts.

Fiscal policy is the government's decisions regarding taxation and spending.

Fiscal stance is the extent to which the government is using fiscal policy to increase or decrease aggregate demand in the economy.

Fixed costs are constant. They remain the same whatever the level of output.

Fixed exchange rate regime, the government fixes the exchange rate between the domestic currency and another strong world currency, such as the US dollar.

Fixed exchange rates have a fixed rate of conversion between currencies.

Floating exchange rate system, the exchange rate is set purely by market forces; there is no market intervention by the government or the central bank.

Foreign direct investment (FDI), the purchase of foreign assets.

Forex market is where different currencies are traded.

Free riders are individuals, or firms, who can benefit from the actions of others without contributing to the effort made by others. They gain benefits from the actions of others for free.

Frictional unemployment refers to individuals who have quit one job and are currently searching for another job. As such, frictional unemployment is temporary.

Full employment, all factors of production that wish to be employed are employed.

Full employment level of the economy is a long-run equilibrium position and the economy operates on its production possibility frontier. The economy is in neither boom nor recession.

Game theory seeks to understand whether strategic interaction will lead to competition or co-operation between rivals.

GDP per capita is the GDP for the economy divided by the population of the economy. GDP per capita provides a measure of average income per person.

Government bonds are a near-cash equivalent and therefore liquid. A government pays the holder of bonds a rate of interest in return for funding the government's debt.

Government deficit is the difference between government spending and tax receipts. Just as students run up overdrafts, spending more than they earn, so too does the government.

Gradient is a measure of the slope of a line.

Gresham's Law states that an increasing supply of bad products will drive out good products from the market.

Gross domestic product (GDP) is a measure of the total output produced by an economy in a given year.

Haircut, the discount required by the buyer of a risky asset. An asset valued at £100 and bought for £80 is said to have suffered a 20 per cent haircut. The haircut will hopefully insure the buyer against any future losses in value of the asset.

Hedging is the transfer of a risky asset for a non-risky asset.

Hold-up problem is the renegotiation of contracts, and is linked to asset specificity.

Horizontal growth occurs when a company develops or grows activities at the same stage of the production process.

Impact analysis is a means of understanding the impact of a policy change on individuals and/or an economy.

Imperfect competition is a highly competitive market where firms may use product differentiation.

Imperfect information exists when a consumer does not have all the facts relating to the key features of a product.

Income elasticity measures the responsiveness of demand to a change in income.

Index numbers are used to transform a data series into a series with a base value of 100.

Index of transnationality is an average of three ratios: foreign assets/total assets, foreign workers/total workers and foreign sales/total sales for the firm.

Industrial clusters occur when related industries co-locate in a region. Examples include Silicon Valley and electronics, Germany and automotives, London and finance.

Inelastic demand is where elasticity $\varepsilon < 1$, or a change in the price will lead to a proportionately smaller change in the quantity demanded.

Inferior goods are demanded more when income levels fall and demanded less when income levels rise.

Infinite wants are the limitless desires to consume goods and services.

Inflation illusion is a confusion of nominal and real changes.

Inflation is the rate of change in the average price level. Inflation of 2 per cent indicates that prices have risen by 2 per cent during the previous 12 months.

Injection into the circular flow is additional spending on goods and services that does not come from the income earned by households in the inner loop. Injections can be investment, government spending and exports.

Input markets are where factor inputs, such as land, labour, capital or enterprise, are traded.

Interest rates are the price of money and are set by the central bank.

Kinked demand curve shows that price rises will not be matched by rivals, but price reductions will be.

Law of comparative advantage states that economies should specialize in the good that they are *comparatively* better at making.

Law of demand states that, *ceteris paribus*, as the price of a product falls, more will be demanded.

Law of diminishing returns states that, as more of a variable factor of production, usually labour, is added to a fixed factor of production, usually capital, then at some point the returns to the variable factor will diminish.

Leakage from the circular flow is income not spent on goods and services within the economy. Leakages can be savings, taxation and imports.

Learning curve suggests that, as cumulative output increases, average costs fall.

Lender of last resort, the central bank if a bank cannot raise funds from any other lender.

Liquidity is the speed, price and ease of access to money.

Long run is a period of time when all factors of production are variable.

M4 takes notes and coins and adds retail and wholesale banking deposits. M4 is, therefore, a broad measure of money.

Macroeconomics is the study of how the entire economy works.

Marginal cost is the cost of creating one more unit.

Marginal private benefit is the benefit to the individual from consuming one more unit of output.

Marginal private cost is the cost to the individual of producing one more unit of output.

Marginal product is the addition to total product after employing one more unit of factor input. In economics, marginal always means 'one more'.

Marginal profit is the profit made on the last unit and is equal to the marginal revenue minus the marginal cost.

Marginal propensity to consume (MPC) is the extra consumption generated by one unit of extra income.

Marginal propensity to save (MPS) is the extra saving generated by one unit of extra income.

Marginal revenue is the change in revenue from selling one more unit.

Marginal social benefit is the benefit to society from the consumption of one more unit of output.

Marginal social cost is the cost to society of producing one more unit of output.

Market economy, the government plays no role in allocating resources. Instead, markets allocate resources to the production of various products.

Market equilibrium occurs at the price where consumers' willingness to demand is exactly equal to firms' willingness to supply.

Market failure, a term used by economists to cover all circumstances in which the market equilibrium is not efficient.

Market structure is the economist's general title for the major competitive structures of a particular marketplace.

Maximum price/price ceiling prevents prices from rising above a set level.

Menu costs are the costs associated with changing prices, which can include updating computer systems, printing new price lists, changing shelf price information.

Merger generally involves two companies agreeing by mutual consent to merge their existing operations.

Merit good provides consumers with more benefits than they expect.

Microeconomics is the study of how individuals make economic decisions within an economy.

Minimum efficient scale (MES) is the output level at which long-run costs are at a minimum.

Minimum price/price floor prevents prices from falling below a set level.

Mixed economy, the government and the private sector jointly solve economic problems.

Models or theories are frameworks for organizing how we think about an economic problem.

Monetary base, or the stock of high-powered money, is the quantity of notes and coins held by private individuals or held by the banking system.

Monetary union is the permanent fixing of exchange rates between member countries.

Monopolistic competition is a highly competitive market where firms may use product differentiation.

Monopoly is a marketplace supplied by only one competitor, so no competition exists.

Monopoly status, a firm has no competition.

Moral hazard occurs when someone agrees to undertake a certain set of actions but then, once a contractual arrangement has been agreed, behaves in a different manner.

Multiplier measures the change in output following a change in autonomous expenditure (the essential or basic amount of consumption plus investment).

Mutual, a financial organization that is owned by its customers. This contrasts with a bank, which is owned by shareholders.

Narrow measure of money, notes and coins held in and outside of the private banking sector.

Nash equilibrium occurs when each player does what is best for themselves, given what their rivals may do in response.

Natural monopoly exists if scale economies lead to only one firm in the market.

Natural rate of unemployment is the level of unemployment when the economy is operating at potential GDP.

Negative externality occurs if production, or consumption, by one group reduces the well-being of third parties.

Negative relationship exists between two variables if the value for one variable increases (decreases) as the value of the other variable decreases (increases).

Net present value is the discounted value of a future cash flow.

Nexus of contracts is a collection of interrelated contractual relationships, where the firm represents a nexus or central point, at which all these interrelated contractual relationships are managed in the pursuit of profit.

N-firm concentration ratio, CR, is a measure of the industry output controlled by the industry's N largest firms.

Nominal prices and wages are not adjusted for inflation.

Nominal wages are earnings unadjusted for inflation. If a worker earns £30 000 per year, this is their nominal wage. If inflation is 5 per cent per year, then at the end of the year the real wage is £30 000/1.05 = £28 571.

Non-excludable, suppliers cannot restrict supply to those consumers who have paid for the good.

Non-rivalrous, the consumption of the good does not prevent consumption by other consumers.

Normal economic profits are equal to the average rate of return which can be gained in the economy.

Normal goods are demanded more when consumer income increases and less when income falls.

Normative economics offers recommendations based on personal value judgements.

Official financing is the extent of government intervention in the forex markets.

Oligopoly is a market that consists of a small number of large players, such as banking, supermarkets and the media.

Open market operations occur when the central bank buys and sells financial assets in return for money.

Opportunity costs are the benefits forgone from the next best alternative.

Optimal currency zone is a group of countries better off with a common currency than keeping separate currencies.

Organic growth is an increase in sales from the same or comparable retail space.

Output gap, the difference between actual and potential GDP.

Panel data combines cross-sectional and time series data.

Pareto efficient means that no one within an economy can be made better off without making some other people worse off. Therefore, the well-being of society is at a maximum.

Participation rate is the percentage of people of working age who are in employment.

Percentage measures the change in a variable as a fraction of 100.

Perfect capital mobility, expected returns on all assets around the world will be zero. If interest rates are 5 per cent higher in New York than in London, then, in order to compensate, the exchange rate will rise by 5 per cent, making dollars more expensive to buy. Therefore, the expected rates of return in London and New York are then identical. Or, in economic terminology, interest parity holds.

Perfect competition is a highly competitive marketplace.

Perfect information assumes that every buyer and every seller knows everything.

Perfectly elastic demand exists when $\varepsilon = \infty$. In other words, demand is very responsive to a change in price.

Perishable good is a good which either decays, for example, fruit and vegetables, or is consumed quickly, for example, wine, Coca-Cola.

Permanent income hypothesis states that consumption is determined by lifetime earnings and not current income.

Phillips curve shows that lower unemployment is associated with higher inflation. Simply, lower unemployment has to be traded for higher inflation.

Piece rates occur when a worker is paid according to the output produced. Under hourly wage rates, workers are paid for time at work.

Planned aggregate expenditure is the total amount of spending on goods and services within the economy that is planned by purchasers.

Planned economy, the government decides how resources are allocated to the production of particular products.

Pooling equilibrium is a market where demand and supply for good and poor products pool into one demand and one supply.

Positive economics studies objective or scientific explanations of how the economy works.

Positive externality occurs if production, or consumption, by one group improves the well-being of third parties.

Positive relationship exists between two variables if the values for both variables increase and decrease together.

Potential GDP is any point on the production possibility frontier.

Precautionary motive for holding money reflects the unpredictability of transactions and the need to hold liquid funds in order to meet these payments.

Price discrimination is the act of charging different prices to different consumers for an identical good or service.

Price expectations are beliefs about how prices in the future will differ from prices today: will they rise or fall?

Price index can be used to deflate current prices into constant prices, where constant prices are prices expressed in the base year.

Price level is the average change in the price of goods and services in an economy. The *change* in the average price level is a measure of inflation, where 5 per cent inflation means that prices on average have changed, i.e. increased, by 5 per cent.

Price taker, a firm that accepts the market price.

Price volatility measures how prices vary over time.

Principal–agent problem refers to the difficulties of a principal or owner in monitoring an agent to whom decisions have been delegated.

Private finance initiatives involve the private sector in financing, building and owning infrastructure projects in return for an annual leasing fee from the government.

Private values means each bidder has a private, subjective, value of an item's worth.

Producer surplus is the difference between the price that a firm is willing to sell at and the price it does sell at.

Product differentiation strategy, a firm will seek a competitive advantage by making its products less substitutable.

Production possibility frontier shows the maximum number of products that can be produced by an economy with a given amount of resources.

Productive efficiency means that the firm is operating at the minimum point on its long-run average cost curve. Moreover, in long-run equilibrium the firm is charging a price that is equal to the marginal cost. This means that the firm is also allocatively efficient.

Profit maximization is the output level at which the firm generates the highest profit.

Protectionist measures seek to lower the competitiveness of international rivals.

Public good is a good that is both non-rivalrous and non-excludable.

Purchasing power parity requires the nominal exchange rate to adjust in order to keep the real exchange rate constant.

Quadratic is generally specified as $Y = a + bX + cX^2$.

Qualitative easing occurs when the central bank swaps high quality assets for poorer quality assets.

Quantitative easing involves the central bank buying government debt, corporate debt and other financial securities. In return, cash is provided to the vendors of these assets.

Quota has the same effect as a tariff. It makes goods more expensive for consumers and it raises the profits of inefficient domestic firms.

Rate of inflation is a measure of how fast prices are rising.

Rationalization is associated with cutbacks in excess resources in the pursuit of increased operational efficiencies.

Reaction function shows that a firm's profit-maximizing output varies with the output decision of its rival.

Real prices and wages are adjusted for inflation.

Real business cycle results from changes in potential GDP.

Real exchange rate is the relative price of domestic and foreign goods measured in a common currency.

Real wages are earnings adjusted for inflation.

Recession is a reduction in national output.

Regulation is the use of rules and laws to limit, control and monitor the activities of banks.

Regulatory capture occurs when the regulated firms have some control or influence over the regulator.

Rent-seeking activities refers to the allocation of resources to non-socially optimal ends.

Rent-seeking behaviour is the pursuit of supernormal profits. An economic rent is a payment in excess of the minimum price at which a good or service will be supplied.

Residual demand is equal to the market demand less the amount produced by the firm's rivals.

Retail bank lends to non-banks, including households and non-bank firms.

Returns to scale simply measure the change in output for a given change in the inputs.

Revenue equivalence theorem states that under private values each auction format will generate the same level of revenue for the seller.

Risk averse means disliking or avoiding risk, an alternative to being risk neutral or risk seeking.

Robustness is a concern with flexibility, or the ability to accommodate change.

Satisficing is the attainment of acceptable levels of performance. Maximizing is the attainment of maximum levels of performance.

Second best solution is the best outcome for an economy when at least one market failure cannot be corrected.

Separating equilibrium is where a market splits into two clearly identifiable sub-markets with separate supply and demand.

Separation of ownership from control exists where the shareholders, who own the company, are a different set of individuals from the managers that control the business on a day-to-day basis.

Short run is a period of time where one factor of production is fixed. We tend to assume that capital is fixed and labour is variable.

Sight deposits provide customers with instant access to cash.

Single-period game is a game that is only played once. In a repeated game, the game is played a number of rounds.

Sources of international competitiveness are likely to stem from the characteristics of the national economy.

Specific asset has a specific use; a general asset has many uses.

Speculative attack, a massive capital outflow from an economy with a fixed exchange rate.

Stackelberg model, similar to the output approach of Cournot, but firms do not make strategic decisions simultaneously.

Standard deviation is a measure of how much a variable differs from its average value over time.

Stock options provide individuals with the *option* to buy shares in the future at a price agreed in the past.

Store of value, something that can be used to make future purchases, e.g. money.

Strategic interdependence exists when the actions of one firm will have implications for its rivals.

Structural unemployment occurs when an industry moves into decline. The structurally unemployed find it difficult to gain employment in new industries because of what is known as a mismatch of skills.

Subsidy is a payment made to producers, by government, which leads to a reduction in the market price of the product.

Substitutes are rival products; for example, a BMW car is a substitute for a Mercedes, or a bottle of wine from France is a substitute for a bottle from Australia.

Sunk cost is an expenditure that cannot be regained when exiting the market.

Supernormal profits are financial returns greater than normal profits.

Supply curve depicts a positive relationship between the price of a product and firms' willingness to supply the product.

Supply-side policies influence aggregate supply.

Systemic risk is a risk which can damage the entire financial system.

Tangency equilibrium occurs when the firm's average revenue line just touches the firm's average total cost line.

Task specialization occurs where the various activities of a production process are broken down into their separate components. Each worker then specializes in one particular task, becoming an expert in the task and raising overall productivity.

Taylor rule links interest rate changes to short-term deviations in both inflation and output from long-term equilibrium values.

Theories (see **Models**).

Time deposits require the customer to give the bank notice before withdrawing cash.

Time series data are the measurements of one variable at different points in time.

Total costs are simply fixed costs plus variable costs.

Total expenditure is equal to consumption, plus investment, plus government spending, plus net exports (exports minus imports).

Total product is the total output produced by a firm's workers.

Total revenue is price multiplied by number of units sold.

Trade bloc is a region or group of countries that have agreed to remove all trade barriers among themselves.

Trade creation occurs when the establishment of a trade bloc facilitates intra-member trade by reducing trade barriers.

Trade deficit is the difference between exported and imported goods and services.

Trade diversion occurs when the establishment of a trade bloc diverts trade from low-cost global suppliers to higher cost member nations.

Transaction costs are the costs associated with organizing the transaction of goods or services.

Transaction motive for holding money recognizes that money payments and money receipts are not perfectly synchronized.

Transmission mechanism is the channel through which monetary policy impacts economic output and prices.

Unemployment is the number of individuals seeking work that do not currently have a job.

Unit elasticity is when $\varepsilon = 1$, or demand is equally responsive to a change in price.

Unit of account is the unit in which prices are quoted.

Value added is net output, after deducting goods and services used up during the production process.

Variable costs change or vary with the amount of production.

Vertical chain of production encapsulates the various stages of production from the extraction of a raw material input, through the production of the product or service, to the final retailing of the product.

Vertical integration refers to owning consecutive stages of the vertical chain.

Volatility is a measure of variability. In the case of exchange rates, a concern over volatility is a concern over how much the exchange rate changes.

Wholesale banks take large deposits and are involved in brokering very large loans to companies.

Winner's curse is where a winning bid exceeds the true value of the sale item.

Index

Note: Glossary terms are in **bold** type

A

accounting profits 115–16
accuracy of measurements, economic
data 269–70
acquisitions *see* **mergers & acquisitions**
activity-based regulation, banks/banking
308
actual GDP, gross domestic product
(GDP) 331–2
adjustment speed, **equilibrium** 340–3
advertising, demand 37–8
agency costs 190
reducing 195–8
stock options 195–8
agents/principals
principal–agent problem 189–90
principal–agent theory 194–5
aggregate demand 230–5, 277–90,
337–9
fiscal policy 281–3
foreign trade 288–90
government 281–3
gross domestic product (GDP) 249,
254
inflation 231–2, 255–60
key components 240–2
UK 240–2
aggregate supply 232–5
gross domestic product (GDP) 249,
254
growth 354–8
inflation 232–3, 255–60
long-run aggregate supply 336–9,
344–5
short-run aggregate supply 336–9
aircraft costs 65–6, 75–7
airline industry 126–7
British Airways, vs. Virgin Atlantic
168
carbon emissions 213
fares, **price discrimination** 52
airports, strategic entry barriers 142
allocative efficiency 118
aluminium industry, Chinese, cost
inefficiency 70
anonymous auctions
see also auctions/auctioning
supermarkets 153–4
supply costs 153–4
Apple Inc.

inelastic demand 105
pricing strategy 51
production techniques 72
profits 105–6
Steve Jobs 7
arithmetic mean 24
asset motive, money 312
assets and liabilities, **inflation** 259
auctions/auctioning
anonymous auctions 153–4
auction formats 156
auction theory 156–9
common values 157–9
private values 157–9
revenue equivalence 159
winner's curse 159
autonomous consumption 277
autonomous expenditure 277
average fixed costs 64–6
average revenue 106–10
monopoly 120–1
perfect competition 113, 114
average total costs 64–6
average variable costs 64–7
averaging, methods of 24

B

balance of payments 382–5
capital account 382–3
current account 382
financial account 383–4
fixed exchange rates 384–5
floating exchange rates 384
manufacturing competitiveness 264–6
official financing 385
policy issues 262–3
balanced budget multiplier 283
Bank of England
financial markets 322–4
inflation 249, 266–9, 340
interest rates 248–9
macroeconomics 248–9
monetary policy 315–16, 339–40
money supply 314–15
policy issues 248–9, 266–9
quantitative easing 322–4
banks/banking
see also Bank of England; **central
banks**
activity-based regulation 308

banking system 302–5
Barings bank 308–9
collateralized debt obligations
(CDOs) 304–5
contagion 305, 309
credit creation 309–11
credit crunch 305
deregulation 321
economic importance 304
European Banking Authority 307–8
financial intermediation 303
government bonds 304
importance to economy 321–2
lender of last resort 309
liquidity 303–5
minimum reserve requirements 307–8
monetary base 310
money multiplier 310
moral hazard 309
mutuals 306
narrow measures of money 310–11
regulation 305–9, 321
retail banks 302
risk-based regulation and monitoring
308
risk pooling 305
risk pricing 305
risk selection/monitoring 305
sight deposits 303–4
systemic risks 305, 309
time deposits 303–4
wholesale banks 303
Barings bank, **regulation** failure 308–9
barriers to entry 112
barter economy 301
Basel III, regulation 307
beer industry, **hold-up problem** 176–7
behavioural theories 193
goal setting 193
target setting 193
Bertrand model, **game theory** 152
Big Mac index, **purchasing power parity**
379
BlackBerry phone 124
Blu-Ray/DVD market, **durable goods**
125–6
boom 234–40
brand and image, globalization 420–1
Brazil, growth 365–7
Bretton Woods 306

BRIC economies, growth 365–7
British Airways, vs. Virgin Atlantic 168
BT, shareholdings analysis 191
bundling/de-bundling, pricing strategy 51
Burj Khalifa, Dubai, construction 73–4
bus market
    competition 154–6
    Competition Commission 154–6
business confidence
    Germany 224, 320
    Ifo Business Climate 320
    investment 319
business cycles
    economic uncertainty 223–4
    gross domestic product (GDP) 249–50, 344–5
    importance to economy 344–5
    national income determination 230–4
    predicting 235–7
    real business cycles 344–5
business data applications
    car market 96–8
    market research 52–4
    soft drinks 52–4
business experience 237
business investment, business outlook 236
business outlook, demand 236–7
business regulation 199–200
buy one get one free, pricing strategy 45–6

C
Canada, exports 413–14
CAP see Common Agricultural Policy
capital
    economic resources 14–17
    factors of production 6
capital account, balance of payments 382–3
capital adequacy ratio, regulation 307
capital formation, growth 367–8
capital input, **short run** 71
car manufacture
    cars vs. TVs, globalization 402–3
    hold-up problem 176
    law of comparative advantage 402–3
car market, demand/supply 96–8
carbon emissions
    airline industry 213
    sustainable growth 252–4
carbon trading 210–13
Carrefour, emerging markets (EMs) 166
cartels
    oligopoly 142–5
    Unilever/Procter & Gamble (P&G) 145
CDOs see **collateralized debt obligations**

central banks 302
    see also Bank of England
    European Central Bank, monetary policy 315–16
    Federal Reserve, **inflation** targeting 268
    financial markets 322–4
    independence 318–19
    inflation targeting 266–9, 339–40
    monetary policy 315–16, 339–40
    money supply 314–15
    policy issues 248–9, 266–9
    quantitative easing 322–4
ceteris paribus
    demand 38
    market equilibrium 87
China
    aluminium industry, cost inefficiency 70
    capital formation 367–8
    economic resources 14–17
    economy 230
    exchange rates 379–80
    exports 276, 413–14
    growth 276, 365–8
    labour costs 422
    labour markets 355
    reform programme 230
circular flow of income 227–9
claimant count, unemployment 261
classical unemployment 260, 261
closed economy 277
co-operation, **game theory** 152–3
Coase conjecture, monopoly 211
collateralized debt obligations (CDOs), banks/banking 304–5
collusion
    vs. competition 142–5
    oligopoly 142–5
command economy see **planned economy**
command GDP
    globalization 403–4
    terms of trade 403–4
commercial environment
    interest rates 300–1
    monetary environment 300–1
Common Agricultural Policy (CAP), European Union (EU) 412
common values, auctions/auctioning 157–9
communication and co-ordination, globalization 420
communications and technology, globalization 402
comparative advantage, globalization 402–5, 420–1
competing perspectives
    equilibrium, adjustment speed 340–3
    extreme Keynesians 341–3

    gradual monetarists 340–1
    macroeconomics 340–3
    moderate Keynesians 341
    new classical economists 340
competition
    bus market 154–6
    vs. collusion 142–5
    forces 127–31
    game theory 152–3
    horizontal growth 168–9
    international competitiveness 264–6
    macroeconomics 264–6
    manufacturing competitiveness 264–6
    markets 12–13
    oligopoly 142–8
    Porter's five forces model 127–31
    rivals 146–8
    service stations, France 127–31
    Spanish invaders 136–7
    supermarkets 129–31
Competition Commission
    bus market 154–6
    competition policy 208–9
competition policy, market power 207–9
competitive issues, productivity 74–5
competitiveness, international, globalization 419–20
complements, demand 36
complete contract
    complexity 172–3
    enforcement 173
    monitoring 173
    nexus of contracts 174–5
    transaction costs 172–3
    uncertainty 173
    vertical growth 172–3
construction, Burj Khalifa, Dubai 73–4
consumer income, demand 36
Consumer Price Index (CPI), **inflation** 257–8
consumer surplus
    price discrimination 49–52
    pricing strategy 49–52
consumption 277–8
    business outlook 236
    monetary policy 316–17
consumption of perquisites, managerial objective 192
contagion
    banks/banking 305, 309
    regulation 305, 309
contestable markets, strategic entry barriers 141–2
control/ownership see **separation of ownership from control**
convergence, growth 358–9
cost–benefit analysis, government intervention 209
cost inefficiency 69–71
    Chinese aluminium industry 70

cost leadership strategy 75
cost-plus pricing 44–5
cost push inflation 255–6
cost structures, pricing 75–7
costs
    see also specific costs
    horizontal growth 169–70
    inflation 258–9
    long run 71–5
    managing, recession 238
    monopoly 120–1
    short run 63–72
Cournot model, game theory 151–2
CPI see Consumer Price Index
creative destruction, monopoly 123–4
credible commitment, game theory 150
credit creation, banks/banking 309–11
credit crisis, deflation 338–9
credit crunch, banks/banking 305
cross-price elasticity 44, 45, 47
cross-sectional data 22–3
crowding out
    debt funding 290–1
    default risk 290–1
    fiscal policy 288, 290–1
culture, globalization 401
cumulative debt 284–5
current account, balance of payments
    382
cycles, business see business cycles
cyclical unemployment 260
Czech Republic, intra-EU trade 411

D
data, economic see business data
    applications; economic data
dead-weight loss, monopoly 208
debt funding, crowding out 290–1
decline, product life cycle 49
default risk, crowding out 290–1
defence, protectionist measures 407
deficits
    government deficit 226, 284–5
    inflation 288
    trade deficit 224–7
deflation
    credit crisis 338–9
    inflation 256–7, 259–60, 268
demand
    see also aggregate demand; supply
    advertising 37–8
    business outlook 236–7
    car market 96–8
    ceteris paribus 38
    changes 87–90
    complements 36
    consumer income 36
    elasticity 39–48
    factors influencing 35–9
    inelastic demand 42

inferior goods 36
law of demand 38–9
Louis Vuitton 39
market equilibrium 86–7
normal goods 36
preferences/tastes 36–40
price expectations 38–9
profit maximization 110
responsiveness 39–44
Starbucks 37
substitutes 36
supply 86–95
tastes/preferences 36–40
demand curve
    elasticity 43–4
    perfect competition 113–14
    pricing 34–5
demand pull inflation 255–6
demand-side policies
    economic stability 275
    macroeconomics 263
demerit goods 204
depreciation, exchange rates 390–1
devaluation, fixed exchange rates 378
Developed OECD, GDP growth rate
    358–9
diagrams 18–19
differentiation 21–2
dirty float 376
discount factor or rate, government
    intervention 209
diseconomies of scale 74
disequilibria, market equilibrium 87,
    90–1
diversification 165–6
    recession 239–40
    risk reduction 178
diversified growth 177–8
    economies of scope 177–8, 182–3
diversified portfolio 178
dominant strategy, game theory 149–
    50
double coincidence of wants 301
drinks, soft
    business data applications 52–4
    market research 52–4
durable goods, monopoly 125–6
DVD/Blu-Ray market, durable goods
    125–6

E
earnings growth, inflation 330–1
East Asia & Pacific, GDP growth rate
    358–9
economic crisis, equilibrium 329–31
economic data 22–3
    accuracy of measurements 269–70
    cross-sectional data 22–3
    economic resources 14–17
    panel data 22–3

time series data 22–3
economic growth
    see also growth
    assessing 352–4
    sustainable 252–4
economic insights 235–7
economic profits 115–16
economic rationales, globalization
    402–3
economic resources, economic data
    14–17
economic terminology 17
economic uncertainty, business cycles
    223–4
economics for business, reasons for
    studying 11–14
economies of scale
    diseconomies of scale 74
    monopoly 122–3
    natural entry barriers 140–1
    production techniques 72
    productivity 72–5
    vertical growth 171
economies of scope
    diversified growth 177–8, 182–3
    globalization 419
EDF Energy, price war 147
education markets, supply-side policies
    360–1
elastic demand 42–3
elasticity
    cross-price elasticity 44, 45, 47
    demand 39–48
    demand curve 43–4
    determinants 40–1
    elastic demand 42–3
    formulae 41–3
    income elasticity 44, 238
    inelastic demand 42
    inelastic supply 89–90
    kinked demand curve 146
    market definition 41
    market equilibrium 89–90
    measuring 41–3
    perfectly elastic demand 42–3
    pricing strategy 44–9
    substitutes 40–1
    time 41
    unit elasticity 42
elasticity of supply 69
electricity/gas metering 213–15
emerging markets (EMs), Carrefour 166
employment 333–5
    see also unemployment
    full employment level 286, 331
    Ireland 334
EMs see emerging markets
endogenized costs, strategic entry
    barriers 141
endogenous growth theory 359–60

enterprise
economic resources 14–17
factors of production 6–7
entry barriers 112
monopoly 120–1
natural entry barriers 140–1
oligopoly 140–2
strategic entry barriers 141–2
supermarkets 139–41
environmental pollution
carbon trading 210–13
sustainable growth 252–4
equation of a straight line 19–20
equilibrium
see also specific equilibria
adjustment 280
adjustment speed 340–3
defining 277
economic crisis 329–31
long-run 116–19, 331–2, 337–9
macroeconomics 233–4, 331–2
money market equilibrium 312–15
short-run 331–2, 337–9
Ericsson vs. Huawei, **horizontal growth**
180–1
EU *see* European Union
euro
membership 375–6, 387–94
monetary sovereignty 390–1
monetary union 387–90, 391–4
real exchange rate 393–4
European Banking Authority, banks/
banking 307–8
European Central Bank, monetary policy
315–16
European Union (EU) 409–13
benefits 410–12
Common Agricultural Policy (CAP)
412
economic resources 14–17
enlargement 412–13
exports 413–14
gross domestic product (GDP) 410
intra-EU trade 410–12
law of comparative advantage 402–3
terms of trade 403–4
trade creation 410–12
trade diversion 410–12
trade issues 412
eurozone
exchange rates 393–4
real exchange rate 393–4
exchange rates 375–82
Bretton Woods 306
China 379–80
depreciation 390–1
dirty float 377
eurozone 393–4
exchange rate regimes 376–80
financial discipline 380, 381–2

fiscal policy 386–7
fixed exchange rates 306, 376, 377–8,
380–2, 384–7
floating exchange rates 376, 378–9,
380–2, 384, 387
government policy 385–7
hedging 391–3
monetary policy 386–7
perfect capital mobility 386
in practice 379–80
real exchange rate 385–6
risk reduction 391–3
robustness 380–1
speculation 393
volatility 380
exit barriers 113
exogenous costs, natural entry barriers
140–1
expectations
inflation 256, 267–8, 345–6
price expectations, demand 38–9
expenditure 275–81
government spending vs. taxation 228,
292–3
planned aggregate expenditure 277
exporters, leading 413–14
exports 228–9
see also foreign trade
business outlook 236–7
China 276
growth 276, 390–1
externalities 200–3
extreme Keynesians, **macroeconomics**
341–3

F
factor abundance, globalization 405
factor inputs, **gross domestic product**
(GDP) 354–5
factors of production 6–7
FDI *see* **foreign direct investment**
Federal Reserve, **inflation** targeting 268
fiat money 302
film and media, globalization 401–2
financial account, balance of payments
383–4
financial discipline, exchange rates 380,
381–2
financial intermediation 303
financial markets
Bank of England 322–4
central banks 322–4
quantitative easing 322–4
financial services, growth 362
finite resources 5–6
production possibility frontier 7–8
firm-specific sources of international
competitiveness, globalization 419
first best solution, government
intervention 210

first-mover advantage, game theory
152–3
fiscal drag, inflation 259
fiscal policy 281–98
aggregate demand 281–3
crowding out 288, 290–1
debt funding 290–1
exchange rates 386–7
fiscal stance 285–6
fixed exchange rates 386–7
floating exchange rates 387
government spending 292–5
government's approach 283–8
implementation problems 286–8
offsetting changes 287–8
spending cuts 287
taxation vs. government spending 228,
292–3
time lags 286–7
uncertainty 287
weaknesses 286
fiscal stance 285–6
fixed costs 59–60, 63–4, 75–7
fixed exchange rate regime 306, 376
fixed exchange rates 306, 376, 377–8
balance of payments 384–5
devaluation 378
fiscal policy 386–7
vs. **floating exchange rates** 380–2
monetary policy 386–7
speculative attack 378
floating exchange rates 376, 378–9
balance of payments 384
fiscal policy 387
vs. **fixed exchange rates** 380–2
monetary policy 387
purchasing power parity 378–9
footballers, employing 59–60, 77
foreign direct investment (FDI)
globalization 416–17
low-carbon technologies 423–5
foreign trade
see also exports
aggregate demand 288–90
forex markets 376–80
France
GDP growth rate 352–4
inflation 387–8
OECD forecasts 240–1
free riders 191
frictional unemployment 260
full employment level 286, 331
future path, **interest rates** 343–4

G
G4S, **mergers & acquisitions** 179
game theory 148–53
Bertrand model 152
co-operation 152–3
competition 152–3

Cournot model 151–2
credible commitment 150
dominant strategy 149–50
first-mover advantage 152–3
Nash equilibrium 149–50
prisoners' dilemma 148–50
reaction function 151–2
residual demand 151
single-period game 150
Sony/Toshiba 152–3
Stackelberg model 152
gas/electricity metering 213–15
GDP *see* **gross domestic product**
GDP per capita 251–2
geometric mean 24
geometric relationships, productivity 74
Germany
business confidence 224, 320
capital formation 367–8
GDP growth rate 352–4
growth 367–8
Ifo Business Climate 320
inflation 387–8
intra-EU trade 411
OECD forecasts 240–1
globalization 13–14, 399–429
brand and image 420–1
cars vs. TVs 402–3
command GDP 403–4
communication and co-ordination 420
communications and technology 402
comparative advantage 402–5, 420–1
competitiveness, international 419–20
culture 401
drivers 401–9
economic rationales 402–3
economies of scope 419
European Union (EU) 409–13
factor abundance 405
film and media 401–2
firm-specific sources of international competitiveness 419
foreign direct investment (FDI) 416–17
global operations 414–17
global product markets 413–14
image and brand 420–1
index of transnationality 415–16
input factors 420
international institutions 408
law of comparative advantage 402–3
legal issues 420
low-carbon technologies 423–5
non-tariff barriers 407
politics 408
pollution 423–5
protectionist measures 405–8, 409
quotas 407

reasons 418–20
revenue growth 418–20
sources of international competitiveness 418–19
tariffs 405–7
technology and communications 402
terms of trade 403–4
trade blocs 408–10
trade restrictions 405–8
travel 401
two-way trade 405
goal setting, behavioural theories 193
Google, **economies of scope** 182
government, **aggregate demand** 281–3
government bonds, banks/banking 304
government deficit 284–5
key macroeconomic inputs 226
government intervention 13
assessing 209–10
impact analysis 209, 213–15
government policy, exchange rates 385–7
government spending
channels of spending 292–3
fiscal policy 292–5
vs. taxation 228, 292–3
government's approach, **fiscal policy** 283–8
gradient 20–2
gradual monetarists, **macroeconomics** 340–1
Greece, OECD forecasts 240–1
Gresham's Law 93
gross domestic product (GDP) 10–11
actual GDP 331–2
aggregate demand 249, 254
aggregate supply 249, 254
business cycles 249–50, 344–5
command GDP 403–4
European Union (EU) 410
factor inputs 354–5
GDP per capita 251–2
growth, economic 252–4, 352–4, 358–9
inflation 254
interest rates 343–4
Italy 332
key macroeconomic outputs 224–7
manufacturing competitiveness 264–6
measuring 249–54, 269–70
output gap 331–2
participation rate 251–2
policy issues 249–54
potential GDP 331–2
productivity 355–7
real business cycles 344–5
recession 332
sustainable growth 252–4
value added 250
variations over time 249–50

growth
see also **horizontal growth; vertical growth**
aggregate supply 354–8
Brazil 365–7
BRIC economies 365–7
capital formation 367–8
China 276, 365–8
convergence 358–9
diversified growth 177–8
earnings growth and **inflation** 330–1
economic growth, assessing 352–4
economic growth, sustainable 252–4
endogenous growth theory 359–60
exports 276, 390–1
financial services 362
Germany 367–8
gross domestic product (GDP) 252–4, 352–4, 358–9
India 365–8
innovation 357–8, 362, 364–5
labour markets 361
neoclassical growth theory 358–9
private finance initiatives (PFIs) 364
privatization 363
product life cycle 48
productivity 355–7
reasons 167
research and development (R&D) 357–8, 362, 364–5
Russia 365–7
strategies 164–87
sustainable 252–4
tax cuts 362–3
taxation 362–3
UK 367–8
growth maximization, managerial objective 192

H
haircut, money supply 314
hedging
exchange rates 391–3
risk reduction 391–3
helicopter money, vs. **quantitative easing** 342
hierarchies, **transaction costs** 174–5
hold-up problem, **vertical growth** 176–7
Hong Kong, China, exports 413–14
horizontal growth 165, 167–70
competition 168–9
costs 169–70
exploiting market growth 169
Huawei vs. Ericsson 180–1
learning curve 169–70
mergers & acquisitions 180–1
rationalization 169
revenue 167–8
Huawei vs. Ericsson, **horizontal growth** 180–1

I

Ifo Business Climate, Germany 320
image and brand, globalization 420–1
impact analysis
   government intervention 209, 213–15
   smart metering 213–15
**imperfect competition, market
      structure** 111–12
imperfect information 204
importers, leading 413–14
imports 228–9
income elasticity 44
   recession 238
index numbers 23–4
index of transnationality, globalization
      415–16
India
   capital formation 367–8
   growth 365–8
indivisibilities, productivity 73–4
industrial clusters
   location benefits 170–1
   vertical growth 170–1
inelastic demand 42
   Apple Inc. 105
inelastic supply 89–90
infant industry, **protectionist measures**
      407
inferior goods, demand 36
infinite wants 5–6
inflation
   aggregate demand 231–2, 255–60
   aggregate supply 232–3, 255–60
   assets and liabilities 259
   Bank of England 249, 266–9, 340
   Consumer Price Index (CPI) 257–8
   cost push inflation 255–6
   costs 258–9
   deficits 288
   deflation 256–7, 259–60, 268, 338–9
   demand pull inflation 255–6
   earnings growth 330–1
   expectations 256, 267–8, 345–6
   fiscal drag 259
   France 387–8
   Germany 387–8
   gross domestic product (GDP) 254
   inflation illusion 259
   investment 319–20
   Italy 387–8
   key macroeconomic outputs 224–7
   manufacturing competitiveness 264–6
   measuring 255–60
   policy issues 255–60, 266–9
   price deflators 258
   price index 257–8
   rate of inflation 255
   Retail Price Index (RPI) 257–8
   Spain 387–8

   targeting 260, 266–9, 339–40
   UK 387–8
   wages 330–1
injections 228–9
innovation
   growth 357–8, 362, 364–5
   monopoly 123–4
   vegetables 365
input factors, globalization 420
input markets 126–7
   labour markets 95–6
interest rates
   Bank of England 248–9
   commercial environment 300–1
   controlling 315
   future path 343–4
   gross domestic product (GDP)
      343–4
   investment 317–20
   investment activity 317–18
   key macroeconomic inputs 226
   macroeconomics 248–9
   monetary environment 300–1
   monetary policy 317–18
   policy issues 248–9
international competitiveness
   macroeconomics 264–6
   **sources of international
      competitiveness** 418–19, 421–3
international institutions, globalization
      408
Interscope Records, Madonna tour
      181–2
intra-EU trade, European Union (EU)
      410–12
investment 278–80
   business confidence 319
   inflation 319–20
   interest rates 317–20
   monetary policy 317–20
investment activity
   interest rates 317–18
   monetary policy 317–18
iPhone
   vs. BlackBerry 124
   production techniques 72
Ireland
   employment 334
   intra-EU trade 411
Italy
   GDP growth rate 352–4
   gross domestic product (GDP) 332
   inflation 387–8
   intra-EU trade 411
   recession 332

J

Japan
   exports 413–14

   OECD forecasts 240–1
Jobs, Steve, Apple Inc. 7

K

kebab shops, **perfect competition** 105,
      118–19
kinked demand curve, oligopoly 146–8
Korea
   exports 413–14
   OECD forecasts 240–1
Kuznets curve, carbon trading 210–11

L

labour
   economic resources 14–17
   factors of production 6
   labour costs, China 422
   productivity 78–80
   wages 78–80
labour markets 95–6
   China 355
   growth 361
   input markets 95–6
   supply-side policies 361
land
   economic resources 14–17
   factors of production 6
language, economic terminology 17
launch, product life cycle 48
law of comparative advantage,
      globalization 402–3
law of demand 38–9
law of diminishing returns, productivity
      62–3
leakages 228–9
learning curve, horizontal growth 169–
      70
least developed countries, GDP growth
      rate 358–9
legal issues, globalization 420
lender of last resort, banks/banking 309
leveraging 343
liabilities and assets, **inflation** 259
licences, **monopoly** 119
liquidity, banks/banking 303–5
location benefits
   industrial clusters 170–1
   vertical growth 170–1
long run 60–1
   costs 71–5
   perfect competition 116–17
   productivity 71–5
long-run aggregate supply 336–9, 344–5
long-run average cost curve (LRAC),
      minimum efficient scale (MES)
      140–1
long-run equilibrium 116–19, 331–2,
      337–9
   monopolistic competition 139

Louis Vuitton, demand 39
low-carbon technologies
  foreign direct investment (FDI) 423–5
  globalization 423–5
LRAC *see* long-run average cost curve

M

M4, measure of money 310–11
Maastricht criteria, monetary union
    388–9
macroeconomics 224–7
  Bank of England 248–9
  changes 226–7
  competing perspectives 340–3
  demand-side policies 263
  equilibrium 233–4, 331–2
  equilibrium, adjustment speed 340–3
  extreme Keynesians 341–3
  gradual monetarists 340–1
  inputs, key macroeconomic 226
  interest rates 248–9
  international competitiveness 264–6
  long-run equilibrium 331–2
  moderate Keynesians 341
  new classical economists 340
  outputs, key macroeconomic 224–6
  policy issues 248–9, 263
  production possibility frontier 8–9
  short-run equilibrium 331–2
  supply-side policies 263
Madonna tour
  Interscope Records 181–2
  pricing 94–5
make or buy? transaction costs 173–4
managerial objectives 192
  consumption of perquisites 192
  growth maximization 192
  sales maximization 192
managers 189–98
  managerial objectives 192
manufacturing competitiveness 264–6
marginal costs (MC) 64–7, 108–11,
    190–1
  oligopoly 142–3
marginal private benefit (MPB) 201–3
marginal private cost (MPC) 200–3
marginal product, productivity 61–3
marginal profit 108–9
marginal propensity to consume
    (MPC) 277–8
marginal propensity to save (MPS)
    277–8
marginal revenue (MR) 106–11, 190–1
  monopoly 120–1
  oligopoly 142–3
  perfect competition 113, 114
marginal social benefit (MSB) 201–3
marginal social cost (MSC) 200–3
market definition, elasticity 41

market economy
  cf. planned economy 10–12
  production possibility frontier 9–10
market equilibrium 86–7
  disequilibria 87, 90–1
  elasticity 89–90
  pop concerts 93–5
  simultaneous equations 87
market failure
  monopoly 200
  perfect competition 200
market power
  competition policy 207–9
  monopolistic competition 139
market research
  business data applications 52–4
  soft drinks 52–4
market structure
  imperfect competition 111–12
  monopoly 111–12
  oligopoly 111–12
  perfect competition 111–12
markets, competition 12–13
maturity, product life cycle 48–9
maximum price/price floor 92
MC *see* marginal costs
mean (average) 24
menu costs 206–7
mergers & acquisitions 167–70, 178–9
  G4S 179
  horizontal growth 180–1
  trends 183–4
merit goods 204
MES *see* minimum efficient scale
Mexico, exports 413–14
microeconomics, production
    possibility frontier 8–9
minimum efficient scale (MES)
  long-run average cost curve (LRAC)
    140–1
  natural entry barriers 140–1
  productivity 74–5
  strategic entry barriers 141
minimum price/price floor 92
minimum reserve requirements, banks/
    banking 307–8
mixed economy 10
models 17, 18
moderate Keynesians, macroeconomics
    341
monetary base, banks/banking 310
monetary environment
  commercial environment 300–1
  interest rates 300–1
monetary policy 315–20
  Bank of England 315–16, 339–40
  central banks 315–16, 339–40
  consumption 316–17
  exchange rates 386–7

fixed exchange rates 386–7
floating exchange rates 387
interest rates 317–18
investment 317–20
investment activity 317–18
net present value 316–17
permanent income hypothesis 317
rules 339–40
Taylor rule 339, 343
transmission mechanism 315–16
monetary sovereignty 390–1
monetary union 387–90, 391–4
  euro 387–90, 391–4
  Maastricht criteria 388–9
  optimal currency zones 389–90
  stability pact 388–9
money 301–2
  asset motive 312
  demand for 311–12
  measures 310–11
  precautionary motive 312
  transaction motive 311
money market equilibrium 312–15
money multiplier, banks/banking 310
money supply
  Bank of England 314–15
  controlling 313–15
monopolistic competition 137–9
  characteristics 139
  excess capacity 139
  long-run equilibrium 139
  market power 139
monopoly 119–27
  average revenue 120–1
  Coase conjecture 211
  costs 120–1
  creative destruction 123–4
  dead-weight loss 208
  durable goods 125–6
  economies of scale 122–3
  entry barriers 120–1
  innovation 123–4
  licences 119
  marginal revenue (MR) 120–1
  market failure 200
  market structure 111–12
  natural monopoly 120
  patents 119–20
  cf. perfect competition 121–2
  perfect competition 126–7, 200
  perishable goods 125–6
  profit maximization 121
  rent-seeking behaviour 123–4
  revenues 120–1
  vertical growth 171
monopoly status 208
moral hazard 190
  banks/banking 309
  regulation 309

movies, price war 148
MPB *see* **marginal private benefit**
MPC *see* **marginal private cost;**
    marginal propensity to consume
MPS *see* **marginal propensity to save**
MR *see* **marginal revenue**
MSB *see* **marginal social benefit**
multiplier 280–1
    balanced budget multiplier 283
    money multiplier, banks/banking 310
mutuals, banks/banking 306

N
N-firm concentration ratio, oligopoly 140
narrow measures of money, banks/banking 310–11
Nash equilibrium, game theory 149–50
national income determination, **business cycles** 230–4
national interest, **protectionist measures** 407
natural entry barriers 140–1
natural monopoly 120
natural rate of unemployment 333
negative externalities 200–3
negative relationship 18–19
neoclassical growth theory 358–9
net present value, monetary policy 316–17
Netflix, price war 148
new classical economists, **macroeconomics** 340
nexus of contracts, transaction costs 174–5
Nintendo, pricing 35
nominal prices 232
nominal wages 232, 334–5
non-excludable goods/services 204
non-rivalrous goods/services 204
non-tariff barriers, globalization 407
normal economic profits 115–16
normal goods, demand 36
normative economics 17–18
North America *see* USA

O
official financing, balance of payments 385
oil, pricing 144, 146
oligopoly 139–48
    cartels 142–5
    collusion 142–5
    competition 142–8
    entry barriers 140–2
    kinked demand curve 146–8
    market structure 111–12
    N-firm concentration ratio 140
    price fixing 143–5

strategic interdependence 137
    supermarkets 111–12
open market operations, money supply 313–14
opportunity cost, production possibility frontier 8
optimal currency zones, monetary union 389–90
organic growth 165
output decisions, **short run** 66–9
output gap, gross domestic product (GDP) 331–2
output markets 126–7
ownership/control *see* **separation of ownership from control**

P
panel data 22–3
Pareto efficient, perfect competition 199
participation rate, gross domestic product (GDP) 251–2
patents, **monopoly** 119–20
percentages 23
perfect capital mobility, exchange rates 386
perfect competition 111–19
    average revenue 113, 114
    demand curve 113–14
    kebab shops 105, 118–19
    long run 116–17
    marginal revenue 114
    marginal revenue (MR) 113
    market failure 200
    market structure 111–12
    cf. **monopoly** 121–2
    monopoly 126–7, 200
    Pareto efficient 199
    profit maximization 114–15
    strategic interdependence 137
perfect information 113
perfectly elastic demand 42–3
performance pay, public sector 198–9
perishable goods, monopoly 125–6
permanent income hypothesis, monetary policy 317
petrol, pricing 146
PFIs *see* **private finance initiatives**
Phillips curve, unemployment 262, 333–6
photovoltaic (PV) industry, **subsidy** 203
piece rates 194–5
planned aggregate expenditure 277
planned economy
    cf. **market economy** 10–12
    production possibility frontier 9–10
Poland, intra-EU trade 411
policy issues
    see also **fiscal policy**
    balance of payments 262–3

Bank of England 248–9, 266–9
    central banks 248–9, 266–9
    gross domestic product (GDP) 249–54
    inflation 255–60, 266–9
    interest rates 248–9
    macroeconomics 248–9, 263
    unemployment 262
politics, globalization 408
pollution
    carbon trading 210–13
    globalization 423–5
    low-carbon technologies 423–5
    sustainable growth 252–4
pooling equilibrium 93
pop concerts
    Madonna tour 94–5
    market equilibrium 93–5
    pricing 93–5
Porter's five forces model
    competition 127–31
    service stations, France 127–31
positive economics 17–18
positive externalities 200–3
positive relationship 18–19
potential GDP, gross domestic product (GDP) 331–2
precautionary motive, money 312
preferences/tastes, demand 36–40
price deflators, **inflation** 258
price discrimination
    airline fares 52
    consumer surplus 49–52
    pricing strategy 49–52
price expectations, demand 38–9
price fixing, **oligopoly** 143–5
price floor/maximum price 92
price floor/minimum price 92
price index, inflation 257–8
price level, macroeconomics 231
price sensitivity, survey data 41
price taker 113–14
price volatility 204–7
price wars
    EDF Energy 147
    movies 148
    Netflix 148
pricing
    best price 33–4
    cost structures 75–7
    demand curve 34–5
    Madonna tour 94–5
    maximum price/price floor 92
    minimum price/price floor 92
    Nintendo 35
    objectives 33–4
    oil 144, 146
    petrol 146
    pop concerts 93–5
    price floor/maximum price 92
    price floor/minimum price 92

product life cycle 48–9
recession 238
standard deviation 206
supermarkets 33–4
total revenue 46
pricing strategy
Apple Inc. 51
bundling/de-bundling 51
buy one get one free 45–6
consumer surplus 49–52
cost-plus pricing 44–5
elasticity 44–9
price discrimination 49–52
principal–agent problem 189–90
principal–agent theory 194–5
prisoners' dilemma, **game theory** 148–50
private finance initiatives (PFIs), growth 364
private values, auctions/auctioning 157–9
privatization, growth 363
Procter & Gamble (P&G)/Unilever, cartel 145
producer surplus 207–8
product differentiation strategy 75
product life cycle, pricing 48–9
production possibility frontier 7–10
production techniques, **economies of scale** 72
productive efficiency 118
productivity
competitive issues 74–5
economies of scale 72–5
geometric relationships 74
gross domestic product (GDP) 355–7
growth 355–7
indivisibilities 73–4
labour 78–80
law of diminishing returns 62–3
long run 71–5
marginal product 61–3
minimum efficient scale (MES) 74–5
short run 61–3
task specialization 61–3
total product 61–3
wages 78–80
products, picking 85–6
profit maximization 106–11, 190–3
demand 110
monopoly 121
perfect competition 114–15
separation of ownership from control 191–2
profits
accounting profits 115–16
Apple Inc. 105–6
economic profits 115–16
normal economic profits 115–16

supernormal profits 115–16
protectionist measures
defence 407
globalization 405–8, 409
infant industry 407
national interest 407
way of life 407–8
public goods 204
public sector, performance pay 198–9
purchasing power parity
Big Mac index 379
floating exchange rates 378–9

Q

quadratic 20–2
qualitative easing, money supply 314
quantitative easing
Bank of England 322–4
central banks 322–4
financial markets 322–4
vs. helicopter money 342
monetary sovereignty 391
money supply 314
quotas, globalization 407

R

R&D *see* research and development
rate of inflation 255
rationalization, **horizontal growth** 169
reaction function, **game theory** 151–2
real business cycles, **gross domestic product** (GDP) 344–5
real exchange rate 385–6
euro 393–4
eurozone 393–4
real prices 232
real wages 232
unemployment 334–5
reasons for studying economics for business 11–14
recession 234–42
costs, managing 238
diversification 239–40
gross domestic product (GDP) 332
income elasticity 238
Italy 332
pricing 238
profiting from 238–40
regulation
activity-based regulation 308
banks/banking 305–9, 321
Basel III 307
capital adequacy ratio 307
contagion 305, 309
deregulation 321
European Banking Authority 307–8
failure 308–9
lender of last resort 309
minimum reserve requirements 307–8

moral hazard 309
risk-based regulation and monitoring 308
systemic risks 305, 309
types 306–8
regulation of business 199–200
regulatory capture, government intervention 210
rent-seeking behaviour, **monopoly** 123–4
research and development (R&D), growth 357–8, 362, 364–5
residual demand, **game theory** 151
resources, economic *see* economic resources
retail banks 302
Retail Price Index (RPI), **inflation** 257–8
returns to scale 71–2
revenue equivalence, auctions/auctioning 159
revenue growth, globalization 418–20
revenues, **monopoly** 120–1
risk averse 197
risk-based regulation and monitoring, banks/banking 308
risk pooling, banks/banking 305
risk pricing, banks/banking 305
risk reduction
diversification 178
exchange rates 391–3
hedging 391–3
risk selection/monitoring, banks/banking 305
robustness, exchange rates 380–1
Royal Mint 302
RPI *see* Retail Price Index
Russia
exports 413–14
growth 365–7

S

sales maximization, managerial objective 192
Samsung
economies of scale 72
products, picking 86
strategy 86
satisficing 193
savings and investments 228
second best solution, government intervention 210
separating equilibrium 93
separation of ownership from control, **profit maximization** 191–2
service stations, France
competition 127–31
Porter's five forces model 127–31
shipping 60
short run 60–1
capital input 71

costs 63–72
　output decisions 66–9
　productivity 61–3
short-run aggregate supply 336–9
short-run equilibrium 331–2, 337–9
sight deposits, banks/banking 303–4
Singapore, exports 413–14
single-period game, game theory 150
smart metering
　gas/electricity metering 213–15
　impact analysis 213–15
soft drinks
　market research 52–4
　substitutes 54
solar panels industry, **subsidy** 203
Sony/Toshiba, **game theory** 152–3
**sources of international
　　competitiveness** 421–3
　globalization 418–19
Spain
　GDP growth rate 352–4
　inflation 387–8
Spanish invaders
　competition 136–7
　game theory 150
specific asset 176
specific assets 176, 419
speculation, exchange rates 393
speculative attack, fixed exchange rates
　377–8
spending cuts, **fiscal policy** 287
stability pact, **monetary union**
　388–9
Stackelberg model, game theory 152
standard deviation, pricing 206
Starbucks
　demand 37
　monopolistic competition 138
stock options, agency costs 195–8
store of value 302
strategic considerations, **vertical growth**
　176–7
strategic direction, Vodafone 197
strategic entry barriers 141–2
strategic interdependence 137
strategy, Samsung 86
structural unemployment 260
subsidy 203
substitutes
　demand 36
　elasticity 40–1
　soft drinks 54
sunk costs, strategic entry barriers 141
supermarkets
　anonymous auctions 153–4
　competition 129–31
　entry barriers 139–41
　oligopoly 111–12
　pricing 33–4
　supply costs 153–4

supernormal profits 115–16
　long-run equilibrium 116–18
supply
　see also **aggregate supply**; demand
　car market 96–8
　changes 87–90
　demand 86–95
　inelastic supply 89–90
　market equilibrium 86–7
supply costs
　anonymous auctions 153–4
　supermarkets 153–4
supply curve 67–9
supply-side policies 360–4
　education markets 360–1
　labour markets 361
　macroeconomics 263
survey data, price sensitivity 41
sustainable growth, **gross domestic
　product** (GDP) 252–4
systemic risks
　banks/banking 305, 309
　regulation 305, 309

T
tangency equilibrium 139
target setting, behavioural theories 193
tariffs, globalization 405–7
task specialization, productivity 61–3
tastes/preferences, demand 36–40
tax cuts, growth 362–3
taxation 202
　vs. government spending 228, 292–3
　growth 362–3
　tax cuts 362–3
Taylor rule, monetary policy 339, 343
technology and communications,
　globalization 402
terms of trade
　command GDP 403–4
　globalization 403–4
Tesco, **economies of scope** 183
theme parks 67
theories 17, 18
time, **elasticity** 41
time deposits, banks/banking 303–4
time lags, **fiscal policy** 286–7
time series data 22–3
timing, government spending vs.
　taxation 228
Toshiba/Sony, **game theory** 152–3
total costs 63–4
total expenditure 229–30
total product, productivity 61–3
total revenue, pricing 45–6
trade blocs
　see also European Union (EU)
　globalization 408–10
trade creation, European Union (EU)
　410–12

trade deficit, key macroeconomic
　outputs 224–7
trade diversion, European Union (EU)
　410–12
trade restrictions, globalization 405–8
transaction costs
　complete contract 172–3
　hierarchies 174–5
　make or buy? 173–4
　markets 174
　nexus of contracts 174–5
　vertical growth 171–6
transaction motive, money 311
transmission mechanism, monetary
　policy 315–16
travel, globalization 401
turning points 20–2
TV manufacture
　law of comparative advantage 402–3
　TVs vs. cars, globalization 402–3
two-way trade, globalization 405

U
UK
　aggregate demand 240–2
　capital formation 367–8
　GDP growth rate 352–4
　growth 367–8
　inflation 387–8
　intra-EU trade 411
　OECD forecasts 240–1
　trade 289
uncertainty
　business cycles 223–4
　complete contract 173
　fiscal policy 287
unemployment 260–2
　categories 260
　claimant count 261
　classical 260, 261
　cyclical 260
　defining 261
　frictional 260
　key macroeconomic outputs 224–7
　manufacturing competitiveness 264–6
　measuring 261
　natural rate of unemployment 333
　Phillips curve 262, 333–6
　policy issues 262
　real wages 334
　structural 260
Unilever/Procter & Gamble (P&G),
　cartel 145
unit elasticity 42
unit of account 301–2
USA
　economic resources 14–17
　exports 413–14
　GDP growth rate 352–4
　OECD forecasts 240–1

V

value added, gross domestic product (GDP) 250
variable costs 59–60, 63–4
vegetables, innovation 365
vertical chain of production 166
vertical growth 170–7, 181–2
    economies of scale 171
    hold-up problem 176–7
    industrial clusters 170–1

location benefits 170–1
    monopoly 171
    strategic considerations 176–7
    transaction costs 171–6
vertical integration 166, 175–7
Virgin Atlantic, vs. British Airways 168
Vodafone
    revenues 279
    strategic direction 197
volatility, exchange rates 380

W

wages
    inflation 330–1
    nominal wages 334–5
    productivity 78–80
    real wages 334–5
way of life, **protectionist measures** 407–8
wholesale banks 303
winner's curse, auctions/auctioning 159